Program Authors

Peter Afflerbach
Camille Blachowicz
Candy Dawson Boyd
Elena Izquierdo
Connie Juel
Edward Kame'enui
Donald Leu
Jeanne R. Paratore
P. David Pearson
Sam Sebesta
Deborah Simmons
Alfred Tatum
Sharon Vaughn
Susan Watts Taffe
Karen Kring Wixson

Glenview, Illinois • Boston, Massachusetts
Chandler, Arizona • Upper Saddle River, New Jersey

We dedicate Reading Street to
Peter Jovanovich.

His wisdom, courage,
and passion for education
are an inspiration to us all.

ISBN-13: 978-0-328-46996-3
ISBN-10: 0-328-46996-3
2 3 4 5 6 7 8 9 10 V064 14 13 12 11 10
CC1

Any Path, Any Pace

Reading Street

Calle de la Lectura

PEARSON

Who said so?

The Leading Researchers,

Program Authors

Peter Afflerbach, Ph.D.
Professor
Department of Curriculum and Instruction
University of Maryland at College Park

Camille L. Z. Blachowicz, Ph.D.
Professor of Education
National-Louis University

Candy Dawson Boyd, Ph.D.
Professor
School of Education
Saint Mary's College of California

Elena Izquierdo, Ph.D.
Associate Professor
University of Texas at El Paso

Connie Juel, Ph.D.
Professor of Education
School of Education
Stanford University

Edward J. Kame'enui, Ph.D.
Dean-Knight Professor of Education and Director
Institute for the Development of Educational Achievement and the Center on Teaching and Learning
College of Education
University of Oregon

Donald J. Leu, Ph.D.
John and Maria Neag Endowed Chair in Literacy and Technology
Director, The New Literacies Research Lab
University of Connecticut

Jeanne R. Paratore, Ed.D.
Associate Professor of Education
Department of Literacy and Language Development
Boston University

P. David Pearson, Ph.D.
Professor and Dean
Graduate School of Education
University of California, Berkeley

Sam L. Sebesta, Ed.D.
Professor Emeritus
College of Education
University of Washington, Seattle

Deborah Simmons, Ph.D.
Professor
College of Education and Human Development
Texas A&M University

Alfred W. Tatum, Ph.D.
Associate Professor and Director of the UIC Reading Clinic
University of Illinois at Chicago

Sharon Vaughn, Ph.D.
H. E. Hartfelder/Southland Corporation Regents Professor
Director, Meadows Center for Preventing Educational Risk
University of Texas

Susan Watts Taffe, Ph.D.
Associate Professor in Literacy
Division of Teacher Education
University of Cincinnati

Karen Kring Wixson, Ph.D.
Professor of Education
University of Michigan

Consulting Authors

Jeff Anderson, M.Ed.
Author and Consultant
San Antonio, TX

Jim Cummins, Ph.D.
Professor
Department of Curriculum, Teaching and Learning
University of Toronto

Lily Wong Fillmore, Ph.D.
Professor Emerita
Graduate School of Education
University of California, Berkeley

Georgia Earnest García, Ph.D.
Professor
Language and Literacy Division
Department of Curriculum and Instruction
University of Illinois at Urbana-Champaign

George A. González, Ph.D.
Professor (Retired)
School of Education
University of Texas-Pan American, Edinburg

Valerie Ooka Pang, Ph.D.
Professor
School of Teacher Education
San Diego State University

Sally M. Reis, Ph.D.
Board of Trustees Distinguished Professor
Department of Educational Psychology
University of Connecticut

Jon Scieszka, M.F.A.
Children's Book Author
Founder of GUYS READ
Named First National Ambassador for Young People's Literature 2008

Grant Wiggins, Ed.D.
Educational Consultant
Authentic Education
Concept Development

Lee Wright, M.Ed.
Pearland, TX

Practitioners, and Authors.

Consultant

Sharroky Hollie, Ph.D.
Assistant Professor
California State University
Dominguez Hills, CA

Teacher Reviewers

Dr. Bettyann Brugger
Educational Support Coordinator—Reading Office
Milwaukee Public Schools
Milwaukee, WI

Kathleen Burke
K–12 Reading Coordinator
Peoria Public Schools, Peoria, IL

Darci Burns, M.S.Ed.
University of Oregon

Bridget Cantrell
District Intervention Specialist
Blackburn Elementary School
Independence, MO

Tahira DuPree Chase, M.A., M.S.Ed.
Administrator of Elementary English Language Arts
Mount Vernon City School District
Mount Vernon, NY

Michele Conner
Director, Elementary Education
Aiken County School District
Aiken, SC

Georgia Coulombe
K–6 Regional Trainer/ Literacy Specialist
Regional Center for Training and Learning (RCTL), Reno, NV

Kelly Dalmas
Third Grade Teacher
Avery's Creek Elementary, Arden, NC

Seely Dillard
First Grade Teacher
Laurel Hill Primary School
Mt. Pleasant, SC

Jodi Dodds-Kinner
Director of Elementary Reading
Chicago Public Schools, Chicago, IL

Dr. Ann Wild Evenson
District Instructional Coach
Osseo Area Schools, Maple Grove, MN

Stephanie Fascitelli
Principal
Apache Elementary, Albuquerque Public Schools, Albuquerque, NM

Alice Franklin
Elementary Coordinator, Language Arts & Reading
Spokane Public Schools, Spokane, WA

Laureen Fromberg
Assistant Principal
PS 100 Queens, NY

Kimberly Gibson
First Grade Teacher
Edgar B. Davis Community School
Brockton, MA

Kristen Gray
Lead Teacher
A.T. Allen Elementary School
Concord, NC

Mary Ellen Hazen
State Pre-K Teacher
Rockford Public Schools #205
Rockford, IL

Patrick M. Johnson
Elementary Instructional Director
Seattle Public Schools, Seattle, WA

Theresa Jaramillo Jones
Principal
Highland Elementary School
Las Cruces, NM

Sophie Kowzun
Program Supervisor, Reading/ Language Arts, PreK–5
Montgomery County Public Schools
Rockville, MD

David W. Matthews
Sixth Grade Teacher
Easton Area Middle School
Easton, PA

Ana Nuncio
Editor and Independent Publisher
Salem, MA

Joseph Peila
Principal
Chappell Elementary School
Chicago, IL

Ivana Reimer
Literacy Coordinator
PS 100 Queens, NY

Sally Riley
Curriculum Coordinator
Rochester Public Schools
Rochester, NH

Dyan M. Smiley
Independent Educational Consultant

Michael J. Swiatowiec
Lead Literacy Teacher
Graham Elementary School
Chicago, IL

Dr. Helen Taylor
Director of English Education
Portsmouth City Public Schools
Portsmouth, VA

Carol Thompson
Teaching and Learning Coach
Independence School District
Independence, MO

Erinn Zeitlin
Kindergarten Teacher
Carderock Springs Elementary School
Bethesda, MD

Animals, Tame and Wild

Key

- SI Strategic Intervention
- OL On-Level
- A Advanced
- ELL ELL

In this Teacher's Edition Unit 1, Volume 2

In the First Stop on Reading Street

- Dear First Grade Teacher
- Research into Practice on Reading Street
- Guide to Reading Street
- Assessment on Reading Street
- Customize Writing on Reading Street
- Differentiated Instruction on Reading Street
- ELL on Reading Street
- Customize Literacy on Reading Street
- Digital Products on Reading Street
- Teacher Resources for Grade 1
- Index

GO Digital!

See It!

- Big Question Video
- Concept Talk Video
- Interactive Sound-Spelling Cards
- Envision It! Animations
- Sing with Me Animations

Hear It!

- Sing with Me Animations
- eSelections
- Grammar Jammer
- eReaders
- Leveled Reader Database

Do It!

- Vocabulary Activities
- Story Sort
- 21st Century Skills Activities
- Online Assessment
- Letter Tile Drag and Drop

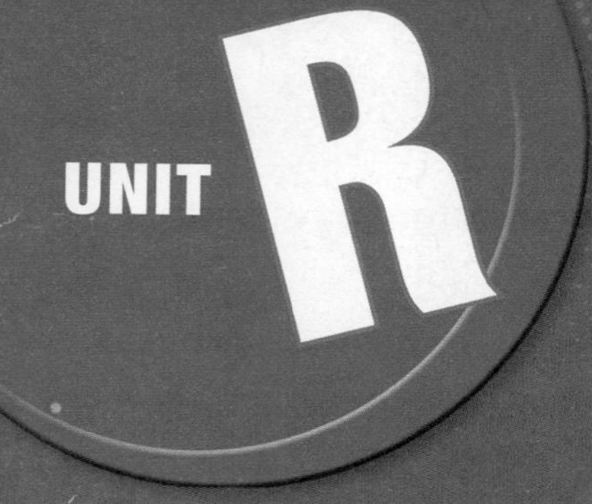

My World

Key
SI Strategic Intervention
OL On-Level
A Advanced
ELL ELL

Animals, Tame and Wild

Key

SI Strategic Intervention
OL On-Level
A Advanced
ELL ELL

Communities

Key
- SI Strategic Intervention
- OL On-Level
- A Advanced
- ELL ELL

Changes

Key
- SI Strategic Intervention
- OL On-Level
- A Advanced
- ELL ELL

Treasures

Key
- SI Strategic Intervention
- OL On-Level
- A Advanced
- ELL ELL

Great Ideas

Key
SI Strategic Intervention
OL On-Level
A Advanced
ELL ELL

Skills Overview

Key
T Tested Skill
◎ Target Skill

	WEEK 1	WEEK 2
	 **Sam, Come Back!** Realistic Fiction pp. 20–29 **"Puppy Games"** Sing-Along pp. 34–35	 **Pig in a Wig** Animal Fantasy pp. 46–57 **"We Are Vets"** Sing-Along pp. 62–63
Get Ready to Read		
Question of the Week	What do pets need?	Who helps animals?
Amazing Words	*needs, responsibility, shelter, cuddle, tickle, faithful, fetch, heel*	*career, service, tool, sloppy, scrub, exercise, comfort, search*
Phonemic Awareness	Distinguish Phonemes, Blend and Segment Phonemes	Count, Segment, and Blend Phonemes, Distinguish /i/
Phonics	T ◎ Short *a* T ◎ Consonant Pattern *-ck* Review Consonant Sounds	T ◎ Short *i* T ◎ Consonant *x* /ks/ Review Short *a*, Consonant Pattern *-ck*
Spelling	Short *a* Words	Short *i* Words
Read and Comprehend		
Comprehension	T ◎ **Skill** Character and Setting ◎ **Strategy** Monitor and Clarify Review **Skill** Plot	T ◎ **Skill** Plot ◎ **Strategy** Summarize Review **Skill** Character
High-Frequency Words	T *my, come, way, on, in*	T *she, take, what, up*
Vocabulary	Words for Location	Alphabetize
Fluency	Accuracy	Accuracy
Language Arts		
Writing	Story Trait: Voice	Fantasy Story Trait: Conventions
Conventions	T Sentences	T Subjects of Sentences
Speaking/Listening	Ask Questions	Share Information About Caring
Research Skills	Selecting Books	Media Center/Library Resources

The Big Question

How are people and animals important to one another?

WEEK 3	WEEK 4	WEEK 5	WEEK 6
The Big Blue Ox Animal Fantasy pp. 74–83 **They Can Help** Photo Essay pp. 88–91	**A Fox and a Kit** Literary Nonfiction pp. 102–111 **The Fox and the Grapes** Fable pp. 116–117	**Get the Egg!** Realistic Fiction pp. 128–137 **Help the Birds** How-to Article pp. 142–143	**Animal Park** Literary Nonfiction pp. 154–163 **Poetry Collection** Poetry pp. 168–169
How do animals help people?	How do wild animals take care of their babies?	Which wild animals live in our neighborhood?	What can we learn about wild animals by watching them?
past, present, produce, transportation, danger, serve, snuggle, enormous, powerful	*observe, wild, parent, canopy, screech, million, reserve, native*	*habitat, hatch, survive, chirp, croak, moist*	*world, forest, desert, chatter, silent, snort, medicine, poisonous*
Count, Segment, and Blend Phonemes	Blend and Segment Phonemes, Onset and Rime	Segment and Blend Phonemes	Segment and Blend Onset and Rime
T Short *o* T Plural *-s*, Consonant *s*/z/ Review Short *a*, *i*, and *o*, Consonant *x*	T Inflected Ending *-s* T Inflected Ending *-ing* Review Short *o*, Plural *-s*	T Short *e* T Initial Consonant Blends Review Inflected Endings *-s*, *-ing*	T Short *u* T Final Consonant Blends Review Short *e*, Initial Consonant Blends
Short *o* Words	Inflected Ending *-s*	Short *e* Words	Short *u* Words with Final Consonant Blends
T **Skill** Character and Setting **Strategy** Visualize Review **Skill** Plot	**Skill** Main Idea and Details **Strategy** Important Ideas Review **Skill** Realism and Fantasy	T **Skill** Main Idea and Details **Strategy** Story Structure Review **Skill** Character	T **Skill** Cause and Effect **Strategy** Text Structure Review **Skill** Main Idea and Details
T *blue, little, from, use, get, help*	T *eat, four, five, her, this, too*	T *saw, tree, your, small*	T *home, many, them, into*
Synonyms	Alphabetize	Sort Words	Antonyms
Appropriate Rate	Accuracy and Appropriate Rate	Appropriate Phrasing	Appropriate Phrasing
Short Poem Trait: Sentences	Personal Narrative Trait: Voice	Realistic Story Trait: Organization	Writing for Tests Brief Composition
T Predicates	T Declarative Sentences	T Interrogative Sentences	T Exclamatory Sentences
Give Introductions	Share Information and Ideas	Give Descriptions	Give Directions
Picture Dictionary	Read a Chart	Lists	Notes

Monitor Progress

Make Data-Driven Decisions

Data Management
- Assess
- Diagnose
- Prescribe
- Disaggregate

Classroom Management
- Monitor Progress
- Group
- Differentiate Instruction
- Inform Parents

Don't Wait Until Friday

SUCCESS PREDICTORS	WEEK 1	WEEK 2	WEEK 3	WEEK 4
Word Reading: **Phonics**	T Short *a* T Consonant Pattern *-ck*	T Short *i* T Consonant *x, /ks/*	T Short *o* T Plural *-s*, Consonant *s/z/*	T Inflected Ending *-s* T Inflected Ending *-ing*
WCPM: **Fluency**	Read with Accuracy	Read with Accuracy	Read with Appropriate Rate	Read with Accuracy and Appropriate Rate
Vocabulary: **High-Frequency Words**	T my T come T way T on T in	T she T take T what T up	T blue T little T from T use T get T help	T eat T four T five T her T this T too
Vocabulary: **Oral Vocabulary/ Concept Development** (assessed informally)	needs responsibility shelter cuddle tickle faithful fetch heel	career service tool sloppy scrub exercise comfort search	past present produce transportation danger serve snuggle enormous powerful	observe wild parent canopy screech million reserve native
Retelling: **Text Comprehension**	T **Skill** Character and Setting **Strategy** Monitor and Clarify	T **Skill** Plot **Strategy** Summarize	T **Skill** Character and Setting **Strategy** Visualize	T **Skill** Main Idea and Details **Strategy** Important Ideas

Key

T Tested Skill

(target icon) Target Skill

WEEK 5	WEEK 6
T (target) Short *e* T (target) Initial Consonant Blends	T (target) Short *u* T (target) Final Consonant Blends
Read with Appropriate Phrasing	Read with Appropriate Phrasing
T saw T tree T your T small	T home T many T them T into
habitat hatch survive chirp croak moist	world forest desert chatter silent snort medicine poisonous
T (target) **Skill** Main Idea and Details (target) **Strategy** Story Structure	T (target) **Skill** Cause and Effect (target) **Strategy** Text Structure

Online Classroom

Manage Data

- Assign the Unit 1 Benchmark Test for students to take online.
- Online Assessment records results and generates reports by school, grade, classroom, or student.
- Use reports to disaggregate and aggregate Unit 1 skills and standards data to monitor progress.
- Based on class lists created to support the categories important for AYP (gender, ethnicity, migrant education, English proficiency, disabilities, economic status), reports let you track adequate yearly progress every six weeks.

Select a Class: Reading 101
Make Assignments | View Reports and Logs
Assign Tests — Search by: Unit — GO!
Class Reports — View by: Standard — GO!
Assignment Log — View by: Entire Class — GO!
Other Resources and Information
Certificates Motivate your students with printable certificates.
The User's Guide and Quick Start Guide get you the help you need fast. Learn how to make the most of the Reading Success Tracker System with our simple to use guides.

Group

- Use results from Unit 1 Benchmark Tests taken online through Online Assessment to measure whether students have mastered the English-Language Arts Content Standards taught in this unit.
- Reports in Online Assessment suggest whether students need Extra Support or Intervention.

Individualized Instruction

- Tests are correlated to Unit 1 tested skills and standards so that prescriptions for individual teaching and learning plans can be created.
- Individualized prescriptions target instruction and accelerate student progress toward learning outcome goals.
- Prescriptions include remediation activities and resources to reteach Unit 1 skills and standards.

Assessment and Grouping

for Data-Driven Instruction

4-Step Plan for Assessment

1 Diagnose and Differentiate
2 Monitor Progress
3 Assess and Regroup
4 Summative Assessment

STEP 1 Diagnose and Differentiate

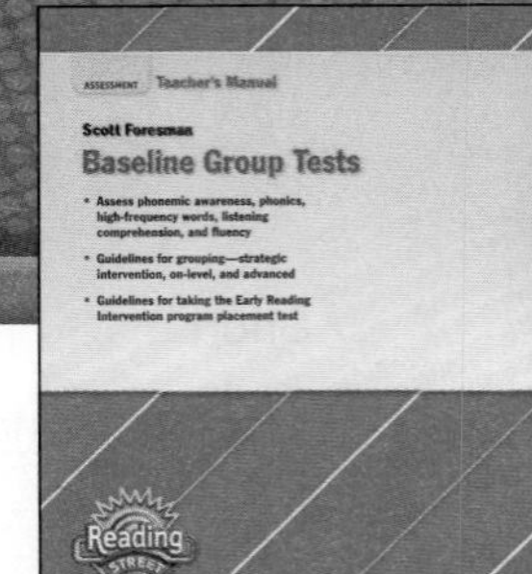

Baseline Group Tests

Diagnose

To make initial grouping decisions, use the Baseline Group Test, the Texas Primary Reading Inventory (TPRI), or another initial placement test. Depending on children's ability levels, you may have more than one of each group.

Differentiate

If... student performance is **SI** **then...** use the regular instruction and the daily **Strategic Intervention** small group lessons.

If... student performance is **OL** **then...** use the regular instruction and the daily **On-Level** small group lessons.

If... student performance is **A** **then...** use the regular instruction and the daily **Advanced** learners small group lessons.

Small Group Time

SI Strategic Intervention

- Daily small group lessons provide more intensive instruction, more scaffolding, more practice, and more opportunities to respond.
- Reteach lessons in the *First Stop on Reading Street* provide additional instructional opportunities with target skills.
- Leveled readers build background and provide practice for target skills and vocabulary.

OL On-Level

- Explicit instructional routines teach core skills and strategies.
- Daily On-Level lessons provide more practice and more opportunities to respond.
- Independent activities provide practice for core skills and extension and enrichment options.
- Leveled reader provides additional reading and practice for core skills and vocabulary.

A Advanced

- Daily Advanced lessons provide instruction for accelerated learning.
- Leveled reader provides additional reading tied to lesson concepts.

Additional Differentiated Learning Options

Reading Street Response to Intervention Kit

- Focused intervention lessons on the five critical areas of reading: phonemic awareness, phonics, vocabulary, comprehension, and fluency

My Sidewalks on Reading Street

- Intensive intervention for struggling readers

STEP 2 Monitor Progress

Use these tools during lesson teaching to **monitor student progress.**

- **Skill and Strategy** instruction during reading
- **Don't Wait Until Friday** boxes to check word reading, retelling, fluency, and oral vocabulary
- **Weekly Assessment** on Day 5 to check phonics and fluency
- **Reader's and Writer's Notebook** pages at point of use
- **Weekly Tests** to assess target skills for the week
- **Fresh Reads for Comprehension and Fluency**

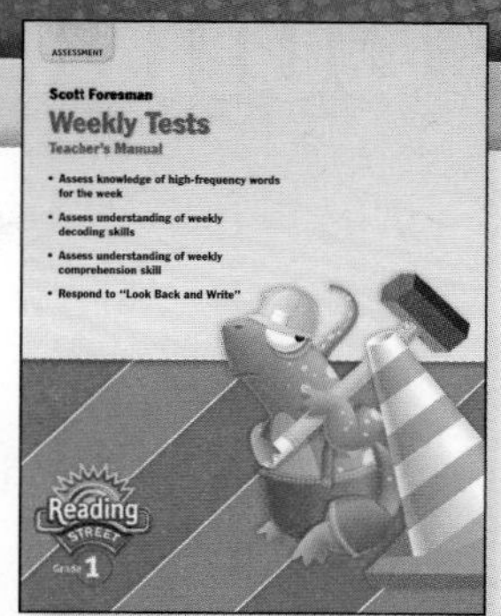

Weekly Tests

Fresh Reads for Fluency and Comprehension

STEP 3 Assess and Regroup

Use these tools during lesson teaching assess and regroup.

- **Weekly Assessments** Record results of weekly assessments in retelling, phonics, and fluency to track student progress.
- **Unit Benchmark Test** Administer this test to check mastery of unit skills.
- **Regroup** We recommend the first regrouping to be at the end of Unit 1. Use weekly assessment information and Unit Benchmark Test performance to inform regrouping decisions. Then regroup at the end of each subsequent unit.

First Stop on Reading Street Assessment Chart

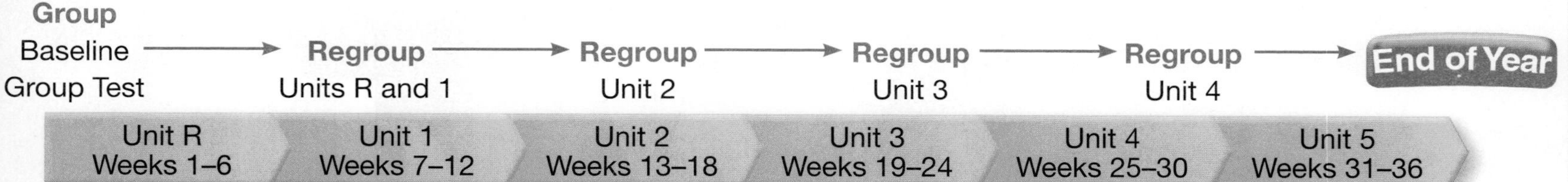

Outside assessments, such as DRA, TPRI, and DIBELS, may recommend regrouping at other times during the year.

STEP 4 Summative Assessment

Use these tools after lesson teaching to assess students.

- **Unit Benchmark Tests** Use to measure a student's mastery of unit skills.
- **End-of-Year Benchmark Test** Use to measure a student's mastery of program skills covered in all six units.

Unit and End-of-Year Benchmark Tests

Concept Launch

Understanding By Design

Grant Wiggins, Ed. D.
Reading Street Author

"We need to go beyond questions answerable by unit facts to questions that burst through the boundaries of the topic. Deep and transferable understandings depend upon framing work around such questions."

Animals, Tame and Wild

Reading Street Online

www.ReadingStreet.com

- Big Question Video
- eSelections
- Envision It! Animations
- Story Sort

How are people and animals important to one another?

Sam, Come Back! REALISTIC FICTION

What do pets need?

Paired Selection
Puppy Games SING-ALONG

Pig in a Wig ANIMAL FANTASY

Who helps animals?

Paired Selection
We Are Vets SING-ALONG

The Big Blue Ox ANIMAL FANTASY

How do animals help people?

Paired Selection
They Can Help PHOTO ESSAY

A Fox and a Kit LITERARY NONFICTION

How do wild animals take care of their babies?

Paired Selection
The Fox and the Grapes FABLE

Get the Egg! REALISTIC FICTION

Which wild animals live in our neighborhood?

Paired Selection
Help the Birds HOW-TO ARTICLE

Animal Park LITERARY NONFICTION

What can we learn about wild animals by watching them?

Paired Selection
"My Dog Rags," "Raccoon," "The Hippo" POETRY

Small Group Time

Flexible Pacing Plans

Small Group Time

Sometimes you have holidays, programs, assemblies, or other interruptions to the school week. This plan can help you make Small Group Time decisions if you have less time during the week.

Key

- SI Strategic Intervention
- OL On-Level
- A Advanced
- ELL ELL

A OL SI

5 Day Plan

DAY 1	• Phonemic Awareness • Phonics • Reading Practice
DAY 2	• Phonemic Awareness • Phonics • Reading Practice
DAY 3	• Phonics • Leveled Reader
DAY 4	• High-Frequency Words • Reading Practice
DAY 5	• Phonics • Comprehension

4 Day Plan

DAY 1	• Phonemic Awareness • Phonics • Reading Practice
DAY 2	• High-Frequency Words • Leveled Reader
DAY 3	• Phonics • Leveled Reader
DAY 4	• High-Frequency Words • Reading Practice

3 Day Plan

DAY 1	• Phonemic Awareness • Phonics • Reading Practice
DAY 2	• Phonics • Leveled Reader
DAY 3	• High-Frequency Words • Reading Practice

ELL

5 Day Plan

DAY 1	• Frontload Concept • Preteach Skills • Conventions and Writing
DAY 2	• Review Concept and Skills • Frontload and Read Main Selection • Conventions and Writing
DAY 3	• Review Concept and Skills • Reread Main Selection • Conventions and Writing
DAY 4	• Review Concept and Skills • Read ELL or ELD Reader • Conventions and Writing
DAY 5	• Review Concept and Skills • Read ELL or ELD Reader • Conventions and Writing

4 Day Plan

DAY 1	• Frontload Concept • Preteach Skills • Conventions and Writing
DAY 2	• Review Concept and Skills • Frontload and Read Main Selection • Conventions and Writing
DAY 3	• Review Concept and Skills • Reread Main Selection • Conventions and Writing
DAY 4	• Review Concept and Skills • Read ELL or ELD Reader • Conventions and Writing

3 Day Plan

DAY 1	• Frontload Concept • Preteach Skills • Conventions and Writing
DAY 2	• Review Concept and Skills • Frontload and Read Main Selection • Conventions and Writing
DAY 3	• Review Concept and Skills • Read ELL or ELD Reader • Conventions and Writing

Common Core Standards
Weekly Planning Guide

Grade 1 • Unit 1 • Week 4
A Fox and a Kit
94j–119k

Selection: A Fox and a Kit
Genre: Literary Nonfiction

Alignment of the Common Core Standards with This Week's Skills and Strategies

This Week's Common Core Standards for English Language Arts	Instructional Summary
Reading Standards for Informational Text	
Informational Text 1. Ask and answer questions about key details in a text. **Informational Text 2.** Identify the main topic and retell key details of a text. **Informational Text 4.** Ask and answer questions to help determine or clarify the meaning of words and phrases in a text.	In this lesson, children are introduced to the concept of **main idea.** Children learn that the main idea is what the story is mostly about. They also learn that **details** help them understand the main idea of a story. This comprehension strategy is called **important ideas.** Children are asked to think about the bigger ideas that the author wants us to know about.
Foundational Skills Standards	
Foundational Skills 3.f. Read words with inflectional endings. **Foundational Skills 4.b.** Read on-level text orally with accuracy, appropriate rate, and expression on successive readings.	This lesson presents the verb endings *-s* and *-ing.* Children are taught to add the endings to words. For the *-s* ending, they practice adding *s* to words such as *hop, dig,* and *sit.* For the *-ing* ending, they add the *ing* to words such as *pack, spill,* and *miss*. The foundational skill related to fluency is practiced as children read for **accuracy** and practice reading at an appropriate **rate.**
Writing Standards	
Writing 3. Write narratives in which they recount two or more appropriately sequenced events, include some details regarding what happened, use temporal words to signal event order, and provide some sense of closure. **Writing 5.** With guidance and support from adults, focus on a topic, respond to questions and suggestions from peers, and add details to strengthen writing as needed.	In this lesson, children write a **personal narrative.** Children learn that a personal narrative is a kind of story that tells about an event in their life. After drafting their narrative, they revise and proofread their writing.
Speaking and Listening Standards	
Speaking/Listening 1.a. Follow agreed-upon rules for discussions (e.g., listening to others with care, speaking one at a time about the topics and texts under discussion). **Speaking/Listening 6.** Produce complete sentences when appropriate to task and situation. (See grade 1 Language standards 1 and 3 on page 26 for specific expectations.)	Children **share information** and **ideas** about zoo animals. Before sharing, the lesson reviews how to be a good speaker and listener.
Language Standards	
Language 2. Demonstrate command of the conventions of standard English capitalization, punctuation, and spelling when writing. **Language 2.b.** Use end punctuation for sentences.	Children work with **declarative sentences.** They learn that a declarative sentence is a sentence that tells about something and it gives a fact or someone's point of view. The instruction includes the use of capital letters and punctuation marks.

Additional Support for a Common Core Standard This Week

Use the following instruction to supplement the teaching of one of this week's Common Core Standards.

Common Core Standard: **Informational Text 4.**
In each lesson, children are introduced to new words on page 101.

- Have children find the word *five* in the story. Ask them to tell how the word is represented on a clock.
- Continue with the words *eat, too, four, her,* and *this.* As each word is found and discussed, have children create new sentences using the word.

ISBN-13: 978-0-328-64366-0 ISBN-10: 0-328-64366-1

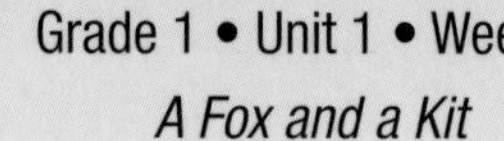

Grade 1 • Unit 1 • Week 4

A Fox and a Kit

Unit 1

How are people and animals important to one another?

Week 1

Sam, Come Back!

Question of the Week

What do pets need?

Concept Talk Guide children as they discuss questions such as:

- What do people do to take care of their pets?

Writing Think about a pet you know. Write a story about the pet playing.

connect to SOCIAL STUDIES

Week 2

Pig in a Wig

Question of the Week

Who helps animals?

Concept Talk Guide children as they discuss questions such as:

- What are some different ways that animals need our help?

Writing Write a fantasy story about a person who helps an animal. Draw a picture for your story.

connect to SOCIAL STUDIES

Week 3

The Big Blue Ox

Question of the Week

How do animals help people?

Concept Talk Guide children as they discuss questions such as:

- What are some ways farm animals help farmers?

Writing Think about a kind of animal you know. Write a two-line poem about that animal.

connect to SOCIAL STUDIES

Common Core Standards and Concept Development

- Introduce and explore this unit's weekly concepts through rich, structured conversations
- Develop complex content knowledge and vocabulary
- Expand on a single concept with engaging literature and nonfiction
- Build better readers in all content areas

Align instruction to **Common Core Anchor Standards**

Week 6

Animal Park

Question of the Week

What can we learn about wild animals by watching them?

Concept Talk Guide children as they discuss questions such as:

- What wild animals have you watched? What did you learn about the food it eats?

Writing Think about wild animals. Write a composition about what people learn by watching wild animals.

Week 5

Get the Egg!

Question of the Week

Which wild animals live in our neighborhood?

connect to SCIENCE

Concept Talk Guide children as they discuss questions such as:

- What are some wild animals you have seen in your neighborhood?

Writing Think about animals in neighborhoods. Write a realistic story about two friends seeing an animal.

You Are Here: Week 4

A Fox and a Kit

Question of the Week

How do wild animals take care of their babies?

As children answer this unit's Big Question and this week's Question of the Week, they will address:

Reading 2. Determine central ideas or themes of a text and analyze their development; summarize the key supporting details and ideas. **(Also Reading 1.)**

Concept Talk Guide children as they discuss questions such as:

- What do some animals do to protect their babies?

As children answer this week's Concept Talk question, they will address:

Speaking/Listening 1. Prepare for and participate effectively in a range of conversations and collaborations with diverse partners, building on others' ideas and expressing their own clearly and persuasively.

Writing Think about a time you watched some animals. Write a narrative about it.

As children write about this week's prompt, they will address:

Writing 3. Write narratives to develop real or imagined experiences or events using effective technique, well-chosen details, and well-structured event sequences. **(Also Writing 5.)**

connect to SCIENCE

Listening and Speaking On page 118, children learn to stay on topic when they speak. By doing so, they address:

Speaking/Listening 1. Prepare for and participate effectively in a range of conversations and collaborations with diverse partners, building on others' ideas and expressing their own clearly and persuasively. **(Also Speaking/Listening 6.)**

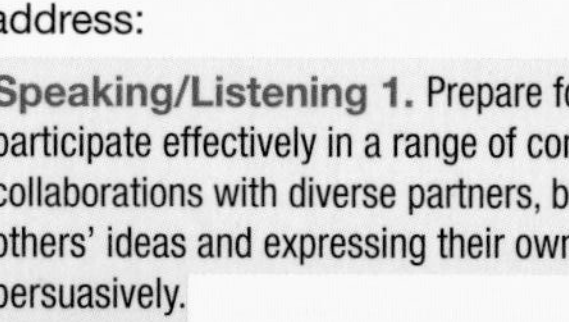

This Week's ELL Overview

Grade 1 • Unit 1 • Week 4
A Fox and a Kit
94a–119l
and DI•75–DI•84

ELL Handbook

- Maximize Literacy and Cognitive Engagement
- Research Into Practice
- Full Weekly Support for Every Selection

A Fox and a Kit
- Multi-Lingual Summaries in Five Languages
- Selection-Specific Vocabulary Word Cards
- Frontloading/Reteaching for Comprehension Skill Lessons
- ELD and ELL Reader Study Guides

- Transfer Activities
- Professional Development

Daily Leveled ELL Notes

ELL notes appear throughout this week's instruction and ELL Support is on the DI pages of your Teacher's Edition. The following is a sample of an ELL note from this week.

English Language Learners

Beginning Children can draw a scene, label the details, and share with a partner, possibly one who speaks the same home language.

Intermediate Have children describe a scene, then write phrases to label details in the scene. Have them describe the scene to other children.

Advanced Have children draw pictures or write short sentences in their story charts. As they share the plan with partners, children can clarify by adding details.

Advanced High Have children write sentences in their story charts. Using their story charts as a guide, have them tell the story events to a partner. Ask them to be sure the story has a beginning, middle, and end.

ELL by Strand

The ELL lessons on this week's Support for English Language Learners pages are organized by strand. They offer additional scaffolding for the core curriculum. Leveled support notes on these pages address the different proficiency levels in your class. See pages DI•75–DI•84.

The Three Pillars of ELL Instruction

ELL Strands	Activate Prior Knowledge	Access Content	Extend Language
Vocabulary p. DI•79	Preteach	Teach/Model	Practice
Reading Comprehension p. DI•80	Preteach	Reteach/Practice	Leveled Practice Activities
Phonics, Spelling, and Word Analysis pp. DI•76–DI•77	Preteach	Listen and Write	Leveled Practice Activities
Listening Comprehension p. DI•78	Prepare for the Read Aloud	First Listening	Second Listening
Conventions and Writing pp. DI•83–DI•84	Preteach/Introduce Terms	Practice/Model	Leveled Practice Activities/ Leveled Writing Activities
Concept Development p. DI•75	Activate Prior Knowledge	Develop Concepts	Review Concepts and Connect to Writing

This Week's Practice Stations Overview

Grade 1 • Unit 1 • Week 4
A Fox and a Kit
94a–119l

Six Weekly Practice Stations with Leveled Activities can be found at the beginning of each week of instruction. For this week's Practice Stations, see pp. 94h–94i.

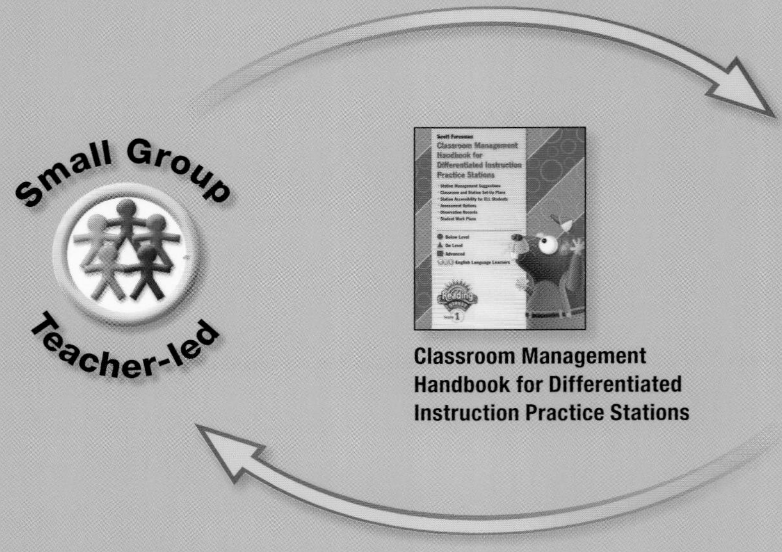

Classroom Management Handbook for Differentiated Instruction Practice Stations

Practice Stations

Daily Leveled Center Activities

Below | Advanced | On-Level | 

Practice Stations Flip Charts

	 **Listen Up**	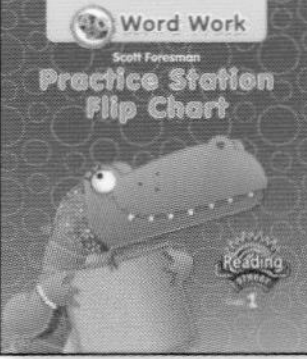 **Word Work**	 **Words to Know**	 **Let's Write**	 **Read for Meaning**	 **Get Fluent**
Objectives	• Identify words with initial and medial sound /o/. • Add final /z/ to spoken words.	• Identify and read words with short *o*. • Identify and read words with *-s* plurals.	• Identify high-frequency words *help, use, from, little, blue, get.* • Write high-frequency words.	• Write complete sentences. • Identify predicates of sentences.	• Identify the characters in a story. • Identify the actions of a character in a story.	• Read aloud at an appropriate rate.
Materials	• *Listen Up* Flip Chart Activity 4 • Picture Cards *block, box, fox, octopus, ox, sock, fan, mug, web*	• *Word Work* Flip Chart Activity 4 • teacher-made Word Cards • T-charts • pencils	• *Words to Know* Flip Chart Activity 4 • High-Frequency Word Cards for Unit 1, Week 3 • paper • pencils • crayons	• *Let's Write* Flip Chart Activity 4 • paper • pencils	• *Read for Meaning* Flip Chart Activity 4 • Leveled Readers • paper • pencils • crayons	• *Get Fluent* Flip Chart Activity 4 • Leveled Readers

This Week on Reading Street!

Animals, Tame and Wild

Question of the Week

How do wild animals take care of their babies?

Daily Plan

Whole Group

- Inflected Ending *-s*
- Inflected Ending *-ing*
- Main Idea and Details
- Fluency
- Vocabulary

Don't Wait Until Friday

MONITOR PROGRESS **Success Predictor**

Day 1	Day 2	Day 3	Day 4	Day 5
Check Word Reading	Check Word Reading	Check High-Frequency Words/Retelling	Check Fluency	Check Oral Vocabulary

Small Group

Teacher-Led

- Reading Support
- Skill Support
- Fluency Practice

Practice Stations

Independent Activities

Customize Literacy More support for a Balanced Literacy approach, see CL•1–CL•47.

Customize Writing More support for a customized writing approach, see CW•11–CW•20.

Whole Group

- Writing: Personal Narrative
- Conventions: Declarative Sentences

Assessment

- Weekly Tests
- Day 5 Assessment
- Fresh Reads

This Week's Reading Selections

Main Selection
Genre: **Literary Nonfiction**

Paired Selection

Decodable Practice Readers

Leveled Readers

ELL and ELD Readers

Resources on Reading Street!

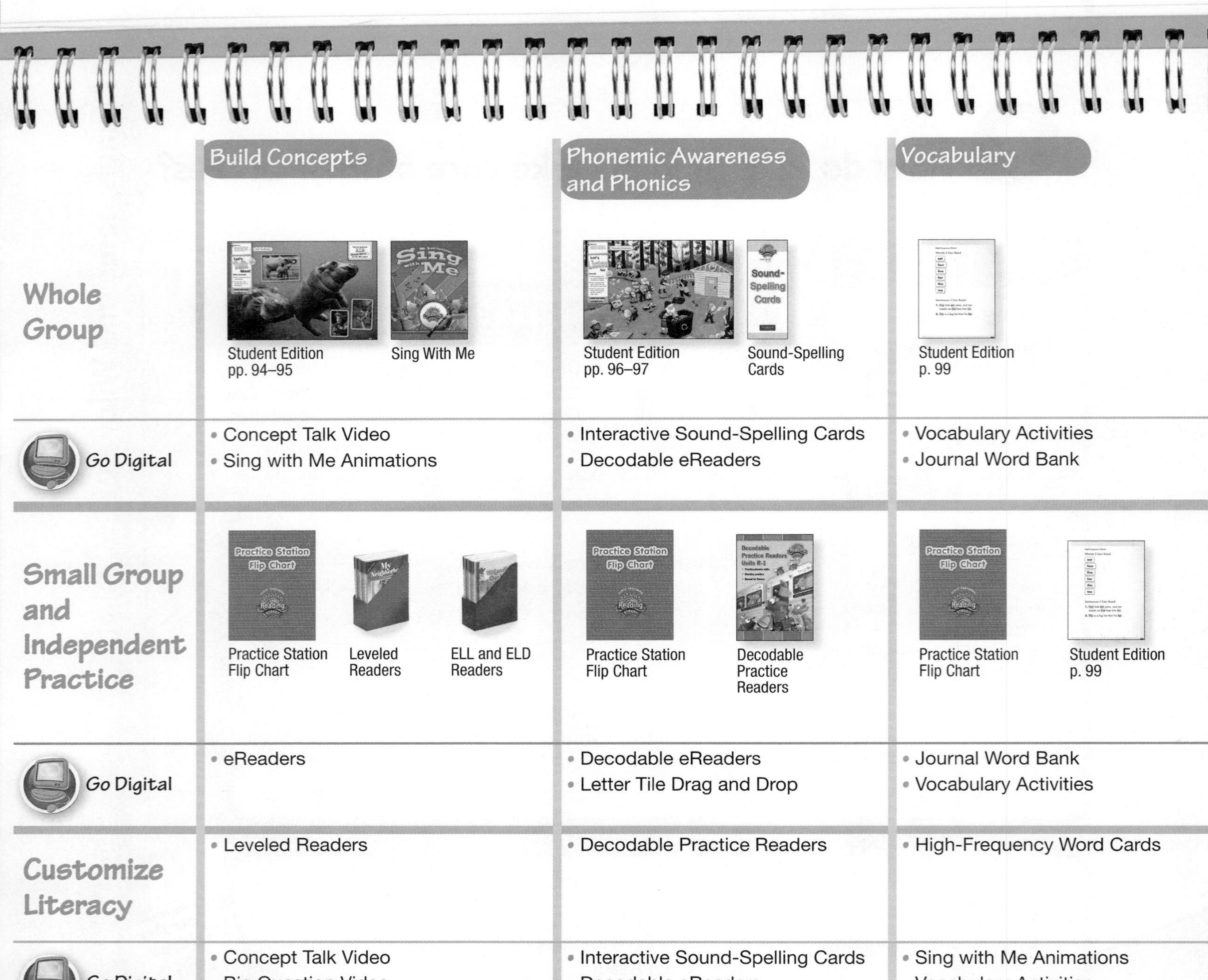

	Build Concepts	Phonemic Awareness and Phonics	Vocabulary
Whole Group	Student Edition pp. 94–95 Sing With Me	Student Edition pp. 96–97 Sound-Spelling Cards	Student Edition p. 99
Go Digital	• Concept Talk Video • Sing with Me Animations	• Interactive Sound-Spelling Cards • Decodable eReaders	• Vocabulary Activities • Journal Word Bank
Small Group and Independent Practice	Practice Station Flip Chart Leveled Readers ELL and ELD Readers	Practice Station Flip Chart Decodable Practice Readers	Practice Station Flip Chart Student Edition p. 99
Go Digital	• eReaders	• Decodable eReaders • Letter Tile Drag and Drop	• Journal Word Bank • Vocabulary Activities
Customize Literacy	• Leveled Readers	• Decodable Practice Readers	• High-Frequency Word Cards
Go Digital	• Concept Talk Video • Big Question Video • eReaders	• Interactive Sound-Spelling Cards • Decodable eReaders	• Sing with Me Animations • Vocabulary Activities

Question of the Week

How do wild animals take care of their babies?

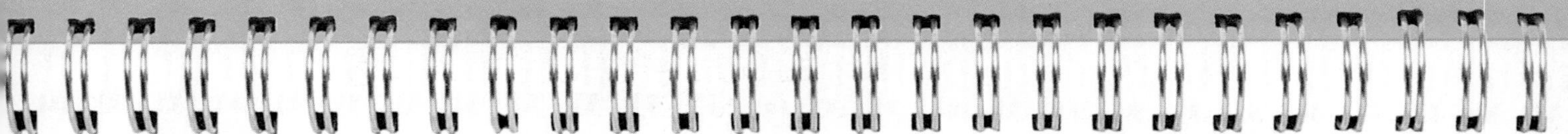

Comprehension	Fluency	Conventions and Writing
 Student Edition pp. 102–111	 Decodable Practice Readers	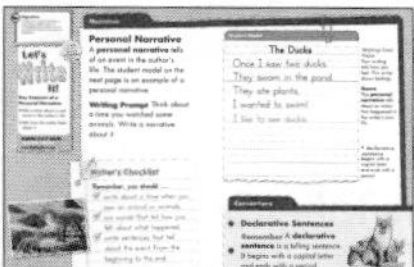 Student Edition pp. 114–115
• Envision It! Animations • eSelections	• eSelections • eReaders	• Grammar Jammer
 Practice Station Flip Chart  Leveled Readers  ELL and ELD Readers	 Practice Station Flip Chart  Decodable Practice Readers	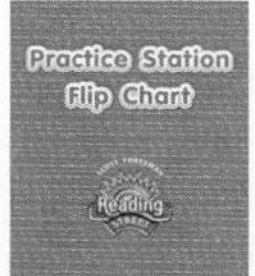 Practice Station Flip Chart  Reader's and Writer's Notebook
• eReaders • Story Sort	• Decodable eReaders	• Grammar Jammer
• Envision It! Skills and Strategies Handbooks • Leveled Readers	• Leveled Readers	• Reader's and Writer's Notebook
• Envision It! Animations • eReaders	• eReaders	• Grammar Jammer

Week 4

My 5-Day Planner for Reading Street!

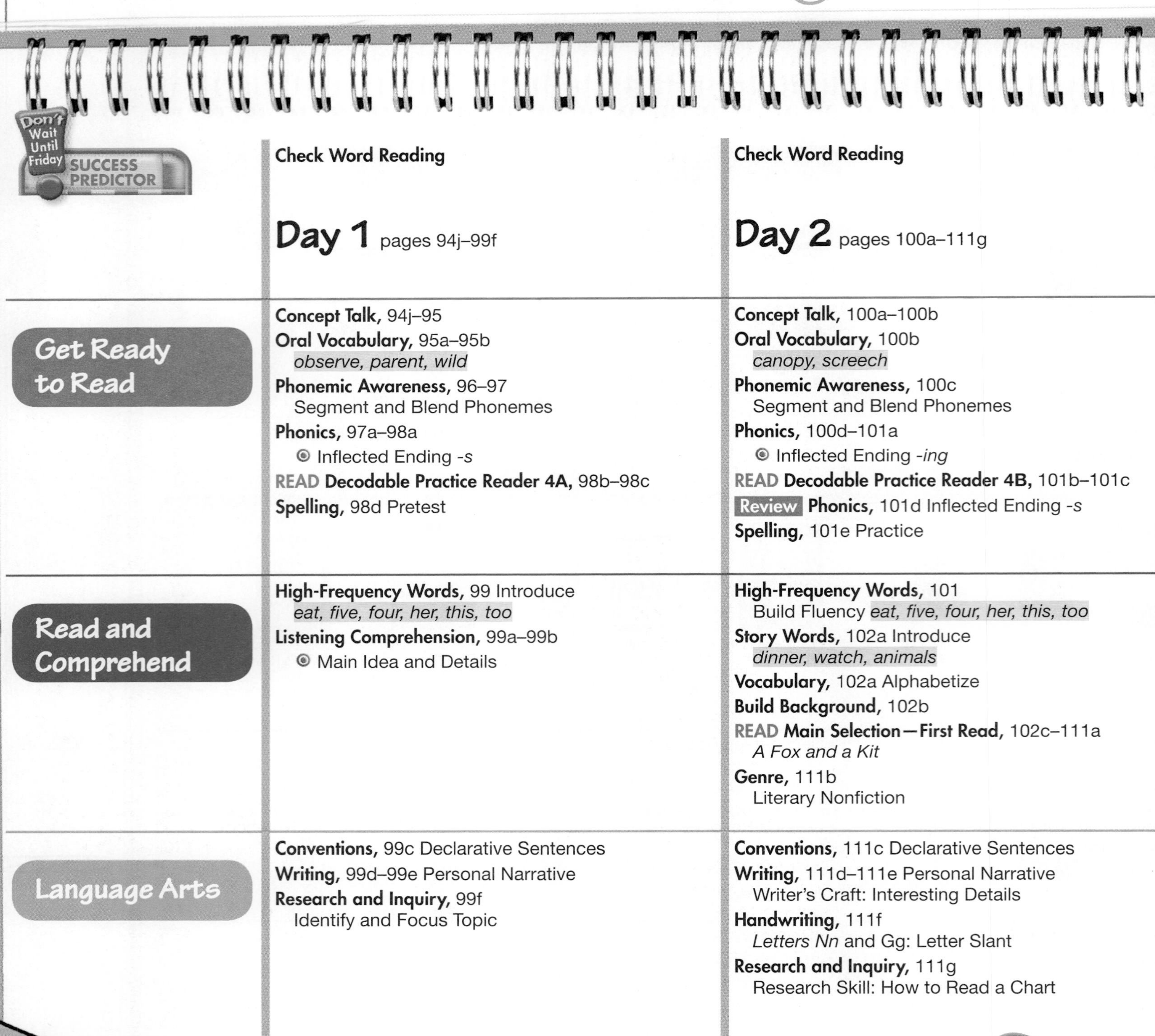

Don't Wait Until Friday SUCCESS PREDICTOR	Check Word Reading **Day 1** pages 94j–99f	Check Word Reading **Day 2** pages 100a–111g
Get Ready to Read	**Concept Talk,** 94j–95 **Oral Vocabulary,** 95a–95b *observe, parent, wild* **Phonemic Awareness,** 96–97 Segment and Blend Phonemes **Phonics,** 97a–98a ◎ Inflected Ending *-s* READ **Decodable Practice Reader 4A,** 98b–98c **Spelling,** 98d Pretest	**Concept Talk,** 100a–100b **Oral Vocabulary,** 100b *canopy, screech* **Phonemic Awareness,** 100c Segment and Blend Phonemes **Phonics,** 100d–101a ◎ Inflected Ending *-ing* READ **Decodable Practice Reader 4B,** 101b–101c Review **Phonics,** 101d Inflected Ending *-s* **Spelling,** 101e Practice
Read and Comprehend	**High-Frequency Words,** 99 Introduce *eat, five, four, her, this, too* **Listening Comprehension,** 99a–99b ◎ Main Idea and Details	**High-Frequency Words,** 101 Build Fluency *eat, five, four, her, this, too* **Story Words,** 102a Introduce *dinner, watch, animals* **Vocabulary,** 102a Alphabetize **Build Background,** 102b READ **Main Selection—First Read,** 102c–111a *A Fox and a Kit* **Genre,** 111b Literary Nonfiction
Language Arts	**Conventions,** 99c Declarative Sentences **Writing,** 99d–99e Personal Narrative **Research and Inquiry,** 99f Identify and Focus Topic	**Conventions,** 111c Declarative Sentences **Writing,** 111d–111e Personal Narrative Writer's Craft: Interesting Details **Handwriting,** 111f *Letters Nn* and *Gg*: Letter Slant **Research and Inquiry,** 111g Research Skill: How to Read a Chart

Question of the Week
How do wild animals take care of their babies?

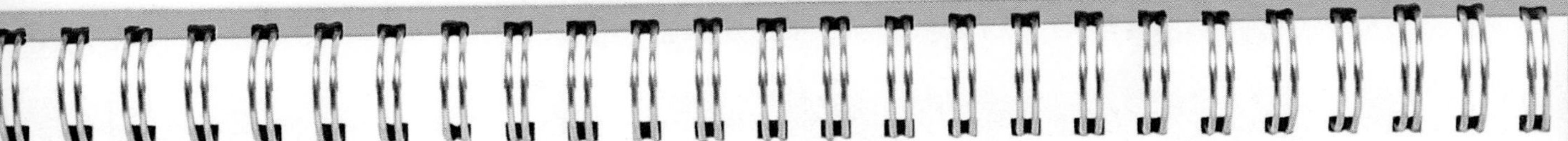

Check High-Frequency Words Check Retelling **Day 3** pages 112a–115c	Check Fluency **Day 4** pages 116a–117f	Check Oral Vocabulary **Day 5** pages 118a–119k
Concept Talk, 112a–112b **Oral Vocabulary,** 112b *million* **Phonological Awareness,** 112c Count Syllables **Phonics,** 112d–112e ◎ Inflected Ending *-s* ◎ Inflected Ending *-ing* **Spelling,** 112f Dictation	**Concept Talk,** 116a–116b **Oral Vocabulary,** 116b *reserve, native* **Phonological Awareness,** 116c Segment and Blend Onset and Rime Review **Phonics,** 116d Short *o* Spelled *o; -s* Plurals READ **Decodable Practice Reader 4C,** 116e–116f **Spelling,** 116h Partner Review	**Concept Wrap Up,** 118a Review **Oral Vocabulary,** 118b **Phonological Awareness,** 118c Segment and Blend Onset and Rime Review **Phonics,** 118c ◎ Inflected Ending *-s* ◎ Inflected Ending *-ing* **Spelling,** 118d Test
Review **High-Frequency Words,** 112g *eat, five, four, her, this, too* Review **Story Words,** 112g *animals, dinner, watch* READ **Main Selection—Second Read,** 102–111, 112h–113a **Fluency,** 113b Accuracy and Appropriate Rate	**Science in Reading,** 116i READ **Paired Selection,** 116–117a "The Fox and the Grapes" **Fluency,** 117b Accuracy and Appropriate Rate	**Listening and Speaking,** 118–119 Share Information and Ideas **Fluency,** 119a Accuracy and Rate Review **Comprehension,** 119b ◎ Main Idea and Details Review **Vocabulary,** 119b High Frequency and Story Words **Genre,** 119c Fable **Assessment,** 119d–119f Monitor Progress
Conventions, 114a–115a Declarative Sentences **Writing,** 114–115a Personal Narrative Writing Trait: Voice **Listening and Speaking,** 115b Share Information and Ideas **Research and Inquiry,** 115c Gather and Record Information	**Conventions,** 117c Declarative Sentences **Writing,** 117d–117e Personal Narrative Revising Strategy **Research and Inquiry,** 117f Review and Revise Topic	Review **Conventions,** 119g Declarative Sentences **Writing,** 119h–119i Personal Narrative Writer's Craft: Declarative Sentences **Research and Inquiry,** 119j **Wrap Up Your Week,** 119k How do wild animals take care of their babies?

Week 4

Grouping Options for Differentiated Instruction
Turn the page for the small group time lesson plan.

Planning Small Group Time on Reading Street!

SMALL GROUP TIME RESOURCES

Look for this Small Group Time box each day to help meet the individual needs of all your children. Differentiated Instruction lessons appear on the DI pages at the end of each week.

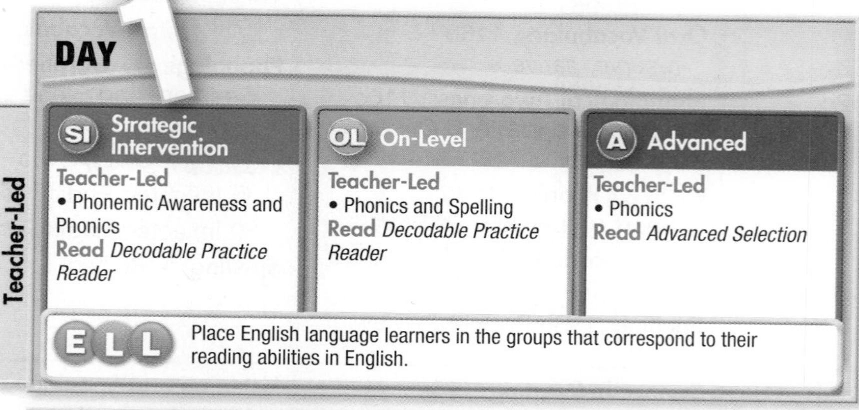

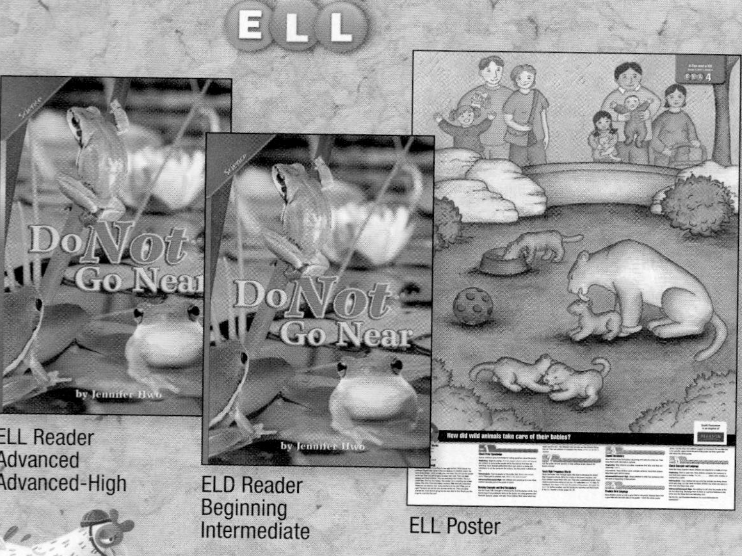

ELL Reader Advanced Advanced-High

ELD Reader Beginning Intermediate

ELL Poster

	Day 1
SI Strategic Intervention	Phonemic Awareness and Phonics, DI•64 Read Decodable Practice Reader 4A, DI•64
OL On-Level	Phonics and Spelling, DI•69 Read Decodable Practice Reader, DI•69
A Advanced	Phonics, DI•72 Read Advanced Selection, DI•72
ELL English Language Learners	DI•75–DI•84 Frontload Concept Practice Skills Writing

You Are Here! Unit 1 Week 4

Reading Street Response to Intervention Kit

Reading Street Leveled Practice Stations Kit

Question of the Week

How do wild animals take care of their babies?

Below-Level Reader

Decodable Practice Readers

Concept Literacy Reader

On-Level Reader

Advanced Reader

Advanced Selection

Small Group Weekly Plan

Day 2	Day 3	Day 4	Day 5
Phonemic Awareness and Phonics, DI•65 Read **Decodable Practice Reader 4B,** DI•65	**Phonemic Awareness and Phonics,** DI•66 Read **Concept Literacy Leveled Reader,** DI•66	**High-Frequency Words,** DI•67 Read **Decodable Practice Reader 4C,** DI•67	**Phonics Review,** DI•68 Read **Below-Level Leveled Reader,** DI•68
Phonics and High-Frequency Words, DI•69 Read **Decodable Practice Reader 4B,** DI•69	Read **On-Level Leveled Reader,** DI•70	**Conventions,** DI•71 Reread **Main Selection,** DI•71	**Phonics Review,** DI•71 Reread **On-Level Leveled Reader,** DI•71
Phonics and Comprehension, DI•72 Read **Main Selection,** DI•72	Read **Advanced Leveled Reader,** DI•73	**Comprehension,** DI•74 Read **Paired Selection,** DI•74 Reread **Leveled Reader,** DI•74	**Fluency and Comprehension,** DI•74 Reread **Advanced Selection,** DI•74
DI•75–DI•84 **Review Concept** **Practice Skills** **Frontload Main Selection** **Writing**	DI•75–DI•84 **Review Concept** **Practice Skills** **Reread Main Selection** **Writing**	DI•75–DI•84 **Review Concept** **Practice Skills** **Read ELL or ELD Reader** **Writing**	DI•75–DI•84 **Review Concept** **Review Skills** **Writing**

Practice Stations for Everyone on Reading Street!

Listen Up!
Match sounds and pictures.

Objectives
- Identify words with initial and medial sound /o/.
- Add final /z/ to spoken words.

Materials
- *Listen Up!* Flip Chart Activity 4
- Picture Cards *block, box, fox, octopus, ox, sock, fan, mug, web*

Differentiated Activities
● Find Picture Cards that have the same beginning sound as *odd.* Find Picture Cards that have the same middle sound as *chop.* Now look at the last three Picture Cards. Say each word, and then add the sound /z/ to each one. What words did you say?

▲ Find Picture Cards that have the same beginning sound as *odd.* Find Picture Cards that have the same middle sound as *chop.* Now look at the last three Picture Cards. Say each word, and then say the word in its plural form. What sound did you add?

■ Look at the Picture Cards. Say the plural of each word, and then place the words whose plurals end with the same ending sound as *drums* in one pile. Place Picture Cards that have the same beginning sound as *odd* in another pile. Place Picture Cards that have the same middle sound as *chop* in another pile.

Technology
- Interactive Sound-Spelling Cards

Word Work
Recognize short *o* and *-s* plurals.

Objectives
- Identify and read words with short *o*.
- Identify and read words with *-s* plurals.

Materials
- *Word Work* Flip Chart Activity 4
- Teacher-made word cards
- T-charts
- pencils

Differentiated Activities
● Pick a card and read the word. If the word has a short *o,* write it on your T-chart in the "Short *o*" column. If it does not have a short *o,* write it in the other column. Repeat the activity for words that are *-s* plurals and words that are not.

▲ Pick a card and read the word. If the word has a short *o,* write it on your T-chart in the "Short *o*" column. If it does not have a short *o,* write it in the other column. Then add your own words to the columns. Repeat the activity for words that are *-s* plurals and words that are not.

■ Pick a card and read the word. If the word has a short *o,* write it on your T-chart in the "Short *o*" column. If it does not have a short *o,* write it in the other column. Repeat the activity for words that are *-s* plurals and words that are not. Write sentences using the words in your charts.

Technology
- Interactive Sound-Spelling Cards

Words To Know
Identify high-frequency words.

Objectives
- Identify high-frequency words *help, use, from, little, blue, get*
- Write high-frequency words.

Materials
- *Words to Know* Flip Chart Activity 4
- High-Frequency Word Cards for Unit 1, Week 3
- paper
- pencils
- crayons

Differentiated Activities
● Use the Word Cards. Write them on your paper. Draw pictures for some of the words.

▲ Use the Word Cards. Write them on your paper. Use two of the words in a sentence. Draw pictures for some of the words.

■ Use the Word Cards. Write sentences using the words, and then draw pictures that describe the sentences.

Technology
- Online Tested Vocabulary Activities

Use this week's materials from the Reading Street Leveled Practice Stations Kit to organize this week's stations.

Key

- ● Below-Level Activities
- ▲ On-Level Activities
- ■ Advanced Activities

Practice Station Flip Chart

Let's Write

Write sentences.

Objectives

- Write complete sentences.
- Identify predicates of sentences.

Materials

- *Let's Write!* Flip Chart Activity 4
- paper
- pencils

Differentiated Activities

- A sentence begins with a capital letter.
- A sentence ends with a period.
- The predicate of a sentence tells what a person or thing does.

● Write a sentence about how an animal might help someone. Start your sentence with a capital letter. End it with a period. Circle the predicate of the sentence.

▲ Write two sentences about how an animal might help someone. Start your sentences with a capital letters. End them with periods. Circle the predicates of the sentences.

■ Write a story about how an animal might help someone. Start your sentences with capital letters. End them with periods. Circle the predicates of the sentences.

Read For Meaning

Identify character.

Objectives

- Identify the characters in a story.
- Identify the actions of a character in a story.

Materials

- *Read for Meaning* Flip Chart Activity 4
- Leveled Readers
- paper
- pencils
- crayons

Differentiated Activities

A **character** is a person or animal in a story.

● Read *On the Farm.* Tell who the characters are. Draw a picture a character and write his or her name.

▲ Read *Where They Live.* Tell who the characters are. Draw a picture of a character and write some words that describe him or her.

■ Read *Loni's Town.* Tell who the characters are. Draw a picture of the characters and write what each character does.

Technology

- Leveled eReaders

Get Fluent

Practice fluent reading.

Objective

- Read aloud at an appropriate rate.

Materials

- *Get Fluent* Flip Chart Activity 4
- Leveled Readers

Differentiated Activities

● Work with a partner. Take turns reading pages from *On the Farm.* Think about what you're reading about. Be sure to read at an appropriate rate. Give your partner feedback.

▲ Work with a partner. Take turns reading pages from *Where They Live.* Think about what you're reading about. Be sure to read at an appropriate rate. Give your partner feedback.

■ Work with a partner. Take turns reading pages from *Loni's Town.* Think about what you're reading about. Be sure to read at an appropriate rate. Give your partner feedback.

Technology

- Reading Street Readers CD-ROM

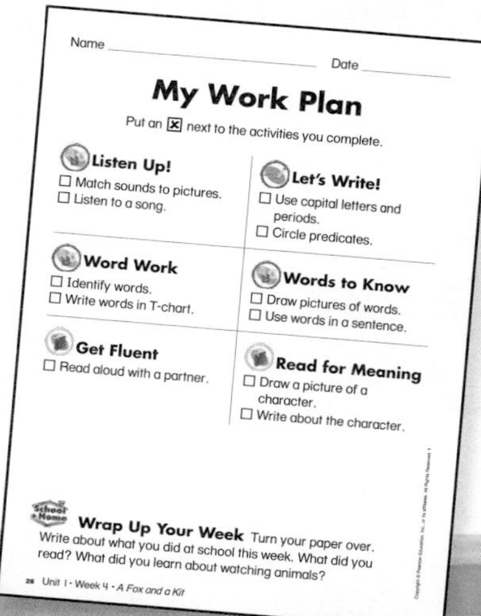

Name ____________ Date ________

My Work Plan

Put an ☒ next to the activities you complete.

Listen Up!
- ☐ Match sounds to pictures.
- ☐ Listen to a song.

Let's Write!
- ☐ Use capital letters and periods.
- ☐ Circle predicates.

Word Work
- ☐ Identify words.
- ☐ Write words in T-chart.

Words to Know
- ☐ Draw pictures of words.
- ☐ Use words in a sentence.

Get Fluent
- ☐ Read aloud with a partner.

Read for Meaning
- ☐ Draw a picture of a character.
- ☐ Write about the character.

Wrap Up Your Week Turn your paper over. Write about what you did at school this week. What did you read? What did you learn about watching animals?

Unit 1 • Week 4 • A Fox and a Kit

My Weekly Work Plan

Week 4

Objectives

- Introduce concepts: wild animals taking care of their babies.
- Share information and ideas about the concept.

Today at a Glance

Oral Vocabulary
observe, wild, parent

Phonemic Awareness
Segment and Blend Phonemes

Phonics and Spelling
◎ Inflected Ending *-s*

Fluency
Oral Rereading

High-Frequency Words
eat, five, four, her, this, too

Comprehension
◎ Main Idea and Details

Conventions
Declarative Sentences

Writing
Personal Narrative: Introduce

Research and Inquiry
Identify and Focus Topic

Concept Talk

Question of the Week

How do wild animals take care of their babies?

Introduce the concept To build concepts and focus children's attention, tell them that this week they will talk, sing, read, and write about wild animals and their babies. Write the Question of the Week and track the print as you read it.

ROUTINE Activate Prior Knowledge **Team Talk**

1. **Think** Have children think for a minute about what they know about wild animals and their babies.
2. **Pair** Have pairs of children discuss the question.
3. **Share** Have children share information and their ideas with the group. Remind them to ask questions to clarify information. Guide discussion and encourage elaboration with prompts such as: What do some animals do to protect their babies?

Routines Flip Chart

Anchored Talk

Develop oral language Have children turn to pages 94–95 in their Student Editions. Read the title and look at the photos. Use these questions to guide discussion and create the "How do wild animals take care of their babies?" concept map (shown on the next page).

- What is the mother chimpanzee doing? (Possible response: She is holding her baby.) Let's add *They hold them* to our map.
- How is the mother hippo helping its baby? (Possible response: She is helping her baby to swim.) Let's add *They teach them new things* to our map.

Amazing Words

You've learned 0 7 2 words so far.

You'll learn 0 0 8 words this week!

observe	screech
wild	million
parent	native
canopy	reserve

Objectives
• Listen closely to speakers and ask questions to help you better understand the topic. • Share information and ideas about the topic. Speak at the correct pace.
Oral Vocabulary
Let's Talk About
Read Together
Wild Animals
• Share information about wild animals.
• Discuss how wild animals take care of their babies.
READING STREET ONLINE
CONCEPT TALK VIDEO
www.ReadingStreet.com
You've learned
0 7 2
Amazing Words
so far this year!
94
95

Student Edition pp. 94–95

Connect to reading Explain that this week, children will read about how a mother fox takes care of its baby. Let's add *They bring them food* to our map.

Writing on Demand

Develop Writing Fluency Ask children to write about what they know about wild animals. Have them write for two to three minutes. Children should write as much as they can. Tell them to try to do their best writing. You may want to discuss what children wrote during writing conferences.

ELL

English Language Learners

Listening Comprehension English learners will benefit from additional visual support to help them understand the key terms in the concept map. Use the pictures on pages 94–95 to scaffold understanding. For example, when talking about how animals take care of their babies, point to the photo of the mother hippo teaching her baby to swim.

Support Additional ELL support and modified instruction are provided in the *ELL Handbook* and in the ELL Support Lessons.

ELL Preteach Concepts Use the Day 1 instruction on ELL Poster 4 to assess and build background knowledge, develop concepts, and build oral vocabulary.

ELL Poster 4

Objectives

- Build oral vocabulary.
- Discuss the concept to develop oral language.
- Share information and ideas about the concept.

Oral Vocabulary

Amazing Words

Introduce Amazing Words

Display page 4 of the *Sing with Me* Big Book. Tell children they are going to sing about a mother and baby squirrel. Ask children to listen for the Amazing Words *observe*, *wild*, and *parent* as you sing. Sing the song again and have children join you.

Sing with Me Big Book Audio

Sing with Me Big Book, p. 4

Teach Amazing Words

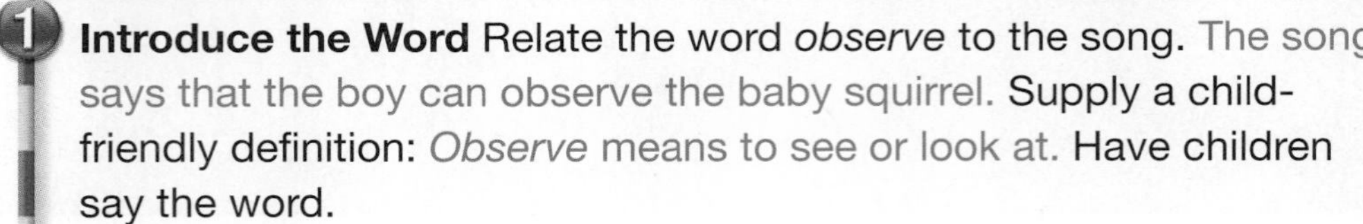

Amazing Words Oral Vocabulary Routine

1. **Introduce the Word** Relate the word *observe* to the song. The song says that the boy can observe the baby squirrel. Supply a child-friendly definition: *Observe* means to see or look at. Have children say the word.
2. **Demonstrate** Provide examples to show meaning: The boy can *observe* the baby squirrel on the ground. You can *observe* your classmates playing a game. Another teacher can *observe* this class.
3. **Apply** Have children demonstrate their understanding: Tell about something you can observe.

See p. OV•1 to teach *wild* and *parent*.

Routines Flip Chart

Check understanding of Amazing Words

Have children look at the picture on page 4. In the song, the boy says he observes the squirrel to learn what *wild* squirrels do. What are some things *wild* squirrels do? Use *wild* in your answer. (Possible response: Wild squirrels climb trees.)

It is exciting to *observe* something you haven't seen before. What is something you would like to *observe*? Use *observe* in your answer. (Possible response: I would like to observe a soccer match.)

What is something a *parent* might help a child learn? Use *parent* in your answer. (Possible response: A parent can help me learn to ride a bike.)

Apply Amazing Words

Have children demonstrate their understanding of the Amazing Words by completing these sentences orally.

I would like to **observe** a ________.

An example of a **wild** animal is ________.

A **parent** can help me learn ________.

Corrective feedback

If… children have difficulty using the Amazing Words,
then… remind them of the definitions and provide opportunities for children to use the words in sentences.

Preteach Academic Vocabulary

Write the following on the board:

- main idea and details
- literary nonfiction
- declarative sentences

Have children share what they know about this week's Academic Vocabulary. Use children's responses to assess their prior knowledge. Preteach the Academic Vocabulary by providing a child-friendly description, explanation, or example that clarifies the meaning of each term. Then ask children to restate the meaning of the Academic Vocabulary in their own words.

Amazing Words

observe	screech
wild	million
parent	native
canopy	reserve

ELL

English Language Learners

Pronunciation Speakers of many languages have trouble pronouncing the initial /r/ sound as in *reserve*. Have children practice the sound alone. Then have children practice words that begin with the initial /r/ sound.

Cognates The words *observe*, *million*, *native*, and *reserve* may have cognates in children's home languages. Invite Spanish speakers to identify cognates *observar* and *millón*. Point out how this prior knowledge can help children with learning new words.

Objectives

- Segment and blend verbs ending in *-s.*
- ◎ Associate the consonant sounds /s/ and /z/ with the spelling *s.*

Skills Trace

◎ **Inflected Ending *-s***
Introduce U1W4D1
Practice U1W4D3; U1W4D4
Reteach/Review U1W4D5; U1W5D4
Assess/Test Weekly Test U1W4
Benchmark Test U1

KEY:
U=Unit W=Week D=Day

Student Edition pp. 96–97

Phonemic Awareness
Segment and Blend Phonemes

Introduce Have children look at the picture on pages 96–97 of the Student Edition. Point out the two little frogs. A frog jumps up. The last sound I hear in *jumps* is /s/. Have children look at the picture to identify other actions that end with the /s/ sound. (dumps, eats, walks, looks) Point out the man on one knee. I can also see a man mending a fence. A man *mends* a fence. The last sound I hear in *mends* is /z/. Again, have children look at the picture, but this time have them identify actions that contain the /z/ sound. (sends, bends, stands, feeds)

Model Listen to the sounds in the word *jumps*: /j/ /u/ /m/ /p/ /s/. There are five sounds in *jumps*. Let's blend those sounds to make a word: /j/ /u/ /m/ /p/ /s/. Continue modeling with *mends*.

Guide practice Guide children as they segment and blend these words from the picture: dumps, eats, stands, feeds, looks, sends, bends.

Corrective feedback **If...** children make an error,
then... model by segmenting the word, and have them repeat the segmenting and blending of the word.

Phonics — Teach/Model
Inflected Ending -s

Sound-Spelling Card 129

ROUTINE Blending Strategy

1. **Connect** Write the words *cats* and *birds*. What do you know about the last sound of these words? (The sound /s/ is spelled *s* at the end of *cats*. The sound /z/ is spelled *s* at the end of *birds*. The *s* makes the words mean "more than one.") Explain that today they will learn more about words with the ending -*s* that don't mean "more than one."
2. **Use Sound-Spelling Cards** Display Card 129. Point to the word *pulls*. We add *s* to *pull* to show that one person is doing something. The *s* has the sound /z/ for this word. Have children say *pulls* with you several times.
3. **Model** Write *hops*. In this word, the letter *s* stands for the sound /s/. Segment and blend *hops*; then have children blend with you: /h/ /o/ /p/ /s/. Follow this procedure to model *digs*.
4. **Guide Practice** Continue the process in step 3. This time have children blend with you. Remind children that *s* can stand for the sound /s/ or the sound /z/.

wags	**sips**	**sees**	**packs**	**gets**	**nods**
fits	**yaps**	**picks**	**digs**	**licks**	**fills**

5. **Review** What do you know about reading these words? (When you see a word that ends with -*s*, you know it might be a base word with an -*s* ending. Look for the base word. The letter *s* can stand for either /s/ or /z/.)

Differentiated Instruction

SI Strategic Intervention

Blend Words with -*s* If children have trouble pronouncing the final -*s* correctly, pronounce final /s/ and /z/ sounds slowly. Then have children practice with words like *stands*, *eats*, and *feeds*.

Vocabulary Support

You may wish to explain the meaning of these words.

wags moves from side to side

yaps barks like a dog

nods moves head up and down

English Language Learners

Pronunciation /s/ Speakers of other languages may need support pronouncing words with the final –*s*. Provide additional practice with words like *dips, mops, dogs*, and *pigs*.

Language Transfer Children who speak Cantonese may have trouble telling the difference between the /s/ and /z/ sounds. Give additional practice with these sounds as needed.

Objectives

- Associate the consonant sounds /s/ and /z/ with the spelling *s*.
- Blend and read words with the inflected ending *-s*.
- Decode words in context and in isolation.

Check Word Reading
SUCCESS PREDICTOR

Phonics — Build Fluency
Inflected Ending *-s*

Model

Envision It!

Have children turn to page 98 in their Student Edition. Look at the picture on this page. I can see someone *pulls* a suitcase in this picture. When I say *pulls*, I hear the sound /z/ at the end of the word. The sound /z/ can be spelled with the letter *s*. We have already learned that the letter *s* can spell the sound /s/ like in the word *sits*. The letter *s* can spell both the sound /z/ and the sound /s/.

Objectives
- Read words that add endings to the main part of the word. • Identify and read at least 100 words from a list of words that you use often.

Envision It! Sounds to Know

pulls

ending -s

READING STREET ONLINE
SOUND-SPELLING CARDS
www.ReadingStreet.com

Phonics

Inflected Ending -s

Words I Can Blend

s i t s

a d d s

t a g s

g r i n s

c l a p s

Sentences I Can Read

1. Lin sits and adds as Pat tags Jill.
2. Kim grins and claps.

98

Student Edition p. 98

Guide practice

For each word in "Words I Can Blend," ask for the sound of each letter or group of letters. Make sure that children identify the correct sound for /s/ or /z/. Then have children blend the whole word.

Corrective feedback

If... children have difficulty blending a word,
then... model blending the word, and then ask children to blend it with you.

Blend and Read

Decode words in isolation

After children can successfully segment and blend the words, point to words in random order and ask children to read them naturally.

Decode words in context

Have children read each of the sentences. Have them identify words in the sentences that have the consonant sound /s/ or /z/.

Team Talk Pair children and have them take turns reading each of the sentences aloud.

On their own

Use *Reader's and Writer's Notebook* p. 169.

A Fox and a Kit

Name ______

Add -s to each word.
Write the new word on the line.

1. hop hops
2. sit sits
3. see sees
4. pat pats
5. help helps

Use the words you wrote to finish the sentences.
Write the words on the lines.

6. Jack sees a big dog.
7. Jack pats the dog.
8. Jack sits on a rock.
9. The dog helps Jack.
10. The dog hops on Jack.

Home Activity Your child added -s to verbs. Have your child write the verbs see, fan, nap, dig, sit, hop, jog, and mop, and add an -s to each verb. Have your child pick a verb and use it in a sentence about you, such as *Mommy hops*. Then act out the sentence.

Phonics Inflected Ending -s 169

Reader's and Writer's Notebook p. 169

Don't Wait Until Friday — MONITOR PROGRESS

Check Word Reading: Inflected Ending -s

Write the following words and have the class read them. Notice which words children miss during the group reading. Call on individuals to read some of the words.

hits	**gabs**	**sits**	**hops**	**wins**
pops	**packs**	**rock**	**jabs**	**bat** ←
comes	**takes**	**sees**	**looks**	**helps** ←

Spiral Review
Row 2 contrasts decodable words with and without ending -*s*.

Row 3 reviews high-frequency words with inflected ending -*s*.

If... children cannot blend words with the inflected ending -*s* at this point,
then... use the Small-Group Time Strategic Intervention lesson, p. DI•64 , to reteach words with inflected ending -s. Continue to monitor children's progress using other instructional opportunities during the week. See the Skills Trace on pp. 96–97.

Day 1	**Day 2**	**Day 3**	**Day 4**	**Day 5**
Check Word Reading	Check Word Reading	Check High-Frequency Words/ Retelling	Check Fluency	Check Vocabulary

Success Predictor

Differentiated Instruction

A Advanced

Extend Blending Provide children who can segment and blend all the words correctly with more challenging words such as: *cuddles*, *serves*, *studies*, and *scrubs*.

Spelling Patterns

***s* /z/** The sound /z/ may be spelled *s*.

DAY 1 Get Ready to Read

Objectives

- Apply knowledge of sound-spellings to decode unknown words when reading.
- Decode words in context and isolation.
- Practice fluency with oral rereading.

Decodable Practice Reader 4A

Inflected Ending *-s*

Decode words in isolation Have children turn to page 169. Have children decode each word.

Big Jobs
Written by Carole Jensen
Decodable Practice Reader 4A

Inflected Ending -s: digs, fills, licks, rocks, naps, picks, packs, mops
Consonant Pattern -ck: Rick, Nick, rocks, picks, Jack, packs, sacks
Word Family -ick: Rick, picks, Nick
Consonant s/z/: fills, digs
High-Frequency Words: a, we, you, the, do, have

169

Decodable Practice Reader 4A

Review High-frequency words Review the previously taught words *a, do, have, the, we,* and *you*. Have children read each word as you point to it on the Word Wall.

Preview Decodable Reader Have children read the title and preview the story. Tell them they will decode words with inflected ending *-s*.

Decode words in context Pair children for reading, and listen as they decode. One child begins. Children read the entire story, switching readers after each page. Partners reread the story. This time the other child begins.

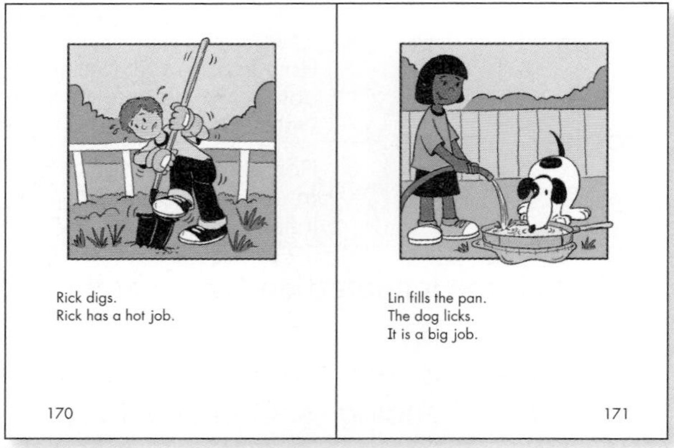
Rick digs.
Rick has a hot job.
170

Lin fills the pan.
The dog licks.
It is a big job.
171

Nick rocks Quin.
Quin naps.
Nick has a big job.
172

Kim picks the pods.
It is a big job.
173

Decodable Practice Reader 4A

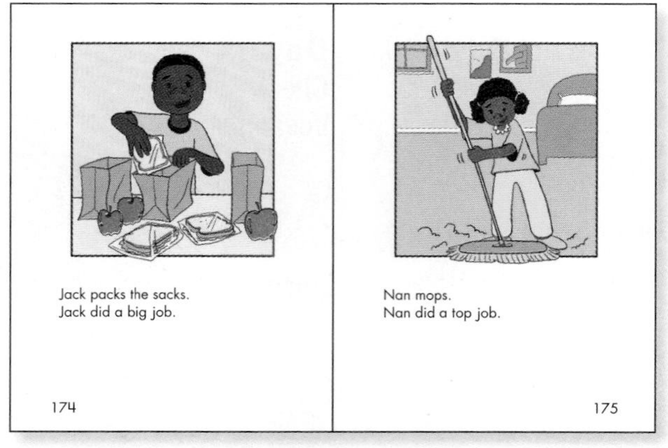
Jack packs the sacks.
Jack did a big job.
174

Nan mops.
Nan did a top job.
175

We did big jobs.
Do you have big jobs?
176

Corrective feedback

If... children have difficulty decoding a word, **then...** refer them to the Sound-Spelling Cards to identify the sounds in the word. Then prompt them to blend the word.

- What is the new word?
- Is the new word a word you know?
- Does it make sense in the story?

Check decoding and comprehension

Have children retell the story to include characters, setting, and events. Then have children find words with the inflected ending *-s* in the story. For each word, have children tell whether the *s* stands for the /s/ sound or the /z/ sound. Children should supply *digs, fills, licks, rocks, naps, picks, packs,* and *mops.*

Reread for Fluency

Have children reread Decodable Practice Reader 4A to develop automaticity decoding words with inflected ending -s.

ROUTINE Oral Rereading

1. **Read** Have children read the entire book orally.
2. **Reread** To achieve optimal fluency, children should reread the text three or four times.
3. **Corrective Feedback** Listen as children read. Provide corrective feedback regarding their fluency and decoding.

Routines Flip Chart

English Language Learners

Beginning Write inflected ending *-s* words from *Big Jobs* on the board. Call on individuals to select a word, read it silently, and then act it out for the group to guess. Have the group pronounce the word and identify the base word and ending.

Intermediate Have children read each sentence with an *-s* word. Have them use pantomime or the picture to help identify each word as a plural noun or verb. Provide assistance with *jobs*.

Advanced/Advanced High Have children sort words from *Big Jobs* that mean "more than one" and words that are verbs with ending *-s* into two lists. Have them pronounce each word and explain how they sorted.

DAY 1 Get Ready to Read

Objectives

- Segment and spell words with the inflected ending *–s*.
- Read high-frequency words.

Spelling Pretest
Inflected Ending *-s*

Dictate spelling words

Dictate the spelling words and read the sentences. Have children write the words. If needed, segment the words for children, clarify the pronunciations, and give meanings of words. Have children check their pretests and correct misspelled words.

1. sit	**Sit** in the front of the classroom.
2. sits*	Tom **sits** next to Mike on the bus.
3. win	The team will **win** the game.
4. wins	Mom **wins** the race.
5. fit	I **fit** into my new pants.
6. fits	The cat **fits** through the little door.
7. hit	I like to **hit** the drum.
8. hits	She **hits** the ball with a bat.
9. nap	I **nap** in the afternoon.
10. naps*	My brother **naps** on the couch.

* Words marked with asterisks come from the selection *A Fox and a Kit*.

On their own

Use Let's Practice It! p. 54 on the *Teacher Resource DVD–ROM*.

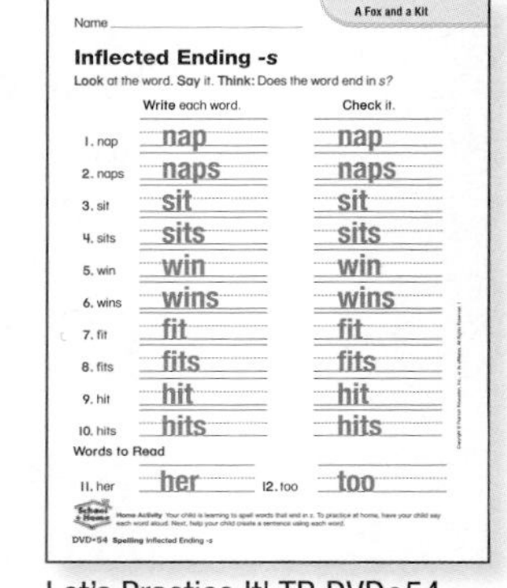

Name ______ A Fox and a Kit

Inflected Ending -s

Look at the word. Say it. Think: Does the word end in *s*?

	Write each word.	Check it.
1. nap	nap	nap
2. naps	naps	naps
3. sit	sit	sit
4. sits	sits	sits
5. win	win	win
6. wins	wins	wins
7. fit	fit	fit
8. fits	fits	fits
9. hit	hit	hit
10. hits	hits	hits

Words to Read

11. her her 12. too too

Home Activity Your child is learning to spell words that end in s. To practice at home, have your child say each word aloud. Next, help your child create a sentence using each word.

DVD•54 **Spelling** Inflected Ending -s

Let's Practice It! TR DVD•54

Small Group Time

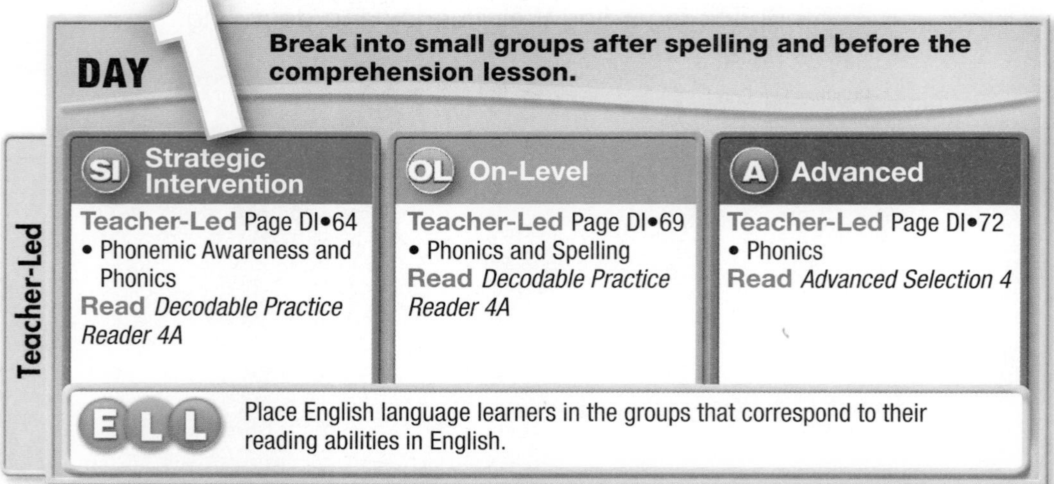

DAY 1 **Break into small groups after spelling and before the comprehension lesson.**

Teacher-Led

SI Strategic Intervention	OL On-Level	A Advanced
Teacher-Led Page DI•64 • Phonemic Awareness and Phonics **Read** *Decodable Practice Reader 4A*	**Teacher-Led** Page DI•69 • Phonics and Spelling **Read** *Decodable Practice Reader 4A*	**Teacher-Led** Page DI•72 • Phonics **Read** *Advanced Selection 4*

ELL Place English language learners in the groups that correspond to their reading abilities in English.

Practice Stations
- Listen Up
- Word Work

Independent Activities
- Read independently/Reading Log on *Reader's and Writer's Notebook* p. RR2
- Concept Talk Video

High-Frequency Words

Introduce

ROUTINE Nondecodable Words

1. **Say and Spell** Look at p. 99. Some words we have to learn by remembering the letters rather than saying the sounds. We will say and spell the words to help learn them. Point to the first word. This word is *eat*. The letters in eat are e-a-t, *eat*. Have children say and spell each word, first with you, and then without you.
2. **Identify Familiar Letter-Sounds** Point to the last letter in *eat*. You know the sound for this letter. What is this letter, and what is its sound? (*t*, /t/)
3. **Demonstrate Meaning** Tell me a sentence using the word *eat*. Repeat this routine with the other Words I Can Read.

Routines Flip Chart

Read words in isolation Have children read the words on p. 99 aloud. Add the words to the Word Wall.

Read words in context Have children read the sentences aloud. Have them identify this week's High-Frequency words in the sentences.

On their own Use *Reader's and Writer's Notebook* p. 170.

Name ______ A Fox and a Kit

Read the words in the box. Pick a word to finish each sentence. Write it on the line. Remember to begin a sentence with a capital letter.

eat four five her this too

1. We see four
2. The eat
3. This is a big cat.
4. This is a big cat too.
5. Can we help her?
6. We see five

170 High-Frequency Words

Reader's and Writer's Notebook p. 170

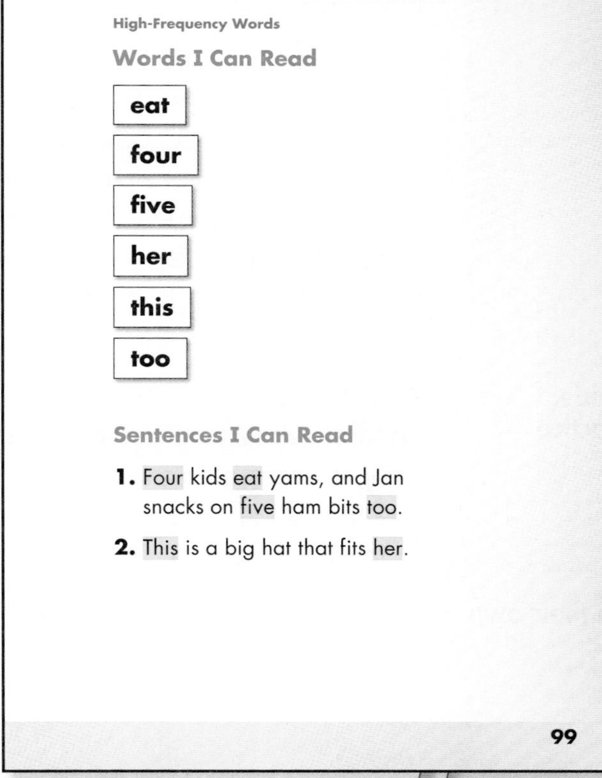

High-Frequency Words

Words I Can Read

eat

four

five

her

this

too

Sentences I Can Read

1. Four kids eat yams, and Jan snacks on five ham bits too.
2. This is a big hat that fits her.

99

Student Edition p. 99

Differentiated Instruction

Advanced

Extend Spelling Challenge children who spell words correctly to spell more difficult words such as: *eats, heats, cats, dogs,* and *tigers*.

Phonics/Spelling Generalization

Each spelling word ends in inflected -*s*, which forms either the present tense or the plural.

ELL

English Language Learners

Frontload Read Aloud Use the modified Read Aloud on p. 72 of the *ELL Support Lessons* to prepare children to listen to "A Rain Forest in the Zoo" on p. 99b.

DAY 1 Read and Comprehend

30–35 min.

Objectives

- Recognize main idea and details in literary nonficition.

Skills Trace

Main Idea and Details

Introduce U1W4D1;U1W5D1; U5W4D1

Practice U1W4D2; U1W4D3; U1W4D4; U1W5D2; U1W5D3; U1W5D4; U5W4D2; U5W4D3' U5W4D4

Reteach/Review U1W4D5; U1W5D5; U1W6D2; U2W3D2; U5W2D2; U5W4D5

Assess/Test Weekly Tests U1W4; U1W5; U5W4

Benchmark Test U1; U5

KEY:

U=Unit W=Week D=Day

Listening Comprehension

Main Idea and Details

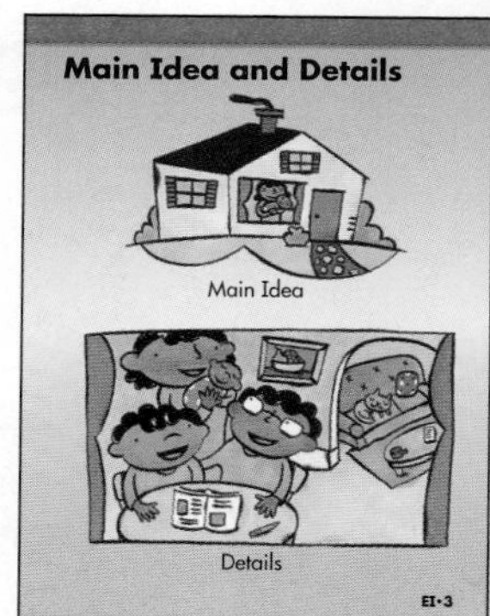

Student Edition EI•3

Introduce

Envision It!

The main idea is what a story is mostly about. Other sentences give details, or small pieces of information, that tell more about the main idea. Good readers pay attention to the details to help them understand the main idea in a story.

Have children turn to page EI•3 in their Student Edition. These pictures show an example of main idea and details. Discuss these questions using the pictures:

- When we look through the window, what details do we see? (a family eating, a table, dishes, a mom holding a sleeping baby, a cat on a couch)
- What do these details show? What details do we see? (All the details show a home. The main idea is home.

Model

Today we will read a story about a girl who goes to the zoo. Read "A Rain Forest in the Zoo" and model how to identify the main idea and details. Use Graphic Organizer Flip Chart 27 to record information.

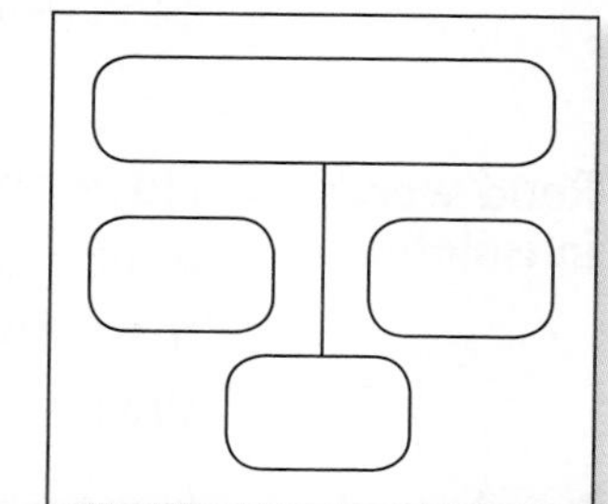

Graphic Organizer Flip Chart 27

When I read, I look for the most important details. A zookeeper tells Erica about the rain forest exhibit. The zoo brings in plants from animals' homes. They bring in rocks for animals to sit on. They change the lights to make it seem like night and day. I ask myself what this story is mainly about. The main idea is making a rain forest in the zoo.

Guide practice

Ask children if they think the title of the selection tells the main idea. Have children explain. (Possible response: Yes, because the selection tells how people brought in things to make a rain forest in the zoo.) What is another title that you could use for this selection? (Possible response: Erica Goes to the Rain Forest)

On their own

Use *Reader's and Writer's Notebook*, p. 171.

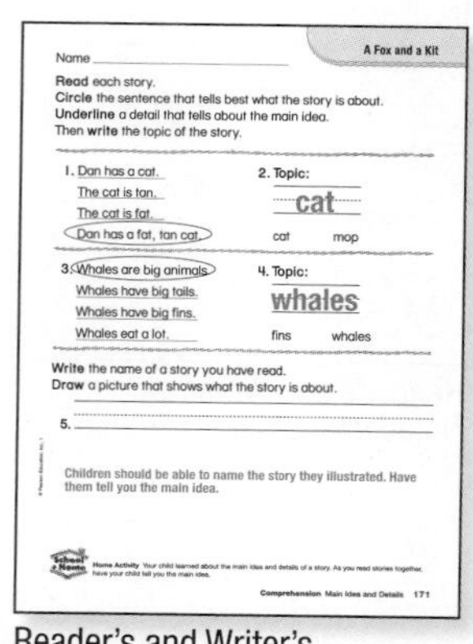

Name ______ A Fox and a Kit

Read each story.
Circle the sentence that tells best what the story is about.
Underline a detail that tells about the main idea.
Then write the topic of the story.

1. Dan has a cat. The cat is tan. The cat is fat. Dan has a fat, tan cat.
2. Topic: cat — cat mop
3. Whales are big animals. Whales have big tails. Whales have big fins. Whales eat a lot.
4. Topic: whales — fins whales

Write the name of a story you have read.
Draw a picture that shows what the story is about.

5. ______

Children should be able to name the story they illustrated. Have them tell you the main idea.

Comprehension Main Idea and Details 171

Reader's and Writer's Notebook, p. 171

Read Aloud

A Rain Forest in the Zoo

Erica was very excited. Today was the day she and her dad were going to the zoo. They had been waiting all month to see the new rain forest exhibit. It finally opened today.

"Tell me about the rain forest again," Erica said to her dad as they walked into the zoo.

"A rain forest is a forest where many trees and plants grow very closely together. It rains a lot. That's why it's called a rain forest. The trees are very tall, and some birds, bugs, and other animals live in the tops of the trees. The largest animals live on the ground under the trees."

"Wow!" Erica said as they entered the exhibit. "This looks like a real forest!"

"It does!" Erica's dad said.

"That's because we try to make everything as real as we can," a zookeeper said. "Today, zoos want to build homes for the animals that look like their homes in the wild. We bring in many plants from the animals' homes. We make rocks for them to sit on. We change the lights to make it seem like night and day."

"That sounds like a lot of work!" exclaimed Erica.

"It is a lot of work," the zookeeper replied. "We do it so the animals feel right at home. We want them to feel safe and happy. Then when you observe them you can learn all about how they really live."

"Let's go look at those monkeys over there first," Erica said. "Look at that little black one. It's riding on the back of another monkey!"

The zookeeper said, "That's called a black spider monkey. Baby black spider monkeys ride on their mothers' tummies until they are about four months old. Then they ride on their mothers' backs. Monkey mothers take very good care of their babies."

"That's cool. I want to learn all about the rain forest!" Erica said.

"Me too," said Erica's dad.

Academic Vocabulary

main idea the big idea that tells what the selection is mainly about

details pieces of information

Objectives

- Identify declarative sentences.
- Understand and recognize the features of personal narrative.

Conventions
Declarative Sentences

Model

Explain that a **declarative sentence** is one that tells about something. It tells a fact or someone's point of view. A declarative sentence begins with a capital letter and ends with a period.

Display Grammar Transparency 4. Read the definition aloud. Model why each example is a declarative sentence. Then read the directions and model number 1.

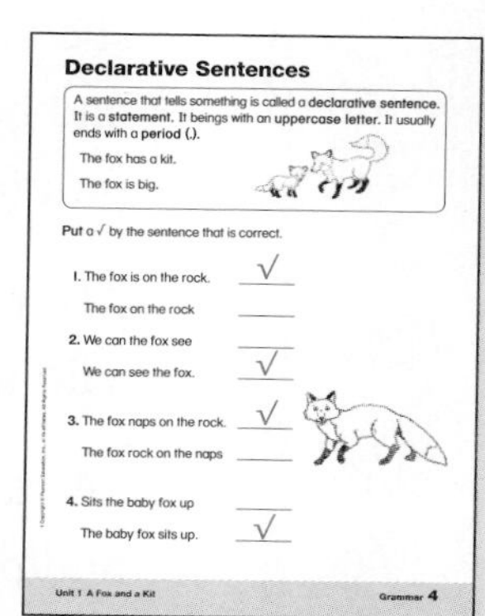

Declarative Sentences
A sentence that tells something is called a declarative sentence. It is a statement. It beings with an uppercase letter. It usually ends with a period (.).
The fox has a kit.
The fox is big.
Put a ✓ by the sentence that is correct.
1. The fox is on the rock. ✓
The fox on the rock
2. We can the fox see
We can see the fox. ✓
3. The fox naps on the rock. ✓
The fox rock on the naps
4. Sits the baby fox up
The baby fox sits up. ✓
Unit 1 A Fox and a Kit
Grammar 4

Grammar Transparency 4
TR DVD

- When I read the first sentence, I see that it tells me a fact. I also notice that it begins with a capital letter and ends with a period.
- When I read the second sentence, I see that it also tells me a fact. But I also notice that it does not begin with a capital letter or end with a period.
- I put a check mark by the first sentence, because it is the correct way to write a declarative sentence. It begins with a capital letter and ends with a period.

Guide practice

Continue with items 2–4, having children put a check mark by the sentence that is written correctly.

Connect to oral language

Have the class complete these sentence frames orally.

1. I can _______ animals to learn about them.

2. A fox is a _______ animal.

3. A _______ is a person with children.

On their own

Write a correct declarative sentence, an unpunctuated declarative sentence, and a sentence fragment on the board.

Team Talk Pair children and have them decide whether each example is a declarative sentence.

MINI-LESSON

5 Day Planner
Guide to Mini-Lessons

DAY 1	• Read Like a Writer
DAY 2	• Interesting details
DAY 3	• Including Feelings
DAY 4	• Revising Strategy: Rearranging Sentences
DAY 5	• Proofread for Declarative Sentences

Writing—Personal Narrative
Introduce

MINI-LESSON

Read Like a Writer

- **Introduce** This week you will write a **personal narrative**. A personal narrative is a kind of story. It tells about an event in your life.

Prompt	Think about a time you watched some animals. Write a narrative about it.
Trait	Voice
Mode	Narrative

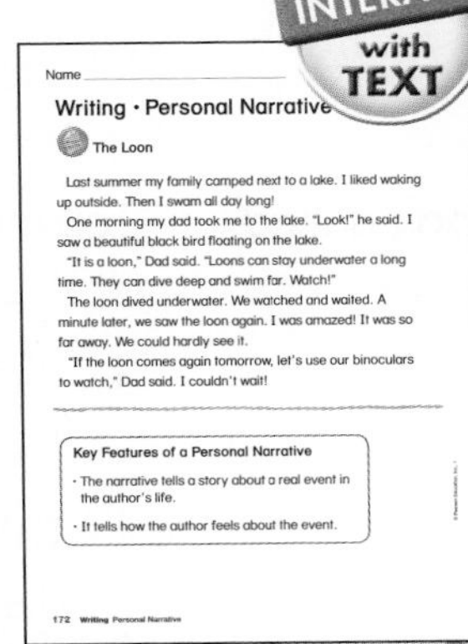

Name ______

Writing • Personal Narrative

The Loon

Last summer my family camped next to a lake. I liked waking up outside. Then I swam all day long!

One morning my dad took me to the lake. "Look!" he said. I saw a beautiful black bird floating on the lake.

"It is a loon," Dad said. "Loons can stay underwater a long time. They can dive deep and swim far. Watch!"

The loon dived underwater. We watched and waited. A minute later, we saw the loon again. I was amazed! It was so far away. We could hardly see it.

"If the loon comes again tomorrow, let's use our binoculars to watch," Dad said. I couldn't wait!

Key Features of a Personal Narrative

- The narrative tells a story about a real event in the author's life.
- It tells how the author feels about the event.

172 Writing Personal Narrative

Reader's and Writer's Notebook, p. 172

- **Examine Model Text** Let's listen to a personal narrative. Track the print as you read aloud "The Loon" on *Reader's and Writer's Notebook* p. 172. Have children follow along.

- **Key Features** What event is this narrative mostly about? (The author and Dad watch a loon.) Help children underline words or short phrases in the story that tell how the author feels about events, such as *liked, amazed,* and *I couldn't wait*.

  Like a story, this personal narrative has a beginning, middle, and end. At the beginning, Dad shows the author a loon. In the middle, they watch the loon. At the end, they decide to use binoculars the next time they see the loon.

  In the personal narrative, the author shares feelings about the events. Does the author feel excited about watching the loon? (yes)

Write Guy
Jeff Anderson

Adjective Strings

As children learn to write, many love to "improve" sentences with adjectives—big adjectives, little adjectives, many adjectives. We don't want to encourage strings of adjectives. On the other hand, this is a problem that can correct itself. Show a sample of a sentence with too many adjectives. Ask which *one* adjective might be unnecessary.

Academic Vocabulary

declarative sentence a group of words that tells

author the person who wrote the text

event an experience

personal narrative a story about an event or events in the author's life

Daily Fix-It

1. Fox napz on her lap
   Fox naps on her lap.
2. frog sitts there too.
   Frog sits there too.

Discuss the Daily Fix-It corrections with children. Review sentence capitalization and punctuation, the inflected ending -*s*, and the spelling of *sits*.

English Language Learners

Conventions To provide children with practice on declarative sentences, use the modified conventions lessons in the *ELL Handbook.*

Language Arts

Objectives

- Understand and recognize the features of a personal narrative.
- Develop an understanding of including feelings in a personal narrative.
- Identify a topic connected to this week's concept.
- Narrow the focus of the topic by formulating inquiry questions related to the topic.
- Explore animal friends.

Writing—Personal Narrative
Introduce, continued

Review Key features

Review key features of a personal narrative with children. You may want to post these key features in the classroom to allow children to refer to them as they work on their narratives.

Key Features of a Personal Narrative

- tells a story about a real event in the author's life
- tells how the author feels about it

Look ahead

Tell children that tomorrow they will plan their own personal narratives.

ROUTINE Quick Write for Fluency — Team Talk

1. **Talk** Read these questions aloud, and give children two minutes to discuss with partners.

   What animals can we see around our school?

   What animals can we see around our community?
2. **Write** Have children write short sentences about their favorite animal among those mentioned.
3. **Share** Partners can read their answers to one another.

Routines Flip Chart

Research and Inquiry
Identify and Focus Topic

Teach Display and review the concept map about this week's question: *How do wild animals take care of their babies?* What are some different wild animals that take care of their babies? Ask children to share their ideas. Help children identify animals they would like to learn about.

Model Think Aloud I love animals, and I would like to learn about all the animals in the world. For now, I will focus on just a few. Bears are one of my favorite animals. I'd like to know more about how they take care of their babies, so I will put bears on my list of animals to learn about. I like foxes because they look like dogs. I wonder how foxes take care of their babies. Foxes go on my list too.

Guide practice Give children time to think of animals they would like to learn about. Record children's suggestions in a list.

Wrap Up Your Day

- ✔ **Phonics: Inflected Ending -*s*** Write *naps*. Have children identify the base word and the ending. (*Nap* is the base word; *s* is the ending.) Continue with *wins, looks,* and *gets*.
- ✔ **Spelling: Inflected Ending -*s*** Have children name the spelling for each sound in *hits*. Write the spelling as children write the letters in the air. Continue with *sits, kicks,* and *locks*.
- ✔ **Build Concepts** Ask children to recall what happened in the Read Aloud, "A Rain Forest in the Zoo." What did Erica and her dad see at the zoo? (Possible response: a monkey and her baby)
- ✔ **Homework** Send home this week's Family Times Newsletter from Let's Practice It! pp. 49–50 on the *Teacher Resource DVD-ROM.*

Let's Practice It!
TR DVD•49–50

Differentiated Instruction

SI Strategic Intervention

Selecting a Topic If children have trouble coming up with wild animals they would like to learn about, have them brainstorm a list of animals they have seen in a zoo, a movie, or on television. Then help them select two or three animals on their list to focus on.

Tell children that tomorrow they will read about how a fox takes care of its baby.

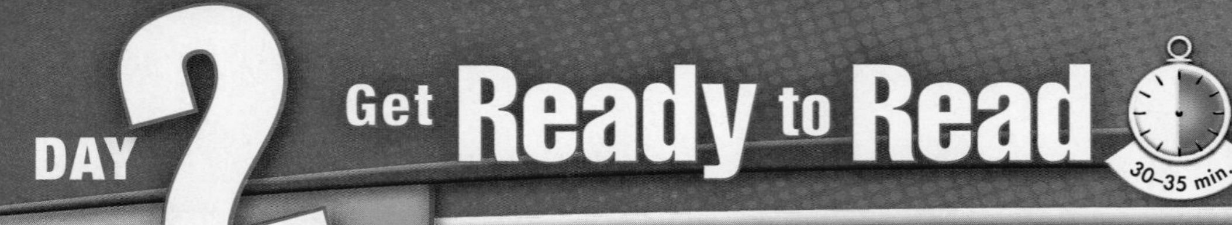

Objectives

- Discuss the concept to develop oral vocabulary.
- Build oral vocabulary.

Today at a Glance

Oral Vocabulary
canopy, screech

Phonemic Awareness
Segment and Blend Phonemes

Phonics and Spelling
◉ Inflected Ending *-s*
◉ Inflected Ending *-ing*

Fluency
Paired Reading

High-Frequency Words

Story Words
dinner

Comprehension
◉ Main Idea and Details
◉ Important Ideas

Vocabulary
Alphabetize

Genre
Literary Nonfiction

Conventions
Declarative Sentences

Writing
Personal Narrative

Handwriting
Letters *Nn, Gg*/Letter Slant

Research and Inquiry
Research Skill: How to Read a Chart

Concept Talk

Question of the Week

How do wild animals take care of their babies?

Build concepts

To reinforce concepts and to focus children's attention, have children sing "Squirrel Song" from the *Sing with Me* Big Book. What does the boy learn about the mother squirrel? (The mother squirrel is watching her baby.)

Sing with Me Big Book Audio

Introduce Amazing Words

Display the Big Book, *Jungle Drum*. Read the title and identify the author. Explain that in the story, the author uses the words *canopy* and *screech*. Have children listen as you read the story to find out where the *canopy* is, and which animals *screech*.

Use the Oral Vocabulary routine on the next page to teach *canopy* and *screech*.

Big Book

ELL Reinforce Vocabulary Use the Day 2 instruction on ELL Poster 4 to reinforce the meaning of high-frequency words.

ELL Poster 4

Oral Vocabulary
Amazing Words

Teach Amazing Words

Amazing Words Oral Vocabulary Routine

1. **Introduce the Word** Relate the word *screech* to the book. We heard the parrot screech "kahroo choo!" Supply a child-friendly definition. To screech means to make a high scream or sound. Have children say the word.
2. **Demonstrate** Provide examples to show meaning. When something frightens you, you may screech, "Help, Help!" A cat might *screech* if it sees a big dog. The tires will *screech* if a bike stops suddenly.
3. **Apply** Have children demonstrate their understanding. If any of the things I name can *screech*, say *screech*; if not, say nothing: a bird, a baby, a pumpkin, a horn, a car.

See p. OV•1 to teach *canopy*.

Routines Flip Chart

Anchored Talk

Add to the concept map

Discuss different ways wild animals take care of their babies.

- In "Squirrel Song," what is Mama Squirrel doing? (Possible response: She is watching her baby.) Let's add *They watch over them* to our map.
- In yesterday's Read Aloud "A Rain Forest in the Zoo," what did Erica see the mother monkey do? (Possible response: She saw the mother monkey carrying her baby on her back.) Let's add *They carry them* to our map.

Amazing Words

observe	screech
wild	million
parent	reserve
canopy	native

Differentiated Instruction

Advanced

Tell children that **onomatopoeia** are words that imitate the sounds they describe. Have children practice saying the words: *blip, blop, mmm,* and *screech.*

Vocabulary Support

You may wish to explain the meaning of these words.

jungle a kind of thick forest where many bushes, vines, and trees grow

drum a musical instrument that makes a sound when you hit it

English Language Learners

Onomatopoeia To help children understand sound words, point to some animals pictured in *Jungle Drum* and say the words that describe the sound they make. Have children repeat each sound word after you and then have them say it on their own.

Objectives

- Blend and read words with the inflected ending *-ing.*
- Associate the sound /ing/ with the spelling of *ing.*

Skills Trace

Inflected Ending *-ing*
Introduce U1W4D2
Practice U1W4D3; U1W4D4
Reteach/Review U1W4D5, U1W5D4
Assess/Test Weekly Test U1W4
Benchmark Test U1

KEY:
U=Unit W=Week D=Day

Phonemic Awareness
Segment and Blend Phonemes

Model isolating sounds Have children look at the picture on pages 96–97 in their Student Editions. I see children *bending* and *feeding* the ducks. The ducks are *eating*. The sound I hear at the end of the words *bending*, *feeding*, and *eating* is *-ing*.

Student Edition pp. 96–97

Model segmenting and blending Listen to the sounds in the word *bending*: /b/ /e/ /n/ /d/ *-ing*. Let's blend those sounds to make a word: /b/ /e/ /n/ /d/ *-ing*. Continue modeling with *feeding* and *eating*.

Guide practice Guide children as they segment and blend these words from the picture: *jumping, dumping, mending, sending, standing, handing,* and *looking*.

If... children make an error, model by segmenting the word,
then... have them repeat the segmenting and blending of the word.

On their own Have children segment and blend the following words.

/d/ /i/ /g/ *-ing* **digging**	/l/ /o/ /k/ *-ing* **locking**
/t/ /o/ /p/ *-ing* **topping**	/w/ /i/ /n/ *-ing* **winning**
/t/ /a/ /p/ *-ing* **tapping**	/n/ /o/ /d/ *-ing* **nodding**

Phonics—Teach/Model
Inflected Ending *-ing*

Sound-Spelling Card 126

ROUTINE Blending Strategy

1. **Connect** Write the words *digs* and *hops*. You studied words like these already. What do you know about reading these words? (The words have -*s* endings.) Today you will learn about words with the ending -*ing*.
2. **Use Sound-Spelling Card** Display Card 126. The sound you hear at the end of *drinking* is -ing. The sound -ing can be spelled *ing*. Have children say /ng/ several times as you point to -*ing*.
3. **Model** Write *fixing*. This word is *fixing*. In this word, the letters *ing* stand for -ing. Segment and blend *fixing*; then have children blend with you: /f/ /i/ /ks/ -ing. Follow this procedure to model blending *rocking*.
4. **Guide Practice** Continue the process in step 3. This time have children blend with you.

picking	**locking**	**seeing**	**packing**
waxing	**looking**	**going**	**doing**

5. **Review** What do you know about reading these words? (When a word ends with -*ing*, you know it might be a base word with an -*ing* ending.)

Routines Flip Chart

Differentiated Instruction

SI Strategic Intervention

Pronounce Inflected Ending *-ing* Some speakers may say *rockin* or *fixin* instead of *rocking* or *fixing* as they might not hear the difference between -*in* and -*ing*. Have children practice pronouncing words with ending -*ing*.

English Language Learners

Pronounce Inflected Ending *-ing* In some languages /ng/ does not exist, so there may be children who need support pronouncing words with the inflected ending -*ing*. Tell children that this sound is made by raising the back part of the tongue toward the roof of the mouth. Then demonstrate and have children follow. Provide practice with words such as *locking, mixing,* and *passing*.

Objectives

- ◎ Blend and read words with the inflected ending *-ing.*
- ◎ Associate the sounds /ing/ with *ing.*
- Decode words in context and isolation.

Check Word Reading
SUCCESS PREDICTOR

Phonics—Build Fluency
Inflected Ending *-ing*

Model

Envision It!

Have children turn to page 100 in their Student Editions. Look at the picture on this page. The word in the picture is *drinking*. When I say *drinking*, I hear the ending -ing. In *drinking*, /i/ /ng/ is spelled *ing*.

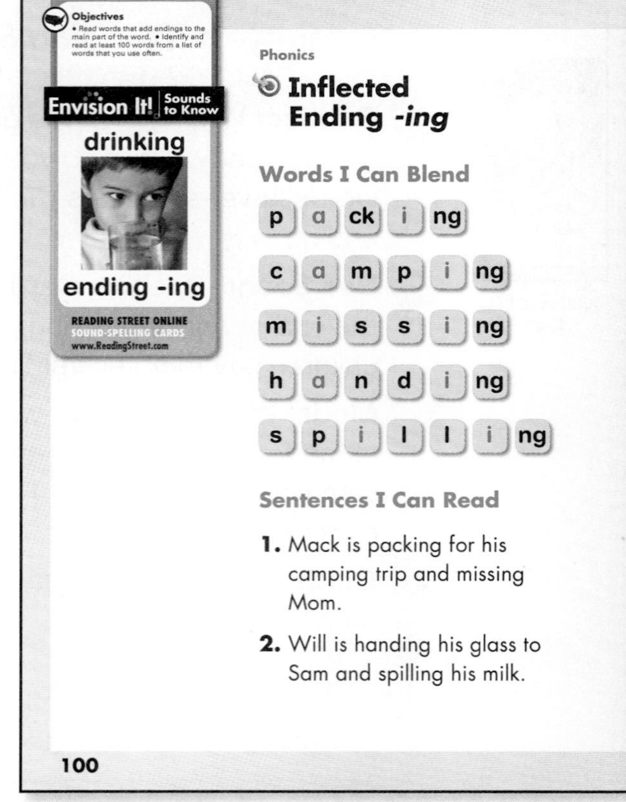

Student Edition p. 100

Guide practice

For each word in "Words I Can Blend," ask for the sound of each letter or group of letters. Make sure that children identify the correct sound for the ending *-ing*. Then have children blend the whole word.

Corrective feedback

If... children have difficulty blending a word,
then... model blending the word, and ask children to blend it with you.

Blend and Read

Decode words in isolation After children can successfully segment and blend the words, ask them to read the words naturally.

Decode words in context Have children read each of the sentences. Have them identify words in the sentences that have the ending *-ing*.

Team Talk Pair children and have them take turns reading each of the sentences aloud.

On their own Use *Reader's and Writer's Notebook* p. 173.

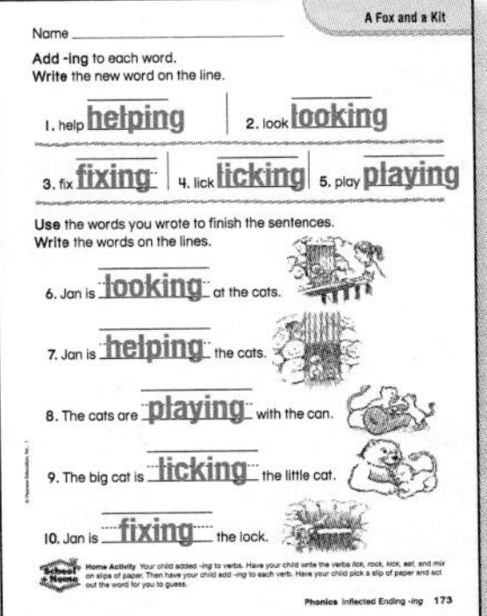
A Fox and a Kit

Name ______

Add -ing to each word.
Write the new word on the line.

1. help helping 2. look looking
3. fix fixing 4. lick licking 5. play playing

Use the words you wrote to finish the sentences.
Write the words on the lines.

6. Jan is looking at the cats.
7. Jan is helping the cats.
8. The cats are playing with the can.
9. The big cat is licking the little cat.
10. Jan is fixing the lock.

Home Activity Your child added -ing to verbs. Have your child write the verbs *lick, rock, kick, eat,* and *mix* on slips of paper. Then have your child add -ing to each verb. Have your child pick a slip of paper and act out the word for you to guess.

Phonics Inflected Ending -ing 173

Reader's and Writer's Notebook, p. 173

MONITOR PROGRESS — Check Word Reading: Inflected Ending *-ing*

Write the following words and have the class read them. Notice which children miss words during the group reading. Call on those individuals to read some of the words.

packing	**ticking**	**locking**	**picking**	**fixing**	**Spiral Review**
wax	**waxing**	**quacking**	**fill**	**filling** ←	Row 2 contrasts decodable words with and without inflected ending -ing
doing	**seeing**	**looking**	**going**	**helping** ←	Row 3 reviews high-frequency words with inflected ending *-ing*.

If… children cannot blend words with the *-ing* ending,
then… use the Small Group Time Strategic Intervention lesson on pg. DI•65 to reteach *-ing* endings. Continue to monitor children's progress using other instructional opportunities during the week. See the Skills Trace on p. 100c.

Day 1	Day 2	Day 3	Day 4	Day 5
Check Word Reading	Check Word Reading	Check High-Frequency Words/ Retelling	Check Fluency	Check Oral Vocabulary

Success Predictor

Differentiated Instruction

A Advanced

Write Inflected Ending *-ing* Have children pick out and then write each word with the inflected ending *-ing* in the sentences. (packing, camping, missing, handing, spilling)

English Language Learners

Pronunciation Children who speak languages without the /ng/ sound may need extra support pronouncing words with the *-ing* ending. Tell children the sound is made by pressing the back part of the tongue toward the roof of the mouth. Then demonstrate and have children follow.

Objectives

- Apply knowledge of sound-spellings to decode unknown words when reading.
- Decode and read words in context and in isolation.
- Practice fluency with oral rereading.

Decodable Practice Reader 4B

Inflected Ending *-ing*

Decode words in isolation Have children turn to page 177. Have children decode each word.

Decodable Practice Reader 4B

Review High-frequency words Review the previously taught word *we*. Have children read the word as you point to it on the Word Wall.

Preview Have children read the title and preview the story. Tell them they will read words that end in *-ing* and *-s*.

Decode words in context Pair children for reading, and listen as they decode. One child begins. Children read the entire story, switching readers after each page.

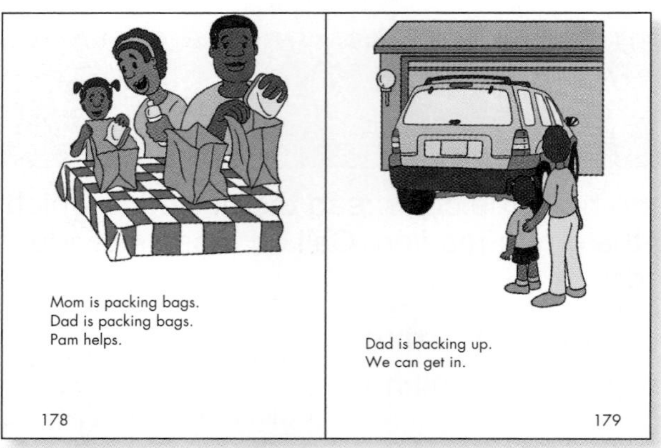

Mom is packing bags.
Dad is packing bags.
Pam helps.
178
Dad is backing up.
We can get in.
179

Decodable Practice Reader 4B

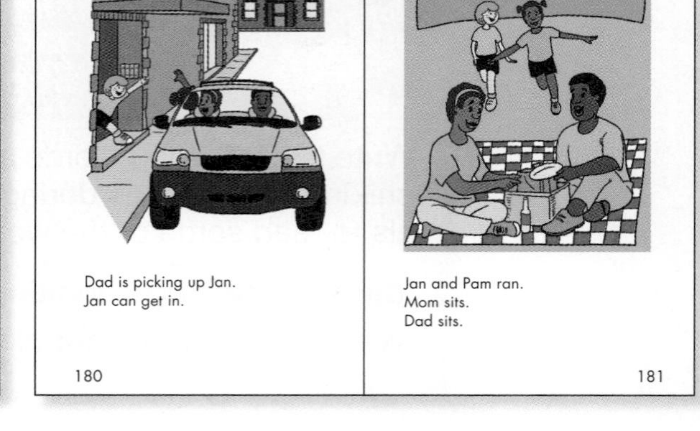

Dad is picking up Jan.
Jan can get in.

Jan and Pam ran.

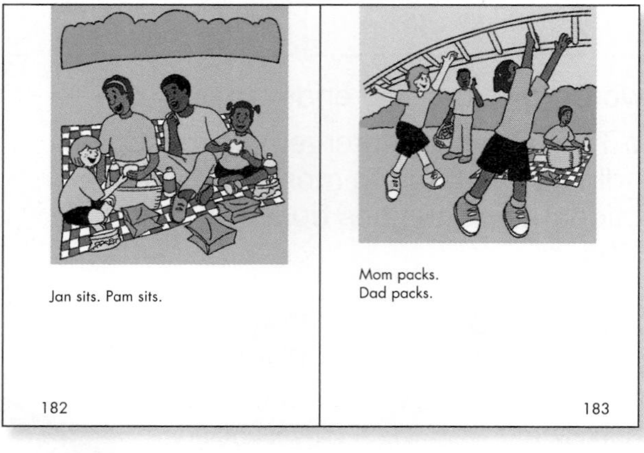

Jan sits. Pam sits.

Mom packs.
Dad packs.

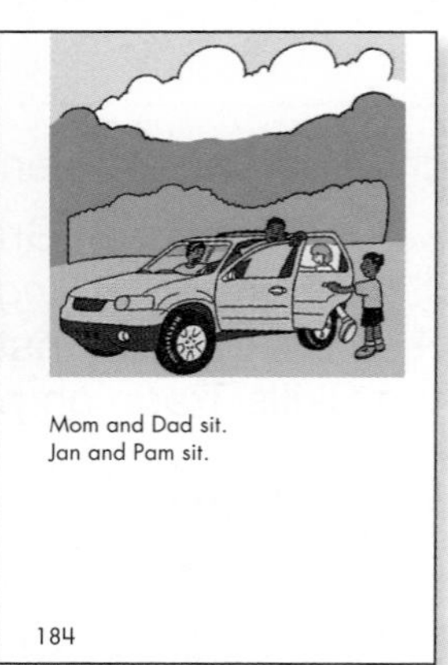

Mom and Dad sit.
Jan and Pam sit.

Corrective feedback

If... children have difficulty decoding a word, **then...** refer them to the Sound-Spelling Cards to identify the sounds in the word. Then prompt them to blend the word.

- What is the new word?
- Is the new word a word you know?
- Does it make sense in the story?

Check decoding and comprehension

Have children retell the story to include characters, setting, and events. Then have children find words with inflected ending *-ing* in the story. Children should supply *packing, backing,* and *picking*.

Reread for Fluency

Have children reread Decodable Practice Reader 4B to develop automaticity decoding words with inflected ending *-ing*.

ROUTINE Paired Reading

1. **Reread** To achieve optimal fluency, have partners reread the text three or four times.

2. **Corrective Feedback** Listen as children read. Provide corrective feedback regarding their fluency and decoding.

Routines Flip Chart

Differentiated Instruction

Strategic Intervention

Retelling If children have difficulty retelling the story, ask them questions regarding the events in the story.

English Language Learners

Inflected Ending *-ing*

Beginning After reading, point out the words with inflected ending *-ing*. Have children read them aloud. Then have children identify the story characters.

Intermediate After reading, have children find words with the inflected ending *-ing* and say them aloud. Have children tell you what each word means.

Advanced/Advanced-High After reading, have children find words that have inflected ending *-ing*. Have them make up questions using the words. For example, *Who is packing?* Allow children to answer the questions.

Objectives

- Apply knowledge of letter-sound correspondences and inflected ending *-s* to decode words in context and in isolation.
- Spell words with the inflected ending *-s*.

Phonics Review
Inflected Ending *-s*

Review Sound–Spelling Review the inflected ending -*s* using Sound-Spelling Card 141.

Decode words in isolation Display these words. Have the class blend the words. Then point to the words in random order and ask children to decode them quickly.

digs	**locks**	**bobs**	**tips**
sits	**naps**	**sips**	**rocks**
taps	**wins**	**nods**	**pods**

Corrective feedback Model blending decodable words and then ask children to blend them with you.

Decode words in context Display these sentences. Have the class read the sentences.

Team Talk Have pairs take turns reading the sentences naturally.

Jan **packs** and then **naps.**

Dad **sits** and **pats** the cat.

The little dog **yips** and **yaps.**

Spelling
Inflected Ending *-s*

Guide practice

Tell children that you will segment the sounds in each spelling word. They should repeat the sounds in each word as they write the word. Check the spelling of each word before saying the next word.

1. /s/ /i/ /t/	**sit**	**6. /f/ /i/ /t//s/**	**fits**
2. /s/ /i/ /t/ /s/	**sits**	**7. /h/ /i/ /t/**	**hit**
3. /w/ /i/ /n/	**win**	**8. /h/ /i/ /t/ /s/**	**hits**
4. /w/ /i/ /n/ /z/	**wins**	**9. /n/ /a/ /p/**	**nap**
5. /f/ /i/ /t/	**fit**	**10. /n/ /a/ /p/ /s/**	**naps**

On their own

Use *Reader's and Writer's Notebook* p. 174.

Small Group Time

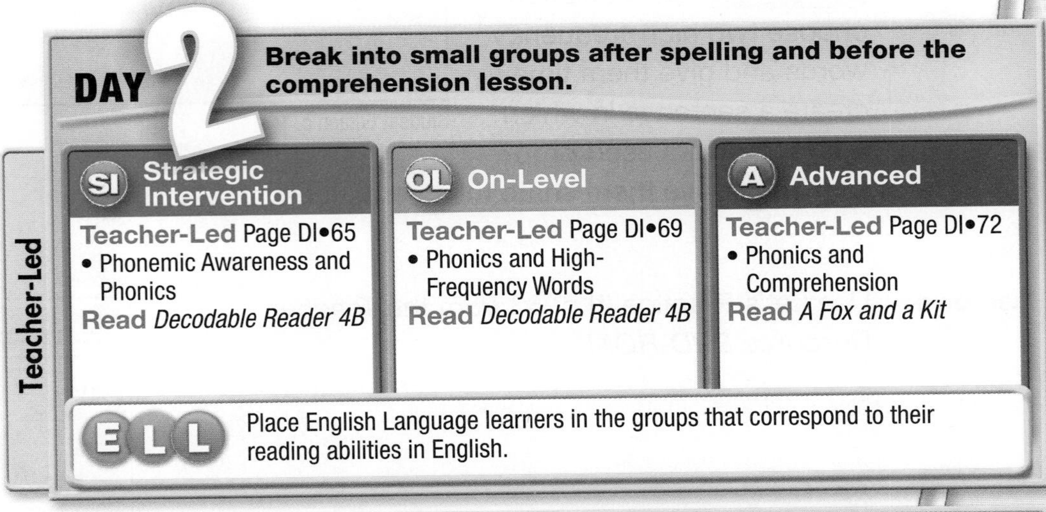

DAY 2 **Break into small groups after spelling and before the comprehension lesson.**

Teacher-Led

SI Strategic Intervention	OL On-Level	A Advanced
Teacher-Led Page DI•65 • Phonemic Awareness and Phonics Read *Decodable Reader 4B*	Teacher-Led Page DI•69 • Phonics and High-Frequency Words Read *Decodable Reader 4B*	Teacher-Led Page DI•72 • Phonics and Comprehension Read *A Fox and a Kit*

ELL Place English Language learners in the groups that correspond to their reading abilities in English.

Practice Stations
- Listen Up
- Word Work

Independent Activities
- Read Independently/Reading Log on *Reader's and Writer's Notebook* p. RR2

Differentiated Instruction

SI Strategic Intervention

Guide Practice To guide practice, have children write the spelling words on their own. Have children sound out the sounds in the words as they write the words. When they have finished, have them confirm their spellings by comparing them to what you have written on the board.

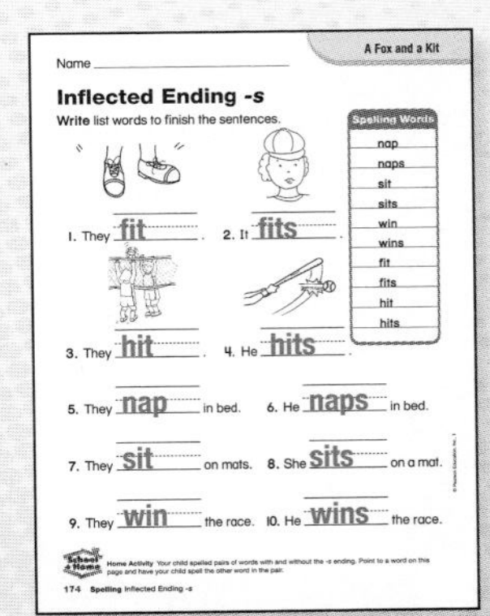

Name ______ A Fox and a Kit

Inflected Ending -s

Write list words to finish the sentences.

Spelling Words: nap, naps, sit, sits, win, wins, fit, fits, hit, hits

1. They fit
2. It fits
3. They hit
4. He hits
5. They nap in bed.
6. He naps in bed.
7. They sit on mats.
8. She sits on a mat.
9. They win the race.
10. He wins the race.

174 Spelling Inflected Ending -s

Reader's and Writer's Notebook, p. 174

English Language Learners

Physical Response Use physical gestures to demonstrate spelling words like *sit, win,* and *nap*. Repeat the words and gestures as needed to help children learn the words.

DAY 2 Read and Comprehend 40–45 min.

Objectives

- Learn story words: *dinner.*
- Review high-frequency words.
- Alphabetize to the second letter.

High-Frequency Words

Build Fluency

Read words in isolation Remind children that there are some words we learn by remembering the letters, rather than by saying the sounds. Then have them read each of the highlighted high-frequency words aloud.

Read words in context Chorally read the I Can Read! passage along with children. Then have them read the passage aloud to themselves. When they are finished, ask children to reread the high-frequency words.

Team Talk Have children choose two high-frequency words and give them time to create a sentence in which both words are used properly. Then have them share their sentence with a partner.

I Can Read!

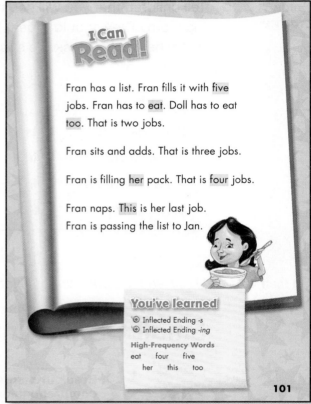

Fran has a list. Fran fills it with five jobs. Fran has to eat. Doll has to eat too. That is two jobs.

Fran sits and adds. That is three jobs.

Fran is filling her pack. That is four jobs.

Fran naps. This is her last job.
Fran is passing the list to Jan.

You've learned

- Inflected Ending *-s*
- Inflected Ending *-ing*

High-Frequency Words

eat four five
her this too

101

Student Edition p. 101

On their own Use Let's Practice It! p. 53 from the *Teacher Resource DVD-ROM.*

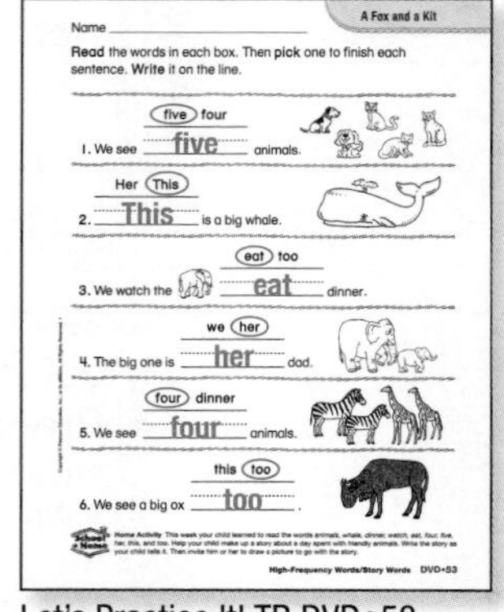

A Fox and a Kit

Name ______________

Read the words in each box. Then **pick** one to finish each sentence. **Write** it on the line.

five four
1. We see five animals.

Her This
2. This is a big whale.

eat too
3. We watch the [elephant] eat dinner.

we her
4. The big one is her dad.

four dinner
5. We see four animals.

this too
6. We see a big ox too.

Home Activity This week your child learned to read the words animals, whale, dinner, watch, eat, four, five, her, this, and too. Help your child make up a story about a day spent with friendly animals. Write the story as your child tells it. Then invite him or her to draw a picture to go with the story.

High-Frequency Words/Story Words DVD•53

Let's Practice It! TR DVD•53

Story Words
A Fox and a Kit

Introduce story word Use Vocabulary Transparency 4 to introduce this week's story words. Read the sentences as you track the print. Frame the underlined word and explain its meaning.

animals	living things that can move around
dinner	the main meal of the day
watch	to look at something

Have children read the sentence with you.

Dinner with the Animals
1. Come see the animals eat.
2. Look, the fox likes her dinner!
3. We can watch her kit eat too.

Unit 1 A Fox and a Kit Vocabulary 4

Vocabulary Transparency 4
TR DVD

Vocabulary
Alphabetize to the Second Letter

Model alphabetizing Explain that words are arranged in a dictionary or glossary according to the letters of the alphabet. Explain that when two or more words begin with the same letter, we need to use the second letter to put them in alphabetical order. Write the following words on the board: *dot*, *dim*, and *dab*.

Think Aloud The first letter of all these words is *d*, so I need to use the second letter to put them in alphabetical order. I can see that the second letters of these words are *o, i,* and *a*. Of these letters, I know that *a* comes first in the alphabet, *i* comes second, and *o* comes third. So the correct alphabetical order is *dab, dim, dot*.

Guide practice Write three words on the board that begin with the same letter and have a different second letter, in non-alphabetical order. What is the second letter of each of these words? Write the letters on the board. Which letter comes first in the alphabet? Which comes second? Which comes third? What is the alphabetical order of these words? Write the words on the board in alphabetical order.

On their own Write three words on the board that begin with the same letter and have a different second letter, in non-alphabetical order. Have children put them in alphabetical order.

Differentiated Instruction

SI Strategic Intervention

Identify High-Frequency and Story Words
Have children practice reading *eat, five, four, her, this, too,* and *dinner*. For corrective feedback, reteach the words using Routine Cards.

Academic Language

alphabetize to put words in order according to the letters of the alphabet

English Language Learners

Multilingual Vocabulary Lists
Children can apply knowledge of their home language to acquire new English vocabulary by using the *Multilingual Vocabulary List* (*ELL Handbook* pp. DI•75–DI•84).

DAY 2 Read and Comprehend

Objectives

- Build background about what zookeepers do.
- Preview and predict.
- Use key structure and elements of literary nonfiction to improve understanding of text.
- Set a purpose for reading text.

Build Background
A Fox and a Kit

Background Building Audio

Have children listen to the CD. Tell them to listen to find out about what zookeepers do.

Background Building Audio

Discuss a zookeeper's job

Team Talk Have children turn to a partner and use these questions for discussion:

- What are some things that zookeepers do?
- Why do zookeepers do all these things?
- What would be important if you wanted to become a zookeeper?

Organize information in a chart

Draw a chart or display Graphic Organizer 17. Write *How Zookeepers Care for Animals* in the circle. Have children recall what they learned from the CD about how zookeepers take care of animals. Record their responses.

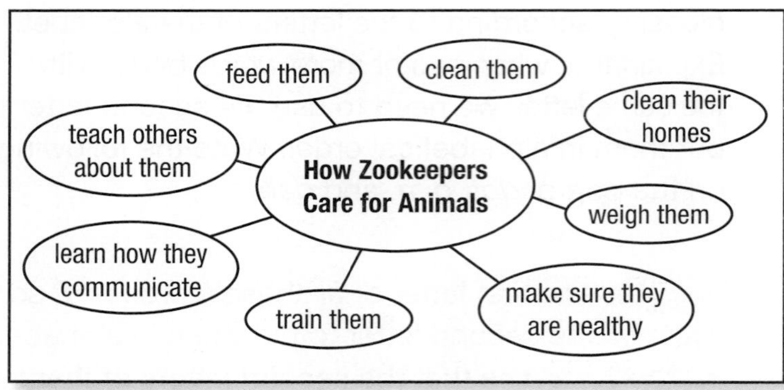

Graphic Organizer 17

Connect to selection

We learned how zookeepers take care of animals that live in zoos. In the story we are about to read, *A Fox and a Kit*, we will learn about a real mother fox and her kit in a zoo. We'll learn about what we might see if we visited them.

Student Edition pp. 102–103

Main Selection — First Read

A Fox and a Kit

Practice the skill

Main Idea and Details Remind children that the main idea is what a story is mostly about. Tell them that good readers pay attention to the details to help them understand the main idea in a story. Remind them of the Main Idea chart they completed after hearing "A Rain Forest in the Zoo."

Introduce the strategy

Important Ideas Explain that good readers think about bigger ideas that the author wants us to think about. Have children turn to page EI•9 in their Student Editions.

In this picture, I can tell that this boy wants to see a panda. The woman is pointing to a sign that says "Giant Panda." I think about what these things mean. They mean that that the boy wants to see a panda and that the zoo has one, so the people will probably visit it.

Student Edition EI•9

Introduce genre

Let's Read Together Literary nonfiction tells about real-life people, animals, or events. The setting is real. As they read *A Fox and a Kit*, ask children to look for clues that tell them that this story is about a real fox and her kit.

Preview and predict

Have children identify the title of the story, the author, and the illustrator. Read aloud the names of the author and illustrator and have children describe the role of each. Help children activate prior knowledge by asking them to look through the selection and use the illustrations to predict what it will be about.

Set a purpose

Good readers read for a purpose. Setting a purpose helps us to think and understand more as we read. We will read this story to find out about the foxes in a zoo.

Tell children that today they will read *A Fox and a Kit* for the first time. Use the Day 2 Guide Comprehension notes to help children develop their comprehension of the selection.

First Read

Continue with DAY 2

For the First Read, use **Guide Comprehension** across the top of pages 102–111.

Strategy Response Log

Background Knowledge Before reading, have children use p. RR16 of their *Reader's and Writer's Notebook* to draw a picture of a fox and a kit.

Academic Vocabulary

author the person who wrote the text

ELL

English Language Learners

Build Background Before children listen to the CD, build background and elicit prior knowledge. On the CD, you will hear about what a zookeeper does. A zookeeper works at a zoo. What are some of the things a zookeeper might do?

Frontload Main Selection Ask children what they already know about foxes using the picture on pp. 106–107. Then do a picture walk of the selection so children can talk about what they see.

Objectives

- Identify important ideas in literary nonfiction.
- Identify main idea and details in literary nonfiction.
- Determine word meaning and use newly acquired vocabulary.
- Discuss ideas related to, but not expressed in the literature.

DAY 2

Guide Comprehension

Skills and Strategies

Connect to Concept

Wild Animals Look at the picture on pages 102 and 103. What wild animals are the people observing? (Possible response: They are observing a fox and her kit.)

Amazing Words Have children continue discussing the concept using the Amazing Words *observe, parent,* and *wild*.

A Fox and a Kit
by Leya Roberts
illustrated by Charles Santore
RED FOX
Genre
Literary nonfiction tells facts about the real world. It is sometimes told like a story. You will read about a fox and her kit at the zoo.
Read Together
Question of the Week
How do wild animals take care of their babies?
102
103

Student Edition pp. 102–103

DAY 3

Extend Thinking

Think Critically

Higher-Order Thinking Skills

Analysis I see in the picture that the mother fox is watching over her kit. Why is it important for the fox to stay close to her kit?

If... children cannot explain why the fox is watching over her kit,
then... encourage them to think about what dangers a baby animal might face.

Strategies

Important Ideas Remind children that good readers look for important ideas as they read. Have them suggest an important idea from what they have seen and read so far. (Possible Response: The fox and her kit do things together. The mother fox stays close to her kit.)

Word Reading

High-Frequency Words Point out the words *four*, *her*, and *too*. Have children practice reading these words.

It is four.
This fox naps on the rocks.
Her kit naps on the rocks too.

104

The kit sits up.
His mom sits up.

105

Student Edition pp. 104–105

Review Realism and Fantasy

Analysis Are the foxes in the story real or make-believe? (They are real.) How do you know this? (Possible response: They live in a zoo. They act like animals, not like people.)

If... children have difficulty answering the question, **then...** model how to use details from the story to distinguish between realism and fantasy.

Skills and Strategies, continued

Skills

Main Idea and Details What happens on these two pages? What details tell us this? (The fox and her kit have dinner. We know this because a man gives them a plate full of food, and then the plate is empty.)

Word Reading

Story Words Have children locate the word *dinner* on page 106. What time of the day do the fox and her kit eat dinner? (They eat dinner at five o'clock.)

It is five.
This man is fixing dinner.
The kit and his mom will eat.

106

The kit is licking his lips.
His mom is licking her lips.

107

Student Edition pp. 106–107

Think Critically, continued

Higher-Order Thinking Skills

Analysis Even though the foxes are wild animals, what tells you that they do not have to find their own food? (The words say that the man is fixing dinner, and the picture shows him giving the foxes dinner.)

Synthesis Do you think the foxes liked their food? How can you tell? (They seem to look forward to eating and then they finish all their food. They lick their lips.)

Skills

Main Idea and Details What is happening on these two pages? What details tell us this? (The mother fox makes sure her kit is happy and safe. We know this because the mother fox plays with her kit, and then she picks him up and takes him away from the rocks.)

If... children have trouble deciding on the main idea and details,
then... ask them to think about what happens on the first page, then what happens on the second page. Then ask them to think about what happens overall, on both pages.

The kit is playing.
His mom is playing.
The kit nips and tags his mom.

108

The kit is on the rocks.
His mom will get him.
She picks him up and takes him back.

109

Student Edition pp. 108–109

Higher-Order Thinking Skills

Evaluation In these pictures, the foxes seem to be behaving as they would in their natural habitat. How can you tell this? (Possible response: They look relaxed and the mother fox protects her kit from the rocks.)

Connect to Science

Animal Environments To stay healthy, animals in a zoo need a habitat similar to their natural one.

Team Talk Have children discuss with a partner things they have observed in zoos that allow animals to behave as they would in the wild.

Skills and Strategies, continued

Strategies

Important Ideas Have children discuss what they see and read on these pages. Have them suggest important ideas. (Possible response: We can observe wild animals, and they can observe us.)

Word Reading

Decoding Have children check their reading of new words:

- Did I blend the sounds to read the word?
- Did the word make sense?

Comprehension Check p. 111a

The kit spots his mom.
His mom spots him.

We like to watch this kit and his mom!
We can watch lots of animals.

110 111

Student Edition pp. 110–111

Think Critically, continued

High-Order Thinking Skills

Evaluation What are some good and bad things about zoos? (Possible response: The foxes are not in their real habitat, but they don't have to find food.)

If... children cannot think of any good and bad things,
then... encourage them to think about where foxes might live if they weren't in a zoo, and what they would eat if they lived there.

Comprehension Check

Have children discuss each question with a partner.
Ask several pairs to share their responses.

- ☑ **Literary nonfiction** Do you think this selection could happen in real life? (Possible response: Yes, there are zoos in real life, and they might have foxes and their kits.)
- ☑ **Main ideas and details** What is this selection mostly about? What are some of the details it tells? (Possible response: The story is about a fox and a kit who live in a zoo. The details tell what they do together, such as napping, eating dinner, and playing.)
- ☑ **Setting** What is the setting of this selection? (a zoo)
- ☑ **Confirm predictions** What did you think this selection would be about from the picture at the beginning? (Possible response: I thought it would be about a fox and her kit who live in a zoo.) Were your predictions correct?
- ☑ **Connect text to self** The foxes in the selection nap, eat dinner, and play. If you have been to a zoo, what did you see the animals do? If not, what do some of the animals you know about do? (Possible response: I have seen animals eat, nap, and play together.)

Think Critically
pp. 112–113a

English Language Learners

Support Discussion Ask yes-or-no questions to start children's responses. For example: Have you been to a zoo? (Yes.) Extend language opportunities for children by asking follow-up questions, such as: What animals did you see? What was their habitat like?

Objectives

- Identify the features of literary nonfiction.
- Recognize and use features of declaritive sentences.

Genre
Literary Nonfiction

Identify features of literary nonfiction

Use *A Fox and a Kit* to have children identify the features of literary nonfiction. Have them use text from the selection to support their answers.

- *A Fox and a Kit* tells about a wild fox and her kit. Where do they live? (They live in a zoo.)
- What is the selection about? (It is about what the fox and her kit do.)
- Do you think this selection is real? How can you tell? (Yes, the selection is real. The foxes live in a zoo. They act like real foxes; they don't talk, or act like humans.)

Guide practice

Explain that the class will now think of all the things that tell the selection is real. Use Graphic Organizer 17, and write *What makes the selection real?* in the circle. Let's begin by thinking about the setting of the selection. Where does it take place? That's right, it takes place in a zoo. Do zoos exist in real life? Yes, zoos exist in real life, so I'll put zoo at the end of this spoke. Repeat this process with the characters and events in the selection. Have children study the finished web. Discuss how all the things are real.

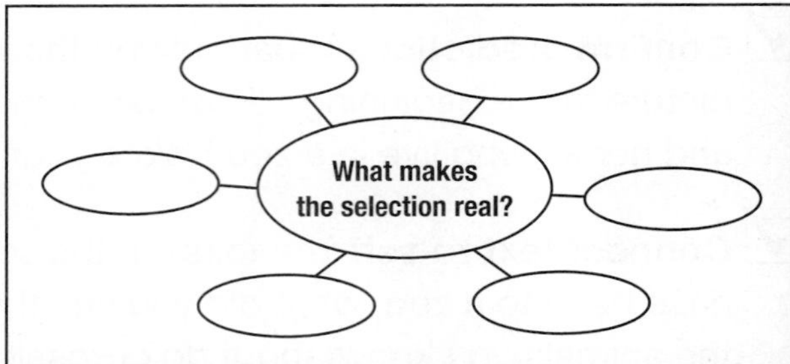

Graphic Organizer Flip Chart 17

On their own

Divide children into small groups. Have each group think about a topic they would like to learn more about. As they share their ideas with the class, reinforce that their topics are main ideas and not details.

Conventions
Declarative Sentences

Model declarative sentences

Write *The green frog flips and flops* on the board. Point to each word as you read it. This is a declarative sentence that tells me that the green frog flips and flops. Ask children to identify the capital letter. Ask them to identify the period.

Guide practice

Write the following sentences on the board. Have children tell you which words should begin with a capital letter and where to put the period in each.

a fox can do a lot
the cat napped on the mat
a tan dog sits on a box

Connect to oral language

Have the class complete these sentence frames orally.

1. I saw a bird ________ from an egg.
2. A green lily pad is a ________'s habitat.
3. I hope the hurt ________ survives.

On their own

Use *Reader's and Writer's Notebook* p. 175.

Name __________ A Fox and a Kit

Declarative Sentences

A **telling sentence** tells something. It is a **declarative sentence**. It begins with a **capital letter**. It usually ends with a **period** (.).

The fox has a kit.
The kit naps.

Find the sentence. **Underline** the sentence.

1. The children see a fox.
   the children see a fox
2. they see the kit
   They see the kit.
3. The kit can run.
   the kit can run
4. the fox and kit play
   The fox and kit play.
5. fox naps on the rocks
   Fox naps on the rocks.

Conventions Declarative Sentences 175

Reader's and Writer's Notebook p. 175

Differentiated Instruction

Advanced

Have children write their own declarative statements about foxes or other animals they know about.

Daily Fix-It

3. the bird's wing is pink
   The bird's wing is pink.
4. i see the foxes eat dinner
   I see the foxes eat dinner.

Discuss the Daily Fix-It corrections with children. Review sentence capitalization and punctuation.

English Language Learners

Support Grammar Reinforce to children that the word order in sentences varies in different languages. In Spanish, for example, the verb can appear before the subject. Provide extra practice with word order in sentences.

Objectives

- Recognize features of a personal narrative.
- Generate personal narrative ideas.
- Use interesting details in writing a plan for a personal narrative.

Writing—Personal Narrative
Writer's Craft: Interesting Details

Introduce the prompt

Review with children the key features of a personal narrative. Assure them that they can write a story based on something they have seen or done themselves. Explain that today children will plan their own personal narrative. Like a made-up story, it will have a beginning, middle, and end. Read aloud the writing prompt.

Writing Prompt

> Think about a time you watched some animals. Write a narrative about it.

Sharing the Writing

Help children generate story ideas

To plan a new personal narrative, think of places where you have seen animals and what animals you have seen there. Let's make a chart of places where you have seen animals and the animals you saw. Display a T-chart. I'll start with the word *school.*

Guide children in identifying animals that children have seen. Possible ideas are shown. Record the responses, and keep the chart so that children can refer to it as they plan and draft their narratives.

Have each child choose an idea for a personal narrative. Circulate to guide them.

Places We Have Seen Animals	Animals We Have Seen
school	robins, squirrels
park	ducks, turtles
woods	foxes, hawks, snakes
zoo	polar bears, monkeys

MINI-LESSON

Interesting Details

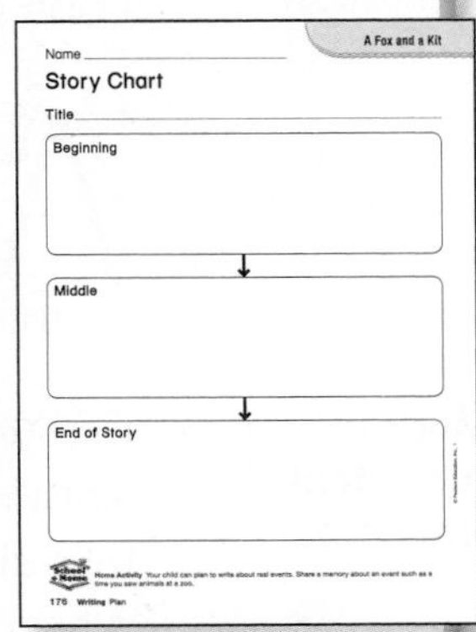

Reader's and Writer's Notebook, p. 176

- **Introduce** Use *Reader's and Writer's Notebook* p. 176 to model planning a personal narrative. Like a made-up story, a personal narrative has a beginning, middle, and end. I can use a chart to plan my personal narrative. I've decided to write about a time I saw a bunny in a garden, so I'll write *The Bunny in the Garden* as my title. Now I will plan what happens in the beginning, middle, and end of my narrative. I want to include interesting details in my plan. Interesting details will bring my narrative to life and keep people reading it.

- **Model** At the beginning, I'll tell about how I like to go to the park. I'll include details about what I do there: sit under an elm tree and walk in the rose garden. Then I will tell about the bunny I saw, and I'll include details about where I saw the bunny: on a grassy path in the rose garden. I'll write that in the Beginning box. In the middle I'll tell what I saw the bunny do. The bunny just watched me while it filled its mouth with grass. I'll write that in the Middle box. I'll also include a detail about how funny it looked with grass sticking out of its mouth! At the end, I'll tell that the bunny hopped away. I'll write that idea in the End of Story box. Now plan for your personal narrative. Circulate to guide and assist children.

ROUTINE

Quick Write for Fluency

Team Talk

1. **Talk** Have children take two minutes to tell the events in their narrative to a partner.
2. **Write** Each child briefly writes about the events at the beginning, middle, and end of the planned narrative.
3. **Share** Each child reads the story ideas to the partner.

Routines Flip Chart

Differentiated Instruction

SI Strategic Intervention

Planning a Topic If children find it difficult to think of a topic for their narrative, discuss any animals that can be seen outside the classroom window. Help them write words such as *bird* or *squirrel*, then have them write what they see the animal doing.

ELL

English Language Learners

Support Prewriting

Beginning Children can draw a scene, label the details, and share with a partner, possibly one who speaks the same home language.

Intermediate Have children describe a scene, then write phrases to label details in the scene. Have them describe the scene to other children.

Advanced/Advanced High Have children draw pictures or write short sentences in their story charts. As they share the plan with partners, children can clarify by adding details.

Objectives

- Write with correct letter slant.
- Understand how to read a chart.

Handwriting

Letters Nn and Gg/Letter Slant

Model letter formation Display upper- and lower-case letters: *Nn* and *Gg*. Use the stroke instructions pictured below to model proper letter formation.

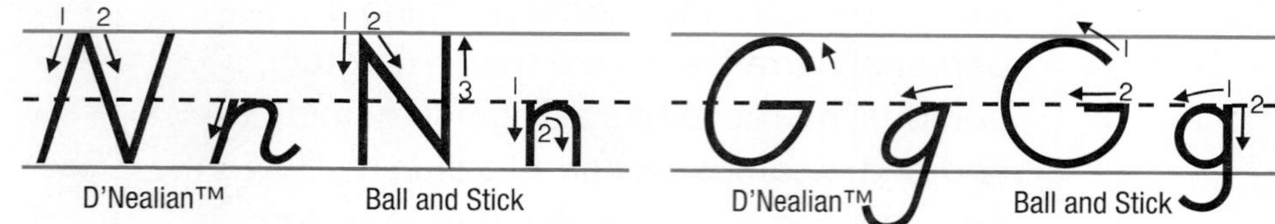

Model consistent letter slant Explain that when we write a word, all the letters in that word should be slanted the same way. Write the word *calling* two times, one with the letters slanted correctly, and one with the letters slanted in various directions. When I write the letters in a word, I need to make sure they all go the same way. By correctly slanting the letters in a word, I make it easier for others to understand what I write.

Guide practice Write the following words, one slanted correctly and the remaining words with letters slanting in various ways.

rolling	packing	camping	stacking

Team Talk Have children work in pairs to discuss which word is slanted correctly and which one is not. Have them discuss how to fix the words that are not slanted correctly. Have them share with the class.

On their own Use the *Reader's and Writer's Notebook* p. 177.

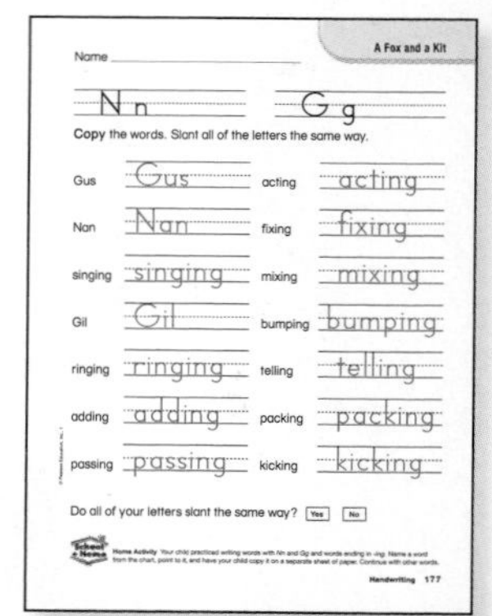

Reader's and Writer's Notebook p. 177

Research and Inquiry
Research Skill: How to Read a Chart

Teach Tell children that a **chart** is a diagram that organizes information and shows how facts are connected. A chart often uses a title, headings, and columns to show how the information is organized.

Model Think Aloud Display Research Transparency 4. This is an example of a chart. Let's see how this chart organizes information. Read aloud the title and the headings. Looking at the title, I can tell that the chart is about wild animals and their babies. On one side are the names of the animals. On the other side are the names of the babies. I see that the animal and the name of its babies are on the same line. Let's read the first animal and baby animal together.

Guide practice Continue reading the names of the animals and their babies. Have children tell how the chart helps them know which baby name goes with which animal name.

Academic Vocabulary

chart a diagram that organizes information and shows how facts are connected

Chart

Animal Name	Baby Name
fox	kit
bear	cub
hippo	calf
seal	pup
goat	kid

Unit 1: A Fox and a Kit — Research 4

Research Transparency 4
TR DVD

Wrap Up Your Day

✔ **Phonics: Inflected Ending *-ing*** Write the words *packing, looking,* and *picking*. Have children identify the base word and the ending.

✔ **High-Frequency Words** Write the following sentence: *This kit eats four or five times a day.* Read the sentence. Then point to the high-frequency words *this*, *eats, four*, and *five*, and have children read them.

✔ **Build Concepts** Monitor children's use of oral vocabulary as they respond. Recall the wild animals children have read about. Ask: What animal lives in the canopy of a jungle? (parrots) What sound do parrots make? (Parrots screech.) What can you learn when you observe wild animals? (how a parent takes care of its babies)

Tell children that tomorrow they will reread *A Fox and a Kit.*

Get Ready to Read

Objectives

- Build oral vocabulary.
- Identify details in text.
- Share information and ideas about the concept.

Today at a Glance

Oral Vocabulary
million

Phonological Awareness
Count Syllables

Phonics and Spelling
Inflected Endings *-s*
Inflected Endings *-ing*

High-Frequency Words
eat, her, five, four, this, too

Story Words
dinner

Comprehension
Plot

Fluency
Accuracy and Appropriate Rate

Conventions
Declarative Sentences

Writing
Personal Narrative
Writing Trait: Voice

Listening and Speaking
Share Information and Ideas

Research and Inquiry
Gather and Record Information

Concept Talk

Question of the Week

How do wild animals take care of their babies?

Build concepts

To reinforce concepts and to focus children's attention, have children sing "Squirrel Song" from the *Sing with Me* Big Book. What are some things that wild squirrels do? (Possible response: They climb trees and gather nuts.)

Sing with Me Big Book Audio

Monitor listening comprehension

Display the Big Book *Jungle Drum*. As children listen to the story, have them think about what sounds they might hear in the jungle. Then read the book aloud.

Big Book

- What sounds can you hear in the jungle? (Drops of water say blip, blop.)
- Why does the jungle sound like a drum? (It has sounds that are repeated over and over.)

ELL **Expand Vocabulary** Use the Day 3 instruction on ELL Poster 4 to expand children's use of English vocabulary to communicate about lesson concepts.

ELL Poster 4

Oral Vocabulary
Amazing Words

Amazing Words

observe	speech
wild	million
parent	reserve
canopy	native

Teach Amazing Words

Amazing Words Oral Vocabulary Routine

1. **Introduce the Word** Relate the word *million* to the book. A million different plants grow in the jungle. Supply a child-friendly definition. A million is a very large number. Have children say the word.
2. **Demonstrate** Provide examples to show meaning. We saw a million stars shining in the night sky. Mom told me a million times not to do that. It would take a long time to count to a million.
3. **Apply** Have children demonstrate their understanding. Would you prefer a million new toys or a million new friends? Why?

Routines Flip Chart

Anchored Talk

Add to the concept map

Use these questions to discuss ideas about how wild animals take care of their babies.

- In *A Fox and a Kit*, we watch the fox nap with her kit. Let's add *They nap with them* to our map.
- How does the mother fox move the kit? She picks him up. Let's add that to the map.

ELL

English Language Learners

Cognates Using the Spanish word *millón* will give Spanish speakers support in learning the English word *million*.

Objectives

- Count syllables in spoken words.
- ◎ Read words with the inflected ending *-s*.

Phonological Awareness
Count Syllables

Model counting syllables Have children look at the picture on pages 96–97 of the Student Edition. Today we are going to use this picture to help us count syllables. Remember that a **syllable** is a word part that has a single vowel sound. When I look at the picture, I see the children bending and feeding bread crumbs to the ducks. *Bending* has two syllables: *bend, ing*. *Feeding* also has two syllables: *feed, ing*.

Student Edition pp. 96–97

Guide practice Guide children to use the picture to say words that have two syllables (bending, feeding).

On their own Have children change each of these single-syllable words into two-syllable words by adding *-ing.*

eat	**look**	**jump**
stand	**mend**	**hand**

Team Talk Allow children the opportunity to say other two-syllable words with a partner.

Phonics
Build Words

Model word building Now we are going to build words that end in *-s*. Write *mend* and blend it. Watch me add *s* to *mend*. Model blending the new word, *mends*.

Guide practice Have children spell *mends* with letter tiles. Monitor children's work as they build words.

- Make the word *bend*. Say the new word together. b e n d
- Add *s* to *bend*. Say the new word together. b e n d s
- Make the word *lend*. Say the new word together. l e n d
- Add *s* to *lend*. Say the new word together. l e n d s

Corrective feedback For corrective feedback, model the correct spelling and have children correct their tiles.

Fluent Word Reading

Model Write *jumps*. I know the sounds for the letters *j, u, m, p*, and *s*. I blend them and read the word *jumps*.

Guide practice Write the words below. Say the sounds in your head for each spelling you see. When I point to the word, we'll read it together. Allow one second per sound-previewing time for the first reading.

sends	dumps	looks	eats	stands	naps

On their own Have children read the list above three or four times, until they can read one word per second.

Differentiated Instruction

 Strategic Intervention

Pronunciation If children have trouble pronouncing words with the inflected ending *-s*, provide additional words and practice opportunities.

Academic Vocabulary

phonics instruction in the relationship between sounds and letters

English Language Learners

Extend Language Help children distinguish between saying singular and plural names for animals in English and in their home languages.

Objectives

- Blend and read words with the inflected endings *-s* and *-ing*.
- Decode words in context and isolation.
- Spell words with the inflected ending *-s*.

Blend and Read

Read words in isolation

Have children turn to pages 179–180 in the *Reader's and Writer's Notebook* and find the first list of words. Each word in this list has either the ending *-s* or the ending *-ing*. Let's blend and read these words. Be sure that children identify the correct sounds in words that end in *-s* or *-ing*.

Next, have children read the high-frequency words.

Read words in context

Chorally read the story along with the children. Have children identify words in the story that have the inflected ending *-s* or *-ing*.

Team Talk Pair children and have them take turns reading the story aloud to each other. Monitor children as they read to check for proper pronunciation and appropriate pacing.

On their own

To further develop automaticity, have children take the story home to reread.

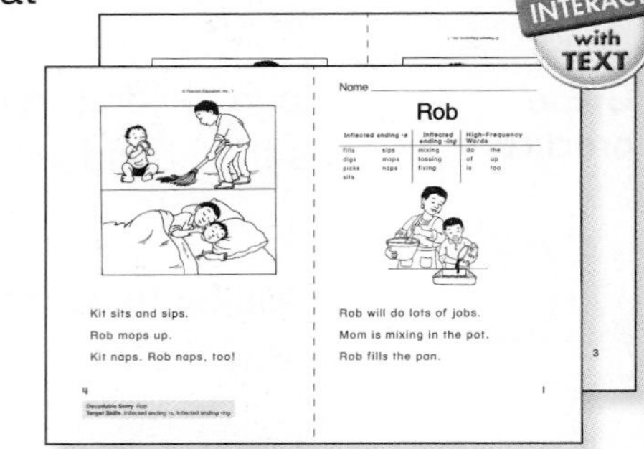

Reader's and Writer's Notebook pp. 179–180

Spelling
Inflected Ending *-s*

Spell high-frequency words Write *her* and *too* and point them out on the Word Wall. Have children say and spell the words with you and then without you.

Dictation Have children write these sentences. Say each sentence. Then repeat it slowly, one word at a time.

1. Emily sits with her.

2. I want to hit the ball too.

3. The dress fits her.

Proofread and correct Write each sentence, spelling words one at a time. Have children circle and rewrite any misspelled words.

On their own Use *Reader's and Writer's Notebook* p. 181.

Reader's and Writer's Notebook, p. 181

Spelling Words

Inflected Ending *-s*

1. sit	**6. fits**
2. sits	**7. hit**
3. win	**8. hits**
4. wins	**9. nap**
5. fit	**10. naps**

High-Frequency Words

11. her	**12. too**

Small Group Time

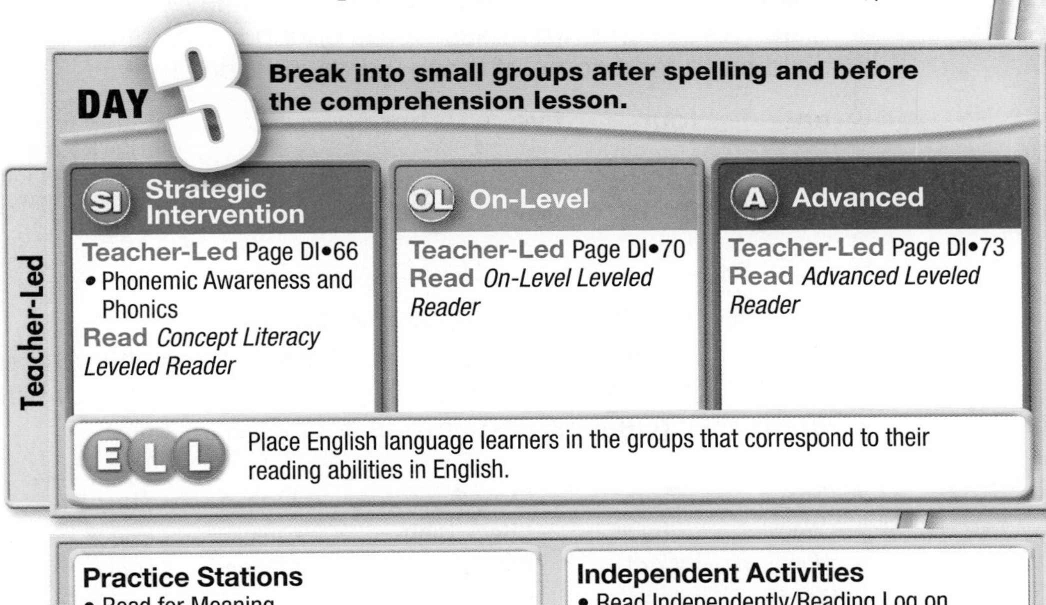

Practice Stations
- Read for Meaning
- Let's Write

Independent Activities
- Read Independently/Reading Log on *Reader's and Writer's Notebook* p. RR2
- AudioText of Main Selection

English Language Learners

Spelling Dictation Children will benefit from hearing each dictated sentence three times. First, have students listen to understand the sentence. The second time, they should write what they hear. The third time, they can check their work.

DAY 3 Read and Comprehend

40–45 min.

Objectives

- Read high-frequency and story words.
- Establish purpose for reading text.
- Review key features of literary nonfiction.

Check High-Frequency Words
SUCCESS PREDICTOR

High-Frequency and Story Words

Read words in isolation Display and review this week's high-frequency words and story words. Have children read the words aloud.

Read words in context Display the following sentence frames. Have children complete the sentences using high-frequency and story words. Have children read each completed sentence with you.

1. The fox and the kit *eat* _______ at *five*. (dinner)

2. We _______ the fox and the kit nap, *too*. (watch)

3. The _______ nap on the rocks. (animals)

4. That man has a cap, and _______ one has a hat. (this)

4. My dad has a hat _______. (too)

5. I *eat* a snack at _______. (four)

6. Sis eats _______ snack, *too*. (her)

Don't Wait Until Friday

MONITOR PROGRESS Check High-Frequency Words

Point to these words on the Word Wall and have the class read them. Listen for children who miss words during the reading. Call on those children to read some of those words individually.

eat	**four**	**five**	**her**	**Spiral Review** Rows 3 and 4 review previously taught high-frequency words.
this	**too**			
blue	**from**	**get**	**help**	←
use				←

If... children cannot read these words,
then... use the Small Group Time Strategic Intervention lesson on p. DI•67 to reteach the words. Monitor children's fluency with these words during reading and provide additional practice.

Day 1	**Day 2**	**Day 3**	**Day 4**	**Day 5**
Check Word Reading	Check Word Reading	Check High-Frequency Words/Retelling	Check Fluency	Check Oral Vocabulary

Success Predictor

Main Selection—Second Read

A Fox and a Kit

Review Realism and fantasy

Recall this week's main selection, *A Fox and a Kit*. Tell children that today they will read the story again. Remind children that this story is nonfiction because the characters, settings, and events are real. We know this story is real because the animals do not talk or behave like people; they act like animals. The setting is a real zoo.

Review Genre: literary nonfiction

Let's Read Together Remind children that literary nonfiction shares information about real people or animals, real places, and real events. Have children recall things in *A Fox and a Kit* that are real. (Possible response: The people and animals are real, zoos are real, and the events that happen in the zoo are real.)

Set a purpose

Remind children that good readers read for a purpose. Guide children to set a new purpose for reading *A Fox and a Kit* today, perhaps to consider what zookeepers do to take care of animals.

Extend thinking

Tell children they will now read *A Fox and A Kit* for the second time. Use the Day 3 Extend Thinking notes to encourage children to use higher order thinking skills to go beyond the details of the story.

Second Read

For the Second Read, use **Extend Thinking** across the bottom of pages 102–111.

Story Words

dinner the main meal of the day

Academic Vocabulary

literary nonfiction shares information about real people and animals, real places, and real events in a story format

ELL

English Language Learners

Activate Prior Knowledge Invite children to share the words for *zoo*, *zookeeper*, *fox*, and *kit* in their home languages and to describe experiences they have had with any of them.

Read and Comprehend

Objectives

- Summarize a nonfiction selection.
- ◎ Identify important ideas in literary nonfiction.
- ◎ Identify main idea and details in literary nonfiction.
- Write clear, coherent sentences.

Check Retelling
SUCCESS PREDICTOR

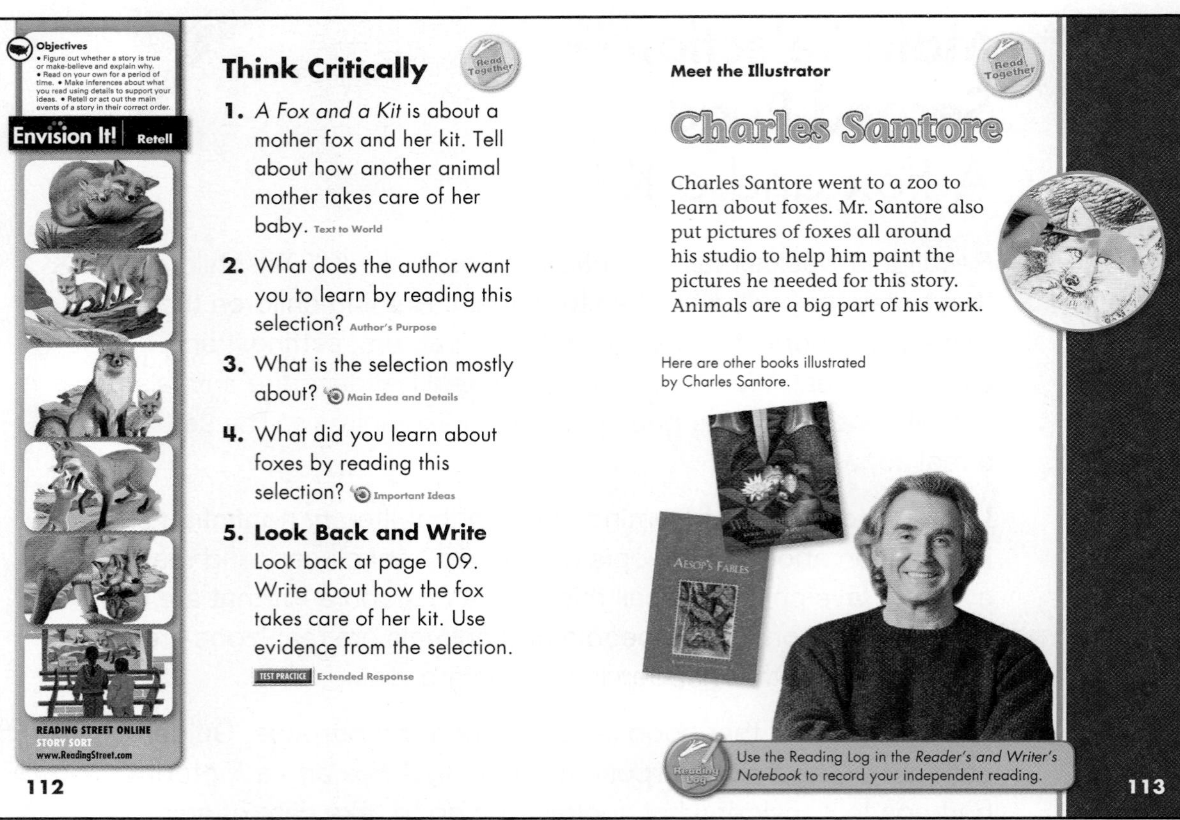

Think Critically
1. A Fox and a Kit is about a mother fox and her kit. Tell about how another animal mother takes care of her baby. Text to World
2. What does the author want you to learn by reading this selection? Author's Purpose
3. What is the selection mostly about? Main Idea and Details
4. What did you learn about foxes by reading this selection? Important Ideas
5. Look Back and Write Look back at page 109. Write about how the fox takes care of her kit. Use evidence from the selection.
Extended Response
Meet the Illustrator
Charles Santore
Charles Santore went to a zoo to learn about foxes. Mr. Santore also put pictures of foxes all around his studio to help him paint the pictures he needed for this story. Animals are a big part of his work.
Here are other books illustrated by Charles Santore.
Use the Reading Log in the Reader's and Writer's Notebook to record your independent reading.
112
113

Student Edition pp. 112–113

Retelling

Have children work in pairs, retelling the story to one another. Remind children that their partners should include the topics, main ideas, and what they learned from the reading. Children should use the retelling strip in the Student Edition as they retell. Monitor children's retelling.

Scoring rubic

Top-Score Response A top-score response makes connections beyond the text, elaborates on the author's purpose, and describes the main ideas and details.

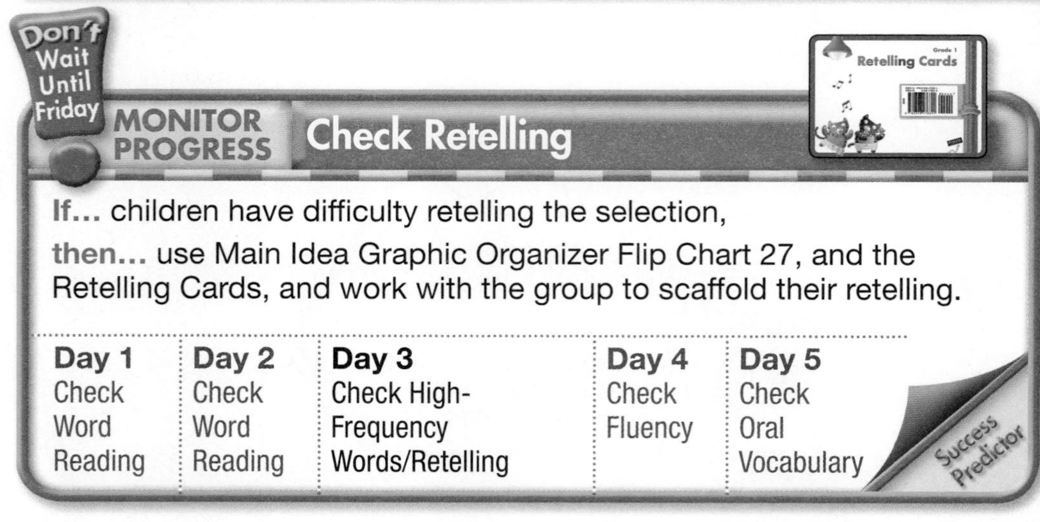

If... children have difficulty retelling the selection,
then... use Main Idea Graphic Organizer Flip Chart 27, and the Retelling Cards, and work with the group to scaffold their retelling.

Day 1	Day 2	Day 3	Day 4	Day 5
Check Word Reading	Check Word Reading	Check High-Frequency Words/Retelling	Check Fluency	Check Oral Vocabulary

Think Critically

Text to World 1. Possible response: Mother cats take care of their babies by feeding them and moving them if they feel they are in danger. Mother cats like to keep their kittens close to them, where they are warm and safe.

Author's Purpose 2. Possible response: The author wants us to learn about how mother foxes take care of their young.

Main idea and details 3. It is mostly about what a wild fox and her kit do. We learn that they nap, eat, and play together.

Important ideas 4. Mother foxes take care of their kits by keeping them close.

Writing on Demand 5. **Look Back and Write** For writing fluency, assign a five-minute time limit. As children finish, encourage them to reread their responses and proofread for errors.

Scoring rubric

> **Top-Score Response** A top-score response uses details from the text and the picture to tell how the fox takes care of her kit. For example:
>
> The fox takes care of her kit by picking him up and moving him if he is on the rocks.

Meet the illustrator Read aloud page 113 as children follow along and track the print. Ask children what an illustrator does.

Read Independently After children enter their independent reading into their Reading Logs, have them paraphrase a portion of the text they have just read. Tell children that when we paraphrase, we express the meaning of what we have just read using our own words.

Differentiated Instruction

A Advanced

Look Back and Write Ask children who show proficiency with the writing prompt to explain what the kit might learn when his mother moves him from the rocks.

INTERACT with TEXT

Strategy Response Log

Important Ideas Have children revisit p. RR16 in their Reader's and Writer's Notebook. Have them draw a picture of what they think was the most important thing that happened in the story.

Plan to Assess Summarizing

- ☐ Week 1: Strategic Intervention
- ☐ Week 2: Advanced
- ☐ Week 3: Strategic Intervention
- ☑ This week assess On-Level children.
- ☐ Week 5: Strategic Intervention
- ☐ Week 6: Assess any children you have not yet checked during this unit.

DAY 3 Read and Comprehend

Objectives

- Read aloud fluently with accuracy and at an appropriate rate.
- Define declarative sentences.

Model Fluency
Accuracy and Appropriate Rate

Model fluent reading Have children turn to Student Edition pages 106–107. Follow along as I read these pages. I will try to read with no mistakes. I want to read just the way I speak.

Guide practice Have children read the pages with you. Then have them reread the pages chorally without you until they read with no hesitation and no mistakes. Continue in the same way with pages 108–109.

Corrective feedback **If...** children have difficulty reading with accuracy and appropriate rate, **then...** prompt:

- Which word is a problem? Let's read it together.
- Read the sentence again to be sure you understand it.
- Tell me the sentence. Now read it as if you are speaking it to me.

Reread for Fluency

ROUTINE **Choral Reading**

1. **Select a Passage** For *A Fox and a Kit*, use pp. 110–111.
2. **Model** First, have children track the print as you read.
3. **Guide Practice** Then have children read along with you.
4. **Corrective Feedback** Have the class read aloud without you. Monitor progress and provide feedback. For optimal fluency, children should reread three to four times.

Routines Flip Chart

Check comprehension Who observes who on these pages? (The fox and her kit observe each other, then they observe the children; the children observe the foxes.)

Conventions
Declarative Sentences

Review Declarative statements Remind children that declarative sentences tell a fact or someone's point of view. They begin with a capital letter and usually end with a period.

Guide practice Write *bird, pig, cat,* and *fox* on the board. Have children supply some declarative sentences about each animal. Write them on the board, asking children how each one should begin and end as you do so.

Team Talk Have children talk in pairs about what each sentence tells.

Connect to oral language Have children complete these sentence frames orally.

1. Sam ________.
2. Pig ________ the mix.
3. Fox ________ her kit.

On their own Use *Reader's and Writer's Notebook* p. 182.

A Fox and a Kit

Name

Declarative Sentences

Which animals have you seen?

squirrel fox kit deer rabbit

Write about an animal you have seen. Begin and end each sentence correctly.

Possible answer: I saw a squirrel last week. It was looking for nuts. I watched it a long time.

182 Conventions Declarative Sentences

Reader's and Writer's Notebook p. 182

Options for Oral Rereading

Use *A Fox and a Kit* or one of this week's Decodable Practice Readers.

Professional Development

Fluency Having children read sentences they have produced builds both their confidence and fluency.

Daily Fix-It

5. a red bird sits in her nest
   A red bird sits in her nest.
6. there are eggs in the nest
   There are eggs in the nest.

Discuss the Daily Fix-It corrections with children. Review sentence capitalization and punctuation.

Objectives

- Write a draft of a personal narrative.
- Include feelings in writing.

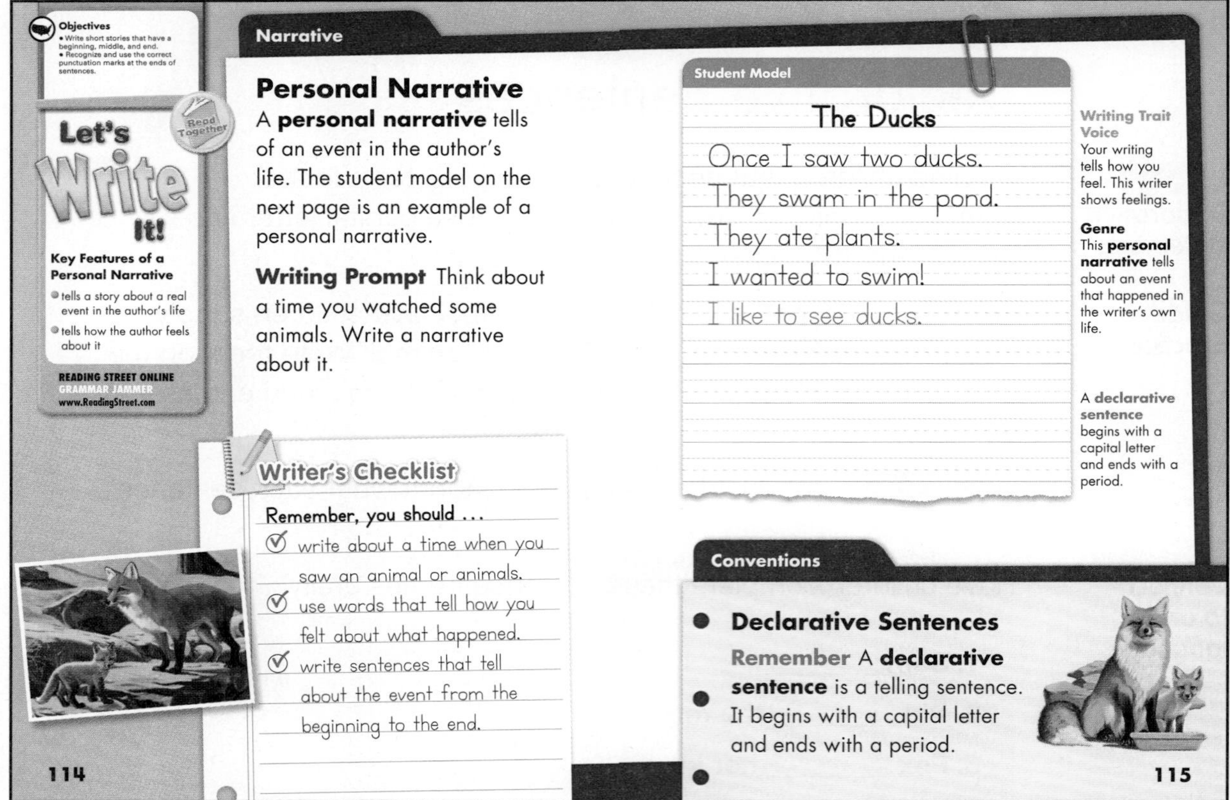

Objectives
• Write short stories that have a beginning, middle, and end. • Recognize and use the correct punctuation marks at the ends of sentences.

Let's Write It! Read Together

Key Features of a Personal Narrative
- tells a story about a real event in the author's life
- tells how the author feels about it

READING STREET ONLINE
GRAMMAR JAMMER
www.ReadingStreet.com

Narrative

Personal Narrative
A **personal narrative** tells of an event in the author's life. The student model on the next page is an example of a personal narrative.

Writing Prompt Think about a time you watched some animals. Write a narrative about it.

Writer's Checklist
Remember, you should ...
- write about a time when you saw an animal or animals.
- use words that tell how you felt about what happened.
- write sentences that tell about the event from the beginning to the end.

114

Student Model

The Ducks
Once I saw two ducks.
They swam in the pond.
They ate plants.
I wanted to swim!
I like to see ducks.

Writing Trait Voice Your writing tells how you feel. This writer shows feelings.

Genre This **personal narrative** tells about an event that happened in the writer's own life.

A **declarative sentence** begins with a capital letter and ends with a period.

Conventions

Declarative Sentences
Remember A **declarative sentence** is a telling sentence. It begins with a capital letter and ends with a period.

115

Student Edition pp. 114–115

Let's Write It! — Personal Narrative

Teach Use pages 114–115 in the Student Edition. Read aloud the Key Features of a Personal Narrative and the definition of a personal narrative. Help children better understand the Writing Prompt by reading it aloud and discussing the Writer's Checklist with children.

Review the student model Then read "The Ducks" on page 115 to children. Ask children to identify what event the narrative is mostly about. (The author watches ducks.) Ask children how the author feels about these events. (The author likes watching the ducks and wants to swim.) Read aloud and briefly discuss the side notes about Genre, the Writing Trait, and declarative sentences to help children understand how an author writes a personal narrative.

Scoring rubric

> **Top-Score Response** Help children understand that a top-score response tells how they feel about what they saw and has words in an order that makes sense. For a complete rubric see Writing Rubric 4 from the Teacher Resource DVD-ROM.

Connect to conventions Read to children the Conventions note about Declarative Sentences. Point out the declarative sentences in the personal narrative.

Writing—Personal Narrative
Writing Trait: Voice

MINI-LESSON

Including Feelings

- **Introduce** Use your story chart from yesterday and Writing Transparency 4A to model including feelings. When I write my narrative, I will use my chart. First, I will tell about going to the park and seeing the bunny in the garden there. I will use voice and show how I feel about my topic. So I'll write I like to go to the park. This sentence tells my feelings. Read aloud the draft on the Transparency and point out other sentences that tell feelings, such as *It looked so funny!* and *I was sorry to see it go*.

The Bunny in the Garden

I like to go to the park. I sit under a big elm tree I walk in the rose garden.

One Saturday I saw a bunny in the rose garden. I looked at the bunny The bunny looked at me. I saw the bunny on the grassy path.

The bunny filled its mouth with grass. It watched me while it stuffed its mouth. The grass stuck out of its mouth. It looked so funny!

Then the bunny hopped away into the rose bushes. I was sorry to see it go.

Writing Transparency 4A
TR DVD

- Explain how children can use story events they planned yesterday to draft the narrative. Remind them to include feelings about the events. Today's goal is to write the story but not to write each word perfectly. They can edit later to correct the words.

Guide story Now it is time to write your narrative. Tell what you saw and how you felt when you watched animals. Have children use their story charts. Help them finish the ideas. Then guide children as they draft the narrative.

ROUTINE Quick Write for Fluency — Team Talk

1. **Talk** Have partners take one minute to talk about an animal that they often see in the schoolyard or near their homes.
2. **Write** Each child writes a sentence telling a feeling about the animal.
3. **Share** Partners point out the words that tell feelings in the others' sentences.

Routines Flip Chart

Differentiated Instruction

Advanced

Developing Voice Ask children to include not just their feelings, but a sentence telling why they feel as they do about the animals and events in their narrative.

Write Guy
Jeff Anderson

Teaching Trait: Focus

In a writing conference, choose one aspect of a child's draft, not many things. This will help the child more than trying to think about multiple writing traits at once. Maybe there is one skill at this child's growing edge of knowledge that I can help him improve. I'd hate to see that lost in a swarm of other comments.

Objectives

- Use good speaking and listening behaviors.
- Share information and ideas.
- Apply knowledge of a chart to an inquiry project.

Listening and Speaking
Share Information and Ideas

Teach sharing information and ideas Remind children that people share information and ideas in order to help each other learn more about a topic. When people share what they know and think, it helps if they speak and listen well.

- Good speakers speak clearly at an appropriate pace. They do not speak too quickly or too slowly. They also use complete sentences that listeners can understand.
- Good listeners pay attention to what the speaker is saying, wait their turn to speak, and make appropriate contributions.

Model Use the passage below to model sharing information.

Bald eagles build nests for their eggs. After the eggs hatch, the babies depend on their parents for food and protection. At first the father collects food for the babies. The mother stays at the nest to protect them. The parents tear the food into small pieces so the babies can eat it.

Guide practice Briefly discuss how other animals care for their babies with the children. Have them share what they know about the birds in their neighborhood or other animals they are familiar with.

On their own Have pairs of children take turns listening to and speaking about how animals take care of their babies. Remind children to listen politely and to speak clearly at an appropriate pace.

Research and Inquiry
Gather and Record Information

Teach Tell children that today they will look through sources of information to find facts about wild animals and their babies. They will use the information to create a chart.

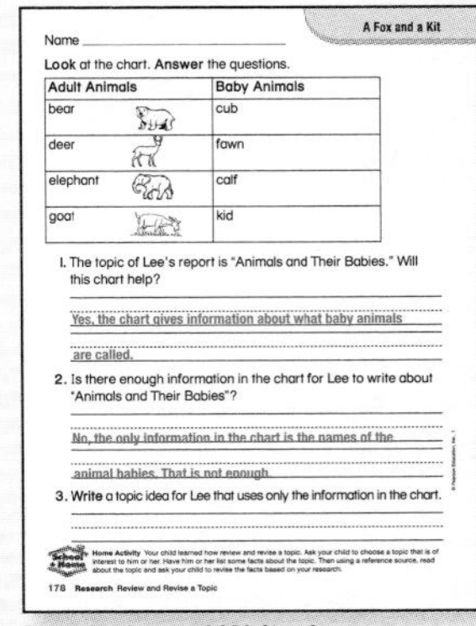

A Fox and a Kit

Name ______

Look at the chart. **Answer** the questions.

Adult Animals	Baby Animals
bear	cub
deer	fawn
elephant	calf
goat	kid

1. The topic of Lee's report is "Animals and Their Babies." Will this chart help?

   Yes, the chart gives information about what baby animals are called.

2. Is there enough information in the chart for Lee to write about "Animals and Their Babies"?

   No, the only information in the chart is the names of the animal babies. That is not enough.

3. Write a topic idea for Lee that uses only the information in the chart.

Home Activity Your child learned how review and revise a topic. Ask your child to choose a topic that is of interest to him or her. Have him or her list some facts about the topic. Then using a reference source, read about the topic and ask your child to revise the facts based on your research.

178 **Research** Review and Revise a Topic

Reader's and Writer's Notebook p. 178

Model Think Aloud Display the list of animals the class created on Day 1. Before we can write a chart, we have to pick animals to include in it. It's best to choose animals you are interested in. So, I'll ask: What are your favorite animals? You can gather information about your animals from sources like books or magazines.

Guide practice Have children use reference works to locate information about different animals that take care of their babies. Encourage children to find information about three or four animals. Suggest they write down the name of the animal and the name of its babies. Explain that they will use this information to write a chart.

On their own Use *Reader's and Writer's Notebook* p. 178.

Wrap Up Your Day

- ✔ **Main Idea and Details** Have children think about *A Fox and a Kit*. What details did you learn about the fox and the kit? What is the main idea these details tell about?
- ✔ **Important Ideas** Remind children that important ideas are the bigger ideas the author wants us to think about. Have children recall why it is helpful to be able to locate bigger ideas.

Tell children that tomorrow they will hear about a special kind of horse.

Objectives

- Discuss the concept to develop oral language.
- Build oral vocabulary.
- Identify details in text.

Today at a Glance

Oral Vocabulary
native, reserve

Phonological Awareness
Segment and Blend Onset and Rime

Phonics and Spelling
Review Short *o* spelled *o*
Review *–s* plurals

High-Frequency Words
Review

Comprehension
◉ Main Idea and Details

Fluency
Accuracy and Appropriate Rate

Conventions
Declarative Sentences

Writing
Personal Narrative

Research and Inquiry
Review and Revise Topic

Concept Talk

Question of the Week

How do wild animals take care of their babies?

Build concepts To reinforce concepts and to focus children's attention, have children sing "Squirrel Song" from the *Sing with Me* Big Book. How can we learn about wild squirrels? (Possible response: We can observe what they do.)

Sing with Me Big Book Audio

Review Genre: literary nonfiction Have children tell the key features of literary nonfiction: it tells about real people, animals, and events. The setting is real. Explain that today you will read about another animal that lives in zoos and in the wild in "Takhi" by Karen Magnuson Beil.

"Takhi"

Monitor listening comprehension Recall how the mother fox and her kit in the zoo were looked after by people. Have children listen to "Takhi" to find out how wild horses were helped by people. Read the selection.

ELL Poster 4

ELL Produce Oral Language Use the Day 4 instruction on ELL Poster 4 to extend and enrich language.

Oral Vocabulary
Amazing Words

Teach Amazing Words

Amazing Words Oral Vocabulary Routine

1. **Introduce the Word** Relate the word *native* to the story. People wanted to return the takhi to their *native* land. Supply a child-friendly definition. *Native* means "from a certain place." Have children say the word.
2. **Demonstrate** Provide examples to show meaning. That man is *native* to New York City. My grandparents decided to return to their *native* land. Spanish is some people's *native* language.
3. **Apply** Have children demonstrate their understanding. Tell something about your *native* country and your *native* language. Use the word *native* when you tell about it.

See p. OV•1 to teach *reserve*.

Anchored Talk

Add to the concept map

Discuss how wild animals take care of their babies.

- We read and sang about how wild animals take care of their babies. In "Squirrel Song," what is Mama Squirrel doing? (Possible response: She is watching over her baby.) Let's add *They watch over their babies* to our map.
- Referring to our concept map, what are some of the ways the takhi horses might take care of their young in the wild? (Possible responses: teach them new things; play with them; nap with them; watch over them.)

Amazing Words

observe	screech
wild	million
parent	native
canopy	reserve

Differentiated Instruction

Advanced

Amazing Words Apply knowledge of oral vocabulary by asking questions that include the Amazing Words, such as: If you hear a wild animal screech, what might have happened? Name some native jungle animals. If you had a million dollars, how might you use it to help wild animals? Encourage children to use the words in discussion and writing.

English Language Learners

Develop Vocabulary Explain that in this selection the word *reserve* means a safe place set aside for animals. For children who need visual support, draw a simple picture to illustrate the meaning.

Objectives

- Segment and blend onset and rime.
- Identify and decode words with short *o* spelled *o*.
- Recognize plurals ending in *-s*.

Phonological Awareness
Segment and Blend Onset and Rime

Model This week we read about a fox and her kit. Listen as I say the first sound in *kit*: /k/. *Kit* ends with the sound *-it.* Now I will blend these sounds together to say the word: /k/ -it, *kit.*

Guide practice I will say the sounds in a word, and you repeat them after me. Then we will say the word together. Say the sounds in each word below, then guide children to say the sounds. Then say the word with the children.

Corrective feedback If children make an error, model the correct response. Return to the word later in the practice.

/s/ -it (sit)	**/d/ -ot** (dot)	**/n/ -ap** (nap)
/h/ -at (hat)	**/s/ /t/ -age** (stage)	**/l/ -og** (log)

On their own Have children segment and blend the following words.

/m/ -an (man)	**/p/ -ick** (pick)	**/p/ -at** (pat)
/k/ -age (cage)	**/p/ -an** (pan)	**/j/ -ot** (jot)

Phonics Review
Short *o* spelled *o*; -*s* plurals

Review Sound-spellings To review last week's phonics skill, write *hop* and *rock*. You studied words like these last week. What do you know about the sound of *o* in a one-syllable word? (The *o* stands for the sound /o/.)

Corrective feedback If children are unable to answer your questions about short *o*, refer them to Sound-Spelling Card 17.

Review Plurals To review last week's second phonics skill, write *kids, caps,* and *socks.* You also studied words like these. What does the letter *s* mean at the end of these words? (It makes the words plural.)

Guide practice Use Graphic Organizer 4. When I say a word, put up your hand if it is plural: *pins, dog, cats, mops, rat, pan, maps, sock.* Write each word in the appropriate column. Then have children read the words. Have them identify words with short *o* (*dog, mops, sock*).

Singular	Plural
dog	pins
rat	cats
pan	mops
sock	maps

On their own Use Let's Practice It! pp. 51–52 on the *Teacher Resource DVD-ROM*.

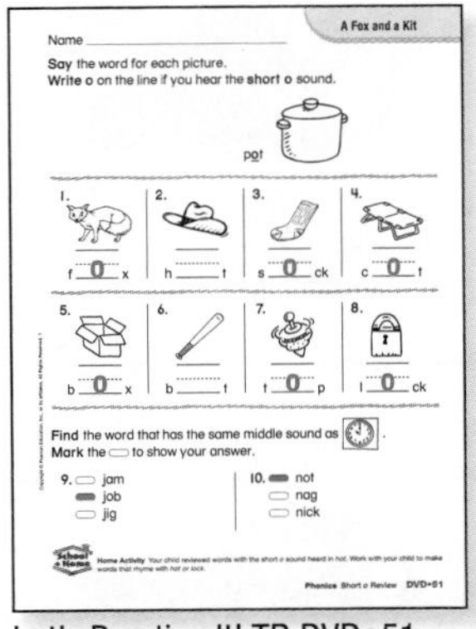

Let's Practice It! TR DVD•51

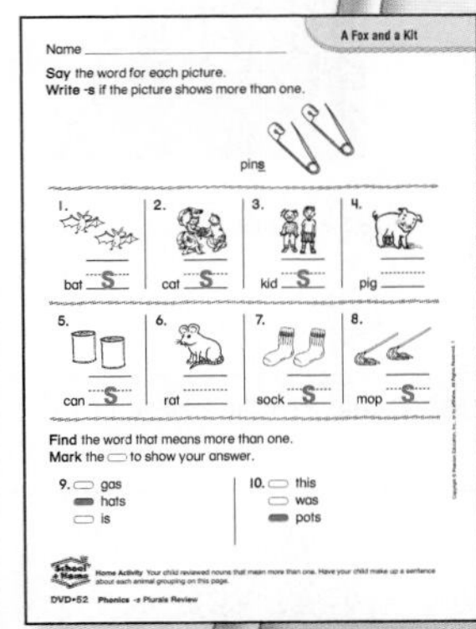

Let's Practice It! TR DVD•52

English Language Learners

Pronounce -*s* plurals Speakers of other languages may have difficulty pronouncing –*s* plurals and may spell them *z.* Provide additional practice with these words.

Objectives

- Apply knowledge of sound-spellings to decode unknown words when reading.
- Decode and read words in context and in isolation.
- Practice fluency with oral rereading.

Decodable Practice Reader 4C

Inflected Ending *-s*; Inflected Ending *-ing*

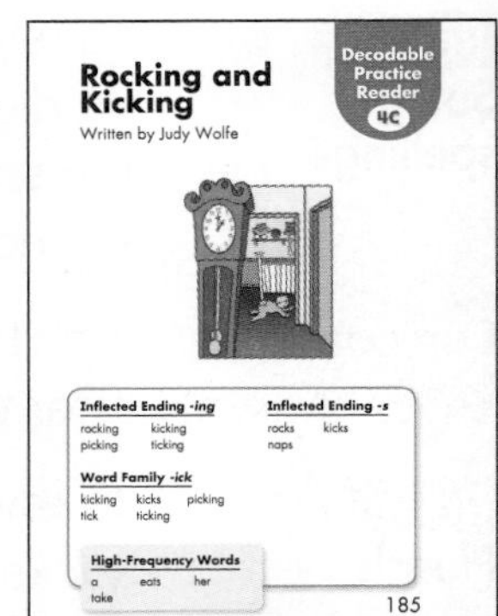

Decodable Practice Reader 4C

Decode words in isolation Have children turn to p. 185. Have children decode each word.

Review High-frequency words Review the previously taught words *a, eats, take,* and *her.* Have children read each word as you point to it on the Word Wall.

Preview Have children read the title and preview the story. Tell them they will read words that end in *–s* and words that end in *–ing.*

Decode words in context Pair children for reading and listen carefully as they decode. One child begins. Children read the entire story, switching readers after each page. Partners reread the story. This time the other child begins.

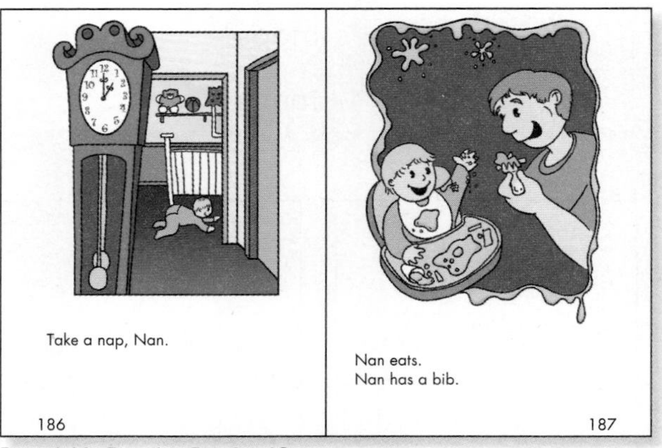

Take a nap, Nan.
186
Nan eats.
Nan has a bib.
187

Decodable Practice Reader 4C

Mom is rocking Nan.
Mom rocks her.
188
Nan is kicking.
Nan kicks.
189

Sam is picking it up.
190
Mom naps.
Dad naps.
Sam naps.
Can Nan nap?
191

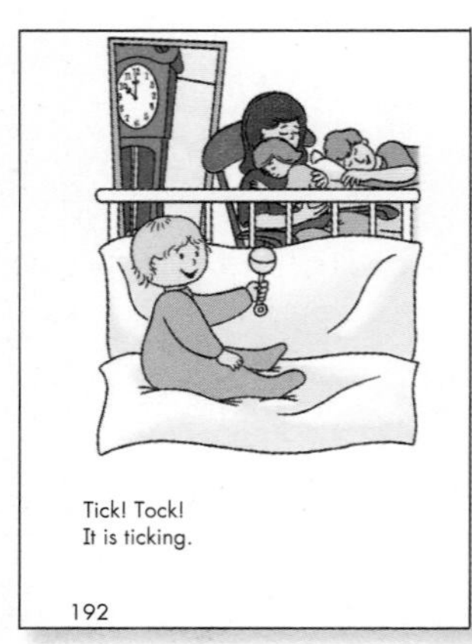

Corrective feedback

If... children have difficulty decoding a word, **then...** refer them to the Sound-Spelling Cards to identify the sounds in the word. Then prompt them to blend the word.

- What is the new word?
- Is the new word a word you know?
- Does it make sense in the story?

Check decoding and comprehension

Have children retell the story to include characters, setting, and events. Then have children find words that end in -*s* and words that end in -*ing* in the story. Children should supply *rocking, rocks, kicking, kicks, eats, picking, naps,* and *ticking.*

Reread for Fluency

Have children reread Decodable Reader 4C to develop automaticity decoding words that end in -*s* and words that end in -*ing.*

ROUTINE Oral Rereading

1. **Read** Have children read the entire book orally.
2. **Reread** To achieve optimal fluency, children should reread the text three or four times.
3. **Corrective Feedback** Listen as children read. Provide corrective feedback regarding their fluency and decoding.

Routines Flip Chart

ELL

English Language Learners

Decodable Practice Reader

Beginning Show children the words with inflected ending –*s* in the story. Break each word into its base word and its –*s* ending. Have children first say each part of a word, and then blend the parts to say the whole word.

Intermediate Have children read each sentence in the story that has a verb with an –*s* ending. Have them pantomime the action as they pronounce the word with the –*s* ending. Monitor children's pronunciation of the words.

Advanced/Advanced High Have children read the sentences in the story with verbs that have the –*s* ending. Then have them produce new sentences using *helps, hits, sits,* and *wins.*

Get Ready to Read

Objectives

- Read words fluently in context and in isolation.
- Spell words with the inflected ending *-s.*
- Spell high-frequency words.

Fluent Word Reading

Spiral Review

Read words in isolation

Display these words. Tell children that they can blend some words on this list and others are Word Wall words.

Have children read the list three or four times until they can read at the rate of two to three seconds per word.

little	**can**	**help**	**Max**	**locks**
sack	**from**	**will**	**for**	**here**
Nick	**me**	**box**	**use**	**is**
blue	**what**	**do**	**lids**	**Dot**

Word Reading

Corrective feedback

If... children have difficulty reading whole words,
then... have them use sound-by-sound blending for decodable words or have them say and spell high-frequency words.

If... children cannot read fluently at a rate of two to three seconds per word,
then... have pairs practice the list until they can read it fluently.

Read words in context

Display these sentences. Call on individuals to read a sentence. Then randomly point to review words and have children read them. To help you monitor word reading, high-frequency words are underlined and decodable words are italicized.

<u>What</u> *can Max* <u>do</u> <u>for</u> <u>me</u>?

***Nick will* <u>help</u> <u>from</u> <u>here</u>.**

<u>Use</u> <u>little</u> *locks on* <u>the</u> *box lids.*

Dot is packing* <u>a</u> <u>blue</u> *sack.

Sentence Reading

Corrective feedback

If... children have difficulty reading an italicized decodable word,
then... guide them in using sound-by-sound blending.

If... children are unable to read an underlined high-frequency word,
then... read the word for them and spell it, having them echo you.

Spelling
Inflected Ending *-s*

Partner Review Supply pairs of children with index cards on which the spelling words have been written. Have one child read a word while the other writes it. Then have children switch roles. Have them use the cards to check their spelling and correct any misspelled words.

On their own Use *Reader's and Writer's Notebook* p. 183.

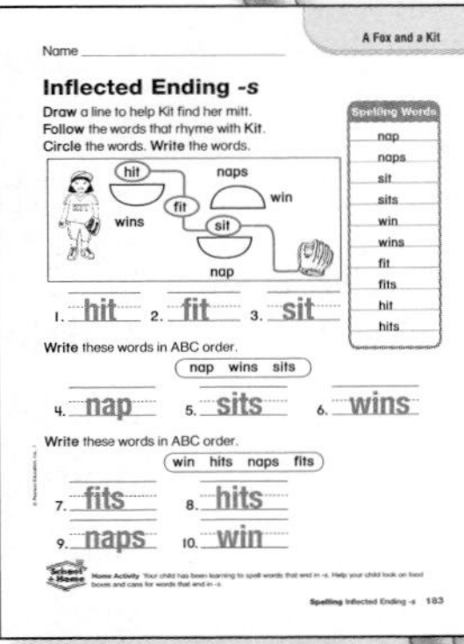

A Fox and a Kit

Name

Inflected Ending -s

Draw a line to help Kit find her mitt.
Follow the words that rhyme with **Kit**.
Circle the words. **Write** the words.

Spelling Words: nap, naps, sit, sits, win, wins, fit, fits, hit, hits

1. hit 2. fit 3. sit

Write these words in ABC order.

nap wins sits

4. nap 5. sits 6. wins

Write these words in ABC order.

win hits naps fits

7. fits 8. hits
9. naps 10. win

Spelling Inflected Ending -s 183

Reader's and Writer's Notebook p. 183

Small Group Time

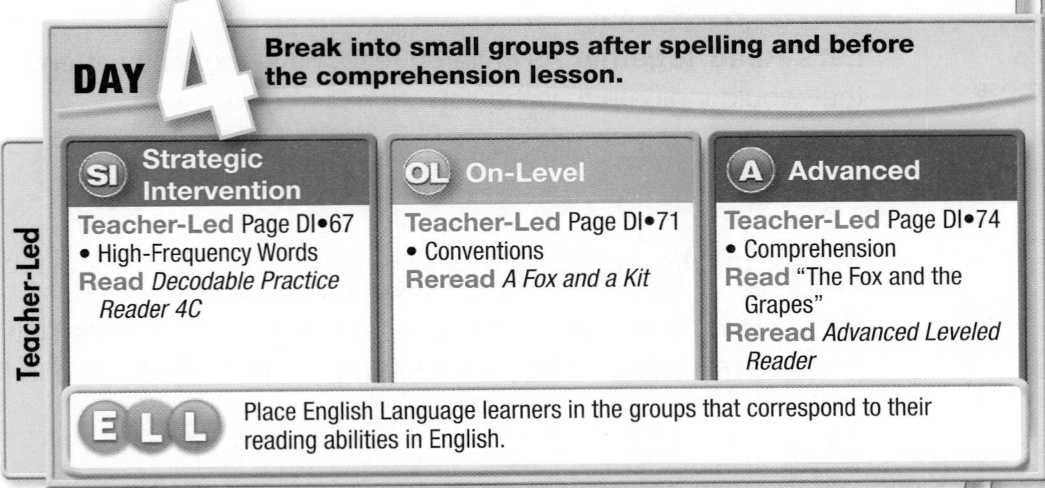

DAY 4 Break into small groups after spelling and before the comprehension lesson.

Teacher-Led

SI Strategic Intervention	OL On-Level	A Advanced
Teacher-Led Page DI•67 • High-Frequency Words **Read** *Decodable Practice Reader 4C*	**Teacher-Led** Page DI•71 • Conventions **Reread** *A Fox and a Kit*	**Teacher-Led** Page DI•74 • Comprehension **Read** "The Fox and the Grapes" **Reread** *Advanced Leveled Reader*

ELL Place English Language learners in the groups that correspond to their reading abilities in English.

Practice Stations
- Words to Know
- Get Fluent

Independent Activities
- Read Independently/Reading Log on *Reader's and Writer's Notebook* p.RR2
- AudioText of Paired Selection

Spiral Review

These activities review
- previously taught high-frequency words *what, help, the, use.*
- short *o* spelled *o,* inflected endings *-s* and *-ing.*

ELL

English Language Learners

Fluent Word Reading Children may benefit from first reading words in pairs to aid their decoding and pronunciation.

Objectives

- ◎ Identify important ideas.
- Recognize structure and elements of a fable.
- Relate prior knowledge to new text.
- Set purpose for reading.

Science in Reading

Preview and predict Read the title and the first sentence of the selection. Have children look through the selection and predict what they might learn. (Possible response: They might learn about a fox and some grapes.) Ask them what clue helped them make that prediction. (Possible response: They might say the title of the selection or the pictures.)

Let's Think About **Genre** **Fable** Tell children that they will read a **fable**. Review the key features of a fable: it is a short story that teaches a lesson, or moral, and it often has animal characters that speak and act like people. Explain that this selection is a fable because it is a short story that teaches a lesson, or moral, and it has an animal character that talks and acts like a person.

Activate prior knowledge Ask children to recall what they have already learned about foxes. (Some foxes live in zoos and some live in the wild; mother foxes take care of their young.)

Set a purpose **Let's Read Together** As children read, have them pay attention to clues that would indicate that the selection is a fable.

As you read "The Fox and the Grapes" together, use Let's Think About in the Student Edition to help children focus on the features of a fable.

Objectives
- Connect the meaning of a famous story or fable to your own experiences.

Science in Reading

Genre
Fable

- A fable is a short story that teaches a lesson, or moral.
- The characters in a fable are often animals that speak and act like people.
- The author wants readers to connect a fable's moral to their personal experiences.
- Read "The Fox and the Grapes." Look for elements that make this story a fable.

Read Together

The Fox and the Grapes
adapted from Aesop

One day, a fox wanted grapes.

But he could not reach them.

The fox tried again and again.

At last, the fox gave up.

"I did not want those sour grapes anyway," he said.

Moral: It is easy to dislike what you cannot get.

Let's Think About...
How do you know this story is a fable? **Fable**

Let's Think About...
What does the moral of the fable mean? How can you connect the meaning to things that have happened to you? **Fable**

Let's Think About...
Reading Across Texts How are the foxes in *A Fox and a Kit* and "The Fox and the Grapes" alike? How are they different?

Writing Across Texts Imagine the foxes in *A Fox and a Kit* could talk to the fox in "The Fox and the Grapes." Write what they would say to him. Write what he would say to them.

116 117

Student Edition pp. 116–117

Academic Vocabulary

moral the lesson or teaching of a fable or story

Science Vocabulary

vine a grape plant, or a long stem that trails along the ground or winds around a support such as the branch of a tree

Guide Comprehension

Important Ideas

Guide practice

Think Aloud: Good readers look for the big or important ideas as they read so that they can have a better understanding of what a story or selection is about. When I finished reading *A Fox and a Kit*, I thought about all the things the mother fox and her kit did together. I will pay attention to what the fox does as I read "The Fox and the Grapes."

Main idea

Think Aloud: I think about the title of this fable — "The Fox and the Grapes." I wonder if the fox will eat the grapes.

Let's Think About... Fables

Possible response: This is a fable because it is a short story that teaches a lesson, or moral, and it has an animal character who speaks and who acts like a human.

Read and Comprehend

Objectives

- Summarize a fable.
- Read aloud fluently with accuracy and at an appropriate rate.

Fluency: WCPM
SUCCESS PREDICTOR

Guide Comprehension, continued

Main Idea and Details What does the fox want to do in this story? It wants to eat the grapes.

Important Ideas What do you think the lesson, or moral, of this story is? It is easy to dislike what you cannot get.

Reading Across Texts Have children find words and sentences in the texts of *A Fox and a Kit* and "The Fox and the Grapes" to tell what the foxes do. How are they different?

Writing Across Texts Children might note that the man in *A Fox and a Kit* brings the foxes their dinner, while the fox in "The Fox and a Grapes" does not get anything to eat.

Fluency
Accuracy and Appropriate Rate

Guide practice

- Have children turn to pages 108–109 in *A Fox and a Kit*.
- Have children follow along as you read the pages accurately and at an appropriate rate.
- Have the class read the pages with you and then reread the pages as a group until they read with no hesitation and no mistakes. To provide additional fluency practice, pair nonfluent readers with fluent readers.

ROUTINE Paired Reading

1. **Select a Passage** For *A Fox and a Kit*, use pp. 110–111.
2. **Model** First, have children track the print as you read.
3. **Guide Practice** Then have children read long with you.
4. **On Their Own** For optimal fluency, have partners reread three or four times.

Routines Flip Chart

MONITOR PROGRESS — Fluency: WCPM

As children reread, monitor their progress toward their individual fluency goals. Beginning in Unit 3, children will be assessed to determine WCPM. Mid-Year Goal: 20–30 words correct per minute. End-of-current Year Goal: 60 words correct per minute.

If... children are not on track to meet benchmark goals,
then... have children practice with text at their independent level.

Day 1	Day 2	Day 3	Day 4	Day 5
Check Word Reading	Check Word Reading	Check High Frequency Words/Retelling	Check Fluency	Check Oral Vocabulary

Success Predictor

Differentiated Instruction

Advanced

WCPM If children already read at 60 words correct per minute, allow them to read independently. See the Books for Independent Reading pages for suggestions.

Options for Oral Rereading

Use *A Fox and a Kit* or one of this week's Decodable Practice Readers.

Fluency WCPM Success Predictor

20–25 min.

Objectives

- Identify declarative sentences.
- Revise narrative by rearranging sentences.

Conventions
Declarative Sentences

Test practice Use Reader's and Writer's Notebook p. 184 to help children understand identifying declarative sentences in test items. Recall that declarative sentences are statements. Model identifying a declarative sentence by writing this sentence on the board, reading it aloud, and underlining the capital letter and period.

A frog flops in the pond.

Then read the *Reader's and Writer's Notebook* p. 184 directions. Guide children as they mark the answer for number 1.

On their own Use *Reader's and Writer's Notebook* p. 184.

Connect to oral language After children mark the answers to numbers 1–6, review the correct choices aloud, and have children read each sentence aloud.

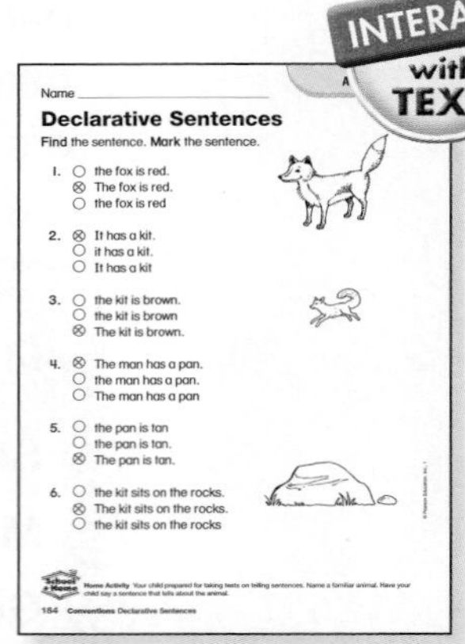

Name ______

Declarative Sentences

Find the sentence. **Mark** the sentence.

1. ○ the fox is red.
   ⊗ The fox is red.
   ○ the fox is red
2. ⊗ It has a kit.
   ○ it has a kit.
   ○ It has a kit
3. ○ the kit is brown.
   ○ the kit is brown
   ⊗ The kit is brown.
4. ⊗ The man has a pan.
   ○ the man has a pan.
   ○ The man has a pan
5. ○ the pan is tan
   ○ the pan is tan.
   ⊗ The pan is tan.
6. ○ the kit sits on the rocks.
   ⊗ The kit sits on the rocks.
   ○ the kit sits on the rocks

Home Activity Your child prepared for taking tests on telling sentences. Name a familiar animal. Have your child say a sentence that tells about the animal.

184 **Conventions** Declarative Sentences

Reader's and Writer's Notebook p. 184

Writing—Personal Narrative
Revising Strategy

MINI-LESSON

Revising Strategy: Rearranging Sentences

- Yesterday we wrote personal narratives about watching animals. Today we will revise. We can help people who read the narratives. We can make them clearer or more interesting. We can make sure the sentences are in an order that makes sense.

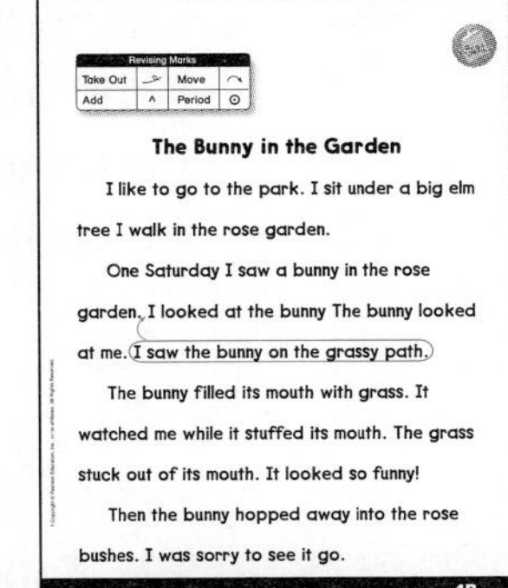

Revising Marks: Take Out | Move | Add | Period

The Bunny in the Garden

I like to go to the park. I sit under a big elm tree I walk in the rose garden.

One Saturday I saw a bunny in the rose garden. I looked at the bunny The bunny looked at me. I saw the bunny on the grassy path.

The bunny filled its mouth with grass. It watched me while it stuffed its mouth. The grass stuck out of its mouth. It looked so funny!

Then the bunny hopped away into the rose bushes. I was sorry to see it go.

Unit 1 A Fox and a Kit — Writing: Revise 4B

Writing Transparency 4B
TR DVD

- Display the Revising Tips. Explain that this is a time for making the narrative clear for anyone who will read it. Tomorrow children will proofread to correct any errors such as misspellings, missing capital letters, or misplaced sentence periods.

Revising Tips

✓ **Make sure you tell your feelings about events.**

✓ **Put sentences in an order that makes sense.**

- Use Writing Transparency 4B to model rearranging sentences. I'll tell about seeing the bunny on the grassy path before I tell about the bunny and me looking at each other. I should tell events in the same order as they happened. On the transparency, show how to use revising marks to rearrange sentences.

Tell children that they can rearrange sentences as they revise.

Peer conferencing

Peer Revision Pair up children and tell half to read the partner's narrative. Allow two minutes. Then have the readers use one or two minutes to tell the events in the narrative in order. Repeat with second partners reading and telling about the other narrative. Have each writer listen for any part of the narrative that seems out of order or that the reader has not understood. Circulate to assist children planning to revise their narratives.

Differentiated Instruction

SI Strategic Intervention

Statements If children are struggling with declarative sentences, have them tell something. Use these sentence frames to have children tell something about themselves:

I am _____.
I like _____.
I live _____.

Daily Fix-It

7. the mix is a hitt.
The mix is a hit.

8. This mix winz too
This mix wins too.

Discuss the Daily Fix-It corrections with children. Review sentence capitalization and punctuation, the *s* spelling of /z/, the inflected ending *-s*, and the spelling of *hit*.

English Language Learners

Past Tense Help children use the inflected ending *–ed* to write their narratives in past tense.

Objectives

- Revise a draft for sequence or clarity.
- Review answers to inquiry questions.

Writing
Personal Narrative, continued

Guide practice Have children revise their personal narratives. For those not sure how to revise, have children refer to the Revising Tips or the Key Features of Personal Narratives.

Corrective Feedback Circulate to monitor and conference with children as they write. Remind them that they will have time to proofread and edit tomorrow. Today they can make their narratives clearer. Help them understand the benefits of rearranging or adding sentences, if necessary. Encourage them to include their feelings about events described in their narratives.

ROUTINE Quick Write for Fluency — Team Talk

1. **Talk** Read these sentences aloud, and have children tell which action should be first and which second.

   The ducks hopped into the water.

   The ducks waddled to the pond.
2. **Write** Have children write two short sentences about two things that happen one after another. Children may write the sentences in order or out of order.
3. **Share** Have children read the sentences to partners and have partners tell which sentence should be first and which should be second.

Routines Flip Chart

Research and Inquiry
Review and Revise Topic

Teach Tell children that the next step in the inquiry project is to review our chart to see if we have the information we set out to find. Or, do we need to do more research?

Model We planned to find out about wild animals and their babies. First, we listed wild animals. Then we picked the ones we were interested in. Last, we gathered information about the animals and their babies. Now I will look at the information I gathered. I will see if I found out enough about the wild animals and their babies. If I did not, I can always look for more information.

Guide practice Have children look at the information they gathered during Day 3. They will decide what kinds of information they want to include in their chart. Guide children to choose the information they want to include and to decide how they want to use a title, columns, and headings to organize this information.

Wrap Up Your Day

✔ **Phonics Review** List several words with the inflected ending *-s*. Have children read each word and identify the base word and the ending.

✔ **Fluency** Write *Will the fox nap? Yes, the fox will nap.* Have the class reread the sentences until they can do so accurately and at an appropriate rate.

Differentiated Instruction

SI Strategic Intervention

Organize Information If children have difficulty organizing information, suggest they ask themselves questions to help figure out what the different pieces of information have in common.

Remind children that they heard about wild horses. Tomorrow they will hear about the horses again.

Objectives

- Review the concept: wild animals taking care of their babies.
- Build oral vocabulary.
- Identify details in text.

Today at a Glance

Oral Vocabulary
Review

Phonics
◎ Review Inflected Ending *-s*
◎ Review Inflected Ending *-ing*

Comprehension
◎ Main Idea and Details

Story Words
Review

High-Frequency Words
Review

Conventions
Declarative Sentences

Writing
Personal Narrative

Research and Inquiry
Communicate

Check Oral Vocabulary
SUCCESS PREDICTOR

Concept Wrap Up

Question of the Week

How do wild animals take care of their babies?

Review Concept

This week we have read and listened to stories about how wild animals take care of their babies. Today you will listen to find out how people helped takhi horses return to the wild. Read the story.

- What is something the takhi needed to learn before returning to the wild? (Possible response: They had to learn how to find food.)

Scott Foresman
Read Aloud
Anthology
"Takhi"

Review Amazing Words

Orally review the meaning of this week's Amazing Words. Then display this week's concept map. Have children use Amazing Words such as *parent, wild,* and *reserve*, as well as the concept map, to answer the question, "How do wild animals take care of their babies?"

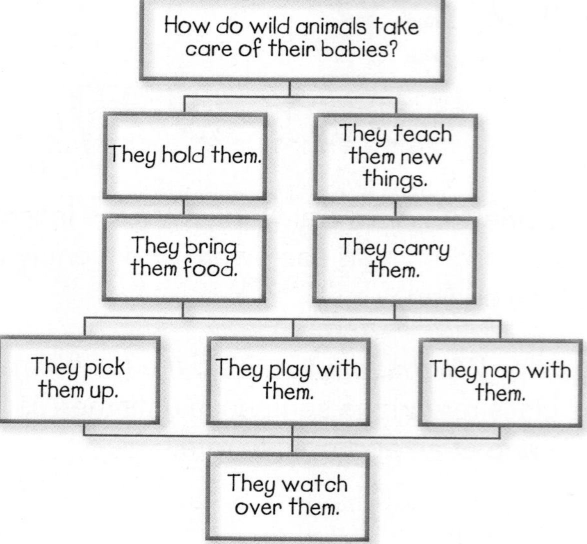
How do wild animals take care of their babies?
They hold them.
They teach them new things.
They bring them food.
They carry them.
They pick them up.
They play with them.
They nap with them.
They watch over them.

ELL Check Concepts and Language Use the Day 5 instruction on ELL Poster 4 to monitor children's understanding of the lesson concept.

ELL Poster 4

Oral Vocabulary
Amazing Ideas

Connect to the Big Question

Team Talk Pair children and have them discuss how the Question of the Week connects to this unit's Big Question, "How are people and animals important to one another?" Tell children to use the concept map and what they've learned from this week's Anchored Talks and reading selections to form an Amazing Idea—a realization or "big idea" about **Animals, Tame and Wild**. Then ask each pair to share their Amazing Idea with the class.

Amazing Ideas might include these key concepts:

- Animal parents take care of their babies.
- People can help wild animals.

It's Friday

MONITOR PROGRESS **Check Oral Vocabulary**

Call on individuals to use this week's Amazing Words to talk about how wild animals take care of their babies. Prompt discussion with the questions below. Monitor children's ability to use the Amazing Words and note which words children are unable to use.

- **What is something you can *observe*?**
- **How is a *wild* animal different from a pet?**
- **What are some things an animal *parent* can do?**
- **Where is the *canopy* in a rain forest?**
- **Why might your little brother or sister *screech?***
- **How long do you think it would take to count to a *million*?**
- **What area is *native* to the takhi?**
- **Why do some wild animals live on a *reserve*?**

If... children have difficulty using the Amazing Words,
then... reteach the unknown words using the Oral Vocabulary Routines, pp. 95a, 100b, 112b, 116b.

Day 1	Day 2	Day 3	Day 4	Day 5
Check Word Reading	Check Word Reading	Check High-Frequency Words/Retelling	Check Fluency	Check Oral Vocabulary

Success Predictor

Amazing Words

observe	screech
wild	million
parent	reserve
canopy	native

ELL

English Language Learners

Amazing Words Rephrase the questions to make true or false statements that use the Amazing Words. Have children repeat the statements before answering. People can count to one *million* very quickly. *Wild* animals are just like pets. Your little brother or sister might *screech* when hiding from you.

Oral Vocabulary Success Predictor

DAY 5 Wrap Up your Week

Objectives

- Review segmenting and blending onset and rime.
- ◎ Review words with the inflected endings -s and *-ing*.

Assess

- Spell words with the inflected ending *-s*.
- Spell high-frequency words.

Phonological Awareness
Segment and Blend Onset and Rime

Review
Segment and blend onset and rime

Have children segment and blend the onset and rime in each word below. If children make an error, model the correct response. Return to the word later in the practice.

/k/ -ap (cap)	**/p/ -age** (page)	**/p/ -ot** (pot)
/b/ -at (bat)	**/s/ -ip** (sip)	**/t/ /r/ -ick** (trick)

Phonics

Inflected Endings *-s* and *-ing*

Review
Inflected endings *-s* and *-ing*

Write the following sentences on the board. Have children read each one, first quietly to themselves and then aloud as you track the print.

1. **Mom pins and tacks the tag on the map.**
2. **Dad is fixing and waxing the van.**
3. **Pam sits and rips the rag.**
4. **Nick is kicking and passing it.**

Team Talk Have children discuss with a partner which words have the ending *-s* and which words have the ending *-ing*. Then call on individuals to share with the class.

Spelling Test
Inflected Ending *–s*

Dictate spelling words

Say each word, read the sentence, repeat the word, and allow time for children to write the word.

1. hit	**Hit** the two lids.
2. hits	Tim **hits** the box.
3. win	Will they **win**?
4. wins	Dad **wins** the top job.
5. sit	**Sit** with me.
6. sits	Max **sits** in the van.
7. nap	I do not like to **nap.**
8. naps	The cat **naps** on the mat.
9. fit	Will this cap **fit**?
10. fits	The wig **fits** Dot.

High-Frequency Words	
11. her	Mom got **her** tan socks wet.
12. too	Did you go **too**?

Differentiated Instruction

Strategic Intervention

Check Spelling Have children choose the correct spelling of each word from three random spellings.

Advanced

Extend Spelling Have children who have demonstrated proficiency in spelling individual words spell each word in a self-made sentence.

Small Group Time

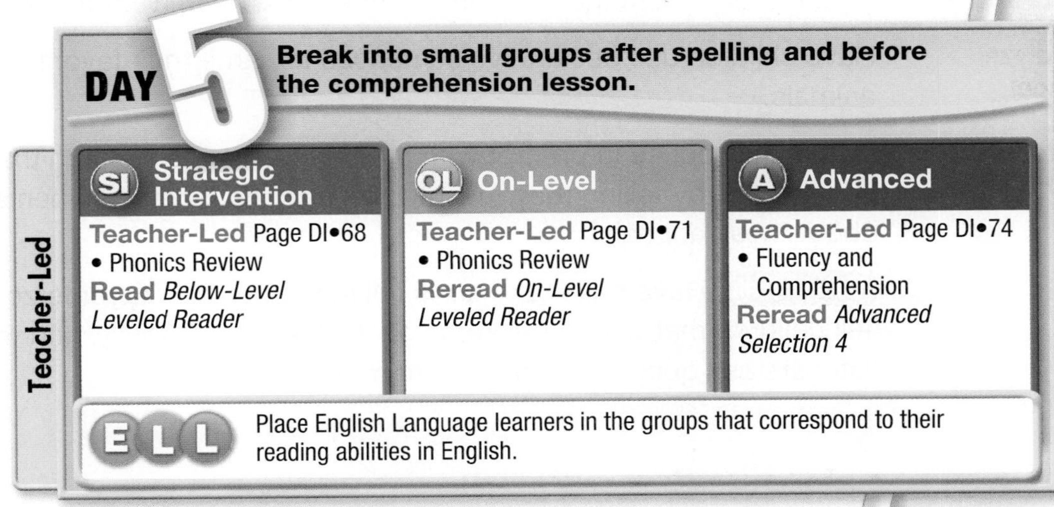

DAY 5 **Break into small groups after spelling and before the comprehension lesson.**

Teacher-Led

SI Strategic Intervention	OL On-Level	A Advanced
Teacher-Led Page DI•68 • Phonics Review **Read** *Below-Level Leveled Reader*	**Teacher-Led** Page DI•71 • Phonics Review **Reread** *On-Level Leveled Reader*	**Teacher-Led** Page DI•74 • Fluency and Comprehension **Reread** *Advanced Selection 4*

ELL Place English Language learners in the groups that correspond to their reading abilities in English.

Practice Stations
- Words to Know
- Read for Meaning

Independent Activities
- Read independently/Reading Log on *Reader's and Writer's Notebook* p. RR2
- Concept Talk Video

DAY 5 Wrap Up your Week

40–45 min.

Objectives

- Use good speaking and listening behaviors.
- Share information and ideas.
- Alphabetize a series of words to the second letter.

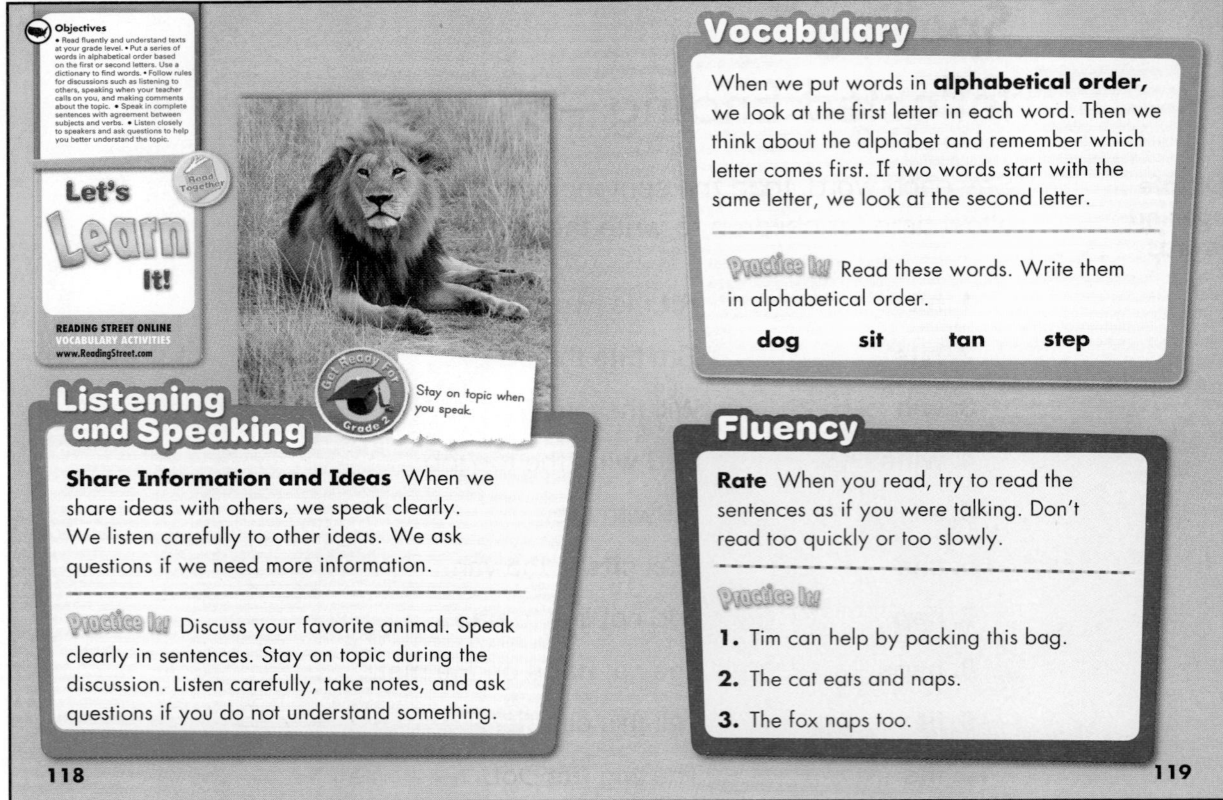

Objectives

• Read fluently and understand texts at your grade level. • Put a series of words in alphabetical order based on the first or second letters. Use a dictionary to find words. • Follow rules for discussions such as listening to others, speaking when your teacher calls on you, and making comments about the topic. • Speak in complete sentences with agreement between subjects and verbs. • Listen closely to speakers and ask questions to help you better understand the topic.

Read Together

Let's Learn It!

READING STREET ONLINE
VOCABULARY ACTIVITIES
www.ReadingStreet.com

Get Ready For Grade 2

Stay on topic when you speak.

Listening and Speaking

Share Information and Ideas When we share ideas with others, we speak clearly. We listen carefully to other ideas. We ask questions if we need more information.

Practice It! Discuss your favorite animal. Speak clearly in sentences. Stay on topic during the discussion. Listen carefully, take notes, and ask questions if you do not understand something.

Vocabulary

When we put words in **alphabetical order,** we look at the first letter in each word. Then we think about the alphabet and remember which letter comes first. If two words start with the same letter, we look at the second letter.

Practice It! Read these words. Write them in alphabetical order.

dog **sit** **tan** **step**

Fluency

Rate When you read, try to read the sentences as if you were talking. Don't read too quickly or too slowly.

Practice It!

1. Tim can help by packing this bag.
2. The cat eats and naps.
3. The fox naps too.

118 119

Student Edition pp. 118-119

Listening and Speaking
Share Information and Ideas

Teach Have children turn to pages 118–119 of the Student Edition. Remind children that good speakers speak clearly, and that good listeners listen carefully. Remind them that we can ask questions if we want more information.

Analyze model Have children use declarative sentences to name their favorite zoo animals.

Introduce prompt Read the Practice It! prompt with the class. Remind children that they should start by telling their favorite zoo animals. They can then add details about these animals.

Team Talk Have pairs take turns talking about their favorite zoo animals. Tell children that good speakers speak clearly and slowly, and that good listeners ask questions if they want more information.

Vocabulary
Alphabetize to Second Letter

Teach Read and discuss the Vocabulary lesson on page 119 of the Student Edition. Alphabetize a series of words to the second letter.

Write these words in order: *band, bed, brick*. Read and point to each word. These words are in alphabetical order. The first letter of all these words is *b*, so we need to use the second letter to put them in alphabetical order. Point to the second letter of each word in order. The second letter of *band* is *a*. The second letter of *bed* is *e*. And the second letter of *brick* is *r*. *A* comes before *e* in the alphabet, so *band* goes before *bed*. *E* comes before *r* in the alphabet, so *bed* goes before *brick*. Point to the second letter of each word. The correct order is: *band, bed, brick*.

Guide practice Read the instructions for the Vocabulary Practice It! activity. Read the first word and then have children repeat after you.

On their own Have pairs continue reading the words and writing them in alphabetical order.

Corrective feedback Circulate around the room and monitor children as they say and write the words. Provide assistance as needed.

Fluency
Accuracy and Rate

Teach Read and discuss the Fluency instructions.

Read words in context Give children a moment to look at the sentences. Then have them read each sentence three or four times until they can read each sentence with accuracy and at an appropriate rate.

Differentiated Instruction

SI Strategic Intervention

Check Alphabetizing Reteach alphabetizing to the first letter, then alphabetizing to the second letter. Ask children to point to the first or second letter of each word as you do so.

A Advanced

Extend Alphabetizing Provide children who can alphabetize to the second letter with ease with some words to alphabetize to the third letter.

ELL

English Language Learners

Pronounce Infected Ending *-ing* Some speakers may say *rockin* and *fixin*, as they may not hear the difference between *-in* and *-ing*. Have these children practice pronouncing words with ending *-ing*.

Objectives

- Identify main idea and details in a story.
- Read high-frequency and story words.
- Identify the features of a fable.

Comprehension

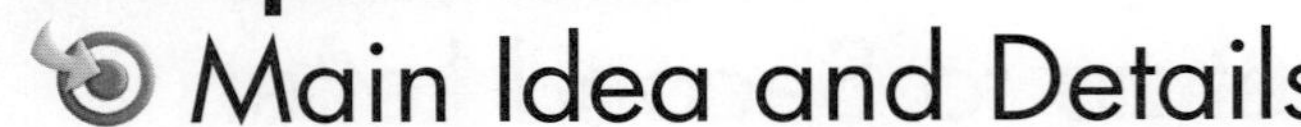

Main Idea and Details

Review Main idea and details

Remember that good readers can tell what a story or selection is mostly about. They can tell us its main idea. What do good readers think about to find the main idea in a story? (the details)

To check understanding of main idea and details, read aloud the following story and have children answer the questions that follow.

> Jasper loves basketball. He watches basketball on TV and sometimes goes to big games with his parents. He goes to basketball practice after school. When he made the school team, he started playing in games on Saturday mornings.

1. What is this passage mostly about? (It is about how Jasper loves basketball.)
2. What tells you this? (He watches basketball on TV and sometimes goes to big games with his parents. He goes to practice after school and plays in games on Saturday mornings.)

Vocabulary

High-Frequency and Story Words

Review High-frequency words

Review this week's high-frequency words: *eat*, *five*, *four*, *her*, *this*, and *too*. Model making up a sentence that tells something about this week's selection and includes a high-frequency word, for example: The man feeds the fox and the kit at *five*.

Team Talk Have children retell *A Fox and a Kit* using declarative sentences. Encourage them to use at least one of the remaining five words in each sentence.

Review Story words

Write the words *dinner, watch,* and *animals*. Read them aloud together. Then have children tell what the words mean.

Corrective feedback

If... children cannot tell what the story words mean,
then... review the definitions on page 102a.

Genre
Fable

Review Genre Review with children that a fable is a short story that teaches a lesson, or moral. The characters in a fable are often animals that speak or act like people. The author wants readers to connect the moral of a fable to their own experience.

Teach In "The Fox and the Grapes," a fox comes across some grapes hanging from a vine. He wants to eat them, but try as he might, he cannot reach them. Finally, he gives up and walks away with his nose in the air. He says, "I did not want those sour grapes anyway."

Model Think Aloud I know that in the story the fox wants something he cannot have, and I know that in real life, we sometimes want things we cannot have. When that happens, we might get annoyed and say we didn't really want the thing anyway because there was something wrong with it.

Guide practice Ask the following questions to guide children in describing a fable and determining its lesson, or moral.

- Who is the character in this story, and what can he do that is different from real life? (Possible response: The character is a fox and he can talk.)
- What happens in the story? (Possible response: The fox sees some grapes. He wants to eat them, but he can't reach them. He says he doesn't want them anyway because they are sour.)

On their own The fox doesn't really know if the grapes are sour. He just decides that they are. Why does he do this? (Possible response: He does this because he is annoyed that he can't eat them. It makes him feel better.)

Differentiated Instruction

SI Strategic Intervention

If children have difficulty understanding why the fox got annoyed, ask them questions that put them in a similar position. For example: If you saw an ice cream vendor and wanted to buy some ice cream, but then discovered you didn't have any money with you, how might you feel? What might you say?

Academic Vocabulary

character one of the people or animals in a story

Wrap Up your Week

Assess

- ◎ Verbs with the Inflected Ending *-s*
- ◎ Words with the Inflected Ending *-ing*
- • High-Frequency Words

Assessment
Monitor Progress

For a written assessment of inflectional endings *-s* and *-ing*, high-frequency words, and main idea and details, use Weekly Test 4, pp. 55–60.

Assess words in isolation

Word reading Use the following reproducible page to assess children's ability to read words in isolation. Call on children to read the words aloud. Start over if necessary.

Assess words in context

Sentence reading Use reproducible page 119f to assess children's ability to read words in context. Call on children to read two sentences aloud. Start over with sentence one if necessary.

MONITOR PROGRESS **Word and Sentence Reading**

If... children have trouble reading words with inflected endings *-s* and *-ing*,
then... use the Reteach Lesson on p. 194–195 of *First Stop*.

If... children cannot read all the high-frequency words,
then... mark the missed words on a high-frequency word list and have the child practice reading the words with a fluent reader.

Success Predictor

Monitor accuracy

Record scores Use the Word/Sentence Reading Chart for this unit in *First Stop*.

Name ______________________________

Read the Words

1. hops
2. four
3. taps
4. eat
5. her
6. kicking
7. naps
8. five
9. packing
10. picking
11. rocking
12. sits
13. this
14. too

MONITOR PROGRESS

- Ending *-s*
- Ending *-ing*
- High-frequency words

Name ______________________________

Read the Sentences

1. Tim hops and Mom is packing this bag.

2. Jack sits packing mix to eat.

3. The cat sits licking mix too.

4. The cat is kicking four pots.

5. The fox is rocking her kit that naps.

6. Five of us can eat the mix Mom is packing.

MONITOR PROGRESS

- Fluency
- Inflected ending *-s*
- Inflected ending *-ing*
- High-frequency words

Objectives
- Identify declarative sentences.

Conventions
Declarative Sentences

Review Remind children that declarative sentences tell a fact or someone's point of view. Have them give some examples of declarative sentences.

Guide practice Write the following sentences on the board. In each case, have children tell you which letter should be a capital and where the period should go.

1. chickens hatch from eggs

2. toads need to be kept moist

3. worms survive in the earth

Connect to oral language Have children form pairs to discuss what each of the sentences tell. Then have them share their responses with the class.

On their own Use *Let's Practice It!* p. 55 on the *Teacher Resource DVD-ROM.*

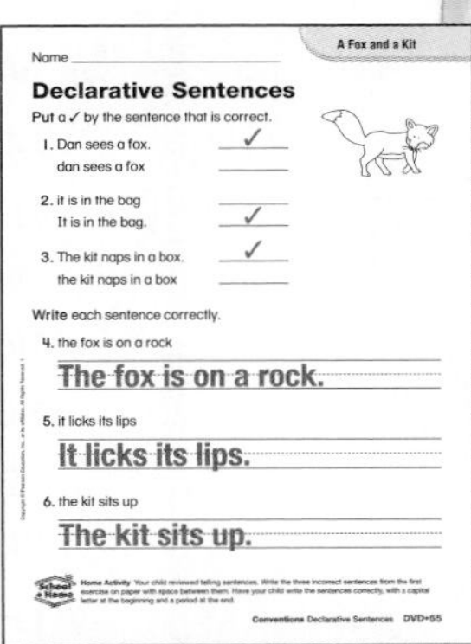
Name
A Fox and a Kit
Declarative Sentences
Put a ✓ by the sentence that is correct.
1. Don sees a fox. ✓
dan sees a fox
2. it is in the bag
It is in the bag. ✓
3. The kit naps in a box. ✓
the kit naps in a box
Write each sentence correctly.
4. the fox is on a rock
The fox is on a rock.
5. it licks its lips
It licks its lips.
6. the kit sits up
The kit sits up.

Let's Practice It! TR DVD•55

Daily Fix-It

9. you can use my net
You can use my net.

10. step up here to see a frog
Step up here to see a frog.

Discuss the Daily Fix-It corrections with children. Review declarative sentences and the use of capital letters and periods.

Objectives

- Edit a draft for spelling, punctuation, and capitalization.
- Create final draft and present.

Writing—Personal Narrative

Writer's Craft: Declarative Sentences

Review Revising Remind children that yesterday they revised their narratives. They may have rearranged sentences to make the events clearer. Today they will proofread their narratives.

MINI-LESSON

Proofread for Declarative Sentences

- **Teach** In our narratives, if we capitalize and punctuate the sentences correctly, readers will know where the sentences begin and end. When we proofread, we check to make sure the sentences are correct.

- **Model** Let's look at my story about the bunny I saw. Display Writing Transparency 4C. I'm going to make sure that each sentence begins with a capital letter and ends with punctuation. I'll check the beginning and end of each sentence. Model checking the beginning and end of each sentence. Look: I forgot the punctuation at the end of the sentence, "I sit under a big elm tree." It's a sentence that tells, so I'll add a period. Add a period after *tree* on the transparency, then continue to check. Look: I forgot the punctuation at the end of the sentence, "I looked at the bunny." It's also a sentence that tells, so I'll add a period. Add a period after *bunny* on the transparency, and then continue to check.

Proofreading Marks

Take Out		Uppercase letter	
Add	^	Lowercase letter	/
Period	⊙	New paragraph	¶
Check spelling	○	Insert apostrophe	

The Bunny in the Garden

I like to go to the park. I sit under a big elm tree I walk in the rose garden.

One Saturday I saw a bunny in the rose garden. The bunny sat on the grassy path. I looked at the bunny The bunny looked at me.

The bunny filled its mouth with grass. It watched me while it stuffed its mouth. The grass stuck out of its mouth. It looked so funny!

Then the bunny hopped away into the rose bushes. I was sorry to see it go.

Unit 1 A Fox and a Kit Writing: Proofread 4C

Writing Transparency 4C
TR DVD

Proofread Display the Proofreading Tips. Have children proofread their narratives to correct any misspellings, missing capital letters, or errors with periods. Circulate to assist children with the punctuation of sentences.

Proofreading Tips

✔ Are words that tell feelings spelled correctly?

✔ Do sentences that *tell* end with a period?

✔ Do all sentences end with punctuation?

✔ Do sentences begin with a capital letter?

Present

Have children make a final draft of their narratives, with their revisions and proofreading corrections. Help as appropriate.

Choose an option for children to present their narratives. They might draw a picture of the animal they saw, to accompany the story in a wall display. They might tell the narrative aloud to a small group. When they have finished, help them complete a Self-Evaluation form.

ROUTINE **Quick Write for Fluency** Team Talk

1. **Talk** Have partners take one minute to find a word that tells feelings in each of their stories.
2. **Write** Each child writes a new short sentence using one of the words.
3. **Share** Partners trade sentences, read them aloud, and determine if the sentences are declarative or not.

Routines Flip Chart

Teacher Note

Self-Evaluation Make copies of the Self-Evaluation form from the Teacher Resource DVD-ROM, and hand them out to children.

Write Guy
Jeff Anderson

Topic Sentence? Really?

Topic sentences are excellent, but many good paragraphs actually don't have topic sentences. We want children to learn how to craft a topic sentence and a paragraph. We also want children to know that not all paragraphs consist of five sentences, beginning with a topic sentence.

ELL

English Language Learners

Support Editing For children to whom the sounds and spelling of English still are not very familiar, look for spelling improvement little by little from week to week rather than rapid development. Help children make progress a word at a time and learn word meanings.

Objectives

- Review concept: how wild animals take care of their babies.
- Organize information.
- Present results of an inquiry project.

Research and Inquiry
Communicate

Teach Tell children that today they will create a chart that tells about animals and their babies. Then they will share the information with others.

Model Think Aloud Display the chart about the topic. I will review my chart and circle the animals and animal babies I would like to tell others about. I liked the idea that a baby cow, a baby whale, and a baby elephant are all called calves. So I will include those facts in my chart. I will write the words *cow, whale*, and *elephant* on the left side of my chart. On the right side, I will write the word *calf* next to each animal name. That means I will write the word *calf* three times. How interesting!

Guide practice Review the animal and animal babies children learned about. Work with them to understand how to organize the information so their charts are easy to read.

On their own Have children choose the information about animals and baby animals they would like to share and create a chart. Have children share their charts in small groups. Remind them how to be good speakers and listeners:

- Good speakers pay close attention to end marks like question marks.
- Good listeners think of questions to ask the speaker when he or she is done talking.

Wrap Up Your Week!

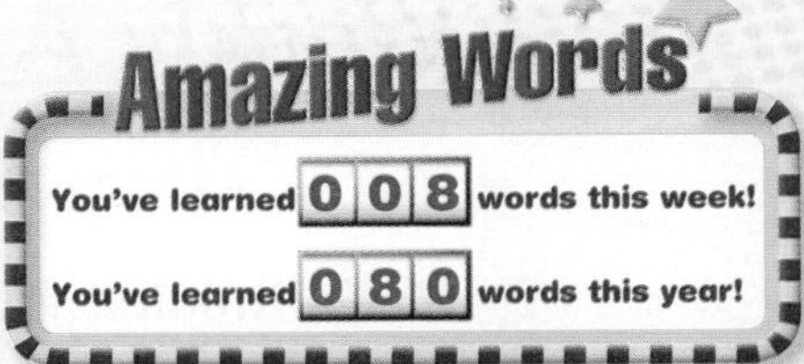
Amazing Words
You've learned 0 0 8 words this week!
You've learned 0 8 0 words this year!

Question of the Week

How do wild animals take care of their babies?

Think Aloud This week we explored the topic of how wild animals take care of their babies. In the story *A Fox and a Kit*, we read about how a mother fox takes care of her kit. In the story "The Fox and the Grapes", we read about a fox who couldn't get what he wanted. Have children recall their Amazing Ideas about wild animals and their babies. Then have children use these ideas to help them demonstrate their understanding of the Question of the Week.

ELL

English Language Learners

Poster Preview Prepare children for next week by using Week 11, ELL Poster 5. Read the Poster Talk-Through to introduce the concept and vocabulary. Ask children to identify and describe objects and actions in the art.

Selection Summary
Send home the summary of *Get the Egg!* in English and the child's home language if available. Children can read the summary with family members.

Preview NEXT WEEK

Tell children that next week they will read about a bird and its eggs.

Assessment Checkpoints for the Week

Weekly Assessment

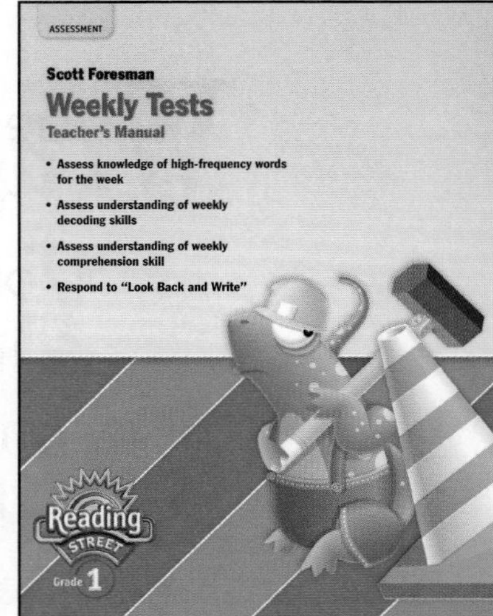

Weekly Tests

Use pp. 55–60 of *Weekly Tests* to check:

- ✔ **Phonics** Inflected Ending *-s*
- ✔ **Phonics** Inflected Ending *-ing*
- ✔ **Comprehension Skill** Main Idea and Details
- ✔ **High-Frequency Words**

eat	her
five	this
four	too

Differentiated Asssessment

Advanced

On-Level

SI Strategic Intervention

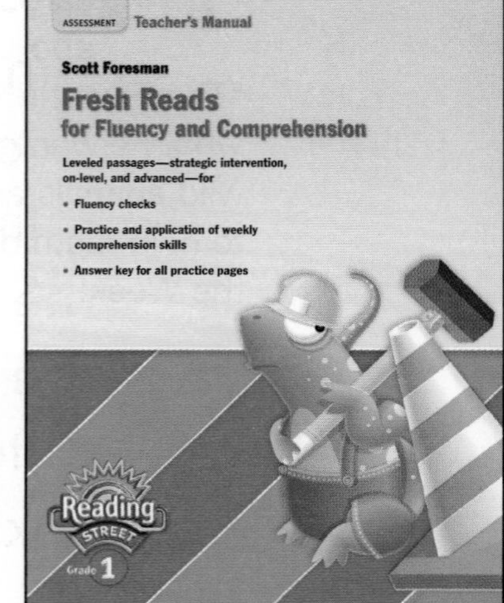

Fresh Reads for Fluency and Comprehension

Use pp. 55–60 of *Fresh Reads for Fluency and Comprehension* to check:

- ✔ **Comprehension Skill** Main Idea and Details
- ✔ Review **Comprehension Skill** Realism and Fantasy

Managing Assessment

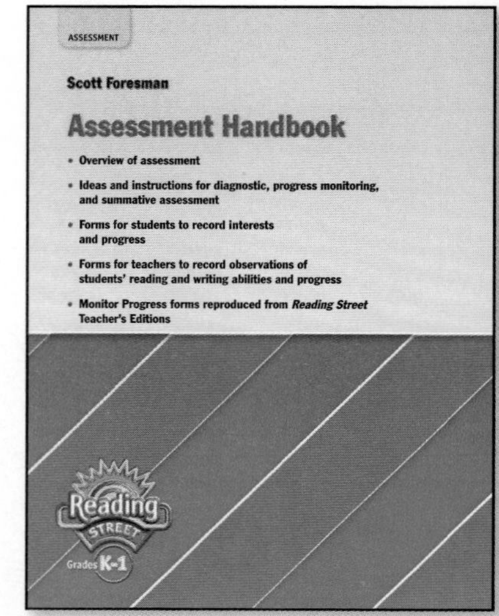

Assessment Handbook

Use *Assessment Handbook* for:

- ✔ **Weekly Assessment Blackline Masters for Monitoring Progress**
- ✔ **Observation Checklists**
- ✔ **Record-Keeping Forms**
- ✔ **Portfolio Assessment**

Panda Peeks at the World

The baby panda peeks out at the world. It is three months old. Its mother holds it. When it was born, it was the size of a stick of butter. A panda grows each day. It is soft now. Its mother licks it and fluffs its black-and-white fur.

Pandas live in just a few places in China. About 1,600 pandas live in the wild. Some pandas live in zoos. Others live in a safe forest called a panda reserve. It is a good place for pandas to have their babies. A baby panda runs and plays with other baby pandas there. There is a giant panda home on the reserve. The home takes pandas that are not able to live in the wild. Maybe one is hurt. Some might be sick. Maybe one was born in a zoo and needs a new home. A panda lives in special rooms while it gets strong. Then it moves from the rooms to the forest.

The panda home uses a camera. Videos of the pandas are fun to watch. A child in another land wants to see pandas. She looks at them on a computer. You can too!

Advanced Selection 4 **Vocabulary:** peeks, reserve

Small Group Time

Pacing Small Group Instruction

5 Day Plan

DAY 1	• Phonemic Awareness/ Phonics • Decodable Reader
DAY 2	• Phonemic Awareness/ Phonics • Decodable Reader
DAY 3	• Phonemic Awareness/ Phonics • Leveled Reader
DAY 4	• High-Frequency Words • Decodable Reader
DAY 5	• Phonics Review • Leveled Reader

3 or 4 Day Plan

DAY 1	• Phonemic Awareness/ Phonics • Decodable Reader
DAY 2	• Phonemic Awareness/ Phonics • Decodable Reader
DAY 3	• Phonemic Awareness/ Phonics • Leveled Reader
DAY 4	• High-Frequency Words • Decodable Reader

3 Day Plan: Eliminate the shaded box.

DAY 1

Phonemic Awareness • Phonics

■ **Segment and Blend Phonemes** Reteach pp. 96–97 of the Teacher's Edition. Model segmenting and blending these words. Then have children practice segmenting and blending on their own.

runs /r/ /u/ n/ /z/ **plays** /p/ /l/ /ā/ /z/ **sits** /s/ /i/ /t/ /s/

■ **Inflected Ending *-s*** Reteach p. 97a of the Teacher's Edition. Then have children spell *packs* using letter tiles. Monitor their work.

- Change the *a* in packs to *i.* What is the new word?

- Change the *p* in picks to *l.* What is the new word?

- Change the *i* in licks to *o.* What is the new word?

Decodable Practice Reader 4A

■ **Review** Review words with inflected ending -s and the high-frequency words *a, we, you, the, do, have.* Then have children blend and read these words from the story: *Rick, Lin, licks, Quin, rocks, pods.*

If... children have difficulty with any of these words, **then...** reteach the word by modeling. Have children practice the words, with feedback from you, until they can read them independently.

Have children reread the text orally. To achieve optimal fluency, children should reread the text three or four times.

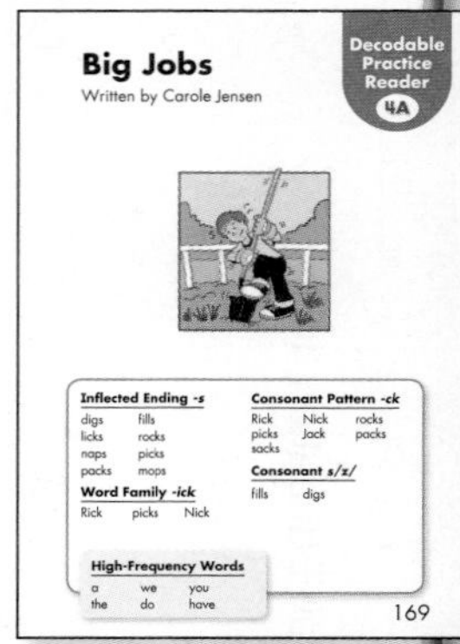

Decodable Practice Reader 4A

Objectives

- Blend spoken phonemes to form one-syllable words, including consonant blends.
- Read base words with inflectional endings.

DAY 2

Phonemic Awareness • Phonics

- **Segment and Blend Phonemes** Reteach p. 100c of the Teacher's Edition. Model segmenting and blending these words. Then have children practice segmenting and blending on their own.

fixing /f/ /i/ /ks/ *-ing* **waiting** /w/ /ā/ /t/ *-ing* **clapping** /k/ /l/ /a/ /p/ *-ing*

- **Inflected Ending *-ing*** Reteach p. 100d of the Teacher's Edition. Then have children spell *kicking* using letter tiles. Monitor their work.
  - Change the *ck* in kicking to *ss*. What is the new word?
  - Change the *k* in kissing to *m*. What is the new word?
  - Change the *ss* in missing to *x*. What is the new word?

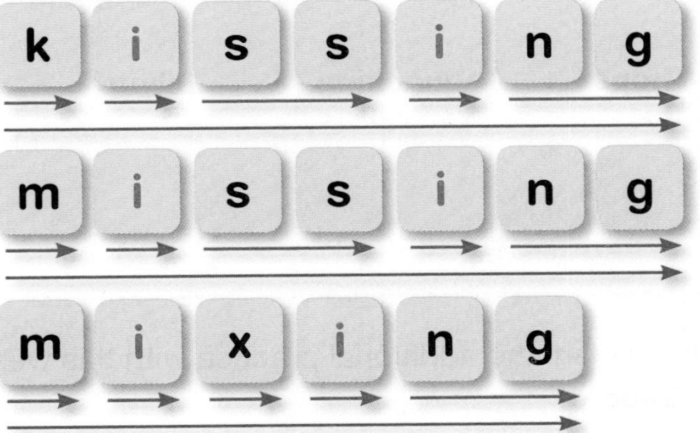

Decodable Practice Reader 4B

- **Review** Review words with inflected ending *-ing* and the high-frequency word *we.* Then have children blend and read these words from the story: *packing, bags, helps, backing.*

If... children have difficulty with any of these words, **then...** reteach the word by modeling. Have children practice the words, with feedback from you, until they can read them independently.

Have children reread the text orally. To achieve optimal fluency, children should reread the text three or four times.

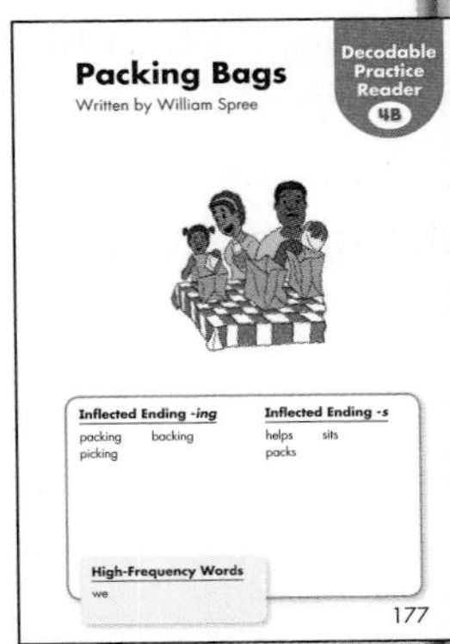

Decodable Practice Reader 4B

More Reading

Use Leveled Readers or other text at children's instructional level to develop fluency.

Objectives
- Blend spoken phonemes to form one-syllable words, including consonant blends.
- Read base words with inflectional endings.

Phonemic Awareness • Phonics

- **Count Syllables** Model counting the syllables in a word. I will say the syllables, or word parts, in the word *flying*. Listen: *fly • ing.* There are two syllables in *flying*. Have children say the syllables with you, and then say the syllables by themselves. Then have children practice saying and counting syllables in words on their own.

helping (help • ing)	**fixing** (fix • ing)	**jumping** (jump • ing)

- **Inflected Ending *-s* and Inflected Ending *-ing*** Reteach p. 112e of the Teacher's Edition. Have children blend and read these additional words to help them practice the target phonics skills.

kicks	**tags**	**hops**	**quacking**	**filling**	**licking**

For a complete literacy instructional plan and additional practice with this week's target skills and strategies, see the **Leveled Reader Teaching Guide.**

Concept Literacy Leveled Reader

- **Preview and Predict** Read the title and the author's name. Have children look at the cover and ask them to describe what they see. Help children activate their prior knowledge by asking them to look through the story and to use the photos to predict things that might take place.
- **Set a Purpose** Remind children that setting a purpose for reading can help them better understand what they read. Guide children to pay attention to what the animals do.
- **Read** Provide corrective feedback as children read the story orally. During reading, ask them if they were able to confirm any of the predictions they made prior to the story.

If... children have difficulty reading the story individually,
then... read a sentence aloud as children point to each word. Then have the group reread the sentences as they continue pointing. Continue reading in this way until children read individually.

- **Retell** Have children take turns retelling the story. Help them identify the things the animals do by asking, What do the animals do? What does the squirrel (deer, horse) do?

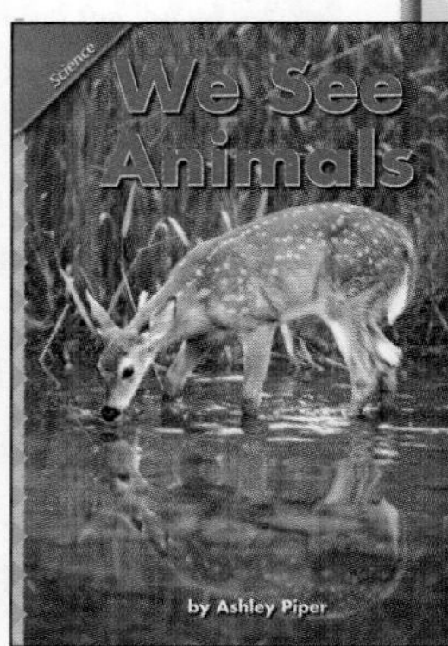

Concept Literacy

Objectives

- Display phonological awareness.
- Read base words with inflectional endings.

High-Frequency Words

- **Review** Write *eat, four, five, her, this, too* on the board. Model saying each word. Then have children read each word, spell each word as you point to each letter, and have them say each word again. Allow time for children to practice reading these high-frequency words using the word cards.

Decodable Practice Reader 4C

- **Review** Use the word lists to review inflected ending *-s* and inflected ending *-ing.* Be sure that children understand that the ending *-s* can make the sound /s/ or /z/ and the ending *-ing* makes the sound /ing/.

  If… children have difficulty reading the story individually, **then…** read a sentence aloud as children point to each word. Then have the group reread the sentences as they continue pointing. Continue reading in this way until children read individually.

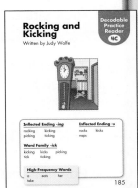

Decodable Practice Reader 4C

Check comprehension by having children retell the story including the characters, plot, and setting. Have children locate words in the story that have inflected ending *-s* and inflected ending *-ing*. List the words children identify. Then have children sort the words in a chart with columns labeled Ending *-s* and Ending *-ing*.

Ending *-s*	Ending *-ing*
eats	rocking
rocks	kicking
kicks	picking
naps	ticking

Objectives

- Read base words with inflectional endings.
- Read at least 100 high-frequency words from a commonly used list.

More Reading

Use Leveled Readers or other text at children's instructional level.

More Reading

Use Leveled Readers or other text at children's instructional level.

Phonics Review

- **Inflected Ending -s and Inflected Ending *-ing*** Write these sentences on the board. Have children read them aloud as you track the print. Then call on individuals to blend and read the underlined words.

Kim naps.

Dad is packing.

Pat is mixing it up.

Rick sits on his mat.

For a complete literacy instructional plan and additional practice with this week's target skills and strategies, see the **Leveled Reader Teaching Guide.**

Below-Level Leveled Reader

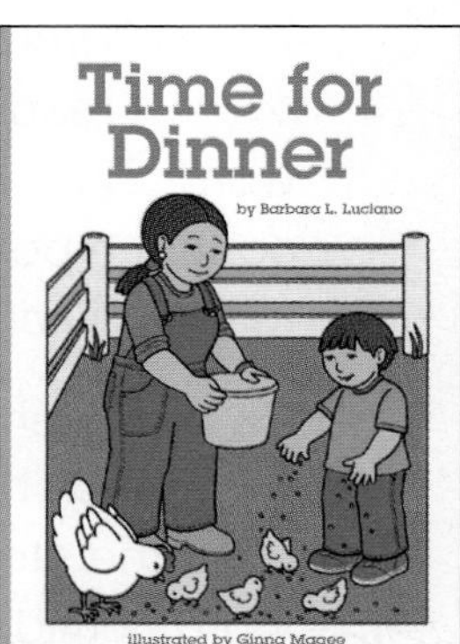

Below-Level Reader

- **Preview and Predict** Read the title, the author's name, and the illustrator's name. Have children look at the cover and ask them to describe what they see. Help children activate their prior knowledge by asking them to look through the story and to use the pictures to predict things that might take place.
- **Set a Purpose** Remind children that setting a purpose for reading can help them better understand what they read. Guide children to identify what the animals and people on the farm do at dinner time.
- **Read** Provide corrective feedback as children read the story orally. During reading, ask them if they were able to confirm any of the predictions they made prior to the story.

  If... children have difficulty reading the story individually,
  then... read each sentence aloud as children point to each word. Then have the group reread the sentences as they continue pointing.

- **Main Idea and Details** Have children name the things that happen in the story. Then prompt them to tell what the story is mostly about.

Objectives

- Read base words with inflectional endings.
- Restate the main idea, read.

DAY 1

Phonics • Spelling

- **Inflected Ending *-s*** Write the following words on the board and have children practice reading words with inflected ending *-s*.

jogs **hits** **wins** **pats**

- **Inflected Ending *-s*** Remind children that some of the spelling words have the ending *-s*, which can spell the sound /s/ or /z/. Clarify the pronunciation and meaning of each word. For example, say: If clothing *fits, it* is the right size. Have children identify which of the following words has the ending sound /s/ and which has the ending sound /z/: *sits, wins, fits, hits, naps.*

Objectives

- Read base words with inflectional endings.

Pacing Small Group Instruction

20–30 min.

5 Day Plan

DAY 1	• Phonics • Spelling • Decodable Reader
DAY 2	• Phonics • High-Frequency Words • Decodable Reader
DAY 3	• Leveled Reader
DAY 4	• Conventions • Main Selection
DAY 5	• Phonics Review • Leveled Reader

DAY 2

Phonics • High-Frequency Words

- **Inflected Ending *-ing*** Write the following words on the board and have children practice reading words with inflected ending *-ing.*

fixing **rocking** **tacking** **passing**

- **High-Frequency Words** Hold up this week's High-Frequency Word Cards *(eat, four, five, her, this, too)* and review proper pronunciation. Continue holding the cards and have children chorally read each word. To help children demonstrate their understanding of the words, provide them with oral sentence frames such as: Let's ___ soup for lunch. (eat)

High-Frequency Word Cards for Grade 1

Objectives

- Read base words with inflectional endings.
- Read at least 100 high-frequency words from a commonly used list.

3 or 4 Day Plan

DAY 1	• Phonics • Spelling • Decodable Reader
DAY 2	• Phonics • High-Frequency Words • Decodable Reader
DAY 3	• Leveled Reader
DAY 4	• Conventions • Main Selection

3 Day Plan: Eliminate the shaded box.

Decodable Practice Reader

For a complete literacy instructional plan and additional practice with this week's target skills and strategies, see the **Leveled Reader Teaching Guide.**

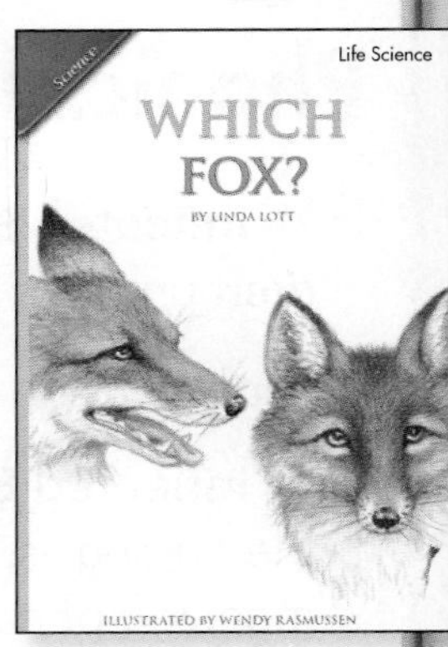

On-Level

On-Level Leveled Reader

- **Preview and Predict** Read the title, the author's name, and the illustrator's name. Have children look at the cover and ask them to describe in detail what they see. Help children preview the story by asking them to look through the story and to use the pictures to predict things that might take place.
- **Main Idea and Details** Before reading, remind children that setting a purpose for reading can help them better understand what they read. Guide children to pay attention to what happens in the story and to think about what the story is mostly about.
- **Read** During reading, monitor children's comprehension by providing higher-order thinking questions. Ask:
  - How are the foxes alike? How are they different?
  - Which fox do you think has an easier life? Why?

  To help children gain a better understanding of the text, build upon their responses with a group discussion.
- **Important Ideas** Discuss with children where they can locate details about foxes.
  - What else would you like to learn about foxes?
  - Where could you learn more about a woods fox and a zoo fox?
  - **Text to Text** Help children make connections to other stories. Ask:
  - What other stories have you read about wild animals?

Objectives
- Locate details about other texts.
- Restate the main idea, read.

eReaders

DAY 4

Conventions

- **Declarative Sentences** Remind children that a telling sentence tells something. It is a statement.
  - A telling sentence begins with a capital letter. It usually ends with a period.
  - Write this sentence: *The fox is in the woods.* This is a telling sentence. Point out the beginning capital letter and the period at the end.
  - Write the following complete and incomplete sentences on the board. Work with children to identify which are complete telling sentences.

The duck.	The duck swims in the pond.
At the farm.	Those brown cows.
A squirrel finds nuts.	The snake is hissing.

Objectives
- Recognize punctuation marks at the end of declarative sentences.

More Reading

Use Leveled Readers or other text at children's instructional level to develop fluency.

DAY 5

Phonics Review

- **Inflected Ending -s and Inflected Ending *-ing*** Have children practice blending and reading words that contain this week's target phonics skills. Write the following words on the board, and say and sound out each word with the children.

digs	**fixing**	**nods**	**fills**	**packing**
kicking	**locks**	**missing**	**rocking**	**taps**

Then have children sort the words according to the ending.

Objectives
- Read base words with inflectional endings.

Pacing Small Group Instruction

20–30 min.

5 Day Plan

DAY 1	• Phonics • Advanced Selection
DAY 2	• Phonics • Comprehension • Main Selection
DAY 3	• Leveled Reader
DAY 4	• Comprehension • Paired Selection
DAY 5	• Fluency • Comprehension • Advanced Selection

3 or 4 Day Plan

DAY 1	• Phonics • Advanced Selection
DAY 2	• Phonics • Comprehension • Main Selection
DAY 3	• Leveled Reader
DAY 4	• Comprehension • Paired Selection

3 Day Plan: Eliminate the shaded box.

A Advanced — DAY 1

Phonics • Advanced Selection

■ **Inflected Ending *-s*** Have children practice with these longer words.

quits	**giggles**	**begins**	**swings**	**feeds**
happens	**swims**	**throws**	**connects**	**scribbles**

Have children write the words on word cards and sort them into groups of one- and two-syllable words. Then have partners use several words in a sentence.

■ **Advanced Selection 4** Before reading, discuss story words *peeks* and *reserve*. Provide oral sentences with the words in context. After reading, have children recall the two most important ideas of the story.

Panda Peeks at the World

Advanced Selection 4

Objectives

- Read base words with inflectional endings.

A Advanced — DAY 2

Phonics • Comprehension

■ **Inflected Ending *-ing*** Have children practice these words.

cracking	**hopping**	**making**	**flying**	**doing**	**helping**

Have children write the words on word cards and sort them into three stacks: words that add *-ing* to the base word without change, words that double the final consonant before adding *-ing,* and words that drop e before adding *-ing.*

■ **Comprehension** Have children silently read *A Fox and a Kit.* Have them retell the story identifying characters, setting, and sequence of events. Discuss what makes *A Fox and a Kit* literary nonfiction. (It is a story that gives facts about foxes.)

A Fox and a Kit

Objectives

- Read base words with inflectional endings.

Advanced

DAY 3

For a complete literacy instructional plan and additional practice with this week's target skills and strategies, see the **Leveled Reader Teaching Guide.**

Science
Life Science
Baby Animals in the Rain Forest
by Melissa Burke
illustrated by Burgandy Beam

Advanced Reader

Advanced Leveled Reader

- **Activate Prior Knowledge** Read the title, the author's name, and the illustrator's name. Have children look at the cover and describe in detail what they see. Remind them that a *rain forest* is a hot, wet place that is home to many plants and animals. Then activate the children's prior knowledge by asking them to share what they know about rain forests.
- **Main Idea and Details** Before reading, remind children that setting a purpose for reading can help them better understand what they read. Guide children to pay attention to what happens in the story and to think about what the story is mostly about.
- **Read** During reading, monitor children's comprehension by providing higher-order thinking questions. Ask:
  - Why do baby animals need their parents?
  - What happens to baby animals when they grow?

  Build on children's answers to help them gain a better understanding of the text.
- **Important Ideas** Discuss with children where they can locate details about baby animals of the rain forest.
  - Which baby animal of the rain forest would you like to learn more about? What would you like to know?
  - Where could you learn more about baby animals of the rain forest?
- **Text to Self** Help children make personal connections to the story. Ask:
  - Would you like to visit a rain forest? Why?

Objectives

- Locate details about other texts.
- Restate the main idea, read.

More Reading

Use Leveled Readers or other text at children's instructional level.

More Reading

Use Leveled Readers or other text at children's instructional level.

Comprehension

The Fox and the Grapes

- **Comprehension** Have children silently read this week's paired selection, "The Fox and the Grapes." Have them retell the story identifying the character, setting, and sequence of events. Then have them summarize what they think was the most important idea from the story.

  Talk about what makes "The Fox and the Grapes" a fable. Ensure that children understand that fables are stories written to teach a lesson.

- **Text to Text** Ask children to name other fables they have heard or read and to tell what lessons the fables taught.

Objectives

- Retell important events in stories in logical order.
- Make connections to ideas in other texts.

DAY 5

Fluency•Comprehension

Advanced Selection 4

- **Fluency** Using the first few sentences of Advanced Selection 4, model reading with accuracy and at an appropriate rate. Then have children read the selection to a partner as you listen to their reading. Provide corrective feedback as needed.

- **Comprehension** After they have finished reading the selection, have children recall what they learned about pandas. Then, on the back of the selection page, have them write three sentences that describe baby pandas.

Objectives

- Read aloud grade-level appropriate text with fluency.

ELL English Language Learners

The ELL lessons are organized by strands. Use them to scaffold the weekly lesson curriculum or during small-group time.

Concept Development

How do wild animals take care of their babies?

- **Activate Prior Knowledge** Write the Question of the Week and read it aloud. Underline the words *take, care,* and *babies*. When someone or something takes care of their baby, they make sure that their baby has everything it needs to be happy and healthy. Display a picture of a mother holding a baby. You were a baby once. How did the grown-ups in your life take care of you? (They made sure you had food, milk, clothing, and so on.)
- **Connect to New Concept** Have children turn to pages 94–95 in the Student Edition. Read the title and have children track the print as you read it. Use pictures to guide a discussion about how wild animals take care of their babies. Point to the mother hippopotamus. How is this mother taking care of her baby? (She is helping it swim.) She is pushing her baby along under the water so it can learn to swim on its own.
- **Develop Concepts** Show this week's Concept Talk Video and ask children to name wild animals. (monkey, whale, squirrels, birds) A reserve is a special place where animals can live. Why are reserves good places for animals to live?
  During a second viewing, stop at appropriate places to build understanding of the concept. Use the leveled prompts below to assess understanding and build oral language.

Beginning Ask yes/no questions, such as Are monkeys wild animals? Can animals live in reserves?

Intermediate Provide sentence frames to help children talk about the video. One wild animal we can help is _____. We can help wild animals by _____.

Advanced/Advanced-High Have children answer the Question of the Week by giving specific examples from the video.

- **Review Concepts and Connect to Writing** Review children's understanding of the concept at the end of the week. Ask them to write in response to these questions: What are some examples of how wild animals take care of their babies? What English words did you learn this week? Write and display key ideas from the discussion.

Objectives

- Use prior knowledge and experiences to understand meanings in English.
- Internalize new basic and academic language by using it and reusing it in meaningful ways in speaking and writing activities that build language attainment.

Content Objectives

- Describe how wild animals take care of their babies.

Language Objectives

- Share information orally.
- Use basic vocabulary for describing how wild animals take care of their babies.

Daily Planner

DAY 1	• **Frontload Concepts** • **Preteach** Comprehension Skill, Vocabulary, Phonemic Awareness/ Phonics, Conventions/ Writing
DAY 2	• **Review** Concepts, Vocabulary, Comprehension Skill • **Frontload Main Selection** • **Practice** Phonemic Awareness/Phonics, Conventions/Writing
DAY 3	• **Review** Concepts, Comprehension Skill, Vocabulary, Conventions/ Writing • **Reread Main Selection** • **Practice** Phonemic Awareness/Phonics
DAY 4	• **Review Concepts** • **Read ELL/ELD Readers** • **Practice** Phonemic Awareness/Phonics, Conventions/Writing
DAY 5	• **Review** Concepts, Vocabulary, Comprehension Skill, Phonemic Awareness/ Phonics, Conventions/ Writing • **Reread ELL/ELD Readers**

*See the ELL Handbook for ELL Workshops with targeted instruction.

ELL Poster 4

Build concept understanding and oral vocabulary throughout the week by using the daily activities on ELL Poster 4.

Language Objectives

- Blend and segment phonemes.

Transfer Skills

The phonemes of certain English consonants may be unfamiliar to English language learners or easily confused with other phonemes. For example, consonant digraphs such as /th/, /sh/, and /ch/ may sound alike to some English learners. Spanish speakers may hear and write /n/ at the end of words ending in /m/.

ELL Teaching Routine

For more practice with blending and segmenting, use the Sound-by-Sound Blending Routine (*ELL Handbook*, page 493).

ELL English Language Learners

Phonemic Awareness: Blend and Segment Phonemes

Preteach the endings *-s* and *-ing*

- Have children open to pages 96–97. What are the skunks doing? (running) I'm going to say the beginning and ending sounds in *running*. Listen for the ending. *Run ing.* The ending sound is *-ing.* Say *ing* with me. Say these words as you point to corresponding pictures: *eating, dumped, swimming, feeding, mail.* Have children repeat each word and raise their hand if they hear the *-ing* at the end of the word.
- What are these animals? (frogs) Listen to the last sound in *frogs*. Slowly segment and blend the sounds: /f/ /r/ /o/ /g/ /z/, *frogs*. What is the last sound in *frogs*? /z/ Yes. Say the last sound in *frogs* with me: /z/.
- Have children point out other words that contain the endings *-ing* and *-s.*

Practice Listen again as I say the beginning and ending sounds of the word *running. Run ing.* Now you try. Have children say each of the following words, emphasizing the ending sounds.

parents	fishing	boys	runs
building	birds	feeding	looking

Phonics: Inflected Endings

Preteach Display Sound-Spelling Card 141. This says *dogs*. What sound do you hear at the end of *dogs*? (/z/) Say it with me: /z/. Point to the *s.* The /z/ sound is spelled *s* in *dogs.*

Listen and Write Distribute Write and Wipe Boards.

- Write the word *runs* on the board. Copy this word. As you write *s,* say the sound to yourself: /z/. Now say the sound aloud. (/z/) Underline the *s* in *runs.* The letter *s* spells /z/ in *beans.*
- Repeat using the word *cars.*

Objectives

- Distinguish sounds and intonation patterns of English with increasing ease.

ELL English Language Learners

■ **Reteach and Practice** Inflected Endings

- Write the following words on the board and have children read them aloud with you: *talks, swims, lifts, farms, writes, learns*. Segment and blend each word with the children. Point out the inflected ending *-s*.
- Write *pick* and *jump* on the board. Have children add the *-s* to the end of the words and pronounce the new words *picks* and *jumps*. Then, have them use the words in a sentence.

Beginning Have children take turns gesturing and naming each word that was written on the board.

Intermediate After children gesture and name the words on the board, have them spell each one.

Advanced/Advanced-High Have children name a word, spell it, and use it in a sentence.

Phonics: Inflected Endings

■ **Preteach** Have children turn to Envision It! on page 100 of the Student Edition.

- The word for the picture is *drinking*. Pantomime drinking a glass of water to indicate the meaning. What sound do you hear at the end of *drinking*? (ing) Say it with me *ing*. The *ing* sound is spelled ing.
- The first word in the list of "Words I Can Blend" is *packing*. What sound do you hear at the end of *packing*? (ing) The *ing* sound is spelled *-ing* in *packing*.
- Repeat with the other words in the list.

■ **Practice** Distribute Letter Tiles, *ng, i, ck, mp, a, o, p*, and *st* to pairs.

1. Blend the sounds in *picking* and have children spell *picking* with their tiles: /p/ /i/ /k/ /i/ /n/ g/
2. Replace the *i*. Spell *packing*.
3. Replace the *p*. Spell *stacking*.
4. Replace the *ck*. Spell *stamping*.
5. Replace the *a*. Spell *stomping*.

Objectives

- Distinguish sounds and intonation patterns of English with increasing ease.
- Use visual, contextual, and linguistic support to enhance and confirm understanding of understanding of increasingly complex and elaborated spoken language.

Language Objectives

- Use inflected endings.
- Read words with inflected endings.

Catch Up

When an ending is inflected, you pronounce it with emphasis. The endings *-s* and *-ing* are both inflected endings.

Transfer Skills

Spanish, like English, has irregular verbs (such as *ser* which means "to be" and *ir* which means "to go.") Challenge children who are literate in Spanish to identify irregular Spanish verbs and see whether English verbs with the same meanings are irregular.

Practice Page

ELL Handbook page 312 provides additional practice for this week's skill.

Content Objectives

- Monitor and adjust oral comprehension.

Language Objectives

- Discuss oral passages.
- Use accessible language to learn new language.
- Use a graphic organizer to take notes.

ELL Teacher Tip

Have children use the web to organize their thoughts. Tell them to focus on what the zookeeper says goes into creating a realistic exhibit.

E L L English Language Learners

Listening Comprehension

A Visit to the Rain Forest

Erica and her dad were going to the zoo. They waited for the rain forest exhibit to open up. Erica's dad told her about the rain forest. "Trees and plants grow close together in the rain forest. It rains a lot too," her dad said. "Some animals live on the ground. Some animals even live in the tops of trees in the rain forest!"

Erica was surprised when she walked into the exhibit. "This looks like a real forest," she said.

A zookeeper heard her. "We try to keep our exhibits as real as we can. We bring in plants from the animals' homes. We build rocks for them. We change the lighting to look like day and night. We want the animals to feel safe and healthy. Just like they would at home."

"Wow!" said Erica. "You work hard. I cannot wait to learn even more about the rain forest!"

"Me too," said Erica's dad.

Prepare for the Read Aloud The modified Read Aloud above prepares children for listening to the oral reading "A Rain Forest in the Zoo" on page 99b.

■ **First Listening: Listen to Understand**

1. Write the title of the Read Aloud on the board. Use accessible language *visit* and *zoo* to connect to students' prior experience. Have you ever visited a zoo? Introduce the new words *rain forest* and *exhibit*. Do you remember visiting any exhibits that looked real? What makes the exhibit look real? Listen to find out what Erica sees and how the zookeepers make sure that exhibits look real.
2. After reading, ask children to recall what Erica learned about how an exhibit is created. What do zookeepers do to create an exhibit? How do they make them realistic?

■ **Second Listening: Listen to Check Understanding** Using the Web graphic organizer (*ELL Handbook*, page 509), work with children to fill in the things zookeepers do to create a new exhibit. Now listen again to check your answers on the Web.

Objectives

- Use accessible language and learn new and essential language in the process.

ELL English Language Learners

High-Frequency Words

- **Preteach** Give each pair of children a set of Word Cards (*ELL Handbook*, p. 83). Read each card. Then write phrases using the words, and explain each with a gesture.
  - Pantomime eating soup. I *eat* soup with a spoon.
  - Put up the correct number of fingers. This is *four*.
  - Put up the correct number of fingers. I have *five* fingers on each hand.
  - Point to a child's desk. This is *her* desk.
  - Point to a book. Whose book is *this*?
  - Follow a child who is walking out the door. I want to go *too*!
- **Practice** Display the words *this, her, too, eat, four,* and *five*. Have children perform actions or respond to questions such as the following, as you direct them. I like to *eat* and drink? Give *this* pencil to *her*. Do you have *four* brothers? Can you jump *five* times? Let me come *too*!
- **Speaking/Writing with High-Frequency Words**
  - **Teach/Model** Review correct pronunciation of the high-frequency words with children.
  - **Practice** Write the sentences on the board with blank spaces 1. ______ is my desk. (this) 2. I have ______ fingers on one hand. (five) 3. Will you come ______? (too) 4. Let ______ sit in the chair. (her) 5. School ends in ______ hours. (four)

Beginning Read the sentences aloud, using a gesture or providing a drawing for each missing word. For example, write the numeral for four and five. Have children hold up the correct Word Card for each sentence.

Intermediate Have children write the sentences from the board adding the missing words. They can use their Word Cards. Then have children read the sentences aloud.

Advanced/Advanced-High Children write the sentences with missing words, and read the sentences aloud.

Objectives

- Speak using learning strategies such as requesting assistance, employing non-verbal cues, and using synonyms and circumlocution (conveying ideas by defining or describing when exact English words are not known).

Language Objectives

- Use accessible language to learn new and essential language.
- Use non-verbal cues to speak.
- Use high-frequency English words.

Transfer Skills

In some languages, such as Spanish, a vowel at the end of a word is not silent. Help children avoid pronouncing words such as *five* with a second vowel sound.

Support for English Language Learners

Content Objectives

- Identify main idea and details.
- Identify the main idea and essential details of a story to aid comprehension.

Language Objectives

- Discuss main ideas and supporting details.
- Expand reading skills by distinguishing main ideas from supporting details in a reading.
- Write main ideas and supporting details from a reading.
- Understand the main ideas in spoken language with familiar topics, language, and context.
- Learn the expressions *main idea* and *details*.

Mini-Lesson: Listening

Use p. EI•3 for listening and speaking practice. Have children examine the scene on the bottom and role-play what the family members might say to each other. Have children demonstrate listening comprehension by summarizing the dialogue they hear. Provide the language structure for summarizing dialogue. *(Mother asks _____. The boys says _____.)*

ELL English Language Learners

Guide Comprehension
Main Idea and Details

■ **Preteach** Model by pantomiming as you define main idea and details. The main idea of a passage or story is what it is mostly about. Details are the parts of the story that make it more interesting and help you understand it better.

■ **Practice** Have children turn to Envision It! on p. EI•3 in the Student Edition. Discuss the pictures with children. Have them identify the main idea. Then have them identify the details that support the main idea. Ask children to work with partners. One partner tells the main ideas, while the other listens to retell and show understanding of spoken language.

■ **Reteach/Practice** Have children complete Picture It! (*ELL Handbook*, p. 84)

- Ask children to describe what is happening in the illustration. Then read the text aloud twice. Prepare children for the second reading by asking them to think about the main idea of the sentences. After reading, put the sentences on sentence strips. Have children help you identify the main idea. Guide children in completing the practice exercises.

Leveled Support

Beginning/Intermediate Have children tell what they see in each picture. Ask yes or no questions to guide them: Did you read about the ocean? Did you read about what whales eat? Did you read about the girl and her father?

Advanced/Advanced-High Ask children to identify details they read about, such as what the father and girl are doing, what they see, and what the girl feels.

MINI-LESSON

Academic Language

Focus on the expressions *main idea* and *details*. Details give you important information about the main idea. When you read a story, you can use the details to help you figure out the main idea. Ask yourself, "What are these details mostly about?" Have children practice identifying essential details using the context and language on p. 106 of the Student Edition. As one child reads, the other can listen for details that support the main idea.

Objectives

- Use accessible language and learn new and essential language in the process.

Reading Comprehension
A Fox and a Kit

Student Edition pp. 102–103

■ **Frontloading**

- **Background Knowledge** Read the title aloud and discuss it. Have you ever gone to a zoo to see the animals? Were there any baby animals when you were there? How did their parents take care of them? Have peers share their background knowledge to support each other's comprehension.
- **Preview** Guide children on a picture walk through the story, asking them to identify people, places, and actions. Reteach these words using visuals in the Student Edition: *kit* (p.104), *dinner* (p. 106), and *playing* (p. 108).
- **Predict** What kinds of things will the mother fox do to take care of her kit?

Sheltered Reading Ask questions such as the following to guide children's comprehension:

- p. 104: Point to the kit. What is this? (a fox kit) What is it doing? (napping)
- p. 107: Point to both foxes. What are they doing? (licking their lips)
- p. 109: Point to the mother fox. What is she doing? (helping the kit by picking it up) Why? (It was on the rocks.)
- p. 111: Point to the kids. What are they doing? (watching the foxes) Why? (They are fun to watch.)

■ **Fluency: Appropriate Accuracy and Rate** Remind children that accuracy means to read the words correctly and rate means to use an appropriate speed. Tell children that they should read like they talk to a friend. Read the sentences on page 105, modeling accuracy and rate. Have pairs choose a sentence on page 107. Have children read accurately and at an appropriate rate as their partner listens and offers feedback. For more practice, use the Fluency: Paired Reading Routine (*ELL Handbook*, page 496).

After Reading Help children summarize the text with the Retelling Cards. Ask questions that prompt children to summarize the important parts of the text. Turn to p. 118 of the Student Edition. Have children share information about their favorite zoo animals. Children can demonstrate listening comprehension by restating what classmates say as well as by asking questions about the information in discussion.

Objectives

- Distinguish sounds and intonation patterns of English with increasing ease.
- Use visual and contextual support and support from peers and teachers to read grade-appropriate content area text, enhance and confirm understanding, and develop vocabulary, grasp of language structures, and background knowledge needed to comprehend increasingly challenging language.

Content Objectives

- Monitor and adjust comprehension.
- Make and adjust predictions.

Language Objectives

- Read with appropriate accuracy and rate.
- Distinguish intonation patterns of English.
- Derive meaning from CD.
- Use support from peers to develop background knowledge.
- Summarize text using visual support.
- Demonstrate listening comprehension.

Audio Support

Children can prepare for reading *A Fox and a Kit* by using the eSelection or the AudioText CD. After listening, ask children to restate the main points of the story to show their attainment of the language.

English Summary

Read the English summary of *A Fox and a Kit* (*ELL Handbook*, page 85). Children can ask questions about ideas or unfamiliar words. Send copies home for children to read with family members.

Support for English Language Learners

ELL English Language Learners

For additional leveled instruction, see the **ELL/ELD Reader Teaching Guide.**

Comprehension: *Do Not Go Near*

- **Before Reading** Distribute copies of the ELL and ELD Readers, *Do Not Go Near*, to children at their reading level.
    - **Preview** Read the title aloud with children: This is a story about different animals and how they live in the wild. Activate prior knowledge about wild animals. The story in our book was about how wild animals take care of their babies. This story is about wild animals too. What should we do when we see a wild animal? Have you ever watched a wild animal?
    - **Set a Purpose for Reading** Let's read to find out what kids do when they see wild animals.

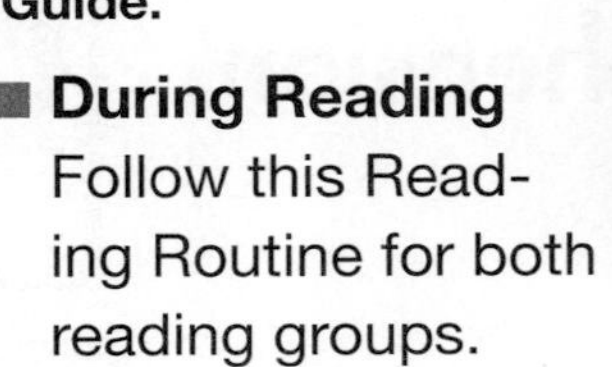

ELL Reader

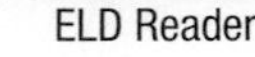

ELD Reader

- **During Reading** Follow this Reading Routine for both reading groups.

    1. Read the entire Reader aloud slowly as children follow along and finger point.
    2. Reread the Reader one sentence at a time. Have the children echo read after you.

- **After Reading** Use the exercises on the inside back cover of *Do Not Go Near* and invite children to share drawings and writing. In a whole-group discussion, ask children to tell what they should do if they see a wild animal close up. Encourage children to think about the animals they are likely to see near their home (birds, ducks, squirrels). Have children point to examples in the book of different situations when children saw wild animals.

ELD Reader Beginning/Intermediate

- **pp. 2–3** Point to the ducks. How does the mother duck take care of her babies? (She leads them)
- **pp. 6–7** Point to the frog. Should the boy touch the frog? (no)

Writing Draw a picture of one of the animals in the story. Ask children to work in pairs and label their picture with a sentence or phrase telling how their animal takes care of its babies. Have them share their drawings with the class.

ELL Reader Advanced/Advanced High

- **pp. 4–5** Point to the nest. This nest fell. Should the girl pick it up? (no) Why? (She may hurt the birds.)
- **p. 8** Point to the bears. How can we help the bears? (by leaving them alone)

Study Guide Distribute copies of the ELL Reader Study Guide (*ELL Handbook*, page 88). Scaffold comprehension by reminding them to focus on the main idea of the story. Review their responses together. (**Answers** See *ELL Handbook*, pp. 245–248.)

Objectives

- Use prior knowledge and experience to understand meanings in English
- Demonstrate comprehension of increasingly complex English by participating in shared reading, retelling or summarizing material, responding to questions, and taking notes commensurate with content area and grade level needs.

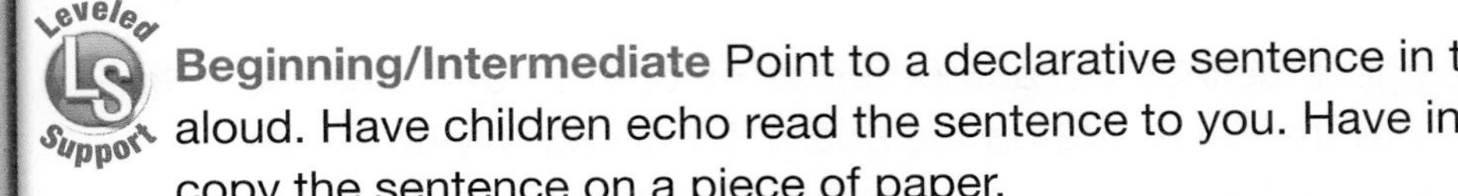

Conventions
Declarative Sentences

- **Preteach** Point to the image on page 105 of the Student Edition. The kit sits up. The period at the end of this sentence lets you know that this is a declarative sentence. A declarative sentence tells you what is happening.
- **Practice** Leaf through the Student Edition and call attention to declarative sentences. Have children do the exercises below according to their proficiency levels.

Leveled Support

Beginning/Intermediate Point to a declarative sentence in the story. Read it aloud. Have children echo read the sentence to you. Have intermediate children copy the sentence on a piece of paper.

Advanced/Advanced-High Have children choose a picture in the story. Then, challenge them to write their own declarative sentence about the picture.

- **Reteach**
  - Write *Birds bring worms to their babies*. This sentence gives information. It ends with a period. This is a declarative sentence. What information is this sentence sharing? (Birds bring their babies food.) What punctuation do we use with a declarative sentence? (period)
  - Write subjects on several note cards and verbs on several others. Have children work in pairs to choose a card from each pile and write a declarative sentence using the subject and verb they chose.
- **Practice** Use the summary of *A Fox and a Kit* (*ELL Handbook*, page 85) to practice identifying and using declarative sentences.

Leveled Support

Beginning Choose simple sentences from the summary to read aloud. Ask children to give a "thumbs up" if the sentence you read is declarative. Have them repeat the sentences.

Intermediate Write several different types of sentences from the summary on sentence strips. Have children work together to sort the sentences—declarative or not.

Advanced/Advanced-High Have children write their own declarative sentences. Check to make sure that they included periods. Have them read their sentences to a partner.

Objectives
- Internalize new basic and academic language by using and reusing it in meaningful ways in speaking and writing activities that build concept and language attainment.
- Demonstrate listening comprehension of increasingly complex spoken English by following directions, retelling or summarizing spoken messages, responding to questions and requests, collaborating with peers, and taking notes commensurate with content and grade-level needs.

Content Objectives
- Identify and use declarative sentences.
- Correctly use declarative sentences.

Language Objectives
- Speak using declarative sentences.
- Write declarative sentences.

Transfer Skills
The typical English sequence of subject then predicate is not standard in some languages. For example, in Spanish the verb often appears before the subject, while in Korean and Hindi the verb typically appears at the end of the sentence.

Mini-Lesson: Speaking
Tell children that we use declarative sentences to answer questions. Have children demonstrate listening comprehension by having them respond to questions. Use questions on p. 112 of the Student Edition. Have children listen to the questions and then answer them orally with complete declarative sentences.

Content Objectives

- Identify words that indicate an author's feelings.
- Identify words that express an author's experiences.

Language Objectives

- Write a personal narrative that expresses your feelings and experiences.
- Share feedback for editing and revising.
- Understand the main points of spoken language and express ideas.
- Monitor written language production.

Mini-Lesson: Listening and Speaking

Ask children to listen as you read p. 111 of the Student Edition. What are the main points of the story that are shown on this page? *(People can watch foxes at the zoo. People can watch many animals at the zoo.)* Ask children if they can support these main ideas with experiences from their own lives. Children should express their ideas in single words and short phrases while discussing animals they can see at the zoo.

ELL English Language Learners

Write a Personal Narrative

- **Introduce Terms** Write *personal narrative* on the board and explain each word as you point to it. A narrative is a story. It is told in words you might use when telling something to a friend. Circle the word *person* inside *personal*. A personal narrative is about things that happened to you. In a personal narrative, the author tells about something that happened in his or her life.
- **Describe feelings and experiences** Explain that a good personal narrative describes how the author feels and about his or her experiences. Write this sentence: *I loved going down the first hill of the roller coaster.*

  Have children suggest feelings the author felt as he or she continued the roller coaster ride. Record their answers on the board. Model supplying the next experience and feeling: *My stomach hurt as the first loop came close.*
- **Writing Model** Draw the graphic organizer below. Label the top circle *topic* and the other two *experiences* and *feelings*. Write *ride the ferris wheel* in the *topic* circle. Encourage children to name feelings they might have on a ferris wheel and things they might experience during their ride. Record their ideas in the circles.

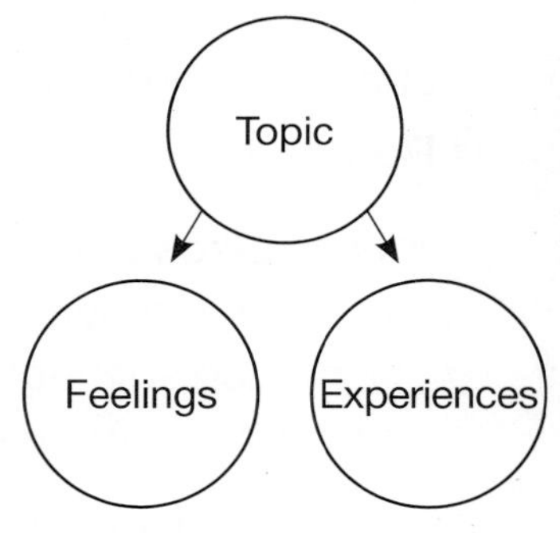

- **Write** Have children copy this story starter: *I went to a* ______. Have them draw three large circles under the sentence and label them *topic, feelings*, and *experiences*. Have children think of a favorite sport or game. What was the topic, how did they feel, and what did they experience?

Leveled Support

Beginning Supply the graphic organizer. Think of something you did this weekend. Draw what you did in the *topic* circle. What feeling did you have? Draw this in the *feelings* circle. What did you experience or what happened? Draw this in the *experiences* circle. Have children tell about their pictures. Supply the feeling words and have children copy them.

Intermediate Guide children's writing. What feeling words will you use? What words can you use to tell more about your experience?

Advanced/Advanced High Have children use the circles for prewriting. Then have them write their sentences in paragraph form. They can monitor their written language production to correct language as necessary.

Objectives

- Narrate, describe, and explain with increasing specificity and detail to fulfill content area writing needs as more English is acquired.

Common Core Standards
Weekly Planning Guide

Selection: Get the Egg!
Genre: Realistic Fiction

Alignment of the Common Core Standards with This Week's Skills and Strategies

This Week's Common Core Standards for English Language Arts	Instructional Summary
Reading Standards for Literature	
Literature 1. Ask and answer questions about key details in a text. **Literature 3.** Describe characters, settings, and major events in a story, using key details. **Literature 4.** Identify words and phrases in stories or poems that suggest feelings or appeal to the senses.	The lesson focuses on the skill of **main idea and details.** Children learn that the main idea is what the story is mostly about and that the details help them understand the main idea of a story. The instruction on the **story structure** strategy helps children understand how a story is organized to know the sequence of events in the story.
Foundational Skills Standards	
Foundational Skills 2.c. Isolate and pronounce initial, medial vowel, and final sounds (phonemes) in spoken single-syllable words. **Foundational Skills 4.b.** Read on-level text orally with accuracy, appropriate rate, and expression on successive readings.	Children segment and blend phonemes to **decode words.** They also work with rhyming words to show the decoding process, where initial sounds are changed to make new words.
Writing Standards	
Writing 5. With guidance and support from adults, focus on a topic, respond to questions and suggestions from peers, and add details to strengthen writing as needed. **Writing 7.** Participate in shared research and writing projects (e.g., explore a number of "how-to" books on a given topic and use them to write a sequence of instructions).	In this lesson, children create a **realistic story** as they follow the steps of the writing process. The how-to article on pages 142 and 143 extends their knowledge as they learn about following the steps given. They also expand their writing in the Research and Inquiry section, where they write about animals in their neighborhood.
Speaking and Listening Standards	
Speaking/Listening 4. Describe people, places, things, and events with relevant details, expressing ideas and feelings clearly.	In the Listening and Speaking sections of the lesson, children focus on giving **descriptions.** They are reminded to tell what something looks like, sounds like, or feels like.
Language Standards	
Language 5.b. Define words by category and by one or more key attributes (e.g., a *duck* is a bird that swims; a *tiger* is a large cat with stripes). **Language 6.** Use words and phrases acquired through conversations, reading and being read to, and responding to texts, including using frequently occurring conjunctions to signal simple relationships (e.g., *I named my hamster Nibblet because she nibbles too much because she likes that*).	Children **sort** words by grouping them in ways that help them remember what the words mean.

Additional Support for a Common Core Standard This Week

Use the following instruction to supplement the teaching of one of this week's Common Core Standards.

Common Core Standard: **Literature 4.**
Display pages 142 and 143 to help children identify sensory details to create pictures in their minds about what they read.

- Review the senses of taste, smell, sight, hearing, and touch.
- Have children look at the peanut butter on page 142 and the coated branch on page 143.
- Ask children to use sensory words to describe what the girl created to help feed the birds.

ISBN-13: 978-0-328-64366-0 ISBN-10: 0-328-64366-1

Grade 1 • Unit 1 • Week 5

Get the Egg!

Unit 1

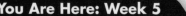

How are people and animals important to one another?

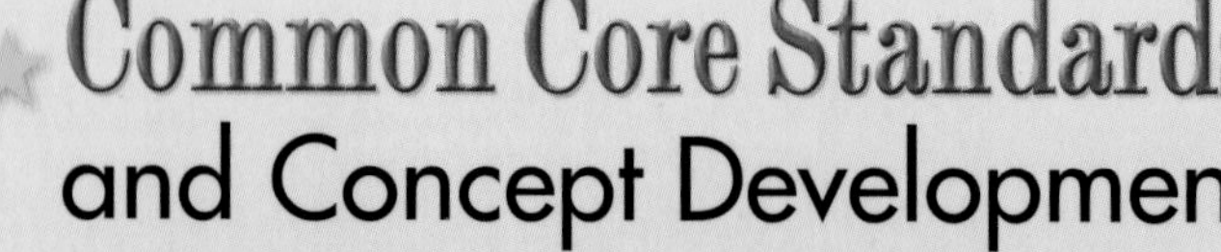

Common Core Standards and Concept Development

- Introduce and explore this unit's weekly concepts through rich, structured conversations
- Develop complex content knowledge and vocabulary
- Expand on a single concept with engaging literature and nonfiction
- Build better readers in all content areas

Align instruction to **Common Core Anchor Standards**

Week 1

Sam, Come Back!

Question of the Week

What do pets need?

connect to SOCIAL STUDIES

Concept Talk Guide children as they discuss questions such as:

- What do people do to take care of their pets?

Writing Think about a pet you know. Write a story about the pet playing.

Week 2

Pig in a Wig

Question of the Week

Who helps animals?

connect to SOCIAL STUDIES

Concept Talk Guide children as they discuss questions such as:

- What are some different ways that animals need our help?

Writing Write a fantasy story about a person who helps an animal. Draw a picture for your story.

Week 3

The Big Blue Ox

Question of the Week

How do animals help people?

connect to SOCIAL STUDIES

Concept Talk Guide children as they discuss questions such as:

- What are some ways farm animals help farmers?

Writing Think about a kind of animal you know. Write a two-line poem about that animal.

Week 4

A Fox and a Kit

Question of the Week

How do wild animals take care of their babies?

connect to SCIENCE

Concept Talk Guide children as they discuss questions such as:

- What do some animals do to protect their babies?

Writing Think about a time you watched some animals. Write a narrative about it.

You Are Here: Week 5

Get the Egg!

Question of the Week

Which wild animals live in our neighborhood?

connect to SCIENCE

As children answer this unit's Big Question and this week's Question of the Week, they will address:

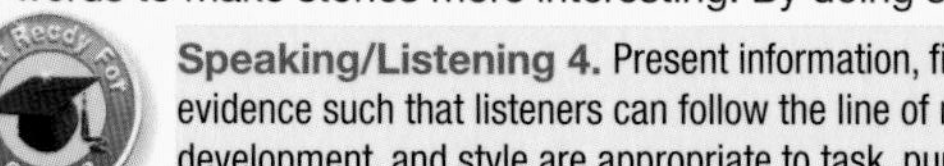

Reading 1. Read closely to determine what the text says explicitly and to make logical inferences from it; cite specific textual evidence when writing or speaking to support conclusions drawn from the text. **(Also Reading 3.)**

Concept Talk Guide children as they discuss questions such as:

- What are some wild animals you have seen in your neighborhood?

As children answer this week's Concept Talk question, they will address:

Speaking/Listening 1. Prepare for and participate effectively in a range of conversations and collaborations with diverse partners, building on others' ideas and expressing their own clearly and persuasively. **(Also Speaking/Listening 4.)**

Writing Think about animals in neighborhoods. Write a realistic story about two friends seeing an animal.

As children write about this week's prompt, they will address:

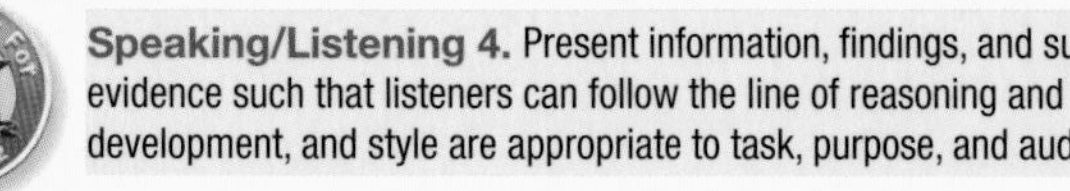

Writing 3. Write narratives to develop real or imagined experiences or events using effective technique, well-chosen details, and well-structured event sequences. **(Also Writing 5.)**

Listening and Speaking On page 144, children learn to use descriptive words to make stories more interesting. By doing so, they address:

Speaking/Listening 4. Present information, findings, and supporting evidence such that listeners can follow the line of reasoning and the organization, development, and style are appropriate to task, purpose, and audience.

Week 6

Animal Park

Question of the Week

What can we learn about wild animals by watching them?

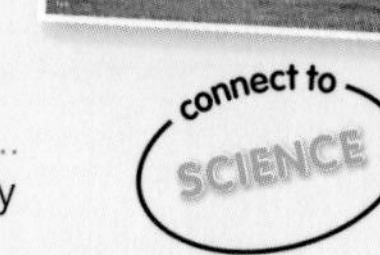

connect to SCIENCE

Concept Talk Guide children as they discuss questions such as:

- What wild animals have you watched? What did you learn about the food it eats?

Writing Think about wild animals. Write a composition about what people learn by watching wild animals.

This Week's ELL Overview

Grade 1 • Unit 1 • Week 5
Get the Egg!
120a–145l and DI•96–DI•105

ELL Handbook

- Maximize Literacy and Cognitive Engagement
- Research Into Practice
- Full Weekly Support for Every Selection

Get the Egg!
- Multi-Lingual Summaries in Five Languages
- Selection-Specific Vocabulary Word Cards
- Frontloading/Reteaching for Comprehension Skill Lessons
- ELD and ELL Reader Study Guides

- Transfer Activities
- Professional Development

Daily Leveled ELL Notes

ELL notes appear throughout this week's instruction and ELL Support is on the DI pages of your Teacher's Edition. The following is a sample of an ELL note from this week.

English Language Learners

Beginning Have children draw and label three story events (beginning, middle, end) and share with a partner, possibly one who speaks the same home language.

Intermediate Have children write phrases to express three story event ideas (beginning, middle, end). Have them describe the story plan to other children.

Advanced Have children write short sentences in their story charts. As they share the plan with partners, children can clarify and add ideas.

Advanced High Have children write sentences in their story charts. As they share the plan with partners, have children add sensory details to make the story more interesting.

ELL by Strand

The ELL lessons on this week's Support for English Language Learners pages are organized by strand. They offer additional scaffolding for the core curriculum. Leveled support notes on these pages address the different proficiency levels in your class. See pages DI•96–DI•105.

The Three Pillars of ELL Instruction

ELL Strands	Activate Prior Knowledge	Access Content	Extend Language
Vocabulary p. DI•100	Preteach	Teach/Model	Practice
Reading Comprehension p. DI•101	Preteach	Reteach/Practice	Leveled Practice Activities
Phonics, Spelling, and Word Analysis pp. DI•97–DI•98	Preteach	Listen and Write	Leveled Practice Activities
Listening Comprehension p. DI•99	Prepare for the Read Aloud	First Listening	Second Listening
Conventions and Writing pp. DI•104–DI•105	Preteach/Introduce Terms	Practice/Model	Leveled Practice Activities/ Leveled Writing Activities
Concept Development p. DI•96	Activate Prior Knowledge	Develop Concepts	Review Concepts and Connect to Writing

This Week's Practice Stations Overview

Six Weekly Practice Stations with Leveled Activities can be found at the beginning of each week of instruction. For this week's Practice Stations, see pp. 120h–120i.

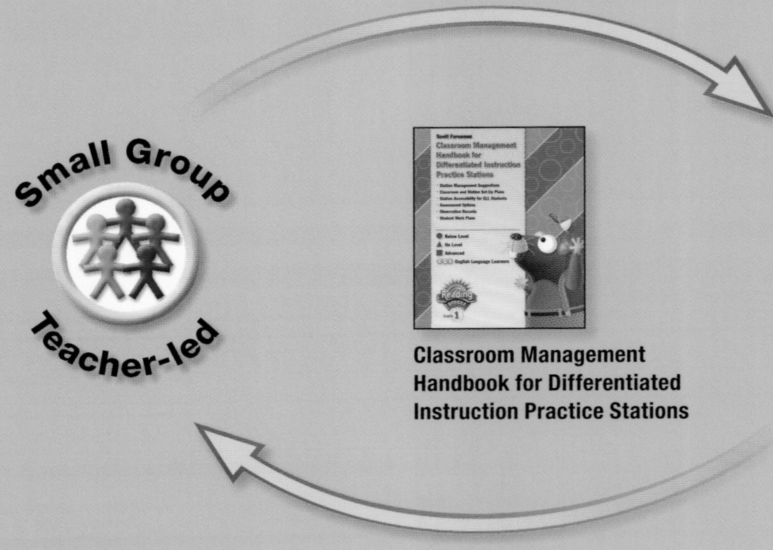

Classroom Management Handbook for Differentiated Instruction Practice Stations

Practice Stations

Daily Leveled Center Activities

 Below
 Advanced
On-Level
ELL

Practice Stations Flip Charts

	 Listen Up	 Word Work	 Words to Know	 Let's Write	 Read for Meaning	 Get Fluent
Objectives	• Add final /s/, final /z/, and /i/ /ng/ to spoken words.	• Add *-s* and *-ing* to verbs. • Read words with inflected endings.	• Identify high-frequency words *eat, her, this, too, four, five.* • Alphabetize words to the first or second letters.	• Write declarative sentences.	• Identify the main idea of a selection. • Identify the details that support the main idea.	• Read aloud with accuracy at an appropriate rate.
Materials	• *Listen Up* Flip Chart Activity 5	• *Word Work* Flip Chart Activity 5 • Letter Tiles	• *Words to Know* Flip Chart Activity 5 • High-Frequency Word Cards for Unit 1, Week 4 • paper • blank cards • pencils	• *Let's Write* Flip Chart Activity 5 • paper • pencils	• *Read for Meaning* Flip Chart Activity 5 • Leveled Readers • paper • pencils	• *Get Fluent* Flip Chart Activity 5 • Leveled Readers

This Week on Reading Street!

Question of the Week

Which wild animals live in our neighborhood?

Daily Plan

Whole Group

- Short *e*: *e*
- Initial Consonant Blends
- Main Idea and Details
- Fluency
- Vocabulary

Don't Wait Until Friday

MONITOR PROGRESS **Success Predictor**

Day 1	Day 2	Day 3	Day 4	Day 5
Check Word Reading	Check Word Reading	Check High-Frequency Words/Retelling	Check Fluency	Check Oral Vocabulary

Small Group

Teacher-Led

- Reading Support
- Skill Support
- Fluency Practice

Practice Stations

Independent Activities

Customize Literacy More support for a Balanced Literacy approach, see CL•1–CL•47.

Customize Writing More support for a customized writing approach, see CW•11–CW•20.

Whole Group

- Writing: Realistic Story
- Conventions: Interrogative Sentences

Assessment

- Weekly Tests
- Day 5 Assessment
- Fresh Reads

This Week's Reading Selections

Main Selection
Genre: **Realistic Fiction**

Paired Selection

Decodable Practice Readers

Leveled Readers

ELL and ELD Readers

Resources on Reading Street!

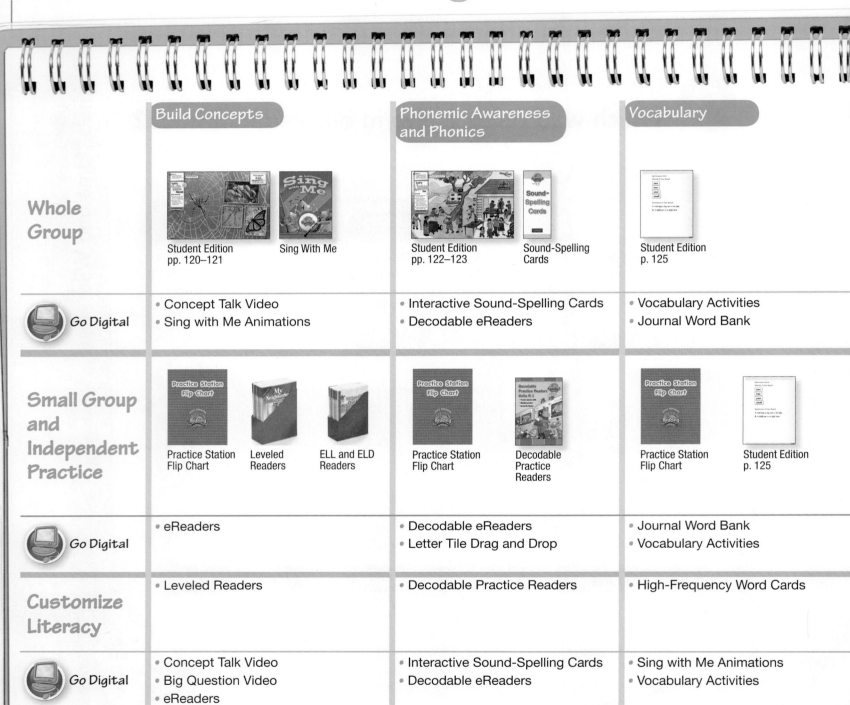

	Build Concepts	Phonemic Awareness and Phonics	Vocabulary
Whole Group	 Student Edition pp. 120–121;  Sing With Me	 Student Edition pp. 122–123;  Sound-Spelling Cards	 Student Edition p. 125
Go Digital	• Concept Talk Video • Sing with Me Animations	• Interactive Sound-Spelling Cards • Decodable eReaders	• Vocabulary Activities • Journal Word Bank
Small Group and Independent Practice	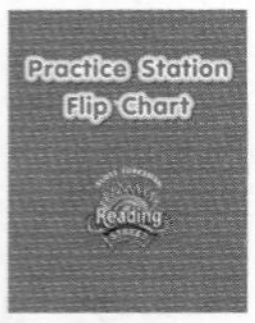 Practice Station Flip Chart;  Leveled Readers;  ELL and ELD Readers	 Practice Station Flip Chart;  Decodable Practice Readers	 Practice Station Flip Chart; 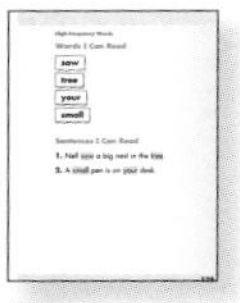 Student Edition p. 125
Go Digital	• eReaders	• Decodable eReaders • Letter Tile Drag and Drop	• Journal Word Bank • Vocabulary Activities
Customize Literacy	• Leveled Readers	• Decodable Practice Readers	• High-Frequency Word Cards
Go Digital	• Concept Talk Video • Big Question Video • eReaders	• Interactive Sound-Spelling Cards • Decodable eReaders	• Sing with Me Animations • Vocabulary Activities

Question of the Week

Which wild animals live in our neighborhood?

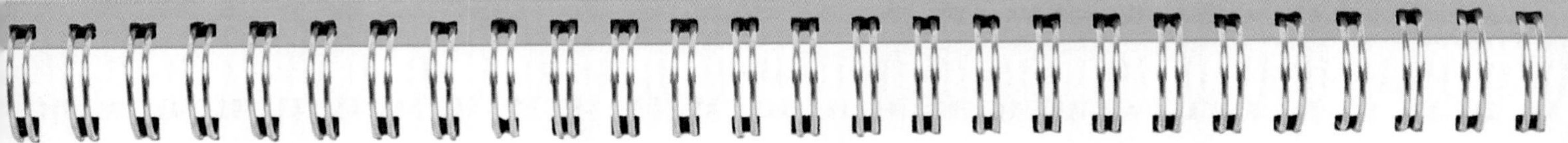

Comprehension	Fluency	Conventions and Writing
 Student Edition pp. 128–137	  Decodable Practice Readers	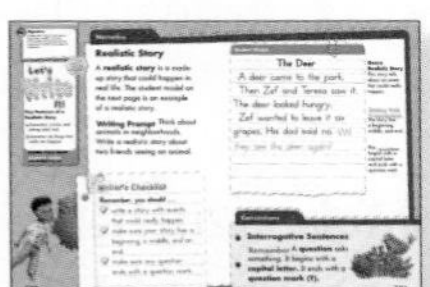 Student Edition pp. 140–141
• Envision It! Animations • eSelections	• eSelections • eReaders	• Grammar Jammer
 Practice Station Flip Chart  Leveled Readers  ELL and ELD Readers	 Practice Station Flip Chart  Decodable Practice Readers	 Practice Station Flip Chart  Reader's and Writer's Notebook
• eReaders • Story Sort	• Decodable eReaders	• Grammar Jammer
• Envision It! Skills and Strategies Handbooks • Leveled Readers	• Leveled Readers	• Reader's and Writer's Notebook
• Envision It! Animations • eReaders	• eReaders	• Grammar Jammer

Week 5

My 5-Day Planner for Reading Street!

Don't Wait Until Friday SUCCESS PREDICTOR

	Check Word Reading **Day 1** pages 120j–125f	Check Word Reading **Day 2** pages 126a–137g
Get Ready to Read	**Concept Talk,** 120j–121 **Oral Vocabulary,** 121a–121b *habitat, hatch, survive* **Phonemic Awareness,** 122–123 Distinguish /e/ **Phonics,** 123a–124a ◉ Short *e: e* READ **Decodable Practice Reader 5A,** 124b–124c **Spelling,** 124d Pretest	**Concept Talk,** 126a–126b **Oral Vocabulary,** 126b *chirp* **Phonemic Awareness,** 126c Segment and Blend Phonemes **Phonics,** 126d–127a ◉ Initial Consonant Blends READ **Decodable Practice Reader 5B,** 127b–127c Review **Phonics,** 127d Short-Vowel Words and Short *e: e* **Spelling,** 127e Practice
Read and Comprehend	**High-Frequency Words,** 125 Introduce *saw, small, tree, your* **Listening Comprehension,** 125a–125b ◉ Main Idea and Details	**High-Frequency Words,** 127 Build Fluency *saw, small, tree, your* **Story Words,** 128a Introduce *bird* **Vocabulary,** 128a Sort Words **Build Background,** 128b READ **Main Selection–First Read,** 128c–137a *Get the Egg!* **Literary Text,** 137b Sensory Details
Language Arts	**Conventions,** 125c Interrogative Sentences **Writing,** 125d–125e Realistic Story **Research and Inquiry,** 125f Identify and Focus Topic	**Conventions,** 137c Interrogative Sentences **Writing,** 137d–137e Realistic Story Writing Trait: Organization **Handwriting,** 137f Letter *E* and *e*: Letter Size **Research and Inquiry,** 137g Research Skill: List

You Are Here! Unit 1 Week 5

Question of the Week
Which wild animals live in our neighborhood?

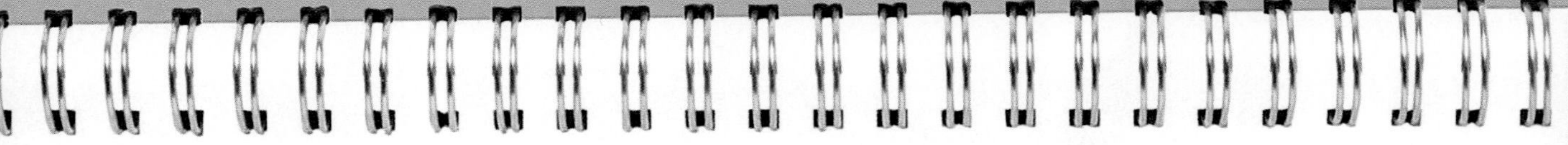

Check High-Frequency Words Check Retelling **Day 3** pages 138a–141c	Check Fluency **Day 4** pages 142a–143f	Check Oral Vocabulary **Day 5** pages 144a–145k
Concept Talk, 138a–138b **Oral Vocabulary,** 138b *croak* **Phonological Awareness,** 138c Rhyming Words **Phonics,** 138d–138e ◎ Short *e: e* ◎ Initial Consonant Blends **Spelling,** 138f Dictation	**Concept Talk,** 142a–142b **Oral Vocabulary,** 142b *moist* **Phonemic Awareness,** 142c Distinguish /e/ Review **Phonics,** 142d Inflected Endings *-s* and *-ing* READ **Decodable Practice Reader 5C,** 142e–142f **Spelling,** 142h Partner Review	**Concept Wrap Up,** 144a Review **Oral Vocabulary,** 144b **Phonemic Awareness,** 144c Segment and Blend Onset and Rime Review **Phonics,** 144c ◎ Short *e: e* ◎ Initial Consonant Blends **Spelling,** 144d Test
Review **High-Frequency Words,** 138g *saw, small, tree, your* Review **Story Words,** 138g *bird* READ **Main Selection—Second Read,** 128–137, 138h–139a **Fluency,** 139b Appropriate Phrasing	**Science in Reading,** 142i READ **Paired Selection,** 142–143a "Help the Birds" **Fluency,** 143b Appropriate Phrasing	**Listening and Speaking,** 144–145 **Vocabulary,** 145a Sort Words **Fluency,** 145a Appropriate Phrasing Review **Comprehension,** 145b ◎ Main Idea and Details Review **Vocabulary,** 145b High-Frequency and Story Words **Procedural Text,** 145c How-to Article **Assessment,** 145d–145f Monitor Progress
Conventions, 140a–141a Interrogative Sentences **Writing,** 140–141a Realistic Story Writer's Craft: Time-Order Words **Listening and Speaking,** 141b Give Descriptions **Research and Inquiry,** 141c Gather and Record Information	**Conventions,** 143c Interrogative Sentences **Writing,** 143d–143e Realistic Story Revising Strategy **Research and Inquiry,** 143f Review and Revise Topic	Review **Conventions,** 145g Interrogative Sentences **Writing,** 145h–145i Realistic Story Writer's Craft: Questions **Research and Inquiry,** 145j Communicate **Wrap Up Your Week,** 145k Which wild animals live in our neighborhood?

Grouping Options for Differentiated Instruction
Turn the page for the small group time lesson plan.

Planning Small Group Time on Reading Street!

Look for this Small Group Time box each day to help meet the individual needs of all your children. Differentiated Instruction lessons appear on the DI pages at the end of each week.

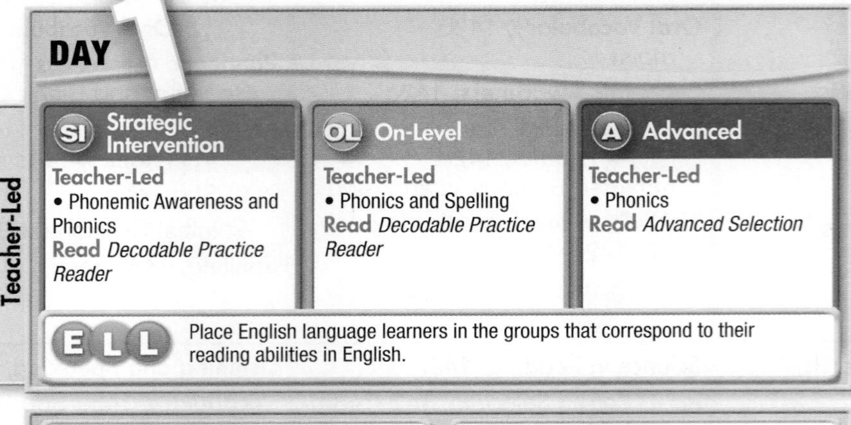

DAY 1

Teacher-Led	SI Strategic Intervention	OL On-Level	A Advanced
	Teacher-Led • Phonemic Awareness and Phonics Read *Decodable Practice Reader*	Teacher-Led • Phonics and Spelling Read *Decodable Practice Reader*	Teacher-Led • Phonics Read *Advanced Selection*

ELL Place English language learners in the groups that correspond to their reading abilities in English.

Practice Stations	Independent Activities
• Listen Up • Word Work	• *Reader's and Writer's Notebook* • Concept Talk Video

ELL Reader Advanced Advanced-High

ELD Reader Beginning Intermediate

ELL Poster

	Day 1
SI Strategic Intervention	**Phonemic Awareness and Phonics,** DI•85 Read **Decodable Practice Reader 5A,** DI•85
OL On-Level	**Phonics and Spelling,** DI•90 Read **Decodable Practice Reader 5A,** DI•90
A Advanced	**Phonics,** DI•93 Read **Advanced Selection,** DI•93
ELL English Language Learners	DI•96–DI•105 **Frontload Concept** **Preteach Skills** **Writing**

You Are Here! Unit 1 Week 5

Reading Street Response to Intervention Kit

Reading Street Leveled Practice Stations Kit

Question of the Week

Which wild animals live in our neighborhood?

Below-Level Reader

Decodable Practice Readers

Concept Literacy Reader

On-Level Reader

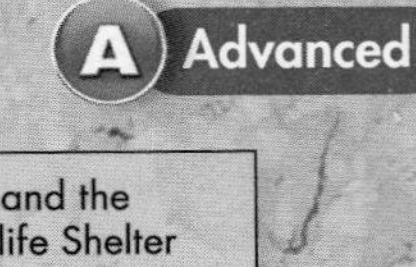

Advanced Reader

Advanced Selection

Small Group Weekly Plan

Day 2	Day 3	Day 4	Day 5
Phonemic Awareness and Phonics, DI•86 Read **Decodable Practice Reader 5B,** DI•86	**Phonemic Awareness and Phonics,** DI•87 Read **Concept Literacy Leveled Reader,** DI•87	**High-Frequency Words,** DI•88 Read **Decodable Practice Reader 5C,** DI•88	**Phonics Review,** DI•89 Read **Below-Level Leveled Reader,** DI•89
Phonics and High-Frequency Words, DI•90 Read **Decodable Practice Reader, 5B,** DI•90	Read **On-Level Leveled Reader,** DI•91	**Conventions,** DI•92 Reread **Main Selection,** DI•92	**Phonics Review,** DI•92 Reread **On-Level Leveled Reader,** DI•92
Phonics and Comprehension, DI•93 Read **Main Selection,** DI•93	Read **Advanced Leveled Reader,** DI•94	**Comprehension,** DI•95 Read **Paired Selection,** DI•95 Reread **Leveled Reader,** DI•95	**Fluency and Comprehension,** DI•95 Reread **Advanced Selection,** DI•95
DI•96–DI•105 **Review Concept** **Practice Skills** **Frontload Main Selection** **Writing**	DI•96–DI•105 **Review Concept** **Practice Skills** **Reread Main Selection** **Writing**	DI•96–DI•105 **Review Concept** **Practice Skills** **Read ELL or ELD Reader** **Writing**	DI•96–DI•105 **Review Concept** **Review Skills** **Writing**

Practice Stations for Everyone on Reading Street!

Listen Up!

Add phonemes to spoken words.

Objective

- Add final /s/, final /z/, and /ing/ to spoken words.

Materials

- *Listen Up!* Flip Chart Activity 5

Differentiated Activities

- A **verb** is a word that tells what someone or something does.

● Work with a partner. Say two verbs. After you say each verb, have your partner repeat the verb, and then add to it the sound you hear at the end of *walks,* the sound you hear at the end of *runs,* or the sounds you hear at the end of *sing.*

▲ Work with a partner. Say five verbs. After you say each verb, have your partner repeat the verb, and then add to it the sound you hear at the end of *walks,* the sound you hear at the end of *runs,* or the sounds you hear at the end of *sing.*

■ Work with a partner. Tell your partner, "I *walk.* He *walks.*" What sound do you hear at the end of *walks?* Repeat with *run, runs,* and *with run, running.* Repeat this activity with other verbs.

Technology

- Interactive Sound-Spelling Cards

Word Work

inflected endings *-s* and *-ing*

Objectives

- Add *-s* and *-ing* to verbs.
- Read words with inflected endings.

Materials

- *Word Work* Flip Chart Activity 5
- Letter Tiles

Differentiated Activities

- A **verb** is a word that tells what someone or something does.

● Build the words *picks, fills,* and *bending* with Letter Tiles. Read the words.

▲ Build the words *pick, fill,* and *bend* with Letter Tiles. Read the words. Now add the consonant *s* to the end of each word. What new words did you make? Next, add the letters *i, n, g* to the end of each word. What new words did you make?

■ Think of six verbs. Build each word with Letter Tiles. Read them. Add the ending *-s* or *-ing* to the verbs. Read the new words.

Technology

- Interactive Sound-Spelling Cards

Words To Know

Alphabetize words.

Objectives

- Identify high-frequency words *eat, her, this, too, four, five.*
- Alphabetize words to the first or second letters.

Materials

- *Words to Know* Flip Chart Activity 5
- High-Frequency Word Cards for Unit 1, Week 4
- paper
- blank cards
- pencils

Differentiated Activities

● Use the Word Cards. Look at the first or second letter of each word. Place the words in alphabetical order.

▲ Use the Word Cards. Place them in alphabetical order. Write the words in a list. Circle the first letter of each word.

■ Use the Word Cards. Place them in alphabetical order. Think of other words you know and write them on blank cards. Arrange them in alphabetical order, along with the Word Card words. Write all the words in a list.

Technology

- Online Tested Vocabulary Activities

Use this week's materials from the Reading Street Leveled Practice Stations Kit to organize this week's stations.

Key

- ● Below-Level Activities
- ▲ On-Level Activities
- ■ Advanced Activities

Practice Station Flip Chart

Let's Write

Write declarative sentences.

Objective

- Write declarative sentences.

Materials

- *Let's Write!* Flip Chart Activity 5
- paper
- pencils

Differentiated Activities

- A **declarative sentence** is a telling sentence.
- A sentence begins with a capital letter.
- A sentence ends with a period.

● Think about a wild animal. Write a declarative sentence about the animal.

▲ Think about a wild animal. Write declarative sentences about the animal.

■ Write a short story about a wild animal. Underline the declarative sentences in your story.

Read For Meaning

Identify main idea.

Objectives

- Identify the main idea of a selection.
- Identify the details that support the main idea.

Materials

- *Read for Meaning* Flip Chart Activity 5
- Leveled Readers
- paper
- pencils

Differentiated Activities

- The **main idea** of a selection tells what the selection is mainly about.
- **Details** are pieces of information that tell more about the main idea.

● Read *Time for Dinner.* Write a sentence that tells the main idea. Then write details.

▲ Read *Which Fox?* Write a sentence that tells the main idea. Then write details.

■ Read *Baby Animals in the Rain Forest.* Write a sentence that tells the main idea. Then write details.

Technology

- Leveled eReaders

Get Fluent

Practice fluent reading.

Objective

- Read aloud with accuracy at an appropriate rate.

Materials

- *Get Fluent* Flip Chart Activity 5
- Leveled Readers

Differentiated Activities

● Work with a partner. Take turns reading pages from *Time for Dinner.* Think about what you're reading about. Be sure to read at an appropriate rate. Read as accurately as you can. Give your partner feedback.

▲ Work with a partner. Take turns reading pages from *Which Fox?* Think about what you're reading about. Be sure to read at an appropriate rate. Read as accurately as you can. Give your partner feedback.

■ Work with a partner. Take turns reading pages from *Baby Animals in the Rain Forest.* Think about what you're reading about. Be sure to read at an appropriate rate. Read as accurately as you can. Give your partner feedback.

Technology

- Reading Street Readers CD-ROM

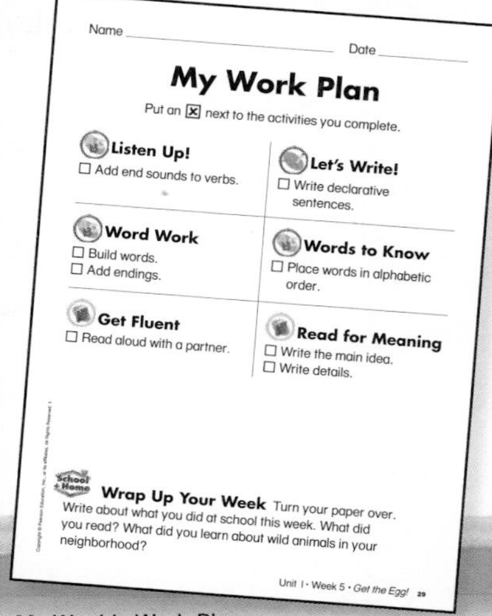

Name ______ Date ______

My Work Plan

Put an ☒ next to the activities you complete.

Listen Up! ☐ Add end sounds to verbs.	**Let's Write!** ☐ Write declarative sentences.
Word Work ☐ Build words. ☐ Add endings.	**Words to Know** ☐ Place words in alphabetic order.
Get Fluent ☐ Read aloud with a partner.	**Read for Meaning** ☐ Write the main idea. ☐ Write details.

Wrap Up Your Week Turn your paper over. Write about what you did at school this week. What did you read? What did you learn about wild animals in your neighborhood?

Unit 1 • Week 5 • Get the Egg! 29

My Weekly Work Plan

Week 5

Objectives

- Introduce concept: wild animals in our neighborhood.
- Share information and ideas about the concept.

Today at a Glance

Oral Vocabulary
habitat, hatch, survive

Phonemic Awareness
Distinguish /e/

Phonics and Spelling
◉ Short *e: e*

Fluency
Oral Rereading

High-Frequency Words
saw, small, tree, your

Comprehension
◉ Main Idea and Details

Conventions
Interrogative Sentences

Writing
Realistic Story: Introduce

Research and Inquiry
Identify and Focus Topic

Concept Talk

Question of the Week

Which wild animals live in our neighborhood?

Introduce the concept To build concepts and focus children's attention, tell them that this week they will talk, sing, read, and write about wild animals that live in their neighborhood. Write the Question of the Week and track the print as you read it.

ROUTINE Activate Prior Knowledge Team Talk

1. **Think** Have children think for a minute about wild animals that live in their neighborhood.
2. **Pair** Have pairs of children discuss the question.
3. **Share** Have children share information and their ideas with the group. Remind children to ask questions to clarify information. Guide discussion and encourage elaboration with prompts such as: What are some wild animals you have seen in your neighborhood?

Routines Flip Chart

Anchored Talk

Develop oral language Have children turn to pages 120–121 in their Student Edition. Read the title and look at the photos. Use these questions to guide discussion and create the "Which wild animals live in our neighborhood?" concept map (shown on next page).

- These photographs show wild animals that may be found in our back-yards. Which animal is building a web? (Possible response: the spider) Which animal makes tunnels in the dirt? (the worm) What emerges from a cocoon? (Possible response: a butterfly) Let's add these animals to our map.
- What other animals do you see in these photographs? (Possible response rabbits) The rabbits survive by digging shallow burrows in the ground to sleep. Let's add *rabbit* to the map too.

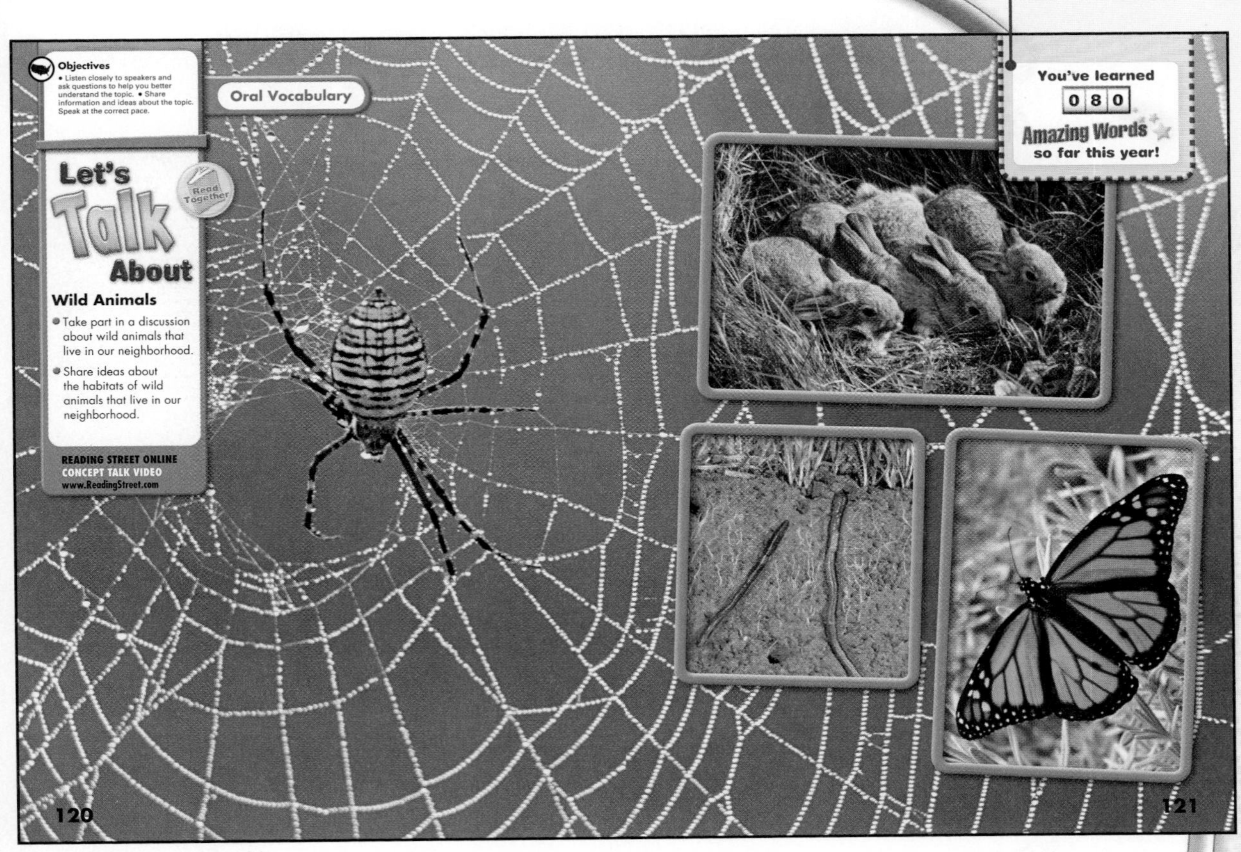

Objectives
• Listen closely to speakers and ask questions to help you better understand the topic. • Share information and ideas about the topic. Speak at the correct pace.
Oral Vocabulary
Let's Talk About
Read Together
Wild Animals
• Take part in a discussion about wild animals that live in our neighborhood.
• Share ideas about the habitats of wild animals that live in our neighborhood.
READING STREET ONLINE
CONCEPT TALK VIDEO
www.ReadingStreet.com
You've learned
0 8 0
Amazing Words
so far this year!
120
121

Student Edition pp. 120–121

Connect to reading Explain that this week, children will read about how two friends help a bird in their neighborhood. Let's add *bird* to our map.

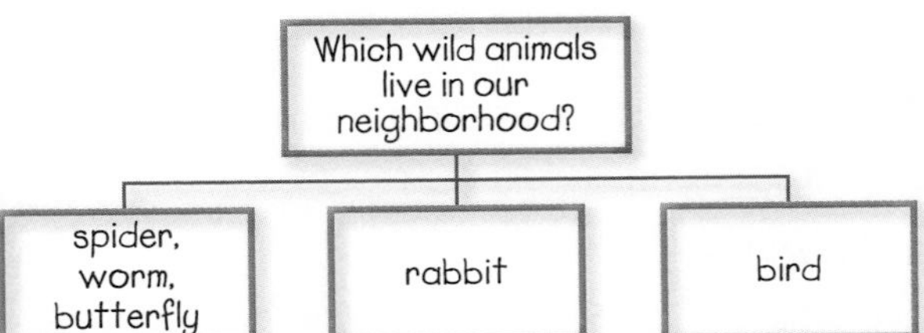

Amazing Words

You've learned 0 8 0 words so far.

You'll learn 0 0 6 words this week!

habitat	chirp
hatch	croak
survive	moist

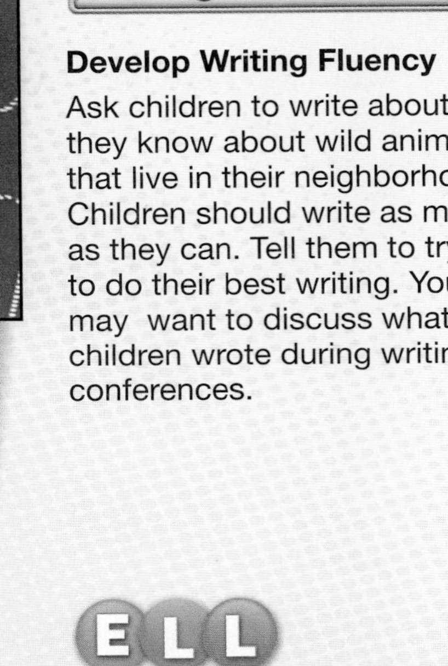

Writing on Demand

Develop Writing Fluency

Ask children to write about what they know about wild animals that live in their neighborhood. Children should write as much as they can. Tell them to try to do their best writing. You may want to discuss what children wrote during writing conferences.

ELL

English Language Learners

Listening Comprehension English learners will benefit from additional visual support to understand the key terms in the concept map. Use the pictures on pp. 120–121 to scaffold understanding. For example, when talking about the different animals, point to the picture of the animal being discussed.

ELL Support Additional ELL support and modified instruction are provided in the *ELL Handbook* and in the ELL Support Lessons on pp. DI•96–DI•105.

ELL **Preteach Concepts** Use the Day 1 instruction on ELL Poster 5 to assess and build background knowledge, develop concepts, and build oral vocabulary.

ELL Poster 5

Objectives

- Build oral vocabulary.
- Discuss the concept to develop oral language.
- Share information and ideas about the concept.

Oral Vocabulary
Amazing Words

Introduce Amazing Words

Display page 5 of the *Sing with Me* Big Book. Tell children they are going to sing "Time to Hatch," a song about how baby birds learn what they need in order to live. Ask children to listen for the Amazing Words *habitat*, *hatch*, and *survive* as you sing. Sing the song again and have children join you.

Sing with Me Big Book Audio

Time to Hatch
Crack! The eggs begin to hatch now.
New birds come alive.
They look at their habitat to
See how they can survive.
Little birdies see a pond and
Feeders filled with seed,
Thorny bushes they can hide in—
Everything they need!

Sing with Me Big Book p. 5

Teach Amazing Words

Amazing Words Oral Vocabulary Routine

1. **Introduce the Word** Relate the word *habitat* to the song. The song says that baby birds look at their *habitat*. Supply a child-friendly definition: A *habitat* is the place where an animal or plant lives. Have children say the word.
2. **Demonstrate** Provide examples to show meaning: Different kinds of animals live in different *habitats*. The *habitat* for a fish may be a lake, or a pond, or the ocean. A forest may be a rabbit's *habitat*. The dirt in a garden may be a worm's *habitat*. Cactus plants live in a desert *habitat*.
3. **Apply** Have children demonstrate their understanding: Name an animal and the *habitat* where that animal lives.

See p. OV•2 to teach *hatch* and *survive*.

Routines Flip Chart

Check understanding of Amazing Words

Have children look at the picture on pp. 120–121. What do you think rabbits eat? What else do they need to live? Use *survive* in your answer. (Possible response: Rabbits eat grass and other plants. They need food, water, and shelter to survive.)

The butterfly hatches from a cocoon. What animal in the picture hatches from an egg? Use the word *hatch*. (Possible response: Spiders hatch from eggs.)

What other animals can you think of that might live in a backyard habitat? Use *habitat* in your answer. (Possible response: Squirrels and mice might live in a backyard habitat.)

Apply Amazing Words

Have children demonstrate their understanding of the Amazing Words by completing these sentences orally.

I watched a ________ **hatch** from an egg.

________ can't **survive** without food or water.

The ocean is a good **habitat** for ________.

Corrective feedback

If... children have difficulty using the Amazing Words,
then... remind them of the definitions and provide opportunities for children to use the words in sentences.

Preteach Academic Vocabulary

Write the following on the board:

- main idea and details
- realistic fiction
- interrogative sentence

Have children share what they know about this week's Academic Vocabulary. Use children's responses to assess their prior knowledge. Preteach the Academic Vocabulary by providing a child-friendly description, explanation, or example that clarifies the meaning of each term. Then ask children to restate the meaning of the Academic Vocabulary in their own words.

Amazing Words

habitat	chirp
hatch	croak
survive	moist

Differentiated Instruction

SI Strategic Intervention

Sentence Production If children's oral sentences lack subject-verb agreement, then say each sentence several times and have children repeat it.

English Language Learners

Pronunciation Children may have difficulty hearing and reproducing stressed and unstressed syllables correctly. If children have difficulty with multi-syllable words, use soft and loud handclaps to help children hear the pacing of stressed and unstressed syllables in words such as *habitat* and *survive*.

Objectives

- Distinguish /e/ in initial and medial positions.
- ◎ Associate the vowel sound /e/ with the spelling *e*.

Skills Trace

◎ **Short *e*: *e***
Introduce U1W5D1
Practice U1W5D3; U1W5D4
Reteach/Review U1W5D5; U1W6D4
Assess/Test Weekly Test U1W5
Benchmark Test U1

KEY:
U=Unit W=Week D=Day

Student Edition pp. 122–123

Phonemic Awareness
Distinguish /e/

Introduce Read together the second bulleted point on pages 122–123 of the Student Edition. What is in the nest? (eggs) The first sound I hear in eggs is /e/. In the picture I also see a bird. What color is the bird? (red) The middle sound I hear in *red* is /e/. Have children look at the picture to identify other items that contain the /e/ sound. (*elf, steps, dress, sled, bell*)

Model Listen to the sounds in the word *red*: /r/ /e/ /d/. There are three sounds in *red*. Let's blend those sounds to make a word: /r/ /e/ /d/, *red*. Continue modeling with *eggs*.

Guide practice Guide children as they look for more words that contain the initial or medial /e/ sound. (*envelope, jet, pet*)

Corrective feedback **If...** children make an error,
then... model by repeating the short *e* sound in other words, and have them repeat the sound and the word after you.

Phonics — Teach/Model

Short e: e

Sound-Spelling Card 6

ROUTINE Blending Strategy

1. **Connect** Write the words *sit* and *hot*. Ask children what they know about the vowel sounds in these words. (The vowel sounds are short. *Sit* has the short vowel sound /i/ and *hot* has the short vowel sound /o/.) Explain that today they will learn how to spell and read words with the short vowel sound /e/.
2. **Use Sound-Spelling Card** Display Card 6. Point to *e*. The short *e* sound, /e/, can be spelled *e*. Have children say /e/ several times as you point to *e*.
3. **Model** Write *ten*. In this word, the letter e stands for the sound /e/. Segment and blend *ten*; then have children blend with you: /t/ /e/ /n/.
4. **Guide Practice** Continue the process in step 3. This time have children blend with you.

beg	vet	deck	sell	mess	red
peg	pen	tell	web	less	get

5. **Review** What do you know about reading these words? (The letter *e* at the beginning or in the middle of a word can spell the sound /e/.)

Routines Flip Chart

Differentiated Instruction

Strategic Intervention

Short Vowel Words If children have difficulty distinguishing the short vowel sounds for *i*, *o*, and *e*, pronounce and then have children repeat words such as *pit*, *pot*, and *pet*.

Advanced

Extend Blending Involve children in a rhyming game by saying a short-vowel word such as *bell* and inviting children to name words that rhyme with it.

Vocabulary Support

You may wish to explain the meaning of these words.

beg ask somebody for something

vet an animal doctor

peg a nail or hook in a wall used to hang things on

English Language Learners

Sound-Symbol Correspondence Double final consonants such as *ss* or *ll* do not exist in Spanish. Speakers of Spanish may need extra spelling practice with words such as *yell, bell, fell, mess,* and *less*.

Pronounce /e/ In Spanish, the letter *e* is pronounced /ā/. If children tend to pronounce short *e* as long *a*, say such words slowly and distinctly, emphasizing the sound /e/, to help children develop the generalization.

Objectives

- ◎ Associate the vowel sound /e/ with the spelling *e*.
- Blend and read words with short vowel sound of *e*.
- Decode words in context and in isolation.

Check Word Reading
SUCCESS PREDICTOR

Phonics — Build Fluency

◎ Short *e*: *e*

Model

Envision It!

Have children turn to page 124 in their Student Edition. Look at the picture on this page. I see a picture of an *elephant*. When I say *elephant*, I hear /e/ at the beginning. In *elephant*, short *e* is spelled *e*.

Guide practice

For each word in "Words I Can Blend," ask for the sound of each letter or group of letters. Make sure that children identify the correct sound for short *e*. Then have children blend the whole word.

Corrective feedback

If... children have difficulty blending a word,
then... model blending the word, and then ask children to blend it with you.

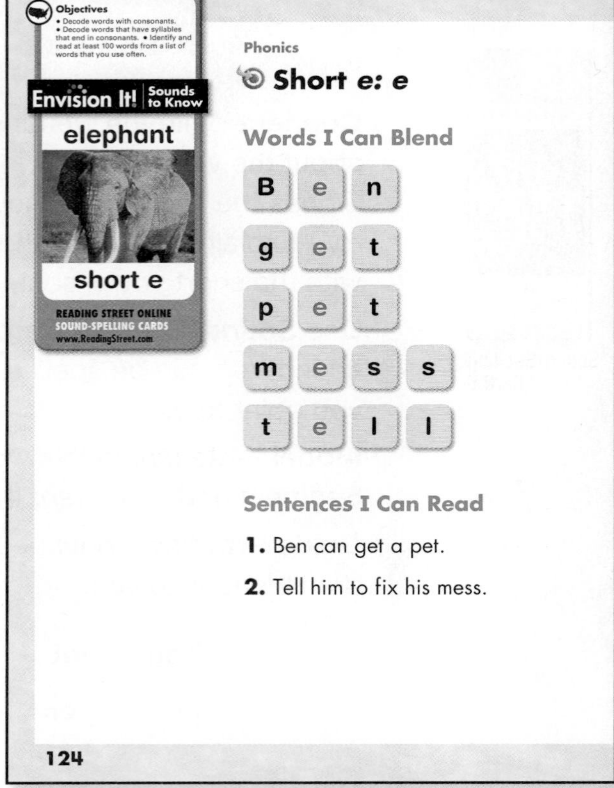

Student Edition p. 124

Blend and Read

Decode words in isolation After children can successfully segment and blend the words, point to words in random order and ask children to read them naturally.

Decode words in context Have children read each of the sentences. Have them identify words in the sentences that have the short *e* sound.

Team Talk Pair children and have them take turns reading each of the sentences aloud.

On their own Use *Reader's and Writer's Notebook* p. 185.

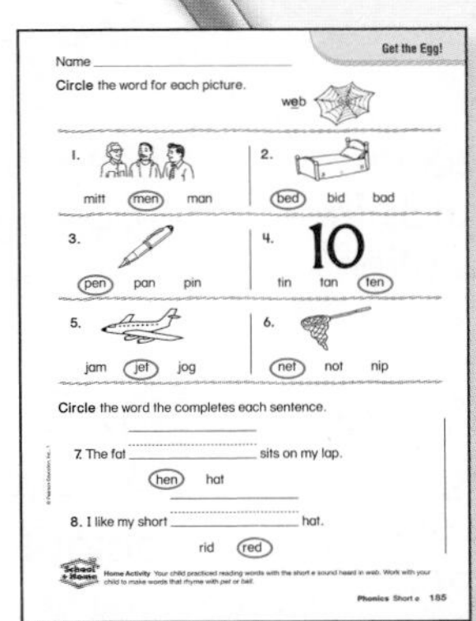
Name
Get the Egg!
Circle the word for each picture.
web
1. mitt men man
2. bed bid bad
3. pen pan pin
4. 10 tin tan ten
5. jam jet jog
6. net not nip
Circle the word that completes each sentence.
7. The fat ______ sits on my lap. hen hat
8. I like my short ______ hat. rid red

Reader's and Writer's Notebook, p. 185

Don't Wait Until Friday — MONITOR PROGRESS — Check Word Reading Short *e*: *e*

Write the following words and have the class read them. Notice which words children miss during the group reading. Call on individuals to read some of the words.

pet	**hen**	**egg**	**bed**	**pen**	
pick	**bell**	**six**	**get**	**miss**	← Spiral Review: Row 2 contrasts short *e* and short *i*.
deck	**rag**	**fell**	**win**	**lock**	← Row 3 reviews short *a*, *e*, *i*, and *o*.

If... children cannot blend words with the short *e* sound at this point,

then... use the Small Group Time Strategic Intervention lesson, p. DI•85, to reteach /e/ spelled *e*. Continue to monitor children's progress using other instructional opportunities during the week. See the Skills Trace on p. 122–123.

Day 1	Day 2	Day 3	Day 4	Day 5
Check Word Reading	Check Word Reading	Check High-Frequency Words/Retelling	Check Fluency	Check Oral Vocabulary

Success Predictor

Differentiated Instruction

SI Strategic Intervention

Pronounce /e/ If children tend to pronounce short *e* as short *i*, especially before the letter *n*, as in *pen, den,* and *Ben,* say such words slowly and distinctly, emphasizing the sound /e/, to help with formal pronunciation.

Advanced

Extend Blending Provide children who can segment and blend all the words correctly with more challenging words such as *pencil, center, pickle,* and *mistake*.

Spelling Patterns

Short *e* Spelled *e* The sound /e/ is usually spelled *e* at the beginning or in the middle of a word.

ELL

English Language Learners

Pronunciation Children whose first language is Spanish may need support with initial short *e* sounds in words such as *egg* and *enter*.

Objectives

- Apply knowledge of sound-spellings to decode unknown words when reading.
- Decode and read words in context and isolation.
- Practice fluency with oral rereading.

Decodable Practice Reader 5A

 Short *e: e*

Decode words in isolation Have children turn to page 193. Have children decode each word.

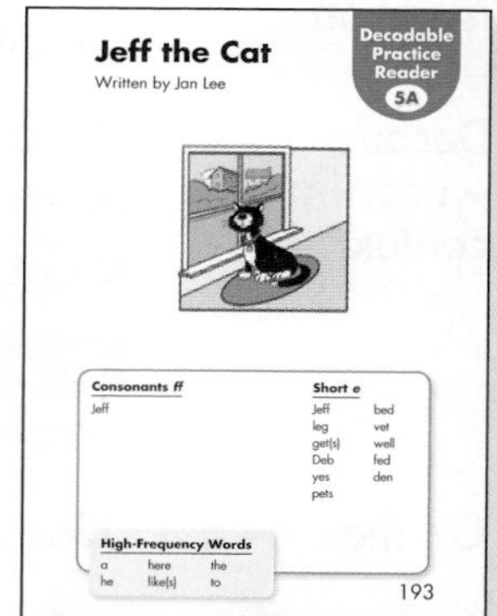

Jeff the Cat

Written by Jan Lee

Decodable Practice Reader 5A

Consonants *ff*

Jeff

Short *e*

Jeff, leg, get(s), Deb, yes, pets, bed, vet, well, fed, den

High-Frequency Words

a, here, the, he, like(s), to

193

Decodable Practice Reader 5A

Review High-frequency words Review the previously taught words *a, here, the, he, like(s)* and *to*. Have children read each word as you point to it on the Word Wall.

Preview Decodable Reader Have children read the title and preview the story. Tell them they will decode words with the short vowel sound *e*.

Decode words in context Pair children for reading and listen as they decode. One child begins. Children read the entire story, switching readers after each page. Partners reread the story. This time the other child begins.

Jeff is a cat.
Jeff sits here.

194

Jeff naps on the bed.
He likes the bed.

195

Decodable Practice Reader 5A

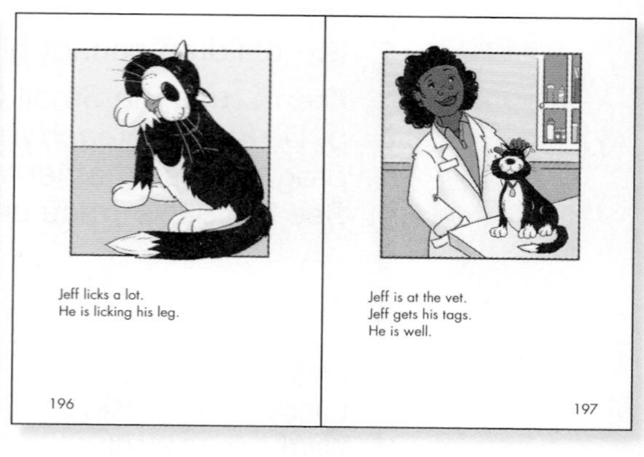

Jeff licks a lot.
He is licking his leg.

196

Jeff is at the vet.
Jeff gets his tags.
He is well.

197

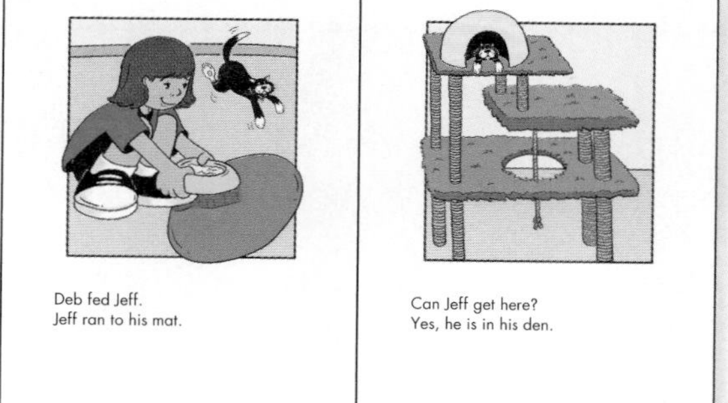

Deb fed Jeff.
Jeff ran to his mat.

198

Can Jeff get here?
Yes, he is in his den.

199

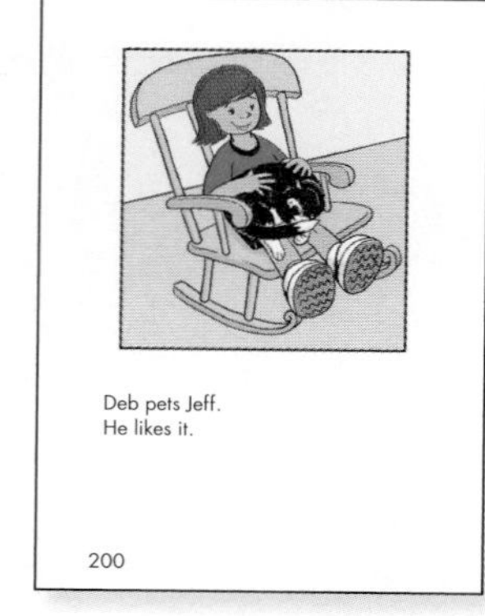

Deb pets Jeff.
He likes it.

200

Corrective feedback

If... children have difficulty decoding a word, **then...** refer them to the Sound-Spelling Cards to identify the sounds in the word. Then prompt them to blend the word.

- What is the new word?
- Is the new word a word you know?
- Does it make sense in the story?

Check decoding and comprehension

Have children retell the story to include characters, setting, and events. Then have children find words with the short *e* sound in the story. Explain that story words with this letter will have the short *e* sound at the beginning or middle of the word. Children should supply *Jeff, bed, leg, vet, gets, well, den, fed, pets, Deb,* and *yes.*

Reread for Fluency

Have children reread Decodable Practice Reader 5A to develop automaticity decoding words with the short *e* sound.

ROUTINE **Oral Rereading**

1. **Read** Have children read the entire book orally.
2. **Reread** To achieve optimal fluency, children should reread the text three or four times.
3. **Corrective Feedback** Listen as children read. Provide corrective feedback regarding their fluency and decoding.

Routines Flip Chart

Differentiated Instruction

 Advanced

Main Idea and Details After reading, have children tell about the main idea of the story, *Jeff the Cat*. Ask them to give a detail from the story that supports the main idea.

English Language Learners

Short *e*: *e*

Beginning Before children read, lead them on a picture walk through the story. Point out and pronounce the words that have the short *e* sound. Then write a pictured word and have children pronounce it and find its picture.

Intermediate After reading, have children read the words with the short *e* sound. Monitor children's pronunciation.

Advanced/Advanced-High After reading, have children find the words with the short *e* sound and use them to make up their own sentences about what they think will happen with Jeff after he comes home form the vet's office.

DAY 1 Get Ready to Read

Objectives
- Segment and spell short *e* words.
- Read high-frequency words.

Spelling Pretest
Short *e* Words

Dictate spelling words

Dictate the spelling words and read the sentences. Have children write the words. If needed, segment the words for children, clarify the pronunciations, and give meanings of words. Have children check their pretests and correct misspelled words.

1. men	The **men** helped us move into the new house.
2. red*	Leah wore a **red** dress.
3. step	My little sister took her first **step** today.
4. ten	We leave in **ten** minutes.
5. net*	I used a **net** to catch a goldfish.
6. leg	An ant crawled up my **leg.**
7. jet	We took a **jet** to visit grandma and grandpa.
8. sled	I love to **sled** down the hill in winter.
9. wet	I fell in the pool and got **wet.**
10. bed	I cleaned my room and made my **bed.**

* Words marked with asterisks come from the selection *Get the Egg!*

On their own

Use Let's Practice It! p. 62 on the *Teacher Resource DVD-ROM.*

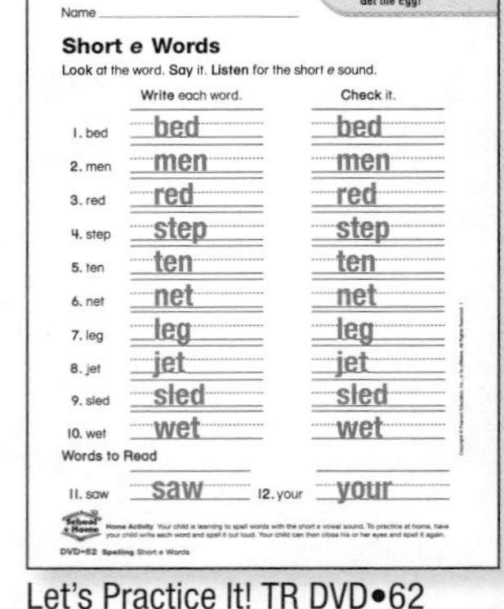
Name ______ Get the Egg!

Short *e* Words

Look at the word. **Say** it. **Listen** for the short *e* sound.

	Write each word.	Check it.
1. bed	bed	bed
2. men	men	men
3. red	red	red
4. step	step	step
5. ten	ten	ten
6. net	net	net
7. leg	leg	leg
8. jet	jet	jet
9. sled	sled	sled
10. wet	wet	wet

Words to Read

11. saw saw 12. your your

Home Activity Your child is learning to spell words with the short e vowel sound. To practice at home, have your child write each word and spell it out loud. Your child can then close his or her eyes and spell it again.

DVD•62 Spelling Short e Words

Let's Practice It! TR DVD•62

Small Group Time

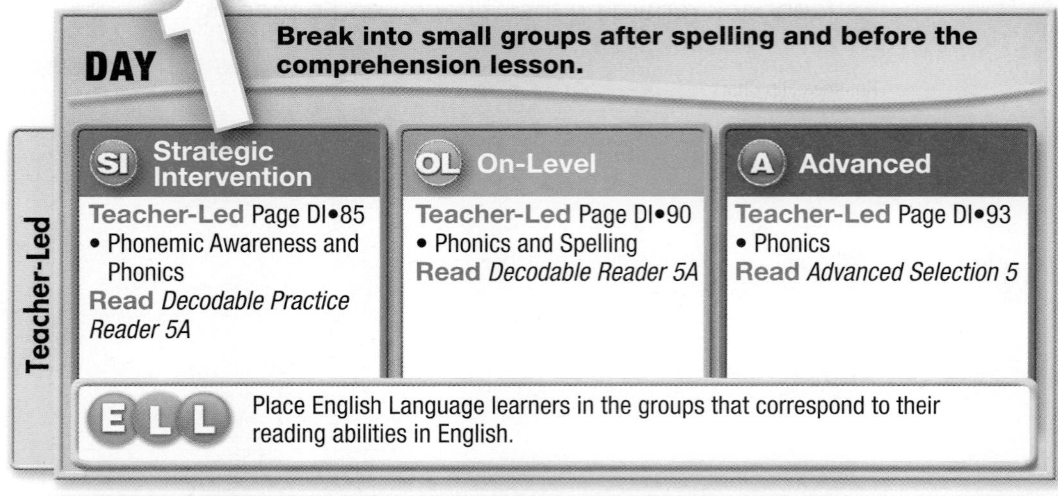

DAY 1
Break into small groups after spelling and before the comprehension lesson.
Teacher-Led
SI Strategic Intervention
Teacher-Led Page DI•85
• Phonemic Awareness and Phonics
Read Decodable Practice Reader 5A
OL On-Level
Teacher-Led Page DI•90
• Phonics and Spelling
Read Decodable Reader 5A
A Advanced
Teacher-Led Page DI•93
• Phonics
Read Advanced Selection 5
ELL
Place English Language learners in the groups that correspond to their reading abilities in English.

Practice Stations
- Listen Up
- Word Work

Independent Activities
- Read independently/Reading Log on *Reader's and Writer's Notebook* p. RR2
- Concept Talk Video

High-Frequency Words

Introduce

ROUTINE **Nondecodable Words**

1. **Say and Spell** Look at p. 125. Some words we have to learn by remembering the letters rather than saying the sounds. We will say and spell the words to help learn them. Point to the first word. This word is *saw*. The letters in *saw* are s-a-w, *saw*. Have children say and spell each word, first with you, and then without you.
2. **Identify Familiar Letter-Sounds** Point to the first letter in *saw*. You know the sound for this letter. What is this letter and what is its sound? (s, /s/)
3. **Demonstrate Meaning** Tell me a sentence using the word *saw*. Repeat this routine with the other Words I Can Read.

Routines Flip Chart

Read words in isolation Have children read the words on p. 125 aloud. Add the words to the Word Wall.

Read words in context Have children read the sentences aloud. Have them identify this week's High-Frequency Words in the sentences.

On their own Use *Reader's and Writer's Notebook* p. 186.

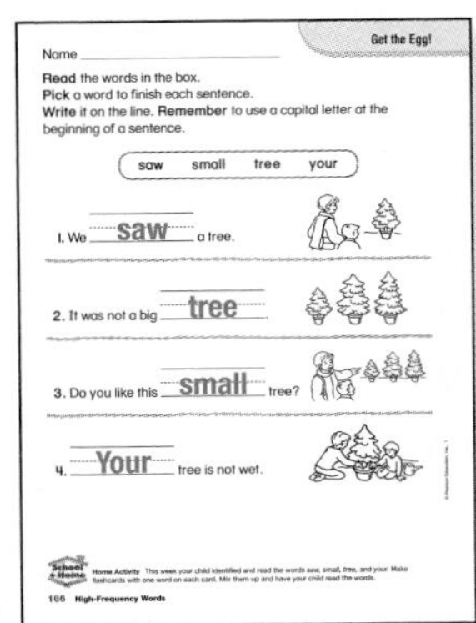
Name
Get the Egg!
Read the words in the box. Pick a word to finish each sentence. Write it on the line. Remember to use a capital letter at the beginning of a sentence.

saw small tree your

1. We saw a tree.
2. It was not a big tree.
3. Do you like this small tree?
4. Your tree is not wet.

Reader's and Writer's Notebook p. 186

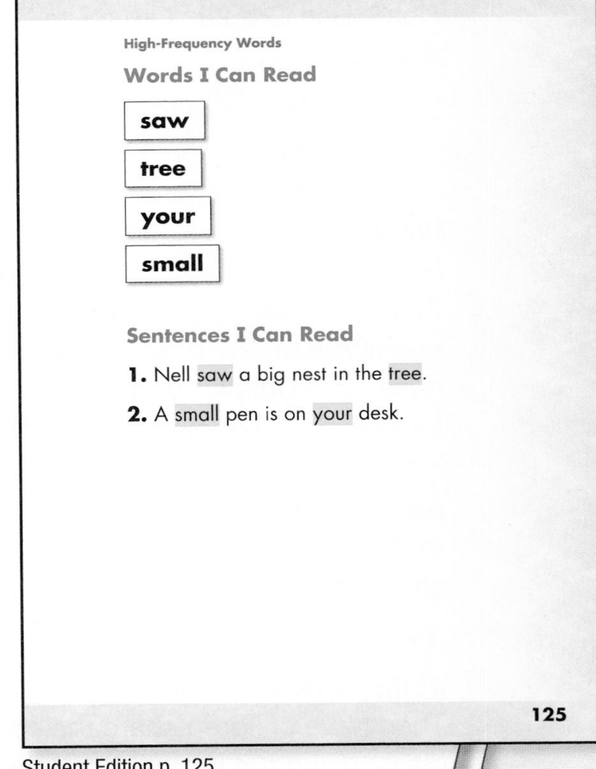
High-Frequency Words

Words I Can Read

saw

tree

your

small

Sentences I Can Read

1. Nell saw a big nest in the tree.
2. A small pen is on your desk.

125

Student Edition p. 125

Differentiated Instruction

Advanced

Extend Spelling Challenge children who spell words correctly to spell more difficult words such as: *denim, dress, exit, speck, tennis* and *welcome.*

Phonics/Spelling Generalization

Each spelling word is a short *e* word, which has the short *e* sound.

ELL

English Language Learners

Survival Vocabulary Have children use the word *saw* to talk about people at school. Children might say, *I* ***saw*** *Mr. Mead on the playground.*

Frontload Read Aloud Use the modified Read Aloud in the *ELL Support* pages to prepare children to listen to "The Pecking Hen" (page 125b).

Objectives

◎ Identify main idea and details.

Skills Trace

◎ **Main Idea and Details**

Introduce U1W4D1; U1W5D1; U5W4D1

Practice U1W4D2; U1W4D3; U1W4D4; U1W5D2; U1W5D3; U1W5D4; U5W4D2; U5W4D3; U5W4D4

Reteach/Review U1W4D5; U1W5D5; U1W6D2; U2W3D2; U5W2D2; U5W4D5;

Assess/Test Weekly Tests U1W4; U1W5; U5W4

Benchmark Tests U1; U5

KEY:

U=Unit W=Week D=Day

Listening Comprehension

◎ Main Idea and Details

Introduce

Envision It!

The **main idea** of a story is what a story is mostly about. Good readers think about the **details**, or small pieces of information, in a story to find the main idea.

Have children turn to p. EI•3 in their Student Edition. These pictures show an example of the main idea and details. Discuss these questions using the pictures:

Main Idea and Details

Main Idea

Details

EI•3

Student Edition EI•3

- What does the "Details" picture show? (the inside of a house, a mother and children, a cat on the couch)
- What does the "Main Idea" picture show? (the outside of a house)
- How do the details connect to the main idea? (They show a family doing things at home.) The main idea is a family doing things at home.

Model

Today we will read a story about a girl named Kashia. Read "The Pecking Hen." Use Graphic Organizer 27 to model how to find the main idea from details.

When I read, I think about the details to find the main idea. In this story, Kashia visits her grandmother and one day, a huge white hen was sitting on a nest. I'll write *hens sit on their eggs* in a "Details" box. When Kashia bends down to get a better look, a hen pecks her on the nose. I'll put *pecks Kashia's nose* in a "Details" box, too. Kashia's grandmother then explains that the hen was protecting herself and her eggs. I'll add *protecting herself and her eggs* in the last details box. From these details, we can tell that the story is mostly about Kashia learning how hens protect themselves. I'll write that in the "Main Idea" box.

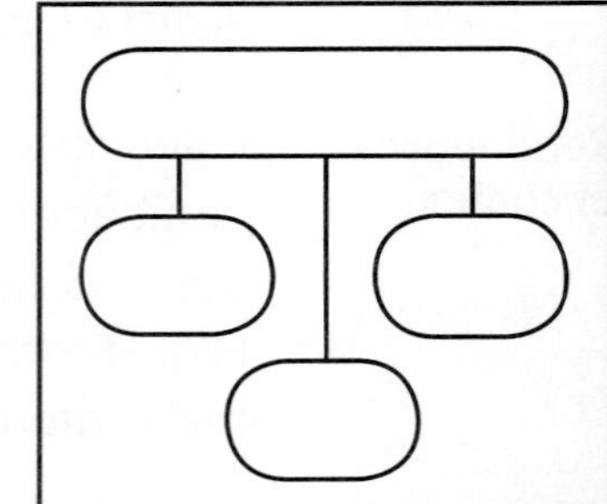

Graphic Organizer Flip Chart 27

Guide practice

After reading the story, have children choose one of the details from the Main Idea chart and draw it. Then have children share their drawings with the class, using the words *details* and *main idea* as they describe their pictures.

On their own

Use *Reader's and Writer's Notebook* p. 187.

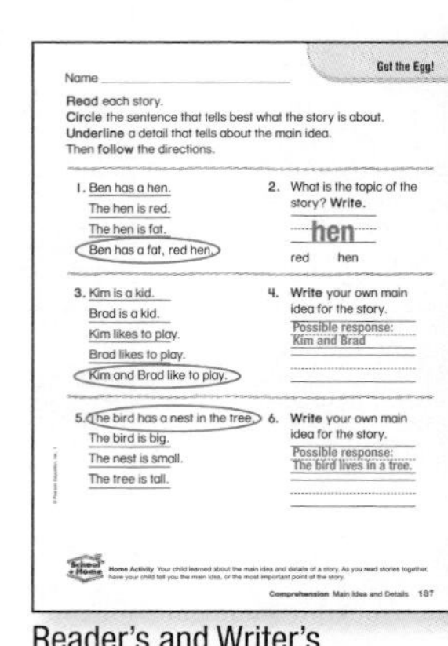

Get the Egg!

Name ______

Read each story.
Circle the sentence that tells best what the story is about.
Underline a detail that tells about the main idea.
Then **follow** the directions.

1. Ben has a hen.
The hen is red.
The hen is fat.
Ben has a fat, red hen.

2. What is the topic of the story? **Write.**
hen
red hen

3. Kim is a kid.
Brad is a kid.
Kim likes to play.
Brad likes to play.
Kim and Brad like to play.

4. **Write** your own main idea for the story.
Possible response: Kim and Brad

5. The bird has a nest in the tree.
The bird is big.
The nest is small.
The tree is tall.

6. **Write** your own main idea for the story.
Possible response: The bird lives in a tree.

Home Activity Your child learned about the main idea and details of a story. As you read stories together, have your child tell you the main idea, or the most important point of the story.

Comprehension Main Idea and Details 187

Reader's and Writer's Notebook p. 187

The Pecking Hen

Grandma Bess lived in a big, old, white house in the country. Kashia, who lived in the city, always learned something new when she visited her grandmother.

Grandma Bess had a wonderful garden. She planted tomatoes, carrots, okra, corn, and green beans. Kashia loved to help her grandmother pick the fresh vegetables. It was like shopping at the grocery store for free!

Grandma Bess also had a pen where she kept hens. Each morning, she went inside the pen and gathered eggs. One morning, Kashia went with her. Kashia saw a huge white hen sitting on a nest, waiting for her eggs to hatch. Kashia bent her head near the hen to get a getter look.

Peck! Peck! Squawk! Squawk!

"Ouch!" cried Kashia.

Grandma Bess turned to Kashia quickly and said, "What's wrong?"

"The hen pecked me on the nose! It hurts!"

Grandma Bess chuckled. "That's what a hen does to survive. She protects herself and her habitat from danger."

"It's not funny!" Kashia said. "And I'm not dangerous!"

"No, you're not, Kashia, but the hen doesn't know that. The same thing happened to me when I was your age. I got too close to a hen too. It pecked me right on the nose," said Grandma Bess. "Hens use their beaks to protect themselves and their eggs."

"I guess I learned my lesson," Kashia said. "From now on, I'll keep my nose out of the hen's business!"

Grandma Bess and Kashia laughed.

Academic Vocabulary

main idea what the story is mostly about

details small pieces of information

DAY 1 Language Arts

20-25 min.

Objectives

- Ask questions with appropriate subject-verb inversion.
- Understand and recognize the features of a realistic story.

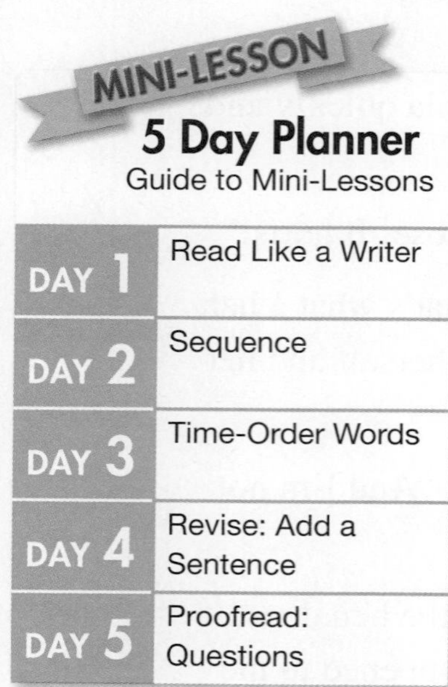

MINI-LESSON

5 Day Planner
Guide to Mini-Lessons

DAY 1	Read Like a Writer
DAY 2	Sequence
DAY 3	Time-Order Words
DAY 4	Revise: Add a Sentence
DAY 5	Proofread: Questions

Conventions
Interrogative Sentences

Model

Explain that an **interrogative sentence** is a sentence that asks something. Interrogative sentences are also called questions. An interrogative sentence begins with a capital letter and ends with a question mark.

Help children recognize that questions use words in a different order than most declarative sentences. Rather than *Pam can run fast,* a question puts a verb before the subject: *Can Pam run fast?* When they practice, help children ask questions with appropriate subject-verb inversion.

Display Grammar Transparency 5. Read the definition aloud. Model why each example is an interrogative sentence. Then read the directions and model number 1.

- The sentence *Can you see zebras?* starts with a capital letter and ends with a question mark, so it is an interrogative sentence, or question. I'll underline it.

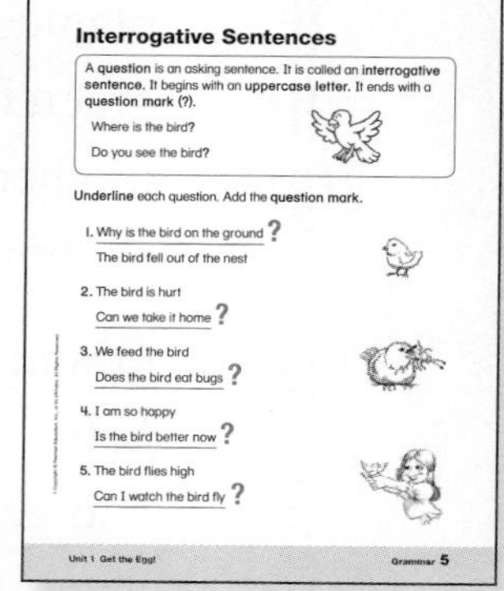

Interrogative Sentences

A **question** is an asking sentence. It is called an **interrogative sentence.** It begins with an **uppercase letter.** It ends with a **question mark** (?).

Where is the bird?

Do you see the bird?

Underline each question. Add the **question mark.**

1. Why is the bird on the ground ?
   The bird fell out of the nest
2. The bird is hurt
   Can we take it home ?
3. We feed the bird
   Does the bird eat bugs ?
4. I am so happy
   Is the bird better now ?
5. The bird flies high
   Can I watch the bird fly ?

Unit 1 Get the Egg! Grammar 5

Grammar Transparency 5
TR DVD

Guide practice

Continue with items 2–5, having children identify which group of words is a question.

Connect to oral language

Have the class complete these sentence frames orally with the words *what, why,* and *where.*

> ________ **do you see wild animals?**
> ________ **do you like to watch animals?**
> ________ **wild animals can you see?**
> ________ **are some wild animals?**

On their own

Team Talk Pair children and have them ask each other questions about animals. Have them say "Question" before they ask a question, and "Answer" before they respond to a question.

Writing—Realistic Story
Introduce

MINI-LESSON

Read Like a Writer

- **Introduce** This week you will write a **realistic story**. A realistic story is made up, but it is like real life. **Characters** in a realistic story do things that real people and animals do.

Prompt	Think about animals in neighborhoods. Write a realistic story about two friends seeing an animal.
Trait	Organization
Mode	Narrative

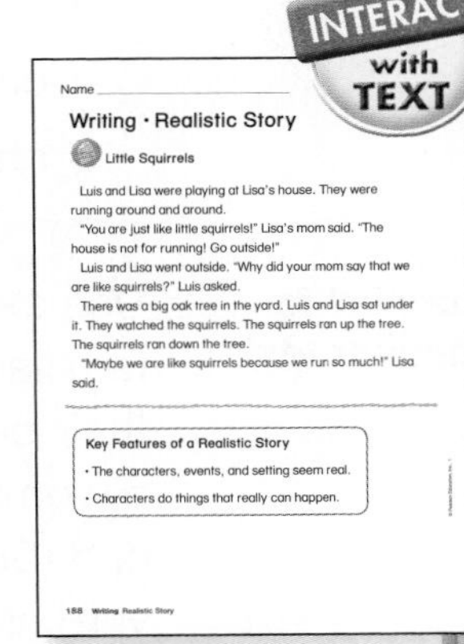
INTERACT with TEXT

Name ____________

Writing • Realistic Story

Little Squirrels

Luis and Lisa were playing at Lisa's house. They were running around and around.

"You are just like little squirrels!" Lisa's mom said. "The house is not for running! Go outside!"

Luis and Lisa went outside. "Why did your mom say that we are like squirrels?" Luis asked.

There was a big oak tree in the yard. Luis and Lisa sat under it. They watched the squirrels. The squirrels ran up the tree. The squirrels ran down the tree.

"Maybe we are like squirrels because we run so much!" Lisa said.

Key Features of a Realistic Story
- The characters, events, and setting seem real.
- Characters do things that really can happen.

188 Writing Realistic Story

Reader's and Writer's Notebook, p. 188

- **Examine Model Text** Let's listen to a realistic story. Track the print as you read aloud "Little Squirrels" on *Reader's and Writer's Notebook* p. 188. Have children follow along.

- **Key Features** Who are the three characters in this story? (Luis, Lisa, and Lisa's mom) Help children find and circle the names. Ask if Luis and Lisa act like real children. (yes) Help children underline short phrases in the story that tell about the characters acting like real children, such as *They were running* and *They sat*. Then ask what the **setting** is—where the story takes place. (Lisa's house and yard) Point out the word *yard.* Ask if yards in real life have big trees and squirrels. (yes)

  This story has characters who are like real people. The writer told events that are like things that can really happen. The place is like someone's real home.

  The story has a beginning, middle, and end. At the beginning, Luis and Lisa play. In the middle, they go outside and watch the squirrels. At the end, Lisa answers Luis's question.

Write Guy
Jeff Anderson

What Do You Notice?

When children are examining the model text, ask, "What do you notice?" By giving children the responsibility of commenting on what they find effective in the text, they build self-confidence and often begin to notice features of the writing they might not have otherwise.

Academic Vocabulary

interrogative sentence a group of words that ask a question

characters the people or animals in a story

realistic story a made-up story that could happen in real life

setting where and when a story takes place

Daily Fix-It

1. ten men sat on a jett.
   Ten men sat on a jet.
2. your redd sled is wet.
   Your red sled is wet.

Discuss the Daily Fix-It corrections with children. Review sentence capitalization and the spelling of words with short *e*, such as *jet* and *red*.

English Language Learners

Conventions To provide children with practice on interrogative sentences, use the modified grammar lessons in the *ELL Handbook.*

Language Arts

Objectives

- Understand and recognize the features of a story.
- Develop an understanding of sequence in a realistic story.
- Identify a topic connected to this week's concept.
- Narrow the focus of the topic by formulating inquiry questions related to the topic.
- Explore animal friends.

Writing—Realistic Story
Introduce, continued

Review key features Review key features of a realistic story with children. You may want to post these key features in the classroom to allow children to refer to them as they work on their stories.

Key Features of a Realistic Story

- characters, events, and setting seem real
- characters do things that really can happen

Connect to familiar texts Use examples from *Sam, Come Back!* (Unit 1) or another realistic story familiar to children. In *Sam, Come Back!*, the characters are people and their pets. There are realistic events at the beginning (Sam the cat sits on a woman's lap), the middle (Sam runs around the yard and house), and the end (Sam comes back to sit on the woman's lap). The setting, a house and yard, is a realistic place for people and their pets.

Look ahead Tell children that tomorrow they will plan their own realistic stories.

ROUTINE **Quick Write for Fluency** **Team Talk**

1. **Talk** Read these questions aloud, and give children two minutes to name as many animals as they can think of.

   What animals live around our school?

   What animals live around your home?

2. **Write** Have children write one short sentence about an animal that lives around the school and one about an animal that lives around their home.
3. **Share** Partners can read their sentences to one another.

Routines Flip Chart

Research and Inquiry
Identify and Focus Topic

Teach Display and review the concept map about this week's question: *Which wild animals live in our neighborhood?* How might you find out which wild animals live in our neighborhood? Ask children to share their ideas. Point out that they can learn about the wild animals in the neighborhood by observing.

Model Think Aloud When I observe, I watch carefully with a purpose in mind. If I want to find out about the wild animals in our neighborhood, I might look out the window and observe the animals that pass by. As I observe the animals, questions come to mind. For example, if I see a bird, I might ask myself, *What kind of nest does this bird have?* If I see a squirrel, I might ask, *What does the squirrel eat?*

Guide practice Give children time to think of questions about the wild animals in their neighborhood. Record children's questions in a chart.

On their own Use *Reader's and Writer's Notebook* p. 194.

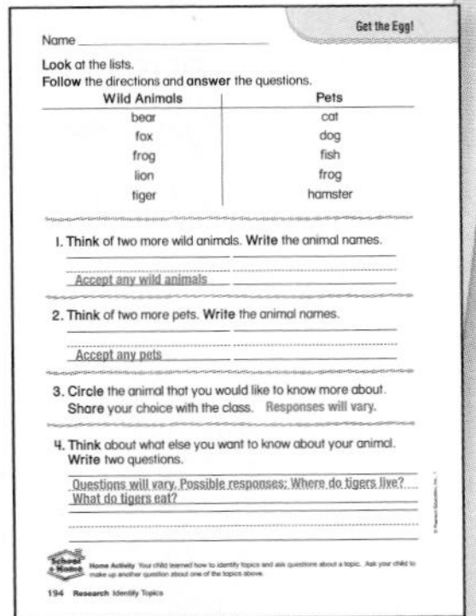
Name ______ Get the Egg!

Look at the lists.
Follow the directions and **answer** the questions.

Wild Animals	Pets
bear	cat
fox	dog
frog	fish
lion	frog
tiger	hamster

1. **Think** of two more wild animals. **Write** the animal names. Accept any wild animals
2. **Think** of two more pets. **Write** the animal names. Accept any pets
3. **Circle** the animal that you would like to know more about. **Share** your choice with the class. Responses will vary.
4. **Think** about what else you want to know about your animal. **Write** two questions. Questions will vary. Possible responses: Where do tigers live? What do tigers eat?

194 Research Identify Topics

Reader's and Writer's Notebook p. 194

Wrap Up Your Day

- ✔ **Phonics: Short *e*: *e*** Write *met* and *egg*. Ask children what sound the *e* in *met* has. (short *e*) Ask children what sound the *e* in *egg* has. (short *e*)
- ✔ **Spelling: Short *e* words** Have children name the letter that spells each sound in *red* and write the word. Continue with *net, leg,* and *bed*.
- ✔ **Build Concepts** Ask children to recall what happened in the Read Aloud, "The Pecking Hen." What animals might you see in a farm neighborhood? (Possible response: chickens, ducks, cows, goats)
- ✔ **Homework** Send home this week's Family Times Newsletter from Let's Practice It! pp. 57–58 on the *Teacher Resource DVD-ROM.*

Let's Practice It! TR DVD•57–58

Differentiated Instruction

SI Strategic Intervention

Selecting a Topic If children have trouble developing questions, write the name of an animal and the question words *what, how,* and *where* on the board. Help them use each word to begin a question sentence about the animal, such as, *What does it eat? How does it find food? Where does it live?*

Academic Vocabulary

observe watch carefully with a purpose in mind

Tell children that tomorrow they will read about two children who help a family of birds that live in their neighborhood.

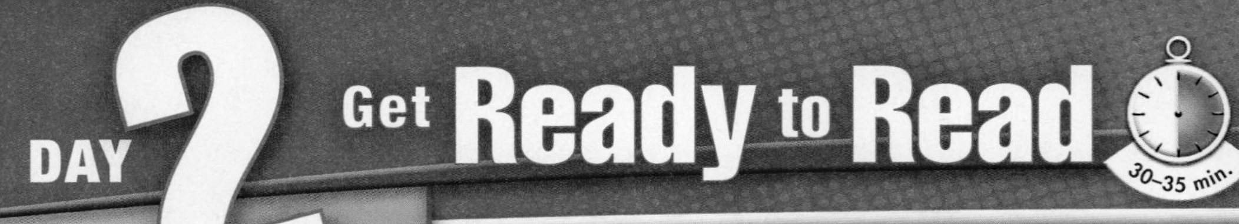

Objectives

- Discuss the concept to develop oral language.
- Build oral vocabulary.

Today at a Glance

Oral Vocabulary
chirp

Phonemic Awareness
Segment and Blend Phonemes

Phonics and Spelling
◉ Short *e: e*
◉ Initial Consonant Blends

Fluency
Paired Reading

High-Frequency Words

Story Words
bird

Comprehension
◉ Main Idea and Details
◉ Story Structure

Vocabulary
Sort Words

Literary Text
Sensory Details

Conventions
Interrogative Sentences

Writing
Realistic Story

Handwriting
Letter *Ee*
Letter Size

Research and Inquiry
Research Skill: List

Concept Talk

Question of the Week

Which wild animals live in our neighborhood?

Build concepts

To reinforce concepts and to focus children's attention, have children sing "Time to Hatch" from the *Sing with Me* Big Book. What do the baby birds see? (a pond, feeders filled with seed, bushes where they can hide)

Sing with Me Big Book Audio

Introduce Amazing Words

Display the Big Book, *Jungle Drum*. Read the title and identify the author. Explain that in the story, the author uses the word *chirp*. Have children listen as you read the story to find out which jungle animals *chirp*.

Big Book

ELL **Reinforce Vocabulary** Use the Day 2 instruction on ELL Poster 5 to reinforce the meanings of high-frequency words.

ELL Poster 5

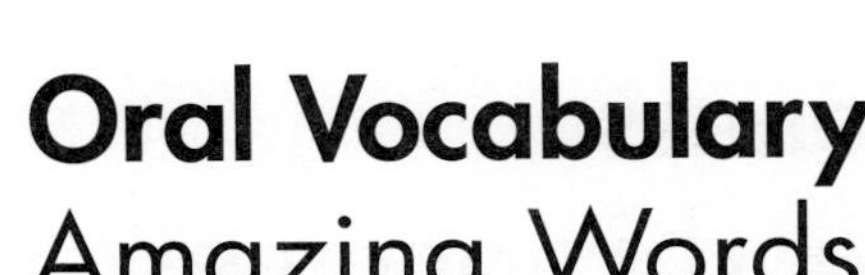

Oral Vocabulary
Amazing Words

Teach Amazing Words

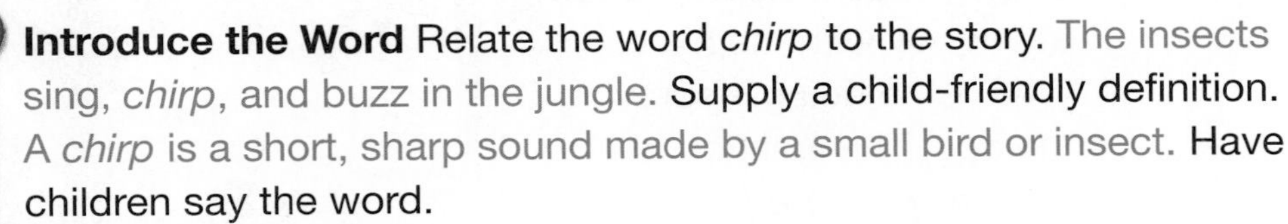

Oral Vocabulary Routine

1. **Introduce the Word** Relate the word *chirp* to the story. The insects sing, *chirp*, and buzz in the jungle. Supply a child-friendly definition. A *chirp* is a short, sharp sound made by a small bird or insect. Have children say the word.
2. **Demonstrate** Provide examples to show meaning. I can hear birds *chirp* in the early morning. Crickets *chirp* in the evening in late summer.
3. **Apply** Have children demonstrate their understanding. What other animals *chirp*? Can you make a *chirping* sound? Let's try it.

Routines Flip Chart

Anchored Talk

Add to the concept map

Discuss what children have learned about the animals that live in their neighborhood.

- Recall the song "Time to Hatch." What kind of habitat do the newly hatched birds live in? (a backyard, a park)
- What do the new birds need to survive? (water, food, shelter) What are some things in their habitat that they need? (pond, bird feeders, bushes to hide in) Let's add *pond for water, bird feeders,* and *bushes to hide in* to our map.
- In yesterday's Read Aloud, "The Pecking Hen," what kind of animal did we read about? (a hen) Let's add *hen* to our map. What kind of habitat do the hens live in? (chicken pen) We can add *chicken pen* to the map. How do you think the hen hatches her eggs? (She sits on them.) Let's add *hatches eggs* to the concept map.

habitat	chirp
hatch	croak
survive	moist

Differentiated Instruction

SI Strategic Intervention

Sentence Production If children do not pronounce the /ėr/ sound in the middle of the word *chirp*, say the sentence containing the word, stressing the sound /ėr/. Have children repeat it.

English Language Learners

Physical Response Teach the word *chirp* by making a chirping sound and having children join you. To reinforce understanding, look for opportunities to recycle language in the day's lessons. For example, invite children to make chirping sounds when they see animals that make chirping sounds outside during recess.

Objectives

- Segment and blend phonemes.
- ◎ Blend and read words with initial consonant blends.

Skills Trace

◎ Initial Consonant Blends
Introduce U1W5D2
Practice U1W5D3; U1W5D4
Reteach/Review U1W5D5; U1W6D4
Assess/Test Weekly Test U1W5
Benchmark Test U1

KEY:
U=Unit W=Week D=Day

Phonemic Awareness
Segment and Blend Phonemes

Model isolating sounds Read together the last bulleted point on pages 122–123 of the Student Edition. Look at the boy with the hose. What is he doing? (spraying the dog) The first sounds I hear in *spray* are /s/ /p/ /r/. Have children look at the picture and find another item whose name begins with /s/ /p/ /r/. (*sprinkler*)

Student Edition pp. 122–123

Model segmenting and blending Listen to the sounds in the word *spray*: /s/ /p/ /r/ /ā/. There are four sounds in *spray*. Let's blend those sounds to make a word: /s/ /p/ /r/ /ā/, *spray*. Continue modeling with *tree* and *steps*.

Guide practice Guide children as they segment and blend these words from the picture: *black, blue, sled, spray, steps, frog,* and *tracks*.

Corrective feedback **If...** children make an error, **then...** model by segmenting the word, and have them repeat the segmenting and blending of the word.

On their own Have children segment and blend the following words.

bread /b/ /r/ /e/ /d/	**neck** /n/ /e/ /k/	**flat** /f/ /l/ /a/ /t/
store /s/ /t/ /ôr/	**speck** /s/ /p/ /e/ /k/	**brown** /b/ /r/ /ou/ /n/
block /b/ /l/ /o/ /k/	**split** /s/ /p/ /l/ /i/ /t/	**spell** /s/ /p/ /e/ /l/

Phonics — Teach/Model
Initial Consonant Blends

Sound-Spelling Chart 41

ROUTINE **Blending Strategy**

1. **Connect** Write *sip* and *lip*. You studied words like this already. What do you know about the beginning sounds of these words? (They are consonant sounds. The sound /s/ is spelled *s*. The sound /l/ is spelled *l*.) Today you will learn to spell and read words that begin with two consonant sounds.
2. **Use Sound-Spelling Card** Display Card 41. The sounds you hear at the beginning of *train* are /t/ /r/. The sounds /t/ /r/ are spelled *tr*. Have children say /t/ /r/ several times as you point to *tr*.
3. **Model** Write *slip*. I see that this word has two consonants at the beginning. (Point to the letters *s* and *l*.) The two sounds /s/ and /l/ are blended together. This is how I blend this word. Segment and blend *slip*. Follow this procedure to model blending *black* and *stop*.
4. **Guide Practice** Continue the process in step 3. This time have children blend with you.

crop	flick	smell	stick	brag	drill
glad	fret	grin	spell	block	prod

5. **Review** What do you know about reading these words? (The two consonant sounds at the beginning of each word are blended together.)

Routines Flip Chart

Differentiated Instruction

 Strategic Intervention

Initial Consonant Blends If children have difficulty blending initial consonant sounds, have them repeat as you pronounce words with initial *bl* and *st* blends, such as *blue* and *stay*, elongating the initial consonant sounds.

A Advanced

Extend Word Blending If children are able to blend words easily and independently, challenge them with more difficult words, such as *snowy, slipper, frightening,* and *broken*.

Vocabulary Support

You may wish to explain the meaning of these words.

fret to worry about something

prod to get someone to do something either by talking to the person or poking the person with your finger

English Language Learners

Visual Support Model isolating sounds while using the pictures on pp. 122–123 of the Student Edition as visual support. For example: /p/ /r/ /i/ /n/ /t/ /s/, *prints*. Who can point to the foot *prints*? Now let's say the sounds of *prints* together: /p/ /r/ /i/ /n/ /t/ /s/.

Objectives

- Blend and read words with initial consonant blends.
- Associate sounds of consonant blends with corresponding letters.
- Read words in context and in isolation.

Check Word Reading
SUCCESS PREDICTOR

Phonics—Build Fluency

Initial Consonant Blends

Model Have children turn to page 126 in their Student Edition. Look at the picture on this page. The picture shows a *train*. When I say *train*, I hear /t/ /r/ at the beginning. The sounds /t/ /r/ are spelled *tr*.

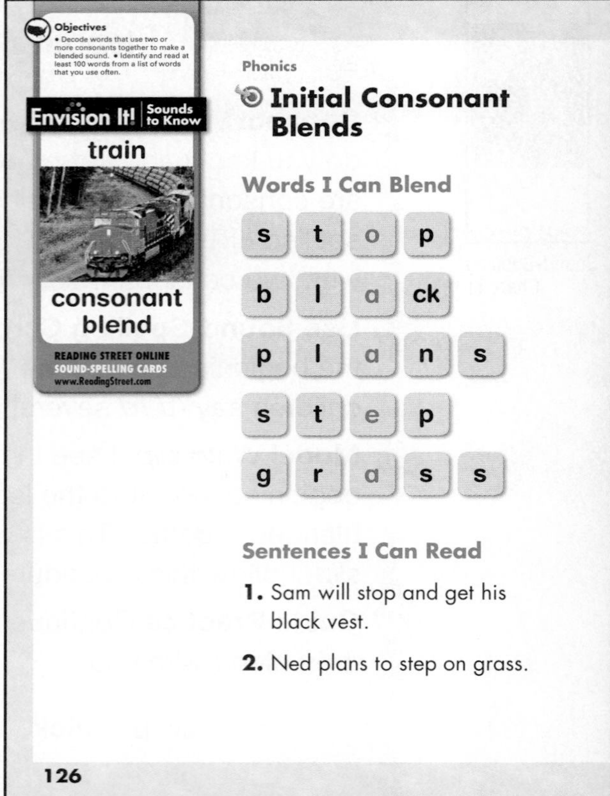

Student Edition p. 126

Guide practice For each word in "Words I Can Blend," ask for the sound of each letter or group of letters. Make sure that children identify the correct sounds for the consonant blends. Then have children blend the whole word.

Corrective feedback **If...** children have difficulty blending a word,
then... model blending the word, and ask children to blend it with you.

Blend and Read

Decode words in isolation After children can successfully segment and blend the words, ask them to read the words naturally.

Decode words in context Have children read each of the sentences. Have them identify words in the sentences that begin with consonant blends.

Team Talk Pair children and have them take turns reading each of the sentences aloud.

On their own Use *Reader's and Writer's Notebook* p. 189.

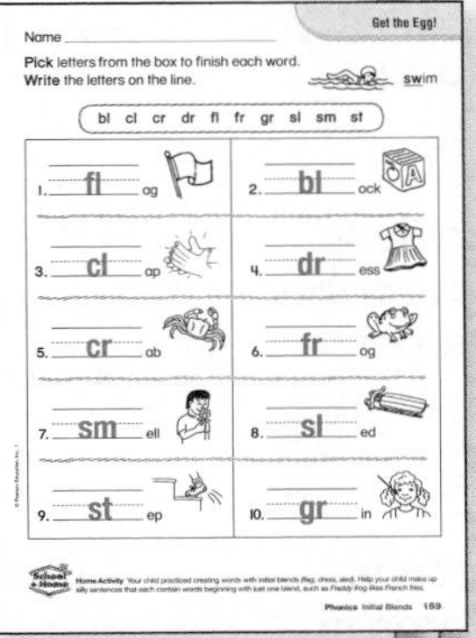
Get the Egg!

Name

Pick letters from the box to finish each word. Write the letters on the line.

bl cl cr dr fl fr gr sl sm st

1. fl ag
2. bl ock
3. cl ap
4. dr ess
5. cr ab
6. fr og
7. sm ell
8. sl ed
9. st ep
10. gr in

Phonics Initial Blends 189

Reader's and Writer's Notebook p. 189

Don't Wait Until Friday — MONITOR PROGRESS
Check Word Reading — Initial Consonant Blends

Write the following words and have the class read them. Notice which children miss words during the group reading. Call on those individuals to read some of the words.

					Spiral Review
flip	**glass**	**clock**	**block**	**slip**	Row 1 reviews initial *l* blends.
grin	**frog**	**track**	**crab**	**dress**	Row 2 reviews initial *r* blends.
skip	**snap**	**stack**	**spot**	**swim**	Row 3 reviews initial *s* blends.

If... children cannot blend words with initial consonant blends,

then... use the Small Group Time Strategic Intervention lesson, p. DI•86, to reteach words with initial consonant blends. Continue to monitor children's progress using other instructional opportunities during the week. See the Skills Trace on p. 126c.

Day 1	Day 2	Day 3	Day 4	Day 5
Check Word Reading	Check Word Reading	Check High-Frequency Words/Retelling	Check Fluency	Check Oral Vocabulary

Success Predictor

Differentiated Instruction

SI Strategic Intervention

Letter Tiles If children have difficulty reading words with initial consonant blends, have them use their letter tiles. For example, they can build and read *lip* and then add *f, c,* and *s*, reading each new word.

Advanced

Extend Blending If children are able to blend initial consonants easily and independently, then have them work with a partner to create short tongue twisters with words that have initial consonant blends. Children can present their tongue twisters to the class.

Academic Vocabulary

consonant blends consonant blends consist of two or more letters whose sounds are blended together when pronouncing a word

English Language Learners

Initial Consonant Blends Initial *s* blends do not appear in Cantonese, Hmong, Khmer, Korean, Spanish, or Vietnamese. Spanish speakers especially may add a short *e* sound at the beginning of words such as *step* and *spin*. Help children practice blending the sounds in words with initial *s* blends, such as *skid, slim, smack, snip, spot, stick,* and *swim.*

Get Ready to Read

Objectives
- Apply knowledge of sound-spellings to decode unknown words when reading.
- Decode words in context and isolation.
- Practice fluency with oral rereading.

Decodable Practice Reader 5B
Initial Consonant Blends

Decode words in isolation

Have children turn to page 201. Have children decode each word.

Decodable Practice Reader 5B

Review High-frequency words

Review the previously taught words *the, you, green* and *a.* Have children read each word as you point to it on the Word Wall.

Preview Decodable Reader

Have children read the title and preview the story. Tell them they will read words with initial consonant blends in this story.

Decode words in context

Pair children for reading and listen as they decode. One child begins. Children read the entire story, switching readers after each page. Partners reread the story. This time the other child begins.

Ted is a frog in the grass.
Fran is a hen in the grass.
202
Ted is green with black spots.
Fran is red.
203

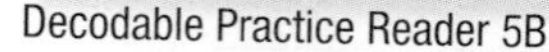
Decodable Practice Reader 5B

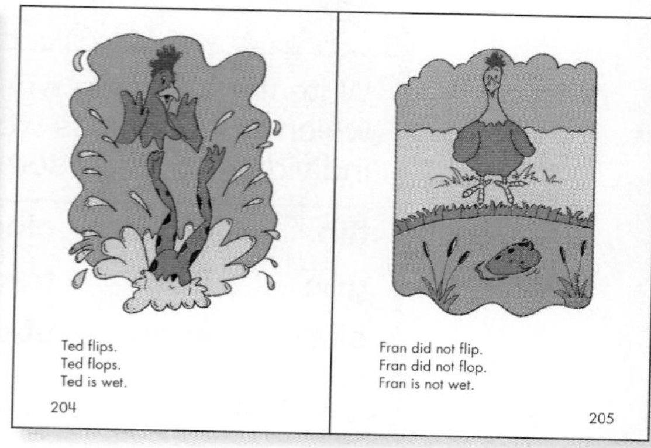

Ted flips.
Ted flops.
Ted is wet.

Fran did not flip.
Fran did not flop.
Fran is not wet.

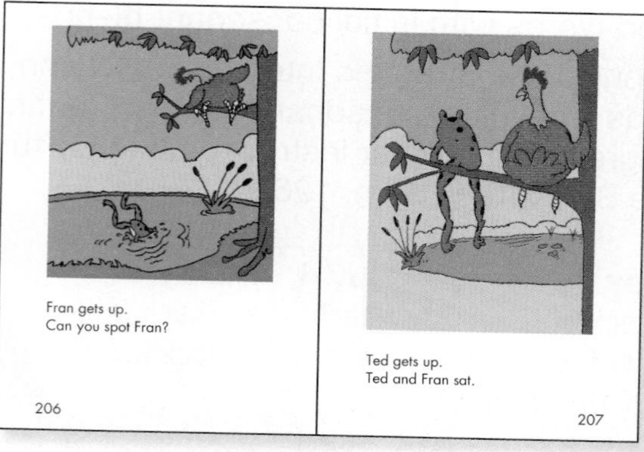

Fran gets up.
Can you spot Fran?

Ted gets up.

Ted did not get wet.
Fran did not get wet.

Corrective feedback

If... children have difficulty decoding a word,
then... refer them to the Sound-Spelling Cards to identify the sounds in the word. Then prompt them to blend the word.

- What is the new word?
- Is the new word a word you know?
- Does it make sense in the story?

Check decoding and comprehension

Have children retell the story to include characters, setting, and events. Then have children locate words that have initial consonant blends in the story. List words that children name. Children should supply *frog, Fran, grass, flip(s), flop(s),* and *spot.* Explain that these words begin with two consonant sounds that are blended together, such as /fr/, /fl/, /gr/, and /sp/, followed by a vowel and another consonant.

Reread for Fluency

Have children reread Decodable Practice Reader 5B to develop automaticity decoding words with initial consonant blends.

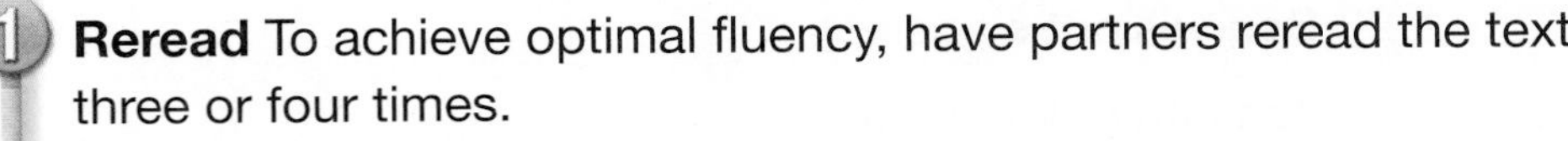

ROUTINE **Paired Reading**

1. **Reread** To achieve optimal fluency, have partners reread the text three or four times.
2. **Corrective Feedback** Listen as children read. Provide corrective feedback regarding their fluency and decoding.

Routines Flip Chart

Differentiated Instruction

SI Strategic Intervention

Retelling If children have difficulty retelling the story, ask them questions regarding events in the story.

English Language Learners

Initial Consonant Blends

Beginning Before children read, lead them on a picture walk through *Ted and Fran.* Point out and pronounce the words that have initial consonant blends such as *frog, flips,* and *flops*. Have children say the words aloud.

Intermediate Before reading, help children pronounce the words with initial consonant blends such as *frog, Fran, grass,* and *flip(s).* Then have them use the word to make a prediction about what the story will be about.

Advanced/ Advanced High After reading, have children use the words with initial consonant blends to create new sentences such as *Fran's pal is a frog named Ted.*

Get Ready to Read

Objectives

- Apply knowledge of letter-sound correspondences to decode words in context and in isolation.
- Spell words with vowel sound /e/.

Phonics Review
Short-Vowel Words and Short *e*: *e*

Review Sound-spellings

Review the short-vowel spelling patterns *a, e, i,* and *o*, using Sound-Spellings Cards 1, 6, 11, and 17.

Decode words in isolation

Display these words. Have the class blend the words. Then point to the words in random order and ask children to decode them quickly.

set	**pill**	**red**
cat	**hot**	**kiss**
ran	**mad**	**pod**
bin	**peck**	**mess**

Corrective feedback

Model blending decodable words and then ask children to blend them with you.

Decode words in context

Display these sentences. Have the class read the sentences.

Team Talk Have pairs take turns reading the sentences naturally.

Ted sat on the **mat.**
Ben will not sit here.
Jan can get a **big pet.**

Spelling

Short *e* Words

Guide practice

Tell children that you will segment the sounds in each spelling word. They should repeat the sounds in each word as they write the word. Check the spelling of each word before saying the next word.

1.	/m/ /e/ /n/	**men**	**6.**	/l/ /e/ /g/	**leg**
2.	/r/ /e/ /d/	**red**	**7.**	/j/ /e/ /t/	**jet**
3.	/s/ /t/ /e/ /p/	**step**	**8.**	/s/ /l/ /e/ /d/	**sled**
4.	/t/ /e/ /n/	**ten**	**9.**	/w/ /e/ /t/	**wet**
5.	/n//e//t/	**net**	**10.**	/b/ /e/ /d/	**bed**

On their own

Use *Reader's and Writer's Notebook* p. 190.

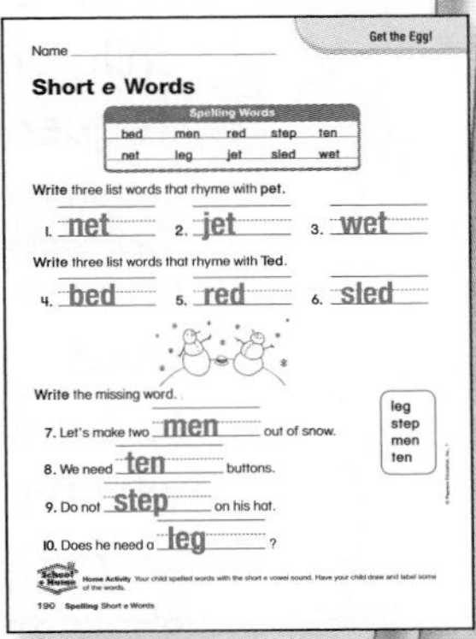
Name ______

Get the Egg!

Short *e* Words

Spelling Words

bed	men	red	step	ten
net	leg	jet	sled	wet

Write three list words that rhyme with **pet**.

1. net 2. jet 3. wet

Write three list words that rhyme with **Ted**.

4. bed 5. red 6. sled

Write the missing word.

leg step men ten

7. Let's make two men out of snow.
8. We need ten buttons.
9. Do not step on his hat.
10. Does he need a leg ?

Home Activity Your child spelled words with the short e vowel sound. Have your child draw and label some of the words.

190 **Spelling** Short e Words

Reader's and Writer's Notebook p. 190

Small Group Time

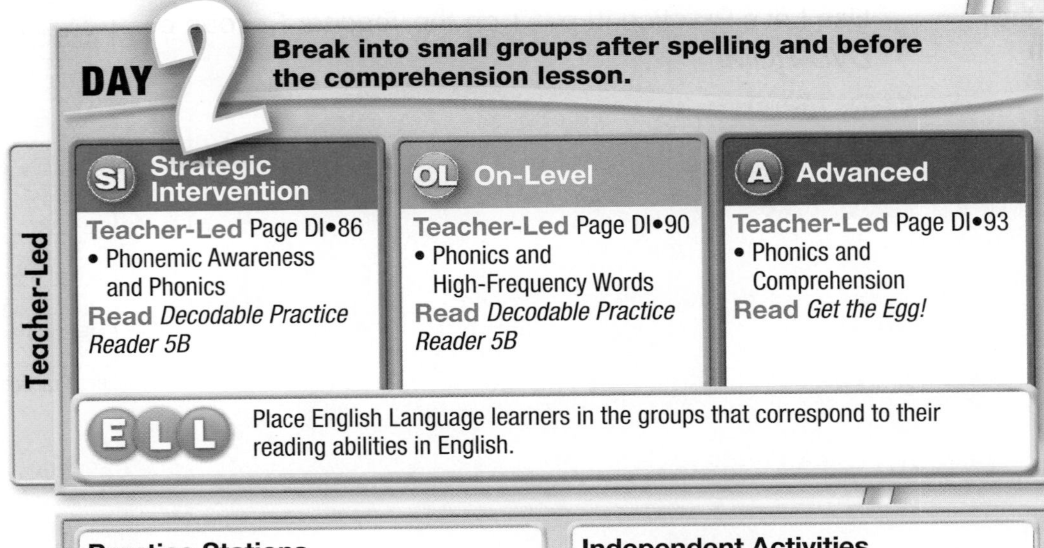
DAY 2 **Break into small groups after spelling and before the comprehension lesson.**

Teacher-Led

SI Strategic Intervention
Teacher-Led Page DI•86
- Phonemic Awareness and Phonics

Read *Decodable Practice Reader 5B*

OL On-Level
Teacher-Led Page DI•90
- Phonics and High-Frequency Words

Read *Decodable Practice Reader 5B*

A Advanced
Teacher-Led Page DI•93
- Phonics and Comprehension

Read *Get the Egg!*

ELL Place English Language learners in the groups that correspond to their reading abilities in English.

Practice Stations
- Listen Up
- Word Work

Independent Activities
- Read independently/Reading Log on *Reader's and Writer's Notebook* p. RR2
- AudioText of Main Selection

ELL

English Language Learners

Word Recognition Write the following words on the board: *peg, got, went, well.* Point to and read each word aloud and have children repeat. Tell children to point to the words that contain /e/.

Objectives

- Learn the story word: *bird.*
- Review high-frequency words.
- Sort words into categories of animals.

High-Frequency Words
Build Fluency

Read words in isolation Remind children that there are some words we learn by remembering the letters, rather than by saying the sounds. Then have them read each of the highlighted high-frequency words aloud.

Read words in context Chorally read the "I Can Read!" passage along with the children. Then have them read the passage aloud to themselves. When they are finished, ask children to reread the high-frequency words.

Team Talk Have children choose two high-frequency words and give them time to create a sentence in which both words are used properly. Then have them share their sentence with a partner.

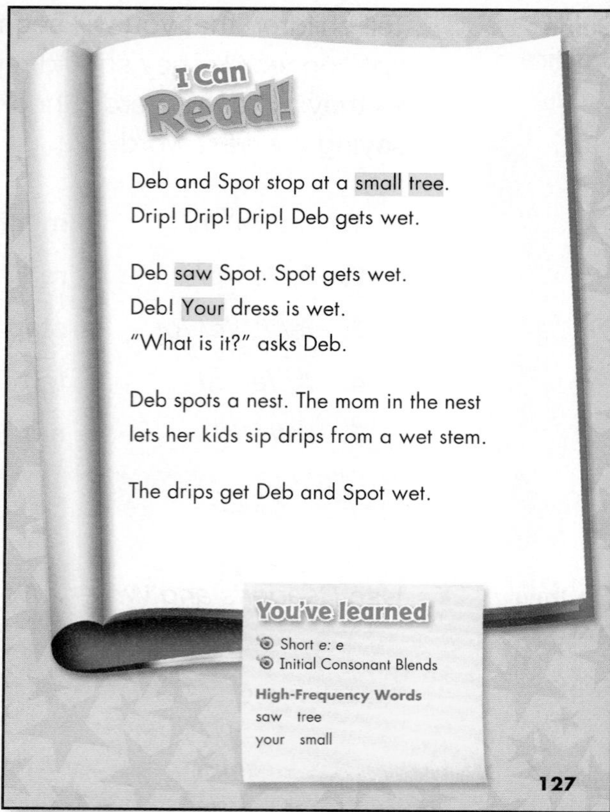

I Can Read!
Deb and Spot stop at a small tree.
Drip! Drip! Drip! Deb gets wet.
Deb saw Spot. Spot gets wet.
Deb! Your dress is wet.
"What is it?" asks Deb.
Deb spots a nest. The mom in the nest lets her kids sip drips from a wet stem.
The drips get Deb and Spot wet.
You've learned
Short e: e
Initial Consonant Blends
High-Frequency Words
saw tree
your small
127

Student Edition p. 127

On their own Use Let's Practice It! p. 61 on the *Teacher Resource DVD-ROM.*

Let's Practice It! TR DVD•61

Story Words
Get the Egg!

Introduce story words

Use Vocabulary Transparency 5 to introduce this week's story word. Read each sentence as you track the print. Frame the underlined word and explain its meaning.

bird	animal covered in feathers that has wings and two legs

Have children read each sentence with you.

Little Bird
1. The little bird is eating dinner.
2. Her nest is in that tree.
Vocabulary 5

Vocabulary Transparency 5
TR DVD

Vocabulary
Sort Words

Model sorting words

Explain that **sort** means to put things into groups. Draw a three-column chart or display Graphic Organizer 5. Put these headings at the top of each column: *Animals with Fur, Animals with Feathers, Animals with Hard Outer Coverings.* Model how to begin adding animals to the chart.

Animals with Fur	Animals with Feathers	Animals with Hard Outer Coverings

Graphic Organizer Flip Chart 5

Think Aloud We are going to sort wild animals by whether they have fur, feathers, or hard outer coverings. I will name an animal and you will tell me what it looks like. Then we will decide what group it belongs in. I'll begin. The red bird in *Get the Egg!* was covered in feathers. So, I'll write *red bird* under *Animals with Feathers.*

Guide practice

Continue naming animals, and have children tell you which column to put them in. If necessary, display the last two pages of *Jungle Drum* to help children think of more animals to sort.

On their own

Work with children to name and sort as many animals as possible.

Differentiated Instruction

SI Strategic Intervention

Selecting a Topic If children pronounce the /s/ sound in *saw* and *small* as /ᴛʜ/, then say each word, clearly pronouncing the /s/, and have children repeat it. If children continue to have trouble, help them practice pronouncing /s/ alone, being certain their tongue is behind their front teeth, not between.

Academic Vocabulary

sort to put things into groups

ELL

English Language Learners

Understand General Meaning Ask children to listen as you read aloud p. 127 in the Student Edition. After reading, have them restate the general ideas in the passage using the familiar language of the high-frequency words. Have them ask questions about any unfamiliar situations in the passage.

Multilingual Vocabulary Lists Children can apply knowledge of their home language to acquire new English vocabulary by using the *Multilingual Vocabulary List* (*ELL Handbook* pp. 465–476).

Objectives

- Build background about birds and their nests.
- Preview and predict.
- Use key structure and elements of realistic fiction to improve understanding of text.
- Set a purpose for reading text.

Build Background
Get the Egg!

Background Building Audio

Have children listen to the CD. Tell them to listen especially for information about why robins are building a nest.

 Background Building Audio

Discuss birds and their nests

Team Talk Have children turn to a partner and use these questions for discussion:

- Where might you find a bird's nest?
- Why do birds build nests?
- How do robins use what they find in their habitats to make nests?
- Why do you think they want the nest to be soft and warm?

Organize information in a chart

Draw a main idea chart or display Graphic Organizer 27. Write "Why Birds Build Nests" in the large box at the top. Ask children to give reasons why birds build nests. Have children recall what was said on the CD about why robins built a nest. After the discussion, add their responses to the smaller boxes.

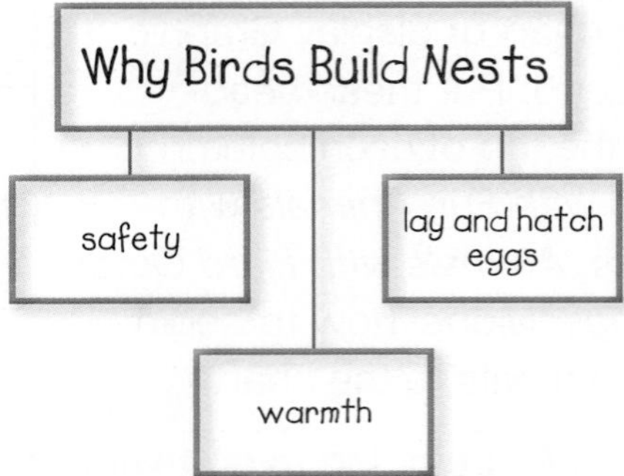

Connect to selection

We learned that birds build nests to make a safe place to lay their eggs. Why do you think they need a safe place for their eggs? (because the eggs are fragile; another animal could get them) Sometimes, things happen to the eggs before they can hatch. Kim and Brad are characters in the story we are about to read. We'll find out what they do to save a red bird's egg.

Student Edition pp. 128–129

Main Selection—First Read
Get the Egg!

Practice the skill

Main Idea and Details Remind children that the main idea is what a story is mostly about. Tell them that good readers pay attention to the details and facts to help them understand the main idea in a story. Remind them of the Main Idea chart they completed after reading "The Pecking Hen."

Introduce the strategy

Story Structure Explain that good readers use many strategies to help them make sense of a story and remember it. One strategy is to look for the most important parts of a story, such as the characters, the setting, and what happens.

Think Aloud: In this cartoon, I can see that the characters include a wolf and three pigs. Three main events happen in the story: the wolf blows down the First Piggy's house, then he blows down the Second Piggy's house, but he can't blow down the Third Piggy's house.

Student Edition EI•14

Introduce genre

Let's Read Together Realistic fiction is a made-up story that could happen in real life. As they read *Get the Egg!,* ask children to look for parts of the story that seem realistic to them.

Preview and predict

Have children identify the title of the story, the author, and the illustrator. Read the names of the author and illustrator, and have children describe the role of each. Have children activate prior knowledge by asking them to look through the selection and use the illustrations to predict what it might be about.

Set a purpose

Good readers read for a purpose. Setting a purpose helps us to think and understand more as we read. We will read this story to find out what happens to the egg.

Tell children that today they will read *Get the Egg!* for the first time. Use the Day 2 Guide Comprehension notes to help children develop their comprehension of the selection.

First Read

For the First Read, use **Guide Comprehension** across the top of pages 128–137.

Strategy Response Log

Genre Have children use page RR 17 in their *Reader's and Writer's Notebook* to draw a picture of what they think will be the setting in the story. Have them discuss why they chose to draw their picture.

Academic Vocabulary

Story Structure the important parts of a story, including the characters, the setting, and the plot

English Language Learners

Build Background Before children listen to the CD, build background and elicit prior knowledge. On the CD, you will hear about birds hatching. They are going to look around and see how they can get the food and water they need. Where do you think they might find what they need?

Frontload Main Selection Ask children what they already know about birds and nests using the picture on pp. 128–129. Then do a picture walk of the selection so children can talk about and see what happens in the nest.

Objectives

- ◎ Identify main idea and details.
- ◎ Recognize story structure.
- Use key features of realistic fiction to improve understanding of the text.
- Determine word meaning and use newly acquired vocabulary.
- Discuss ideas related to, but not expressed in the literature.

Guide Comprehension

Skills and Strategies

Connect to Concept

Wild Animals Look at the picture on pages 128 and 129. What wild animal do you see? (a bird)

Amazing Words Have children continue discussing the concept using the Amazing Words *habitat, hatch, survive,* and *chirp* as they read.

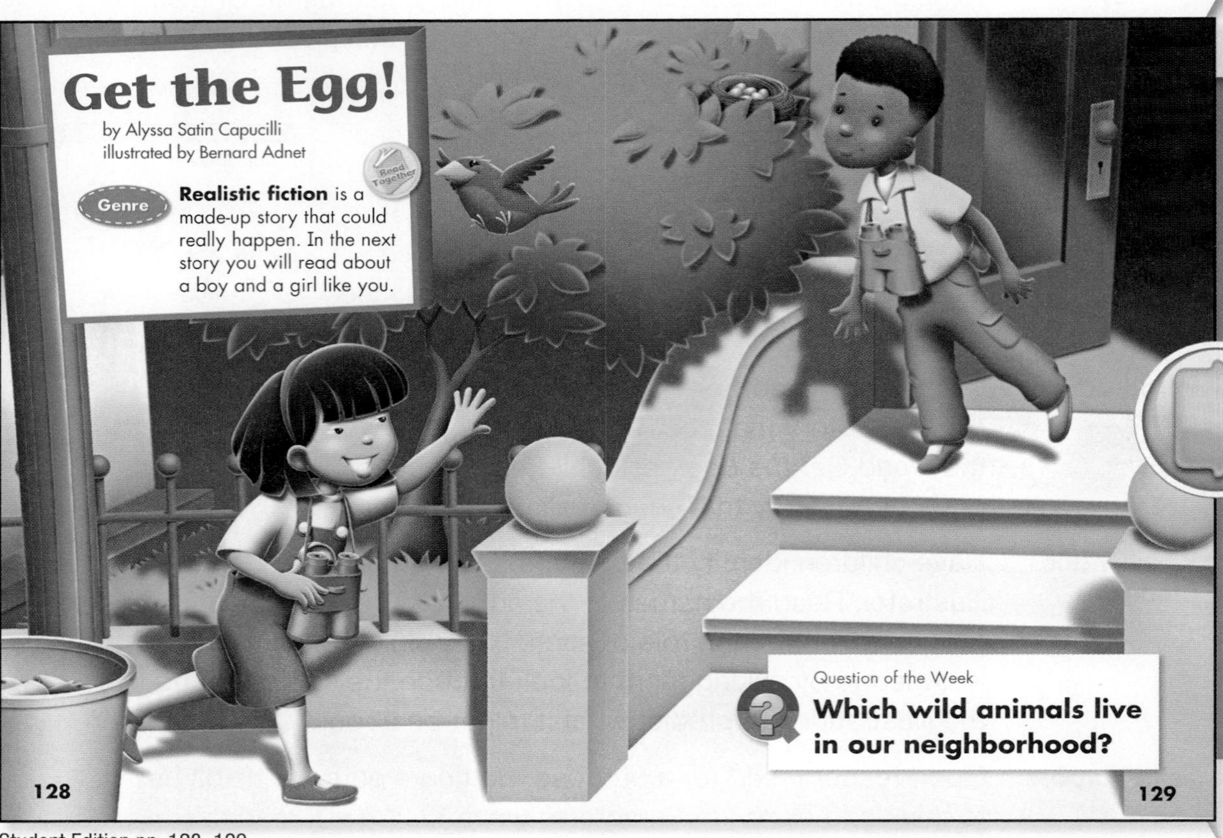

Get the Egg!
by Alyssa Satin Capucilli
illustrated by Bernard Adnet
Read Together
Genre
Realistic fiction is a made-up story that could really happen. In the next story you will read about a boy and a girl like you.
Question of the Week
Which wild animals live in our neighborhood?
128
129

Student Edition pp. 128–129

Extend Thinking

Think Critically

DAY 3

Higher-Order Thinking Skills

Analysis I see in the picture that the red bird is leaving its nest. I wonder what will happen to one of the eggs while the red bird is away. Explain what you think may happen to the egg.

If... children cannot suggest what may happen to the egg while the red bird is away,
then... ask children what might happen if an egg fell out of the nest or was stolen by another animal.

Strategies

Story Structure Remind children that good readers look for the important parts of a story—the characters, the setting, and the plot. Have children name the characters and the setting of the story.

Word Reading

High-Frequency Words Point out the words *saw* and *tree* on page 130. Have children practice reading these words.

Kim saw Brad at the tree.
A big red bird is in its nest, Kim.

130

Yes, Brad.
Six eggs sit in the nest.

131

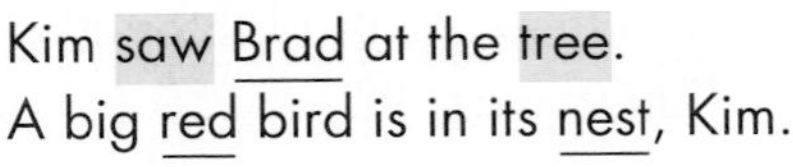

Student Edition pp. 130–131

Higher-Order Thinking Skills

Analysis I see in the illustration that Brad is holding his finger to his lips. What do you think he means when he does that? (He wants Kim to be quiet and not talk.) Why do you think Brad feels it's important for them not to talk? (If they talk, they might scare away the bird.)

Connect to Science

Habitats Explain that a habitat is where an animal lives. It provides the animal with what it needs to survive, including food, water, and shelter.

Team Talk Have children discuss how the red bird gets what she needs from her habitat.

Skills and Strategies, continued

Skills

Main Idea and Details What are these pages of the story mostly about? What details tell you this? (Brad tries to save an egg that has fallen out of the nest. We know this because a twig hits the egg. Then Brad tries to grab the egg from where it has fallen.)

Vocabulary

Sort Have children recall the animals in *Get the Egg!* and *Jungle Drum.* Discuss how children might sort these animals. Explain that **sort** means to put things into groups.

Snap! A big twig hit the nest!
Snap, snap!
The big twig hit an egg!

132

Stop the egg, Brad. Stop it!
Can you get it?

133

Student Edition pp. 132–133

Think Critically, continued

Review Setting

Analysis I see Brad in the picture on page 133. Where do you think he is?

If... children have difficulty using the picture on page 133 to explain where Brad is,
then... direct their attention to the leaves in the picture and have them find earlier pictures with leaves like these.

Skills

Main Idea and Details What is the main idea of this story? What details tell you this? (The story is about how Kim and Brad save a bird's egg. We know that the egg falls from the nest, that Brad uses his net to get it, and that Kim puts it back in the nest.)

Strategies

Story Structure What happens in this part of the story? What do Brad and Kim do? (Brad gets the egg in his net. Kim sets the egg back in the nest.)

The net! Get your net, Brad.
You can help.
Get the egg in your net.
134
Yes! You did it, Brad.
You can help, Kim.
Set the egg back in its nest.
135

Student Edition pp. 134–135

Higher-Order Thinking Skills

Evaluation Do you think it was a good idea for Brad and Kim to try to save the bird's egg? (Possible response: Yes, because if they hadn't saved the egg, a bird might not have hatched from it. No, because people should not get in the way of what happens in nature.)

Review Character

Analysis What words would you use to describe Brad and Kim? (kind, careful, interested in nature, helpful) Have children give examples of the characters' actions and words to support their ideas.

Skills and Strategies, continued

DAY 2

Vocabulary

Story Words Have children locate the story word *bird* on page 136. Where is the bird in this part of the story? (back in the nest)

Strategy Self Check

Story Structure Have children name the characters in the story. Ask them to describe the setting. Then have them retell the plot.

Continue to DAY 2
Comprehension Check p. 137a

Brad is at the tree.
The big red bird is back, Kim.
136

Yes, Brad.
It is in its nest.
Six small birds sit in the nest!

137

Student Edition pp. 136–137

Think Critically, continued

DAY 3

Higher-Order Thinking Skills

Synthesis How can you tell that all the red bird's eggs have hatched? (Possible response: There were six eggs, and now there are six baby birds.)

If... children can not explain how they know the eggs hatched,
then... have them count eggs in the beginning, and how many birds there are in the end.

Comprehension Check

Have children discuss each question with a partner. Ask several pairs to share their responses.

✓ **Realistic fiction** Do you think this story could happen in real life? (Possible response: Yes, eggs can fall out of nests, and people can return the eggs safely to their nests if they're careful.)

✓ **Character** How do you think Brad and Kim feel at the end of the story? Why? (Possible response: They're happy because all the eggs hatched safely, even the one that fell.)

✓ **Plot** What was the main problem in this story? How was it solved? (Possible response: The main problem was that an egg fell out of the red bird's nest. It was solved when Brad got the egg into his net and Kim set the egg back in the nest.)

✓ **Confirm predictions** How did you use pictures or story clues to predict what would happen next in the story? (Possible response: The pictures showed what was happening in the story, especially the picture that showed Brad reaching for the egg.)

✓ **Connect text to self** In the story, Brad and Kim see a red bird and its nest in their neighborhood. What wild animals have you seen in your neighborhood? (Possible response: I see squirrels and many kinds of birds in my neighborhood.)

Think Critically
pp. 138–139a

Differentiated Instruction

SI Strategic Intervention

Story Structure If children have trouble discussing story structure, write *Characters*, *Setting*, and *Plot* as headings and read them aloud. As each is discussed, write notes under the appropriate heading.

English Language Learners

Support Discussion Ask yes-or-no questions to start children's responses. For example: Are Brad and Kim happy at the end of the story? (Yes.) Extend language opportunities for children by asking follow-up questions, such as: Why? What has made them happy?

Objectives

- Identify sensory details.
- Recognize and use punctuation marks at the end of interrogative sentences.

Literary Text
Sensory Details

Identify sensory details in a story

Use the story *Get the Egg!* to have children identify sensory details in a story.

- In *Get the Egg!* we read about a bird. What color is the bird? (red)
- Is the bird big or small? (big)
- These details paint a picture of what the bird looks like. They help us see the bird in our mind's eye. Good readers use details from a story to help them visualize, or see, the characters, objects and setting in their minds.

Guide practice

Explain that the class will now think of other examples of details that paint a picture. Use Graphic Organizer 4, and write the heading Eggs in the top left column. Let's begin by thinking about the eggs in the nest. How many eggs were there? That's right, there were six. I'll write *six* under the heading Eggs. Were the eggs large or small? Yes, the eggs were small, so I'll write *small* in the same column. Repeat this process by directing children's attention to page 132. Write the heading Twig in the top right column. Have children identify the words that help them *hear* what happened to the twig. Authors sometimes use words that help us hear what happens. What words would we put in this column? (Possible response: Snap, snap!)

Eggs	Twig

Graphic Organizer Flip Chart 4

On their own

Divide children into small groups and assign each group a previously read story from the Student Edition. Have them identify the details in the story that paint a picture in their minds. Have them share their information with the class.

Go Digital!

Grammar Jammer 

Conventions
Interrogative Sentences

Model interrogative sentences

Write *Where were you born? I was born in New York.* on the board. Point to each word as you read it. Have children identify which sentence is a question. (Where were you born?) Continue with *I am six years old. How old are you?* (How old are you?) A question is an asking sentence. It begins with a capital letter. It ends with a question mark. Write a question mark.

Guide practice

Write the following sentences on the board. Have children tell you which words should begin with a capital letter and where to put the question mark in each case.

1. do you have a pet
2. have you seen a bird's nest
3. what animals do you like
4. have you been to a zoo

Point out the word order in the questions, such as *Do you have,* rather than *You do have*. As children ask questions, guide them by encouraging appropriate word order in each question.

Connect to oral language

Have the class ask questions for which these statements could be answers.

I like a tiger the best.
Many wild animals have fur.
Some wild animals sleep in trees.

On their own

Use *Reader's and Writer's Notebook* p. 191.

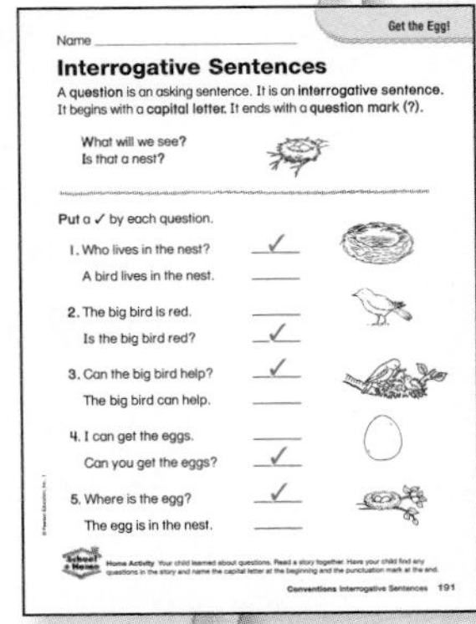
Name ______

Get the Egg!

Interrogative Sentences

A **question** is an asking sentence. It is an **interrogative sentence.** It begins with a **capital letter.** It ends with a **question mark (?).**

What will we see?
Is that a nest?

Put a ✓ by each question.

1. Who lives in the nest? ✓
   A bird lives in the nest. ___
2. The big bird is red. ___
   Is the big bird red? ✓
3. Can the big bird help? ✓
   The big bird can help. ___
4. I can get the eggs. ___
   Can you get the eggs? ✓
5. Where is the egg? ✓
   The egg is in the nest. ___

Conventions Interrogative Sentences 191

Reader's and Writer's Notebook p. 191

Differentiated Instruction

 Strategic Intervention

Interrogative Sentences If children have difficulty forming questions, make statements about animals and then transform the statements into questions.

Daily Fix-It

3. what did you see
   What did you see?
4. where is Lisa
   Where is Lisa?

Discuss the Daily Fix-It corrections with children. Review sentence capitalization and punctuation.

English Language Learners

Questions Unlike English, in Spanish questions begin and end with a question mark. Read the interrogative sentences on the board. Point out that in English questions end with a question mark, but do not begin with a question mark. Have children identify where the question mark belongs in each question.

Objectives

- Recognize features of a realistic story.
- Generate realistic story ideas.
- Use sequence in writing a plan for a story.

Writing—Realistic Story
Writing Trait: Organization

Introduce the prompt

Review with children the key features of a realistic story. Point out that *Get the Egg!* is a realistic story. Assure them that they can make up a brief story with characters that seem real and a setting like a real place. Explain that today children will plan their own story with events that really could happen. It will be a story with a beginning, middle, and end. Read aloud the writing prompt.

Writing Prompt

Think about animals in neighborhoods. Write a realistic story about two friends seeing an animal.

Sharing the Writing

Help children generate story ideas

To plan a new story, think of animals in our neighborhoods. Let's make a chart of animals and where they live in our neighborhoods. Display a T-chart. I'll start with the word *squirrel*.

Animals in Our Neighborhoods	Where They Live
squirrel	nest, hollow
butterfly	garden
bird	nest
toad	pond
rabbit	warren

Guide children in identifying animals and where they live in their neighborhoods. Possible ideas are shown. Record the responses, and keep the chart so that children can refer to it as they plan and draft their stories.

Have each child choose an animal for a new story. Circulate to guide them. Have them make up names for children who will be their characters.

MINI-LESSON

Sequence

INTERACT with TEXT

Introduce Use *Reader's and Writer's Notebook* p. 192 to model story planning. To plan a story, I can use a chart. I want to write about a butterfly, so I'm going to call my story *The Butterfly.* My characters will be a girl and boy who find a butterfly cocoon in a garden. I'll call my characters Ava and Tyler. I'll write the names in the Characters box. In the Setting box, I'll write *garden*. Now I will plan what happens in the beginning, middle, and end of my story. I will use the chart to help me put my story ideas in order.

Name
Story Chart
Title
Characters
Setting
Beginning
Middle
End of Story

Reader's and Writer's Notebook, p. 192

Model At the beginning, Ava and Tyler will find a cocoon in the garden. I'll write that in the Beginning box. In the middle of the story, they will put the cocoon in a big jar. They will watch the cocoon break open. I'll write that in the Middle box. At the end, They will let the butterfly go. Now I'll write that idea in the End of Story box. The chart has helped me put my ideas for the beginning, middle, and end of my story in order. Now plan for your story. Circulate to guide and assist children.

ROUTINE **Quick Write for Fluency** Team Talk

1. **Talk** Have children take two minutes to tell their story events to a partner.
2. **Write** Each child writes one short sentence for the beginning, one for the middle, and one for the end of the planned story.
3. **Share** Each child reads the story ideas to the partner.

Routines Flip Chart

Write Guy
Jeff Anderson

Writers Write!

Young writers succeed in classrooms where they write. Children need to read every day and to write every day. Teachers do not need to read and assess everything that children write.

Differentiated Instruction

Strategic Intervention

Planning Story Ideas If children find it difficult to think of a story idea, have them think about times they have seen an animal in their neighborhood. They can base their story idea on something that really happened.

English Language Learners

Support Prewriting

Beginning Have children draw and label three story events (beginning, middle, end) and share with a partner, possibly one who speaks the same home language.

Intermediate Have children write phrases to express three story event ideas (beginning, middle, end). Have them describe the story plan to other children.

Advanced/Advanced High Have children write short sentences in their story charts. As they share the plan with partners, children can clarify and add ideas.

Objectives
- Write with consistent letter size.
- Make a list about a topic.

Handwriting
Letter *E* and *e*/Letter Size

Model letter formation Display upper- and lower-case letters: *Ee*. Use the stroke instructions pictured below to model proper letter formation.

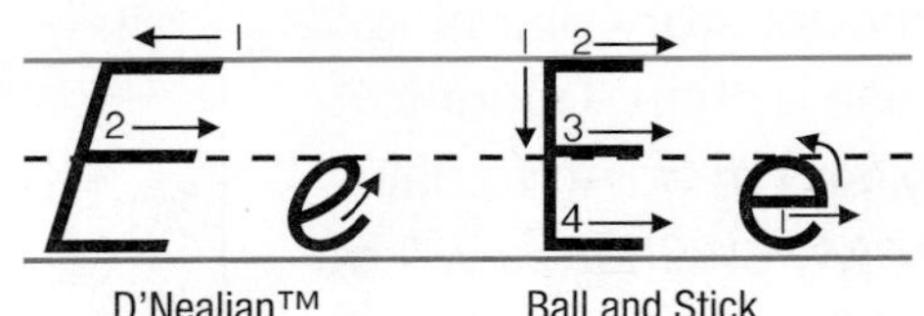

Model consistent letter size Explain that when we write a word, all the letters in that word should be the same size. Write the word *man* using different letter sizes. When I write the letters in a word, I need to make sure they all are the same size. Write another example of the word *man* with different letter sizes. One letter should not be bigger or smaller than another. Write the word *man* again, with letters the same size. When the letters are the same size, the word is easier to read. Ask children which of the three writing samples is easiest to read and why.

Guide practice Write the following words, two with letters of different sizes and two with letters of the same size.

run **mess** **men** **win**

On their own Team Talk Have children work in pairs to discuss which words are written with letters of the same size and which ones are not. Have them discuss how the words need to be fixed. Have them share with the class.

Use the *Reader's and Writer's Notebook* p. 193.

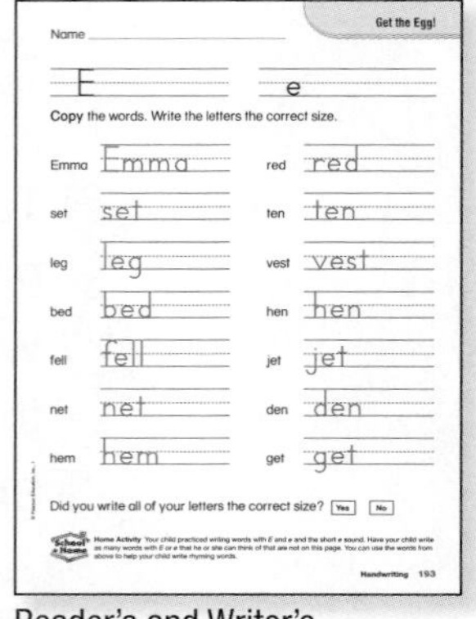

Reader's and Writer's Notebook p. 193

Research and Inquiry
Research Skill: List

Teach Tell children that a **list** is a group of words about a topic arranged in order one after the other. Explain that sometimes people make lists to keep track of things to do. Point out that people write lists using words, phrases, or sentences and that lists may be numbered. Write *Books in Our Classroom* and list book titles under the heading. Read the list aloud. Then explain that some lists group things that are alike. Write subheadings such as *Fiction* and *Nonfiction*, and reorganize the titles under the appropriate subheadings.

Model Think Aloud First, I read the title of the list. The title tells me what the list is about. I see that the list must be read from top to bottom. So, I start by reading the name at the top. Then I read the rest of the names.

Guide practice Write the heading *Places Where We Might Find Wild Animals*. Read the heading aloud. Have partners work together to make a list of places to look for wild animals.

Wrap Up Your Day

- ✔ **Consonant Blends** Write the words *grass* and *spot*. Have children identify the blend at the beginning of each word.
- ✔ **High-Frequency Words** Write the following sentence: *We saw a small bird in your tree.* Ask children to read the sentence. Ask questions to elicit the high-frequency words, such as *Where was the bird?* (in the tree) *What size was the bird?* (small)
- ✔ **Build Concepts** Monitor children's use of oral vocabulary as they respond. What are some habitats in our neighborhood where we might find wild animals? (trees, soil) What do wild animals need in order to survive? (food, water, place to live)

Academic Vocabulary

list words about a topic arranged in order one after the other

Tell children that tomorrow they will reread *Get the Egg!*

Get Ready to Read

30–35 min.

Objectives

- Build oral vocabulary.
- Identify details in text.
- Share information and ideas about the concept.

Today at a Glance

Oral Vocabulary
croak

Phonological Awareness
Generate Rhyming Words

Phonics and Spelling
◉ Short *e: e*
◉ Initial Consonant Blends

High-Frequency Words
saw, small, tree, your

Story Words
bird

Comprehension
Review Character

Fluency
Appropriate Phrasing

Conventions
Interrogative Sentences

Writing
Realistic Story

Listening and Speaking
Give Descriptions

Research and Inquiry
Gather and Record Information

Concept Talk

Question of the Week

Which animals live in our neighborhood?

Build concepts

To reinforce concepts and to focus children's attention, have children sing "Time to Hatch" from the *Sing with Me* Big Book. How will the pond help the baby birds survive? (The pond has water, which the baby birds need.)

Sing with Me Big Book Audio

Monitor listening comprehension

Display the Big Book, *Jungle Drum*. As children listen to the story, have them think about the sounds in the jungle and who or what makes the sounds. Then read the book aloud.

- What makes the "Blip!" and "Blop!" sounds? (water drops)
- What animal makes the growling sound? (jaguar)
- What animal croaks in the jungle? (tree frog)

Big Book

ELL Expand Vocabulary Use the Day 3 instruction on ELL Poster 5 to help children expand vocabulary.

ELL Poster 5

Oral Vocabulary
Amazing Words

Teach Amazing Words

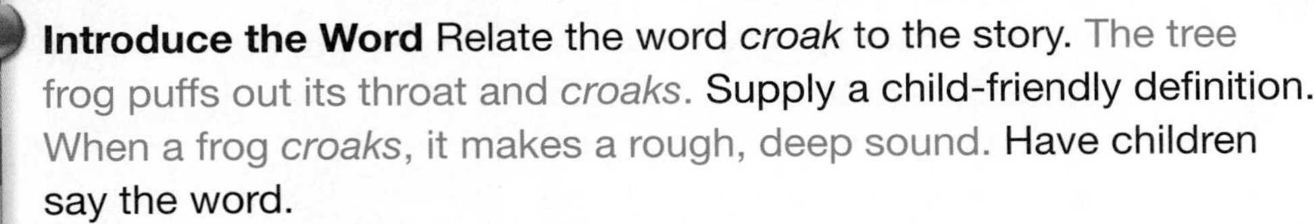

1. **Introduce the Word** Relate the word *croak* to the story. The tree frog puffs out its throat and *croaks*. Supply a child-friendly definition. When a frog *croaks*, it makes a rough, deep sound. Have children say the word.
2. **Demonstrate** Provide examples to show meaning. Frogs *croak* as they sit by the pond. I hear frogs *croak* when it's starting to get dark. Toads make a *croaking* sound too.
3. **Apply** Have children demonstrate their understanding. Have you heard a frog *croak*? What does it sound like?

Routines Flip Chart

Anchored Talk

Add to the concept map

Use these questions to discuss wild animals that live in our neighborhood as you add to the concept map.

- In *Get the Egg!* Kim and Brad found an animal that we have listed on our map. What is it? (a bird) What is the red bird's habitat? (It lives in a tree in the yard.) Let's add *lives in tree* to our map.
- The red bird is in a nest. What else is in the nest? (the red bird's eggs) Let's add *nest and eggs* to our map.

Amazing Words

habitat	chirp
hatch	croak
survive	moist

Differentiated Instruction

Advanced

Amazing Words Allow children to show an understanding of the word *croak* by demonstrating a croaking sound and naming animals that croak.

English Language Learners

Pronunciation Assist children with the articulation of phonemes as they blend sounds, particularly initial consonant blends. Focus on tongue and lip positions when saying words such as *croak*.

Vocabulary Help children understand that the story words *blip* and *blop* are words that sound like what they mean. If possible, demonstrate the sound by dripping water into a bowl. Talk about other words that sound like what they mean, such as *croak*.

Objectives

- Identify and generate words that rhyme.
- ◎ Read words with initial consonant blends.

Phonological Awareness
Rhyming Words

Model producing rhyming words

Read together the first bullet point on pages 122–123 of the Student Edition. Today we are going to use this picture to help us produce rhyming words. Remember that **rhyming words** are words that end with the same sounds. The directions tell us to find three things that rhyme with *tack*. When I look at the picture, I see a cat with *black* fur, a *stack* of books, and a *track* left by the cat. *Black*, *stack*, and *track* rhyme with *tack*. Repeat by reading the third bullet point and finding the rhyming word for *best* (*nest*).

Student Edition pp. 122–123

Guide practice

Guide children to use the picture to produce words that rhyme with *red*. (*sled, bread*)

On their own

Have children orally generate words starting with consonant blends that rhyme with the following words. Sample responses are given.

top (stop, drop, plop, crop)	**fill** (still, grill)
sack (stack, black, track)	**due** (blue, true)
bee (tree, flee)	**day** (play, stay, tray, gray)

Team Talk Allow children the opportunity to create pairs of rhyming words with a partner.

Phonics
Build Words

Model word building Now we are going to build words with beginning consonant blends. Write *lip* and blend it. Watch me add *f* to the beginning of *lip*. Model blending the new word, *flip*.

Guide practice Have children spell *flip* with letter tiles. Monitor children's work as they build words.

- Change the *f* in *flip* to *c*. Say the new word together.
- Change the *c* in *clip* to *s*. Say the new word together.

- Change the *l* in *slip* to *n*. Say the new word together.

- Change the *n* in *snip* to *k*. Say the new word together.

Corrective feedback For corrective feedback, model the correct spelling and have children correct their tiles.

Fluent Word Reading

Model Write *step*. I know the sounds for *s, t, e,* and *p*. I blend them and read the word *step*.

Guide practice Write the words below. Say the sounds in your head for each spelling you see. When I point to the word, we'll read it together. Allow one second per sound-previewing time for the first reading.

sped	Fred	dress	stress	sled

On their own Have children read the list above three or four times, until they can read one word per second.

Differentiated Instruction

Advanced

Blend Words If children are able to blend words with initial consonant blends easily and independently, have them use letter tiles to build these more difficult words with initial blends: *trap, drop, slam, flop* and *grand*.

Academic Vocabulary

blend combine a series of sounds in sequence without pausing between them

rhyming words words that end with the same sound

English Language Learners

Produce Initial Blends Children whose first language is Spanish may need support with words with initial *s* blends, such as *slip*. Model the formal pronunciation and have children repeat the words.

DAY 3 Get Ready to Read

Objectives

- Distinguish /e/ in initial and medial positions.
- ◎ Blend and read words with short /e/ and initial consonant sounds.
- Decode words in context and in isolation.
- Spell words with short /e/.

Blend and Read

Decode words in isolation

Have children turn to page 195 in the *Reader's and Writer's Notebook* and find the first list of words. Each word in this list either contains the short *e* sound or begins with two consonants that are blended together. Let's blend and read these words. Be sure that children distinguish the short *e* sound or pronounce the consonant blend correctly in each word.

Reader's and Writer's Notebook pp. 195–196

Next, have children read the high-frequency words.

Decode words in context

Chorally read the story along with children. Have children identify words in the story that contain the short *e* sound or begin with two consonants that are blended together.

Team Talk Pair children and have them take turns reading the story aloud to each other. Monitor children as they read to check for proper pronunciation and appropriate pacing.

On their own

To further develop automaticity, have children take the story home to reread.

Spelling
Short *e* Words

Spell high-frequency words Write *your* and *saw* and point them out on the Word Wall. Have children say and spell the words with you and then without you.

Dictation Have children write these sentences. Say each sentence. Then repeat it slowly, one word at a time.

1. **Get your hat.**
2. **I saw Sam and his cat.**
3. **Kim and Kit use the net.**

Proofread and correct Write each sentence, spelling words one at a time. Have children circle and rewrite any misspelled words.

On their own Use *Reader's and Writer's Notebook* p. 197.

Reader's and Writer's Notebook p. 197

Small Group Time

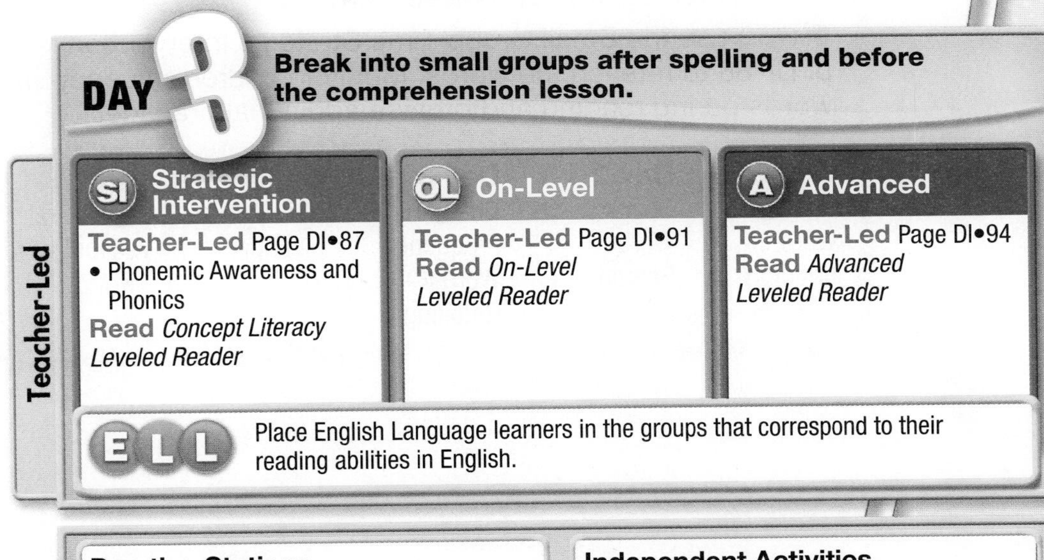
DAY 3
Break into small groups after spelling and before the comprehension lesson.
Teacher-Led
SI Strategic Intervention
Teacher-Led Page DI•87
• Phonemic Awareness and Phonics
Read Concept Literacy Leveled Reader
OL On-Level
Teacher-Led Page DI•91
Read On-Level Leveled Reader
A Advanced
Teacher-Led Page DI•94
Read Advanced Leveled Reader
ELL
Place English Language learners in the groups that correspond to their reading abilities in English.
Practice Stations
• Read for Meaning
• Let's Write
Independent Activities
• Read independently/Reading Log on Reader's and Writer's Notebook p. RR2
• AudioText of Main Selection

Spelling Words
Short *e* Words

1. men	**6. leg**
2. red	**7. jet**
3. step	**8. sled**
4. ten	**9. wet**
5. net	**10. bed**

High-Frequency Words

11. your	**12. saw**

ELL

English Language Learners

Spelling Dictation Children will benefit from hearing each dictated sentence read three times. First, have children listen to understand the sentence. The second time, they should write what they hear. The third time, they can check their work.

DAY 3 Read and Comprehend

40–45 min.

Objectives

- Read high-frequency words.
- Establish purpose for reading text.
- Review key features of realistic fiction.

Check High-Frequency Words
SUCCESS PREDICTOR

High-Frequency and Story Words

Read words in isolation Display and review this week's high-frequency words and story words. Have children read the words aloud.

Read words in context Display the following sentence frames. Have children complete the sentences using high-frequency and story words. Have the children read each completed sentence with you.

1. **We ________ the blue eggs in the nest. (saw)**
2. **The nest was up in the ________. (tree)**
3. **A baby ________ hatched from the egg in the nest. (bird)**
4. **The baby was so ________ it fit in my hand. (small)**
5. **Tell Nat about ________ pal Bud. (your)**

Don't Wait Until Friday

MONITOR PROGRESS Check High-Frequency Words

Point to these words on the Word Wall and have the class read them. Listen for children who miss words during the reading. Call on those children to read some of the words individually.

saw	**small**	**tree**	**your**	**Spiral Review**
are	**the**	**too**	**you** ←	Row 2 reviews previously taught high-frequency words.

If... children cannot read these words,

then... use the Small Group Time Strategic Intervention lesson on p. DI•88 to reteach the words. Monitor children's fluency with these words during reading and provide additional practice.

Day 1	**Day 2**	**Day 3**	**Day 4**	**Day 5**
Check Word Reading	Check Word Reading	Check High-Frequency Words/ Retelling	Check Fluency	Check Oral Vocabulary

Success Predictor

Main Selection— Second Read
Get the Egg!

Review Character and setting

Recall this week's main selection, *Get the Egg!* Tell children that today they will read the story again. Remind children that **characters** are the people and animals in a story. Remind them that the **setting** is where and when the story takes place. Readers better understand a story when they can describe the reasons for a character's actions or feelings, as well as the setting of the story.

Review Genre: realistic fiction

Let's Read Together Remind children that realistic fiction is a made-up story about events that could happen in real life. Have children recall facts from *Get the Egg!* that indicate that this story could happen in real life. (An egg can fall out of a bird's nest. People can help return the egg safely to the nest.)

Set a purpose

Remind children that good readers read for a purpose. Guide children to set a new purpose for reading *Get the Egg!* today, perhaps to consider what else Brad and Kim might have done.

Extend thinking

Tell children they will now read *Get the Egg!* for the second time. Use the Day 3 Extend Thinking notes to encourage children to use higher-order thinking skills to go beyond the details of the story.

Second Read

Continue to DAY 3

For the Second Read, use **Extend Thinking** across the bottom of pages 128–137.

Story Word

bird an animal covered in feathers that has wings and two legs

Academic Vocabulary

character the people and animals in a story

setting where and when a story takes place

English Language Learners

Phonics Clues Provide support for children during the sentence frames review activity on page 138g by supplying the initial consonant or consonant blend of the word that completes the sentence.

High-Frequency Words Success Predictor

Read and Comprehend

Objectives

- Retell a narrative.
- ◎ Identify the main idea and details of a story.
- Explain a story's structure.
- Write clear, coherent sentences.

Check Retelling
SUCCESS PREDICTOR

138

Think Critically

1. In *Get the Egg!*, Brad and Kim have an adventure. Find and read one part of the story that reminds you of something exciting that has happened to you. Text to Self
2. Why did the author write this story? Author's Purpose
3. What is this story about? ◎ Main Idea and Details
4. Does this story have a happy ending? Explain. ◎ Story Structure
5. **Look Back and Write** Look back at pages 134 and 135. Write about how Brad and Kim save the red bird's egg. Provide evidence from the story. Discuss what you wrote with a partner. TEST PRACTICE Extended Response

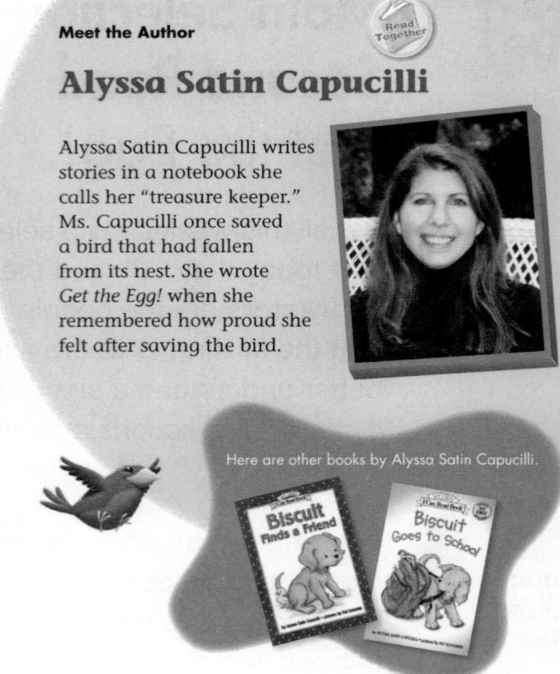

Meet the Author

Alyssa Satin Capucilli

Alyssa Satin Capucilli writes stories in a notebook she calls her "treasure keeper." Ms. Capucilli once saved a bird that had fallen from its nest. She wrote *Get the Egg!* when she remembered how proud she felt after saving the bird.

Here are other books by Alyssa Satin Capucilli.

Use the Reading Log in the *Reader's and Writer's Notebook* to record your independent reading.

139

Student Edition pp. 138-139

Retelling

Have children work in pairs, retelling the story to one another. Remind children that their partners should include the characters, setting, and events from the beginning, middle, and end of the story. Children should use the retelling strip in the Student Edition as they retell. Monitor children's retelling.

Scoring rubric

Top-Score Response A top-score response makes connections beyond the text, elaborates on the author's purpose, and describes in detail the characters, setting, and plot.

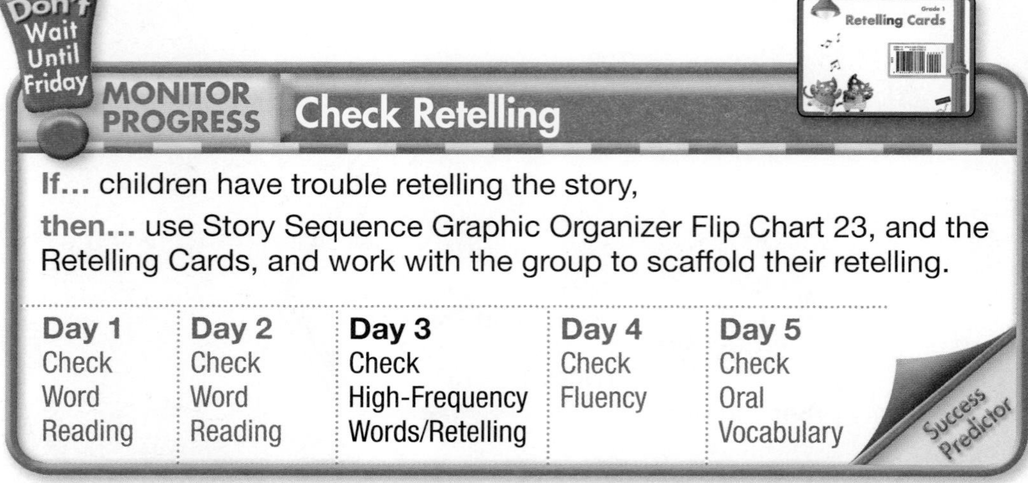

Don't Wait Until Friday

MONITOR PROGRESS **Check Retelling**

If... children have trouble retelling the story,
then... use Story Sequence Graphic Organizer Flip Chart 23, and the Retelling Cards, and work with the group to scaffold their retelling.

Day 1	Day 2	Day 3	Day 4	Day 5
Check Word Reading	Check Word Reading	**Check High-Frequency Words/Retelling**	Check Fluency	Check Oral Vocabulary

Success Predictor

Think Critically

Text to Self

1. Possible response: I once found a bird's nest with eggs in it in my neighborhood.

Author's Purpose

2. Possible response: The author wants us to see that we can care for animals.

Main Idea and Details

3. The story is about how Kim and Brad save a bird's egg. They discover that a red bird had a nest in a tree. The nest has eggs in it, and one of them falls out.

Story Structure

4. Yes. The story has a happy ending because Brad and Kim are able to save the egg and put it back in the nest.

Writing on Demand

5. **Look Back and Write** For writing fluency, assign a five-minute time limit. As children finish, encourage them to reread their response and proofread for errors.

Scoring rubric

> **Top-Score Response** A top-score response uses details from the text and the pictures to tell how Brad and Kim saved the egg. For example:
>
> Brad and Kim used the net to get the egg. Then they put the egg back in the nest.

Meet the author Read aloud page 139 as children follow along. Ask children what authors do.

Read independently After children enter their independent reading into their Reading Logs, have them paraphrase a portion of the text they have just read. Tell children that when we paraphrase, we express the meaning of what we have just read using our own words.

Differentiated Instruction

A Advanced

Look Back and Write Ask children who show proficiency with the writing prompt to explain why they think Brad and Kim did not touch the egg.

INTERACT with TEXT

Strategy Response Log

Story Structure Have children use p. RR17 in their *Reader's and Writer's Notebook* to draw a picture of the most important event in the story. Remind children to include the main characters and the setting in their pictures.

Plan to Assess Retelling

- ☐ Week 1: Strategic Intervention
- ☐ Week 2: Advanced
- ☐ Week 3: Strategic Intervention
- ☐ Week 4: On-Level
- ☑ This Week: Assess Advanced children.
- ☐ Week 6: Assess any children you have not yet checked during this unit.

Retelling
Success Predictor

Objectives

- Read aloud fluently with appropriate phrasing.
- Recognize and use question marks at the end of interrogative sentences.

Model Fluency

Appropriate Phrasing

Model fluent reading Have children turn to Student Edition page 130. Point to the periods at the end of each sentence. A period shows that it is the end of a sentence. I stop when I come to a period.

Guide practice Have children read the page with you. Then have them reread the page as a group until they read with appropriate phrasing, paying attention to punctuation. Encourage them to read stopping for each period. Continue in the same way with page 131.

Corrective feedback **If…** children have difficulty reading with appropriate phrasing, **then…** prompt:

- Do all of the sentences end in a period?
- Try to read the sentences, pausing when you come to each period.

Reread for Fluency

ROUTINE Choral Reading

1. **Select a Passage** For *Get the Egg!* use pp. 132–133.
2. **Model** First, have children track the print as you read.
3. **Guide Practice** Then have children read along with you.
4. **Corrective Feedback** Have the class read aloud without you. Monitor progress and provide feedback. For optimal fluency, children should reread three to four times.

Routines Flip Chart

Check comprehension What did Brad do to help Kim? (Possible response: He got the egg in his net and Kim put it back in the nest.)

Conventions
Interrogative Sentences

Review Interrogative sentences Remind children that an interrogative sentence, or question is an asking sentence. It begins with a capital letter and ends with a question mark.

Guide practice Write this sentence on the board and have children read it aloud.

what do birds eat

How should our question begin? (with a capital letter) Write a capital letter. How should our question end? (with a question mark) Write a question mark.

Team Talk Have children suggest other questions about birds.

Connect to oral language Have children complete these sentence frames orally. Then have them turn each statement into a question.

1. **I want to know why a zebra ________.**
2. **I want to know how a hippo ________.**
3. **I want to know if an elephant can ________.**

Make sure children ask questions with appropriate subject-verb inversion. For example, rather than *An elephant can run,* a speaker asks *Can an elephant run?*

On their own Use *Reader's and Writer's Notebook* p. 198.

Name ________ Get the Egg!

Interrogative Sentences

Finish the question. Write an animal name.

a bird a cat a dog an elephant an ostrich

What does Answers will vary. look like?

Read the sentence. Change the words to make a question. Write the question.

The bird is red.

Is the bird red?

150 Conventions Interrogative Sentences

Reader's and Writer's Notebook p. 198

Options for Oral Rereading

Use *Get the Egg!* or one of this week's Decodable Practice Readers.

Professional Development

Questions Using printed materials to identify interrogative sentences helps children recognize them. Provide newspapers or children's magazines for children to use to find questions.

Daily Fix-It

5. what does a dog eat
   What does a dog eat?
6. have you seen a zebra
   Have you seen a zebra?

Discuss the Daily Fix-It corrections with children. Review sentence capitalization and punctuation.

English Language Learners

Interrogative Sentences English language learners may benefit from focusing on question words and their use in interrogative sentences. List question words on the board and read them aloud. Invite children to say or write interrogative sentences that begin with the question words.

Objectives

- Write a draft of a realistic story.
- Use time-order words in writing.

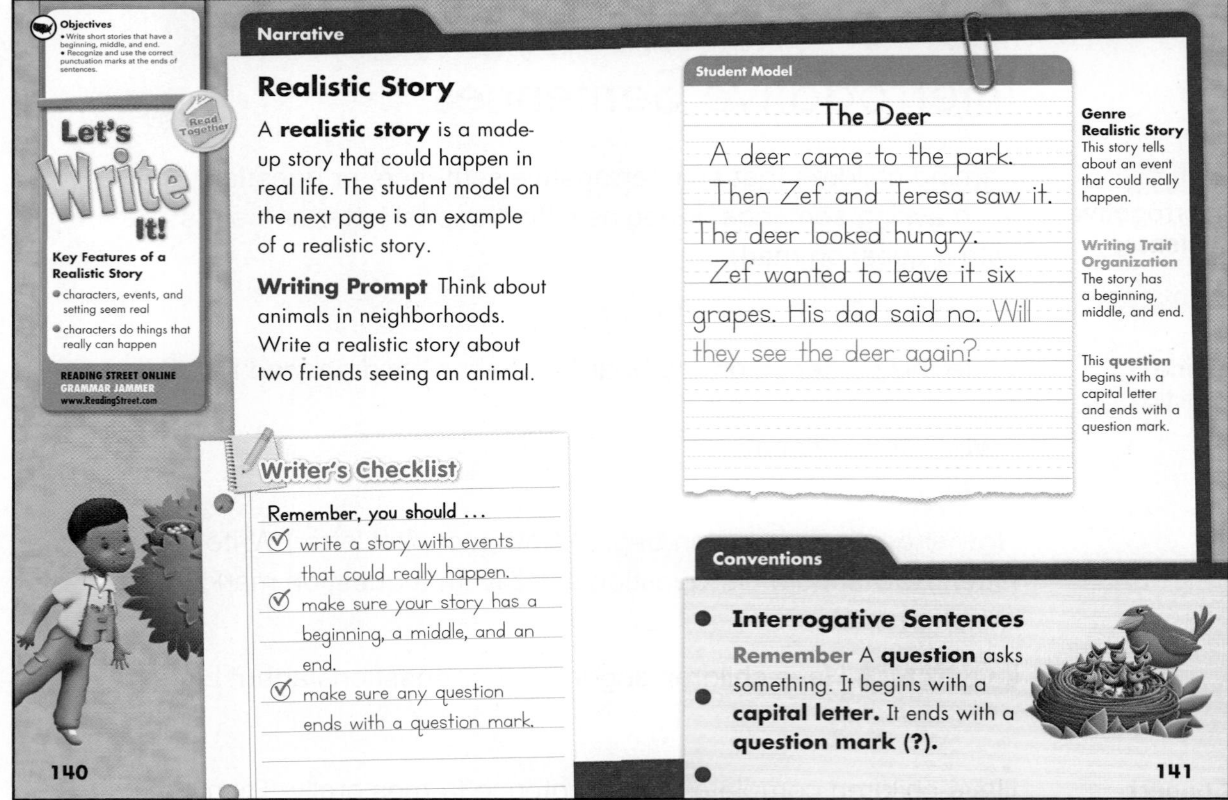

Student Edition pp. 140–141

Let's Write It!—Realistic Story

Teach Use pages 140–141 in the Student Edition. Read aloud the Key Features of a Realistic Story and the definition of a realistic story. Help children better understand the Writing Prompt by reading it aloud and discussing the Writer's Checklist with children.

Review the student model Then read "The Deer" on page 141 to children. Point out the realistic characters and events in the story. Ask children to identify the setting. (a park) Use time-order transition words such as *First, Then,* and *At last* when discussing the story to help children recognize the beginning, middle, and end. Read aloud and briefly discuss the side notes about Genre, the Writing Trait, and questions to help children understand how an author writes a realistic story.

Scoring rubric

> **Top-Score Response** Help children understand that a top-score response has events that could really happen; a beginning, middle, and end; and sentences that are capitalized and punctuated correctly. For a complete rubric see Writing Rubric 5 from the *Teacher Resource DVD-ROM*.

Connect to conventions Read to children the Conventions note about Questions. Point out the question in the model story.

Writing—Realistic Story
Writer's Craft: Time-Order Words

MINI-LESSON

Time-Order Words

- **Introduce** Use your story chart from yesterday and Writing Transparency 5A to model using time-order words when writing story events in sequence. When I write my story, I will use my chart. Yesterday the chart helped me put my ideas for the beginning, middle, and end of my story in order. Today I will write each event in order. I can also use time-order words like *first, next,* and *last* to make the order of events clear. After Ava wonders what is in the cocoon, *then* they will put it in a big glass jar. *Later,* they will watch the cocoon open. I will use the words *then* and *later* to tell the order of events. Read aloud the draft on the Transparency and discuss the order of story events.

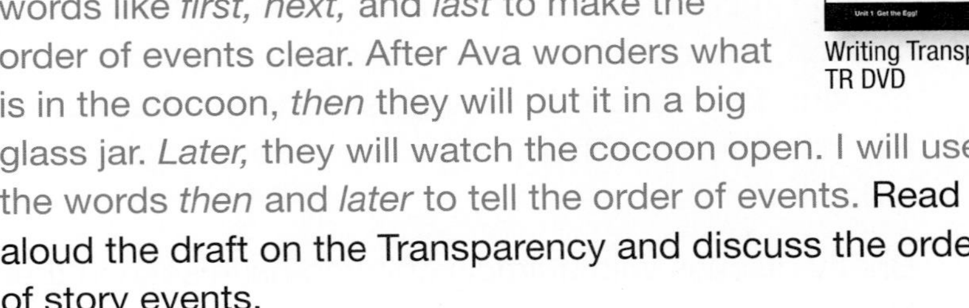

The Butterfly

Tyler and Ava were playing in Ava's garden. They found a cocoon on a flower stem.

Ava asked, "What is inside this cocoon."

Then they put it in a big glass jar. Later, they watched the cocoon open. Out came a beautiful butterfly!

When its wings got strong, Tyler and Ava let it go. They watched it fly away.

Unit 1: Get the Egg! Writing: Model 5A

Writing Transparency 5A
TR DVD

- Explain how children can use story events they planned yesterday to draft the story: beginning, middle, and end. Today's goal is to write the story but not to rewrite each word perfectly. They can edit later to correct the words.

Guide story Now it is time to write your story. Tell about your characters' seeing a neighborhood animal. Have children use their story charts. Help them finish the ideas. Then guide children as they draft the stories.

ROUTINE **Quick Write for Fluency** Team Talk

1. **Talk** Have partners take one minute to talk about what children might do with a neighborhood dog.
2. **Write** Each child writes two sentences about children and a dog.
3. **Share** Partners can add time-order words to each other's sentences.

Routines Flip Chart

Differentiated Instruction

 Advanced

Developing Sequence Children may include more than one story event in the beginning, middle, or end of the story.

Academic Vocabulary

time-order transition words words that show readers the order of events or steps: *first, next, then, later, now, tomorrow, last, finally* (and others)

Objectives

- Use descriptive words when speaking.
- Listen attentively as others give descriptions.
- Express ideas through speaking and writing.
- Gather and record information about the topic.

Listening and Speaking
Give Descriptions

Teach giving descriptions Ask children what they know about giving descriptions. Remind them that good descriptions tell what something looks like, sounds like, or feels like. Tell children that people often give descriptions of things they have seen or experiences they have had.

- Good speakers choose descriptive words that help listeners better understand an experience.
- Good listeners pay attention as others give descriptions so they can better understand the experience.
- Good speakers speak clearly and at an appropriate pace.

Model Use the passage below to model giving a description.

Once I saw a cardinal in my back yard. It was hopping from branch to branch in the tall tree by the fence. It was bright red, so I could see it easily as it moved among the green leaves. All of a sudden, whoosh! The cardinal swooped down to the ground and started pecking for seeds in the tall grass. Then, I heard tap, tap, tap! It was coming from the tree. There was a tiny woodpecker pecking at the trunk. What a day for birds!

Guide practice Briefly discuss wild animals children have seen in their neighborhood. Invite children to suggest words that describe the animals. Make a list of animals and related descriptive words on the board. Have children use the words in sentences describing the animals.

On their own Have pairs of children take turns listening to and giving descriptions of wild animals in their neighborhood. Remind children to follow the rules established in Week 1.

Research and Inquiry
Gather and Record Information

Teach Tell children that today they will write a list of the wild animals they could observe in their neighborhood.

Model Think Aloud Display the list of places to look for wild animals created on Day 2. Now it's time to make a list of the wild animals we might see in one place in our neighborhood. Think about the list we made yesterday of places where we could see wild animals. Which place do you think would be the best to see animals?

Guide practice Guide children to choose one of the locations they listed to watch for wild animals. Encourage children to write the names of wild animals they would see in that location. Point out that children may think of dogs and other pets, but they should not write the names of these animals because they are not wild animals. Remind children that wild animals live outdoors, not with people. Explain to children that they will use what they write down to make their lists.

Wrap Up Your Day

- ✓ **Main Ideas and Details** Have children think about the main ideas and details of *Get the Egg!* What details did you read about in *Get the Egg!*? What is the story mostly about?
- ✓ **Story Structure** Have children recall the main characters from *Get the Egg!* What did the characters do? How does remembering the characters and events help you enjoy the story?

Differentiated Instruction

SI Strategic Intervention

Making Lists Some children may have trouble making a list. Tell these children that they do not need to write the names of the animals. They can draw pictures of what they observe and write the names later in the week.

Tell children that tomorrow they will read about something that they can do to help wild birds in the neighborhood.

Objectives

- Discuss the concept to develop oral language.
- Build oral vocabulary.
- Identify details in text.

Today at a Glance

Oral Vocabulary
moist

Phonemic Awareness
Distinguish /e/

Phonics and Spelling
Review Inflected Endings

Comprehension
◉ Main Idea and Details

Fluency
Appropriate Phrasing

Conventions
Interrogative Sentences

Writing
Realistic Story

Research and Inquiry
Review and Revise Topic

Concept Talk

Question of the Week

Which wild animals live in our neighborhood?

Build concepts

To reinforce concepts and to focus children's attention, have children sing "Time to Hatch" from the *Sing with Me* Big Book. How will the bird feeders help the baby birds survive? (Possible response: The feeders have food, which the birds need.)

Sing with Me Big Book Audio

Review Genre: realistic fiction

Have children tell the key features of realistic fiction: it is a made-up story about people and animals doing things that could really happen. Explain that today you will read about Maisie and her toad in "Maisie Caught a Toad Today" by Tryn Paxton.

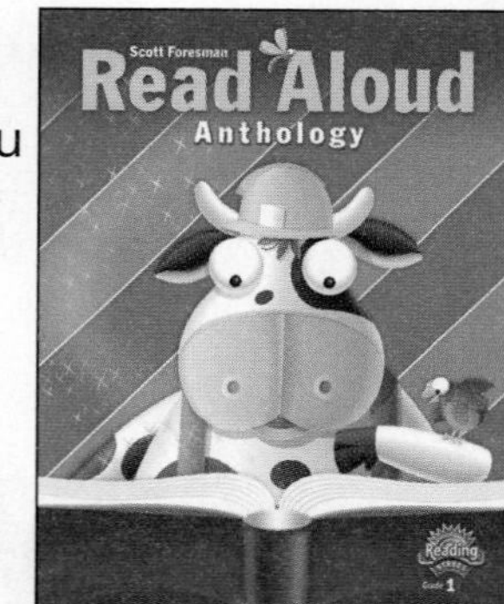

"Maisie Caught a Toad Today"

Monitor listening comprehension

Recall that Brad and Kim discovered a red bird living in its natural habitat, a tree. Have children listen to "Maisie Caught a Toad Today" to find out about a toad's habitat. Read the selection.

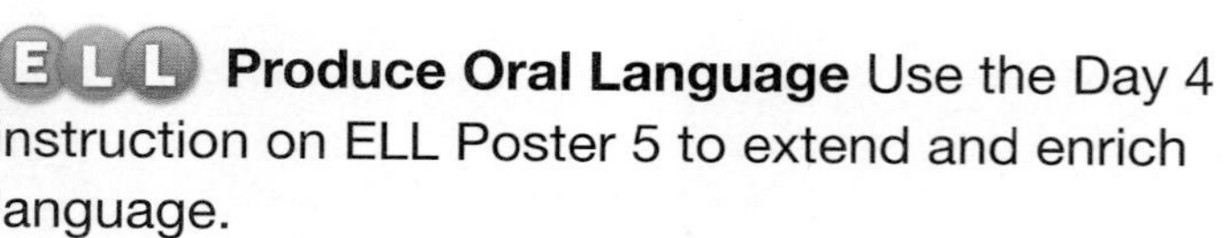
ELL Produce Oral Language Use the Day 4 instruction on ELL Poster 5 to extend and enrich language.

Poster 5

Oral Vocabulary
Amazing Words

Teach Amazing Words

Amazing Words Oral Vocabulary Routine

1. **Introduce the Word** Relate the word *moist* to the story. Maisie used a bucket and *moist* dirt to make a shelter for the toad. Supply a child-friendly definition. When something is *moist*, it is slightly wet or damp. Have children say the word.
2. **Demonstrate** Provide examples to show meaning. The sand was *moist* after it rained. I used a *moist* sponge to clean up the mess. My mom added milk to the oatmeal to make it *moist*.
3. **Apply** Have children demonstrate their understanding. How does something *moist* feel? How do things in nature become *moist*?

Routines Flip Chart

Anchored Talk

Add to the concept map

Discuss wild animals in our neighborhood.

- What did Maisie do with the toad she caught? (Possible response: She put it in a bucket with mud and rocks.) What did Maisie's parents tell her a toad needs? (bugs to eat, water to stay moist) Where can we add these to our concept map?

Amazing Words

habitat	chirp
hatch	croak
survive	moist

Differentiated Instruction

Advanced

Amazing Words Allow children who demonstrate an understanding of the word *moist* to name things that are moist and explain how they might have become moist.

English Language Learners

Frontload Listening Use the *Sing With Me* illustration to review the idea of birds being wild animals that live in many neighborhoods. Before reading, ask children: What other wild animals live in the neighborhood? Record their answers on the board.

Objectives

- Distinguish /e/ in initial and medial positions.
- Read and identify words with inflected endings *-s* and *-ing*.

Phonemic Awareness
Distinguish /e/

Model

This week we read about Maisie and a toad. The toad hops out of Maisie's hand and finds a shady spot to *rest*. Listen as I say the sounds in *rest*. Slowly model the sounds in *rest*, /r/ /e/ /s/ /t/. The middle sound in *rest* is /e/.

Guide practice

I will say some words, and you can tell me if they have the /e/ sound in the middle or at the beginning. Say each word below, then guide children to decide whether the /e/ sound is in the middle or at the beginning of each one.

Corrective feedback

If children make an error, model the correct response. Return to the word later in the practice.

nest	**edge**	**step**
Ben	**empty**	**ten**

On their own

Have children tell you which of the following words contain the /e/ sound.

dress	**deck**	**clam**
luck	**toy**	**egg**

Phonics Review
Inflected Endings -*s* and -*ing*

Review Inflected ending -*s*

To review last week's first phonics skill, write *naps* and *tags*. You studied words like these already. What do you know about the ending of these words? (They end in the letter s. The letter *s* can stand for the /s/ or the /z/ sound.) When you see a word that ends with -*s*, you know it might be a base word with an -*s* ending.

Corrective feedback

If children are unable to answer the questions about the inflected ending -*s*, refer them to Sound-Spelling Card 129.

Review Inflected ending -*ing*

To review last week's second phonics skill, write *mixing*. You also studied words like this one. When a word ends with -*ing*, you know it might be a base word with an -*ing* ending. In this word, the base word is *mix* and it has an -*ing* ending. What is the word? (*mixing*)

Guide practice

Draw a T-chart. When I say a word, hold a hand up high if it has an -*s* ending or down low if it has an -*ing* ending: *yelling, packs, hits, resting, passing, naps, wags, helping, taps, licking*. Write each word in the appropriate column. Read the lists together. Then call on individuals to use words in sentences.

-*s*	-*ing*
packs	yelling
hits	resting
naps	passing
wags	helping
taps	licking

On their own

Use Let's Practice It! pp. 59–60 on the *Teacher Resource DVD-ROM*.

Name ______ Get the Egg!

Use the word in ( ) to finish each sentence.
Write it on the line.
Add -s if needed.

Mom sits.
Mick and Bess swim.

1. Bess (hop) hops up the hill.
2. She (dig) digs
3. Mom and Mick (play) play with her.
4. Mick (get) gets wet.

Find the sentence that tells about the picture.
Mark the ⬭ to show your answer.

5. ⬭ Moms sees Bess and Mick.
⬭ Mom see Bess and Mick.
⬬ Mom sees Bess and Mick.

School + Home Home Activity Your child reviewed verbs that end in -s that describe what one person or thing does. Have your child create sentences about one person and more than one person, using correct verbs.

Phonics Inflected Ending -s Review DVD•59

Let's Practice It!
TR DVD•59

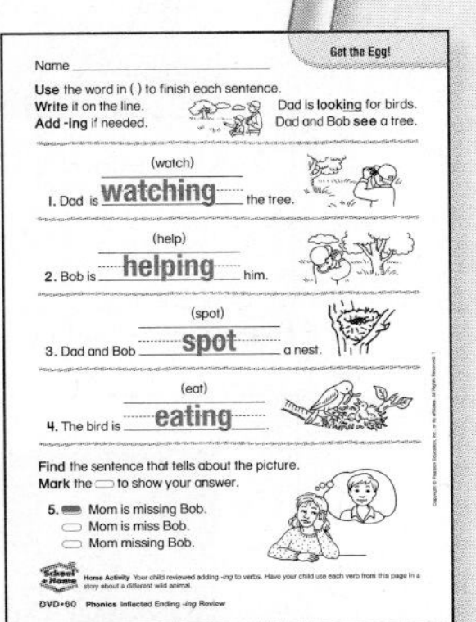
Name ______ Get the Egg!

Use the word in ( ) to finish each sentence.
Write it on the line.
Add -ing if needed.

Dad is looking for birds.
Dad and Bob see a tree.

1. Dad is (watch) watching the tree.
2. Bob is (help) helping him.
3. Dad and Bob (spot) spot a nest.
4. The bird is (eat) eating.

Find the sentence that tells about the picture.
Mark the ⬭ to show your answer.

5. ⬬ Mom is missing Bob.
⬭ Mom is miss Bob.
⬭ Mom missing Bob.

School + Home Home Activity Your child reviewed adding -ing to verbs. Have your child use each verb from this page in a story about a different wild animal.

DVD•60 Phonics Inflected Ending -ing Review

Let's Practice It!
TR DVD•60

Differentiated Instruction

SI Strategic Intervention

Inflected Ending -*s* If children do not pronounce the inflected ending -*s*, then say each word with and without the inflected ending and have children repeat it.

 Advanced

Using Inflected Endings If children are able to produce words with inflected endings easily and with understanding, give them a base word, such as *pack*, and ask them to create a sentence that has the word with either the inflected ending -*s* or the inflected ending -*ing*.

Get Ready to Read

Objectives

- Apply knowledge of sound-spellings to decode unknown words when reading.
- Decode and read words in context and isolation.
- Practice fluency with oral rereading.

Decodable Practice Reader 5C

Short *e: e;* Initial Consonant Blends

Decode words in isolation Have children turn to page 209. Have children decode each word.

The Sleds
Written by Alphie Heart
Decodable Practice Reader 5C

Short e
Peg get sled Meg
red Ned Fred
Consonants qu
Quin
Initial Consonant Blends
sled sleds Fred
High-Frequency Words
a little the

209

Decodable Practice Reader 5C

Review High-frequency words Review the previously taught words *little, the,* and *a.* Have children read each word as you point to it on the Word Wall.

Preview Decodable Reader Have children read the title and preview the story. Tell them they will read words with short *e* and initial consonant blends in this story.

Decode words in context Pair children for reading and listen as they decode. One child begins. Children read the entire story, switching readers after each page. Partners reread the story. This time the other child begins.

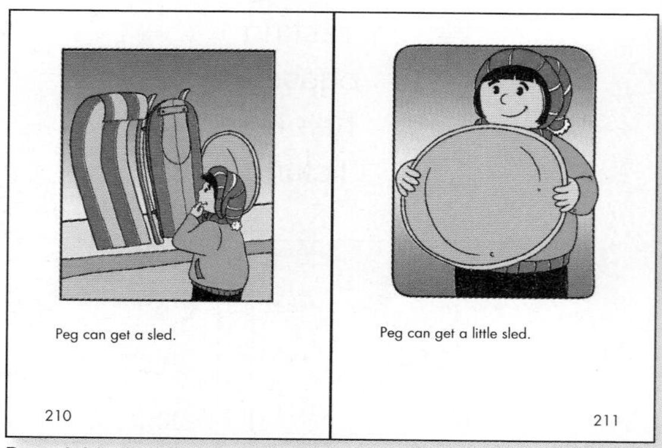

Peg can get a sled.
210
Peg can get a little sled.
211

Decodable Practice Reader 5C

Meg can get a sled.
212
Meg can get a big sled.
213

Quin can get a sled.
214
Quin can get a red sled.
215

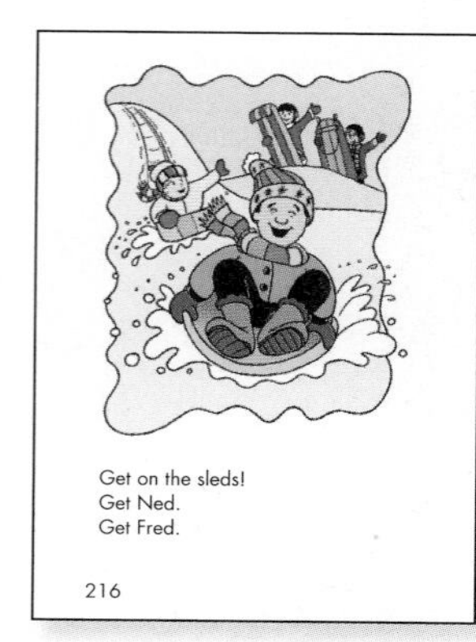

Get on the sleds!
Get Ned.
Get Fred.
216

Corrective Feedback

If... children have difficulty decoding a word, **then...** refer them to the Sound-Spelling Cards to identify the sounds in the word. Then prompt them to blend the word.

- What is the new word?
- Is the new word a word you know?
- Does it make sense in the story?

Check decoding and comprehension

Have children retell the story to include characters, setting, and events. Then point to a word in the story that has a consonant blend and ask children to say the word. List words that children name. Children should supply *Fred, sled,* and *sleds*. Explain that these words begin with two consonant sounds that are blended together. Point to a word that has a short *e* sound and ask children to say the word. List the words that children name.

Reread for Fluency

Have children reread Decodable Practice Reader 5C to develop automaticity decoding words with the short *e* sound and initial consonant blends.

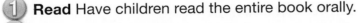

ROUTINE Oral Rereading

1. **Read** Have children read the entire book orally.
2. **Reread** To achieve optimal fluency, children should reread the text three or four times.
3. **Corrective Feedback** Listen as children read. Provide corrective feedback regarding their fluency and decoding.

Routines Flip Chart

ELL

English Language Learners

Decodable Practice Reader

Beginning. Have children point out the words in the story with initial consonant blends. Have them practice saying the blend sounds together and then say the whole word: *sled* and *sleds*. Have them point out the words with the short *e* sound such as *Tex* and *Lex*. Ask them to say the words aloud.

Intermediate Have children say other words with the short *e* sound such as *web* and *bed* and words with initial consonant blends such as *friend, frog, free, fry, slip, slide, slam.*

Advanced/Advanced High After reading, have children think of words with initial consonant blends and words with the short *e* sound and ask them to create sentences with them.

DAY 4 Get Ready to Read

Objectives

- Read words fluently in context and in isolation.
- Spell words with vowel sound /e/ spelled *e*.
- Spell high-frequency words.

Fluent Word Reading

Spiral Review

Read words in isolation

Display these words. Tell children that they can blend some words on this list, and others are Word Wall words.

Have children read the list three or four times until they can read at the rate of two to three seconds per word.

too	**five**	**this**	**are**	**her**
can	**nap**	**four**	**packing**	**eats**
Tom	**Mom**	**black**	**locking**	**hops**
sit	**will**	**pots**	**vans**	**missing**

Word Reading

Corrective feedback

If... children have difficulty reading whole words,
then... have them use sound-by-sound blending for decodable words, or have them say and spell high-frequency words.
If... children cannot read fluently at a rate of two to three seconds per word,
then... have pairs practice the list until they can read it fluently.

Read words in context

Display these sentences. Call on individuals to read a sentence. Then randomly point to review words and have children read them. To help you monitor word reading, high-frequency words are underlined and decodable words are italicized.

Where ***can Tom sit and nap?***

Mom will **take** ***six black pots.***

Ten men **are** ***packing and locking vans.***

Sal **eats** ***less and less.***

Sentence Reading

Corrective feedback

If... children are unable to read an underlined high-frequency word,
then... read the word for them and spell it, having them echo you.
If... children have difficulty reading an italicized decodable word,
then... guide them in using sound-by-sound blending.

Spelling
Short *e* Words

Partner review

Supply pairs of children with index cards on which the spelling words have been written. Have one child read a word while the other writes it. Then have children switch roles. Have them use the cards to check their spelling and correct any misspelled words.

On their own

Use *Reader's and Writer's Notebook* p. 199.

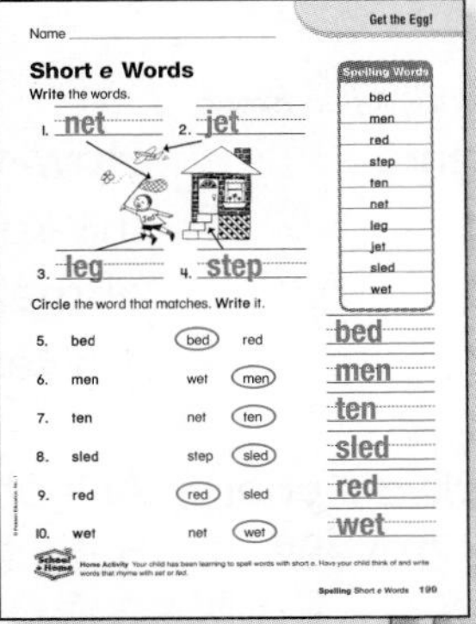
Name
Get the Egg!
Short e Words
Write the words.
1. net 2. jet
3. leg 4. step

Circle the word that matches. Write it.

5.	bed	bed	red	bed
6.	men	wet	men	men
7.	ten	net	ten	ten
8.	sled	step	sled	sled
9.	red	red	sled	red
10.	wet	net	wet	wet

Spelling Words: bed, men, red, step, ten, net, leg, jet, sled, wet

Spelling Short e Words 199

Reader's and Writer's Notebook p. 199

Spiral Review

These activities review

- previously taught high-frequency words *eat, four, five, her, this, too, where, take, are.*
- inflected endings *-s, -ing*; /a/ spelled *a*, /i/ spelled *i*, /o/ spelled *o*.

Small Group Time

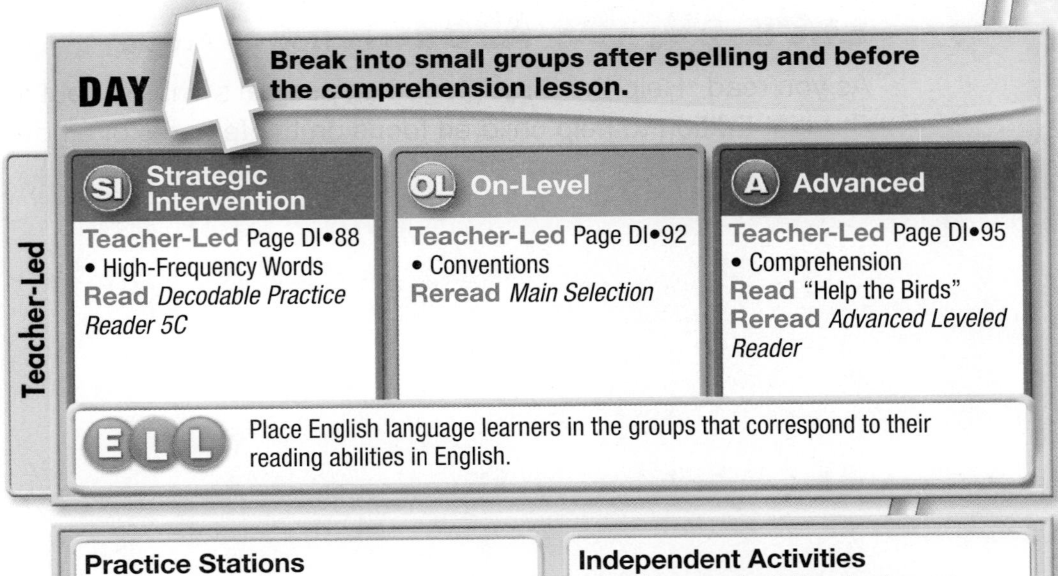

DAY 4 **Break into small groups after spelling and before the comprehension lesson.**

Teacher-Led

SI Strategic Intervention	OL On-Level	A Advanced
Teacher-Led Page DI•88 • High-Frequency Words **Read** *Decodable Practice Reader 5C*	**Teacher-Led** Page DI•92 • Conventions **Reread** *Main Selection*	**Teacher-Led** Page DI•95 • Comprehension **Read** "Help the Birds" **Reread** *Advanced Leveled Reader*

ELL Place English language learners in the groups that correspond to their reading abilities in English.

Practice Stations
- Words to Know
- Get Fluent

Independent Activities
- Read independently/Reading Log on *Reader's and Writer's Notebook* p. RR2
- AudioText of Paired Selection

English Language Learners

Fluent Word Reading Have children listen to a more fluent reader say the words. Then have them repeat the words.

DAY 4 Read and Comprehend

40–45 min.

Objectives

- Identify main idea and details.
- Recognize structure and elements of a how-to article.
- Relate prior knowledge to new text.
- Set purpose for reading.

Science in Reading

Preview and predict

Explain that a how-to article gives directions on how to do or make something. The directions often have more than one step. Usually the steps are numbered to show the order in which they should be followed.

Read the title and the first two sentences of the selection. Have children look through the selection and predict what they might learn. (Possible response: They might learn how to help birds get food to eat.) Ask them what clue helped them make that prediction. (Possible response: They might say the title of the selection or the pictures.)

Let's Think About **Genre**

How-to Article Tell children that they will read a **how-to article**. Review the key features of a how-to article: it is a set of instructions for how to do or make something. Explain that this selection is a how-to article because it gives directions for how to make a feeder for birds.

Activate prior knowledge

Ask children to recall what they have already learned about birds. (They build their nests in trees. They lay eggs in their nests.)

Set a purpose

Let's Read Together As children read, have them pay attention to clues that indicate that the selection is a how-to article.

Let's Think About... How-to Article

As you read "Help the Birds" together, use Let's Think About in the Student Edition to help children focus on the features of a how-to article.

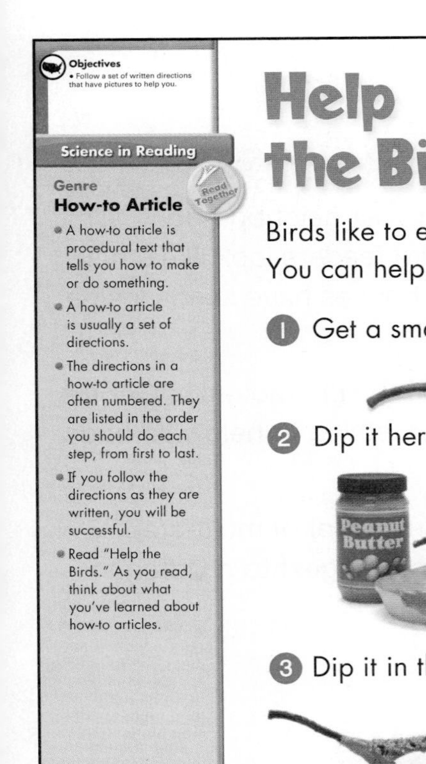

Objectives
- Follow a set of written directions that have pictures to help you.

Science in Reading

Genre
How-to Article

Read Together

- A how-to article is procedural text that tells you how to make or do something.
- A how-to article is usually a set of directions.
- The directions in a how-to article are often numbered. They are listed in the order you should do each step, from first to last.
- If you follow the directions as they are written, you will be successful.
- Read "Help the Birds." As you read, think about what you've learned about how-to articles.

Help the Birds

Birds like to eat.
You can help.

1 Get a small twig.

2 Dip it here.

3 Dip it in this.

142

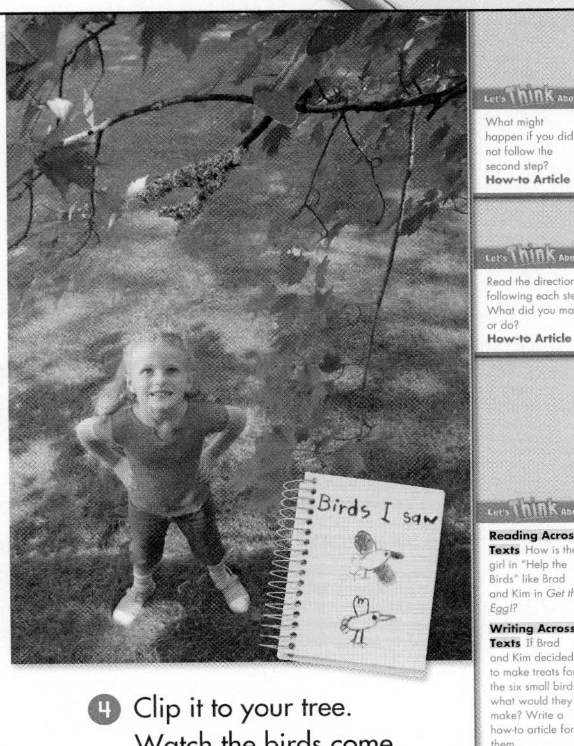

4 Clip it to your tree.
Watch the birds come.

Let's Think About...
What might happen if you did not follow the second step?
How-to Article

Let's Think About...
Read the directions, following each step. What did you make or do?
How-to Article

Let's Think About...
Reading Across Texts How is the girl in "Help the Birds" like Brad and Kim in *Get the Egg!*?

Writing Across Texts If Brad and Kim decided to make treats for the six small birds, what would they make? Write a how-to article for them.

143

Student Edition pp. 142–143

Academic Vocabulary

how-to article writing made up of numbered instructions for how to do or make something

Science Vocabulary

twig a small branch of a tree

Guide Comprehension

Guide practice

Main Idea and Details

Think Aloud The **main idea** is what a selection is mostly about. **Details**, or small pieces of information, tell more about the main idea. In *Get the Egg!* some details were a red bird had a nest in a tree, the nest had eggs in it, and one of the eggs fell out of the nest. The main idea was Kim and Brad saved the egg. As I read "Help the Birds" I will pay attention to the details so I can better understand the main idea.

Multi-Step Directions

Think Aloud When I read the title of the article and see the numbered steps, I wonder what I will learn to do or make to help birds. Since there are numbers, I know the numbers are in a certain order. I know if I want to learn how to do something. I must follow the steps in the correct order. If I don't, then things will not work out.

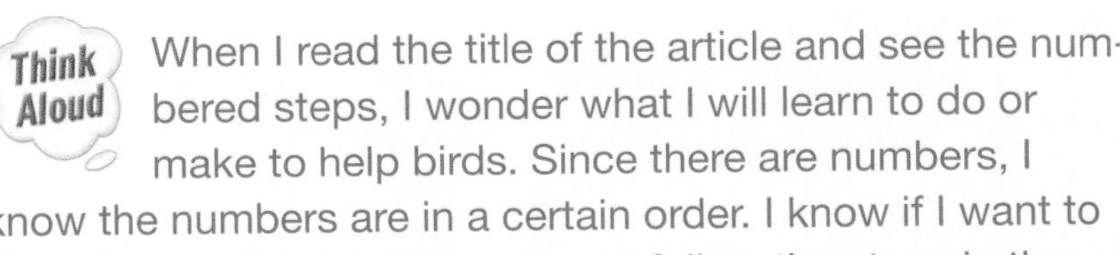

How-to Article

Possible response: The seeds won't stick on the twig. I would make a bird feeder.

Objectives

- Summarize the multi-step directions in a how-to article.
- Read aloud fluently with accuracy and appropriate phrasing.

Check Fluency WCPM
SUCCESS PREDICTOR

Guide Comprehension, continued

Connect to Self Have you seen bird feeders in your neighborhood? What do they look like? (Possible response: Some bird feeders look like small houses hanging from the branch of a tree. The houses have seeds inside and a place for birds to land.)

Reading Across Texts Children might note that the characters in *Get the Egg!* and the girl in "Help the Birds" both do something to help wild birds in their neighborhood.

Writing Across Texts Children might write a similar set of multi-step directions that they read in their Student Edition. Suggest to children to draw a picture to go with each step.

Fluency
Appropriate Phrasing

Guide practice

- Have children turn to pp. 134–135 in *Get the Egg!*
- Have children follow along as you read the pages with appropriate phrasing, stopping at each period.
- Have the class read the pages with you and then reread the pages as a group without you until they read with appropriate phrasing, stopping at each period. To provide additional fluency practice, pair nonfluent readers with fluent readers.

ROUTINE Paired Reading

1. **Select a Passage** For *Get the Egg!* use pages 136–137.
2. **Model** First, have children track the print as you read.
3. **Guide Practice** Then have children read along with you.
4. **On Their Own** For optimal fluency, have partners reread three or four times.

Routines Flip Chart

Don't Wait Until Friday — MONITOR PROGRESS — Fluency WCPM

As children reread, monitor their progress toward their individual fluency goals. Mid-Year Goal: 20–30 words correct per minute. End-of-Year Goal: 60 words correct per minute. Beginning in Unit 3, children will be assessed to determine WCPM.

If... children are not on track to meet benchmark goals,
then... have children practice with text at their independent level.

Day 1	Day 2	Day 3	Day 4	Day 5
Check Word Reading	Check Word Reading	Check High-Frequency Words/ Retelling	Check Fluency	Check Oral Vocabulary

Success Predictor

Differentiated Instruction

A Advanced

WCPM If children already read at 60 words correct per minute, allow them to read independently.

Options for Oral Rereading

Use *Get the Egg!* or one of this week's Decodable Practice Readers.

Fluency WCPM Success Predictor

Objectives

- Identify interrogative sentences.
- Revise a draft of a realistic story.

Conventions
Interrogative Sentences

Test practice Use *Reader's and Writer's Notebook* p. 200 to help children understand identifying interrogative sentences in test items. Recall that a question is an asking sentence that begins with a capital letter and ends with a question mark. Model identifying an interrogative sentence by writing this sentence on the board, reading it aloud, and underlining the capital letter and the question mark.

Where do squirrels live?

Then read the *Reader's and Writer's Notebook* p. 200 directions. Guide children as they mark the answer for number 1.

On their own Use *Reader's and Writer's Notebook* p. 200.

Connect to oral language After children mark the answers to numbers 1–6, review the correct choices aloud, and have children read each interrogative sentence.

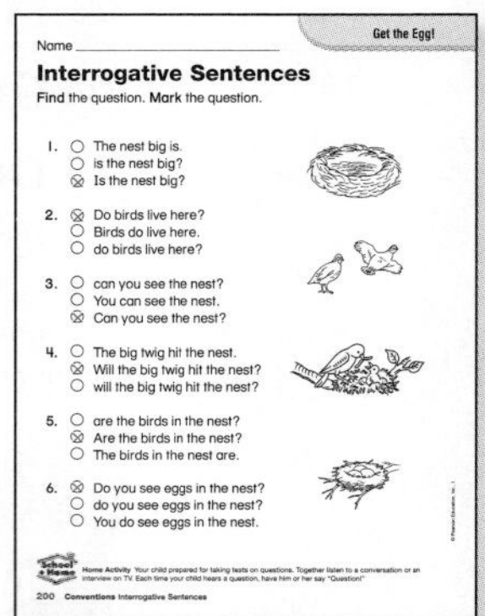
Name ______ Get the Egg!

Interrogative Sentences

Find the question. Mark the question.

1. ○ The nest big is. ○ is the nest big? ⊗ Is the nest big?
2. ⊗ Do birds live here? ○ Birds do live here. ○ do birds live here?
3. ○ can you see the nest? ○ You can see the nest. ⊗ Can you see the nest?
4. ○ The big twig hit the nest. ⊗ Will the big twig hit the nest? ○ will the big twig hit the nest?
5. ○ are the birds in the nest? ⊗ Are the birds in the nest? ○ The birds in the nest are.
6. ⊗ Do you see eggs in the nest? ○ do you see eggs in the nest? ○ You do see eggs in the nest.

200 Conventions Interrogative Sentences

Reader's and Writer's Notebook p. 200

Writing—Realistic Story
Revising Strategy

MINI-LESSON

Revising Strategy: Adding a Sentence

- Yesterday we wrote realistic stories about children seeing an animal. Today we will revise to help people who read the stories. One way to make the stories clearer is to add a sentence.

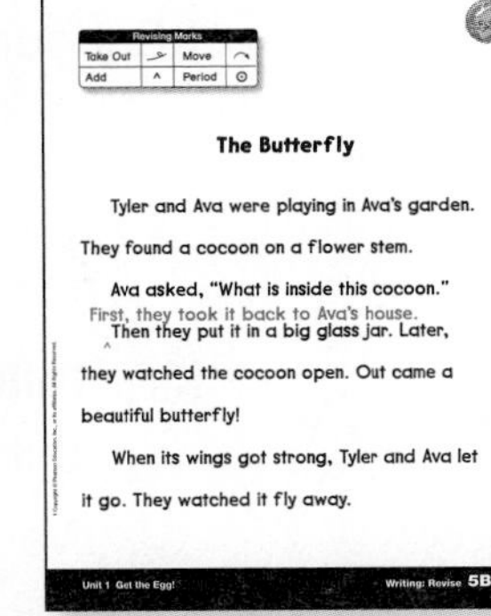

Revising Marks			
Take Out		Move	
Add	^	Period	⊙

The Butterfly

Tyler and Ava were playing in Ava's garden. They found a cocoon on a flower stem.

Ava asked, "What is inside this cocoon." First, they took it back to Ava's house. Then they put it in a big glass jar. Later, they watched the cocoon open. Out came a beautiful butterfly!

When its wings got strong, Tyler and Ava let it go. They watched it fly away.

Unit 1 Get the Egg! Writing: Revise 5B

Writing Transparency 5B
TR DVD

- Display the Revising Tips. Explain that this is a time for making the story clear for anyone who will read it. Tomorrow children will proofread to correct any errors such as misspellings, missing capital letters, or misplaced sentence periods.

Revising Tips

✓ Make sure your story events could really happen.

✓ Add sentences to make the story clearer.

- Use Writing Transparency 5B to model adding sentences. In my realistic story "The Butterfly," Tyler and Ava find a cocoon. I'm going to add the sentence *First, they took it back to Ava's house*. Now it is clearer that part of the story happens in Ava's house, not in her garden. Add the sentence to the transparency. Tell children that they can add sentences to their story as they revise.

Peer conferencing

Peer Revision Pair up children and tell half to read the partner's story. Allow one to two minutes. Then have the readers ask the writers one question about the story. Repeat with second partners reading and asking a question about the other story. Have each writer consider whether a sentence should be added, based on the readers' questions. Circulate to assist children planning to revise their stories. As appropriate, suggest adding sentences to make stories clearer.

Differentiated Instruction

SI Strategic Intervention

Sentence Production If children have difficulty asking questions during peer conferencing, ask them questions about classroom items. For example: *What is this? How many blocks do we have?* Then encourage pairs to ask each other questions about classroom items.

Daily Fix-It

7. the mix is a hitt.
   The mix is a hit.
8. This mix winz too
   This mix wins too.

Discuss the Daily Fix-It corrections with children. Review sentence capitalization and punctuation, the *s* spelling of /z/, the inflected ending -*s*, and the spelling of *hit*.

English Language Learners

Subject-Verb Agreement Be sure children understand that plural forms differ from singular forms.

Objectives

- Revise a draft for clarity.
- Review answers to inquiry questions.

Writing
Realistic Story, continued

Guide practice Have children revise their stories. For those not sure how to revise, have children refer to the Revising Tips or the Key Features of Realistic Stories.

Corrective feedback Circulate to monitor and conference with children as they write. Remind them that they will have time to proofread and edit tomorrow. Today they can make changes in story events or make sentences clearer. Help them understand the benefits of adding or changing words or sentences. Encourage them to make the beginning, middle, and end interesting.

ROUTINE **Quick Write for Fluency** **Team Talk**

1. **Talk** These sentences tell part of a story. Read them aloud, and have children tell what event could be missing from the story.

   We woke up and opened the shades.

   We were going to need our umbrellas!
2. **Write** Have children write a sentence that could be added to the story to make it clearer.
3. **Share** Partners can read the sentences to one another.

Routines Flip Chart

Research and Inquiry
Review and Revise Topic

Teach Tell children that the next step in their project is to review the lists they made to see if they have the information they set out to find. Or, do their lists have information that is not about their topic?

Model We wanted to make a list of wild animals in our neighborhood. First, we picked a place to watch for animals. Then we wrote the names or drew pictures of the animals we would see there. Now I will look at the list I made. I will see if all the animals on the list are wild animals, not pets. If some of the animals are pets, I can cross them off the list. I will also check the spelling of the animal names on my list. If a word is spelled wrong, I will write the word again with the correct spelling.

Guide practice Have children look at the lists they made during Day 3. Instruct them to work with a partner to go over their lists. If necessary, they can look out the classroom window to look for more wild animals. Finally, tell children that tomorrow they will organize their lists in order to share them with others.

Wrap Up Your Day

- ✔ **Phonics Review** List several words with the short *e* sound spelled e, such as *get, bed,* and *step*. Have children read each word and identify the letter that spells the sound /e/.
- ✔ **Fluency** Write *Mom did hop. Stan can run.* Have the class reread the sentences until they can do so with appropriate phrasing.

Differentiated Instruction

Advanced

Information Sources Give children time to check the spelling of animal names on their lists by providing reference books about animals, such as encyclopedias, nonfiction books, or magazines.

Remind children that they heard about Maisie, a girl who caught a toad. Tomorrow they will hear about Maisie and the toad again.

Objectives

- Review the concept: which wild animals live in our neighborhood.
- Build oral vocabulary.
- Identify details in text.

Today at a Glance

Oral Vocabulary
Review

Phonics
◉ Review Short *e: e*
◉ Review Initial Consonant Blends

Comprehension
◉ Main Idea and Details

Story Words
Review

High-Frequency Words
Review

Conventions
Interrogative Sentences

Writing
Realistic Story

Research and Inquiry
Communicate

Check Oral Vocabulary
SUCCESS PREDICTOR

Concept Wrap Up

Question of the Week

Which wild animals live in our neighborhood?

Review Concept

This week we have read and listened to stories about animals that live in different habitats. Today you will listen to find out if you might be able to find a toad, like Maisie's, in your backyard. Read the story.

- Where did Maisie catch the toad? (Possible response: in the garden)
- Why does Maisie use moist dirt for the toad's home? (Possible response: Toads need the moisture to keep from getting dehydrated.)

Review Amazing Words

Orally review the meaning of this week's Amazing Words. Then display this week's concept map. Have children use Amazing Words such as *habitat, survive,* and *moist,* as well as the concept map, to answer the question, "Which wild animals live in our neighborhood?"

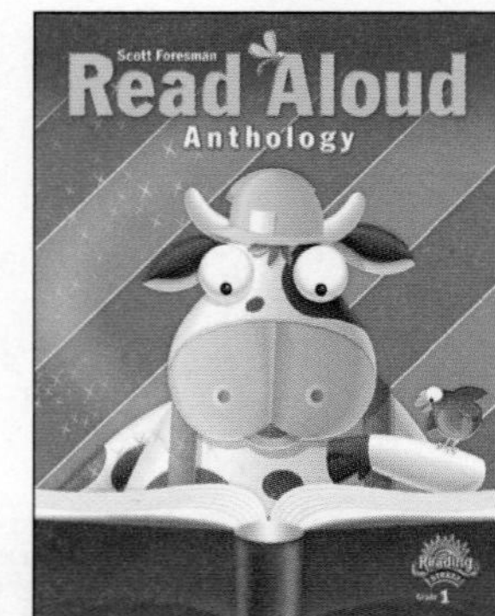

"Maisie Caught a Toad Today"

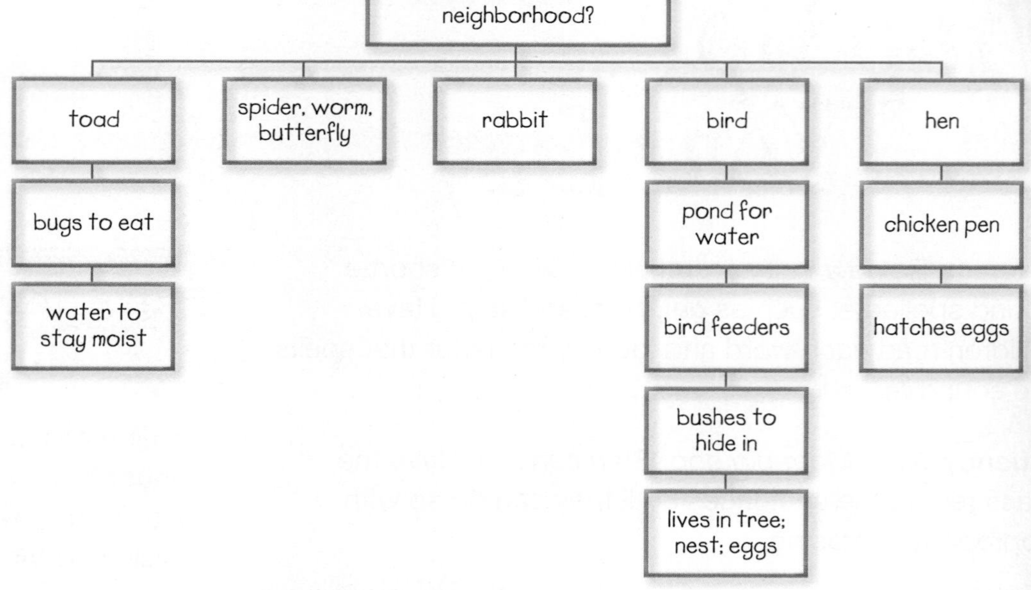

ELL Check Concepts and Language Use the Day 5 instruction on ELL Poster 5 to monitor children's understanding of the lesson concept.

ELL Poster 5

Oral Vocabulary
Amazing Ideas

Connect to the Big Question

Team Talk Pair children and have them discuss how the Question of the Week connects to this unit's Big Question, "Which wild animals live in our neighborhood?" Tell children to use the concept map and what they've learned from this week's Anchored Talks and reading selections to form an Amazing Idea—a realization or "big idea" about **Animals, Tame and Wild**. Then ask each pair to share their Amazing Idea with the class.

Amazing Ideas might include these key concepts:

- Wild animals need food, water, and shelter.
- You can help protect wild animals from danger.

MONITOR PROGRESS **Check Oral Vocabulary**

Call on individuals to use this week's Amazing Words to talk about which wild animals live in our neighborhood. Prompt discussion with the questions below. Monitor children's ability to use the Amazing Words and note which words children are unable to use.

- **What do birds need in their *habitat* to *survive*?**
- **What do you think happens when baby birds *hatch* from their eggs?**
- **How can you help keep a toad *moist* so it won't get too dry?**
- **Where might you hear birds *chirp*?**
- **What does a toad's *croak* sound like?**

If... children have difficulty using the Amazing Words,
then... reteach the unknown words using the Oral Vocabulary Routines, pp. 121a, 126b, 138b, 142b.

Day 1	Day 2	Day 3	Day 4	Day 5
Check Word Reading	Check Word Reading	Check High-Frequency Words/Retelling	Check Fluency	Check Oral Vocabulary

Success Predictor

Amazing Words

habitat	chirp
hatch	croak
survive	moist

ELL

English Language Learners

Amazing Words Give children the initial consonant, consonant blend or digraph (chirp) as clues when you review the Amazing Words.

Objectives

- Segment and blend onset and rime.
- ◎ Review words with vowel sound /e/.
- ◎ Review words with initial consonant blends.

Assess

- Spell words with vowel sound /e/.
- Spell high-frequency words.

Phonological Awareness
Segment and Blend Onset and Rime

Review **Onset and rime**

Have children segment and blend the onset and rime in each word below. If children make an error, model the correct response. Return to the word later in the practice.

/b/ -ed **bed**	/m/ -iss **miss**	/p/ -ig **pig**
/s/ -ad **sad**	/f/ -ox **fox**	/r/ -ug **rug**
/d/ -ish **dish**	/j/ -et **jet**	/v/ -an **van**

Phonics

Short *e*: *e*; Initial Consonant Blends

Review **Target phonics skills**

Write the following sentences on the board. Have children read each one, first quietly to themselves and then aloud as you track the print.

1. **The crab will get wet.**
2. **Meg has ten blocks and six bricks.**
3. **Get on the black sled.**
4. **Glen can skip and Ben can swim.**

Team Talk Have children discuss with a partner which words have the short *e* sound and which words have initial consonant blends. Then call on individuals to share with the class.

Spelling Test
Words with Short *e*

Dictate spelling words

Say each word, read the sentence, repeat the word, and allow time for children to write the word.

1. men	The **men** will fix the deck.
2. red	Lisa fed the red **hen**.
3. step	**Step** on the dock.
4. ten	**Ten** kids are going.
5. net	Get the bird with a **net**.
6. leg	I hit my **leg** on the rocks.
7. jet	Will you get on the big **jet**?
8. sled	Dad is fixing my **sled**.
9. wet	The dog got **wet**.
10. bed	I nap in my **bed**.

High-Frequency Words

11. saw	I **saw** a big cat.
12. your	Kick the ball with **your** foot.

Small Group Time

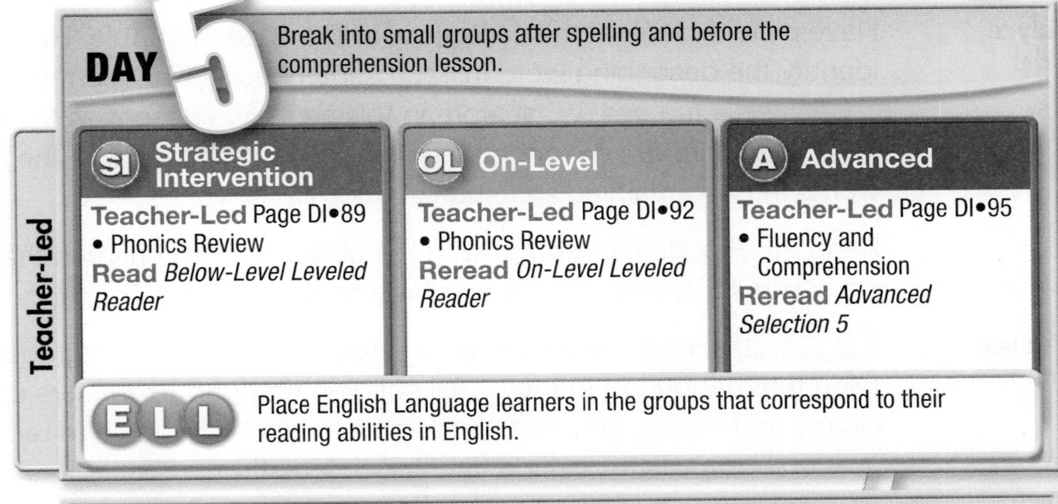
DAY 5 Break into small groups after spelling and before the comprehension lesson.

Teacher-Led

SI Strategic Intervention	OL On-Level	A Advanced
Teacher-Led Page DI•89 • Phonics Review **Read** *Below-Level Leveled Reader*	**Teacher-Led** Page DI•92 • Phonics Review **Reread** *On-Level Leveled Reader*	**Teacher-Led** Page DI•95 • Fluency and Comprehension **Reread** *Advanced Selection 5*

ELL Place English Language learners in the groups that correspond to their reading abilities in English.

Practice Stations
- Words to Know
- Read for Meaning

Independent Activities
- Read independently/Reading Log on *Reader's and Writer's Notebook* p. RR2
- Concept Talk Video

Differentiated Instruction

SI Strategic Intervention

High-Frequency Words To help children recognize the high-frequency words, use them in everyday short sentences that children hear often, such as *Where is your_________?*

English Language Learners

Pronunciation If children tend to pronounce short /e/ as short /i/, especially before the letter *n,* as in *pen*, *den*, and *Ben*, say such words slowly and distinctly, emphasizing the sound /e/ to help with correct pronunciation.

Objectives

- Relate an experience using describing words.
- Speak clearly and accurately.
- Listen attentively.
- Identify describing words.
- Sort words.
- Read aloud fluently and with appropriate phrasing.

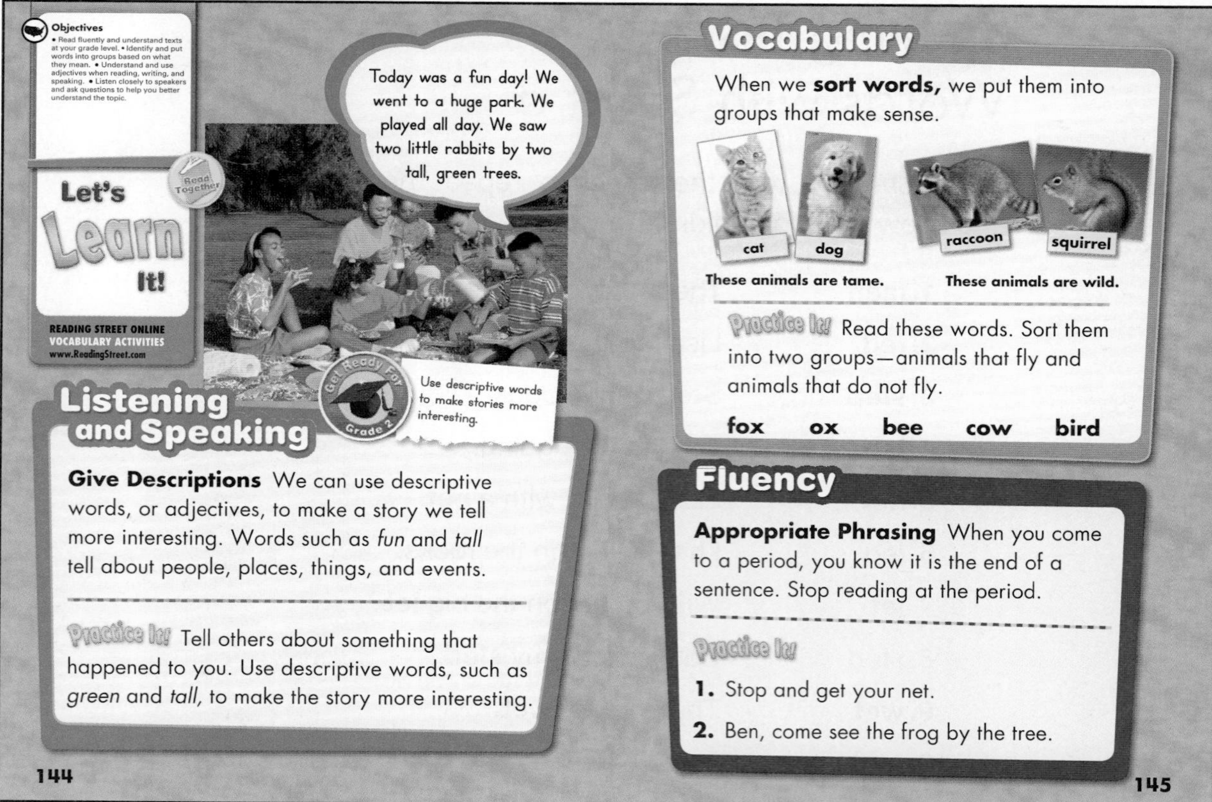

Today was a fun day! We went to a huge park. We played all day. We saw two little rabbits by two tall, green trees.
Let's Learn It!
READING STREET ONLINE VOCABULARY ACTIVITIES www.ReadingStreet.com
Listening and Speaking
Use descriptive words to make stories more interesting.
Give Descriptions We can use descriptive words, or adjectives, to make a story we tell more interesting. Words such as fun and tall tell about people, places, things, and events.
Practice It! Tell others about something that happened to you. Use descriptive words, such as green and tall, to make the story more interesting.
Vocabulary
When we sort words, we put them into groups that make sense.
cat
dog
raccoon
squirrel
These animals are tame.
These animals are wild.
Practice It! Read these words. Sort them into two groups—animals that fly and animals that do not fly.
fox ox bee cow bird
Fluency
Appropriate Phrasing When you come to a period, you know it is the end of a sentence. Stop reading at the period.
Practice It!
1. Stop and get your net.
2. Ben, come see the frog by the tree.
144
145

Student Edition pp. 144–145

Listening and Speaking
Give Descriptions

Teach Have children turn to page 144 of the Student Edition. Read and discuss what members of the family said about their picnic. Remind children that good speakers use describing words to make a story more interesting.

Analyze model Have children look at the sentences in the speech bubble. Help children identify the describing word in each sentence. The first sentence says *Today was a fun day!* What word in this sentence describes the day? That's right. The word *fun* describes the day. Have children name the describing words in the remaining sentences.

Read the Practice It! prompt with the class. Remind children that their story should use describing words to make it interesting.

Introduce prompt **Team Talk** Have pairs take turns listening to and speaking about something that happened to them. Tell children that good speakers speak clearly and slowly, and that good listeners should be able to remember the describing words that made the story interesting.

Vocabulary
Sort Words

Teach Read and discuss the Vocabulary lesson on page 145 of the Student Edition. Use the model to explain that words can be sorted, or put into groups that make sense.

Model Point to the pictures of the cat and the dog. Why do the cat and the dog go together? The cat and the dog go together because they are both tame. Point to the other pictures. Do the squirrel and the raccoon go together? Yes, because both the squirrel and the raccoon are wild animals, not tame.

Guide practice Read the instructions for the Vocabulary Practice It! activity. Then write the headings "Animals that fly" and "Animals that do not fly." Read the first word and have children repeat after you.

Can a fox fly? No, a fox can't fly. So I will say and write *fox* under the heading *Animals that do not fly*.

On their own Have children continue saying and writing the other words under the appropriate heading.

Corrective feedback Circulate around the room and listen as children say and sort the words. Provide assistance as needed.

Fluency
Appropriate Phrasing

Teach Read and discuss the Fluency instructions.

Read words in context Give children a moment to look at the sentences. Then have them read each sentence three or four times until they can read each sentence with appropriate phrasing.

Differentiated Instruction

Strategic Intervention

Visualize Skills Some children might find it helpful to see additional visual representations of the vocabulary skill, sort.

Give Descriptions

In addition to using descriptive words to make a story more interesting, children at Grade 2 should also be able to speak clearly at an appropriate rate, sharing ideas that are focused and to the point.

English Language Learners

Activate Prior Knowledge Ask children to recall some important skills they have learned. Children can identify these skills in their home language and then in English, or demonstrate them using pantomime.

Language Production Have children point to each photo and complete this sentence frame: The child learns to ______.

Objectives

- Identify the main idea and details.
- Read high-frequency and story words.
- Understand the features of a how-to article.

Comprehension

Review **Main idea and details**

Remember that good readers can tell what a story or selection is mostly about. They can tell us its main idea. What do good readers think about to find the main idea in a story? (the details)

To check understanding of main idea and details, read aloud the following story and have children answer the questions that follow.

> Malia found a beautiful rock to add to her rock collection. But where should she put it? She kept all her round rocks in one bag and all her flat rocks in another bag. Malia also had a bag of rough rocks and a bag of black rocks. Malia's new rock was smooth and black, so she put it in the bag with the other black rocks. What a big rock collection she had!

1. What is this story mostly about? (It is mostly about Malia deciding how to add a new rock to her rock collection.)
2. What tells you this? (Malia has a rock collection. She finds a new rock. She has different types of rocks in different bags. Her new rock is smooth and black.)

Vocabulary
High-Frequency and Story Words

Review **High-frequency words**

Review this week's high-frequency words: *saw, small, tree,* and *your*. Provide an example of a rhyming riddle for one of the words for the class to solve, such as: I'm thinking of a word that rhymes with *paw*. (*saw*)

Team Talk Have children work with a partner to trade rhyming riddles for the remaining three words.

Review **Story words**

Write the word *bird*. Read it aloud together. Have children tell what the word means.

Corrective feedback

If... children cannot tell what the story word means,
then... review the definition on page 128a.

Procedural Text
How-to Article

Review Procedural text Review with children that a how-to article gives step-by-step directions for making or doing something. The steps are numbered to show the order in which they should be followed, and most steps have pictures to help readers understand what to do. The author of a how-to article wants readers to follow the steps carefully and in order.

Teach In "Help the Birds," the author tells how to make a bird feeder. The steps are numbered, so it's clear what to do first, second, third, and so on. Each step has a picture that shows what to do.

Model 

When I look at this article, I see there are four steps altogether. The steps are numbered, so I will read and follow Step 1 first. After I read what to do, I look at the picture. Looking at the picture helps me understand exactly what the author wants me to do. The first picture shows me the kind of stick I should get.

Guide practice Ask the following questions to guide children in understanding a how-to article.

- What do the directions in Step 2 say to do? (Possible response: Dip the stick.)
- Why is the picture especially important in Step 2? (Possible response: The picture is important because it shows what to dip the stick in. The words do not give this information.)

On their own Remember, there are four steps in this how-to article. What are the last two steps? (Possible response: Dip the stick in bird seed. Put it up in a tree.)

Differentiated Instruction

 Strategic Intervention

Connect Text to Pictures If children have difficulty understanding the connection between the text and the picture, ask them questions that help clarify the relationship. For example: What is being dipped in peanut butter? Then where is the twig being dipped? What is being clipped on to the tree? Help children understand that, in each case, the word *it* in the text refers to the twig.

Academic Vocabulary

how-to article writing that gives step-by-step instructions for making or doing something

Assess

- ◎ Words with Short *e*
- ◎ Initial Consonant Blends
- • High-Frequency Words

Assessment
Monitor Progress

For a written assessment of short *e*, initial consonant blends, high-frequency words, and identifying main ideas and details, use Weekly Test 5, pages 61–66.

Assess words in isolation

Word reading Use the following reproducible page to assess children's ability to read words in isolation. Call on children to read the words aloud. Start over if necessary.

Assess words in context

Sentence reading Use the reproducible page on page 145f to assess children's ability to read words in context. Call on children to read two sentences aloud. Start over with sentence one if necessary.

MONITOR PROGRESS **Word and Sentence Reading**

If... children have trouble reading words with short *e* and initial consonant blends,
then... use the Reteach Lessons on pp. 188 and 196 in *First Stop*.

If... children cannot read all the high-frequency words,
then... mark the missed words on a high-frequency word list and have the child practice reading the words with a fluent reader.

Monitor accuracy

Record Scores Use the Word/Sentence Reading Chart for this unit in *First Stop.*

Name ______________________________

Read the Words

1. bed
2. Ben
3. small
4. frog
5. block
6. net
7. saw
8. sled
9. stop
10. tree
11. wet
12. your

MONITOR PROGRESS

- Fluency
- Short *e*: *e*
- Initial consonant blends
- High-frequency words

Name ___

Read the Sentences

1. Pop saw six red blocks.

2. Ken, your pet can sit.

3. Ten small frogs will hop.

4. Mom saw red and black dots on hats.

5. Bill, grab six small nets.

6. Jeff will let us sit in a big tree.

MONITOR PROGRESS

- Fluency
- Short *e*: *e*
- Initial consonant blends
- High-frequency words

Objectives

- Identify interrogative sentences.
- Use correct punctuation for interrogative sentences.

Conventions
Interrogative Sentences

Review Remind children that interrogative sentences begin with a capital letter and end with a question mark. Have children give examples of questions.

Guide practice Write the following interrogative sentences. Have children write capital letters and question marks where they belong.

> **1. where is the red bird**
> **2. what does a toad eat**
> **3. when does an owl sleep**

Connect to oral language Display and read the following sentence. Have children work in pairs to ask questions for which the statement could be the answer. Then have them share their responses with the class.

> **The tiger eats dinner after dark.**

On their own Use Let's Practice It! p. 63 from the *Teacher Resource DVD-ROM.*

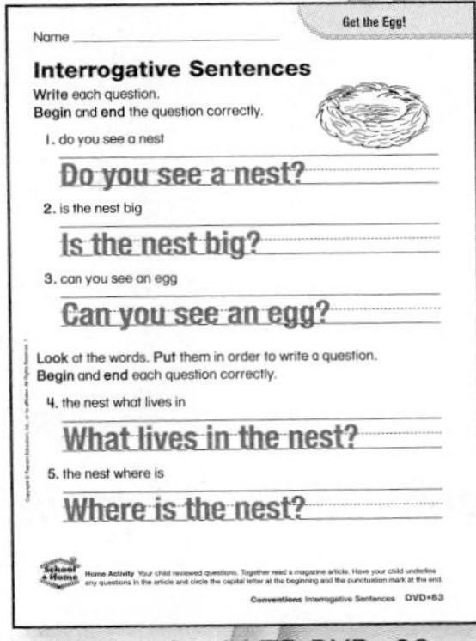
Get the Egg!

Name ______

Interrogative Sentences

Write each question.
Begin and **end** the question correctly.

1. do you see a nest
   Do you see a nest?
2. is the nest big
   Is the nest big?
3. can you see an egg
   Can you see an egg?

Look at the words. **Put** them in order to write a question.
Begin and **end** each question correctly.

4. the nest what lives in
   What lives in the nest?
5. the nest where is
   Where is the nest?

Home Activity Your child reviewed questions. Together read a magazine article. Have your child underline any questions in the article and circle the capital letter at the beginning and the punctuation mark at the end.

Conventions Interrogative Sentences DVD•63

Let's Practice It! TR DVD•63

Daily Fix-It

9. what do frogs eat
What do frogs eat?

10. have you seen a fox
have you seen a fox?

Discuss the Daily Fix-It corrections with children. Review sentence capitalization and punctuation.

English Language Learners

Word Order Point out that in English, questions usually have a different word order than statements. In a question, the auxiliary verb often comes before the subject. Provide additional practice forming statements and questions with the correct word order by having children turn statements such as *The bird flies to the nest.* into questions, such as *Where does the bird fly?*

Objectives

- Edit a draft for spelling, punctuation, and capitalization.
- Create final draft and present.

Writing—Realistic Story

Writer's Craft: Questions

Review Revising Remind children that yesterday they revised their stories. They may have added sentences to make the events clearer. Today they will proofread their stories.

MINI-LESSON

Proofread for Questions

- **Teach** In our stories, if we capitalize and punctuate the sentences correctly, readers will know where the sentences begin and end. They will also be able to tell if a sentence is a telling sentence or a sentence that asks a question. When we proofread, we check to make sure the sentences are correct.
- **Model** Let's look at my story about Tyler and Ava. Display Writing Transparency 5C. I'm going to make sure that each sentence begins with a capital letter and ends with punctuation. I'll check the beginning and end of each sentence. Model checking the beginning and end of each sentence. Look: Ava asks a question, but I ended the sentence with a period. I will delete the period and replace it with a question mark. Use a deletion mark to show that the period should be removed from the end of Ava's question, add a question mark, then continue to check.

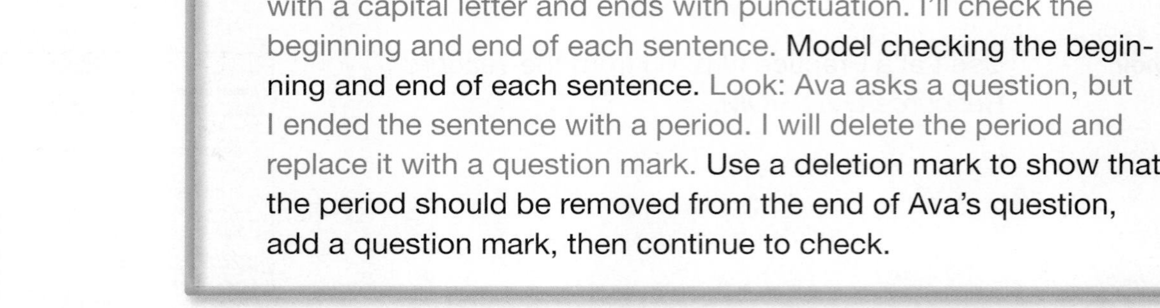

Writing Transparency 5C
TR DVD

Proofread Display the Proofreading Tips. Have children proofread their stories to correct any misspellings, missing capital letters, or errors with periods. Circulate to assist children.

Proofreading Tips

- ✔ Are words such as *first, then,* and *last* spelled correctly?
- ✔ Do sentences that ask end with a question mark?
- ✔ Do sentences that tell end with a period?
- ✔ Do all sentences end with punctuation?

Present

Have children make a final draft of their stories, with their revisions and proofreading corrections. Help as appropriate.

Choose an option for children to present their stories. They might make a book out of each story by writing the title and drawing an illustration on a separate sheet of paper to create a cover. When they have finished, help them complete a Self-Evaluation form.

ROUTINE Quick Write for Fluency — Team Talk

1. **Talk** Have partners take one minute to tell each other about their stories.
2. **Write** Have children write a sentence about what might happen next in their partners' stories.
3. **Share** Partners trade sentences and read them aloud.

Routines Flip Chart

Teacher Note

Self-Evaluation Make copies of the Self-Evaluation form from the *Teacher Resource DVD-ROM*, and hand them out to children.

ELL

English Language Learners

Support Editing For children to whom the sounds and spelling of English still are not very familiar, look for spelling improvement little by little from week to week rather than rapid development. Help children make progress a word at a time and learn word meanings.

Objectives

- Review concept: wild animals that live in our neighborhood.
- Organize information.
- Present results of an inquiry project.

Research and Inquiry
Communicate

Teach

Tell children that today they will finish their lists about wild animals that live in the neighborhood and share the list with others.

Model

Think Aloud Display the list of wild animals that live in the neighborhood. I will review my list and circle the animals that live in the neighborhood. Those will be the animals I will include in my final list. My list is about wild animals that live in the neighborhood. I will start by writing *Wild Animals That Live in the Neighborhood* as the title of my list. I will write the title at the top of my page. Before I write my list, I will make sure I know that all the animal names on my list are spelled correctly. If I have questions about spelling, I will use books and magazines we have in the classroom to find the correct spelling.

Guide practice

Review children's lists. Work with them to write the title of the list at the top of their page and be sure the names of the animals on the list are spelled correctly.

On their own

Have children write a list to share with the class. Suggest they write the title at the top of a sheet of paper and then list the animals. Have children break themselves into groups. Instruct them to read aloud their lists to one another so they can compare the animals they saw. Remind children how to be good speakers and listeners:

- Good speakers speak clearly so their listeners can understand what they are saying.
- Good listeners pay attention to the speaker and do not talk while someone else is speaking.

Wrap Up Your Week!

Question of the Week

Which wild animals live in our neighborhood?

Think Aloud This week we explored the topic of wild animals in our neighborhood. In the story *Get the Egg!* we read about two children who helped save a bird's egg that had fallen out of a nest in a tree. In the how-to article *Help the Birds,* we read directions for how to make a bird feeder. Both reading selections told of ways we can help wild animals in our neighborhood. Have children recall their Amazing Ideas about animals. Then have children use these ideas to help them demonstrate their understanding of the Question of the Week.

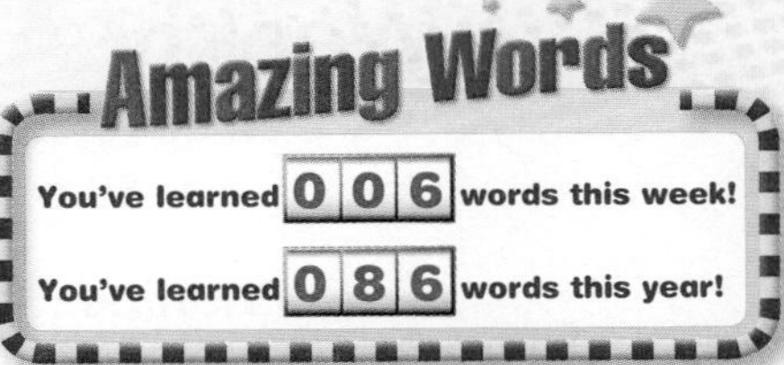
Amazing Words
You've learned 006 words this week!
You've learned 086 words this year!

ELL

English Language Learners

Poster Preview Prepare children for next week by using Week 6, ELL Poster 6. Read the Poster Talk-Through to introduce the concept and vocabulary. Ask children to identify and describe objects and actions in the art.

Selection Summary
Send home the summary of *Animal Park* in English and the child's home language if available. Children can read the summary with family members.

Preview NEXT WEEK

Tell children that next week they will read about ways we can learn about animals by watching them.

DAY 5 Assessment Checkpoints for the Week

Weekly Assessment

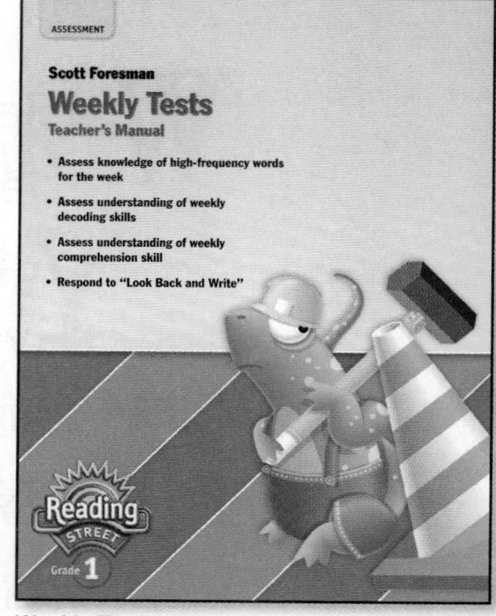

Weekly Tests

Use pp. 61–66 of *Weekly Tests* to check:

- ✔ **Phonics** Short *e: e*
- ✔ **Phonics** Initial Consonant Blends
- ✔ **Comprehension Skill** Main Idea and Details
- ✔ **High-Frequency Words**

saw	tree
small	your

Differentiated Asssessment

Advanced

On-Level

Strategic Intervention

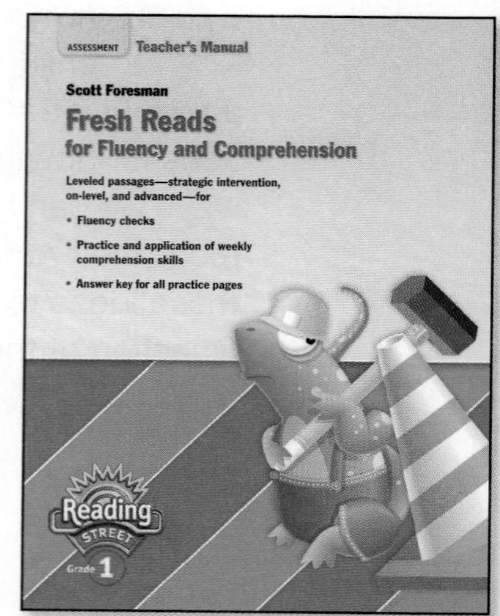

Fresh Reads for Fluency and Comprehension

Use pp. 61–66 of *Fresh Reads for Fluency and Comprehension* to check:

- ✔ **Comprehension Skill** Main Idea and Details
- ✔ Review **Comprehension Skill** Character and Setting

Managing Assessment

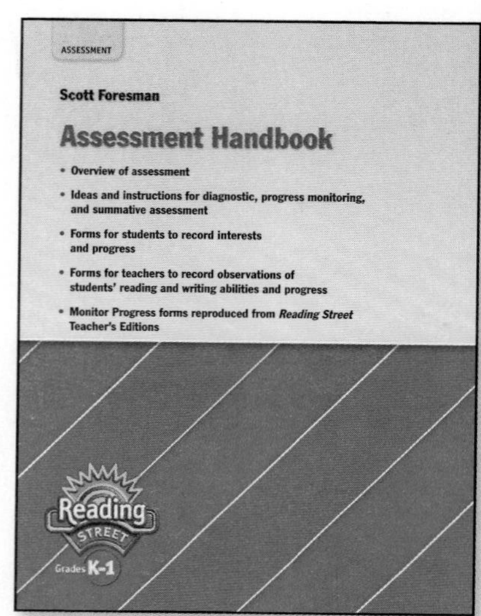

Assessment Handbook

Use *Assessment Handbook* for:

- ✔ **Weekly Assessment Blackline Masters for Monitoring Progress**
- ✔ **Observation Checklists**
- ✔ **Record-Keeping Forms**
- ✔ **Portfolio Assessment**

Why Woodpeckers Peck

Listen! Do you hear a pecking sound? A woodpecker might be living in a tree near you. Some woodpeckers live deep in the forest. Others live near people. Woodpeckers might live in a tree next to your home!

Can you picture this bird? Red feathers stick up on top of its head. Its neck and the rest of its body are covered with black and white feathers. You might see a woodpecker using its tail and strong legs to help it stand on the side of a tree. Its long feet let it walk up and down the tree trunk.

What do woodpeckers do when they are hanging on trees? They peck! They tap hard with their long, pointy beaks. They peck to get the bugs that live in the tree trunk. Then they eat the bugs.

Woodpeckers can send a signal. They make loud sounds by hitting their beaks on things. The loud pecking tells other birds to stay away.

Woodpeckers also peck to make places to live. They peck, peck, peck very hard. They make a hole in the side of a tree! Then, they nest in the hole. It is their home. Woodpeckers are the best at pecking!

Advanced Selection 5 **Vocabulary:** beaks, signal

Pacing Small Group Instruction

5 Day Plan

DAY 1	• Phonemic Awareness/ Phonics • Decodable Reader
DAY 2	• Phonemic Awareness/ Phonics • Decodable Reader
DAY 3	• Phonemic Awareness/ Phonics • Leveled Reader
DAY 4	• High-Frequency Words • Decodable Reader
DAY 5	• Phonics Review • Leveled Reader

3 or 4 Day Plan

DAY 1	• Phonemic Awareness/ Phonics • Decodable Reader
DAY 2	• Phonemic Awareness/ Phonics • Decodable Reader
DAY 3	• Phonemic Awareness/ Phonics • Leveled Reader
DAY 4	• High-Frequency Words • Decodable Reader

3 Day Plan: Eliminate the shaded box.

SI Strategic Intervention — DAY 1

Phonemic Awareness • Phonics

- **Distinguish /e/** Reteach pp. 122–123 of the Teacher's Edition. Model identifying short *e*. I hear the sound /e/ at the beginning of the word *egg*. I hear the sound /e/ in the middle of the word *bed*. Then have children practice identifying short *e* on their own.

set	**edge**	**bell**
elf	**web**	**ten**

- **Short *e*: *e*** Reteach p. 123a of the Teacher's Edition. Then have children spell *get* using letter tiles. Monitor their work.
  - Change the *g* in *get* to *p*. What is the new word?

  - Change the *t* in *pet* to *n*. What is the new word?

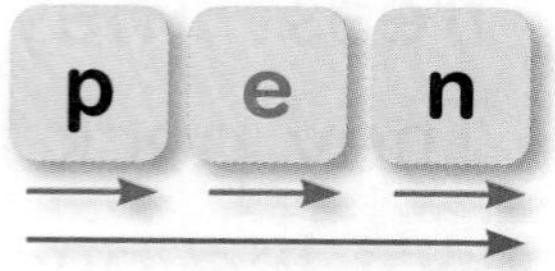

  - Change the *p* in *pen* to *h*. What is the new word?

Decodable Practice Reader 5A

- **Review** Review words with short *e* and the high-frequency words *a, here, the, he, like(s), to*. Then have children blend and read these words from the story: *naps, vet, tags, well, den.*

  If... children have difficulty with any of these words, **then...** reteach the word by modeling. Have children practice the words, with feedback from you, until they can read them independently.

Have children reread the text orally. To achieve optimal fluency, children should reread the text three or four times.

Decodable Practice Reader 5A

Objectives
- Isolate medial sounds in one-syllable spoken words.
- Decode words in isolation by applying common letter-sound correspondences, including: single letters (vowels) including short e.

DAY 2

Phonemic Awareness • Phonics

■ **Segment and Blend Phonemes** Reteach p. 126c of the Teacher's Edition. Model segmenting and blending these words. Then have children practice segmenting and blending on their own.

black /b/ /l/ /a/ /k/ **stop** /s/ /t/ /o/ /p/ **truck** /t/ /r/ /u/ /k/

■ **Initial Consonant Blends** Reteach p. 126d of the Teacher's Edition. Then have children spell *flip* using letter tiles. Monitor their work.

- Change the *f* in *flip* to *c*. What is the new word?

- Change the *i* in *clip* to *a*. What is the new word?

- Change the *c* in *clap* to *s*. What is the new word?

Decodable Practice Reader 5B

■ **Review** Review words with initial consonant blends and the high-frequency words *a, the, green, you*. Then have children blend and read these words from the story: *frog, grass, spot*.

If... children have difficulty with any of these words,
then... reteach the word by modeling. Have children practice the words, with feedback from you, until they can read them independently.

Have children reread the text orally. To achieve optimal fluency, children should reread the text three or four times.

Decodable Practice Reader 5B

More Reading

Use Leveled Readers or other text at children's instructional level to develop fluency.

Objectives

- Blend spoken phonemes to form one-syllable words, including consonant blends.
- Decode words in isolation by applying common letter-sound correspondences, including: consonant blends.

Phonemic Awareness • Phonics

- **Generate Rhyming Words** Model generating rhyming words. Say each sound in the word *red:* /r/ /e/ /d/. Have children say the sounds with you and then say the sounds by themselves. Now listen as I say another word with the same ending sounds as *red*. Model the sounds of the word *bed*. Have children say the sounds with you and then say the sounds by themselves. Point out that *red* and *bed* are rhyming words.

  Work with children to generate rhyming words for the following words.

  - **men** (ten, hen, when, pen)
  - **net** (set, jet, bet, let)

- **Short *e*: *e* and Initial Consonant Blends** Reteach p. 138e of the Teacher's Edition. Have children blend and read these additional words to help them practice the target phonics skills.

met	glad	step	ten	neck	trip

For a complete literacy instructional plan and additional practice with this week's target skills and strategies, see the **Leveled Reader Teaching Guide.**

Concept Literacy Leveled Reader

- **Preview and Predict** Read the title and the author's name. Have children look at the cover and ask them to describe what they see. Help children activate their prior knowledge by asking them to look through the story and to use the photos to predict things that might take place.
- **Set a Purpose** Remind children that setting a purpose for reading can help them better understand what they read. Guide children to pay attention to the kinds of animals that can be found in a neighborhood.
- **Read** Provide corrective feedback as children read the story orally. During reading, ask them if they were able to confirm any of the predictions they made prior to the story.

If... children have difficulty reading the story individually,
then... read a sentence aloud as children point to each word. Then have the group reread the sentences as they continue pointing. Continue reading in this way until children read individually.

Concept Literacy

- **Retell** Have children take turns retelling the story. Help them identify the neighborhood animals by asking, What animals can be found in the neighborhood? Which animals are found in the air (on the ground)?

Objectives

- Orally generate a series of original rhyming words using a variety of phonograms.
- Decode words in isolation by applying common letter-sound correspondences, including: single letters (vowels) including short e.

DAY 4

High-Frequency Words

- **Review** Write *saw, tree, your, small* on the board. Model saying each word. Then have children read each word, spell each word as you point to each letter, and have them say each word again. Allow time for children to practice reading these high-frequency words using the word cards.

Decodable Practice Reader 5C

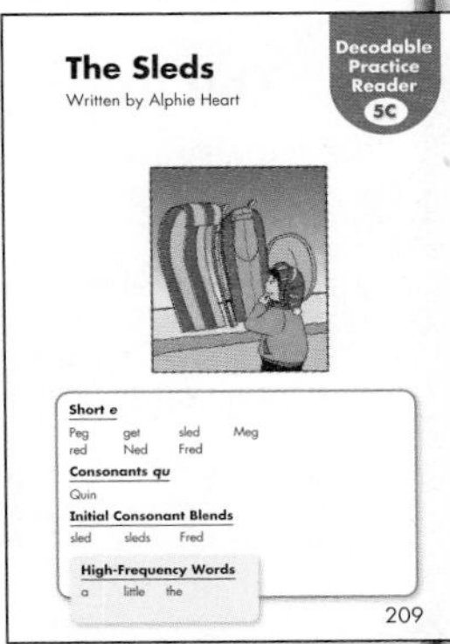

Decodable Practice Reader 5C

- **Review** Use the word lists to review short *e* and initial consonant blends. Be sure that children understand that the letter *e* can make the sound /e/ and that the sounds of the letters in a consonant blend are blended together.

  If... children have difficulty reading the story individually, **then...** read a sentence aloud as children point to each word. Then have the group reread the sentences as they continue pointing. Continue reading in this way until children read individually.

Check comprehension by having children retell the story including the characters, plot, and setting. Have children locate words in the story that have short *e* and initial consonant blends. List the words children identify. Then have children sort the words in a chart with columns labeled Short *e* and Initial Consonant Blends. Point out that some words can be sorted into more than one group.

Short *e*	Initial Consonant Blends
Peg	sled
red	sleds
get	Fred
Ned	
sled	
Meg	

Objectives

- Decode words in context by applying common letter-sound correspondences, including: single letters (vowels) including short e.
- Read at least 100 high-frequency words from a commonly used list.

More Reading

Use Leveled Readers or other text at children's instructional level.

More Reading

Use Leveled Readers or other text at children's instructional level.

Phonics Review

- **Short *e*: *e* and Initial Consonant Blends** Write these sentences on the board. Have children read them aloud as you track the print. Then call on individuals to blend and read the underlined words.

Can <u>Jed</u> <u>spell</u>?

<u>Peg</u> has a <u>red</u> <u>dress</u>.

His <u>pet</u> dog is <u>black</u>.

The <u>frog</u> will hop in <u>grass</u>.

For a complete literacy instructional plan and additional practice with this week's target skills and strategies, see the **Leveled Reader Teaching Guide.**

Below-Level Leveled Reader

Below-Level Reader

- **Preview and Predict** Read the title, the author's name, and the illustrator's name. Have children look at the cover and ask them to describe what they see. Help children activate their prior knowledge by asking them to look through the story and to use the pictures to predict things that might take place.
- **Set a Purpose** Remind children that setting a purpose for reading can help them better understand what they read. Guide children to pay attention to the animals that need help from the vet.
- **Read** Provide corrective feedback as children read the story orally. During reading, ask them if they were able to confirm any of the predictions they made prior to the story.

  If... children have difficulty reading the story individually,
  then... read each sentence aloud as children point to each word. Then have the group reread the sentences as they continue pointing.

- **Story Structure** Have children identify the characters, setting, and events of the story.

Objectives

- Decode words in context by applying common letter-sound correspondences, including: single letters (vowels) including short e.
- Describe characters in a story.

DAY 1

Phonics • Spelling

- **Short *e*: *e*** Write the following words on the board and have children practice reading words with short *e*.

  hen **bell** **fed** **stem**

- **Short *e* Words** Remind children that each spelling word has the letter *e*, which spells the /e/ sound. Clarify the pronunciation and meaning of each word. For example, say: *Men* means more than one man. Have children identify which of the following words begin with a consonant blend: *red, ten, step, net, sled, wet*.

Objectives

- Decode words in isolation by applying common letter-sound correspondences, including: single letters (vowels) including short e.

DAY 2

Phonics • High-Frequency Words

- **Initial Consonant Blends** Write the following words on the board and have children practice reading words with initial consonant blends.

  drip **stack** **trim** **block**

- **High-Frequency Words** Hold up this week's High-Frequency Word Cards *(saw, tree, your, small)* and review proper pronunciation. Continue holding the cards and have children chorally read each word. To help children demonstrate their understanding of the words, provide them with oral sentence frames such as: The squirrel climbs a _______. (tree)

High-Frequency Word Cards for Grade 1
Reading
PEARSON

Objectives

- Decode words in isolation by applying common letter-sound correspondences, including: consonant blends.
- Read at least 100 high-frequency words from a commonly used list.

Pacing Small Group Instruction

20-30 min.

5 Day Plan

DAY 1	• Phonics • Spelling • Decodable Reader
DAY 2	• Phonics • High-Frequency Words • Decodable Reader
DAY 3	• Leveled Reader
	• Conventions • Main Selection
DAY 5	• Phonics Review • Leveled Reader

3 or 4 Day Plan

DAY 1	• Phonics • Spelling • Decodable Reader
DAY 2	• Phonics • High-Frequency Words • Decodable Reader
DAY 3	• Leveled Reader
DAY 4	• Conventions • Main Selection

3 Day Plan: Eliminate the shaded box.

Decodable Practice Readers Units R-1
Reading Street
Practice phonics skills
Blending practice
Reread for fluency

Decodable Practice Readers

On-Level

For a complete literacy instructional plan and additional practice with this week's target skills and strategies, see the **Leveled Reader Teaching Guide.**

On-Level Leveled Reader

On-Level

- **Preview and Predict** Read the title, the author's name, and the illustrator's name. Have children look at the cover and ask them to describe in detail what they see. Help children preview the story by asking them to look through the story and to use the pictures to predict things that might take place.
- **Main Idea and Details** Before reading, remind children that setting a purpose for reading can help them better understand what they read. Guide children to pay attention to what happens in the story and to think about what the story is mostly about.
- **Read** During reading, monitor children's comprehension by providing higher-order thinking questions. Ask:
  - How do you think Fran feels about seeing the animals? Why do you think so?
  - Is your neighborhood like Fran's or is it different? Tell how.

  To help children gain a better understanding of the text, build upon their responses with a group discussion.
- **Story Structure** With a partner, have children name the characters and setting and take turns telling the story events in order.
  - Who is the story about?
  - Where and when does the story take place?
- **Text to Self** Help children make personal connections to the story. Ask:
  - If you went for a walk in your neighborhood, what animals might you see?

Objectives
- Locate details about stories.
- Make connections to own experiences.

DAY 4

Conventions

- **Interrogative Sentences** Remind children that a question is an asking sentence.
  - A question begins with a capital letter. It ends with a question mark.
- Write this question: *Where is the bird?* This is a question. Point out the beginning capital letter and the question mark at the end.

  Ask children to dictate questions. Write the questions and have children identify each beginning capital letter and question mark.

Objectives

- Recognize punctuation marks at the end of interrogative sentences.

More Reading

Use Leveled Readers or other text at children's instructional level to develop fluency.

Phonics Review

- **Short *e*: *e* and Initial Consonant Blends** Have children practice blending and reading words that contain this week's target phonics skills. Write the following words on the board, and say and sound out each word with the children.

plan	**snap**	**jet**	**smell**	**press**
drop	**tell**	**frog**	**spot**	**wet**

Then have children circle the words with short *e*.

Objectives

- Decode words in isolation by applying common letter-sound correspondences, including: single letters (vowels) including short e.
- Decode words in isolation by applying common letter-sound correspondences, including: consonant blends.

Pacing Small Group Instruction

20–30 mins.

5 Day Plan	
DAY 1	• Phonics • Advanced Selection
DAY 2	• Phonics • Comprehension • Main Selection
DAY 3	• Leveled Reader
DAY 4	• Comprehension • Paired Selection
DAY 5	• Fluency • Comprehension • Advanced Selection

3 or 4 Day Plan	
DAY 1	• Phonics • Advanced Selection
DAY 2	• Phonics • Comprehension • Main Selection
DAY 3	• Leveled Reader
DAY 4	• Comprehension • Paired Selection

3 Day Plan: Eliminate the shaded box.

A Advanced — DAY 1

Phonics • Advanced Selection

- **Short *e*: *e*** Have children practice with longer words containing short *e*.

enter	**head**	**meadow**	**ever**	**empty**
weather	**explain**	**edge**	**breakfast**	**feather**

Have children write the words on word cards and sort the words by the spelling of the short *e* sound (*e* or *ea*). Then have partners choose several words to use in sentences.

Advanced Selection 5

- **Advanced Selection 5** Before reading, have children identify these story words: *beaks* and *signal*. If they do not know these words, provide oral sentences with the words in context to help children determine their meaning. After reading, have children recall the two most important ideas of the story.

Objectives

- Decode words in isolation by applying common letter-sound correspondences, including: single letters (vowels) including short e.

A Advanced — DAY 2

Phonics • Comprehension

- **Initial Consonant Blends** Have children practice with longer words containing initial consonant blends.

broken	**smudge**	**skillet**	**blanket**
freedom	**pleasant**	**clever**	**grandpa**

Have children write the words on word cards and sort by blends with *s*, *l*, and *r*. Ask children to use each word in a sentence.

- **Comprehension** Have children silently read this week's main selection, *Get the Egg!*. Have them retell the story identifying characters, setting, and sequence of events. Discuss what makes *Get the Egg!* realistic fiction. Point out that story events could happen in real life.

Get the Egg!

Objectives

- Decode words in isolation by applying common letter-sound correspondences, including: consonant blends.

DAY 3

For a complete literacy instructional plan and additional practice with this week's target skills and strategies, see the **Leveled Reader Teaching Guide.**

Advanced Leveled Reader

Cary and the Wildlife Shelter
by Libby McCord
illustrated by Aleksey Ivanov

Advanced Reader

- **Activate Prior Knowledge** Read the title, the author's name, and the illustrator's name. Have children look at the cover and describe in detail what they see. Remind them that a *habitat* is a place where plants and animals live. Then activate the children's prior knowledge by asking them to name and describe some *habitats* they know about.
- **Main Idea and Details** Before reading, remind children that setting a purpose for reading can help them better understand what they read. Guide children to pay attention to what happens in the story and to think about what the story is mostly about.
- **Read** During reading, monitor children's comprehension by providing higher-order thinking questions. Ask:
  - Why is the work done at the Wildlife Shelter important for animals?
  - What else might Cary and Mom do to help wild animals?

  Build on children's answers to help them gain a better understanding of the text.
- **Story Structure** With a partner, have children name the characters and setting and take turns telling the story events in order.
  - What happens at the beginning of the story? in the middle?
  - How does the story end?
- **Text to Self** Help children make personal connections to the story. Ask:
  - What could you do to help wild animals?

Objectives

- Locate details about stories.
- Retell a story's beginning, with attention to sequence of events.

More Reading

Use Leveled Readers or other text at children's instructional level.

More Reading

Use Leveled Readers or other text at children's instructional level.

Comprehension

Help the Birds

- **Comprehension** Have children silently read this week's paired selection, "Help the Birds." Have them recall the sequence of steps. Then have them state the purpose of the selection.

  Talk about what makes "Help the Birds" a how-to article. Ensure that children understand that a how-to article gives directions for how to make or do something.

- **Text to Self** Besides making a birdfeeder, have children name other ways they might help birds.

Objectives

- Retell the order of events in a text by referring to words.
- Retell the order of events in a text by referring to illustrations.

A Advanced DAY 5

Fluency • Comprehension

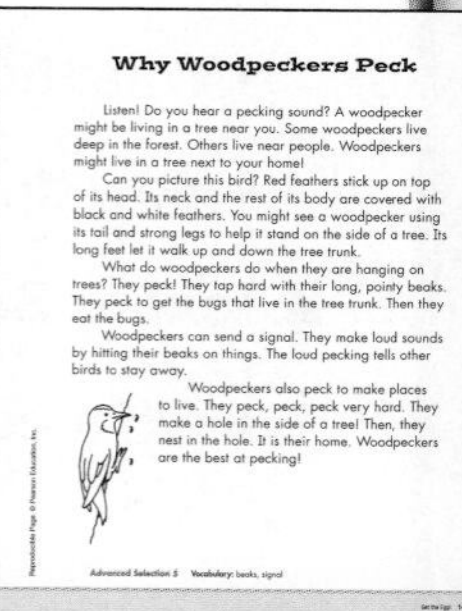

Advanced Selection 5

- **Fluency** Using the first few sentences of Advanced Selection 5, model reading with appropriate expression. Then have children read the selection to a partner as you listen to their reading. Provide corrective feedback as needed.
- **Comprehension** After they have finished reading the selection, have children recall what they learned about woodpeckers. Then, on the back of the selection page, have them write three sentences that describe what woodpeckers look like and what they do.

Objectives

- Read aloud grade-level appropriate text with fluency.

The ELL lessons are organized by strands. Use them to scaffold the weekly lesson curriculum or during small-group time.

Concept Development

Which wild animals live in our neighborhood?

- **Activate Prior Knowledge** Write the Question of the Week and read it aloud. Underline the word *neighborhood* and have children say it with you. Neighborhood is where you live. Display a picture of a suburban or city street with houses, apartments or condos, whichever is more common to your school district. Even though people are most common in a neighborhood, there are still animals that live there. What wild animals have you seen in your neighborhood? (birds, squirrels, mice, raccoons, and so on.)
- **Connect to New Concept** Have children turn to pages 120–121 in the Student Edition. Read the title and have children track the print as you read it. Point to the pictures one at a time and use them to guide a discussion about the types of wild animals that children can find in their neighborhood. For example, point to the butterfly. What is this? (a butterfly) You may not think about a butterfly as a wild animal, but insects are animals. So are worms, spiders, and rabbits.
- **Develop Concepts** Display ELL Poster 5 and have children identify the animals they know. (rabbit, dog, cat) What do the children use to take care of their pets? Have children point to things pets need on the Poster. (food, water, cage, leash, bed) Use the leveled prompts below to assess understanding and build oral language. Point to pictures on the poster as you guide discussion.

Beginning Ask yes/no questions, such as, Is the rabbit getting fed? Is the cat on a leash?

Intermediate Ask children questions that can be answered with simple sentences. What is the cat doing? Why is the dog on a leash? How do the boys take care of the rabbit?

Advanced/Advanced-High Have children answer the Question of the Week by giving specific examples from the poster and their own experiences.

- **Review Concepts and Connect to Writing** Review children's understanding of the concept at the end of the week. Ask them to write in response to these questions: What wild animals have you seen near your home? What English words did you learn this week? Write and display key ideas from the discussion.

Objectives

- Use prior knowledge and experiences to understand meanings in English.
- Internalize new basic and academic language by using it and reusing it in meaningful ways in speaking and writing activities that build language attainment.
- Use visual, contextual, and linguistic support to enhance and confirm understanding of increasingly complex and elaborated spoken language.

Content Objectives

- Describe the wild animals that live in the neighborhood.

Language Objectives

- Share information orally.
- Use academic language for identifying local wild animals.

Daily Planner

DAY 1	• **Frontload Concepts** • **Preteach** Comprehension Skill, Vocabulary, Phonemic Awareness/ Phonics, Conventions/ Writing
DAY 2	• **Review** Concepts, Vocabulary, Comprehension Skill • **Frontload Main Selection** • **Practice** Phonemic Awareness/Phonics, Conventions/Writing
DAY 3	• **Review** Concepts, Comprehension Skill, Vocabulary, Conventions/ Writing • **Reread Main Selection** • **Practice** Phonemic Awareness/Phonics
DAY 4	• **Review Concepts** • **Read ELL/ELD Readers** • **Practice** Phonemic Awareness/Phonics, Conventions/Writing
DAY 5	• **Review** Concepts, Vocabulary, Comprehension Skill, Phonemic Awareness/ Phonics, Conventions/ Writing • **Reread ELL/ELD Readers**

**See the* ELL Handbook for *ELL Workshops with targeted instruction.*

Concept Talk Video

Use this week's Concept Talk Video to help children build background knowledge. See the Conept Talk Video Routine (*ELL Handbook,* page 500) for suggestions.

Language Objectives

- Segment and blend phonemes.

Transfer Skills

Short vowels may be difficult for many English language learners because in many languages, short vowel sounds may not exist or may only have approximations. For example, English language learners from various language backgrounds may pronounce short *i* like the *ee* in *see*.

ELL Teaching Routine

For more practice with the sound /e/, use the Sound-by-Sound Blending Routine (*ELL Handbook*, page 493).

ELL English Language Learners

Phonemic Awareness: Distinguish /e/ in Initial and Medial Positions

■ **Preteach words with the sound /e/**

- Have children open to pages 122–123. What is nestled in the tree? (nest) Say the word *nest* slowly. I'm going to say the sounds in *nest*. Listen for the /e/ sound: /n/ /e/ /s/ /t/. I hear the /e/ sound in the middle of the word *nest*. Say /e/ with me. Say these words as you point to corresponding pictures: *egg, elf, pet, send, bell.* Have children repeat each word and raise their hand if they hear the /e/ sound in the middle of the word.
- What is this woman wearing? (dress) Listen to the /e/ sound in *dress*. Slowly segment and blend the sounds: /d/ /r/ /e/ /s/, *dress*. What is the middle sound in *dress?* /e/ Yes, say the middle sound in *dress* with me: /e/.
- Have children point out other words that contain the short *e* sound /e/.

Phonics: Short *e*

■ **Preteach** Display Sound-Spelling Card 6. This is an elephant. What sound do you hear at the beginning of *elephant*? (/e/) Say it with me: /e/. Point to the *e*. The /e/ sound is spelled *e* in *elephant*.

■ **Listen and Write** Distribute Write and Wipe Boards.

- Write the word *bell* on the board. Copy this word. As you write *e*, say the sound to yourself: /e/. Now say the sound aloud. (/e/) Underline the *e* in *bell*. The letter *e* spells /e/ in *bell*.
- Repeat using the word *elevator*.

Objectives

- Distinguish sounds and intonation patterns of English with increasing ease.

ELL English Language Learners

Reteach and Practice Short *e*

- Write the following words on the board and have children read them aloud with you: *best, yes, neck, rest, best, lent.* Segment and blend each word with the children. Point out the short *e* sound in each word.
- Leave the words on the board and help children understand the words with sentences and gestures, such as *Your neck is here*. (Point to your neck.); *Yes, I want to play*. (Shake your head *yes*.) Have children read the words with you, repeating each word.

Leveled Support

Beginning Have children chant, *Yes, yes, we are the best!*
Intermediate Have children write the words *yes* and *best*.
Advanced/Advanced-High Have children write *best* and the word that rhymes with it. (*rest*)

Phonics: Initial Consonant Blends

Preteach Have children turn to Envision It! on page 126 of the Student Edition.

- The word for the picture is *train*. Point to the train to show meaning. What sound do you hear at the beginning of *train*? (/t/ /r/) Say it with me: /t/ /r/. The sounds /t/ /r/ are spelled *tr*.
- The first word in the list of Words I Can Blend is *stop*. What sounds do you hear at the beginning of *stop*? (/s/ /t/) The sounds /s/ /t/ are spelled *st* in *stop*.
- Repeat with the other words in the list.

Practice Distribute Letter Tiles *s, t, p, l, t, r, m, o, p,* and *t* to pairs.

1. Blend the sounds in *stomp* and have children spell *stomp* with their tiles: /s/ /t/ /o/ /m/ /p/
2. Drop the *m*. Spell *stop*.
3. Replace the *st*. Spell *plop*.
4. Replace the *p*. Spell *plot*.
5. Replace the *pl*. Spell *trot*.

Objectives

- Distinguish sounds and intonation patterns of English with increasing ease.
- Use visual, contextual, and linguistic support to enhance and confirm understanding of increasingly complex and elaborated spoken language.

Language Objectives

- Learn the initial consonant blend sounds *bl* and *st*.
- Read words containing initial consonant blends.

Catch Up

Consonant blends are formed when two or more consonants are next to each other in a word. Each letter produces its own sound so when we say the word, we hear each consonant sound.

Transfer Skills

When a word begins with two consonants like *c* and *r*, you blend the sounds of the two consonants together. In the word *crib*, take the /k/ sound and /r/ sound and put them together: /kr/. Try it: /kr/, /kr/, *crib*.

Practice Page

ELL Handbook pages 276 and 285 provide additional practice for this week's skills.

Content Objectives

- Monitor and adjust oral comprehension.

Language Objectives

- Discuss oral passages.
- Use a graphic organizer to take notes.

ELL Teacher Tip

Have students use the Cause and Effect organizer to process what happens to Kashia and why. Remind them that most things happen for a reason and when they can figure out the cause of each effect, they will be able to understand things that they read and learn better.

ELL English Language Learners

Listening Comprehension

A Peck on the Nose

Kashia loved to visit her grandmother in the country. Kashia lived in the city. She always learned a lot when she visited her Grandma Bess.

Grandma Bess planted a large garden. There were tomatoes, okra, carrots, and much more. Kashia liked picking the vegetables. She thought it was like shopping at the store for free.

Grandma Bess also had hens. She had a pen where she kept them. Each morning she went to gather their eggs. One morning Kashia went with her. She saw a large hen sitting on eggs. Kashia bent down to get a closer look and—OUCH! The hen had pecked her right on the nose!

Grandma Bess laughed. She told Kashia that pecking was how hens protected themselves and their eggs from danger. The hen did not know Kashia would not hurt her, so it pecked when she got too close. Kashia learned her lesson. She would never stick her nose too close to a hen again!

Prepare for the Read Aloud The modified Read Aloud above prepares children for listening to the oral reading "The Pecking Hen" on page 125b.

- **First Listening: Listen to Understand**

1. Write the title of the Read Aloud on the board. Have you ever been to a farm? Have you ever read a book about a farm? What kinds of animals are there on the farm? I am going to read a story about a little girl's visit to her grandmother's house. What happens to her? Listen to find out what happens to Kashia as she helps her grandmother gather eggs one morning.
2. After reading, ask children to recall what Kashia learned about how hens protect themselves. What do hens do to protect themselves? (They peck with their beak.) What happened to Kashia? (She was pecked on the nose.)

- **Second Listening: Listen to Check Understanding** Using the Cause and Effect graphic organizer (*ELL Handbook*, page 512), work with children to fill in what happened to Kashia and why.

Objectives

- Demonstrate listening comprehension of increasingly complex spoken English by following directions, retelling or summarizing spoken messages, responding to questions and requests, collaborating with peers, and taking notes commensurate with content and grade-level needs.

ELL English Language Learners

High-Frequency Words

- **Preteach** Distribute copies of this week's Word Cards (*ELL Handbook,* p. 89). Have children point to or hold up the corresponding card when you say a word in a sentence or make a gesture. When appropriate, use opposites to reinforce meaning.
  - The word saw is used when telling about something you looked at in the past. Point to the children. I *saw* you yesterday.
  - A *tree* is a large plant with a trunk. Draw a picture on the board of a tree. This is a *tree*.
  - *Your* is a word used when telling about something that belongs to you. Point to the child's feet. *Your* shoes are on *your* feet. *Your* name is [will vary]. (my)
  - With your hands, pantomime *small* and *big*. The pencil is *small*. The board is big.
- **Practice** Give each pair of children a set of the Word Cards. Pantomime the meaning of each word. For example, stand like a tree and use your arms as branches. Point to a *tree* and say *tree*.
- **Speaking/Writing with High-Frequency Words**
  - **Teach/Model** Write the following sentences on the board. Model filling in the missing word from the first sentence. 1. I ________ the red bird. (saw) 2. The bug is ________. (small) 3. The ________ is big. (tree) 4. This is ________ desk. (your)
  - **Practice** Give each pair of children a set of the Word Cards. Have them work together to find the correct word for each sentence you read.

Leveled Support

Beginning Read the sentences aloud, using a gesture for each missing word. Have children hold up the correct Word Card for each sentence. Then have them write each word.

Intermediate Have children write the missing words. Have them use the Word Cards as a spelling resource.

Advanced/Advanced-High Have children write the high-frequency words. Children can make up a sentence with a partner.

Objectives

- Internalize new basic and academic language by using and reusing it in meaningful ways in speaking and writing activities that build concept and language attainment.
- Understand the general meaning, main points, and important details of spoken language ranging from situations in which topics, language, and contexts are familiar to unfamiliar.

Language Objectives

- Use accessible language to learn new and essential language.
- Internalize new basic language with writing.
- Use high-frequency English words.
- Understand the general meaning of spoken language as well as the important details.

Transfer Skills

Many factors can influence a child's understanding of print conventions. As you write sentences on the board, emphasize that you are starting at the top and left and continuing across and down.

Mini-Lesson: Listening and Speaking

Turn to p. 127 in the Student Edition. Ask children to listen as you read aloud. After reading, have them restate the general ideas in the passage using the familiar language of the high-frequency words. Then focus on important ideas by asking questions that prompt deeper thinking.

Content Objectives

- Identify main idea and details.
- Identify and retell the main idea and essential details of a story to aid comprehension.

Language Objectives

- Use accessible language to discuss main ideas and supporting details.
- Retell and write main ideas and details from reading.
- Understand the main points of spoken language.

Mini-Lesson: Listening

Turn to p. 142 of the Student Edition. Have children listen as you read the text aloud, with context and topic that may be familiar or unfamiliar. After reading, ask children to retell the steps to show their understanding of the text's general meaning.

Mini-Lesson: Environmental Print

Point out the sign on Envision It! p. EI•9 as you focus on important ideas. Ask children what kinds of signs they see at school. Point out a sign in the classroom and ask children to state its meaning. Continue with other signs in the room or school or with pictures of common signs.

ELL English Language Learners

Guide Comprehension
Main Idea and Details

- **Preteach** Remember that the main idea of a passage or story is what it is mostly about. Stories also contain details. Details support the main idea.
- **Practice** Have children turn to Envision It! on page EI•3 in the Student Edition. Discuss the pictures with children. Have them identify the main idea. (This is a home.) Then have them identify essential details that support the main idea. (family lives together in the house, making it a home). Children can summarize the main points of the page as partners listen. Partners can then retell or summarize the spoken message about the Student Edition page to demonstrate their comprehension.
- **Reteach/Practice** Work with children to complete Picture It! (*ELL Handbook*, p. 90)

Ask children to describe what is happening in the illustration. Then read the text aloud twice. Prepare children for the second reading by asking them to think about the main idea of the sentences. After reading, guide children to use the pictures and words to identify the main idea according to their proficiency level.

Leveled Support

Beginning/Intermediate Reread the story aloud. Have children draw a picture in the box to show the main idea. Then have them write a word or phrase beneath their picture.

Advanced/Advanced-High Read the directions. Tell children to read the story and draw a picture in the box to answer the question. Then have them write an answer in a sentence beneath the picture.

MINI-LESSON

Academic Language

When you look at a story, you can get a good understanding of the main idea by reading the details of the story carefully. The details help you understand the main idea better. Have children practice identifying main ideas in short paragraphs in books they are reading by first identifying the details.

Objectives

- Use accessible language and learn new and essential language in the process.
- Respond orally to information presented in a wide variety of print, electronic, audio, and visual media to build and reinforce concept and language attainment.

ELL
English Language Learners

Reading Comprehension
Get the Egg!

Get the Egg!
Which wild animals live in our neighborhood?
Student Edition pp. 128–129

■ **Frontloading**

- **Background Knowledge** Read the title aloud and discuss it. Have you ever seen a bird's nest? Did you see birds fly back and forth to it? What did you learn from watching it?
- **Preview** Guide children on a picture walk through the story, asking them to identify people, places, and actions. Reteach these words using visuals in the Student Edition: *twig* (p. 132), *net* (p. 134), and *small* (p. 137).
- **Predict** What will happen to the eggs in the nest?

Sheltered Reading Ask questions such as the following to guide children's comprehension:

- p. 130: Point to the nest. What did Brad find? (a nest) What is in it? (eggs)
- p. 132: Point to the twig. What hit the nest? (a twig) What happened then? (an egg fell out)
- p. 135: Point to the net. What did Brad use to get the egg? (net)
- p. 111: Point to the birds. What happened to the eggs? (They hatched.) What is there now? (baby birds)

■ **Fluency: Appropriate Phrasing** Remind children that phrasing means to read punctuation correctly and carefully. They should pay attention to whether periods or question marks are used. Read the sentences on page 131, modeling phrasing with periods at the end of the sentence. Have pairs read page 136. Have children read with appropriate phrasing as their partner listens and offers feedback. For more practice, use the Fluency: Paired Reading Routine (*ELL Handbook*, page 496).

After Reading Help children summarize the text with the Retelling Cards. Ask questions that prompt children to summarize the important parts of the text. Then turn to p. 144 of the Student Edition. Ask children to share information cooperatively by telling each other in small groups about something that happened to them. They should use descriptive words as they share information about their experiences.

Objectives

- Develop and expand repertoire of learning strategies such as reasoning inductively or deductively, looking for patterns in language, and analyzing sayings and expressions commensurate with grade-level learning expectations.
- Understand implicit ideas and information in increasingly complex spoken language commensurate with grade-level learning expectations.
- Narrate, describe, and explain with increasing specificity and detail as more English is acquired.
- Use visual and contextual support and support from peers and teachers to read grade-appropriate content area text, enhance and confirm understanding, and develop vocabulary, grasp of language structures, and background knowledge needed to comprehend increasingly challenging language.

Content Objectives

- Monitor and adjust comprehension.
- Make and adjust predictions.

Language Objectives

- Read with appropriate phrasing.
- Summarize text using visual support.
- Share information in cooperative learning interactions.

Audio Support

Children can prepare for reading *Get the Egg!* by using the eSelection or the AudioText CD. See the AudioText CD Routine (*ELL Handbook*, page 500) for suggestions on using these learning tools.

ELL Teaching Routine

For more practice summarizing, use the Retelling/Summarizing Narrative Routine (*ELL Handbook*, page 499).

English Summary

Read the English summary of *Get the Egg!* (*ELL Handbook*, page 91). Children can ask questions about ideas or unfamiliar words.

For additional leveled instruction, see the **ELL/ELD Reader Teaching Guide.**

Comprehension: *Who Lives Here?*

- **Before Reading** Distribute copies of the ELL and ELD Readers, *Who Lives Here?*, to children at their reading level.
  - **Preview** Read the title aloud with children: This is a story about different animal homes. Activate prior knowledge about animal homes. The story in our book was about children finding a bird nest. This story is about wild animal homes too. Have you ever found a wild animal's home in your neighborhood?
  - **Set a Purpose for Reading** Let's read to find out what kinds of homes animals live in.

ELL Reader

ELD Reader

- **During Reading** Follow this Reading Routine for both reading groups.
  1. Read the entire Reader aloud slowly as children follow along and finger point.
  2. Reread the Reader one sentence at a time. Have the children echo read after you.
- **After Reading** Use the exercises on the inside back cover of *Who Lives Here?* and invite children to share drawings and writing. In a whole-group discussion, ask children to tell about different animal homes they've seen. Encourage children to think about the animals they are likely to see near their home (birds, ducks, insects, squirrels). Have children point to examples in the book of different types of animal homes.

ELD Reader Beginning/Intermediate

- **p. 4** Point to the beehive. What is this? (beehive) What animals live there? (bees)
- **p. 5** Point to the nest. What lives here? (bird) What is this home called? (nest)

Writing Draw a picture of one of the animal homes in the story. Ask children to work in pairs and label their picture with a sentence or phrase telling what their animal home is made out of and what lives there. Have them share their drawings with the class.

ELL Reader Advanced/Advanced-High

- **p. 3** Point to the beaver lodge. What animal made this home? (beaver) What is it called? (lodge)
- **p. 7** Point to the anthill. What is this anthill made out of? (dirt) What animals' home is it? (ants)

Study Guide Distribute copies of the ELL Reader Study Guide (*ELL Handbook*, page 94). Scaffold comprehension by reminding them to focus on the main idea and details of the story. Review their responses together. (**Answers** See *ELL Handbook*, pp. 245–248.)

Objectives

- Use prior knowledge and experience to understand meanings in English.
- Demonstrate comprehension of increasingly complex English by participating in shared reading, retelling or summarizing material, responding to questions, and taking notes commensurate with content area and grade level needs.

eReaders

ELL English Language Learners

Conventions

Interrogative Sentences

- **Preteach** Point to the image on page 133 of the Student Edition. *Can you get it?* The question mark at the end of this sentence lets you know that this is an interrogative sentence. An interrogative sentence asks a question. Kim is asking Brad if he can get the egg.
- **Practice** Leaf through the Student Edition and call attention to interrogative sentences. Have children do the exercises below according to their proficiency level.

Beginning/Intermediate Point to an interrogative sentence in the story. Read it aloud. Have children echo read the sentence to you. Have intermediate children copy the sentence on a sheet of paper.

Advanced/Advanced-High Have children choose a picture in the story. Then, challenge them to write their own interrogative sentence that asks about the picture. Have partners read their sentences aloud to each other.

- **Reteach**
  - Write "What is in the nest?" on the board. This sentence asks a question. It ends in a question mark. This is an interrogative sentence. What is this sentence asking about? (what can be found in the nest) What punctuation do we use with an interrogative sentence? (question mark)
  - Write subjects on several note cards. Have children work in pairs to choose a card from the pile and write an interrogative sentence using the subject they chose.
- **Practice** Use the student edition story *Get the Egg!* to practice identifying interrogative sentences.

Beginning Choose simple sentences from the story to read aloud. Ask children to give a "thumbs up" if the sentence you read is interrogative. Have them repeat the sentences.

Intermediate Write several different types of sentences from the story on sentence strips. Have children work together to sort the sentences—interrogative or not.

Advanced/Advanced-High Have children write their own interrogative sentences. Check to make sure that they included question marks. Have them share their sentences with a partner.

Objectives

- Internalize new basic and academic language by using and reusing it in meaningful ways in speaking and writing activities that build concept and language attainment.
- Speak using a variety of grammatical structures, sentence lengths, sentence types, and connecting words with increasing accuracy and ease as more English is acquired.

Content Objectives

- Identify and use interrogative sentences.
- Correctly use interrogative sentences.

Language Objectives

- Speak using interrogative sentences.
- Write using the pattern of interrogative sentences.
- Ask for information.

Transfer Skills

Speakers of Chinese, Vietnamese, and other Asian languages often form questions by adding words to statements, comparable to *The food is hot, no?* or *You see or not see the bird?* Provide model English questions for children to understand and follow the patterns.

Mini-Lesson: Speaking

Interrogative sentences are used to ask for information. Have students practice saying questions they might ask in social situations *(Where can I find the milk?)* and academic situations *(What page should we turn to now?).* They can work with partners to ask and answer questions.

Content Objectives

- Identify words that indicate beginning, middle, and end.
- Identify characteristics that show the beginning, middle, and end of a story.

Language Objectives

- Write realistic fiction that progresses from beginning to middle and end.
- Share feedback for editing and revising.

ELL Teaching Routine

For practice spelling words related to homework, use the Spelling Routine (*ELL Handbook*, page 499).

ELL English Language Learners

Write Realistic Fiction

- **Introduce Terms** Write *realistic fiction* on the board and explain each word as you point to it. Fiction is made up. It comes from your mind. Circle the word *real* inside *realistic*. See the word *real*? *Real* means that it is not make-believe. Realistic fiction is about things that could really happen. In realistic fiction, a bird could not moo. In realistic fiction, a bird could build a nest.
- **Describe Story Parts** Explain that a good story has a beginning, middle, and end. Write this sentence on the board: *The bird built its nest*.

  Have children suggest things the bird would need to do to build a nest. Record their answers on the board. Model supplying the first action: *The bird gathered twigs*.
- **Writing Model**

  Draw three large boxes connected with arrows on the board. Label them *First, Next*, and *Last*. Engage children in naming three things that the bird would do when it built its nest. Write sentences for each action in the boxes.

- **Write** Have children copy this story starter: *Janna did her homework.* Have them draw three large boxes under the sentence and label them *First, Next*, and *Last*. Have partners work together to think of the things Janna would need to do to complete her homework. What would happen first, next, and last while she worked?

Beginning Supply the graphic organizer. Write the words *First, Next*, and *Last* in your boxes. Think of what Janna would need to do her homework. Draw three things that she would do. Have children tell about their pictures. Supply the action words and have children copy them in the appropriate boxes.

Intermediate Guide children's writing. What action words will you use? What words can you use to tell more about what Janna did? Help children with their spelling.

Advanced/Advanced-High Have children use the boxes for prewriting. Then have them write their sentences in paragraph form.

Objectives

- Write using newly acquired basic vocabulary and content-based vocabulary.
- Narrate, describe, and explain with increasing specificity and detail to fulfill content area writing needs as more English is acquired.

This Week on Reading Street!

Animals, Tame and Wild

Question of the Week

What can we learn about wild animals by watching them?

Daily Plan

Whole Group

- Short *u*: *u*
- Final Consonant Blends
- Cause and Effect
- Fluency
- Vocabulary

Don't Wait Until Friday — MONITOR PROGRESS — Success Predictor

Day 1	Day 2	Day 3	Day 4	Day 5
Check Word Reading	Check Word Reading	Check High-Frequency Words/Retelling	Check Fluency	Check Oral Vocabulary

Small Group

Teacher-Led

- Reading Support
- Skill Support
- Fluency Practice

Practice Stations

Independent Activities

Customize Literacy More support for a Balanced Literacy approach, see CL•1–CL•47.

Customize Writing More support for a customized writing approach, see CW•11–CW•20.

Whole Group

- Writing for Tests: Brief Composition
- Conventions: Exclamatory Sentences

Assessment

- Weekly Tests
- Day 5 Assessment
- Fresh Reads

You Are Here! Unit 1 Week 6

This Week's Reading Selections

Main Selection
Genre: **Literary Nonfiction**

Paired Selection

Decodable Practice Readers

Leveled Readers

ELL and ELD Readers

Resources on Reading Street!

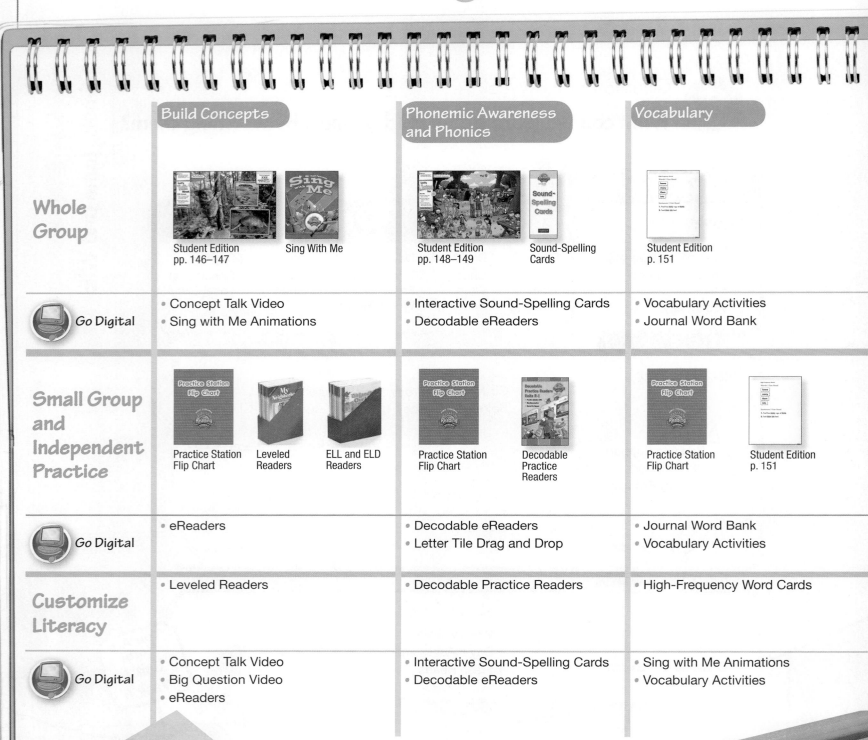

	Build Concepts	Phonemic Awareness and Phonics	Vocabulary
Whole Group	 Student Edition pp. 146–147;  Sing With Me	 Student Edition pp. 148–149;  Sound-Spelling Cards	 Student Edition p. 151
Go Digital	• Concept Talk Video • Sing with Me Animations	• Interactive Sound-Spelling Cards • Decodable eReaders	• Vocabulary Activities • Journal Word Bank
Small Group and Independent Practice	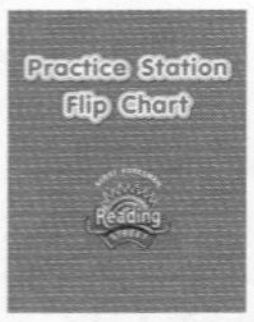 Practice Station Flip Chart;  Leveled Readers;  ELL and ELD Readers	 Practice Station Flip Chart;  Decodable Practice Readers	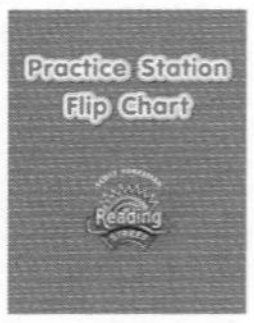 Practice Station Flip Chart;  Student Edition p. 151
Go Digital	• eReaders	• Decodable eReaders • Letter Tile Drag and Drop	• Journal Word Bank • Vocabulary Activities
Customize Literacy	• Leveled Readers	• Decodable Practice Readers	• High-Frequency Word Cards
Go Digital	• Concept Talk Video • Big Question Video • eReaders	• Interactive Sound-Spelling Cards • Decodable eReaders	• Sing with Me Animations • Vocabulary Activities

Question of the Week

What can we learn about wild animals by watching them?

Week 6

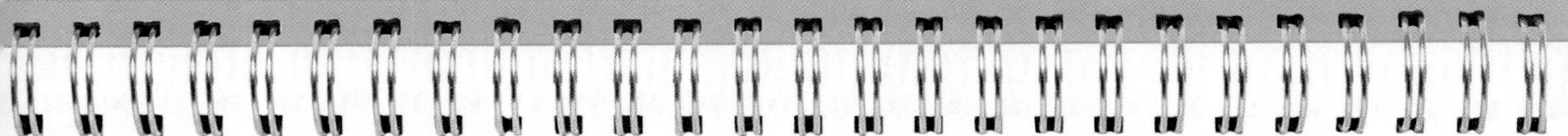

Comprehension	Fluency	Conventions and Writing
 Student Edition pp. 154–163	 Decodable Practice Readers	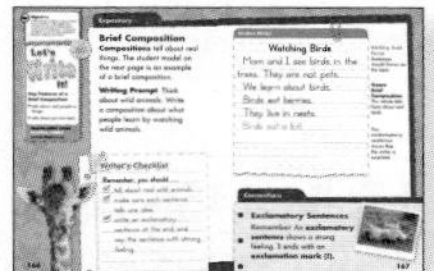 Student Edition pp. 166–167
• Envision It! Animations • eSelections	• eSelections • eReaders	• Grammar Jammer
 Practice Station Flip Chart  Leveled Readers  ELL and ELD Readers	 Practice Station Flip Chart  Decodable Practice Readers	 Practice Station Flip Chart  Reader's and Writer's Notebook
• eReaders • Story Sort	• Decodable eReaders	• Grammar Jammer
• Envision It! Skills and Strategies Handbooks • Leveled Readers	• Leveled Readers	• Reader's and Writer's Notebook
• Envision It! Animations • eReaders	• eReaders	• Grammar Jammer

My 5-Day Planner for Reading Street!

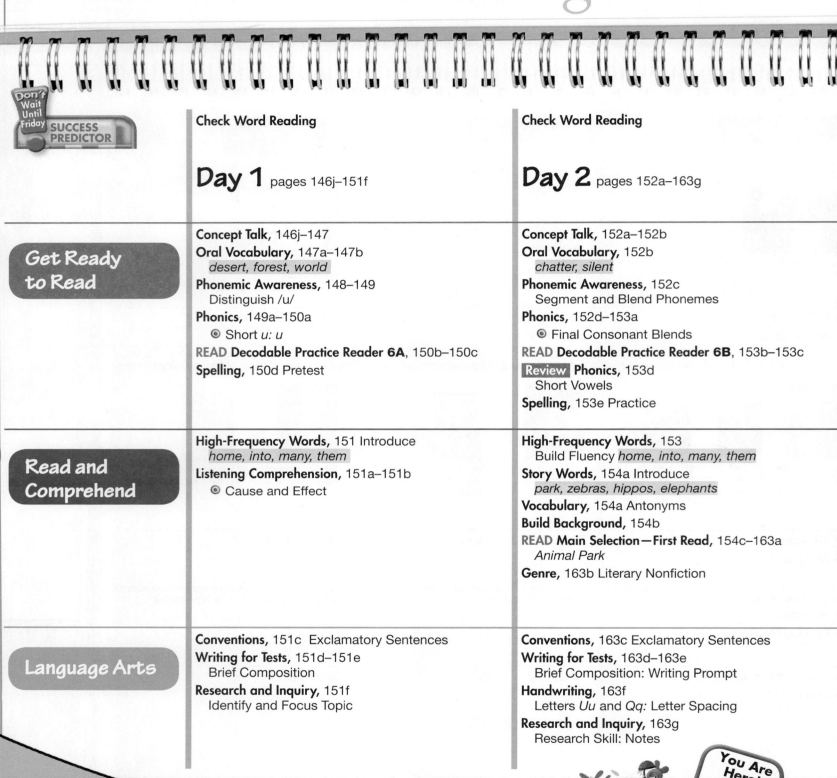

Don't Wait Until Friday SUCCESS PREDICTOR

	Check Word Reading **Day 1** pages 146j–151f	Check Word Reading **Day 2** pages 152a–163g
Get Ready to Read	**Concept Talk,** 146j–147 **Oral Vocabulary,** 147a–147b *desert, forest, world* **Phonemic Awareness,** 148–149 Distinguish /u/ **Phonics,** 149a–150a ◎ Short *u: u* READ **Decodable Practice Reader 6A,** 150b–150c **Spelling,** 150d Pretest	**Concept Talk,** 152a–152b **Oral Vocabulary,** 152b *chatter, silent* **Phonemic Awareness,** 152c Segment and Blend Phonemes **Phonics,** 152d–153a ◎ Final Consonant Blends READ **Decodable Practice Reader 6B,** 153b–153c Review **Phonics,** 153d Short Vowels **Spelling,** 153e Practice
Read and Comprehend	**High-Frequency Words,** 151 Introduce *home, into, many, them* **Listening Comprehension,** 151a–151b ◎ Cause and Effect	**High-Frequency Words,** 153 Build Fluency *home, into, many, them* **Story Words,** 154a Introduce *park, zebras, hippos, elephants* **Vocabulary,** 154a Antonyms **Build Background,** 154b READ **Main Selection—First Read,** 154c–163a *Animal Park* **Genre,** 163b Literary Nonfiction
Language Arts	**Conventions,** 151c Exclamatory Sentences **Writing for Tests,** 151d–151e Brief Composition **Research and Inquiry,** 151f Identify and Focus Topic	**Conventions,** 163c Exclamatory Sentences **Writing for Tests,** 163d–163e Brief Composition: Writing Prompt **Handwriting,** 163f Letters *Uu* and *Qq:* Letter Spacing **Research and Inquiry,** 163g Research Skill: Notes

You Are Here! Unit 1 Week 6

Question of the Week

What can we learn about wild animals by watching them?

Check High-Frequency Words Check Retelling **Day 3** pages 164a–167c	Check Fluency **Day 4** pages 168a–169f	Check Oral Vocabulary **Day 5** pages 170a–171k
Concept Talk, 164a–164b **Oral Vocabulary,** 164b *snort* **Phonological Awareness,** 164c Rhyming Words **Phonics,** 164d–164e ◎ Short *u: u* ◎ Final Consonant Blends **Spelling,** 164f Dictation	**Concept Talk,** 168a–168b **Oral Vocabulary,** 168b *medicine, poisonous* **Phonemic Awareness,** 168c Distinguish /u/ Review **Phonics,** 168d Short *e* Spelled *e;* Initial Consonant Blends READ **Decodable Practice Reader 6C,** 168e–168f **Spelling,** 168h Partner Review	**Concept Wrap Up,** 170a Review **Oral Vocabulary,** 170b **Phonological Awareness,** 170c Segment and Blend Onset and Rime Review **Phonics,** 170c ◎ Short *u: u* ◎ Final Consonant Blends **Spelling,** 170d Test
High-Frequency Words, 164g Review *home, into, many, them* **Story Words,** 164g Review *elephants, hippos, park, zebras* READ **Main Selection—Second Read,** 154–163, 164h–165a **Fluency,** 165b Appropriate Phrasing	**Science in Reading,** 168i READ **Paired Selection,** 168–169a Poetry Collection **Fluency,** 169b Appropriate Phrasing	**Listening and Speaking,** 170–171 Give Directions **Vocabulary,** 171a Antonyms **Fluency,** 171a Appropriate Phrasing Review **Comprehension,** 171b ◎ Cause and Effect Review **Vocabulary,** 171b High-Frequency and Story Words **Poetry,** 171c Rhyme and Rhythm **Assessment,** 171d–171f Monitor Progress
Conventions, 166a–167a Exclamatory Sentences **Writing for Tests,** 166–167a Brief Composition: Evaluation **Listening and Speaking,** 167b Give Directions **Research and Inquiry,** 167c Gather and Record Information	**Conventions,** 169c Exclamatory Sentences **Writing for Tests,** 169d–169e Brief Composition Writing Prompt **Research and Inquiry,** 169f Review and Revise Topic	Review **Conventions,** 171g **Writing for Tests,** 171h–171i Brief Composition: Evaluation **Research and Inquiry,** 171j Communicate **Wrap Up Your Week,** 171k What can we learn about wild animals by watching them?

Grouping Options for Differentiated Instruction
Turn the page for the small group time lesson plan.

Planning Small Group Time on Reading Street!

Look for this Small Group Time box each day to help meet the individual needs of all your children. Differentiated Instruction lessons appear on the DI pages at the end of each week.

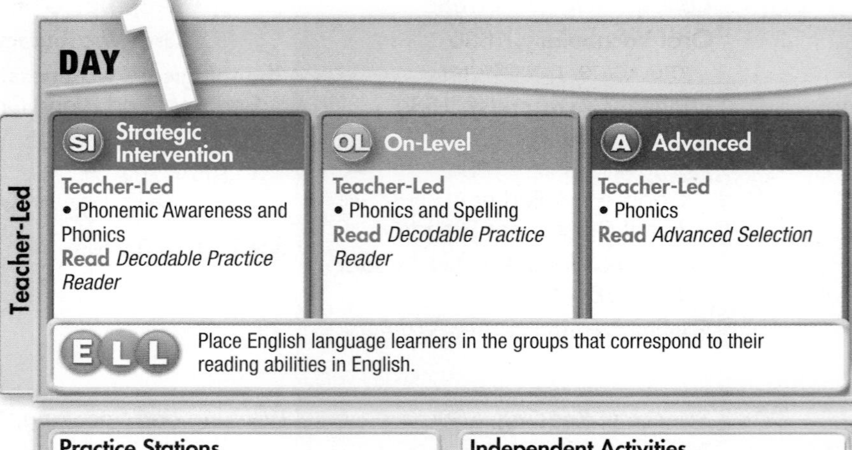

ELL

ELL Reader
Advanced
Advanced-High

ELD Reader
Beginning
Intermediate

ELL Poster

	Day 1
SI Strategic Intervention	**Phonemic Awareness and Phonics**, DI•106 Read **Decodable Practice Reader 6A**, DI•106
OL On-Level	**Phonics and Spelling**, DI•111 Read **Decodable Practice Reader 6A**, DI•111
A Advanced	**Phonics**, DI•114 Read **Advanced Selection**, DI•114
ELL English Language Learners	DI•117–DI•126 **Frontload Concept** **Preteach Skills** **Writing**

You Are Here! Unit 1 Week 6

Reading Street Response to Intervention Kit

Reading Street Leveled Practice Stations Kit

Question of the Week

What can we learn about wild animals by watching them?

Below-Level Reader

Decodable Practice Readers

Concept Literacy Reader

On-Level Reader

A Advanced

Advanced Reader

Fun with Ducks

Advanced Selection

Small Group Weekly Plan

Day 2	Day 3	Day 4	Day 5
Phonemic Awareness and Phonics, DI•107 Read **Decodable Practice Reader 6B,** DI•107	**Phonemic Awareness and Phonics,** DI•108 Read **Concept Literacy Leveled Reader,** DI•108	**High-Frequency Words,** DI•109 Read **Decodable Practice Reader 6C,** DI•109	**Phonics Review,** DI•110 Read **Below-Level Leveled Reader,** DI•110
Phonics and High-Frequency Words, DI•111 Read **Decodable Practice Reader 6B,** DI•111	Read **On-Level Leveled Reader,** DI•112	**Conventions,** DI•113 Reread **Main Selection,** DI•113	**Phonics Review,** DI•113 Reread **On-Level Leveled Reader,** DI•113
Phonics and Comprehension, DI•114 Read **Main Selection,** DI•114	Read **Advanced Leveled Reader,** DI•115	**Comprehension,** DI•116 Read **Paired Selection,** DI•116 Reread **Leveled Reader,** DI•116	**Fluency and Comprehension,** DI•116 Reread **Advanced Selection,** DI•116
DI•117–DI•126 **Review Concept** **Practice Skills** **Frontload Main Selection** **Writing**	DI•117–DI•126 **Review Concept** **Practice Skills** **Reread Main Selection** **Writing**	DI•117–DI•126 **Review Concept** **Review Skills** **Read ELL or ELD Reader** **Writing**	DI•117–DI•126 **Review Concept** **Review Skills** **Writing**

Week 6

Practice Stations for Everyone on Reading Street!

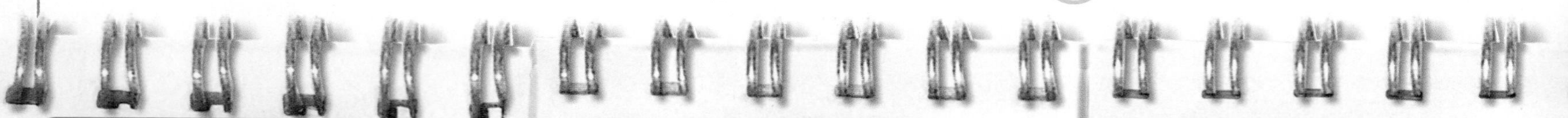

Listen Up!

Match sounds and pictures.

Objectives

- Identify words with initial and medial sound /e/.
- Identify words with initial consonant blends.

Materials

- *Listen Up!* Flip Chart Activity 6
- Picture Cards *egg, elbow, elephant, escalator, bed, ten, flag, grape, snail, playground*

Differentiated Activities

● Find Picture Cards that have the same beginning sound as *echo.* Find Picture Cards that have the same middle sound as *pet.* Find Picture Cards that begin with consonant blends.

▲ Find Picture Cards that have the same beginning sound as *echo.* Find Picture Cards that have the same middle sound as *pet.* Find Picture Cards that begin with consonant blends.

■ Find Picture Cards that have the same beginning sound as *echo.* Find Picture Cards that have the same middle sound as *pet.* Find Picture Cards that begin with consonant blends. Now think of other words with these sounds.

Technology

- Interactive Sound-Spelling Cards

Word Work

short *e,* consonant blends

Objectives

- Write and read words with short *e.*
- Write and read words with initial consonant blends.

Materials

- *Word Work* Flip Chart Activity 6
- pre-cut paper strips
- scissors
- blue and red markers

Differentiated Activities

● Work with a partner. Write these words on paper strips: *egg, wet, glad.* Use a red marker to write each *e* and for the consonant blend *gl.* Use a blue marker for the other letters. Have your partner read the words.

▲ Work with a partner. Write these words on paper strips: *egg, wet, glad.* Use a red marker to write each *e* and for the consonant blend *gl.* Use a blue marker for the other letters. Now cut the strips so each letter is separate. Have your partner build the words and read them.

■ Work with a partner. Write short *e* words and words with initial consonant blends on paper strips. Use a red marker to write each *e* and for the consonant blends. Use a blue marker for the other letters. Now cut the strips so each letter is separate. Have your partner build the words and read them.

Technology

- Interactive Sound-Spelling Cards

Words To Know

Sort words.

Objectives

- Identify high-frequency words *small, tree, your, saw.*
- Sort words with initial consonant blends.

Materials

- *Words to Know* Flip Chart Activity 6
- High-Frequency Word Cards for Unit 1, Week 5
- paper
- pencils

Differentiated Activities

● Use the Word Cards. Read the words. Sort them into two piles: words with initial consonant blends and words without initial consonant blends. Write the words and underline the initial consonant blends.

▲ Use the Word Cards. Read the words. Sort them into two piles: words with initial consonant blends and words without initial consonant blends. Write the words and underline the initial consonant blends.

■ Use the Word Cards. Read the words. Write the words with initial consonant blends in one column and words without initial consonant blends in another column. Underline the initial consonant blends. Write sentences using the words.

Technology

- Online Tested Vocabulary Activities

Use this week's materials from the Reading Street Leveled Practice Stations Kit to organize this week's stations.

Key

● Below-Level Activities

▲ On-Level Activities

■ Advanced Activities

Practice Station Flip Chart

Let's Write!

Write interrogative sentences.

Objective

- Write interrogative sentences.

Materials

- *Let's Write!* Flip Chart Activity 6
- paper
- pencils

Differentiated Activities

- An **interrogative sentence** is an asking sentence.
- A sentence begins with a capital letter.
- An interrogative sentence ends with a question mark.

● Think about what you might want to know about an animal in your neighborhood. Write an interrogative sentence about the animal. Be sure to end your sentence with a question mark.

▲ Think about what you might want to know about an animal in your neighborhood. Write interrogative sentences about the animal. Be sure to end your sentences with question marks.

■ Think about what you might want to know about an animal in your neighborhood. Write interrogative sentences about the animal. Be sure to end your sentences with question marks. Now read your sentences to a partner and see if he or she knows the answers.

Read For Meaning

Identify the main idea of a story.

Objectives

- Identify the main idea of a story.
- Identify the details that support the main idea.

Materials

- *Read for Meaning* Flip Chart Activity 6
- Leveled Readers
- paper
- pencils

Differentiated Activities

- The **main idea** of a story tells what the story is mainly about.
- **Details** tell more about the main idea.

● Read *At Your Vet.* Write a sentence that tells the main idea. Then write details.

▲ Read *What Animals Can You See?* Write a sentence that tells the main idea. Then write details.

■ Read *Cary and the Wildlife Shelter.* Draw a circle. Inside the circle, write a sentence that tells the main idea. Draw lines coming out of the circle and write details on the lines.

Technology

- Leveled eReaders

Get Fluent

Practice fluent reading.

Objective

- Read aloud with appropriate phasing.

Materials

- *Get Fluent* Flip Chart Activity 6
- Leveled Readers

Differentiated Activities

● Work with a partner. Take turns reading pages from *At Your Vet.* As you read, look at how words are grouped and read with appropriate phrasing. Punctuation can help you read with appropriate phrasing. Give your partner feedback.

▲ Work with a partner. Take turns reading pages from *What Animals Can You See?* As you read, look at how words are grouped and read with appropriate phrasing. Punctuation can help you read with appropriate phrasing. Give your partner feedback.

■ Work with a partner. Take turns reading pages from *Cary and the Wildlife Shelter.* As you read, look at how words are grouped and read with appropriate phrasing. Punctuation can help you read with appropriate phrasing. Give your partner feedback.

Technology

- Reading Street Readers CD-ROM

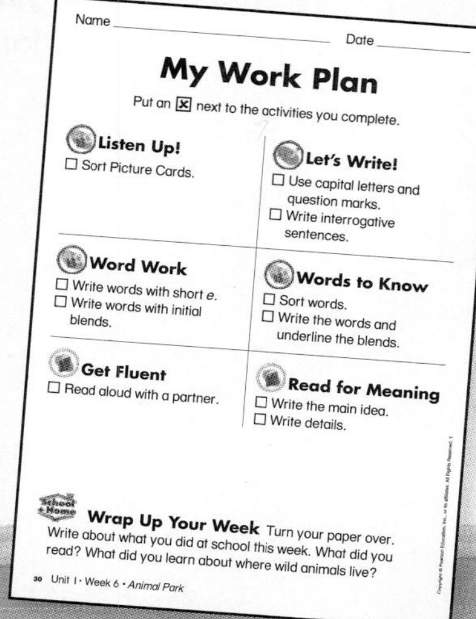

Name ____ Date ____

My Work Plan

Put an ☒ next to the activities you complete.

Listen Up!
☐ Sort Picture Cards.

Let's Write!
☐ Use capital letters and question marks.
☐ Write interrogative sentences.

Word Work
☐ Write words with short *e*.
☐ Write words with initial blends.

Words to Know
☐ Sort words.
☐ Write the words and underline the blends.

Get Fluent
☐ Read aloud with a partner.

Read for Meaning
☐ Write the main idea.
☐ Write details.

Wrap Up Your Week Turn your paper over. Write about what you did at school this week. What did you read? What did you learn about where wild animals live?

30 Unit 1 • Week 6 • Animal Park

My Weekly Work Plan

Week 6

Objectives

- Introduce concept: what we learn about wild animals by watching them.
- Share information and ideas about the concept.

Today at a Glance

Oral Vocabulary
desert, forest, world

Phonemic Awareness
Distinguish /u/

Phonics and Spelling
◎ Short *u: u*

Fluency
Oral Rereading

High-Frequency Words
home, into, many, them

Comprehension
◎ Cause and Effect

Conventions
Exclamatory Sentences

Writing
Writing for Tests: Brief Composition

Research and Inquiry
Identify and Focus Topic

Concept Talk

Question of the Week

What can we learn about wild animals by watching them?

Introduce the concept To build concepts and to focus children's attention, tell them that this week they will talk, sing, read, and write about what people learn about wild animals by watching them. Write the Question of the Week and track the print as you read it.

ROUTINE Activate Prior Knowledge Team Talk

1. **Think** Have children think for a minute about what they have learned by watching wild animals.
2. **Pair** Have pairs of children discuss the question.
3. **Share** Have children share information and their ideas with the group. Remind children to ask questions to clarify information. Guide discussion and encourage elaboration with prompts such as: What wild animal have you watched? What did you learn about the food it eats?

Routines Flip Chart

Anchored Talk

Develop oral language Have children turn to pages 146–147 in their Student Editions. Read the title and look at the photos. Use these questions to guide discussion and create the "What can we learn about wild animals by watching them?" concept map (shown on the next page).

- One thing we can learn by watching animals is how they move. How is the snake in the picture moving? (Possible response: It is wriggling forward.) Let's add *wriggling* to our map.
- The animal in the tree is a tarsier. How can it move? (Possible response: It can climb.) Let's add *climb* to our map.

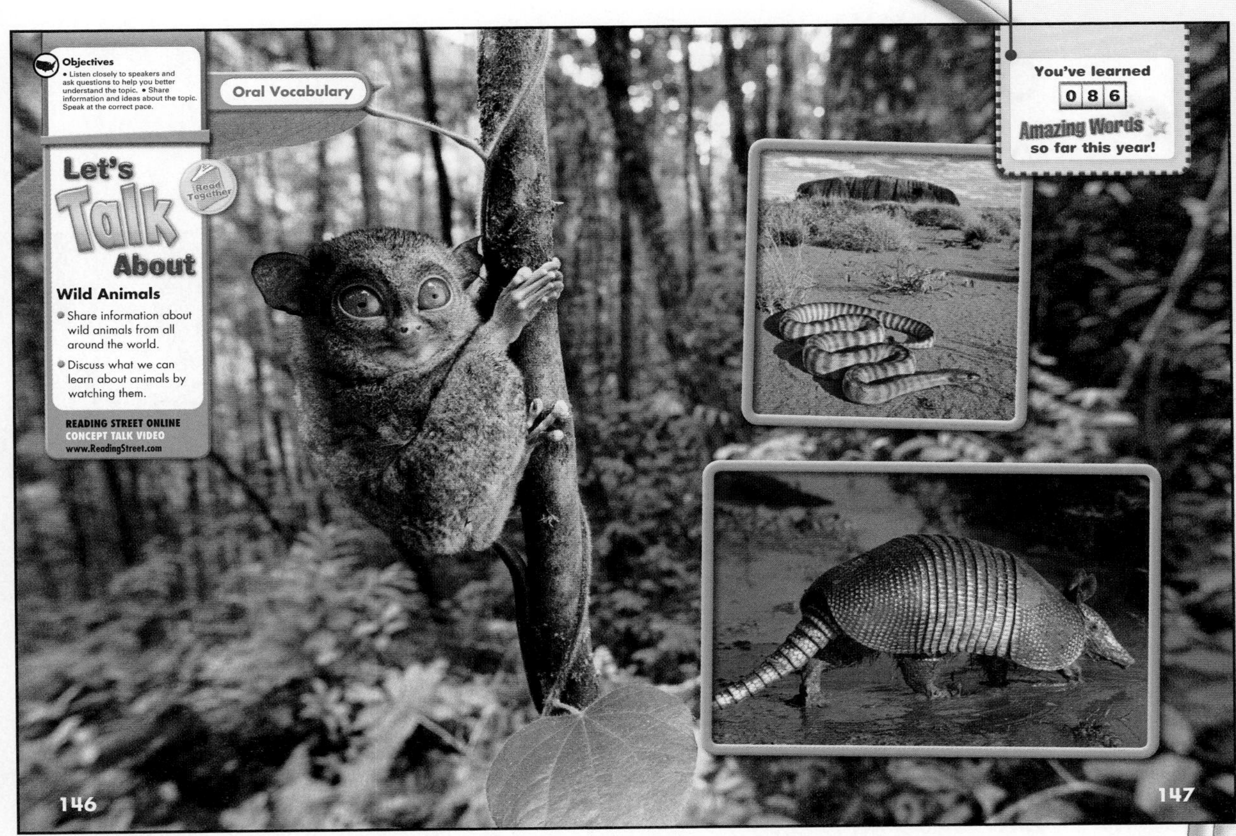
Objectives
• Listen closely to speakers and ask questions to help you better understand the topic. • Share information and ideas about the topic. Speak at the correct pace.
Oral Vocabulary
Let's Talk About
Read Together
Wild Animals
• Share information about wild animals from all around the world.
• Discuss what we can learn about animals by watching them.
READING STREET ONLINE
CONCEPT TALK VIDEO
www.ReadingStreet.com
You've learned
0 8 6
Amazing Words
so far this year!
146
147
Student Edition pp. 146–147

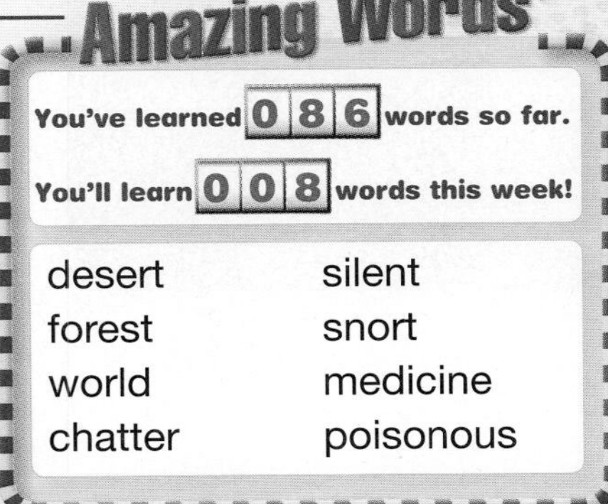
Amazing Words
You've learned 0 8 6 words so far.
You'll learn 0 0 8 words this week!
desert
forest
world
chatter
silent
snort
medicine
poisonous

Writing on Demand

Develop Writing Fluency
Ask children to write what they know about the kinds of things people can learn by watching wild animals. Have them write for two or three minutes. Children should write as much as they can. Tell them to try to do their best writing. You may want to discuss what children wrote during writing conferences.

Connect to reading Explain that this week, they will read about wild animals that live in a special park and what the animals there do all day. Let's add *We learn what animals do all day* to our map.

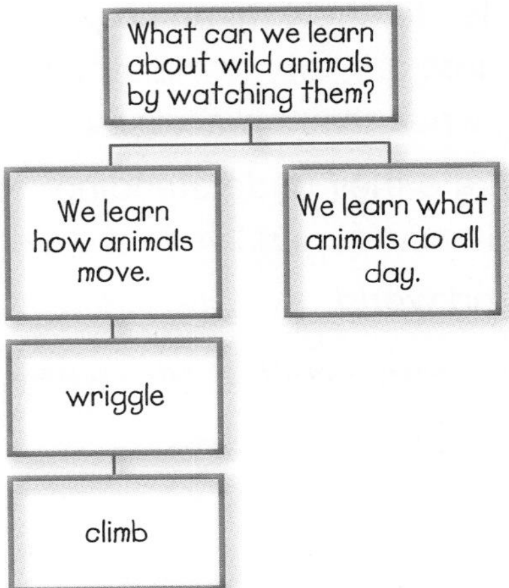
What can we learn about wild animals by watching them?
We learn how animals move.
We learn what animals do all day.
wriggle
climb

English Language Learners
Listening Comprehension English learners will benefit from additional visual support to understand the key terms in the concept map. Use the pictures on pp. 146–147 to scaffold understanding. For example, when talking about the different animals and how they move, point to the corresponding pictures.

ELL Support Additional ELL support and modified instruction are provided in the *ELL Handbook* and in the ELL Support Lessons on pp. DI•117–DI•126.

ELL **Preteach Concepts** Use the Day 1 instruction on ELL Poster 6 to assess and build background knowledge, develop concepts, and build oral vocabulary.

Poster 6

Objectives

- Build oral vocabulary.
- Discuss the concept to develop oral language.
- Share information and ideas about the concept.

Oral Vocabulary

Amazing Words

Introduce Amazing Words

Display p. 6 of the *Sing with Me* Big Book. Tell children they are going to sing about some wild animals and the places where they live. Ask children to listen for the Amazing Words *desert, forest,* and *world* as you sing. Sing the song again and have children join you.

Sing with Me Big Book Audio

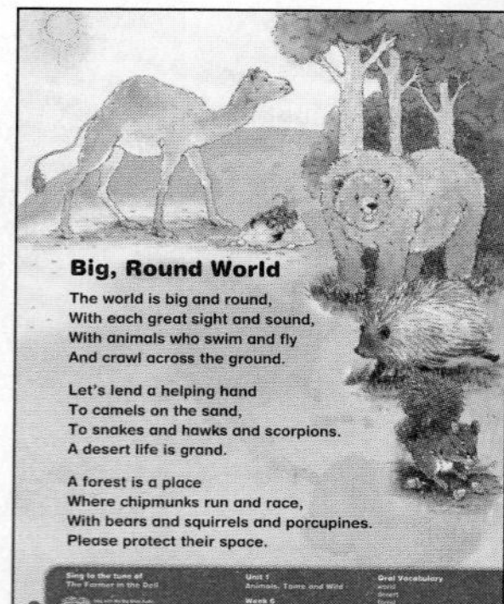

Sing with Me Big Book p. 6

Amazing Words Oral Vocabulary Routine

Teach Amazing Words

1. **Introduce the Word** Relate the word *desert* to the song. We know from the song that camels and snakes live in the *desert*. Supply a child-friendly definition: A *desert* is a dry area of land that has very little rain. Have children say the word.
2. **Demonstrate** Provide examples to show meaning: A *desert* is often hot and covered with sand. There are very few plants in a *desert*. People bring water with them when they go across a *desert*.
3. **Apply** Have children demonstrate their understanding: Explain why only some kinds of plants and animals can live in a *desert*.

See p. OV•3 to teach *forest* and *world*.

Routines Flip Chart

Check understanding of Amazing Words

Have children look at the picture on p. 6. Which three animals in the picture live in the *forest*? (bear, porcupine, squirrel) What other wild animals might you see in a *forest*? Use *forest* in your answer. (Possible response: I might see deer and birds in a forest.)

Some animals live in many parts of the *world* and some live in only a few places. What is an animal that lives in a different part of the *world* from you? Use the word *world* in your answer. (Possible response: Elephants live in a different part of the world.)

What might you learn by watching an animal in the *desert*? Use *desert* in your answer. (Possible response: I might learn how animals find food in the desert.)

Apply Amazing Words

Have children demonstrate their understanding of the Amazing Words by completing these sentences orally.

Our **world** is home to many ________.

If I go to the **desert**, I will probably see ________.

The **forest** is a great place to ________.

Corrective feedback

If... children have difficulty using the Amazing Words, **then...** remind them of the definitions and provide opportunities for children to use the words in sentences.

Preteach Academic Vocabulary

Write the following on the board:

- cause and effect
- literary nonfiction
- exclamatory sentences

Have children share what they know about this week's Academic Vocabulary. Use children's responses to assess their prior knowledge. Preteach the Academic Vocabulary by providing a child-friendly description, explanation, or example that clarifies the meaning of each term. Then ask children to restate the meaning of the Academic Vocabulary in their own words.

Amazing Words

desert	silent
forest	snort
world	medicine
chatter	poisonous

English Language Learners

Visual Support Use the illustrations on p. 6 of the Big Book to support children's understanding of animal names and the Amazing Words. Have children name each animal as you point to its picture. Then say and have children repeat these sentences: *The camel and scorpion live in the desert. The bear, porcupine, and squirrel live in the forest.*

Objectives

- Distinguish /u/ in initial and medial positions.
- ◎ Associate the vowel sound /u/ with the spelling *u*.

Skills Trace

◎ **Short *u*: *u***
Introduce/Teach U1W6D1
Practice U1W6D3; U1W6D4
Reteach/Review U1W6D5; U2W1D4
Assess/Test Weekly Test U1W6
Benchmark Test U1

KEY:
U=Unit W=Week D=Day

Student Edition pp. 148–149

Phonemic Awareness
Distinguish /u/

Introduce Read together the second bulleted point on p. 148. In the picture, what is shining up in the sky? (sun) The middle sound I hear in *sun* is /u/. The sound /u/ is called the short *u* sound.

Model Listen as I say the short *u* sound: /u/, /u/, /u/. There are two sounds in *up:* /u/ /p/. The first sound in *up* is /u/.

Guide practice Have children identify other items or actions in the picture with the short *u* sound, /u/. (Possible responses: *mug, skunk, hug, cup, bug*) Read the following words: *us, egg, ugly, untie, inch*. Have children raise their hands if they hear the /u/ sound at the beginning of the word.

Model Listen as I say the word *sun*. There are three sounds in *sun:* /s/ /u/ /n/. The middle sound in *sun* is /u/.

Guide practice Read the following words: *cut, bug, bag, rest, rust.* Have children raise their hands if they hear /u/ sound in the middle of the word.

Corrective feedback **If...** children make an error,
then... model by segmenting the word, and have them repeat the segmenting of the word.

Phonics—Teach/Model

Short *u*: *u*

Sound-Spelling Card 24

ROUTINE Blending Strategy

1. **Connect** Write the words *top* and *jet*. Ask children what they know about the vowel sounds in these words. (The vowel sounds are short. Short *o* is spelled *o*. Short *e* is spelled *e*.) Explain that today they will learn how to spell and read words with short *u*, /u/, spelled *u*.
2. **Use Sound-Spelling Cards** Display Card 24. Point to *u*. The short *u* sound, /u/, is usually spelled *u*. Have children say /u/ several times as you point to *u*.
3. **Model** Write *bug*. In this word, the letter *u* stands for the sound /u/. Segment and blend *bug*; then have children blend with you: /b/ /u/ /g/. Follow this procedure to model *bud* and *mug*.
4. **Guide Practice** Continue the process in step 3. This time have children blend with you. Remind children that *u* usually spells the short *u* sound, /u/.

cut	**rug**	**mud**	**tub**	**run**	**but**
rub	**cup**	**sun**	**nut**	**dud**	**luck**

5. **Review** What do you know about reading these words? (The letter *u* can spell the short *u* sound, /u/.)

Routines Flip Chart

Differentiated Instruction

Strategic Intervention

Distinguish /u/ If children have difficulty hearing short *u* at the beginning of a word, have them repeat the word *umbrella*. Then ask, Does our new word have the same sound you hear at the beginning of *umbrella*?

Vocabulary Support

You may wish to explain the meaning of this word.

dud something that doesn't work the way it should

English Language Learners

Produce /u/ Because English short vowel sounds do not exist or have only approximations in many languages, English learners may have a hard time hearing the difference between, for example, short *u* and short *o*. Demonstrate the position of the mouth when saying /u/ versus /o/. Provide additional phonemic awareness activities to help children hear and pronounce words with short *u*.

Pronounce /u/ In Spanish, the letter *u* spells the sound /ü/ heard in *ruby*. Spanish-speaking children may therefore read a word like *mud* as *mood*. Provide extra practice pronouncing /u/ and associating the short *u* sound with the letter *u*.

Objectives

- ◎ Associate the vowel sound /u/ with the spelling *u*.
- Blend and read words with the short *u* sound.
- Decode words in context and in isolation.

Check Word Reading
SUCCESS PREDICTOR

Phonics—Build Fluency

Short *u*: *u*

Model

Envision It!

Have children turn to page 150 in their Student Edition. Look at the picture on this page. I see a picture of an *umbrella*. When I say *umbrella*, I hear the short *u* sound, /u/, at the beginning. The /u/ sound is spelled *u*.

Student Edition p. 150

Guide practice

For each word in "Words I Can Blend," ask for the sound of each letter or group of letters. Make sure that children identify the correct sound for *u*. Then have children blend the whole word.

Corrective feedback

If... children have difficulty blending a word,
then... model blending the word, and then ask children to blend it with you.

Blend and Read

Decode words in isolation

After children can successfully segment and blend the words, point to words in random order and ask children to read them naturally.

Decode words in context

Have children read each of the sentences. Have them identify words in the sentences that have the short *u* sound, /u/.

Team Talk Pair children and have them take turns reading each of the sentences aloud.

On their own

Use *Reader's and Writer's Notebook* p. 201.

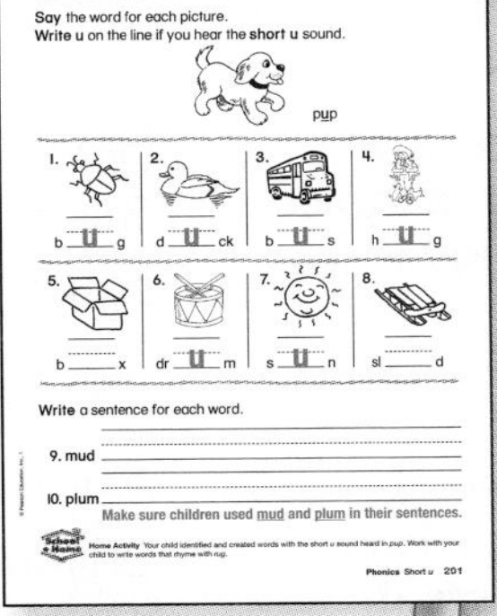
Animal Park

Name

Say the word for each picture.
Write u on the line if you hear the short u sound.

pup

b u g, d u ck, b u s, h u g

b __ x, dr u m, s u n, sl __ d

Write a sentence for each word.

9. mud

10. plum

Make sure children used mud and plum in their sentences.

Phonics Short u 201

Reader's and Writer's Notebook p. 201

Don't Wait Until Friday — MONITOR PROGRESS

Check Word Reading — Short *u*: *u*

Write the following words and have the class read them. Notice which words children miss during the group reading. Call on individuals to read some of the words.

hum	**jug**	**tub**	**pup**	**fun**	
box	**job**	**hut**	**mop**	**gum**	← Row 2 contrasts short *o* and short *u* words.
hid	**ten**	**pot**	**cup**	**bat**	← Row 3 reviews short vowels.

Spiral Review

If… children cannot blend short *u* words at this point,

then… use the Small-Group Time Strategic Intervention lesson, p. DI•106, to reteach short *u* spelled *u*. Continue to monitor children's progress using other instructional opportunities during the week. See the Skills Trace on p. 148–149.

Day 1	**Day 2**	**Day 3**	**Day 4**	**Day 5**
Check Word Reading	Check Word Reading	Check High-Frequency Words/Retelling	Check Fluency	Check Oral Vocabulary

Success Predictor

Differentiated Instruction

Advanced

Extend Blending Provide children who can segment and blend all the words correctly with more challenging words such as: *uncle, summer, funny, study, sunshine,* and *bunch*.

Spelling Patterns

/u/ Spelled *u* The sound /u/ is usually spelled *u* at the beginning or in the middle of a word.

DAY 1 Get Ready to Read

Objectives

- Apply knowledge of sound-spellings to decode unknown words when reading.
- Decode and read words in context and isolation.
- Practice fluency with oral rereading.

Decodable Practice Reader 6A

Short *u: u*

Decode words in isolation

Have children turn to page 217. Have children decode each word.

Duck Has Fun
Written by Elena Mays
Decodable Practice Reader 6A
Short u
Duck fun runs
mud tub hum
Cub up nuts
cups Pup cut
suns Bug rug
tucks
Initial Consonant Blends
Frog
flop
drop
spin
High-Frequency Words
like(s) to they the
with too a
217

Decodable Practice Reader 6A

Review High-frequency words

Review the previously taught words *like, they, with, too, to, the,* and *a*. Have children read each word as you point to it on the Word Wall.

Preview Decodable Reader

Have children read the title and preview the story. Tell them they will read words with the short vowel sound *u.*

Decode words in context

Pair children for reading and listen as they decode. One child begins. Children read the entire story, switching readers after each page. Partners reread the story. This time the other child begins.

Duck likes fun.
218
Duck runs to Frog.
They flop in mud.
219

Decodable Practice Reader 6A

Duck hops in the tub.
Frog hops in too.
They hum.
220
Duck runs with Cub.
They pick up nuts.
They drop nuts in the cups.
221

Duck sits with Pup.
They cut suns.
222
Duck spots Bug.
They sit on a rug.
They spin tops.
223

Duck gets in bed.
Mom tucks Duck in.
Duck had fun.
224

Corrective feedback

If... children have difficulty decoding a word, **then...** refer them to the Sound-Spelling Cards to identify the sounds in the word. Then prompt them to blend the word.

- What is the new word?
- Is the new word a word you know?
- Does it make sense in the story?

Check decoding and comprehension

Have children retell the story to include characters, setting, and events. Then have children locate short *u* words in the story. List words that children name. Children should supply *Duck, fun, runs, mud, tub, hum, Cub, up, nuts, cups, Pup, cut, suns, Bug, rug,* and *tucks*.

Reread for Fluency

Have children reread Decodable Practice Reader 6A to develop automaticity decoding words with the short *u* sound.

ROUTINE Oral Rereading

1. **Read** Have children read the entire book orally.
2. **Reread** To achieve optimal fluency, children should reread the text three or four times.
3. **Corrective Feedback** Listen as children read. Provide corrective feedback regarding their fluency and decoding.

Routines Flip Chart

Differentiated Instruction

Strategic Intervention

Guide Writing After reading, write the following short *u* words on the board and ask children to pronounce them after you: *mud, tub, gum,* and *hut*. Ask children to write their own sentences using these words. Monitor children's use of each word within their sentences.

English Language Learners

Short *u*: /u/

Beginning Before children read, lead them through *Duck Has Fun*, identifying Duck, Cub, Pup, and Bug. Point out short *u* words, such as *rug*, *mud*, and *tub* and the drawing that illustrates each. Have children say each word aloud.

Intermediate After reading, have children find short *u* words in the story. Ask them to use one or more of the words in a sentence—for example, *It's fun to hum in the tub.* Monitor children's pronunciation.

Advanced/High Advanced After reading, have children act out some of the ways Duck has fun. Have them explain what they are doing. Monitor children's pronunciation.

Objectives

- Segment and spell short *u* words with final consonant blends.
- Read high-frequency words.

Spelling Pretest
Short *u* Words with Final Consonant Blends

Dictate spelling words

Dictate the spelling words. Have children write the words. If needed, segment the words for children, clarify the pronunciations, and give meanings of words. Have children check their pretests and correct misspelled words.

1. crust	Mom can cut the **crust** off my sandwich.
2. bump*	The road has a big **bump** in it.
3. jump	I can **jump** up and down.
4. must	I **must** do my homework.
5. just	I **just** finished reading the book.
6. dust	Look at the **dust** on the table!
7. trust	I **trust** you to tell the truth.
8. dusk	It is **dusk** just before the sun sets.
9. hunt	I have to **hunt** for my mop.
10. lump	The cat made a **lump** under the blanket.

Let's Practice It! TR DVD•70

* Words marked with asterisks come from the selection *Animal Park*.

On their own

Use Let's Practice It! p. 70 on the *Teacher Resource DVD-ROM.*

Small Group Time

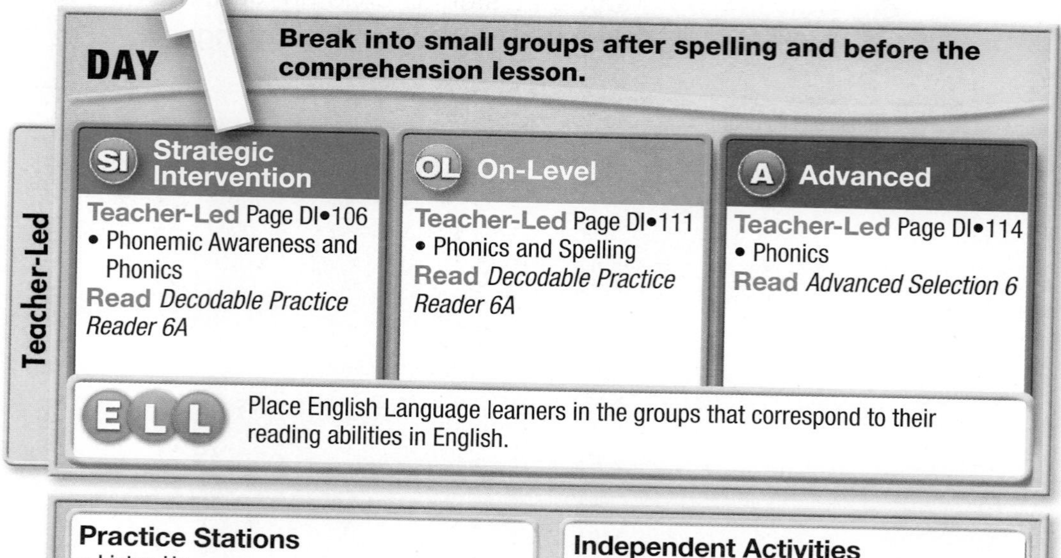

DAY 1
Break into small groups after spelling and before the comprehension lesson.
Teacher-Led
SI Strategic Intervention
Teacher-Led Page DI•106
• Phonemic Awareness and Phonics
Read Decodable Practice Reader 6A
OL On-Level
Teacher-Led Page DI•111
• Phonics and Spelling
Read Decodable Practice Reader 6A
A Advanced
Teacher-Led Page DI•114
• Phonics
Read Advanced Selection 6
ELL
Place English Language learners in the groups that correspond to their reading abilities in English.

Practice Stations
- Listen Up
- Word Work

Independent Activities
- Read independently/Reading Log on *Reader's and Writer's Notebook* p. RR2
- Concept Talk Video

High-Frequency Words

Introduce

ROUTINE **Nondecodable Words**

1. **Say and Spell** Look at p. 151. Some words we have to learn by remembering the letters rather than saying the sounds. We will say and spell the words to help learn them. Point to the first word. This word is *home*. The letters in *home* are h-o-m-e, *home*. Have children say and spell each word, first with you, and then without you.
2. **Identify Familiar Letter-Sounds** Point to the first letter in *home*. You know the sound for this letter. What is this letter and what is its sound? (*h*, /h/)
3. **Demonstrate Meaning** Tell me a sentence using the word *home*. Repeat this routine with the other Words I Can Read.

Routines Flip Chart

Read words in isolation Have children read the words on p. 151 aloud. Add the words to the Word Wall.

Read words in context Have children read the sentences aloud. Have them identify this week's High-Frequency Words in the sentences.

On their own Use *Reader's and Writer's Notebook* p. 202.

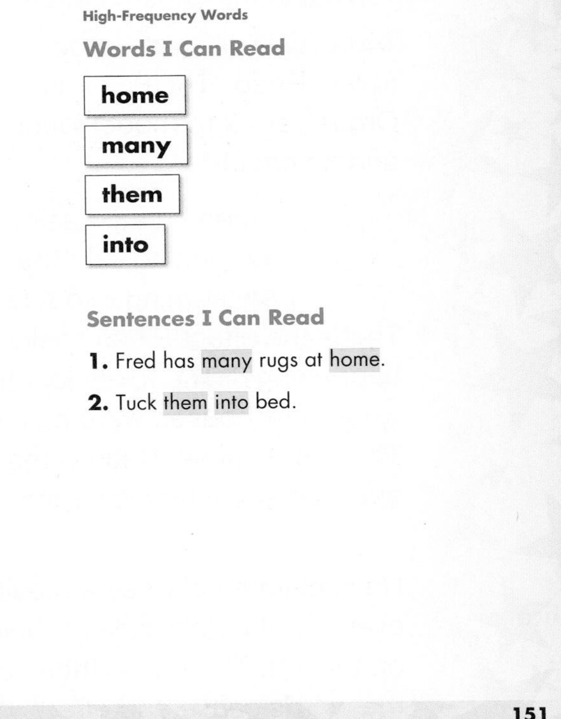
High-Frequency Words

Words I Can Read

home

many

them

into

Sentences I Can Read

1. Fred has many rugs at home.
2. Tuck them into bed.

151

Student Edition p. 151

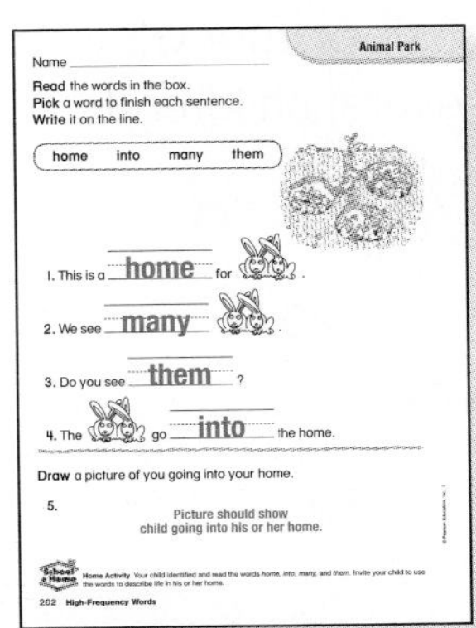
Animal Park

Name ______

Read the words in the box.
Pick a word to finish each sentence.
Write it on the line.

home into many them

1. This is a home for [rabbits].
2. We see many [rabbits].
3. Do you see them?
4. The [rabbits] go into the home.

Draw a picture of you going into your home.

5. Picture should show child going into his or her home.

Home Activity Your child identified and read the words *home, into, many,* and *them*. Invite your child to use the words to describe life in his or her home.

202 High-Frequency Words

Reader's and Writer's Notebook p. 202

Differentiated Instruction

Advanced

Extend Spelling Challenge children who spell words correctly to spell more difficult words such as: *plump, tusk, pumpkin, stunt, grump,* and *uncle*.

Phonics/Spelling Generalization

Short *u* Each spelling word is a short *u* word, which has the short *u* sound.

English Language Learners

Survival Vocabulary Have children use the word *home* to talk about where they live. Children might say, *My **home** is nice.*

Frontload Read Aloud Use the modified Read Aloud in the *ELL Support Lessons* to prepare students to listen to "The Fox Family" (page 151b).

DAY 1 Read and Comprehend

30–35 min.

Objectives

◎ Identify cause and effect in narrative text.

Skills Trace

◎ Cause and Effect

Introduce U1W6D1; U2W2D1; U4W6D1
Practice U1W6D2; U1W6D3; U1W6D4; U2W2D2; U2W2D3; U2W2D4; U4W6D2; U4W6D3; U4W6D4
Reteach/Review U1W6D5; U2W1D2; U2W2D5; U2W4D2; U2W5D2; U4W1D2; U4W6D5
Assess/Test Weekly Tests U1W6; U2W2; U4W6
Benchmark Tests U1

KEY:
U=Unit W=Week D=Day

Listening Comprehension
◎ Cause and Effect

Introduce

Many things happen for a reason. The reason, or why something happens, is called the **cause**. The thing that is made to happen is the **effect**. Good readers ask themselves what happens and why because it helps them understand what they are reading. Display the words *because, so,* and *since*. Authors may use clue words like these to help readers figure out the cause and effect.

Student Edition EI•2

Have children turn to p. EI•2 in their Student Edition. These pictures show an example of cause and effect. Discuss these questions using the pictures:

- What do you see in the first picture? (a rain cloud)
- What do you see in the second picture? (a wet girl)
- What is the cause and effect? (Rain is the cause; a wet girl is the effect)

Model

Today we will read a story about some wild foxes. Read "The Fox Family." Use Graphic Organizer 29 to model identifying a cause and its effect.

When I read, I ask myself, "What is happening?" In the story, wild foxes are coming into a family's backyard. That's the effect. Then I ask, "Why is this happening?" The foxes lost their homes when new houses were built in the woods. That's the cause. Record the cause and effect on the Graphic Organizer.

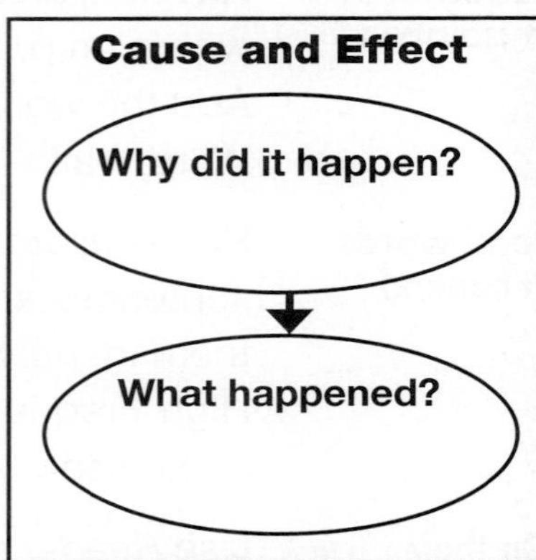

Graphic Organizer Flip Chart 29

Guide practice

Have children choose a previously read story. Ask them to draw one story event on the right side of their paper and its cause on the left. Then have them label their picture with the words *cause* and *effect*. Ask several children to share their pictures with the class.

On their own

Use *Reader's and Writer's Notebook* p. 203.

Reader's and Writer's Notebook p. 203

Read Aloud

The Fox Family

"Mom! Mom!" Jake cried when he saw the red and white furry animal that sat on the grass. "Look at that funny little dog in the backyard!"

Jake's mom moved to the window and looked out.

"Now there are two of them! One is small, and one is big! Maybe one is the mother and one is the baby!"

Jake's mom said, "Those aren't dogs, Jake. Those are foxes. And yes, one is the parent, and the smaller one is the baby. We call a baby fox a kit."

"But why is a wild fox in our backyard?"

Jake's mom looked sad. "We live in a place that was once country and forests. Every year more and more people are building houses here. When people build houses, the foxes lose their homes. We have so many trees in our backyard, I guess they feel safe here."

"Are they dangerous?"

"Not really. They eat beetles, earthworms, mice, and sometimes rabbits."

"What else do they do?"

"Watch and find out," Jake's mom said.

"Can I pet them?"

"No, Jake, foxes are not pets. It's okay to observe them, but we should always remember they are wild animals."

Academic Vocabulary

cause why something happens

effect what happens

Language Arts

Objectives

- Identify and use exclamatory sentences.
- Recognize and use correct capitalization and punctuation for exclamatory sentences.
- Identify key features of a brief composition.

MINI-LESSON

5 Day Planner
Guide to Mini-Lessons

DAY 1	• Read Like a Writer
DAY 2	• Brief Composition: Narrowing Your Topic
DAY 3	• Evaluation
DAY 4	• Know Your Purpose
DAY 5	• Proofread: Sentences

Conventions
Exclamatory Sentences

Model

Review that a declarative sentence tells something and ends with a period and that an interrogative sentence asks something and ends with a question mark. Explain that an **exclamatory sentence** shows strong feeling and ends with an exclamation mark. *That is the biggest bird I ever saw!* is an exclamatory sentence.

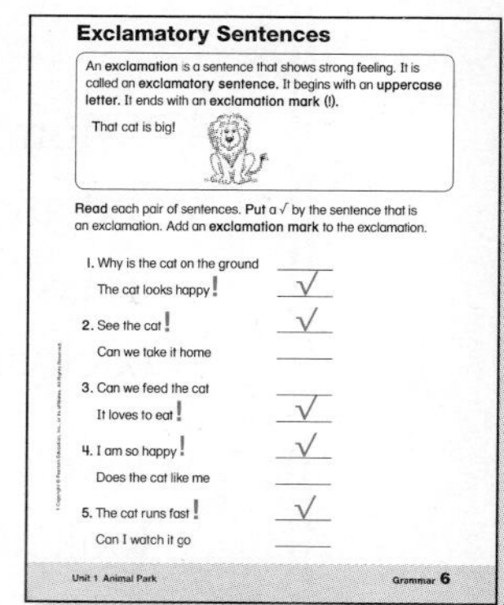

Exclamatory Sentences

An **exclamation** is a sentence that shows strong feeling. It is called an **exclamatory sentence.** It begins with an **uppercase letter.** It ends with an **exclamation mark (!).**

That cat is big!

Read each pair of sentences. **Put** a √ by the sentence that is an exclamation. Add an **exclamation mark** to the exclamation.

1. Why is the cat on the ground ____
   The cat looks happy! √
2. See the cat! √
   Can we take it home ____
3. Can we feed the cat ____
   It loves to eat! √
4. I am so happy! √
   Does the cat like me ____
5. The cat runs fast! √
   Can I watch it go ____

Unit 1 Animal Park — Grammar 6

Grammar Transparency 6
TR DVD

Display Grammar Transparency 6. Read the definition and example aloud. Point out the capital letter and exclamation mark. Then read the directions and model number 1.

- The sentence *Why is the cat on the ground* asks a question and should end with a question mark. This sentence is an interrogative sentence.
- The sentence *Wow, that cat can jump* shows strong feeling, so I will add an exclamation mark. This sentence is an exclamatory sentence.

Guide practice

Continue with items 2–5, having children identify the exclamatory sentence in each pair and write the exclamation mark.

Connect to oral language

Read each sentence below. Have children identify the sentence type and name the end punctuation mark. Then have children discuss why these end marks are used.

Did his cat nap in the sun?
Jen has a big dog.
That dog can swim fast!

On their own

Team Talk Pair children and have them talk about some amazing things they have seen animals do. Have them make up and write two exclamatory sentences about the animals. Remind them to use an exclamation mark at the end of each sentence.

Writing for Tests
Brief Composition

MINI-LESSON

Read Like a Writer

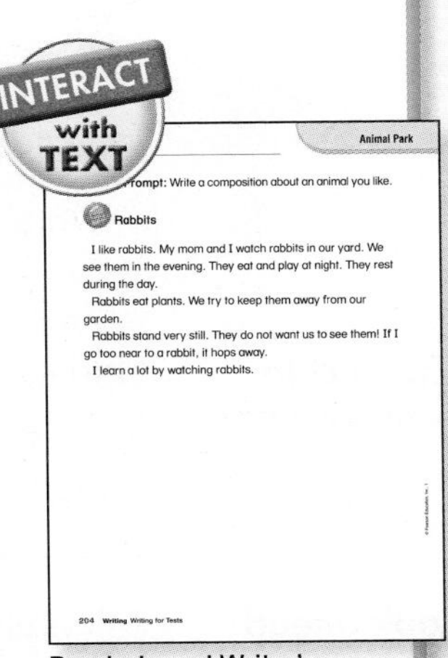
INTERACT with TEXT

Animal Park

Prompt: Write a composition about an animal you like.

Rabbits

I like rabbits. My mom and I watch rabbits in our yard. We see them in the evening. They eat and play at night. They rest during the day.

Rabbits eat plants. We try to keep them away from our garden.

Rabbits stand very still. They do not want us to see them! If I go too near to a rabbit, it hops away.

I learn a lot by watching rabbits.

204 Writing Writing for Tests

Reader's and Writer's Notebook p. 204

■ **Introduce** This week you will write a brief **composition**. A composition tells about real things.

Genre	Brief Composition
Trait	Focus/Ideas
Mode	Expository

■ **Examine Model Text** Let's listen to a brief composition. This composition is written to answer a test question. Track the print as you read aloud "Rabbits" on *Reader's and Writer's Notebook* p. 204. Have children follow along.

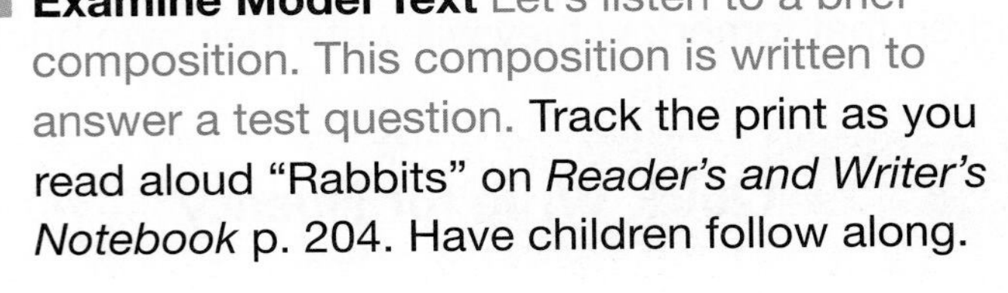

■ **Key Features** What is the topic of this composition? (rabbits) Help children find and underline sentences that tell real things about rabbits, such as *They eat and play at night* and *Rabbits eat plants*. Ask children if they can find any made-up things in the composition. (no)

This composition tells real things about rabbits. It tells when rabbits eat and play. It tells what they eat. It tells that they like to be left alone.

The author of this composition tells about only one topic. The composition is only about rabbits. The author also tells only real things, not made-up things.

Write Guy
Jeff Anderson

The Sunny Side

I like to look for what's *right* in students' writing rather than looking for things I can edit or fix. Most students don't write flawlessly, but they will learn what they are doing well if we point it out.

Academic Vocabulary

exclamatory sentence a group of words that shows a strong feeling

brief composition writing that tells about real things

topic what the composition is all about

Daily Fix-It

1. jump onto a bus to go home.
   Jump onto a bus to go home.
2. many of them sit in sunn.
   Many of them sit in sun.

Discuss the Daily Fix-It corrections with children. Review sentence capitalization, the difference between *m* and *n,* and the spelling of *sun*.

English Language Learners

Conventions To provide children with practice on exclamatory sentences, use the modified grammar lessons in the *ELL Handbook*.

Objectives

- Understand and recognize the features of a brief composition.
- Identify a topic connected to this week's concept.
- Narrow the focus of the topic by formulating inquiry questions related to the topic.
- Explore animals, tame and wild.

Writing for Tests
Brief Composition, continued

Introduce key features Introduce the key features of a brief composition with children. You may want to post these key features in the classroom to allow children to refer to them as they work on their compositions.

Key Features of a Brief Composition

- tells about real people, animals, or things
- tells about one topic

Connect to familiar texts Use examples from *A Fox and a Kit* (Unit 1) or another nonfiction text familiar to children. *A Fox and a Kit* tells about real animals. It tells real things about a fox and her kit. It tells how the fox takes care of her baby. It does not tell made-up things.

Look ahead Tell children that tomorrow they will write their own brief compositions.

ROUTINE Quick Write for Fluency Team Talk

1. **Talk** Read these titles aloud, and have children discuss which one sounds like the title of a composition and why.

   Penguin Babies

   The Penguin that Flew Around the World
2. **Write** Have children write a sentence explaining what kinds of things a composition might tell about.
3. **Share** Partners can read their sentences to one another.

Routines Flip Chart

Research and Inquiry
Identify and Focus Topic

Teach

Display and review the concept map about this week's question: *What can we learn about wild animals by watching them?* What would you like to learn about an animal by watching it? Ask children to share their ideas. Point out that they can learn about an animal in the neighborhood by observing.

Model

Think Aloud One way to learn about an animal is to spend time observing it. When I find an animal I want to watch, I don't look away even for a second. I stay very still and quiet. As I am watching my animal, I ask myself questions about my animal. I keep watching to find the answers to my questions. Later, I will share these answers with other people.

Guide Practice

Give children time to think about an animal to observe and questions about the animal. Record children's questions in a chart.

Wrap Up Your Day

- **Phonics: Short *u*: *u*** Write *cup* and *ugly*. Ask children what sound the letter *u* spells in each word. (short *u*).
- **Spelling: Short *u* Words with Final Consonant Blends** Have children name the letter or letters that spell each sound in *dunk* and write the word. Continue with *rust, sunk,* and *pump*.
- **Build Concepts** Ask children to recall what happened in the Read Aloud, "The Fox Family." What do you think Jake will learn if he observes the fox and kit in his yard? (Possible response: What they do during the day, what they eat, where they go.)
- **Homework** Send home this week's Family Times Newsletter from Let's Practice It! pp. 65–66 on the *Teacher Resource DVD-ROM*.

Let's Practice It!
TR DVD•65–66

Differentiated Instruction

SI Strategic Intervention

Selecting a Topic If children have trouble deciding on an animal to write about, write the names of several neighborhood animals on the board. Invite them to pick an animal and tell what they know about it and what more they would like to find out. Tell children they can find out more by observing the animal.

Tell children that tomorrow they will read about wild animals that live in an animal park.

Objectives

- Discuss the concept to develop oral vocabulary.
- Build oral vocabulary.

Today at a Glance

Oral Vocabulary
chatter, silent

Phonemic Awareness
Segment and Blend Phonemes

Phonics and Spelling
- Short *u: u*
- Final Consonant Blends

Fluency
Paired Reading

High-Frequency Words

Story Words
elephants, hippos, park, zebras

Comprehension
- Cause and Effect
- Text Structure

Vocabulary
Antonyms

Genre
Literary Nonfiction

Conventions
Exclamatory Sentences

Writing
Brief Composition: Narrowing Your Topic

Handwriting
Letters *Uu* and *Qq*/Letter Spacing

Research and Inquiry
Research Skill: Notes

Concept Talk

Question of the Week

What can we learn about wild animals by watching them?

Build concepts

To reinforce concepts and to focus children's attention, have children sing "Big, Round World" from the *Sing with Me* Big Book. Where do the chipmunks in the song live? (in the forest) What could you watch them do there? (run and race)

Sing with Me Big Book Audio

Introduce Amazing Words

Display the Big Book, *Jungle Drum*. Read the title and identify the author. Explain that in the story, the author uses the words *chatter* and *silent*. Have children listen as you read the story to find out who likes to *chatter* and when the animals in the jungle are *silent*.

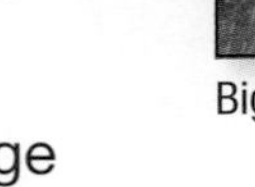

Big Book

Use the Oral Vocabulary routine on the next page to teach *chatter* and *silent*.

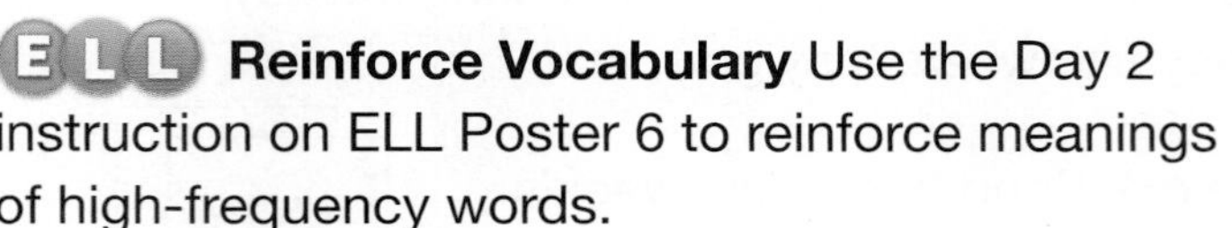
ELL **Reinforce Vocabulary** Use the Day 2 instruction on ELL Poster 6 to reinforce meanings of high-frequency words.

ELL Poster 6

Oral Vocabulary
Amazing Words

Teach Amazing Words

Amazing Words Oral Vocabulary Routine

1. **Introduce the Word** Relate the word *silent* to the book. When the drum plays, the animals are *silent*. Supply a child-friendly definition. *Silent* means "quiet." It means "not making a sound." Have children say the word.
2. **Demonstrate** Provide examples to show meaning. An empty house is *silent*. Your room at night is *silent*. When you turn the TV off, it is *silent*.
3. **Apply** Have children demonstrate their understanding. Name some times when you try to be *silent*.

See p. OV•3 to teach *chatter*.

Routines Flip Chart

Anchored Talk

Add to the concept map

Discuss how watching wild animals can help us learn where animals live and what sounds they make.

- What does the song "Big, Round World" tell us about the places animals live? (They live in the desert and in the forest.) Let's add *We learn where animals live* to our map. Then I'll write *desert* and *forest* under that.
- The book *Jungle Drum* describes another place that animals live. Where do the animals in that story live? (They live in the jungle.) Let's add *jungle* to our map.
- What sounds do the parrots in the jungle make? (They screech.) What sounds do the monkeys make? (They chatter.) Let's add *We learn what sounds animals make* to our map. Then I'll write *parrots screech* and *monkeys chatter*.

Amazing Words

desert	silent
forest	snort
world	medicine
chatter	poisonous

Differentiated Instruction

Advanced

Using Amazing Words Have children fold a piece of drawing paper in half. Ask them to draw a desert on one side and a forest on the other, including the appropriate plants and animals. Have children add the labels *desert* and *forest*. Then have them add speech balloons to show what sounds the animals make. For example, they might write "chatter" above a squirrel.

English Language Learners

Physical Response Teach the words *chatter* and *silent* by acting them out and having children join you. To reinforce understanding, look for opportunities to recycle the words during the day. For example, you might note that children are *chattering* during peer writing conferences or that they should be *silent* when you are giving instructions.

Objectives

- Segment and blend words with final consonant blends.
- ◎ Blend and read words with final consonant blends.
- ◎ Associate consonants with their corresponding sounds.

Skills Trace

◎ **Final Consonant Blends**
Introduce/Teach U1W6D2
Practice U1W6D3; U1W6D4
Reteach/Review U1W6D5; U2W1D4
Assess/Test Weekly Test U1W6
Benchmark Test U1

KEY:
U=Unit W=Week D=Day

Phonemic Awareness
Segment and Blend Phonemes

Model isolating sounds Have children look at the picture on pages 148–149 in their Student Edition. I see a boy who has a bug crawling on his *wrist*. I hear two consonant sounds at the end of *wrist*, /s/ and /t/. I also see a *tent*. I hear the two consonant sounds /n/ and /t/ at the end of *tent*.

Student Edition pp. 148–149

Model segmenting and blending Listen to the sounds in the word *wrist*: /r/ /i/ /s/ /t/. There are four sounds in *wrist*. Let's blend those sounds to make a word: /r/ /i/ /s/ / t/. Continue modeling with *tent*.

Guide practice Guide children as they segment and blend these words from the picture: *crust, bump, camp, last, dump,* and *rust*.

Corrective Feedback **If...** children make an error,
then... model by segmenting the word, and have them repeat the segmenting and blending of the word.

On their own Have children segment and blend the following words.

/f/ /a/ /s/ /t/ **fast**	/b/ /e/ /l/ /t/ **belt**	/m/ /i/ /s/ /t/ **mist**
/l/ /a/ /m/ /p/ **lamp**	/n/ /e/ /s/ /t/ **nest**	/b/ /l/ /o/ /n/ /d/ **blond**
/d/ /e/ /s/ /k/ **desk**	/g/ /r/ /u/ /n/ /t/ **grunt**	/g/ /i/ /f/ /t/ **gift**

Phonics—Teach/Model

Final Consonant Blends

Sound-Spelling Card 38

ROUTINE Blending Strategy

1. **Connect** Write the word *ten*. You studied words like this already. What is the consonant sound at the end of *ten*? (/n/) Today you will learn about words that have two consonant sounds at the end.
2. **Use Sound-Spelling Card** Display Card 38. Point to the word *lamp*. The letters *mp* at the end of *lamp* stand for the sounds /m/ /p/. Have children say /m/ /p/ several times as you point to *mp*. Explain that the letters *mp* make a consonant blend whose sounds blend together at the end of a word.
3. **Model** Write *tent*. In this word, the letters *nt* stand for the sounds /n/ /t/. Segment and blend *tent*; then have children blend with you: /t/ /e/ /n/ /t/. Follow this procedure to model *fast*.
4. **Guide Practice** Continue the process in step 3. This time have children blend with you. Remind children to blend the sounds of the last two consonants together.

rust	**pant**	**romp**	**gift**	**bend**
milk	**belt**	**camp**	**pond**	**desk**

5. **Review** What do you know about reading these words? (The sounds of the two consonant letters at the end of each word are blended together.)

Routines Flip Chart

Differentiated Instruction

Advanced

Extend Blending Provide children who can segment and blend all the words correctly with more challenging words such as: *friend, shrimp, myself, August, frost,* and *spent*.

Vocabulary Support

You may wish to explain the meaning of these words.

rust a reddish-brown coating on metal that is caused by air and water

romp to play in a way that is lively

English Language Learners

Visual Support Model isolating sounds while using the pictures on pp. 148–149 of the Student Edition as visual support. For example: /b/ /u/ /m/ /p/, *bump*. Who can point to a bump on the tree trunk? Now let's say the sounds of *bump* together: /b/ /u/ /m/ /p/.

Objectives

- ◎ Blend and read words with final consonant blends.
- ◎ Associate consonant sounds with consonant blends.
- Decode words in context and in isolation.

Check Word Reading
SUCCESS PREDICTOR

Phonics—Build Fluency
Final Consonant Blends

Model

Envision It!

Have children turn to page 152 in their Student Edition. Look at the pictures on this page. I see a picture of a *lamp*. The word *lamp* ends with two consonants, *m* and *p*. When I say *lamp*, I blend the two consonant sounds together, /m/ /p/.

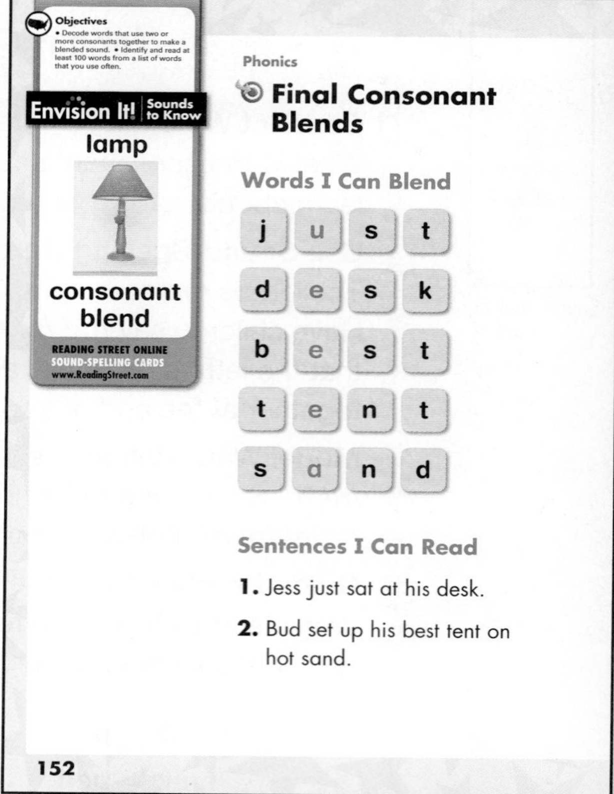

Student Edition p. 152

Guide practice

For each word in "Words I Can Blend," ask for the sound of each letter or group of letters. Make sure that children identify the correct sounds for each final consonant blend. Then have children blend the whole word.

Corrective feedback

If... children have difficulty blending a word,
then... model blending the word, and ask children to blend it with you.

Blend and Read

Decode words in isolation After children can successfully segment and blend the words, ask them to read the words naturally.

Decode words in context Have children read each of the sentences. Have them identify words with final consonant blends in the sentences.

Pair children and have them take turns reading each of the sentences aloud.

On their own Use *Reader's and Writer's Notebook* p. 205.

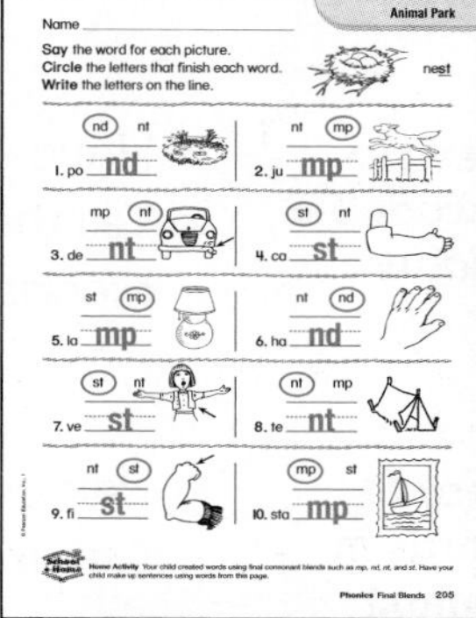
Reader's and Writer's Notebook p. 205

MONITOR PROGRESS — Check Word Reading: Final Consonant Blends

Write the following words and have the class read them. Notice which children miss words during the group reading. Call on those individuals to read some of the words.

bend	**help**	**stump**	**pond**	**last**
truck	**raft**	**sick**	**black**	**held**
drift	**plan**	**clasp**	**must**	**stamp**

Spiral Review
Row 2 contrasts final consonant blends and final *-ck*.
Row 3 reviews initial and final consonant blends.

If... children cannot blend words with final consonant blends,
then... use the Small Group Time Strategic Intervention lesson, p. DI•107, to reteach final consonant blends. Continue to monitor children's progress using other instructional opportunities during the week. See the Skills Trace on p. 152C.

Day 1	Day 2	Day 3	Day 4	Day 5
Check Word Reading	**Check Word Reading**	Check High-Frequency Words/Retelling	Check Fluency	Check Oral Vocabulary

Success Predictor

Differentiated Instruction

A Advanced

Listing Words with Blends Give children one or two common final consonant blends, such as *-st*. Have partners list as many words as they can that end with that blend. For example, children might list *fast, last, nest, chest, first, worst, feast, beast, mist, twist, lost, frost, most, toast, just,* and *trust*.

Academic Vocabulary

consonant blend two or more letters whose sounds are blended together when pronouncing a word

Word Reading Success Predictor

Objectives

- Apply knowledge of sound-spellings to decode unknown words when reading.
- Decode words in context and isolation.
- Practice fluency with oral rereading.

Decodable Practice Reader 6B

Final Consonant Blends

Decode words in isolation

Have children turn to page 225. Have children decode each word.

Decodable Practice Reader 6B

Review High-frequency words

Review the previously taught words *see, small,* and *that*. Have children read each word as you point to it on the Word Wall.

Preview Decodable Reader

Have children read the title and preview the story. Tell them they will read words with final consonant blends.

Decode words in context

Pair children for reading and listen as they decode. One child begins. Children read the entire story, switching readers after each page.

The sun is up.
Frog sits on a stump.
226
Frog can bend his legs.
Frog can jump in the pond.
227

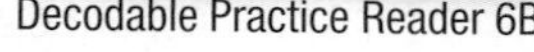
Decodable Practice Reader 6B

Frog can see a bug.
Flick!
Stop that bug!
228
Frog can see a nest.
It has small ducks in it.
229

A big duck swims at him.
230
Frog must jump.
Frog gets back on the stump.
231

At last, Frog can rest!
Frog is on his stump.
232

Corrective feedback

If... children have difficulty decoding a word, **then...** refer them to the Sound-Spelling Cards to identify the sounds in the word. Then prompt them to blend the word.

- What is the new word?
- Is the new word a word you know?
- Does it make sense in the story?

Check decoding and comprehension

Have children retell the story to include characters, setting, and events. Then have children locate words that end with consonant blends in the story. List words that children name. Children should supply *stump, bend, jump, pond, nest, must, last,* and *rest*.

Reread for Fluency

Have children reread Decodable Practice Reader 6B to develop automaticity decoding words with final consonant blends.

ROUTINE Paired Reading

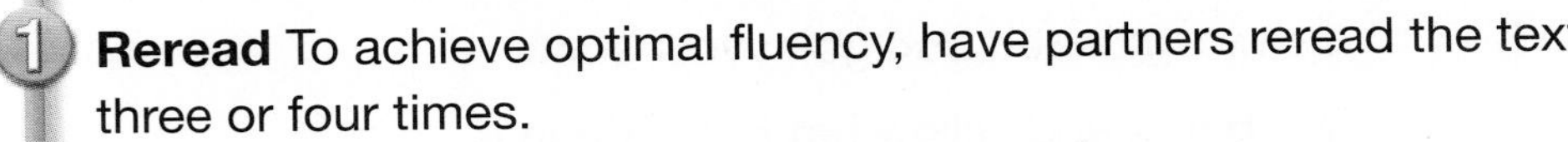

1. **Reread** To achieve optimal fluency, have partners reread the text three or four times.
2. **Corrective Feedback** Listen as children read. Provide corrective feedback regarding their fluency and decoding.

Routines Flip Chart

Differentiated Instruction

SI Strategic Intervention

Retelling If children have difficulty retelling the story, ask them questions regarding events in the story.

ELL English Language Learners

Final Consonant Blends

Beginning Before children read, lead them on a picture walk through the story. Point out and pronounce the words that end with consonant blends. Then write a pictured word and have children pronounce it and find its picture.

Intermediate Write words with final consonant blends on the board, such as *dust, rust, milk,* and *pond*. Say them aloud and then ask children to repeat them after you.

Advanced/Advanced High Have children find words that end with consonant blends in the story and use them in sentences.

Get Ready to Read

Objectives

- Apply knowledge of letter-sound correspondences and short vowels to decode words in context and in isolation.
- Spell words with short *u* and final consonant blends.

Phonics
Short Vowels

Review Sound-spellings Review the short-vowel spelling patterns *a, e, i, o,* and *u,* using Sound-Spelling Cards 1, 6, 11, 17, and 24.

Decode words in isolation Display these words. Have the class blend the words. Then point to the words in random order and ask children to read them quickly.

wet	**tag**	**dot**	**spin**
twig	**job**	**flap**	**pup**
drum	**truck**	**men**	**quick**

Corrective feedback Model blending decodable words and then ask children to blend them with you.

Decode words in context Display these sentences. Have the class read the sentences.

Team Talk Have pairs take turns reading the sentences naturally.

I saw a little **red bug** go **in** your **sock**.

My **black and** yellow **hat has** a **rip in it**.

It is too **hot** to **run**, **but** we **can still** have **fun**.

Spelling
Short *u* Words with Final Consonant Blends

Guide practice Tell children that you will segment the sounds in each spelling word. They should repeat the sounds in each word as they write the word. Check the spelling of each word before saying the next word.

1. /k/ /r/ /u/ /st/	**crust**	**6.** /d/ /u/ /s/ /t/	**dust**
2. /b/ /u/ /m//p/	**bump**	**7.** /tr/ /u/ /s/ /t/	**trust**
3. /j/ /u/ /m/ /p/	**jump**	**8.** /d/ /u/ /s/ /k/	**dusk**
4. /m/ /u/ /s/ /t/	**must**	**9.** /h/ /u/ /n/ /t/	**hunt**
5. /j/ /u/ /s/ /t/	**just**	**10.** /l/ /u/ /m/ /p/	**lump**

On their own Use *Reader's and Writer's Notebook* p. 206.

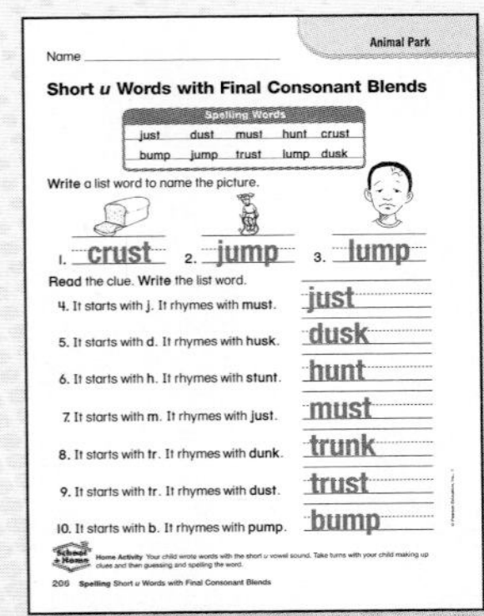
Name ______ Animal Park

Short *u* Words with Final Consonant Blends

Spelling Words: just dust must hunt crust bump jump trust lump dusk

Write a list word to name the picture.

1. crust 2. jump 3. lump

Read the clue. Write the list word.

4. It starts with j. It rhymes with must. just
5. It starts with d. It rhymes with husk. dusk
6. It starts with h. It rhymes with stunt. hunt
7. It starts with m. It rhymes with just. must
8. It starts with tr. It rhymes with dunk. trunk
9. It starts with tr. It rhymes with dust. trust
10. It starts with b. It rhymes with pump. bump

Reader's and Writer's Notebook p. 206

Small Group Time

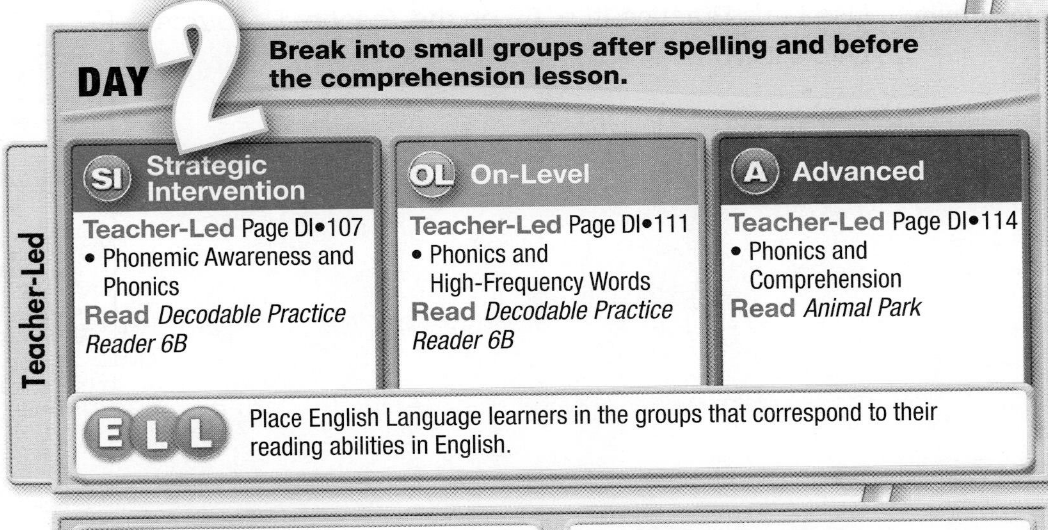

DAY 2
Break into small groups after spelling and before the comprehension lesson.
Teacher-Led
SI Strategic Intervention
Teacher-Led Page DI•107
• Phonemic Awareness and Phonics
Read Decodable Practice Reader 6B
OL On-Level
Teacher-Led Page DI•111
• Phonics and High-Frequency Words
Read Decodable Practice Reader 6B
A Advanced
Teacher-Led Page DI•114
• Phonics and Comprehension
Read Animal Park
ELL
Place English Language learners in the groups that correspond to their reading abilities in English.

Practice Stations
- Listen Up
- Word Work

Independent Activities
- Read Independently/Reading Log on *Reader's and Writer's Notebook* p. RR2
- AudioText of Main Selection

English Language Learners

Pronunciation Remind children that when they pronounce short *u*, the mouth is open, and the tongue is down. Have children practice saying the sound in isolation. Then have them practice with the spelling words, if needed.

Objectives

- Learn story words: *park, zebras, hippos, elephants.*
- Review high-frequency words.
- Identify antonyms.

High-Frequency Words
Build Fluency

Read words in isolation Remind children that there are some words we learn by remembering the letters, rather than by saying the sounds. Then have them read each of the highlighted high-frequency words aloud.

Read words in context Chorally read the "I Can Read!" passage along with the children. Then have them read the passage aloud to themselves. When they are finished, ask children to reread the high-frequency words.

Team Talk Have children choose two high-frequency words and give them time to create a sentence in which both words are used properly. Then have them share their sentence with a partner.

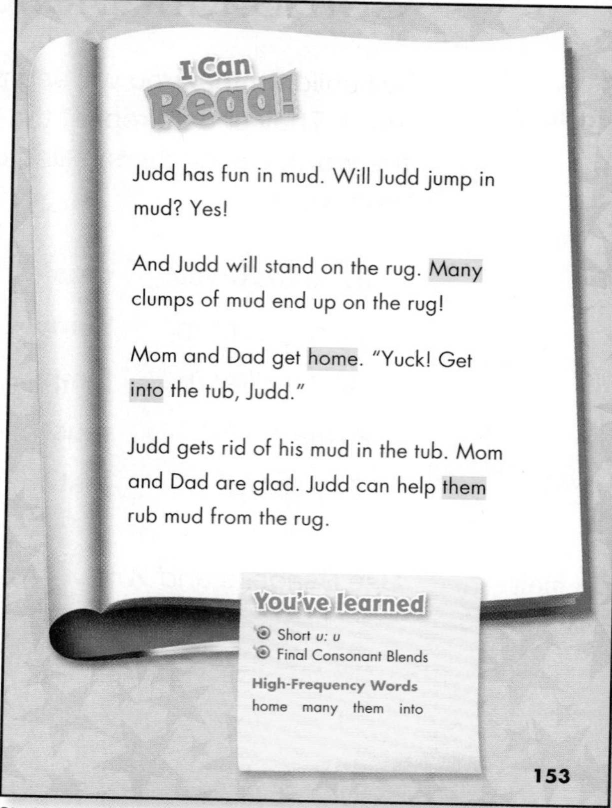

I Can Read!
Judd has fun in mud. Will Judd jump in mud? Yes!
And Judd will stand on the rug. Many clumps of mud end up on the rug!
Mom and Dad get home. "Yuck! Get into the tub, Judd."
Judd gets rid of his mud in the tub. Mom and Dad are glad. Judd can help them rub mud from the rug.
You've learned
Short u: u
Final Consonant Blends
High-Frequency Words
home many them into
153

Student Edition p. 153

On their own Use Let's Practice It! p. 69 on the *Teacher Resource DVD-ROM.*

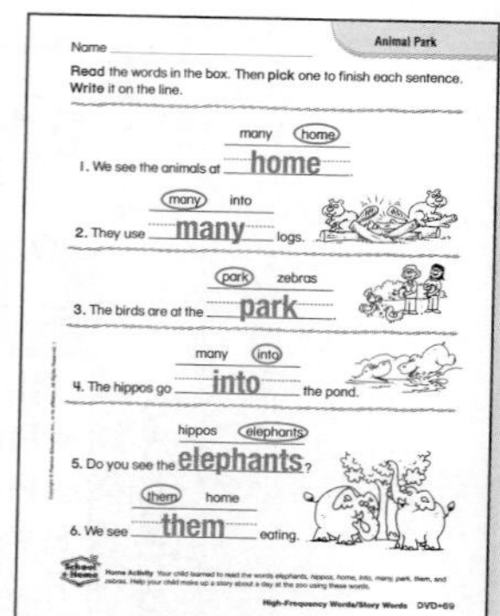

Let's Practice It!
TR DVD•69

Story Words
Animal Park

Introduce story words

Use Vocabulary Transparency 6 to introduce this week's story words. Read each sentence as you track the print. Frame each underlined word and explain its meaning.

park	land set aside for people to enjoy nature
elephants	huge, strong land animals with gray skin and long trunks
zebras	black-and-white striped animals that look like horses
hippos	a short word for hippopotamuses, which are large animals with short legs, thick skin, and wide mouths

At the Park

1. We like to go to the park.
2. The elephants are big.
3. The zebras are fast.
4. Three hippos sit in the mud.

Unit 1 Animal Park Vocabulary 6

Vocabulary Transparency 6
TR DVD

Have children read each sentence with you.

Vocabulary
Antonyms

Model antonyms

Explain that **antonyms** are words that have opposite meanings. Draw a T-chart or display Graphic Organizer 4. List these words in the left column: *stop, win, top, sad,* and *pull.* Explain that each word in the left column has an antonym.

stop	go
win	lose
top	bottom
sad	happy
pull	push

Graphic Organizer Flip Chart 4

I see the word *stop.* The opposite of *stop* is *go*. So *stop* and *go* are antonyms. I'll write *go* in the right column, so I can see the antonyms together.

Guide practice

Have a volunteer give the antonym for *win* and write it in the right column (lose). Repeat the procedure for the remaining words.

On their own

Have children think of and write pairs of antonyms on cards, writing one word on each card. Then have partners switch card sets and see if they can match the words that are antonyms.

Differentiated Instruction

Strategic Intervention

Word Reading If children have difficulty reading the high-frequency words, have them write each word on a card and practice reading the words aloud either to you or to a partner. Later today, have children match each card to a word on the pages of the main selection *Animal Park.*

Academic Vocabulary

antonym a word that means the opposite of another word

English Language Learners

Multilingual Vocabulary Lists
Children can apply knowledge of their home languages to acquire new English vocabulary by using the *Multilingual Vocabulary Lists* (*ELL Handbook* pp. 465–476).

Objectives

- Build background about safaris and wild-animal preserves.
- Preview and predict.
- Use key structure and elements of literary nonfiction to improve understanding of text.
- Set a purpose for reading text.

Build Background
Animal Park

Background Building Audio

Have children listen to the CD. Tell them to listen to find out what a safari is and the kinds of animals you might see and hear on a safari.

Background Building Audio

Discuss going on a safari

Team Talk Have children turn to a partner and use these questions for discussion:

- What would you most like to see or do on a safari?
- How might going on a safari make you want to protect wild animals?

Organize information in a web

Draw a web or display Graphic Organizer 17. Write "Safaris" in the center. Ask children to name wild animals that people on a safari might see. Add their responses to the web.

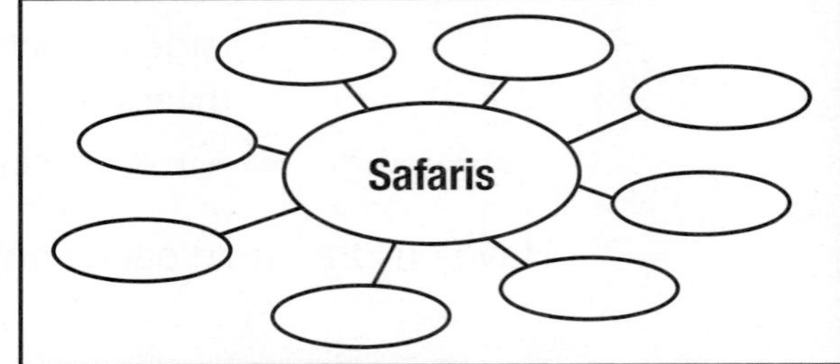

Graphic Organizer Flip Chart 17

Connect to selection

We learned that there are many kinds of wild animals and that they live in different places. In the story we are about to read, *Animal Park,* we'll find out about a big animal park that has been set aside to protect some animals. We'll find out what kinds of animals call the big park home.

Student Edition pp. 154–155

Main Selection—First Read
Animal Park

Practice the skill

Cause and Effect Review that a **cause** is why something happens. An **effect** is what happens. Ask children to imagine that a new highway covered a pond in the forest. Have them tell what effect that might have on the wild animals that live there.

Introduce the strategy

Text Structure Explain that one way good readers understand what they are reading is to think about how a story is organized. They look at titles, labels, diagrams, maps, pictures, and the order that the author tells readers information. Have children turn to page EI•16 in their Student Edition.

Envision It!

Think Aloud What is happening in the first set of pictures? (A tadpole changes into a frog.) What happens in the second set of pictures? (The seed changes into a plant.) As I read *Animal Park*, I will pay attention to how the selection is organized.

Student Edition EI•16

Introduce genre

Read Together Literary **nonfiction** tells about real-life people, animals, or events. The setting is real. As they read *Animal Park*, ask children to identify text features that indicate this is a true story about real people, animals, events, and places.

Preview and predict

Have children read the title of the story. Read the names of the author and illustrator, and have children describe the role of each. Have children activate prior knowledge by looking through the selection and predicting what visitors see in the animal park.

Set a purpose

Good readers read for a purpose. Setting a purpose helps us to think and understand more as we read. Guide children to set a purpose for reading the selection.

Tell children that today they will read *Animal Park* for the first time. Use the Day 2 Guide Comprehension notes to help children develop their comprehension of the selection.

First Read

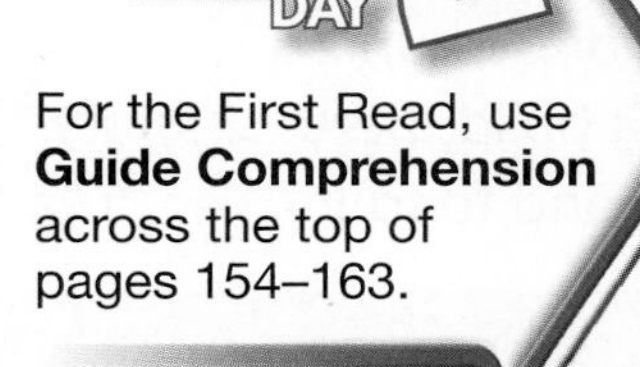

For the First Read, use **Guide Comprehension** across the top of pages 154–163.

Strategy Response Log

Genre Have children use p. RR18 in their *Reader's and Writer's Notebook* to identify the characteristics of literary nonfiction.

Academic Vocabulary

author a person who writes books, stories, poems, or plays

cause why something happens

effect what happens

nonfiction writing that tells facts about something real

English Language Learners

Build Background Before children listen to the CD, build background and elicit prior knowledge. On the CD, you will hear about animals people might see and hear on a safari. Name some of those animals, and tell what they look like.

Frontload Main Selection Ask children what they already know about wild animals in Africa, using the picture on pp. 154–155. Then do a picture walk of the selection so children can talk about and see the animals in one African animal preserve.

DAYS 2 & 3 Read and Comprehend

Objectives

- Make inferences using textual evidence.
- ◎ Use text features to locate information.
- Determine word meaning and use newly acquired vocabulary.
- Discuss ideas related to but not expressed in the literature.

Guide Comprehension
Skills and Strategies

Connect to Concept

Watching Wild Animals Look at the pictures on pages 154 and 155. What is one thing you might learn about these elephants by watching them? (Possible response: We might learn what they eat.)

Amazing Words Have children continue discussing the concept using the Amazing Words *desert, forest, world, chatter,* and *silent* as they read.

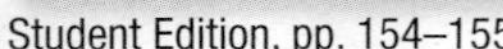
Student Edition, pp. 154–155

Extend Thinking
Think Critically

Higher-Order Thinking Skills

Synthesis *Animal Park* tells about a special park where wild animals are protected. How can a park like this help keep animals safe? (Possible response: Animals cannot be hunted in the park. People can't build there, so animals have homes and food.)

If... children cannot identify ways an animal preserve protects animals, **then...** encourage them to think about what they learned about animals' homes in the Read Aloud story "The Fox Family."

Strategies

Text Structure Remind children that good readers look at titles, labels, maps, and pictures to help them understand what they are reading. Have children tell what they know so far about the story: What will it be about? Where does it take place? Which animals live in the park? Ask children to explain which text features provide this information.

If... children have trouble identifying their sources of information,
then... point out the selection title, the labeled map on page 155, and the various photographs. Explain what information readers can learn from each.

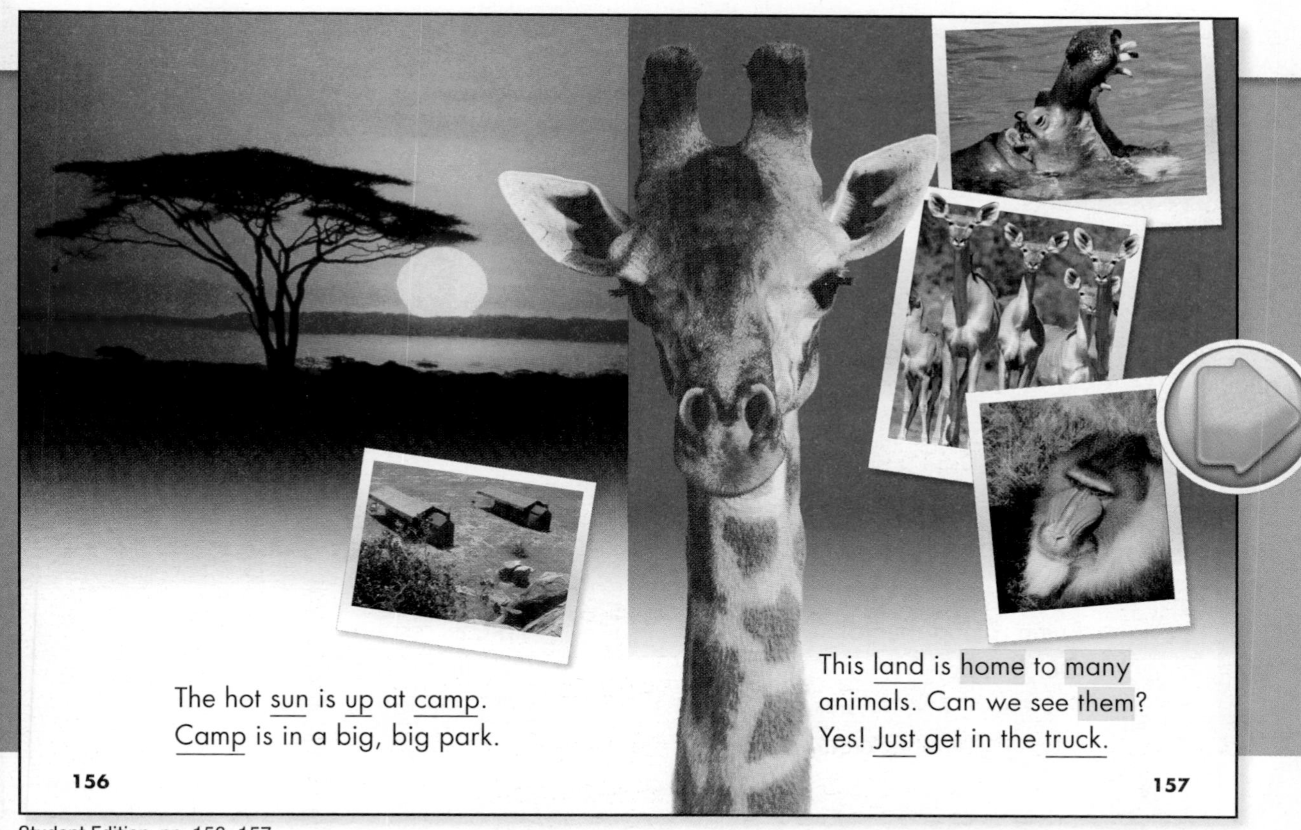

The hot sun is up at camp.
Camp is in a big, big park.
156
This land is home to many animals. Can we see them? Yes! Just get in the truck.
157

Student Edition, pp. 156–157

Higher-Order Thinking Skills

Analysis What kind of camp is the author writing about on page 156? How can you tell? (Possible response: I can tell from the small photograph that this isn't a summer camp. It's the kind of camp people stay in when they visit the park.)

Synthesis The author says that this is a "big, big park." Why do you think the park is so big? (Possible response: The park must have room for many animals, some of which are very big and need lots of space.)

Skills and Strategies, continued

DAY 2

Strategies

Text Structure Remind children to pay attention to the order an author tells events. Describe what has happened so far, in order. (Possible response: The visitors are staying in a camp. They get into a truck. They see a band of zebras. Then they see big cats and cubs.)

Skills

Cause and Effect The big cats are resting on part of a tree. What caused them to be so tired? (They are tired from hunting.)

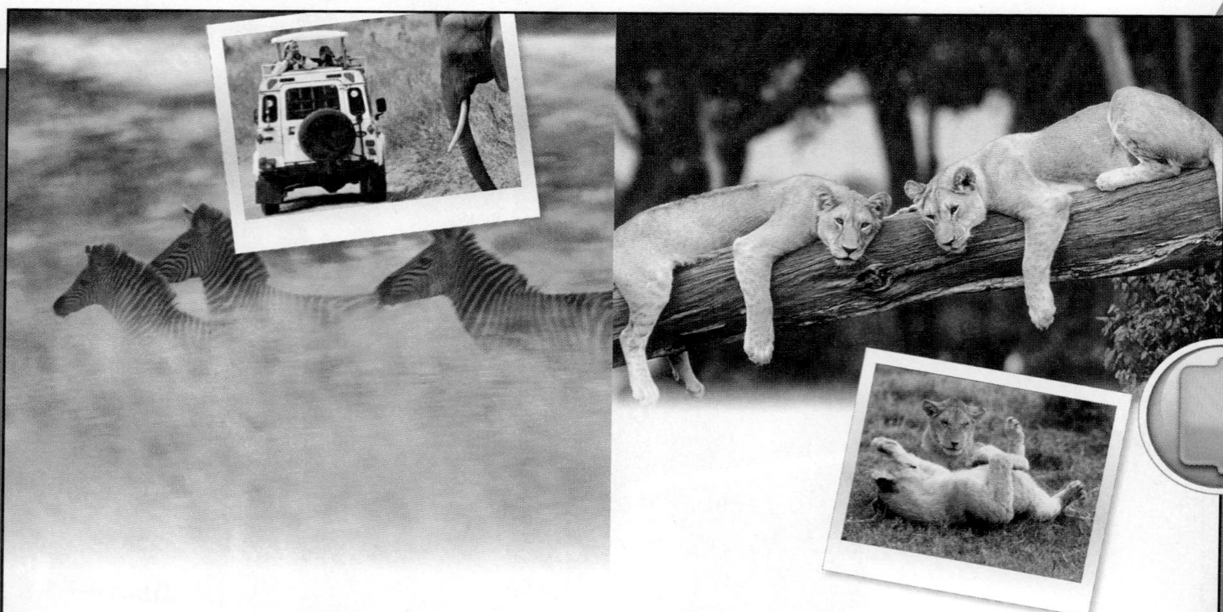

Bump, bump, bump!
Quick, stop!
A band of zebras runs past us.
They blend into the grass.
158
Big cats rest up.
They had a big hunt.
Cubs can bat at bugs.
159

Student Edition pp. 158–159

Think Critically, continued

DAY 3

Connect to Science

Animal Adaptations Many animals have developed features that help protect them. The vertical stripes of a zebra, for example, help it hide in the tall grass of the African savanna.

Team Talk Have children discuss other animals whose coloring helps them hide.

Higher-Order Thinking Skills

Analysis Look at the photograph on page 158. Why do you think the truck goes "bump, bump, bump"? (Possible response: The road is dirt, so it is probably bumpy, not smooth.)

Vocabulary

Antonyms I know that the words *stand* and *sit* on pages 160 and 161 are opposites. Words that are opposites are called antonyms. What word on page 160 is the antonym, or opposite, of *slow*? (fast) What word on page 161 is the antonym of *dry*? (wet) What word on page 161 is the antonym of *cold*? (hot)

Skills

Cause and Effect The hot sun has caused the air in the animal park to be very warm. What effect does this have on the hippos? (They sit in mud to try to cool off.)

Big birds stand in tan grass.
They can run fast!
160
Big hippos sit in wet mud.
It is hot, but mud is not hot!
161

Student Edition pp. 160–161

Higher-Order Thinking Skills

Evaluation The animals in the park do different things. Compare what the big birds are doing with what the hippos are doing. (The big birds are active. They're running fast. The hippos are not active. They're resting.)

If... children cannot easily compare the behavior of the two kinds of animals,
then... encourage them to reread the text and to look carefully at the photographs.

Skills and Strategies, continued

DAY 2

Word Reading

High-Frequency Words Point out the words *home, many,* and *them* on page 163. Have children practice reading these words.

Strategy Self-Check

Text Structure Have children explain how they used the title, map, photographs, and the order of events to help them understand the author's trip to the animal park.

Continue to DAY 2
Comprehension Check p. 163a

Big elephants stand and sip in the pond.
They can stomp and swim in it.

162

Bump, bump, bump!
The truck is back at camp.

This park is home to many animals.
It was fun to see them!

163

Student Edition pp. 162–163

Think Critically, continued

DAY 3

Higher-Order Thinking Skills

Analysis The author says that the elephants sip, stand in, stomp in, and swim in the pond. Why do you think they are doing this? (Because it is very hot out, the elephants are thirsty and they want to cool off in the water.)

Review **Main Idea and Details**

Evaluation What is the topic of the selection we just read? (an animal park) The main idea is the one big idea the author tells about the topic. What is the main idea? (People see many animals at the park) A detail is often a fact. What are some facts that we read on pages 162–163?

Comprehension Check

Have children discuss each question with a partner. Ask several pairs to share their responses.

☑ **Literary nonfiction** How is *Animal Park* different from a fantasy story about animals? (Possible response: In *Animal Park*, the animals are real, and the author tells about things that really happened.)

☑ **Confirm predictions** How did you use pictures or other clues to predict what visitors see at the animal park? (Possible response: I could tell what animals the visitors see by looking at the pictures.)

☑ **Setting** What is the setting for the selection *Animal Park?* (The setting is a hot day in an African animal preserve.)

☑ **Summarize** Summarize what happens in the selection. (Possible response: People go to an animal park in Africa to see wild animals. They get in a truck and drive through the park. They see giraffes, hippos, zebras, lions, hippos, and many other animals.)

☑ **Connect text to world** Do you think it's important to have parks like this one in different places in the world? Tell why or why not. (Possible response: I think it's important to have animal parks because animals need safe places to live, and people can learn about wild animals by going to the parks.)

Think Critically
pp. 164–165

English Language Learners

Support Discussion Help children state their opinions by providing them with this sentence frame: *I think* _____ *because* _____. Explain that first children should tell their opinion and that after the word *because* they should give their reason or reasons.

DAY 2 Read and Comprehend

Objectives

- Identify the features of literary nonfiction.
- Recognize and use correct capitalization and punctuation for exclamatory sentences.
- Say exclamatory sentences using the proper intonation.

Genre
Literary Nonfiction

Identify features of literary nonfiction

Use *Animal Park* to have children identify the features of literary nonfiction.

- *Animal Park* tells about real people and animals. Who are the people in the selection? (the author and other park visitors) What kinds of big animals do they see in the park? (Possible response: elephants, hippos)
- The setting of the selection is real too! Where is this animal park? (It is in Africa.)
- The selection tells about real events. How do the visitors travel around in the park? (They ride in a truck on bumpy roads.)

Guide practice

Explain that the class will now compare two nonfiction texts that the class has read. Display T-chart Graphic Organizer 4. Write the titles *Animal Park* and *A Fox and a Kit* at the tops of the columns. Record real-life people, animals, places, and events for each selection. Ask children to tell you what to write in each column. Once the chart is complete, have children compare and contrast the selections, discussing how the two selections are alike and different.

Animal Park	A Fox and a Kit

Graphic Organizer Flip Chart 4

On their own

Divide children into small groups and assign each group a previously read nonfiction selection. Have them identify the features that tell the selection really happened. Have them share their information with the class.

Conventions
Exclamatory Sentences

Model! exclamatory sentences

Write *His frog is the best pet!* on the board. Point to each word as you read it. Ask children to identify the end punctuation mark. (exclamation mark) An exclamatory sentence begins with a capital letter and ends with an exclamation mark. What does the exclamation mark tell us about the writer's feelings? (They are strong feelings.)

Guide Practice

Discuss feelings. Have children suggest the kinds of feelings that might cause someone to exclaim. List the feelings on the board. Then have children brainstorm events that might make them feel that way. Record what children might exclaim next to the appropriate emotion and event, for example:

Feeling	Event	Exclamatory Sentence
happy	winning a game	We won!

Connect to oral language

Explain that some declarative sentences can be changed to exclamatory sentences by changing the end punctuation. Have the class say these sentences once as a declarative sentence and once as an exclamatory sentence. Have them listen to the difference in their voices.

A black bug is on his leg.	**A black bug is on his leg!**
It is hot in here.	**It is hot in here!**

On their own

Use *Reader's and Writer's Notebook* p. 207.

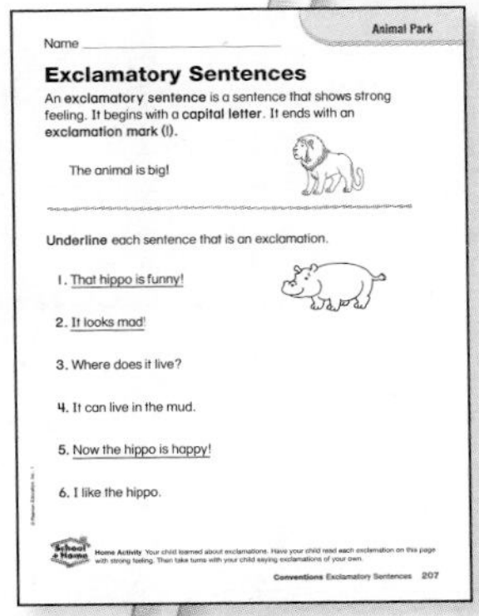
Animal Park

Name ______

Exclamatory Sentences

An **exclamatory sentence** is a sentence that shows strong feeling. It begins with a **capital letter**. It ends with an **exclamation mark (!)**.

The animal is big!

Underline each sentence that is an exclamation.

1. That hippo is funny!
2. It looks mad!
3. Where does it live?
4. It can live in the mud.
5. Now the hippo is happy!
6. I like the hippo.

Home Activity Your child learned about exclamations. Have your child read each exclamation on this page with strong feeling. Then take turns with your child saying exclamations of your own.

Conventions Exclamatory Sentences 207

Reader's and Writer's Notebook p. 207

Differentiated Instruction

SI Strategic Intervention

Support Conventions Ask children to draw a favorite scene from the Big Book *Jungle Drum.* Below their drawing, have them write two simple exclamatory sentences about their illustration. Ask them to explain what strong feeling each sentence shows and what punctuation mark they used at the end of each sentence.

Daily Fix-It

3. The bus hit a big bemp
The bus hit a big bump!

4. did frogs swim in the pont?
Did frogs swim in the pond?

Discuss the Daily Fix-It corrections with children. Review sentence capitalization and punctuation, the *u* spelling of /u/, and the *d* spelling of /d/.

English Language Learners

Intonation If English learners have difficulty making declarative and exclamatory sentences sound different, model the sentences for them. Then have them sit when they say a statement and stand up when they say an exclamation.

DAY 2 Language Arts

20–25 min.

Objectives

- Choose a topic for a brief composition.
- Write a brief composition.

Writing for Tests
Brief Composition

Introduce the prompt Review with children the key features of a composition. Explain that today children will write their own composition. Read aloud the writing prompt.

Writing Prompt

> Think about wild animals. Write a composition about what people learn by watching wild animals.

MINI-LESSON

Narrowing Your Topic

- **Teach** A good composition tells about just one topic. By writing about just one topic, the author helps readers understand the ideas in the composition. All the ideas are about one thing. To write an answer to the prompt, first we should choose just one topic to write about. One way to do this is to list the topics we could write about, then choose just one from the list.

- **Model** Let's write a list of topics we could write about. Write *Wild Animals We Watch* as a heading for the list. I'll think of wild animals I have seen. I see birds everywhere. I'll write *birds* at the top of my list. Add *squirrels, lizards, raccoons, deer, frogs, spiders,* and other animals children suggest to the list. Next I'll reread the prompt. The prompt asks me to write about what people learn by watching wild animals. So I should write about an animal that I know about. I know things about deer. I can tell what people learn by watching deer. I know that they live in the woods. I know that they eat plants. So I will write about deer. Circle *deer* on the list.

Discuss rubric Explain the rubric on *Reader's and Writer's Notebook* p. 208. Tell children that their writing this week will be evaluated using the rubric. Track the print as you read aloud the rubric, focusing on the trait of Focus/Ideas. Have children follow along.

Sample test Have children get paper and pencil ready to take a writing test. Display the writing prompt and give children time to write to the prompt. Remind children to allow themselves a few minutes after writing to reread what they have written and make changes or additions.

INTERACT with TEXT

Focus/Ideas	A good composition tells about one topic.
Organization	A good composition tells important ideas in an order that makes sense.
Voice	A good composition tells about the topic in a way that is interesting.
Word Choice	A good composition uses clear words.
Sentences	A good composition is written in complete sentences.
Conventions	A good composition has sentences that are punctuated correctly.

Reader's and Writer's Notebook p. 208

ROUTINE Quick Write for Fluency — Team Talk

1. **Talk** Have partners take two minutes to tell what they did to narrow their topic.
2. **Write** Have children write one sentence telling what they did to narrow their topic.
3. **Share** Partners trade sentences and read them aloud.

Routines Flip Chart

Differentiated Instruction

SI Strategic Intervention

Writing for Tests If children are overwhelmed by the task, tell them that writing even just one sentence is good. They will be able to practice again later in the week.

English Language Learners

Support Writing

Beginning Have children write one sentence telling about their topic.

Intermediate Have children write one sentence telling what their topic is and at least one more sentence telling about their topic.

Advanced/Advanced High Have children write one sentence telling what their topic is and at least two more sentences telling about their topic.

Objectives

- Write letters legibly and with proper spacing.
- Understand the features of notes.
- Take notes based on personal observations.

Handwriting
Letters *Uu* and *Qq*/Letter Spacing

Model letter formation Display upper- and lower-case letters: *Uu, Qq*. Use the stroke instructions pictured below to model proper letter formation.

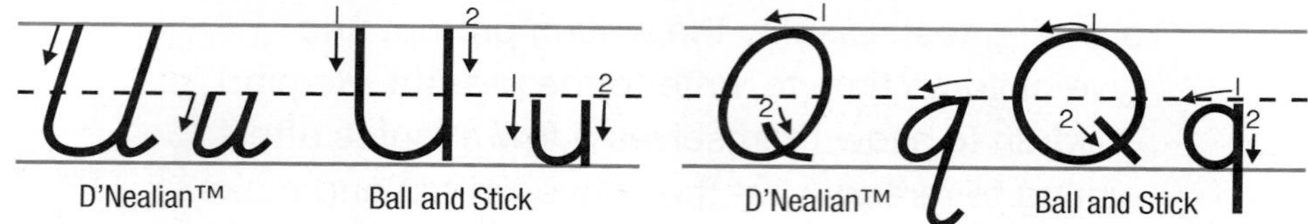

Model letter spacing Remind children that when they write a word, all the letters should be evenly spaced. Write the word *bump* using correct spacing. When I write a word, I write the letters with just a small space separating them. I make sure I'm leaving the same amount of space between my letters. Write *bump* again, making some letters touch. The letters shouldn't be so close that they touch one another. Write *bump* a third time with the letters too far from one another. When I make my letters too far apart, it's hard to tell that they spell a word. Write *bump* a fourth time, using inconsistent letter spacing. Point out the places where the letter spacing is too large or too small.

Guide practice Write the following sentence, using letter spacing that is inconsistent: *Gus the duck runs and quacks*.

Team Talk Have children work in pairs to discuss what is wrong with the sentence and how it needs to be fixed. Have them share with the class.

On their own Use the *Reader's and Writer's Notebook* p. 209.

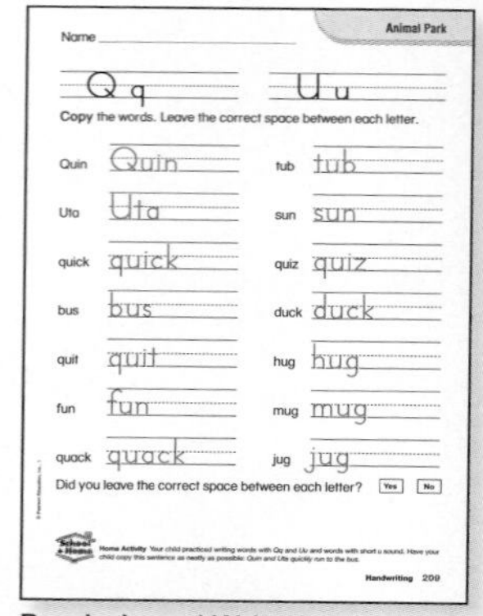
Reader's and Writer's Notebook p. 209

Research and Inquiry
Research Skill: Notes

Teach Tell children that **notes** are words and groups of words written about a topic. Explain that people make notes so they can remember information about the topic. Notes may be words, phrases, sentences, or drawings. Write *Our Classroom* on the board. Add two or three notes that describe the room, such as the number of seats, the color of the walls and so forth. Read the notes aloud as children track the print.

Model Think Aloud When I write notes, I always start by writing the topic of my notes. The topic tells me what the notes are about. My notes may be words, groups of words, or even drawings. Each note is a bit of information about my topic, so I write each note on a separate line.

Guide practice Have children work with a partner to write two or three more notes about the classroom. As children share their notes, add them to those already on the board.

Academic Vocabulary

notes words and groups of words written about a topic so information about the topic can be remembered

Wrap Up Your Day

- ✔ **Final Consonant Blends** Write the words *last* and *rest*. Have children identify the blend at the end of each word.
- ✔ **High-Frequency Words** Point to these words on the Word Wall: *home, many, them* and *into*. Have children read each word and use it in a sentence.
- ✔ **Build Concepts** Monitor children's use of oral vocabulary as they respond. Ask: Is it better to chatter or be silent when you observe animals? (It is better to be silent so you don't scare away the animals.) Why would you observe an animal you are curious about? (to learn about the animal) What could you learn by observing a parent animal? (how it takes care of its babies)

Tell children that tomorrow they will reread *Animal Park*.

Get Ready to Read

Objectives

- Build oral vocabulary.
- Identify details in text.
- Share information and ideas about the concept.

Today at a Glance

Oral Vocabulary
snort

Phonological Awareness
Rhyming Words

Phonics and Spelling
◎ Short *u*: *u*
◎ Final Consonant Blends

High-Frequency Words
home, into, many, them

Story Words
elephants, hippos, park, zebras

Comprehension
Review Main Idea and Details

Fluency
Appropriate Phrasing

Conventions
Exclamatory Sentences

Writing
Brief Composition: Evaluation

Listening and Speaking
Give Directions

Research and Inquiry
Gather and Record Information

Concept Talk

Question of the Week

What can we learn about wild animals by watching them?

Build concepts

To reinforce concepts and to focus children's attention, have children sing "Big, Round World" from the *Sing with Me* Big Book. How can watching wild animals help us know how to protect the places where they live? (Possible response: We can learn what they need to eat and how they make their homes.)

Sing with Me Big Book Audio

Monitor listening comprehension

Review that yesterday the class read the Big Book, *Jungle Drum,* to find out which animals chatter and when the jungle animals are silent. Ask children to listen today to find out what other sounds jungle animals make. Read the book, and then ask children the following questions.

Big Book

- What sound does the mosquito make? (She says, "Hmmmmmmmm.")
- Who puffs out his throat and croaks? (a tree frog)
- Which animal growls? (a jaguar)

ELL Poster 6

ELL Expand Vocabulary Use the Day 3 instruction on ELL Poster 6 to help students expand vocabulary.

Oral Vocabulary
Amazing Words

Teach Amazing Words

Amazing Words Oral Vocabulary Routine

1. **Introduce the Word** Relate the word *snort* to the book. The wild boars in the jungle *snort*. Supply a child-friendly definition: When you *snort*, you make a sound through your nose. Have children say the word.
2. **Demonstrate** Provide examples to show meaning. A pig *snorts*. Sometimes people *snort* when they laugh. The angry horse *snorted* and kicked.
3. **Apply** Have children demonstrate their understanding. Make a *snorting* sound. What other animal might *snort* at you?

Routines Flip Chart

Anchored Talk

Add to the concept map

Use these questions to discuss what we can learn by observing animals as you add to the concept map.

- In *Animal Park*, the visitors see some big cats resting after a long hunt. Let's add *big cats hunt* to our concept map.
- What do the visitors see the hippos doing? (They are sitting in wet mud.) Let's add *hippos sit in mud* to our concept map.
- Next, the visitors watch some elephants in a pond. What do the elephants do there? (The elephants sip, stomp in, and swim in the pond.) Let's add that to our concept map, too.

Amazing Words

desert	silent
forest	snort
world	medicine
chatter	poisonous

English Language Learners

Physical Response To support children's understanding of what the animals in the park do, pantomime the animals' actions and have children join you. For example, pantomime *sip, stomp*, and *swim* to demonstrate what the elephants do in the pond.

DAY 3 Get Ready to Read

Objectives

- Identify and generate words that rhyme.
- Build words with final consonant blends.
- ◎ Read words with short *u* and final consonant blends.

Phonological Awareness
Rhyming Words

Model producing rhyming words

Read together the first bullet point on pp. 148–149 of the Student Edition. Today we are going to use this picture to help us produce rhyming words. Remember that **rhyming words** are words that end with the same sounds. The directions tell us to find two things that rhyme with *trust*. When I look at the picture, I see a *crust* of bread, and I see some old trucks with *rust* on them. The words *crust* and *rust* rhyme with *trust*.

Student Edition pp. 148–149

Guide practice

Guide children to use the picture to produce words that rhyme with *dunk*. (*skunk, trunk, junk*)

On their own

Have children produce words that rhyme with the following words.

bug	**tub**	**dump**
cut	**must**	**fun**

Team Talk Allow children the opportunity to create pairs of rhyming words with a partner.

Phonics
Build Words

Model word building Now we are going to build words that end with a consonant blend. Write *hand* and blend it. Watch me change *h* to *b*. Model blending the new word, *band*.

Guide practice Have children spell *band* with letter tiles. Monitor children's work as they build words.

- Change the *a* in *band* to *e*. Say the new word together. **b e n d**
- Change the *d* in *bend* to *t*. Say the new word together. **b e n t**
- Change the *n* in *bent* to *s*. Say the new word together. **b e s t**
- Change the *b* in *best* to *r*. Say the new word together. **r e s t**

Corrective feedback For corrective feedback, model the correct spelling and have children correct their tiles.

Fluent Word Reading

Model Write *hunt*. I know the sounds for *h, u, n,* and *t*. I blend them and read the word *hunt*.

Guide practice Write the words below. Say the sounds in your head for each spelling you see. When I point to the word, we'll read it together. Allow one second per sound-previewing time for the first reading.

mud	dust	pup	tusk	lump	bunt

On their own Have children read the list above three or four times, until they can read one word per second.

Differentiated Instruction

 Advanced

Build Rhyming Words If children are able to rhyme words easily and independently, ask partners to use letter tiles to build a word with short *u*. Then have them see how many rhyming words they can build by changing the first letter tile to another consonant or consonant blend.

Academic Vocabulary

rhyming words words that end with the same sounds

English Language Learners

Pronounce Final Blends Final consonant blends may be challenging for speakers of Greek, Italian, Spanish, and some other languages. Provide additional practice in segmenting and blending words with final blends.

Get Ready to Read

Objectives

- ◎ Associate the sound /u/ with the spelling *u*, and correctly pronounce words with final consonant blends.
- Blend and read words with short *u* or final consonant blends.
- Decode words in context and isolation.
- Spell words with short *u* and a final consonant blend.

Blend and Read

Decode words in isolation

Have children turn to pages 211–212 in the *Reader's and Writer's Notebook* and find the first list of words. Each word in this list has either the short *u* sound or a final consonant blend. Let's blend and read these words. Be sure that children identify the correct sounds in short *u* words and words that end with a consonant blend.

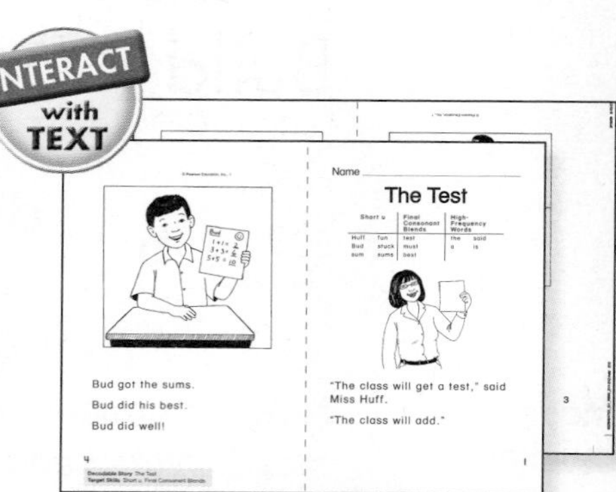

Reader's and Writer's Notebook pp. 211-212

Next, have children read the high-frequency words.

Decode words in context

Chorally read the story along with the children. Have children identify words in the story that have short *u* and/or a final consonant blend.

Team Talk Pair children and have them take turns reading the story aloud to each other. Monitor children as they read to check for proper pronunciation and appropriate pacing.

On their own

To further develop automaticity, have children take the story home to reread.

Spelling
Short *u* Words with Final Consonant Blends

Spell high-frequency words Write *many* and *into* and point them out on the Word Wall. Have children say and spell the words with you and then without you.

Dictation Have children write these sentences. Say each sentence. Then repeat it slowly, one word at a time.

1. **The cat ran into the net.**
2. **I sat in the dust.**
3. **I just got many rocks on the walk.**

Proofread and correct Write each sentence, spelling words one at a time. Have children circle and rewrite any misspelled words.

On their own Use *Reader's and Writer's Notebook* p. 213.

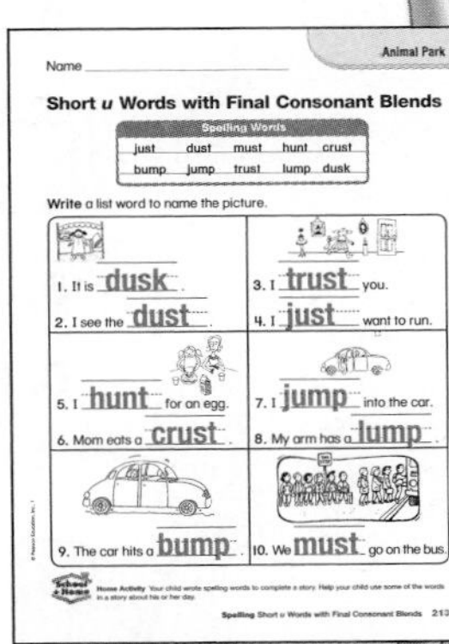

Name ______ Animal Park

Short *u* Words with Final Consonant Blends

Spelling Words				
just	dust	must	hunt	crust
bump	jump	trust	lump	dusk

Write a list word to name the picture.

1. It is dusk.
2. I see the dust.
3. I trust you.
4. I just want to run.
5. I hunt for an egg.
6. Mom eats a crust.
7. I jump into the car.
8. My arm has a lump.
9. The car hits a bump.
10. We must go on the bus.

Home Activity Your child wrote spelling words to complete a story. Help your child use some of the words in a story about his or her day.

Spelling Short *u* Words with Final Consonant Blends 213

Reader's and Writer's Notebook p. 213

Spelling Words

Short *u* Words with Final Consonant Blends

1. crust	**6. dust**
2. bump	**7. trust**
3. jump	**8. dusk**
4. must	**9. hunt**
5. just	**10. lump**

High-Frequency Words

11. many	**12. into**

Small Group Time

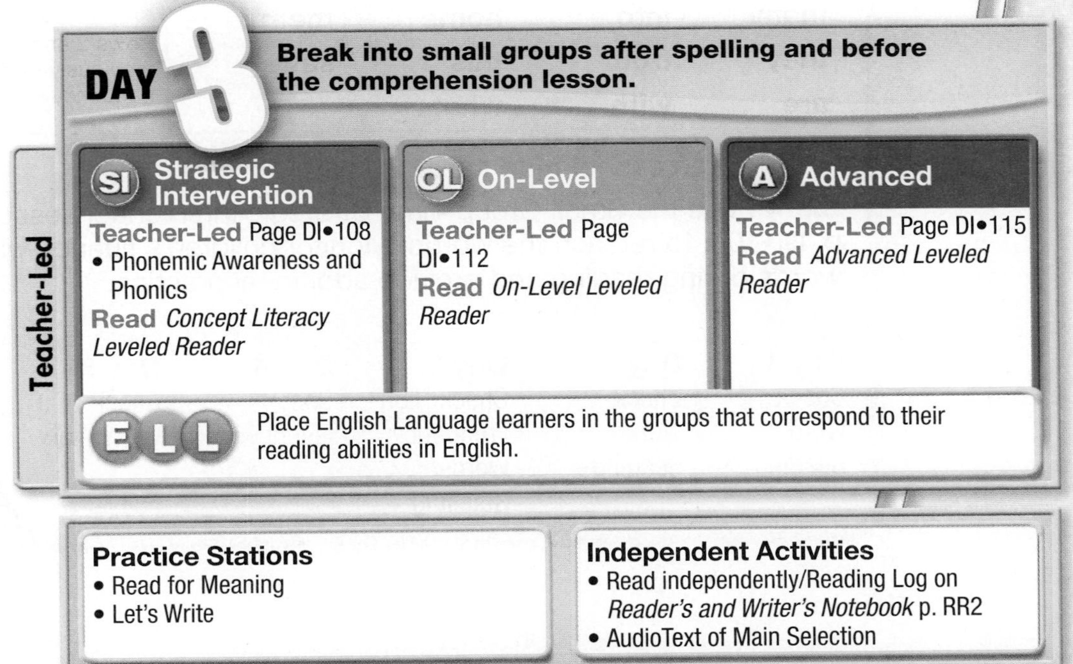

DAY 3 **Break into small groups after spelling and before the comprehension lesson.**

Teacher-Led

SI Strategic Intervention	OL On-Level	A Advanced
Teacher-Led Page DI•108 • Phonemic Awareness and Phonics **Read** *Concept Literacy Leveled Reader*	**Teacher-Led** Page DI•112 **Read** *On-Level Leveled Reader*	**Teacher-Led** Page DI•115 **Read** *Advanced Leveled Reader*

ELL Place English Language learners in the groups that correspond to their reading abilities in English.

Practice Stations
- Read for Meaning
- Let's Write

Independent Activities
- Read independently/Reading Log on *Reader's and Writer's Notebook* p. RR2
- AudioText of Main Selection

English Language Learners

Spelling Dictation Children will benefit from hearing each dictated sentence read three times. First, have children listen to understand the sentence. The second time, they should write what they hear. The third time, they can check their work.

Read and Comprehend

Objectives

- Read high-frequency words.
- Establish purpose for reading text.
- Review key features of literary nonfiction.

Check High-Frequency Words
SUCCESS PREDICTOR

High-Frequency and Story Words

Read words in isolation Display and review this week's high-frequency words and story words. Have children read the words aloud.

Read words in context Display the following sentence frames. Have children complete the sentences using high-frequency and story words. Have the children read each completed sentence with you.

1. **Nan and Ken got ________ his black truck. (into)**
2. **Yes, *many* fast ________ ran past Mom and Dad. (zebras)**
3. **Big ________ can stomp and swim in the *park*. (elephants)**
4. **Will ________ sit in mud if the sun is hot? (hippos)**
5. **Jack went ________ and fed his dog. (home)**
6. **Kim gets six blocks and stacks ________. (them)**

Don't Wait Until Friday

MONITOR PROGRESS — **Check High-Frequency Words**

Point to these words on the Word Wall and have the class read them. Listen for children who miss words during the reading. Call on those children to read some of the words individually.

many	**into**	**home**	**them**	
they	**from**	**this**	**saw**	←
are	**with**	**what**		←

Spiral Review
Rows 2 and 3 review previously taught high-frequency words.

If... children cannot read these words,
then... use the Small Group Time Strategic Intervention lesson, p. DI•109, to reteach the words. Monitor children's fluency with these words during reading and provide additional practice.

Day 1	Day 2	Day 3	Day 4	Day 5
Check Word Reading	Check Word Reading	Check High-Frequency Words/ Retelling	Check Fluency	Check Oral Vocabulary

Success Predictor

Main Selection—Second Read
Animal Park

Review Main idea and details

Recall this week's main selection, *Animal Park*. Tell children that today they will read the selection again. Remind children that the **main idea** of a selection is what the selection is mainly, or mostly, about. Paying attention to the main idea helps us understand the information we are reading. What is the selection *Animal Park* mostly about? (It is about seeing wild animals that live in an animal park.) What detail, or fact, did we learn about some big birds that live in the park? (Possible response: They can run fast.)

Review Genre: literary nonfiction

Let's Read Together Remind children that literary nonfiction tells about real-life people, animals, or events and that the setting is real. Have children point out text features that helped them know that *Animal Park* is about real people, animals, events, and places. (Possible response: The pictures show real animals and the words tell what real animals do.)

Set a purpose

Remind children that good readers read for a purpose. Guide children to set a new purpose for reading *Animal Park* today, perhaps to consider why visitors might come to a park like this one.

Extend thinking

Tell children they will now read *Animal Park* for the second time. Use the Day 3 Extend Thinking notes to encourage children to use higher order thinking skills to go beyond the details of the selection.

Second Read

Continue to DAY 3

For the Second Read, use **Extend Thinking** across the bottom of pages 154–163.

Story Words

park land set aside for people to enjoy nature

elephants huge, strong land animals with gray skin and long trunks

zebras black-and-white striped animals that look like horses

hippos a short word for hippopotamuses, which are large animals with short legs, thick skin, and wide mouths

Academic Vocabulary

main idea tells what the selection is mainly about

ELL

English Language Learners

Sentence Production In preparation for their second reading of *Animal Park*, have children choose two or three animals pictured in the text. Ask them to point to a photo and say a short sentence that explains what the animals are doing. For example, children might point to the elephants on p. 162 and say, "The elephants are sipping water from the pond."

DAY 3 Read and Comprehend

Objectives

- Retell a nonfiction selection.
- Identify author's purpose.
- ◎ Identify text structure.
- Write clear, coherent sentences.

Check Retelling
SUCCESS PREDICTOR

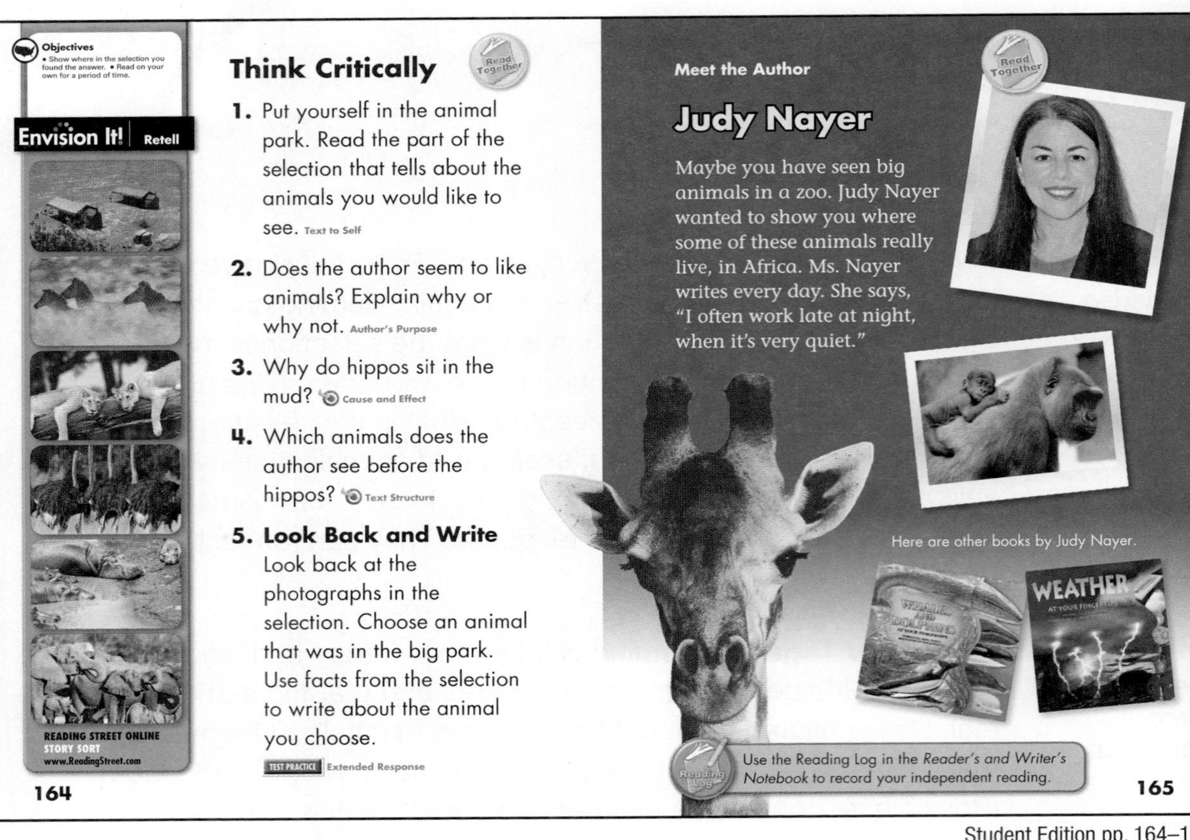

Objectives
• Show where in the selection you found the answer. • Read on your own for a period of time.

Envision It! Retell

READING STREET ONLINE
STORY SORT
www.ReadingStreet.com

Think Critically Read Together

1. Put yourself in the animal park. Read the part of the selection that tells about the animals you would like to see. Text to Self
2. Does the author seem to like animals? Explain why or why not. Author's Purpose
3. Why do hippos sit in the mud? Cause and Effect
4. Which animals does the author see before the hippos? Text Structure
5. **Look Back and Write** Look back at the photographs in the selection. Choose an animal that was in the big park. Use facts from the selection to write about the animal you choose. TEST PRACTICE Extended Response

164

Meet the Author Read Together

Judy Nayer

Maybe you have seen big animals in a zoo. Judy Nayer wanted to show you where some of these animals really live, in Africa. Ms. Nayer writes every day. She says, "I often work late at night, when it's very quiet."

Here are other books by Judy Nayer.

Reading Log Use the Reading Log in the *Reader's and Writer's Notebook* to record your independent reading.

165

Student Edition pp. 164–165

Retelling

Envision It! Have children work in pairs, retelling the reading to one another. Remind children that their partners should include the topics, main ideas, and what they learned from the reading. Children should use the retelling strip in the Student Edition as they retell. Monitor children's retelling.

Scoring rubric

Top-Score Response A top-score response makes connections beyond the text, elaborates on the topics, main ideas, and what children learned from the reading.

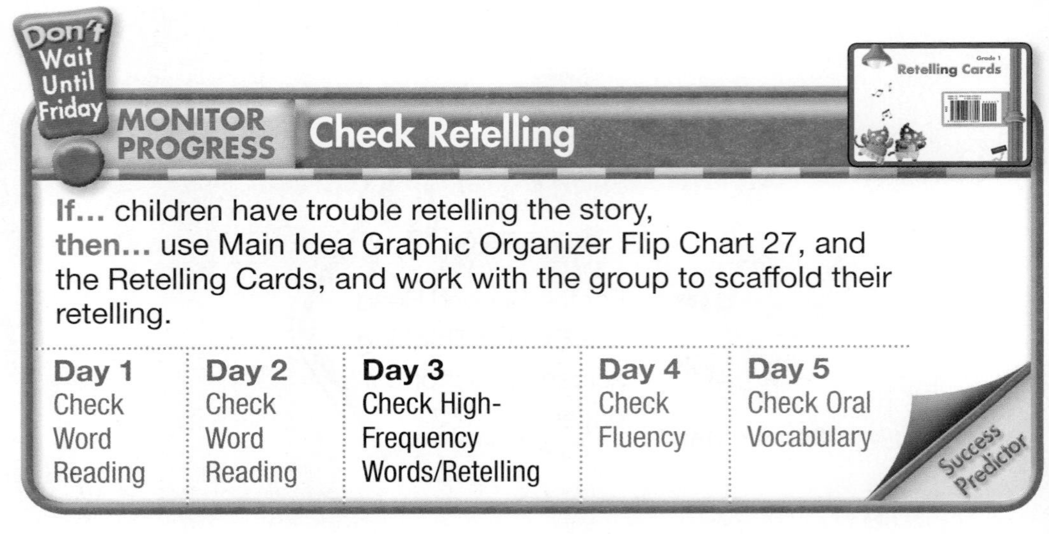

Don't Wait Until Friday **MONITOR PROGRESS** **Check Retelling**

If… children have trouble retelling the story,
then… use Main Idea Graphic Organizer Flip Chart 27, and the Retelling Cards, and work with the group to scaffold their retelling.

Day 1	Day 2	Day 3	Day 4	Day 5
Check Word Reading	Check Word Reading	Check High-Frequency Words/Retelling	Check Fluency	Check Oral Vocabulary

Success Predictor

Think Critically

Text to Self 1. Possible response: I would like to see the elephants on p. 162 stomping and swimming in the pond.

Author's Purpose 2. Possible response: The author really likes animals. She goes on a special trip to see them and is happy when she spots different kinds.

Cause and Effect 3. Hippos sit in the mud because it helps them stay cool in the hot sun.

Text Structure 4. She sees some big birds just before she sees the hippos.

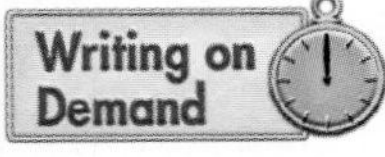

5. **Look Back and Write** For writing fluency, assign a five-minute time limit. As children finish, encourage them to reread their response and proofread for errors.

Scoring rubric

> **Top-Score Response** A top-score response uses details from the text and the pictures to tell about an animal pictured in the selection. For example:
>
> Some big hippos are sitting in mud. It is hot out. The wet mud keeps the hippos cool.

Meet the author Read aloud page 165 as children follow along. Ask children what authors do.

Read independently After children enter their independent reading into their Reading Logs, have them paraphrase a portion of the text they have just read. Tell children that when we paraphrase, we express the meaning of what we have read using our own words.

Differentiated Instruction

A Advanced

Look Back and Write Ask children who show proficiency with the writing prompt to explain how they think the elephants in the park stay cool.

Strategy Response Log

Text Structure Have children use p. RR18 in their *Reader's and Writer's Notebook* to draw and write what the author saw at the animal park right after she saw the zebras.

Plan to Assess Retelling

- ☐ Week 1: Strategic Intervention
- ☐ Week 2: Advanced
- ☐ Week 3: Strategic Intervention
- ☐ Week 4: On-Level
- ☐ Week 5: Strategic Intervention
- ☑ This week: Assess any children you have not yet checked during this unit.

Retelling Success Predictor

Objectives

- Read aloud fluently and appropriate phrasing.
- Review use of exclamation marks.

Model Fluency
Appropriate Phrasing

Model fluent reading Have children turn to Student Edition page 158. Point to an exclamation mark. This is an exclamation mark. It tells me that I should read this sentence with excitement.

Guide practice Have children read the page with you. Then have them reread the page as a group until they read with appropriate phrasing, paying attention to the exclamation. Point out how your voice changes when you read the exclamation. Continue in the same way with page 160.

Corrective feedback **If...** children have difficulty reading with appropriate phrasing, **then...** prompt:

- Did you look at the end marks?
- How should your voice sound when you read a sentence that ends with an exclamation mark?
- Read the sentence as if you are very excited.

Reread for Fluency

ROUTINE **Choral Reading**

1. **Select a Passage** For *Animal Park,* use pp. 159–160.
2. **Model** First, have children track the print as you read.
3. **Guide Practice** Then have children read along with you.
4. **Corrective Feedback** Have the class read aloud without you. Monitor progress and provide feedback. For optimal fluency, children should reread three to four times.

Routines Flip Chart

Check comprehension How are the big birds different from the big cats? (Possible response: The big cats are resting and the big birds are running.)

Conventions

Exclamatory Sentences

Review Exclamatory sentences Remind children that an exclamatory sentence shows strong feeling and ends with an exclamation mark: *Those giraffes are so tall! I love watching animals!*

Guide practice Write this sentence on the board and have children read it aloud.

Big cats can run fast!

Guide children in describing the sentence. What kind of sentence is this? (an exclamatory sentence) What punctuation mark is at the end? (an exclamation mark) What does that punctuation mark tell you about the writer's feelings? (The writer has a strong feeling about something.)

Team Talk Have pairs look at the photographs in the selection *Animal Park.* Ask them to generate exclamations they might have said if they had been riding on the truck and seeing these animals.

Connect to oral language Have children say these sentences with the appropriate intonation.

That was such a great surprise!

I am so excited!

I'm very worried about the test!

On their own Use *Reader's and Writer's Notebook* p. 214.

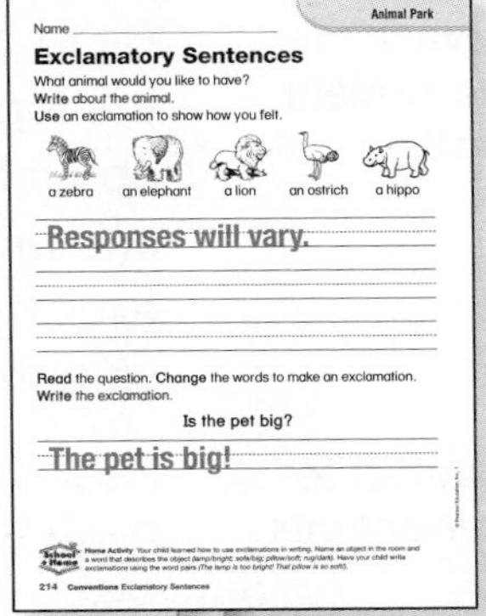
Animal Park

Name

Exclamatory Sentences

What animal would you like to have?
Write about the animal.
Use an exclamation to show how you felt.

a zebra · an elephant · a lion · an ostrich · a hippo

Responses will vary.

Read the question. **Change** the words to make an exclamation. **Write** the exclamation.

Is the pet big?

The pet is big!

School + Home **Home Activity** Your child learned how to use exclamations in writing. Name an object in the room and a word that describes the object (lamp/bright; sofa/big; pillow/soft; rug/dark). Have your child write exclamations using the word pairs (The lamp is too bright! That pillow is so soft!).

214 **Conventions** Exclamatory Sentences

Reader's and Writer's Notebook p. 214

Options for Oral Rereading

Use *Animal Park* or one of this week's Decodable Practice Readers.

Professional Development

Fluency Children who are able to mark sentence endings with pauses and appropriate pitch are better able to comprehend what they are reading.

Daily Fix-It

5. Jummp up for a nutt
Jump up for a nut.

6. she kut a rug up
She cut a rug up.

Discuss the Daily Fix-It corrections with children. Review sentence capitalization and punctuation, the *m* spelling of /m/, the *t* spelling of /t/, and the *c* spelling of /k/.

English Language Learners

Punctuation Children with literacy skills in Spanish may be accustomed to writing an introductory (upside-down) exclamation mark at the beginning of an exclamation. Point out that in English, the exclamation mark appears only at the end.

Objectives

- Evaluate a brief composition.

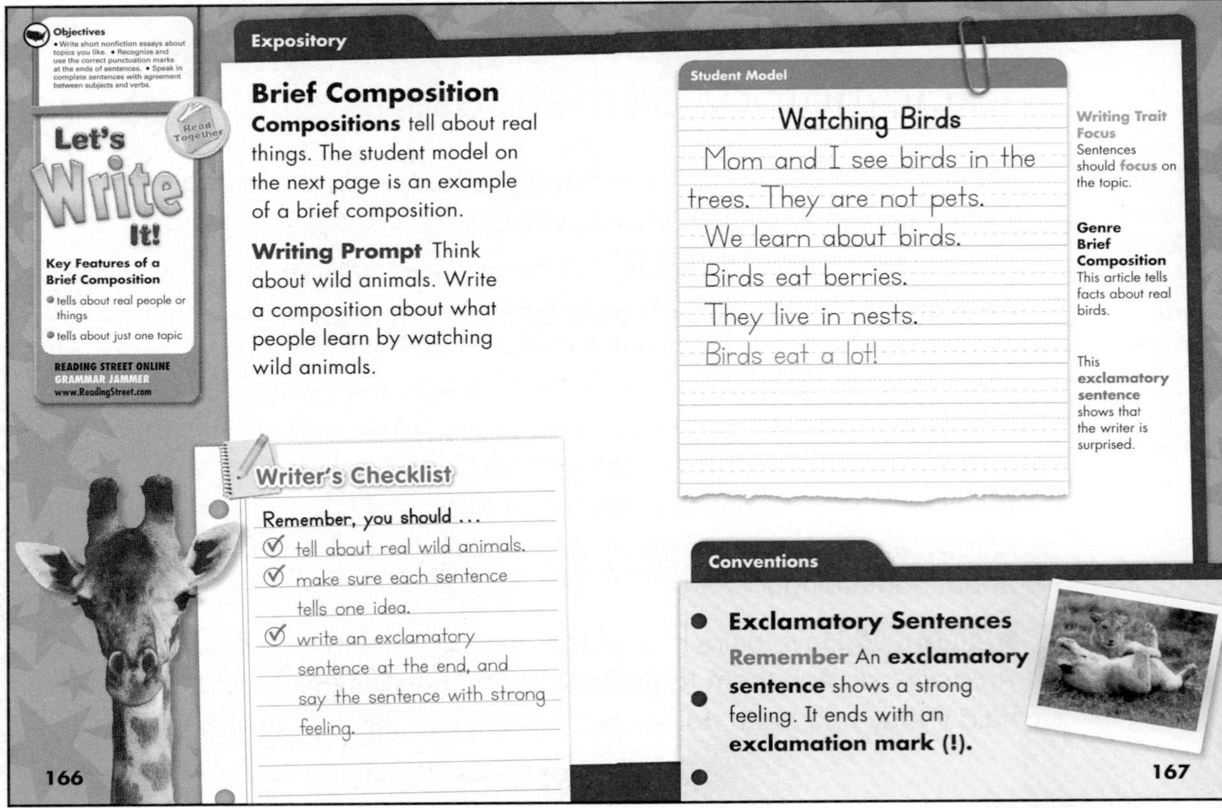
Objectives
• Write short nonfiction essays about topics you like. • Recognize and use the correct punctuation marks at the ends of sentences. • Speak in complete sentences with agreement between subjects and verbs.

Read Together

Let's Write It!

Key Features of a Brief Composition
- tells about real people or things
- tells about just one topic

READING STREET ONLINE
GRAMMAR JAMMER
www.ReadingStreet.com

Expository

Brief Composition

Compositions tell about real things. The student model on the next page is an example of a brief composition.

Writing Prompt Think about wild animals. Write a composition about what people learn by watching wild animals.

Writer's Checklist

Remember, you should ...
- tell about real wild animals.
- make sure each sentence tells one idea.
- write an exclamatory sentence at the end, and say the sentence with strong feeling.

166

Student Model

Watching Birds

Mom and I see birds in the trees. They are not pets. We learn about birds. Birds eat berries. They live in nests. Birds eat a lot!

Writing Trait Focus Sentences should **focus** on the topic.

Genre Brief Composition This article tells facts about real birds.

This **exclamatory sentence** shows that the writer is surprised.

Conventions

Exclamatory Sentences

Remember An **exclamatory sentence** shows a strong feeling. It ends with an **exclamation mark (!)**.

167

Student Edition pp.166–167

Let's Write It!
Brief Composition

Teach Use pages 166–167 in the Student Edition. Read aloud the Key Features of a Brief Composition and the definition of compositions. Discuss the Writing Prompt and Writer's Checklist with children.

Review the student model Read "Watching Birds" on page 167 to children. Ask children to identify the topic. (birds) Ask them to identify the real things the composition tells about birds. (They live in nests, eat berries, and eat a lot.) Read aloud and briefly discuss the side notes about Genre, the Writing Trait, and the exclamatory sentence to help children understand how an author writes a composition.

Connect to conventions Read to children the Conventions note about Exclamatory Sentences. Point out the exclamatory sentence in the model composition.

Writing for Tests
Brief Composition, continued

MINI-LESSON

Evaluation

INTERACT with TEXT

- **Introduce** Have students turn again to the rubric on *Reader's and Writer's Notebook* p. 208. Track the print as you read aloud the description of a top-score response for the trait of Focus/Ideas. Have children follow along.

Reader's and Writer's Notebook p. 208

- **Teach** When I evaluate a composition, I check that all of the ideas are about the topic of the composition. I reread each sentence, then ask myself if the sentence tells about my topic.
- Explain that children can follow a similar process to check their compositions for Focus/Ideas or for other traits. They can reread each sentence, then ask themselves if the composition matches the trait.
- Your composition may receive a high score for each trait. Or you may need to try to improve one or some of the traits. Different scores on the traits will help you see which parts of your writing you should give more attention.
- Now it is time to evaluate your compositions. Have children use the rubric to evaluate their compositions. Circulate to guide children.

Evaluate

ROUTINE **Quick Write for Fluency** Team Talk

1. **Talk** Have partners take two minutes to discuss the best part of the writing they did.
2. **Write** Have each child write a sentence about one strength of their composition.
3. **Share** Partners can read their sentences to one another.

Routines Flip Chart

Differentiated Instruction

Advanced

Developing Evaluation Children may share their compositions with a partner and identify one strength in their partners' compositions. Based on this evaluation, have them tell how they could improve their own compositions.

Write Guy
Jeff Anderson

Life in a Fishbowl

When a teacher can't conference with every student, a "fishbowl conference" with one willing student can allow other children to observe, listen, and learn. It's important to reflect what the student is doing well and how a draft might be revised and improved.

Objectives

- Give a short set of directions with the correct sequence of steps.
- Gather and record information for an inquiry project.

Listening and Speaking
Give Directions

Introduce giving directions

Explain that people often give each other directions for how to do something.

- Good directions are given step by step. Each step is short and simple, and it stays on topic.
- Good directions put the steps in the correct order.
- When good speakers give directions, they speak clearly and slowly.
- They speak even more slowly and loudly when they are saying words that are really important to remember.

Model

Explain that you are going to give two sets of directions for how to open a drawer. The first time you will give bad directions, and the second time you will give good directions.

Slide the drawer open with your hand. Put your fingers on the knob. It's the thing on the front of the drawer, and it's made of metal or wood, which comes from a factory where lots of people work.

Here's the second set of directions. Step 1: With your hand, grab the *knob*. This is the piece of wood or metal sticking out from the front, flat part. Step 2: *pull* the knob *toward* you gently. Step 3: Stop pulling when the drawer is open far enough that you can see what's inside.

Discuss the differences between the two sets of directions.

Guide practice

Divide the children into pairs. Draw a T-chart on the board, and have each pair draw their own T-chart on a piece paper. Label the columns "Good Directions" and "Bad Directions." Work with children to write words or phrases to fill each column to give directions for writing capital *A*. Then have children work in pairs to add to their own charts. Walk around the room and provide feedback as needed. Then have volunteers share their work with the class.

On their own

Have children practice giving directions for how to make their favorite snack or sandwich.

Research and Inquiry
Gather and Record Information

Teach Tell children that today they will think about an animal they have observed in the neighborhood and write notes about what they observed. The notes they make will help them remember what they learned.

Model Think Aloud Display the list of questions the class created on Day 1. When we write about our animals, we will need the list of questions we made two days ago. We will think about whether we can use what we saw to answer any of our questions. We will write notes that will answer the questions.

Guide practice Tell children that they will now write notes about the animals they observed. Suggest that children write the name of the animal they observed at the top of their paper. Remind children that their notes can be words, groups of words, or drawings. Have them write any bits of information they remember from when they observed their animals. Explain to children that they will use the notes they write about their animal later.

Wrap Up Your Day

- ✔ **Cause and Effect** Why might it be harder to observe animals in the winter than in the summer?
- ✔ **Text Structure** Have children explain how the picture on each page of *Animal Park* helps them know, in advance, what they will be reading about on that page.

Differentiated Instruction

Strategic Intervention

Writing Notes Some children may have trouble writing notes. Tell these children that they can draw pictures of what they observe instead of writing words. Later in the week they can use the pictures to write their notes.

Tell children that tomorrow they will read poems about more animals, including a dog, a raccoon, and a hippopotamus.

DAY 4 Get Ready to Read

30–35 min.

Objectives

- Discuss the concept to develop oral language.
- Build oral vocabulary.
- Identify details in text.

Today at a Glance

Oral Vocabulary
medicine, poisonous

Phonemic Awareness
Distinguish /u/

Phonics and Spelling
Review Short *e*: *e*
Review Initial Consonant Blends

High-Frequency Words
Review

Comprehension
Genre: Poetry

Fluency
Appropriate Phrasing

Conventions
Exclamatory Sentences

Writing
Brief Composition: Know Your Purpose

Research and Inquiry
Review and Revise Topic

Concept Talk

Question of the Week

What can we learn about wild animals by watching them?

Build concepts

To reinforce concepts and to focus children's attention, have children sing "Big, Round World" from the *Sing with Me* Big Book. What are some great animal sights and sounds you might notice in a desert? (Possible response: I might see huge camels and hear snakes hiss.)

Sing with Me Big Book Audio

Review Genre: expository text

Have children tell the key features of expository text: it tells facts about something real. Explain that today you will read about how some real animals take care of themselves in "When Animals Are Doctors," by Deborah Churchman.

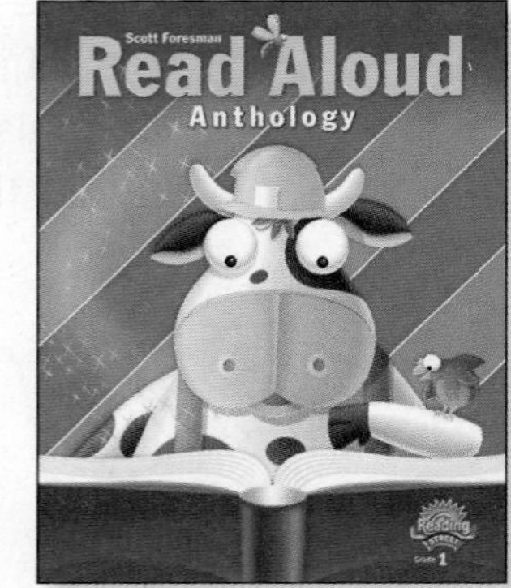

Read Aloud Anthology
"When Animals Are Doctors"

Monitor listening comprehension

Recall that in *Animal Park*, the wild animals do things like run fast, hunt, and swim. Have children listen to "When Animals Are Doctors" to find out what some other wild animals do to stay healthy. Read the selection.

ELL Produce Oral Language Use the Day 4 instruction on ELL Poster 6 to extend and enrich language.

ELL Poster 6

Oral Vocabulary
Amazing Words

Amazing Words Oral Vocabulary Routine

Teach Amazing Words

1. **Introduce the Word** Relate the word *medicine* to the story. A doctor gives you *medicine* if you're sick. Supply a child-friendly definition. *Medicine* is something that helps you feel better or makes you well. Have children say the word.
2. **Demonstrate** Provide examples to show meaning. My doctor gave me *medicine* for my sore throat. Never take *medicine* without an adult present. Scientists work to discover new *medicines*.
3. **Apply** Have children demonstrate their understanding. Describe a time when your parents helped you take *medicine*.

See p. OV•3 to teach *poisonous.*

Routines Flip Chart

Anchored Talk

Add to the concept map

Discuss how animals take care of themselves.

- We just read about something else we can find out about wild animals by watching them. We can learn how they stay healthy. Where can we add that to our concept map?
- What unusual thing do elephants eat? (mud) Why do they eat it? (to get minerals) Let's add to our concept map *elephants eat mud*.
- What unusual thing do macaws eat? (clay) Why do they eat that? (The clay keeps poisonous food from harming them.) Let's add *macaws eat clay* to our concept map.

Amazing Words

desert	silent
forest	snort
world	medicine
chatter	poisonous

Differentiated Instruction

A Advanced

Extend Amazing Words Ask questions such as the following:

- Why do scientists work to discover new *medicines* for animals?
- Why is it important to keep animals away from *poisonous* plants?

Encourage children to use the words in discussion and writing.

English Language Learners

Frontload Listening To prepare children for vocabulary they will encounter in "When Animals Are Doctors," demonstrate the words *swallow*, *nibble*, and *chew*. Then point out and/or explain *foot*, *stomach*, and *bone*. Have children repeat the words after you.

DAY 4 Get Ready to Read

Objectives

- Distinguish /u/ in initial and medial positions.
- Identify and decode words with short *e* spelled *e* and words with initial consonant blends.

Phonemic Awareness
Distinguish /u/

Model This week we read about how hippos sit in mud. Listen as I say the three sounds in *mud*. Slowly model the sounds in *mud*: /m/ /u/ /d/. The middle sound in *mud* is /u/. Now, we're going to say some other words and listen for the sound /u/.

Guide practice I will say a word. Repeat the word after me. Raise your hand if you hear the /u/ sound at the beginning of the word.

Corrective feedback If children make an error, segment the word and model the correct response. Return to the word later in the practice.

up	**it**	**uneven**	**ever**	**umpire**
apple	**uncle**	**odd**	**unsafe**	**use**

Guide practice Now I will say some more words. Repeat each word after me. Raise your hand if you hear the /u/ sound in the middle of the word.

Corrective feedback If children make an error, segment the word and model the correct response. Return to the word later in the practice.

tub	**nest**	**tusk**	**dunk**	**milk**
mat	**stuck**	**club**	**stop**	**bud**

On their own Have children say each word and tell if they hear the /u/ sound at the beginning or in the middle of the word.

hut	**undo**	**trust**	**upon**	**hunt**
us	**brush**	**run**	**usher**	**skunk**

Phonics Review
Short *e* Spelled *e*; Initial Consonant Blends

Review Sound-spellings To review last week's first phonics skill, write *pen*. You studied words like this one last week. What do you know about the vowel sound you hear in *pen*? (The vowel sound is /e/ spelled *e*.)

Corrective feedback If children are unable to answer your question about the short *e* sound in *pen*, refer them to Sound-Spelling Card 6.

Review Initial blends To review last week's second phonics skill, write *flag*. You also studied words like this. What do you know about the consonant sounds you hear at the beginning of *flag*? (You blend the sounds /f/ and /l/ together.)

Corrective feedback If children are unable to answer your question about the initial consonant blend in *flag*, refer them to Sound-Spelling Card 41.

Guide practice Draw a T-chart or use Graphic Organizer 4. Write Short *e* and Not Short *e* as headings. When I say a word, hold a hand up high if it has a short *e* sound, or shake your head no if it does not have a short *e*: *net, six, sled, dress, bug, grill, step, black, ten, snap*. Write each word in the appropriate column. Then have children identify which words have initial consonant blends and underline them. Finally, have children read the lists aloud.

Short *e*	Not Short *e*
net	six
sled	bug
dress	grill
step	black
ten	snap

Graphic Organizer Flip Chart 4

On their own Use Let's Practice It! pp. 67-68 on the *Teacher Resource DVD-ROM.*

Let's Practice It! TR DVD•67

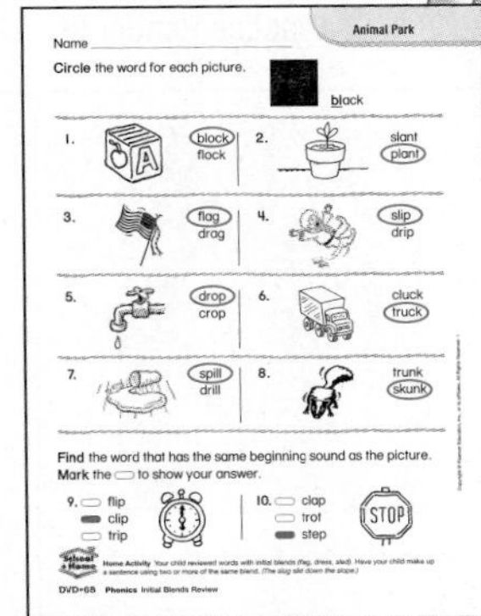

Let's Practice It! TR DVD•68

English Language Learners

Initial Consonant Blends Consonant blends in English words are often challenging for English learners because their home languages may not combine consonant phonemes in similar ways at the beginnings of words. For example, Spanish speakers may add the sound /e/ at the beginning of words with *s*-blends, saying "esled, estep," etc.

Objectives

- Apply knowledge of sound-spellings to decode unknown words when reading.
- Decode and read words in context and isolation.
- Practice fluency with oral rereading.

Decodable Practice Reader 6C

Short *u*: *u*; Final Consonant Blends

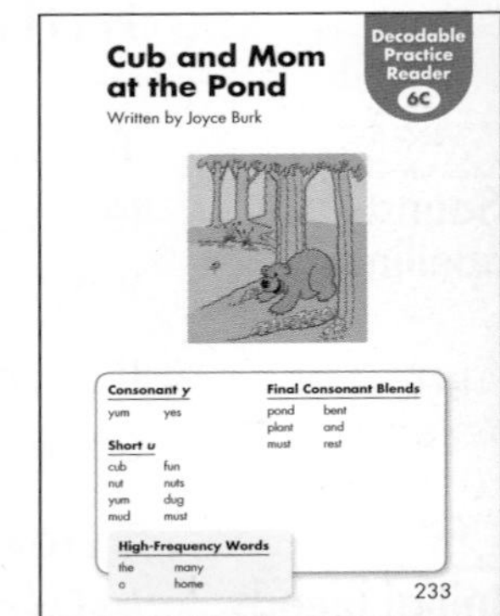

Decodable Practice Reader 6C

Decode words in isolation Have children turn to page 233. Have children decode each word.

Review High-frequency words Review the previously taught words *a, the, home,* and *many*. Have children read each word as you point to it on the Word Wall.

Preview Decodable Reader Have children read the title and preview the story. Tell them they will read words with the short *u* sound and consonant blends in the story.

Decode words in context Pair children for reading and listen as they decode. One child begins. Children read the entire story, switching readers after each page. Partners reread the story. This time the other child begins.

Cub has fun at the pond.
234
Cub picks up a nut. Yum!
235

Decodable Practice Reader 6C

Mom has many nuts. Yum! Yum!
236
Mom bent.
Mom dug in the mud.
237

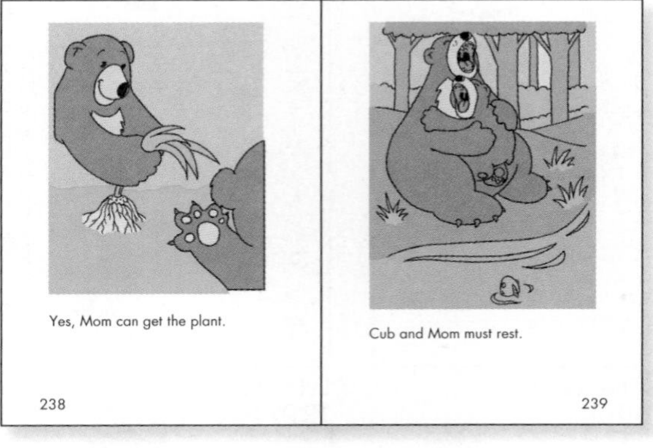

Yes, Mom can get the plant.
238
Cub and Mom must rest.
239

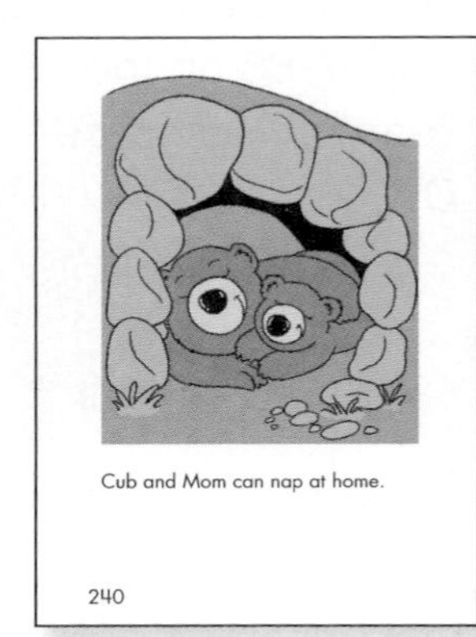

Cub and Mom can nap at home.
240

Corrective feedback

If... children have difficulty decoding a word, **then...** refer them to the Sound-Spelling Cards to identify the sounds in the word. Then prompt them to blend the word.

- What is the new word?
- Is the new word a word you know?
- Does it make sense in the story?

Check decoding and comprehension

Have children retell the story to include characters, setting, and events. Then have children locate words that have the short *u* sound and end with consonant blends in the story. List words that children name. Children should supply *Cub, fun, nut, rest, must, yum, dug, mud, plant, bent,* and *pond*. Ask children how they know that some of these words end with consonant blends and some have the short *u* sound. (There are two consonants together at the end of some of the words and some words have the letter *u* in them.)

Reread for Fluency

Have children reread Decodable Practice Reader 6C to develop automaticity decoding words with the short *u* sound and final consonant blends.

ROUTINE Oral Rereading Team Talk

1. **Read** Have children read the entire book orally.
2. **Reread** To achieve optimal fluency, children should reread the text three or four times.
3. **Corrective Feedback** Listen as children read. Provide corrective feedback regarding their fluency and decoding.

Routines Flip Chart

English Language Learners

Decodable Practice Reader

Beginning. Before children read, lead them through *Cub and Mom at the Pond.* Ask them to identify Cub and Mom. Point out words with the short *u* sound and those with final consonant blends and say them aloud. Have children repeat them after you.

Intermediate Refer children to the list of words with final consonant blends and those with the short *u* sound. Have them choose words and ask them to use them in sentences.

Advanced/Advanced High

Have children read a sentence and then use an illustration to elaborate on it. For example, "Cub and his mom have had a busy day. They are both tired because they are yawning. They will take a nap now."

DAY 4 Get Ready to Read

Objectives

- Read words fluently in context and in isolation.
- Spell words with short *u* and final consonant blends.
- Spell high-frequency words.

Fluent Word Reading

Spiral Review

Read words in isolation

Display these words. Tell children that they can blend some words on this list, and others are Word Wall words.

Have children read the list three or four times until they can read at the rate of two to three seconds per word.

cluck	**saw**	**red**	**small**	**was**
that	**big**	**tree**	**your**	**sled**
five	**green**	**like**	**pond**	**hens**
stuck	**see**	**frogs**	**Fran**	**where**

Word Reading

Corrective feedback

If... children have difficulty reading whole words,
then... have them use sound-by-sound blending for decodable words, or have them say and spell high-frequency words.

If... children cannot read fluently at a rate of two to three seconds per word,
then... have pairs practice the list until they can read it fluently.

Read words in context

Display these sentences. Call on individuals to read a sentence. Then randomly point to review words and have children read them. To help you monitor word reading, high-frequency words are underlined and decodable words are italicized.

I like to see *frogs at* the *pond*.

***Fran* saw your small green tree.**

"*Cluck*, *cluck*," *went* the five *red hens*.

Where was that *big sled stuck*?

Sentence Reading

Corrective feedback

If... children are unable to read an underlined high-frequency word,
then... read the word for them and spell it, having them echo you.

If... children have difficulty reading an italicized decodable word,
then... guide them in using sound-by-sound blending.

Spelling

Short *u* Words with Final Consonant Blends

Partner review Supply pairs of children with index cards on which the spelling words have been written. Have one child read a word while the other writes it. Then have children switch roles. Have them use the cards to check their spelling and correct any misspelled words.

On their own Use *Reader's and Writer's Notebook* p. 215.

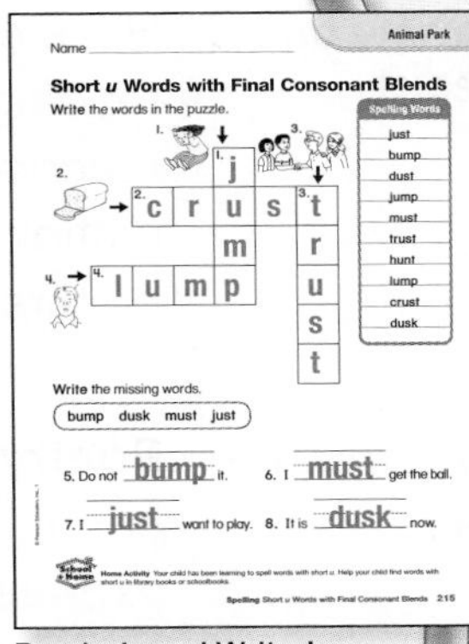

Animal Park

Name

Short *u* Words with Final Consonant Blends

Write the words in the puzzle.

Spelling Words: just, bump, dust, jump, must, trust, hunt, lump, crust, dusk

1. jump 2. crust 3. trust 4. lump

Write the missing words.

bump dusk must just

5. Do not bump it.
6. I must get the ball.
7. I just want to play.
8. It is dusk now.

Home Activity Your child has been learning to spell words with short u. Help your child find words with short u in library books or schoolbooks.

Spelling Short u Words with Final Consonant Blends 215

Reader's and Writer's Notebook p. 215

Spiral Review

These activities review

- previously taught high-frequency words *like, saw, your, small, green, tree, five, where, was.*
- short vowels, initial blends, and /k/ spelled *–ck*.

Small Group Time

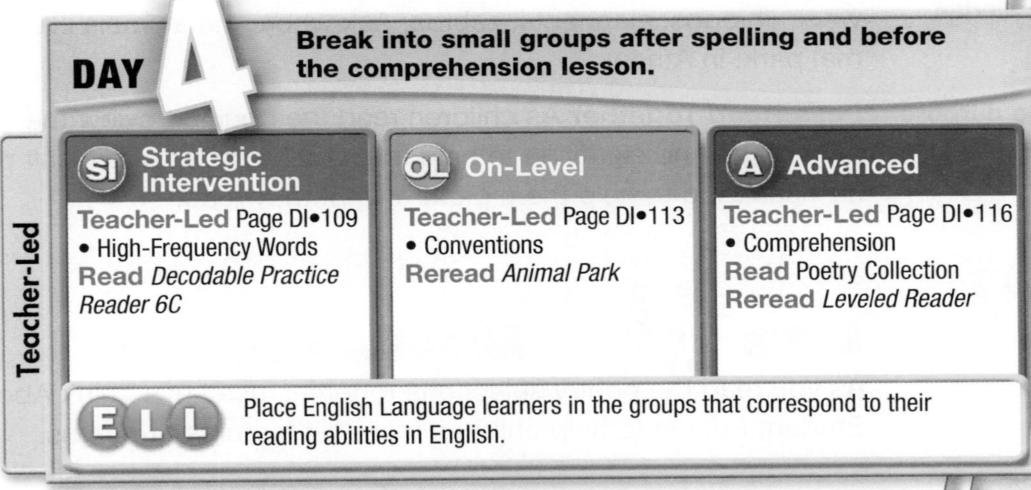

DAY 4 **Break into small groups after spelling and before the comprehension lesson.**

Teacher-Led

SI Strategic Intervention	OL On-Level	A Advanced
Teacher-Led Page DI•109 • High-Frequency Words **Read** *Decodable Practice Reader 6C*	**Teacher-Led** Page DI•113 • Conventions **Reread** *Animal Park*	**Teacher-Led** Page DI•116 • Comprehension **Read** Poetry Collection **Reread** *Leveled Reader*

ELL Place English Language learners in the groups that correspond to their reading abilities in English.

Practice Stations
- Words to Know
- Get Fluent

Independent Activities
- Read independently/Reading Log on *Reader's and Writer's Notebook* p. RR2
- AudioText of Paired Selection

ELL

English Language Learners

Fluent Word Reading Have children listen to a more fluent reader say the words. Then have them repeat the words.

Objectives

- Recognize rhythm and rhyme in poetry.
- Scan a reading selection to predict what it is about.
- Recognize structure and elements of poetry.
- Relate prior knowledge to new text.
- Set a purpose for reading.

Science in Reading

Use poetry Recite the first stanza of the nursery rhyme "Hickory Dickory Dock" (Hickory Dickory Dock, the mouse ran up the clock). Ask children which words rhyme. Then have them clap the rhythm of the words.

Preview and predict Have children look through the selection and predict what they might be reading about. (Possible response: They might say: Poems about a dog, a raccoon, and a hippo.) Ask them what clues helped them make their predictions. (Possible response: They might say the titles of the poems or the pictures and recall some of the elements of poetry.)

Let's Think About Genre **Poetry** Tell children that they will read poetry. *Poetry* is another word for *poems*. The author of a poem is called a poet. A poem tells a story or expresses the poet's feelings about something. A poem is written in lines. Often the words at the ends of some lines rhyme. A poem usually has a rhythm, or a regular pattern of beats.

Activate prior knowledge Ask children to recall and name some of the animals they read about this week. (hippos, elephants, zebras) Ask where the animals lived. (in an animal park; in Africa)

Set a purpose **Let's Read Together** As children read the poems, review the strategies of monitoring and clarifying to help them make sense of difficult parts as well as visualizing to help them picture what they read.

Let's Think About... Poetry

As you read the poetry selections together, use Let's Think About in the Student Edition to help children focus on features of poems.

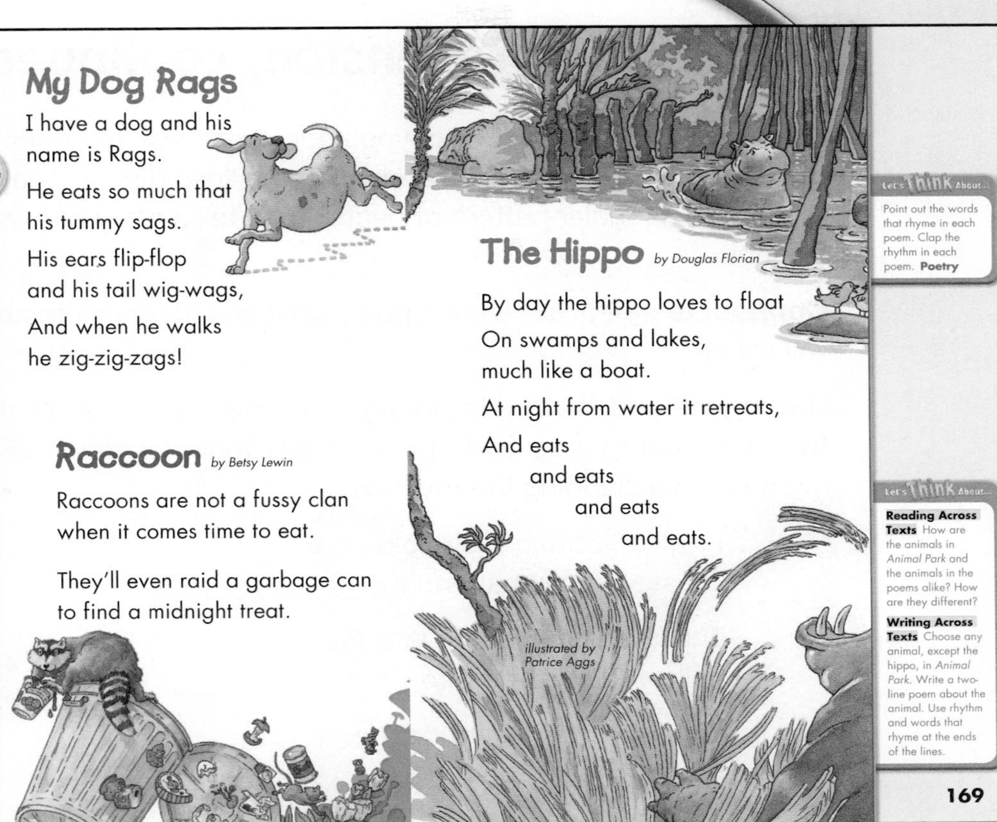

Objectives
• Describe and use rhythm and rhyme in poetry.

Genre
Poetry
- *Poetry* is another word for *poems*. The author of a poem is called a poet.
- A poem tells a story or expresses the poet's feelings about something.
- A poem is written in lines. Often the words at the ends of the lines rhyme.
- A poem usually has a rhythm, or a regular pattern of beats.
- Some poems have alliteration, or words close to each other with the same beginning sound.
- As you read "My Dog Rags," "Raccoon," and "The Hippo," look for elements of poetry.
- Find the alliteration in "My Dog Rags." Which words begin with the same sound?

Read Together

My Dog Rags

I have a dog and his
name is Rags.
He eats so much that
his tummy sags.
His ears flip-flop
and his tail wig-wags,
And when he walks
he zig-zig-zags!

Raccoon by Betsy Lewin

Raccoons are not a fussy clan
when it comes time to eat.
They'll even raid a garbage can
to find a midnight treat.

168

The Hippo by Douglas Florian

By day the hippo loves to float
On swamps and lakes,
much like a boat.
At night from water it retreats,
And eats
and eats
and eats
and eats.

illustrated by Patrice Aggs

Let's Think About...
Point out the words that rhyme in each poem. Clap the rhythm in each poem. **Poetry**

Let's Think About...
Reading Across Texts How are the animals in *Animal Park* and the animals in the poems alike? How are they different?
Writing Across Texts Choose any animal, except the hippo, in *Animal Park*. Write a two-line poem about the animal. Use rhythm and words that rhyme at the ends of the lines.

169

Student Edition pp. 168–169

Academic Vocabulary

rhythm a strong beat

Science Vocabulary

swamp wetlands with trees and grass growing out of water

Guide Comprehension

Guide practice

Think Aloud When I read "My Dog Rags," I wonder what "he zig-zig-zags" means. How can I find out? I look at the picture for a clue. I see that Rags walks first one way, then the other way, then back again, over and over. Which words rhyme in "My Dog Rags"? **(Possible response: rags, sags, wags, zags)**

Let's clap the rhythm in this poem together.

Monitor and clarify

When I read "The Hippo," I imagine what the hippo looks like. I see a picture in my mind of a happy hippo floating on a swamp.

Poetry

Possible response: In the poem "Raccoon", the words *clan* and *can* rhyme. So do *eat* and *treat*.

Objectives

- Confirm a prediction.
- Compare and contrast two different reading selections.
- Write a poem.
- Read aloud fluently, attending to punctuation.

Fluency: WCPM
SUCCESS PREDICTOR

Guide Comprehension, continued

Confirm predictions How do you know that these are poems? Because they are written in lines. The ends of some lines rhyme. They have a rhythm, or a regular pattern of beats. They tell a story or express the poet's feelings.

Connect to self If you were a poet, what would you write about? (Answers will vary.)

Use rhyme and rhythm in poetry Have children complete the following two-line poems using rhythm and rhyme. Together, read the completed rhymes while clapping the rhythms.

> I walked onto the big, old boat
> Dressed in my hat and my ______________.
>
> The big black cat ran into the fog
> Followed by large, brown ______________.
>
> You will never, ever find me
> Hiding behind the big oak ______________.

Reading Across Texts How are the animals in *Animal Park* and the animals in the poems alike? How are they different? Possible response: The animals in *Animal Park* all live in the same place. The animals in the poems live in different places.

Writing Across Texts Choose any animal, except the hippo, in *Animal Park.* Write a two-line poem about the animal. Use rhythm and words that rhyme at the end of the line. Example: Big birds run; in the hot sun!

Fluency

Appropriate Phrasing

Guide practice

- Have children turn to page 161 in *Animal Park*.
- Have children follow along as you read the page with appropriate phrasing.
- Have the class read the page with you and then reread the page as a group without you until they read with appropriate phrasing. To provide additional fluency practice, pair nonfluent readers with fluent readers.

ROUTINE Paired Reading

1. **Select a Passage** For *Animal Park*, use page 162.
2. **Model** First, have children track the print as you read.
3. **Guide Practice** Then have children read along with you.
4. **On Their Own** For optimal fluency, have partners reread three or four times.

Routines Flip Chart

Don't Wait Until Friday — MONITOR PROGRESS — Fluency: WCPM

As children reread, monitor their progress toward their individual fluency goals. Mid-Year Goal: 20–30 words correct per minute. End-of-Year Goal: 60 words correct per minute. Beginning in Unit 3, children will be assessed to determine WCPM.

If... children are not on track to meet benchmark goals,
then... have children practice with text at their independent level.

Day 1	Day 2	Day 3	Day 4	Day 5
Check Word Reading	Check Word Reading	Check High-Frequency Words/Retelling	Check Fluency	Check Oral Vocabulary

Success Predictor

Differentiated Instruction

 Advanced

WCPM If children already read at 60 words correct per minute, allow them to read independently.

Options for Oral Rereading

Use *Animal Park* or one of this week's Decodable Practice Readers.

Objectives

- Identify exclamatory sentences.
- Recognize and use correct capitalization and punctuation for exclamatory sentences.
- Revise draft of brief composition.

Conventions
Exclamatory Sentences

Test practice Use *Reader's and Writer's Notebook* p. 216 to help children understand exclamatory sentences in test items. Recall that an exclamatory sentence shows strong feeling. It begins with a capital letter and ends with an exclamation mark: *That baby elephant is so cute!* Model identifying an exclamatory sentence by writing this sentence on the board, reading it aloud, and underlining the capital letter and the exclamation mark.

My truck got stuck in mud!

Then read the *Reader's and Writer's Notebook* p. 216 directions. Guide children as they mark the answer for number 1.

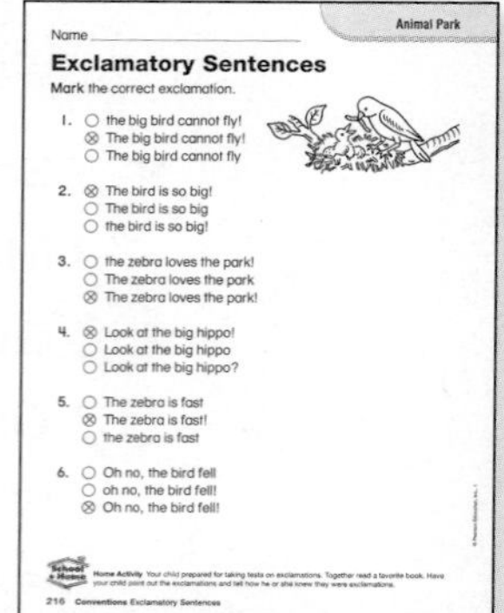
Animal Park

Name

Exclamatory Sentences

Mark the correct exclamation.

1. ○ the big bird cannot fly!
   ⊗ The big bird cannot fly!
   ○ The big bird cannot fly
2. ⊗ The bird is so big!
   ○ The bird is so big
   ○ the bird is so big!
3. ○ the zebra loves the park!
   ○ The zebra loves the park
   ⊗ The zebra loves the park!
4. ⊗ Look at the big hippo!
   ○ Look at the big hippo
   ○ Look at the big hippo?
5. ○ The zebra is fast
   ⊗ The zebra is fast!
   ○ the zebra is fast
6. ○ Oh no, the bird fell
   ○ oh no, the bird fell!
   ⊗ Oh no, the bird fell!

School + Home **Home Activity** Your child prepared for taking tests on exclamations. Together read a favorite book. Have your child point out the exclamations and tell how he or she knew they were exclamations.

216 **Conventions** Exclamatory Sentences

Reader's and Writer's Notebook p. 216

On their own Use *Reader's and Writer's Notebook* p. 216.

Connect to oral language After children mark the answers to numbers 1–6, review the correct choices aloud. Have children read each exclamatory sentence with the proper intonation.

Writing for Tests
Brief Composition

MINI-LESSON

Know Your Purpose

- Yesterday we evaluated brief compositions about what people learn by watching wild animals. Today we will use what we learned from our evaluations to write another brief composition.

- **Teach** When you don't have a lot of time to plan, write, revise, and edit a composition, it helps to know your **purpose**, or reason for writing. For example, my reason for writing a composition is to tell real things about a topic.

- **Think Aloud** Let's say I am choosing a topic for a composition about what people learn by watching wild animals. I am interested in writing about lions or about turtles. How can I choose which topic to write about? I know that my reason for writing a composition is to tell real things about my topic. I've never seen a lion. I like stories about lions, but I don't know many real things about them. Lions are probably not a good topic. What about turtles? I have seen turtles. I also know a few real things about them. I know that they have shells. I know that they live all over the world. I know that many of them live in water. Turtles would be a good topic for me.

Differentiated Instruction

Strategic Intervention

Test Formats Help children understand and follow the directions on the Reader's and Writer's Notebook test-practice page. Children will practice both the conventions skill and test-taking skills.

Academic Vocabulary

purpose reason for writing

Daily Fix-It

7. did you jump onto the bus
Did you jump onto the bus?

8. Can you take the bus heme.
Can you take the bus home?

Discuss the Daily Fix-It corrections with children. Review the capitalization and punctuation of questions and the spelling of *home.*

English Language Learners

Capitalization of Titles Tell children that the title of a composition tells its topic. Be sure they understand that important words in a title are capitalized.

Objectives

- Understand the purpose of a brief composition.
- Write a brief composition.
- Review answers to inquiry questions.

Writing for Tests
Brief Composition, continued

Write Review with children the key features of a brief composition. Then have children get paper and pencil ready to take a writing test. Display the writing prompt and give children time to write to it. Remind children to allow themselves a few minutes after writing to reread what they have written and make changes or additions.

Writing Prompt

Write a composition telling what you know about a kind of animal you have seen outside or at a zoo.

ROUTINE Quick Write for Fluency Team Talk

1. **Talk** Have children discuss which animals they would like to see at an animal park.
2. **Write** Have each child write a sentence about the animal they would most like to see.
3. **Share** Partners trade sentences and read them aloud.

Routines Flip Chart

Research and Inquiry
Review and Revise Topic

Teach Tell children that the next step in their project is to review their notes to see if they have the information they set out to find. Or, do their notes contain information that is not about their animal.

Model We observed an animal and wrote notes about what we observed to help us remember. Now I will look at the notes I made. I will see if all my notes are about my animal. If some of the notes are about other animals or other things I observed, I will cross them out. I will also check my spelling. If a word is not spelled correctly, I will write the word again with the correct spelling.

Guide practice Have children look at the notes they made during Day 3. Instruct them to work with a partner to go over their notes. Remind children to be sure all their notes are about their animal and that the words are spelled correctly. Finally, tell children that tomorrow they will organize their notes in order to share them with others.

On their own Use *Reader's and Writer's Notebook* p. 210.

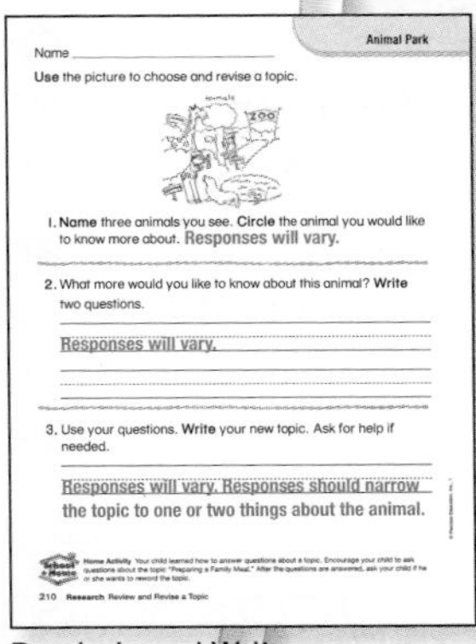
Animal Park

Name

Use the picture to choose and revise a topic.

1. **Name** three animals you see. **Circle** the animal you would like to know more about. Responses will vary.

2. What more would you like to know about this animal? **Write** two questions.

Responses will vary.

3. Use your questions. **Write** your new topic. Ask for help if needed.

Responses will vary. Responses should narrow the topic to one or two things about the animal.

210 Research Review and Revise a Topic

Reader's and Writers Notebook p. 210

Wrap Up Your Day

- ✔ **Phonics Review** List several words with the short *u* sound spelled *u* and final consonant blends, such as *must* and *dump.* Have children read each word and identify the letter that spells the sound /u/.
- ✔ **Fluency** Write *Can Bud run back? At last!* Have the class reread the sentences until they can do so with appropriate phrasing.

Differentiated Instruction

SI Strategic Intervention

Check Spelling If children have difficulty deciding if a word is spelled correctly, give them time to check the spelling by looking up the word in a dictionary.

Remind children that they heard about animals that are like doctors. Tomorrow they will hear about these animals again.

Objectives

- Review the concept: what we learn about wild animals by watching them.
- Build oral vocabulary.
- Identify details in text.

Today at a Glance

Oral Vocabulary
Review

Phonics
◎ Review Short *u*: *u*
◎ Review Final Consonant Blends

Comprehension
◎ Cause and Effect

Story Words
Review

High-Frequency Words
Review

Conventions
Exclamatory Sentences

Writing
Writing for Tests: Brief Composition

Research and Inquiry
Communicate

Check Oral Vocabulary SUCCESS PREDICTOR

Concept Wrap Up

Question of the Week

What can we learn about wild animals by watching them?

Review Concept

This week we have read and listened to stories about wild animals and the things they do. Today you will listen to find out how watching what wild animals eat helps us understand more about them. Read the article.

- Why won't most wild animals eat unripe fruit? (Animals won't eat unripe fruit because it can be poisonous.)

Read Aloud Anthology

"When Animals Are Doctors"

Review Amazing Words

Orally review the meaning of this week's Amazing Words. Then display this week's concept map. Have children use Amazing Words such as *desert, snort,* and *poisonous*, as well as the concept map, to answer the question, "What can we learn about wild animals by watching them?"

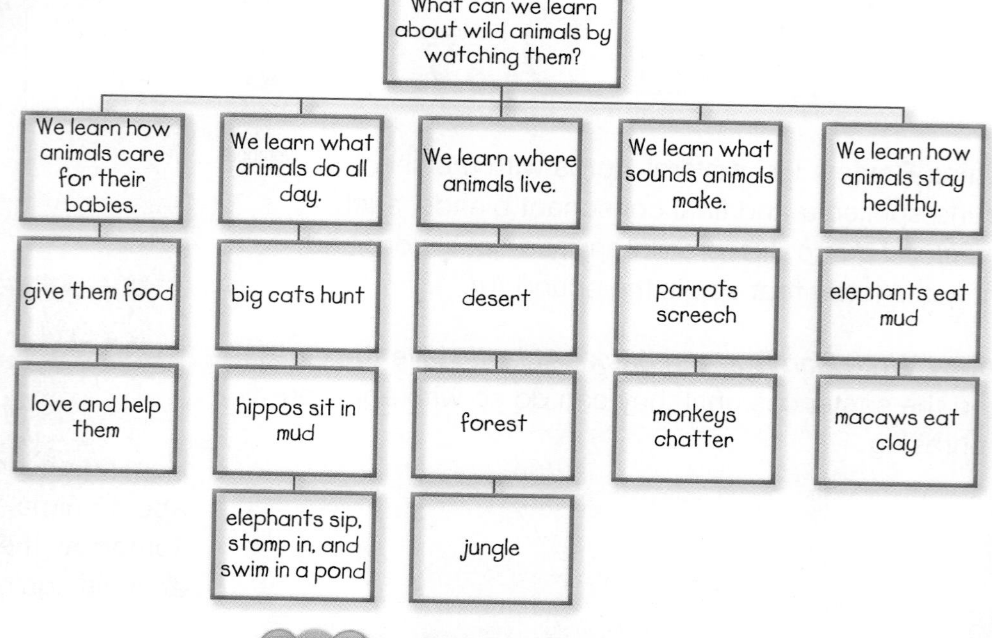
What can we learn about wild animals by watching them?
We learn how animals care for their babies.
give them food
love and help them
We learn what animals do all day.
big cats hunt
hippos sit in mud
elephants sip, stomp in, and swim in a pond
We learn where animals live.
desert
forest
jungle
We learn what sounds animals make.
parrots screech
monkeys chatter
We learn how animals stay healthy.
elephants eat mud
macaws eat clay

ELL Check Concepts and Language Use the Day 5 instruction on ELL Poster 6 to monitor children's understanding of the lesson concept.

ELL Poster 6

Oral Vocabulary
Amazing Ideas

Connect to the Big Question

Team Talk Pair children and have them discuss how the Question of the Week connects to this unit's Big Question, "How are people and animals important to one another?" Tell children to use the concept map and what they've learned from this week's Anchored Talks and reading selections to form an Amazing Idea—a realization or "big idea" about **Animals, Tame and Wild**. Then ask each pair to share their Amazing Idea with the class.

Amazing Ideas might include these key concepts:

- People can protect the places where wild animals live.
- Knowing what plants are poisonous to animals can help people stay safe, too.

It's Friday

MONITOR PROGRESS

Check Oral Vocabulary

Call on individuals to use this week's Amazing Words to talk about what we learn by watching wild animals. Prompt discussion with the questions below. Monitor children's ability to use the Amazing Words and note which words children are unable to use.

- **What animals could you observe in a *forest*? in a *desert*?**
- **Where in the *world* would you go to see zebras and hippos?**
- **Why do you think some animals *chatter*?**
- **When are animals likely to be *silent*?**
- **What would you do if you heard an animal *snort* nearby?**
- **What kinds of *medicine* do some animals use to protect themselves from *poisonous* foods?**

If... children have difficulty using the Amazing Words,
then... reteach the unknown words using the Oral Vocabulary Routines, pp. 147a, 152b, 164b, 168b.

Day 1	Day 2	Day 3	Day 4	Day 5
Check Word Reading	Check Word Reading	Check High Frequency Words/Retelling	Check Fluency	Check Oral Vocabulary

Success Predictor

desert	silent
forest	snort
world	medicine
chatter	poisonous

ELL

English Language Learners

Amazing Words Provide a sentence frame to help children answer each question, for example: I could see animals in a ____.

DAY 5 Wrap Up your Week

Objectives

- ◎ Review words with short *u*.
- ◎ Review words with final consonant blends.
- Segment and blend onset and rime.

Assess

- Spell words with short *u* and final consonant blends.
- Spell high-frequency words.

Phonological Awareness

Segment and Blend Onset and Rime

Review
Onset and rime

Have children repeat the onset and rime for each word. Then have them blend the sounds to say the word. If children make an error, model the correct response. Return to the word later in the practice.

/b/-ug **bug**	/t/ /r/-ust **trust**	/h/-elp **help**
/s/ /t/-ump **stump**	/b/-and **band**	/k/-ut **cut**
/d/-esk **desk**	/f/-un **fun**	/m/-ilk **milk**

Phonics

Short *u*: *u*; Final Consonant Blends

Review
Target phonics skills

Write the following sentences on the board. Have children read each one, first quietly to themselves and then aloud as you track the print.

1. **His pup can run fast.**
2. **An ant will step in sand.**
3. **The small bug will drift in the tub.**
4. **Six frogs rest at the pond.**

Team Talk Have children discuss with a partner which words have short *u* spelled *u* and which words have a final consonant blend. Then call on individuals to share with the class.

Spelling Test
Short *u* Words with Final Consonant Blends

Dictate spelling words

Say each word, read the sentence, repeat the word, and allow time for children to write the word.

1. crust	The **crust** is the best part of the pie!
2. bump	I fell and got a **bump** on my head.
3. jump	How high can you **jump?**
4. must	I **must** study for the test.
5. just	It is **just** a movie.
6. dust	Can you **dust** the books?
7. trust	I **trust** you to be fair.
8. dusk	It is **dusk** after the sun sets.
9. hunt	Can we **hunt** for my blue socks?
10. lump	I fell on a **lump** of dirt in my yard.

High-Frequency Words

11. many	I saw **many** animals at the zoo.
12. into	I put my toys **into** the box.

Small Group Time

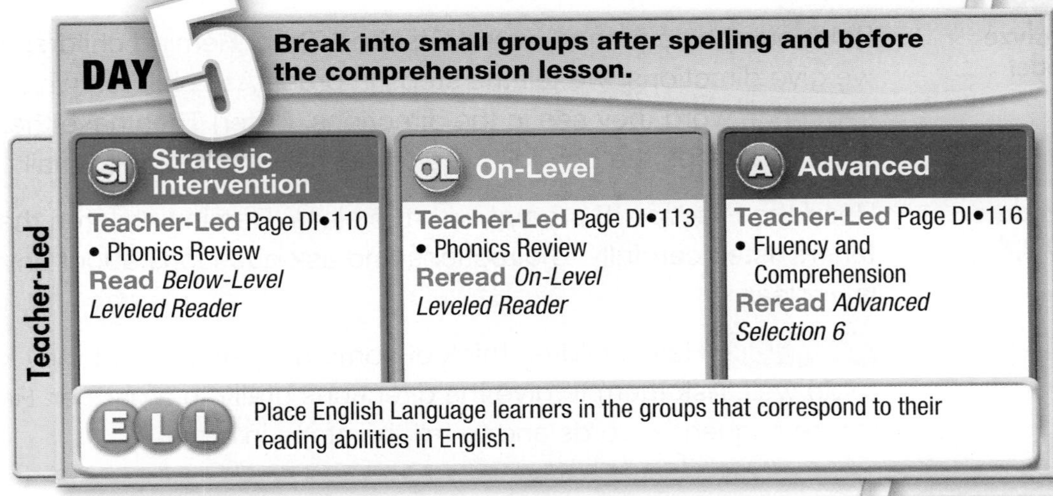

DAY 5
Break into small groups after spelling and before the comprehension lesson.
Teacher-Led
SI Strategic Intervention
Teacher-Led Page DI•110
• Phonics Review
Read Below-Level Leveled Reader
OL On-Level
Teacher-Led Page DI•113
• Phonics Review
Reread On-Level Leveled Reader
A Advanced
Teacher-Led Page DI•116
• Fluency and Comprehension
Reread Advanced Selection 6
ELL
Place English Language learners in the groups that correspond to their reading abilities in English.

Practice Stations
- Words to Know
- Read for Meaning

Independent Activities
- Read independently/Reading Log on *Reader's and Writer's Notebook* p. RR2
- Concept Talk Video

Differentiated Instruction

Strategic Intervention

Reteach Use sound-to-sound spelling to model blending *bug.* Write *b* and say its sound /b/. Then write *u* and say its sound /u/. Write *g* and say its sound /g/. Then blend the whole word, pointing to each letter as you say its sound.

Advanced

Extend Spelling Have children look through the main selection and find as many words as they can with final consonant blends. List the words that children find. Then ask children to write a sentence for each word.

Objectives

- Give oral instructions in sequence.
- Speak clearly, using complete sentences.
- Listen attentively and ask relevant questions.
- Identify antonyms.
- Read aloud fluently with appropriate phrasing.

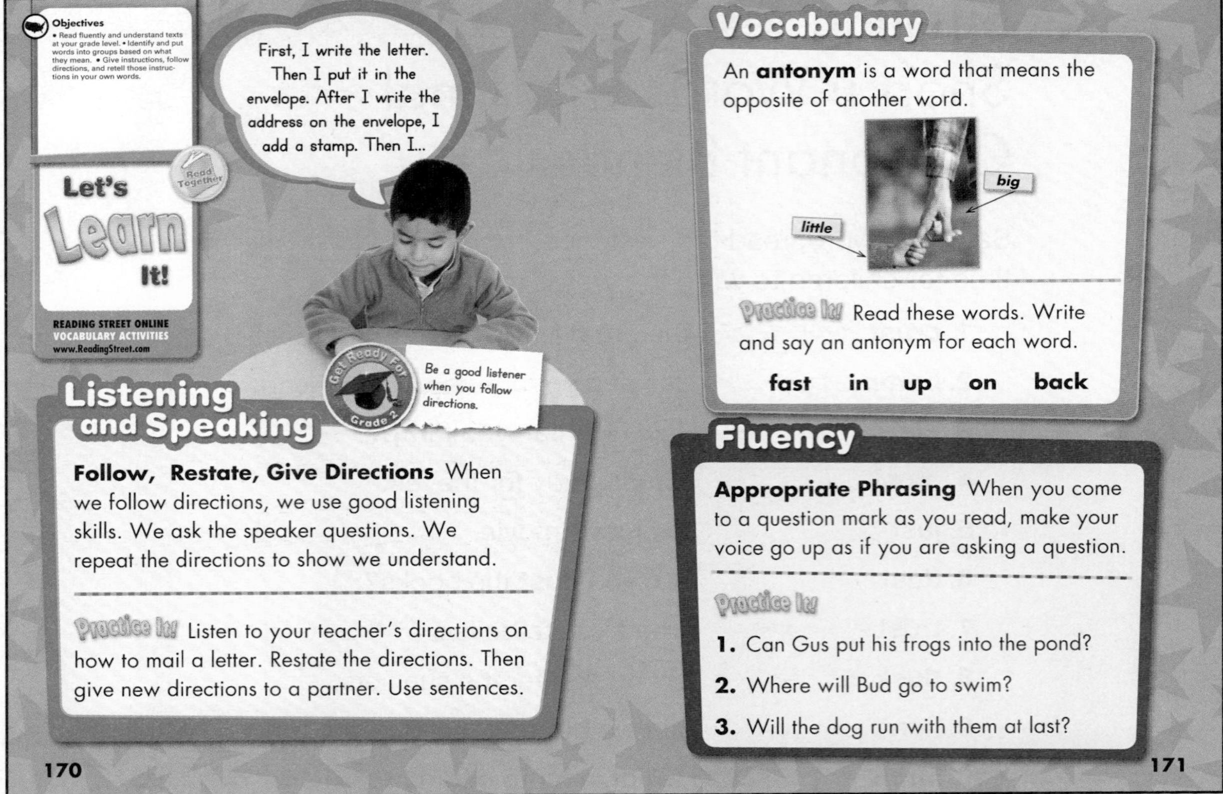

First, I write the letter. Then I put it in the envelope. After I write the address on the envelope, I add a stamp. Then I...
Let's Learn It!
Read Together
READING STREET ONLINE VOCABULARY ACTIVITIES www.ReadingStreet.com
Be a good listener when you follow directions.
Listening and Speaking
Follow, Restate, Give Directions When we follow directions, we use good listening skills. We ask the speaker questions. We repeat the directions to show we understand.
Practice It! Listen to your teacher's directions on how to mail a letter. Restate the directions. Then give new directions to a partner. Use sentences.
Vocabulary
An antonym is a word that means the opposite of another word.
big
little
Practice It! Read these words. Write and say an antonym for each word.
fast in up on back
Fluency
Appropriate Phrasing When you come to a question mark as you read, make your voice go up as if you are asking a question.
Practice It!
1. Can Gus put his frogs into the pond?
2. Where will Bud go to swim?
3. Will the dog run with them at last?
170
171

Student Edition pp. 170–171

Listening and Speaking
Give Directions

Teach Have children turn to page 170 of the Student Edition. Read and discuss the directions the child in the photo is giving. Remind children that good speakers speak in complete sentences.

Analyze model Point out the sequence words *First* and *Then*. Remind children that when we give directions, we tell the steps in order. Ask children what other sequence word they see in the directions. (After) Then have them tell, in order, the steps the boy followed to get his letter ready to mail.

Introduce prompt Read the Practice It! prompt with the class. Remind children that good listeners listen carefully to directions and ask questions about anything that is unclear.

Team Talk Have children think of something simple that they know how to do well. Ask them to give the directions orally to a partner. Remind them to use sequence words and to tell the steps in order.

Vocabulary
Antonyms

Teach Read and discuss the Vocabulary lesson on page 171 of the Student Edition. Use the model to explain that antonyms are words that are opposites.

Model Point to the photograph. What word describes the size of the adult's hand? (big) What word describes the size of the child's hand? (little) Because *big* and *little* have opposite meanings, we call them antonyms.

Guide practice Read the instructions for the Vocabulary Practice It! Activity. Read the first word and then have children repeat after you.

I need to think of an antonym for the word *fast*. The opposite of *fast* is *slow*. So, I will write and say the word *slow*.

On their own Have partners continue writing and saying antonyms for the remaining words in the list.

Corrective feedback Circulate around the room and listen as children say the antonyms. Provide assistance as needed.

Fluency
Appropriate Phrasing

Teach Read and discuss the Fluency instructions.

Read words in context Give children a moment to look at the sentences. Then have them read each sentence three or four times until they can read each sentence with appropriate phrasing.

Differentiated Instruction

Strategic Intervention

Visual Support Help children understand antonyms by demonstrating the meanings of opposites, such as *in/out, up/down, stop/go, under/over, left/right, open/close, give/take*.

Give and Follow Directions

Children at Grade 2 should be able to give and follow directions of four or more steps.

English Language Learners

Physical Response Ask children to demonstrate their understanding of antonyms by physically showing the meanings of the words in each pair. Then have children use this sentence frame to structure their oral response: *The opposite of ____ is ____.*

Objectives

- ◎ Identify cause and effect in narrative nonfiction.
- Review high-frequency and story words.
- Identify and use rhythm and rhyme in poems.

Comprehension
Cause and Effect

Review **Cause and effect**

Remember that good readers ask themselves what happens and why it happens. What do we call the reason, or why something happens? (the cause) What do we call the result of what happened? (the effect)

To check understanding of cause and effect, read aloud the following story and have children answer the questions that follow.

> Diego hung two big birdfeeders in his backyard and filled them with different seeds. Many wild birds came to the feeders, and Diego would watch the birds for hours. One day Diego noticed that the feeders were suddenly empty. Where had all his seeds gone so quickly? Diego became a detective. What did he discover? Squirrels were leaping off the fence onto his feeders. They gobbled up all the birdseed!

1. What is the cause of the disappearing birdseed? (The squirrels are eating it.)
2. What is the effect on the birds? (The birds don't have anything to eat.)

Vocabulary
High-Frequency and Story Words

Review **High-frequency words**

Review this week's high-frequency words: *home*, *into*, *many*, and *them*. Write each word on a card. Place the cards in a box or bag. Model pulling out a card, reading the word, and using it in a sentence about wild animals. For example: Camels are at *home* in the desert.

Team Talk Have partners make their own card sets. Ask them to take turns choosing and reading a word and then creating an original sentence.

Review **Story words**

Write the words *park*, *zebras*, *hippos*, and *elephants*. Read them aloud together. Then ask children questions that use the words. For example: What color are *zebras*? Have children respond in complete sentences that include the story words.

Corrective feedback

If… children cannot use the story words correctly,
then… review the definitions on page 154a.

Poetry
Rhythm and Rhyme

Review Poetry Review with children that a poem is writing that may say things in an unusual way. The words in a poem are usually organized in lines, and some lines may repeat. A poem has a **rhythm**, or beat. And the words often **rhyme**—they end with the same sound.

Teach Listen as I read the poem "My Dog Rags." Read the poem on page 168 aloud. When I read, I noticed that the words at the end of each line of the poem rhyme. Write *Rags*, *sags*, *wags*, and *zags* on the board. Have children read the rhyming words with you.

Model  I'm going to read the poem again. This time, I'll clap out the rhythm as I read. Clap out the rhythm as you reread the poem. I can hear that there are four beats in each line of this poem.

Guide practice Use the poem "The Hippo" on page 169 to guide children in understanding rhythm and rhyme in poetry.

- Follow along as I read the poem. Read the poem aloud. Which words rhyme? (float/boat, retreats/eats)
- What line in this poem repeats? ("and eats") How many times is this line in the poem? (four times)
- Listen as I read the first two lines again. I'll clap out the rhythm as I read. How many beats do you hear in each line? (four)

On their own Have children read the poem "Raccoon" on page 168. Ask them to clap out the rhythm as they read. Then have children find and write the words that rhyme (clan/can, eat/treat). Finally, ask children to write and illustrate their own rhyming couplet about a favorite animal.

Differentiated Instruction

 **Strategic Intervention**

To help children think of rhyming words, have them use letter tiles to spell a familiar phonogram such as *-ag, -ut,* or *-in.* Then ask them to place tiles for different consonants and consonant blends before the phonograms to create rhyming words.

Academic Vocabulary

rhythm a beat that repeats

rhyme ending with the same sounds

Assess
- ◎ Words with Short *u:u*
- ◎ Final Consonant Blends
- • High-Frequency Words

Assessment
Monitor Progress

For a written assessment of short *u: u*, final consonant blends, high-frequency words, and cause and effect, use Weekly Test 6, pages 67–72.

Assess words in isolation

Word reading Use the following reproducible page to assess children's ability to read words in isolation. Call on children to read the words aloud. Start over if necessary.

Assess words in context

Sentence reading Use the reproducible page on page 171f to assess children's ability to read words in context. Call on children to read two sentences aloud. Start over with sentence one if necessary.

MONITOR PROGRESS **Word and Sentence Reading**

If... children have trouble reading words with short *u: u* and final consonant blends,
then... use the Reteach Lessons in *First Stop*.

If... children cannot read all the high-frequency words,
then... mark the missed words on a high-frequency word list and have the child practice reading the words with a fluent reader.

Monitor accuracy

Record scores Use the Word/Sentence Reading Chart for this unit in *First Stop.*

Name ______________________________

Read the Words

1. home
2. bus
3. into
4. rest
5. jump
6. many
7. pond
8. hugs
9. stump
10. mud
11. them
12. grunt

MONITOR PROGRESS

- Fluency
- Short *u: u*
- Final Consonant Blends
- High-frequency words

Name ____________________

Read the Sentences

1. Dogs ran into the pond.

2. Gus has many pets.

3. Mom is helping them pick plums.

4. Tim can rest at home.

5. Many trucks stop on the hill.

6. Will Nan get them a gift?

MONITOR PROGRESS

- Fluency
- Short *u: u*
- Final Consonant Blends
- High-frequency words

Objectives

- Identify and use exclamatory sentences.
- Recognize and use correct punctuation for exclamatory sentences.

Conventions
Exclamatory Sentences

Review Remind children that an exclamatory sentence shows strong feeling and ends with an exclamation mark. Have them give several examples of exclamatory sentences.

Guide practice Write the following sentences without end punctuation. Have children tell you what end punctuation to add and why. If they choose an exclamation mark, have them say what emotion the sentence shows. There will be more than one correct response.

1. Mom is so mad at Ben
2. A big dog bit Brad
3. Fran just got a new red sled

Connect to oral language Display and read the following sentence frame. Have children work in pairs to think of as many ways as they can to complete the exclamatory sentence. Then have children share their responses with the class.

__________ is the best __________!

On their own Use Let's Practice It! p. 71 on the *Teachers Resource DVD-ROM.*

Name ____________ Animal Park

Exclamatory Sentences

Read each pair of sentences.
Write the exclamation on the line.

1. The hippo sat in the mud. The hippo is big!
The hippo is so big!
2. Where is the hippo? Look at it run!
Look at it run!
3. The lion is in the park. I like the lion!
I like the lion!

Write each exclamation correctly.

4. the animal is mad
The animal is mad!
5. the lion is the best
The lion is the best!

Home Activity Your child reviewed exclamations. With your child, look through newspaper and magazine ads. Have your child highlight the exclamations he or she finds.

Conventions Exclamatory Sentences DVD•71

Let's Practice It! TR DVD•71

Daily Fix-It

9. Did the bus hit a rok.
Did the bus hit a ro<u>ck?</u>

10. Can you see the elephants ruun
Can you see the elephants r<u>u</u>n<u>?</u>

Discuss the Daily Fix-It corrections with children. Review sentence punctuation, the *ck* spelling of final /k/, and the *u* spelling of /u/.

Objectives

- Evaluate a brief composition.

Writing for Tests
Brief Composition

Review Evaluating Remind children that yesterday they learned more about writing brief compositions and they wrote to a second prompt. Today they will evaluate their writing from yesterday.

MINI-LESSON

Proofread for Sentences

- **Teach** In our compositions, we must capitalize and punctuate each sentence correctly, so that readers know where the sentence begins and ends. This will also help readers tell what kind of sentence it is. If it is a telling sentence, it should end with a period. If it is a sentence that asks a question, it should end with a question mark. If it is a sentence that shows a strong feeling, it should end with an exclamation point.
- **Think Aloud** Write the sentence, *How funny the giraffes look with their long necks.* I put a period at the end of this sentence. Is it a telling sentence, a question, or a sentence that shows a strong feeling? I think that this sentence shows a strong feeling. It is an exclamation about how funny the giraffes look. I will change the period at the end to an exclamation point. Use a deletion mark and a caret to delete the period and add an exclamation point.
- Explain that when editing compositions, children should check each sentence, think about what kind of sentence it is, and then check the end punctuation.

Evaluate Now it is time to evaluate your compositions. First, have children evaluate their compositions to make sure their purpose is clear. Then have children use the rubric on *Reader's and Writer's Notebook* p. 208 to evaluate their compositions. If helpful, they can share their compositions and work with a partner. Circulate to guide children.

ROUTINE **Quick Write for Fluency** Team Talk

1. **Talk** Have partners take two minutes to discuss what they learned from writing their brief compositions this week.
2. **Write** Have each child write a sentence about what they learned from writing their brief compositions this week.
3. **Share** Partners can read their sentences to one another.

Routines Flip Chart

Teacher Note

Self-Evaluation Make copies of the Self-Evaluation form from the Teacher Resource DVD-ROM, and guide children as they use it.

English Language Learners

Support Editing For children to whom the sounds and spelling of English still are not very familiar, look for spelling improvement little by little from week to week rather than rapid development. Help children make progress a word at a time and learn word meanings.

Objectives

- Review concept: what we can learn about wild animals by watching them.
- Organize information.
- Present results of an inquiry project.

Research and Inquiry

Communicate

Teach Tell children that today they will finish the notes about their animal and share the notes with others.

Model Think Aloud Display the notes about animals in the neighborhood. I will review my notes and circle the words and drawings about my animal. Those will be the notes I will include in my final work. My notes are about the animal I watched. I will start by writing the name of the animal as the title of my notes. Before I write my notes, I will make sure that all the words are spelled correctly. If I have questions about spelling, I will use the dictionaries we have in the classroom to find the correct spelling. I will write each note on its own line. My final work will look a little like a list.

Guide practice Review children's notes. Work with them to write the name of their animal at the top of their page and to be sure the words in the notes are spelled correctly.

On their own Have children write notes to share with the class. Suggest they write the title at the top of a sheet of paper and each note on its own line. Have children break themselves into groups. Instruct them to read aloud their notes to one another so they can learn about other animals. Remind children how to be good speakers and listeners:

- Good speakers speak clearly so their listeners can understand what they are saying.
- Good listeners pay attention to the speaker and do not talk while someone else is speaking.

Visual display Display children's notes on the classroom bulletin board.

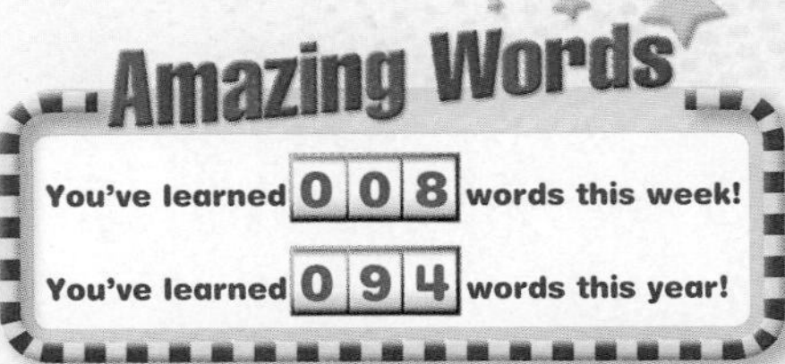

Amazing Words
You've learned 008 words this week!
You've learned 094 words this year!

Wrap Up Your Week!

Question of the Week

What can we learn about wild animals by watching them?

Think Aloud This week we explored what we can learn about wild animals by watching them. In the nonfiction story *Animal Park*, we found out what wild animals that live in a special park do. In the poems "Raccoon" and "The Hippo," we learned more about how wild animals behave. Have children recall their Amazing Ideas about wild animals. Then have children use these ideas to help them demonstrate their understanding of the Question of the Week.

ELL

English Language Learners

Poster Preview Prepare children for next week by using Week 13, ELL Poster 7. Read the Poster Talk-Through to introduce the concept and vocabulary. Ask children to identify and describe objects and actions in the art.

Selection Summary
Send home the summary of *A Big Fish for Max* in English and the child's home language if available. Children can read the summary with family members.

Preview NEXT WEEK

Tell children that next week they will read about a family of rabbits.

Unit Wrap-Up

The Big Question

How are people and animals important to one another?

Understanding By Design

Grant Wiggins, Ed. D.
Reading Street Author

"A big idea is not necessarily vast in the sense of a vague phrase covering lots of content. Nor is a big idea a 'basic' idea. Rather, big ideas are at the 'core' of the subject; they need to be uncovered; we have to dig deep until we get to the core."

WEEK 1

Question of the Week

What do pets need?

Concept Knowledge

Children will understand that pets:

- need food and water
- need shelter
- need exercise
- need love

WEEK 2

Question of the Week

Who helps animals?

Concept Knowledge

Children will understand that:

- pet owners help animals
- vets help animals
- trainers help animals

Discuss the Big Question

Help children relate the concept question for this unit to the selections and their own experiences. Write the question and prompt discussion with questions such as the following:

How are people important to animals?
Possible answers:

- *Sam, Come Back!* The lady's yarn keeps Sam busy.
- *Pig in a Wig* The lady helps Pig get well.
- *The Big Blue Ox* Mom and Pop give Ox something to do.
- *A Fox and a Kit* Animals can get protection from people.

WEEK 3

Question of the Week

How do animals help people?

Concept Knowledge

Children will understand that animals provide:

- food for people
- transportation for people
- services to people

WEEK 4

Question of the Week

How do wild animals take care of their babies?

Concept Knowledge

Children will understand that wild animals

- provide food for their babies
- protect their babies from harm

WEEK 5

Question of the Week

Which wild animals live in our neighborhood?

Concept Knowledge

Children will understand that:

- all kinds of animals live in our neighborhood
- neighborhood animals need different kinds of food and shelter

WEEK 6

Question of the Week

What can we learn about wild animals by watching them?

Concept Knowledge

Children will understand that:

- we can learn about animals by watching them
- wild animals need food, water, and shelter
- we protect animals from danger

How are animals important to people?

- *Sam, Come Back!* Sam keeps the lady company.
- *Pig in a Wig* Pig dances and is funny.
- *The Big Blue Ox* Ox helps Mom and Pop.
- *A Fox and a Kit* People watch the fox and kit.
- *Get the Egg!* Brad and Kim get to watch the baby birds.
- *Animal Park* People see the animals in a more natural setting.

Tell about an animal that is important to you. What can you do to help that animal?

Responses will vary.

Assessment Checkpoints for the Week

Weekly Assessment

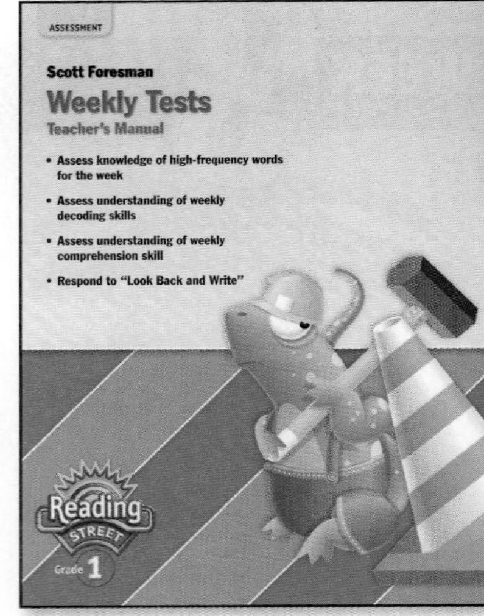
Weekly Tests

Use pp. 67–72 of *Weekly Tests* to check:

- ✔ **Phonics** Inflected Ending *u: u*
- ✔ **Phonics** Final Consonant Blends
- ✔ **Comprehension Skill** Cause and Effect
- ✔ **High-Frequency Words**

home	many
into	them

Differentiated Asssessment

Advanced

On-Level

Strategic Intervention

Fresh Reads for Fluency and Comprehension

Use pp. 67–72 of *Fresh Reads for Fluency and Comprehension* to check:

- ✔ **Comprehension Skill** Cause and Effect
- ✔ Review **Comprehension Skill** Main Idea and Details

Unit Assessment

Unit and End-of-Year Benchmark Tests

Use the Unit 1 Benchmark Test to check progress in:

- ✔ **Passage Comprehension**
- ✔ **High-Frequency Words**
- ✔ **Phonics**
- ✔ **Writing Conventions**
- ✔ **Writing**
- ✔ **Fluency**

Fun with Ducks

Mom led the family up the path. Gus was happy. The forest was beautiful. The sun felt good. Family hikes were fun.

The path ended at a large pond. Near the pond was a picnic table. It was under a tree with a big trunk. "Let's rest here," said Mom. "I have nuts and a bunch of grapes for us to munch. We can drink cups of water."

As the family ate, they saw a mother duck and four little ducks. The ducks marched to the pond in a line. At the muddy edge, the mother duck jumped into the pond. Then she looked back at the little ducks and quacked. The little ducks jumped in, too. They each quacked as they jumped.

The mother duck paddled. Then three little ducks paddled in a line. The mother duck looked back. One little duck was not keeping up. The mother duck quacked at it. The little duck quacked and caught up. Gus and his family grinned. The ducks were funny.

Soon the family got up and started to hike again. But Gus was still looking at the ducks. Mom looked back. "Gus!" said Mom. "Quack!"

"Quack!" Gus grinned and ran to catch up.

Advanced Selection 6 **Vocabulary:** munch, paddled

Pacing Small Group Instruction

20–30 min.

5 Day Plan

DAY 1	• Phonemic Awareness/ Phonics • Decodable Reader
DAY 2	• Phonemic Awareness/ Phonics • Decodable Reader
DAY 3	• Phonemic Awareness/ Phonics • Leveled Reader
DAY 4	• High-Frequency Words • Decodable Reader
DAY 5	• Phonics Review • Leveled Reader

3 or 4 Day Plan

DAY 1	• Phonemic Awareness/ Phonics • Decodable Reader
DAY 2	• Phonemic Awareness/ Phonics • Decodable Reader
DAY 3	• Phonemic Awareness/ Phonics • Leveled Reader
DAY 4	• High-Frequency Words • Decodable Reader

3 Day Plan: Eliminate the shaded box

DAY 1

Phonemic Awareness • Phonics

- **Distinguish /u/** Reteach p. 148–149 of the Teacher's Edition. Model identifying short *u*. I hear the sound /u/ at the beginning of the word *us*. I hear the sound /u/ in the middle of the word *cup*. Then have children practice identifying short *u* on their own.

sun	**cut**	**hum**
mug	**up**	**luck**

- **Short *u*: *u*** Reteach p. 149a of the Teacher's Edition. Then have children spell *hug* using letter tiles. Monitor their work.
  - Change the *h* in *hug* to *b*. What is the new word?
  - Change the *g* in *bug* to *n*. What is the new word?
  - Change the *b* in *bun* to *f*. What is the new word?

Decodable Practice Reader 6A

- **Review** Review words with short *u* and the high-frequency words *like(s), to, they, the, with, too, a*. Then have children blend and read these words from the story: *flop, drop, spots, spin.*

  If... children have difficulty with any of these words, **then...** reteach the word by modeling. Have children practice the words, with feedback from you, until they can read them independently.

  Have children reread the text orally. To achieve optimal fluency, children should reread the text three or four times.

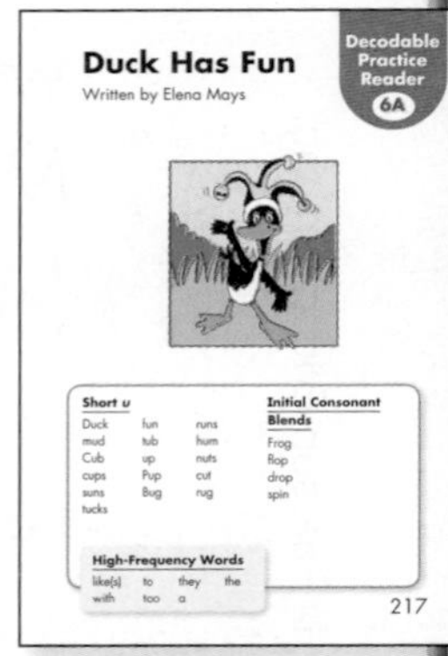

Decodable Practice Reader 6A

Objectives

- Isolate medial sounds in one-syllable spoken words.
- Decode words in isolation by applying common letter-sound correspondences, including: single letters (vowels) including short u.

DAY 2

Phonemic Awareness • Phonics

- **Segment and Blend Phonemes** Reteach p. 152c of the Teacher's Edition. Model segmenting and blending these words. Then have children practice segmenting and blending on their own.

last /l/ /a/ /s/ /t/ **jump** /j/ /u/ /m/ /p/ **belt** /b/ /e/ /l/ /t/

- **Final Consonant Blends** Reteach p. 152d of the Teacher's Edition. Then have children spell *band* using letter tiles. Monitor their work.

- Change the *a* in *band* to *e*. What is the new word?

- Change the *d* in *bend* to *t*. What is the new word?

- Change the *b* in *bent* to *w*. What is the new word?

w e n t

Decodable Practice Reader 6B

- **Review** Review words with final consonant blends and the high-frequency words *the, a, see, that, small.* Then have children blend and read these words from the story: *bend, pond, flick.*

If... children have difficulty with any of these words, **then...** reteach the word by modeling. Have children practice the words, with feedback from you, until they can read them independently.

Have children reread the text orally. To achieve optimal fluency, children should reread the text three or four times.

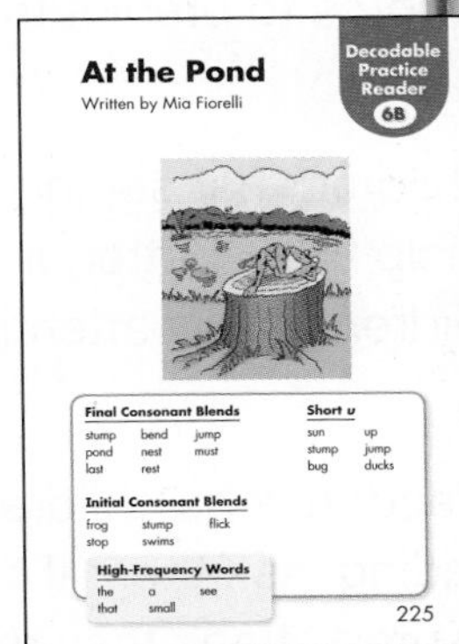

Decodable Practice Reader 6B

More Reading

Use Leveled Readers or other text at children's instructional level to develop fluency.

Objectives

- Blend spoken phonemes to form one-syllable words, including consonant blends.
- Decode words in isolation by applying common letter-sound correspondences, including: consonant blends.

DAY 3

Phonemic Awareness • Phonics

■ **Generate Rhyming Words** Model generating rhyming words. Say each sound in the word /r/ /u/ /b/. Have children say the sounds with you and then say the sounds by themselves. Now listen as I say another word with the same ending sounds as *rub*. Model the sounds of the word *tub*. Have children say the sounds with you and then say the sounds by themselves. Point out that *rub* and *tub* are rhyming words.

Work with children to generate rhyming words for the following words.

- **nut** (cut, but, shut, hut)
- **bug** (rug, hug, tug, plug)

■ **Short *u*: *u* and Final Consonant Blends** Reteach p. 164e of the Teacher's Edition. Have children blend and read these additional words to help them practice the target phonics skills.

drum	just	run	tent	camp	mud

For a complete literacy instructional plan and additional practice with this week's target skills and strategies, see the **Leveled Reader Teaching Guide.**

Concept Literacy Leveled Reader

■ **Preview and Predict** Read the title and the author's name. Have children look at the cover and ask them to describe what they see. Help children activate their prior knowledge by asking them to look through the story and to use the photos to predict things that might take place.

■ **Set a Purpose** Remind children that setting a purpose for reading can help them better understand what they read. Guide children to pay attention to the different kinds of animals.

■ **Read** Provide corrective feedback as children read the story orally. During reading, ask them if they were able to confirm any of the predictions they made prior to the story.

If... children have difficulty reading the story individually,
then... read a sentence aloud as children point to each word. Then have the group reread the sentences as they continue pointing. Continue reading in this way until children read individually.

■ **Retell** Have children take turns retelling the story. Help them identify the animals by asking, What wild animals did you see? Which animal has stripes (spots, feathers)?

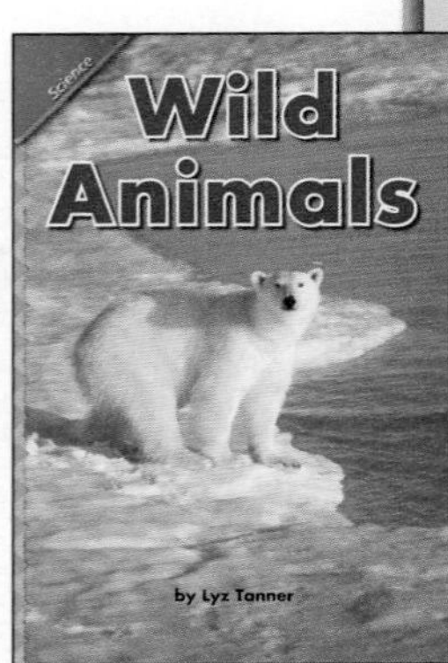

Concept Literacy

Objectives

- Orally generate a series of original rhyming words using a variety of phonograms.
- Decode words in isolation by applying common letter-sound correspondences, including: single letters (vowels) including short u.

DAY 4

More Reading

Use Leveled Readers or other text at children's instructional level.

High-Frequency Words

- **Review** Write *home, many, them, into* on the board. Model saying each word. Then have children read each word, spell each word as you point to each letter, and have them say each word again. Allow time for children to practice reading these high-frequency words using the word cards.

Decodable Practice Reader 6C

Decodable Practice Reader 6C

- **Review** Use the word lists to review short *u* and final consonant blends. Be sure that children understand that the letter *u* can make the sound /u/ and that the sounds of the letters in a consonant blend are blended together.

  If... children have difficulty reading the story individually, **then...** read a sentence aloud as children point to each word. Then have the group reread the sentences as they continue pointing. Continue reading in this way until children read individually.

Check comprehension by having children retell the story including the characters, plot, and setting. Have children locate words in the story that have short *u* and final consonant blends. List the words children identify. Then have children sort the words in a chart with columns labeled Short *u* and Final Consonant Blends.

Short u	Final Consonant Blends
cub	pond
nut	plant
yum	must
mud	bent
mud	and
dug	rest

Objectives

- Decode words in context by applying common letter-sound correspondences, including: single letters (vowels) including short u.
- Read at least 100 high-frequency words from a commonly used list.

More Reading

Use Leveled Readers or other text at children's instructional level.

Phonics Review

- **Short *u*: *u* and Final Consonant Blends** Write these sentences on the board. Have children read them aloud as you track the print. Then call on individuals to blend and read the underlined words.

Nan will rest in the sun.

Bud can jump in the sand.

The cub went in its den.

Gus kept gum in his bag.

For a complete literacy instructional plan and additional practice with this week's target skills and strategies, see the **Leveled Reader Teaching Guide.**

Below-Level Leveled Reader

Below-Level Reader

Preview and Predict Read the title and the author's name. Have children look at the cover and ask them to describe what they see. Help children activate their prior knowledge by asking them to look through the story and to use the photos to predict things that might take place.

- **Set a Purpose** Remind children that setting a purpose for reading can help them better understand what they read. Guide children to pay attention to what the animals do.
- **Read** Provide corrective feedback as children read the story orally. During reading, ask them if they were able to confirm any of the predictions they made prior to the story.

  If... children have difficulty reading the story individually,
  then... read each sentence aloud as children point to each word. Then have the group reread the sentences as they continue pointing.

- **Cause and Effect** Have children explain why the animals go into the pond.

Objectives

- Decode words in context by applying common letter-sound correspondences, including: single letters (vowels) including short u.
- Make inferences about text.

eReaders

DAY 1

Phonics • Spelling

- **Short *u*: *u*** Write the following words on the board and have children practice reading words with short *u*.

bug **plus** **dust** **fun**

- **Short *u* Words with Final Consonant Blends** Remind children that each spelling word has the letter *u*, which spells the /u/ sound, and a final consonant blend. Clarify the pronunciation and meaning of each word. For example, say: *Dusk* is the time of evening just before dark.

Objectives

- Decode words in isolation by applying common letter-sound correspondences, including: single letters (vowels) including short u.

Pacing Small Group Instruction

20–30 min.

5 Day Plan

DAY 1	• Phonics • Spelling • Decodable Reader
DAY 2	• Phonics • High-Frequency Words • Decodable Reader
DAY 3	• Leveled Reader
DAY 4	• Conventions • Main Selection
DAY 5	• Phonics Review • Leveled Reader

3 or 4 Day Plan

DAY 1	• Phonics • Spelling • Decodable Reader
DAY 2	• Phonics • High-Frequency Words • Decodable Reader
DAY 3	• Leveled Reader
DAY 4	• Conventions • Main Selection

3 Day Plan: Eliminate the shaded box

DAY 2

Phonics • High-Frequency Words

- **Final Consonant Blends** Write the following words on the board and have children practice reading words with final consonant blends.

hand **best** **sent** **lamp**

- **High-Frequency Words** Hold up this week's High-Frequency Word Cards and review proper pronunciation. Continue holding the cards and have children chorally read each word. To help children demonstrate their understanding of the words, provide them with oral sentence frames such as: There are __________ stars in the sky. (many)

High-Frequency Word Cards for Grade 1

Objectives

- Decode words in isolation by applying common letter-sound correspondences, including: consonant blends.
- Read at least 100 high-frequency words from a commonly used list.

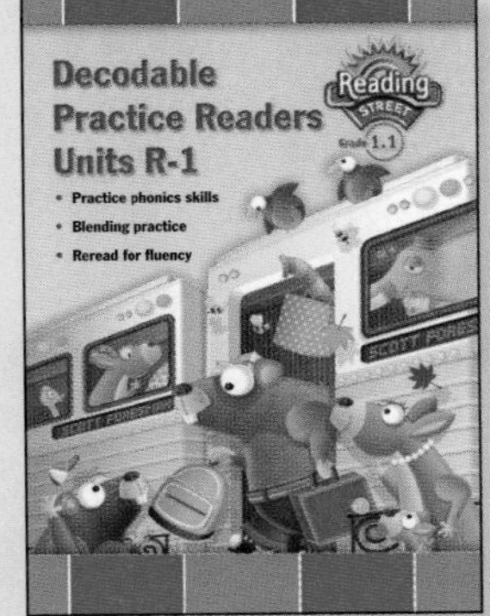

Decodable Practice Readers Units R-1
Practice phonics skills
Blending practice
Reread for fluency

Decodable Practice Readers

For a complete literacy instructional plan and additional practice with this week's target skills and strategies, see the **Leveled Reader Teaching Guide.**

On-Level Leveled Reader

Which Animals Will We See?
by Megan Litwin

On-Level

- **Preview and Predict** Read the title and the author's name. Have children look at the cover and ask them to describe in detail what they see. Help children preview the story by asking them to look through the story and to use the photos to predict things that might take place.
- **Cause and Effect** Before reading, remind children that setting a purpose for reading can help them better understand what they read. Guide children to think about why things happen in the story.
- **Read** During reading, monitor children's comprehension by providing higher-order thinking questions. Ask:
  - Why do you think the family went on a hike in the woods?
  - Do you think the family enjoyed their hike? Why?

  To help children gain a better understanding of the text, build upon their responses with a group discussion.
- **Text Structure** Discuss with children how they gained information from text features of the story.
  - What information does the title give you about this story?
  - What can you learn from the photos?
- **Text to Self** Help children make personal connections to the story. Ask:
  - Have you ever been on a hike in the woods? What did you see?

Objectives

- Use text features to locate specific information in text.
- Make connections to own experiences.

DAY 4

Conventions

- **Exclamatory Sentences** Remind children that an exclamation is a sentence that shows strong feeling.
  - An exclamation begins with a capital letter. It ends with an exclamation mark.
  - Write this exclamation: *Look out for the car!* This is an exclamation. Point out the beginning capital letter and the exclamation mark at the end.

  Continue modeling in the same way with other exclamations. Have children identify the beginning capital letter and exclamation mark in each exclamation.

Objectives
- Recognize punctuation marks at the end of exclamatory sentences.

More Reading

Use Leveled Readers or other text at children's instructional level to develop fluency.

DAY 5

Phonics Review

- **Short *u*: *u* and Final Consonant Blends** Have children practice blending and reading words that contain this week's target phonics skills. Write the following words on the board, and say and sound out each word with the children.

club	**must**	**wilt**	**melt**	**rug**
duck	**ant**	**sub**	**list**	**pump**

Then have children circle the words with short *u*.

Objectives
- Decode words in isolation by applying common letter-sound correspondences, including: single letters (vowels) including short u.
- Decode words in isolation by applying common letter-sound correspondences, including: consonant blends.

Small Group Time

Pacing Small Group Instruction

5 Day Plan

DAY 1	• Phonics • Advanced Selection
DAY 2	• Phonics • Comprehension • Main Selection
DAY 3	• Leveled Reader
DAY 4	• Comprehension • Paired Selection
DAY 5	• Fluency • Comprehension • Advanced Selection

3 or 4 Day Plan

DAY 1	• Phonics • Advanced Selection
DAY 2	• Phonics • Comprehension • Main Selection
DAY 3	• Leveled Reader
DAY 4	• Comprehension • Paired Selection

3 Day Plan: Eliminate the shaded box

DAY 1

Phonics • Advanced Selection

Advanced Selection 6

- **Short *u*: *u*** Have children practice with longer words containing short *u*.

  uncle **suddenly** **unhappy** **fuzzy** **summer**

  Have children write the words on word cards and sort into groups of two- and three-syllable words. Then have partners use several words in a sentence.

- **Advanced Selection 6** Before reading, have children identify these story words: *munch* and *paddled*. If they do not know these words, provide oral sentences with the words in context to help children determine their meaning. After reading, have children recall the two most important ideas of the story.

Objectives

- Decode words in isolation by applying common letter-sound correspondences, including: single letters (vowels) including short u.

DAY 

Phonics • Comprehension

Animal Park

- **Final Consonant Blends** Have children practice with longer words containing final consonant blends.

stamp	**myself**	**child**	**friend**	**unwind**
find	**behind**	**shelf**	**cold**	**shrimp**

  Have children write the words on word cards and sort by final consonant blend. Ask children to use each word in a sentence.

- **Comprehension** Have children silently read this week's main selection, *Animal Park.* Have them retell the story identifying animals, setting, and sequence of events. Discuss what makes *Animal Park* literary nonfiction. Point out that it is a story that gives facts about real animals living in a special park.

Objectives

- Decode words in isolation by applying common letter-sound correspondences, including: consonant blends.

DAY 3

For a complete literacy instructional plan and additional practice with this week's target skills and strategies, see the **Leveled Reader Teaching Guide.**

Advanced Leveled Reader

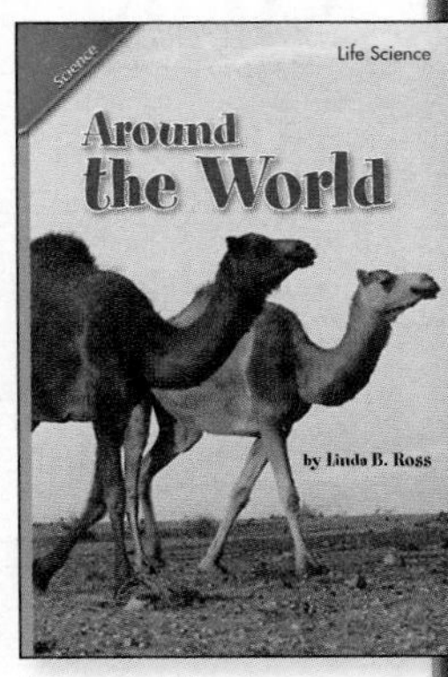

Advanced Reader

- **Activate Prior Knowledge** Read the title and the author's name. Have children look at the cover and describe in detail what they see. Remind them that the *world* is the planet Earth where we all live. Then activate the children's prior knowledge by asking them to name places they know about in the *world*.
- **Cause and Effect** Before reading, remind children that setting a purpose for reading can help them better understand what they read. Guide children to pay attention to things that happen and why they happen.
- **Read** During reading, monitor children's comprehension by providing higher-order thinking questions. Ask:
  - How is each animal suited to the place in which it lives?
  - Could a polar bear live in the desert? Why? Could a toad live at the North Pole? Why?

  Build on children's answers to help them gain a better understanding of the text.
- **Text Structure** Discuss with children how they gained information from text features of the story.
  - What information does the title give you about this story?
  - What can you learn from the photos and captions?
- **Text to Text** Help children make connections to the story. Ask:
  - What other books have you read about wild animals and their habitats? Tell how the animals are suited to places where they live.

Objectives

- Use text features to locate specific information in text.
- Use textual evidence to support understanding.

More Reading

Use Leveled Readers or other text at children's instructional level.

More Reading

Use Leveled Readers or other text at children's instructional level.

Comprehension

Poetry Collection

- **Comprehension** Have children silently read the poems in this week's paired selection. Have them summarize what happens in each poem.

  Talk about what makes these selections poems. Ensure that children understand that poems use rhythm and rhyme.

- **Text to Self** Ask children to identify which poem they liked best and to give reasons for their choice.

Objectives
- Respond to rhythm in poetry.
- Respond to rhyme in poetry.

Fluency • Comprehension

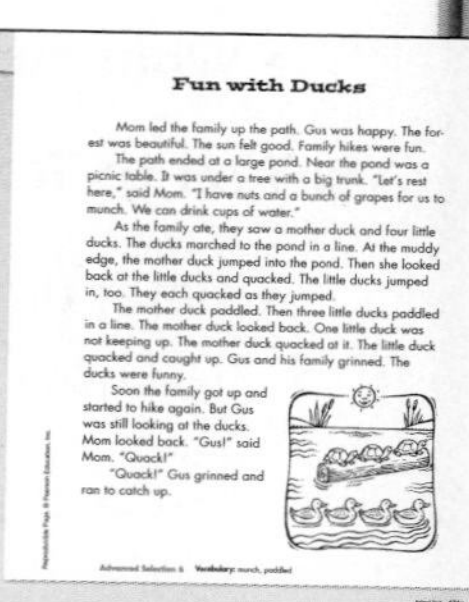
Advanced Selection 6

- **Fluency** Using the first few sentences of Advanced Selection 6, model reading with appropriate phrasing. Then have children read the selection to a partner as you listen to their reading. Provide corrective feedback as needed.
- **Comprehension** After they have finished reading the selection, have children retell what happened by stating the story events in sequence. Then, on the back of the selection page, have them write three sentences that describe what they would like to do on a family hike.

Objectives
- Read aloud grade-level appropriate text with fluency.

The ELL lessons are organized by strands. Use them to scaffold the weekly lesson curriculum or during small-group time.

Concept Development

What can we learn about wild animals by watching them?

- **Activate Prior Knowledge** Write the Question of the Week and read it aloud. Underline the words *learn* and *watching* and have children say them with you. Watching, or observing something, is a great way to learn about animals. Display a picture of a scientist or naturalist sitting outdoors. Scientists learn about nature by watching what happens. What can you learn about by watching? (nature, sports, and so on)
- **Connect to New Concept** Have children turn to pages 146–147 in the Student Edition. Read the title and have children track the print as you read it. Use pictures to guide a discussion about the things that can be learned by watching wild animals. For example, point to the picture of the snake. What is this? (snake) You can learn a lot about this snake by watching it. You can learn what it eats, how it moves, and how it protects itself from danger.
- **Develop Concepts** Show this week's Concept Talk Video and ask children to name some animals in the video. (monkey, dolphin, giraffe) What can we learn about animals by watching them? During a second viewing, stop at appropriate places to discuss things children can learn about wild animals. Use the leveled prompts below to assess understanding and build oral language.

Beginning Ask yes/no questions, such as Can wild animals get medicine when they are sick? Do hippos live in Africa?

Intermediate Ask simple questions that can be answered in a word or two. What do hippos like to eat? Where do hippos live?

Advanced/Advanced-High Have children answer the Question of the Week by giving specific examples from the video.

- **Review Concepts and Connect to Writing** Review children's understanding of the concept at the end of the week. Ask them to write in response to these questions: What can you learn about wild animals by watching them? What English words did you learn this week? Write and display key ideas from the discussion.

Objectives

- Use prior knowledge and experiences to understand meanings in English.
- Internalize new basic and academic language by using it and reusing it in meaningful ways in speaking and writing activities that build language attainment.
- Listen to and derive meaning from a variety of media such as audiotape, video, DVD, and CD ROM to build and reinforce concept and language attainment.

Content Objectives

- Describe what people can learn from watching animals.

Language Objectives

- Share information orally.
- Use video to reinforce concept.
- Use basic vocabulary for describing wild animals.

Daily Planner

DAY 1	• **Frontload Concepts** • **Preteach Comprehension** Skill, Vocabulary, Phonemic Awareness/ Phonics, Conventions/ Writing
DAY 2	• **Review** Concepts, Vocabulary, Comprehension Skill • **Frontload Main Selection** • **Practice** Phonemic Awareness/Phonics, Conventions/Writing
DAY 3	• **Review** Concepts, Comprehension Skill, Vocabulary, Conventions/ Writing • **Reread Main Selection** • **Practice** Phonemic Awareness/Phonics
DAY 4	• **Review Concepts** • **Read ELL/ELD Readers** • **Practice** Phonemic Awareness/Phonics, Conventions/Writing
DAY 5	• **Review** Concepts, Vocabulary, Comprehension Skill, Phonemic Awareness/ Phonics, Conventions/ Writing • **Reread ELL/ELD Readers**

**See the* ELL Handbook for *ELL Workshops with targeted instruction.*

ELL Poster 6

Build concept understanding and oral vocabulary throughout the week by using the daily activities on ELL Poster 6.

Support for English Language Learners

Language Objectives

- Distinguish /u/ in initial and medial positions.

Transfer Skills

The writing systems of languages such as Arabic and Hebrew focus on consonant sounds and long vowels. Short vowels are indicated with separate marks that are often optional. Speakers of these languages may need extra help in spelling words with short vowels or multiple vowel sounds.

ELL Teaching Routine

For more practice with the short *u*, use the Sound-by-Sound Blending Routine (*ELL Handbook*, page 493).

Phonemic Awareness: Distinguish /u/ in Initial and Medial Positions

■ **Preteach words with the sound /u/**

- Have children open to pages 148–149. What is swarming around the kids? (bugs) Say the word *bugs* slowly. I am going to say the sounds in *bugs*. Listen for the /u/ sound: /b/ /u/ /g/ /z/. I hear the /u/ sound in the middle of the word *bugs*. Say /u/ with me. Say these words as you point to corresponding pictures: *hug, skunk, under, fun, truck*. Have children repeat each word and raise their hand if they hear the /u/ sound in the middle of the word. Ask partners to say each word. Have them listen carefully for the /u/ sound in each word.
- What are the men drinking out of? (mugs) Listen to the /u/ sound in *mugs*. Slowly segment and blend the sounds: /m/ /u/ /g/ /z/, *mugs*. What is the middle sound in *mugs*? (/u/) Yes. Say the middle sound in *mugs* with me: /u/.
- Have children point out other words that contain the short *u* sound /u/.

Phonics: Short *u*

■ **Preteach** Display Sound-Spelling Card 24. This is an umbrella. What sound do you hear at the beginning of *umbrella*? (/u/) Say it with me: /u/. Point to the *u*. The /u/ sound is spelled *u* in *umbrella*.

■ **Listen and Write** Distribute Write and Wipe Boards.

- Write the word *rub* on the board. Copy this word. As you write *u*, say the sound to yourself: /u/. Now say the sound aloud. (/u/) Underline the *u* in *rub*. The letter *u* spells /u/ in *rub*.
- Repeat using the word *dug*.

For more practice pronouncing this sound, use the Modeled Pronunciation Audio CD Routine (*ELL Handbook*, page 501).

Objectives

- Monitor oral and written language production and employ self-corrective techniques or other resources.
- Distinguish sounds and intonation patterns of English with increasing ease.

ELL English Language Learners

■ **Reteach and Practice** Short *u*

- Write the following words on the board and have children read them aloud with you: *cut, sun, run, cup, but, mug*. Segment and blend each word with the children. Point out the short *u* sound.
- Leave the words on the board and help children understand the words with sentences and gestures, such as *I can drink from a cup*. (Pretend to tip a cup toward your mouth.); *I cut paper*. (cut a piece of paper with scissors) Have children read the words with you, repeating each word.

Beginning Have children chant *Run to the sun!*
Intermediate Have children write the words *run* and *sun*.
Advanced/Advanced High Have children write the word *run* and the word that rhymes with it. (sun) Then have them write the word *cut* and the word that rhymes with it. (but)

Phonics: Final Consonant Blends

■ **Preteach** Have children turn to Envision It! on page 152 of the Student Edition.

- The word for the picture is *lamp*. Point to the picture of the lamp. What sounds do you hear at the end of *lamp*? (/m/ /p/) Say it with me: /m/ /p/. The sounds /m/ /p/ are spelled *mp*.
- The first word in the list of Words I Can Blend is *just*. What sounds do you hear at the end of *just*? (/s/ /t/) The sounds /s/ /t/ are spelled *st* in *just*.
- Repeat with the other words in the list.

■ **Practice** Distribute Letter Tiles *n, u, e, j, b, t, t,* and *s* to pairs.

1. Blend the sounds in *just* and have children spell *just* with their tiles: /j/ /u/ /s/ /t/
2. Replace the *u*. Spell *jest*.
3. Replace the *j*. Spell *best*.
4. Replace the *st*. Spell *bent*.
5. Replace the *b*. Spell *tent*.

Objectives

- Distinguish sounds and intonation patterns of English with increasing ease.
- Use visual, contextual, and linguistic support to enhance and confirm understanding of increasingly complex and elaborated spoken language.

Language Objectives

- Learn the final consonant blend sound -*st*.
- Read words containing final consonant blends.
- Use linguistic support.
- Distinguish sounds of English.

Transfer Skills

Consonant blends in English words are often challenging for English language learners because their home language may not combine consonant phonemes in similar ways at the beginnings and ends of words. For example, consonant blends with *l* and *r* can be particularly difficult for speakers of Asian languages such as Chinese, Korean, and Vietnamese. Speakers of Arabic may insert vowel sounds between the consonants in a word.

Practice Page

ELL Handbook pages 277, 283, and 288 provide additional practice for this week's skills.

Content Objectives

- Monitor and adjust oral comprehension.

Language Objectives

- Discuss oral passages.
- Use a graphic organizer to take notes.

ELL Teacher Tip

Have children use the Story Map organizer to identify the things that happen in the beginning, middle, and end of the story. This sequencing activity can help them make sense of the story.

ELL English Language Learners

Listening Comprehension

A Furry Kit

Jake yelled for his mom. He watched the red and white furry animal sit in his backyard. "What a funny looking dog, Mom," he said.

"That's not a dog, Jake," said Mom. "That's a fox. Here comes its parent. A baby fox is called a kit."

Jake wondered why there would be foxes in his backyard. They were wild animals, weren't they? Jake's mom told him that his house was not always on this land. Once the land was country and forests. People came in and built homes. The foxes and other animals lost their homes. "They probably feel comfortable in our backyard because of all the trees," said Mom.

"Can I pet them, Mom?" asked Jake.

"No," said Mom. "They are wild animals. You never know what they will do. You can watch them and you can learn all about them."

Prepare for the Read Aloud The modified Read Aloud above prepares children for listening to the oral reading "The Fox Family" on page 151b.

- **First Listening: Listen to Understand**

  1. Write the title of the Read Aloud on the board. Have you ever seen a wild animal up close? Have you seen one in your backyard? I am going to read a story about a little boy who watches a fox kit in his backyard. What will he do? Listen to find out what Jake does when he sees the fox kit.
  2. After reading, ask children to recall what Jake learned about observing wild animals. Why couldn't Jake pet the foxes? (They are wild animals.) Why shouldn't people approach wild animals? (They can be unpredictable.)

- **Second Listening: Listen to Check Understanding** Using the Story Map A graphic organizer (*ELL Handbook*, page 506), work with children to fill in the different things that happen in the story.

Objectives

- Demonstrate listening comprehension of increasingly complex spoken English by following directions, retelling or summarizing spoken messages, responding to questions and requests, collaborating with peers, and taking notes commensurate with content and grade-level needs.

English Language Learners

High-Frequency Words

- **Preteach** Distribute copies of this week's Word Cards (*ELL Handbook*, p. 95). Teach the words and how to use them by using the following gestures:
  - Make a roof with your arms for *home*. I go *home* after school.
  - Put a book into a bag. I am putting a book *into* a bag.
  - Hold up many pencils. I am holding *many* pencils.
  - Point to several of the children. I want to go to lunch with *them*.
- **Practice** Have children use high-frequency words to discuss common items in the classroom. Children might say, "We put the books *into* our desks" or "We have *many* children in the classroom." Use the accessible language to learn the essential high-frequency words.
- **Speaking/Writing with High-Frequency Words**
  - **Teach/Model** Review correct pronunciation of the high-frequency words with children. Give each pair of children a set of the Word Cards. Have them work together to find the correct word for each sentence you read.
  - **Practice** Write the sentences on the board. Model filling in the missing word from the first sentence. 1. I go _______ for dinner. (home) 2. The dog ran _______ the house. (into) 3. There are _______ animals at the zoo. (many) 4. Please give _______ the toys. (them)

Beginning Read the sentences aloud, using a gesture or providing a drawing for each missing word. For example, hold up five fingers for *many*, or point to three children for *them*. Have children hold up the correct Word Card for each sentence. Then have them write the word.

Intermediate Have children write the sentences from the board, adding the missing words. They can copy the Word Cards if necessary.

Advanced/Advanced-High Have children write the sentences, including the missing words, and read the sentences aloud.

Objectives

- Internalize new basic and academic language by using and reusing it in meaningful ways in speaking and writing activities that build concept and language attainment.
- Speak using grade-level content area vocabulary in context to internalize new English words and build academic language proficiency.

Language Objectives

- Use accessible language to learn new and essential language.
- Internalize new basic language with speaking.
- Use high-frequency English words.
- Speak using grade-level content area vocabulary.

Transfer Skills

Speakers of some languages, such as Chinese, may be unfamiliar with blending adjacent consonant sounds. Guide children in blending sounds such as /th/ smoothly, without inserting a vowel sound in between the two consonants.

Mini-Lesson: Speaking and Listening

Turn to p. 153 in the Student Edition. Read the selection aloud as children listen. Then give children the Word Cards. Have them speak, summarizing p. 153, as they use the high-frequency words on the cards in their summaries.

Content Objectives

- Identify cause and effect.
- Identify the causes and their effects to aid comprehension.
- Use the basic reading skill of determining cause and effect to demonstrate comprehension.

Language Objectives

- Discuss cause and effect.
- Retell causes and their effects from reading.
- Write causes and effects.

Beginning Learners

Directionality As you read a book aloud put your finger on the starting point in the text on each page. Show that you read from left to right and from top to bottom by moving your finger along lines of text. Have children use their finger to show the correct movement as you read the text aloud again.

ELL English Language Learners

Guide Comprehension
Cause and Effect

- **Preteach** Model by pantomiming as you define *cause* and *effect*. Things happen for a reason. The reason is the cause. The thing that happens is the effect.
- **Practice** Have children turn to Envision It! on page EI•2 in the Student Edition. Discuss the pictures with children. Discuss their comprehension of the events on the page. Have them identify the effect. (The girl got wet.) Then have them identify the cause. (It was raining.) Ask questions as necessary: What happened? Why did it happen?
- **Reteach/Practice** Work with children to complete Picture It! (*ELL Handbook*, p. 96)
  - Ask children to describe what is happening in each illustration. Then read the text aloud twice. Prepare children for the second reading by asking them to think about why it would be important to have the zoo exhibit look like a real rain forest. After reading, guide children to use the pictures and words to identify a cause-and-effect relationship.

Leveled Support

Beginning/Intermediate Reread the story aloud, then read the questions. Have children use short phrases to answer the questions.

Advanced/Advanced-High Read the directions. Have children read the story and answer the questions. Provide help as needed.

MINI-LESSON

Academic Language

Words in a story, such as *why, so,* and *because*, can help you find a cause-and-effect relationship. Listen to this sentence: *The chalk fell because I didn't put it on the table carefully.* What happened? (The chalk fell.) Why? (Because it wasn't put down carefully.) Have children practice saying sentences that contain a cause and effect.

Objectives

- Understand the general meaning, main points, and important details of spoken language ranging from situations in which topics, language, and contexts are familiar to unfamiliar.

Reading Comprehension
Animal Park

Animal Park
What can we learn about wild animals by watching them?

Student Edition pp. 154–155

Frontloading

- **Background Knowledge** Read aloud the title and discuss it. What do you think an animal park is? What would you probably see there? What would it be like to visit?
- **Preview** Guide children on a picture walk through the story, asking them to identify people, places, and actions. As you read, support children's understanding of the pictures. Reteach these words using visuals in the Student Edition: *camp* (p. 156), *rest* (p. 159), and *stomp* (p. 162).
- **Predict** What types of animals will the campers see?

Sheltered Reading Ask questions such as the following to guide children's comprehension:

- p. 158: Point to the zebras. What are these? (zebras) Why are they hard to see? (They blend with the grass.)
- p. 159: Point to the lions. What are they doing? (resting) Why? (They had a big hunt.)
- p. 161: Point to the hippos. What are they doing? (laying in mud) Why? (to cool off)
- p. 162: Point to the elephants. Where are they? (in the pond) Why? (They are drinking.)

Fluency: Appropriate Phrasing

Fluency: Appropriate Phrasing Phrasing means to read punctuation correctly and carefully. They should pay attention to punctuation. Read the sentences on p. 157, modeling different phrasing with periods and question marks at the end of the sentence. Have pairs share the reading of p. 157. Have children read with appropriate phrasing as their partner listens and offers feedback. They should also focus on comprehension of the text, sharing information and asking questions after reading for fluency. For more practice, use the Fluency: Paired Reading Routine (*ELL Handbook*, page 496).

After Reading Help children summarize the text with the Retelling Cards. Ask questions that prompt children to summarize the important parts of the text.

Objectives

- Ask and give information ranging from using a very limited bank of high-frequency, high-need, concrete vocabulary, including key words and expressions needed for basic communication in academic and social contexts, to using abstract and content-based vocabulary during extended speaking assignments.
- Use visual and contextual support and support from peers and teachers to read grade-appropriate content area text, enhance and confirm understanding, and develop vocabulary, grasp of language structures, and background knowledge needed to comprehend increasingly challenging language.

Content Objectives

- Monitor and adjust comprehension.
- Make and adjust predictions.

Language Objectives

- Read with appropriate phrasing.
- Summarize text using visual support.
- Participate in shared reading.

Audio Support

Children can prepare for reading *Animal Park* by using the eSelection or the AudioText CD. See the AudioText CD Routine (*ELL Handbook*, page 500) for suggestions on using these learning tools.

English Summary

Read the English summary of *Animal Park* (*ELL Handbook*, page 97). Children can ask questions about ideas or unfamiliar words. Send copies home for children to read with family members.

ELL English Language Learners

For additional leveled instruction, see the **ELL/ELD Reader Teaching Guide.**

Comprehension: *Animals of Africa*

- **Before Reading** Distribute copies of the ELL and ELD Readers, *Animals of Africa*, to children at their reading level.
- **Preview** Read the title aloud with children: This is a story about different animals that live in Africa. Activate prior knowledge about wild animals. The story in our book was about a wild animal park in Africa. This story is about African wild animals too. What can we learn from watching wild animals in their habitats?
- **Set a Purpose for Reading** Let's read to find out about the different animals in Africa.
- **During Reading** Follow this Reading Routine for both reading groups.

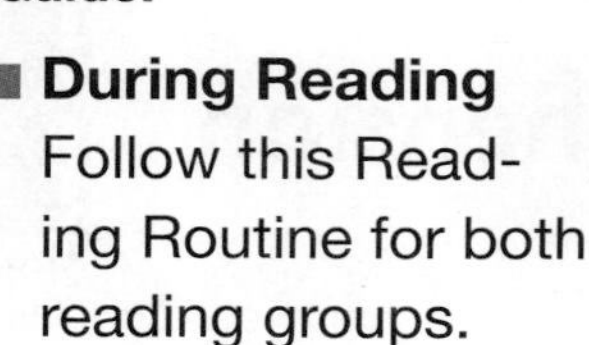

ELL Reader

ELD Reader

1. Read the entire Reader aloud slowly as children follow along and finger point.
2. Reread the Reader one sentence at a time. Have the children echo read after you.

- **After Reading** Use the exercises on the inside back cover of *Animals of Africa* and invite children to share drawings and writing. In a whole-group discussion, ask children to tell one animal that lives in Africa. Encourage children to think about the animals they read about and what they can learn from observing wild animals. Have children point to examples in the book of different animals and what they do.

ELD Reader Beginning/Intermediate

- **pp. 2–3** Point to the zebras. What are the zebras eating? (grass)
- **p. 7** Point to the elephant. What does the elephant use to help it pick things up? (its trunk)

Writing Draw a picture of one of the animals in the story. Ask children to work in pairs and label their picture with a sentence or phrase telling how their animal takes care of itself. Have them share their drawings with the class.

ELL Reader Advanced/Advanced-High

- **p. 5** Point to the ostrich. What type of animal is this? (bird) Can it fly? (no)
- **p. 6** Point to the hippos. What are the hippos doing? (swimming) Why? (to keep cool)

Study Guide Distribute copies of the ELL Reader Study Guide (*ELL Handbook*, page 100). Scaffold comprehension by reminding them to focus on different things the animals they read about do. Review their responses together. (**Answers** See *ELL Handbook*, pp. 245–248.)

Objectives

- Use prior knowledge and experience to understand meanings in English.
- Demonstrate comprehension of increasingly complex English by participating in shared reading, retelling or summarizing material, responding to questions, and taking notes commensurate with content area and grade level needs.

ELL English Language Learners

Conventions
Exclamatory Sentences

■ **Preteach** Point to the image on page 158 of the Student Edition. Bump, bump, bump! Quick, stop! The exclamation marks at the end of these sentences let you know that these are exclamatory sentences. An exclamatory sentence tells you something using emotion, like being excited or surprised. It can also be a command that tells you to do something.

■ **Practice** Leaf through the Student Edition and call attention to exclamatory sentences. Have children do the exercises below according to their language proficiency level.

Leveled Support

Beginning/Intermediate Point to an exclamatory sentence in the story. Read it aloud. Have children echo read the sentence to you. Have intermediate children copy the sentence on a sheet of paper.

Advanced/Advanced High Have children choose a picture in the story. Then, challenge them to write their own exclamatory sentence about the picture.

■ **Reteach**

- Write *Look at that huge lion!* on the board. This sentence calls your attention to something. It ends in an exclamation mark. It is said with emotion. This is an exclamatory sentence. What is this sentence telling about? (There is a huge lion.) What punctuation do we use with an exclamatory sentence? (exclamation mark)
- Write subjects on several note cards. Have children work in pairs to choose a card from the pile and write an exclamatory sentence using the subject they chose.

■ **Practice** Use the summary of "Animal Park" (*ELL Handbook*, page 97) to practice identifying and using exclamatory sentences.

Leveled Support

Beginning Choose simple sentences from the summary to read aloud. Ask children to give a "thumbs up" if the sentence you read is exclamatory. Have them repeat the sentences.

Intermediate Write several different types of sentences from the summary on sentence strips. Have children work together to sort the sentences—exclamatory or not.

Advanced/Advanced High Have children write their own exclamatory sentences. Check to make sure that they included exclamation marks. Have them share their sentences with a partner.

Objectives

- Internalize new basic and academic language by using and reusing it in meaningful ways in speaking and writing activities that build concept and language attainment.

Content Objectives

- Identify and use exclamatory sentences.
- Correctly use exclamatory sentences.

Language Objectives

- Speak using exclamatory sentences.
- Write exclamatory sentences.

Transfer Skills

Help children see that word order strongly affects meaning in English. *Tony thanked Lee* is very different than *Lee thanked Tony.*

Grammar Jammer

For more practice with sentences use the Grammar Jammer for this target skill. See the Grammar Jammer Routine (*ELL Handbook*, page 501) for suggestions on using this learning tool.

Content Objectives

- Identify words that indicate things in the real world.
- Identify characteristics that show a story is about the real world.
- Take notes from spoken information.

Language Objectives

- Write a brief composition that tells about the real world.
- Share feedback for editing and revising.
- Explain with increasing specificity and detail.

Mini-Lesson: Taking Notes

Explain to children that taking notes can help them write compositions. Sometimes notes come from information they hear. Read aloud p, 161 from the Student Edition. Ask children to write notes about hippos as they listen. (*sit, wet mud, sit in mud to stay cool*) Discuss how these notes might help them write a composition.

ELL English Language Learners

Write a Brief Composition

- **Introduce Terms** Write *brief composition* on the board and explain each word as you point to it. *Brief* means something is short. See the word *composition*? A composition gives facts about a topic. You can learn a great deal from reading a brief composition.

- **Describe characteristics that show realism** Explain that a good composition gives details that tell about the topic. Write this sentence: *Elephants are interesting animals.*

  Have children suggest information that would be good to know about elephants. Record their answers on the board. Use the student edition, p. 162, to help children explain facts about elephants with increasing specificity and detail: *Elephants can stand and sip at the same time. Elephants have trunks.*

- **Writing Model**

  Draw three large boxes with a smaller box above them on the board. Label the top box *topic* and draw three arrows from the topic box to the other boxes. Write *elephants* in the topic box. Label those Fact *One, Fact Two,* and *Fact Three*. Engage children in naming three facts about elephants. Write sentences for each fact in the boxes.

Fact One	Fact Two	Fact Three

- **Write** Have children choose an animal that they are familiar with. Have them draw the graphic organizer and write their animal in the topic box. Have partners work together to think of facts about the animal.

Leveled Support

Beginning Supply the graphic organizer. Write your topic in the top box. Think of three facts. Draw them in the boxes. Have children tell about their pictures. Supply the action words and have children copy them in the appropriate boxes.

Intermediate Guide children's writing. What descriptive words will you use? What words can you use to tell more about your animal? Help children with their spelling.

Advanced/Advanced High Have children use the boxes for prewriting. Then have them write their sentences in paragraph form.

Objectives

- Internalize new basic and academic language by using and reusing it in meaningful ways in speaking and writing activities that build concept and language attainment.
- Use visual and contextual support and support from peers and teachers to read grade-appropriate content area text, enhance and confirm understanding, and develop vocabulary, grasp of language structures, and background knowledge needed to comprehend increasingly challenging language.

Customize Your Writing

Weekly Writing Focus

Writing Forms and Patterns

- Instruction focuses on a different **product** each week.
- Mini-lessons and models help children learn key features and **organizational patterns**.

Grade 1 Products poetry, personal narrative, realistic story, play scene, letter, and so on

Grade 1 Organization Patterns beginning, middle, and end, main idea and details, sequence, and so on

Daily Writing Focus

Quick Writes for Fluency

- Writing on Demand Use the Quick Write routine for **writing on demand**.
- The Quick Write **prompt and routine** extend skills and strategies from daily writing lessons.

Unit Writing Focus

Writing Process 1 2 3 4 5

- Six **writing process** lessons provide structure to move children through the steps of the writing process.
- One-week and two-week pacing allows lessons to be used in **Writing Workshop**.

Steps of the Writing Process Plan and Prewrite, Draft, Revise, Edit, Publish and Present

Grade 1 Writing Process Products personal narrative, letter, expository article, realistic story, short report

MINI-LESSON

- Daily 10-minute mini-lessons focus instruction on the **traits** and **craft** of good writing.
- Instruction focuses on one writing trait and one writer's craft skill every week.

Traits focus/ideas, organization, voice, word choice, sentences, conventions

Craft drafting strategies, revising strategies, editing strategies

Read Like a Writer

- Use **mentor text** every week as a model to exemplify the traits of good writing.
- **Interact with text** every week to learn the key features of good writing.

Mentor Text Examine literature in the Student Edition.

INTERACT with TEXT Underline, circle, and highlight model text in the *Reader's and Writer's Notebook.*

Write Guy
Jeff Anderson

Need Writing Advice?

Writing instruction is all about creating effective writers. We don't want to crush the inner writer in a child by over-correcting and over-editing. What makes effective writing instruction? Children need to write, write, write! But is that enough? Probably not. All kinds of instruction and guidance go into making an effective writer.

The Write Guy offers advice on teacher and peer conferencing, focusing on writing traits, revising strategies, editing strategies, and much, much more.

Customize Your Writing

Alternate Pacing Plan for Unit Writing Projects

Sometimes you want to spend more time on writing—perhaps you do a **Writing Workshop**. This one- or two-week plan for the unit level writing projects can help.

1 Week Plan	Day 1	Day 2	Day 3	Day 4	Day 5
1 Plan and Prewrite	■	■			
2 Draft			■		
3 Revise				■	
4 Edit					■
5 Publish					■

2 Week Plan	Day 1	Day 2	Day 3	Day 4	Day 5	Day 6	Day 7	Day 8	Day 9	Day 10
1 Plan and Prewrite	■	■	■	■						
2 Draft					■	■	■			
3 Revise								■		
4 Edit									■	
5 Publish										■

Grade 1 Unit Writing Projects

Internet Guy
Don Leu

Unit Writing Project 1–21st Century Project

Unit 1 Trading Card
Unit 2 Pen Pal E-mail
Unit 3 Photo Essay
Unit 4 Story Exchange
Unit 5 E-Newsletter

Unit Writing Project 2–Writing Process

Unit 1 Personal Narrative
Unit 2 Letter
Unit 3 Expository Article
Unit 4 Realistic Story
Unit 5 Short Report

Customize Your Writing

Common Core Standards and the Writing Process

Process Writing and the Common Core Standards for English Language Arts

This unit's Writing Process assignment will provide you with opportunities to instruct children in the steps of process writing: Plan and Prewrite, Draft, Revise, Edit, and Publish. Discuss these tips with children before they begin writing.

Process Writing Steps	Common Core Standards for English Language Arts	Tips for Unit 1 Process Writing
1 **Plan and Prewrite**	**Writing 3.**	As children prepare to prewrite, remind them that they will be writing personal narratives.
2 **Draft**	**Writing 3.**	As children draft their personal narratives, show them how to use a Story Chart to organize their ideas.
3 **Revise**	**Writing 5.**	Before children revise their drafts, refer them to the Revising Checklist.
4 **Edit**	**Language 1.; Language 2.**	As children edit their writing, suggest that they look for one kind of mistake at a time as they review their work.
5 **Publish**	**Writing 6.**	When children are ready to publish their writing, have them use the Scoring Rubric to evaluate their own writing.

Writing Trait Skills Trace

All of the writing traits taught in Scott Foresman *Reading Street* are dimensions of good writing. In this unit's Writing Process project, children will write a Personal Narrative. The chart below shows you how the writing traits taught each week of the unit match the elements of the Scoring Rubric for Personal Narratives and criteria from the highest score point of the rubric.

	Writing Trait of the Week/ Weekly Selection	Scoring Rubric Top Score Point Criteria (The complete Personal Narrative Scoring Rubric is located on page CW•15.)
Week 1	• Voice *Sam, Come Back!*	Clearly shows how you feel
Week 2	• Conventions *Pig in a Wig*	Uses good spelling and capitalization
Week 3	• Sentences *The Big Blue Ox*	Sentences not all alike
Week 4	• Voice *A Fox and a Kit*	Clearly shows how you feel
Week 5	• Organization *Get the Egg!*	Has a good beginning, middle, and end
Week 6	• Focus/Ideas *Animal Park*	Reader can understand the story about you

Writing Resources

Use the resources to the right to build writing skills during and after the teaching of Unit 1.

Writing Resources

Reader's and Writer's Notebook

Writing Rubrics and Anchor Papers

Digital Resources
- Online Writing Transparencies

Teacher Resources DVD-ROM
- Reader's and Writer's Notebook
- Let's Practice It!
- Graphic Organizers
- Writing Transparencies

ISBN-13: 978-0-328-64366-0
ISBN-10: 0-328-64366-1

Personal Narrative

Writing Prompt

Write about something funny that happened to you and a pet or another animal.

Purpose Entertain

Audience A friend

Introduce genre and prompt

Tell children that in this lesson they will learn about a kind of story called a personal narrative. A personal narrative is a story about you. When you write a personal narrative, you tell a story about something that happened to you.

Introduce key features

Key Features of a Personal Narrative

- tells about an interesting event in your life
- gives details that help readers understand
- uses the words *I, me,* and *my*
- has a beginning, middle, and end

Academic Vocabulary

Personal Narrative In a personal narrative, the writer tells about something that happened in his or her own life.

English Language Learners

Introduce Genre Point out that a personal narrative is a story that a writer writes about his or her own experience. Explain that the writer uses the words *I, me,* and *my.* Discuss with children the key features of a personal narrative that appear on this page.

UNIT 1 Writing Process

Objectives

- Understand and identify the key features of a personal narrative.
- Generate ideas for writing by drawing, sharing ideas, and listing key ideas.
- Select a topic.

Plan and Prewrite

MINI-LESSON

Reading Like a Writer

- **Examine Model Text** Let's look at an example of a personal narrative. Display and read aloud to children "My Dog Jet" on Writing Transparency WP1. Point out the words *I* and *My*. Explain that these pronouns show that the writer is writing a personal narrative, or a story about himself. Point out the beginning, middle, and end of the personal narrative. Read aloud the sentences that tell how the writer feels: *I was scared! I was happy!* Ask children why he felt first scared and then happy.

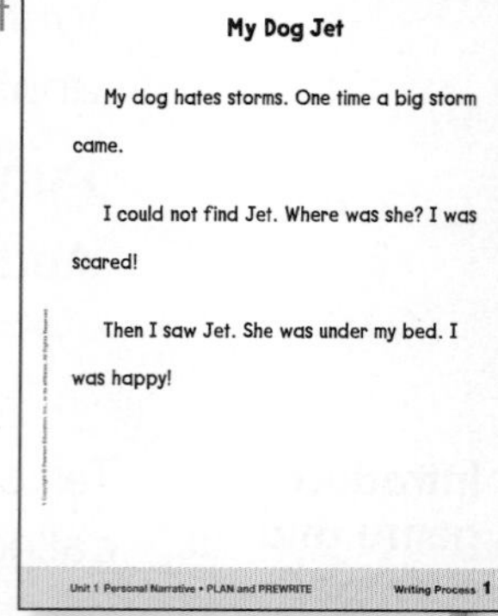

My Dog Jet

My dog hates storms. One time a big storm came.

I could not find Jet. Where was she? I was scared!

Then I saw Jet. She was under my bed. I was happy!

Unit 1 Personal Narrative • PLAN and PREWRITE Writing Process 1

Writing Transparency WP1
TR DVD

- **Explore Model Text** Display "Traits of a Good Personal Narrative" on Writing Transparency WP2. Discuss each trait with children. First read the name of the trait and remind children what it means. Then read aloud the statement, explaining any unfamiliar words. Finally, help children understand how the statement applies to the model personal narrative.

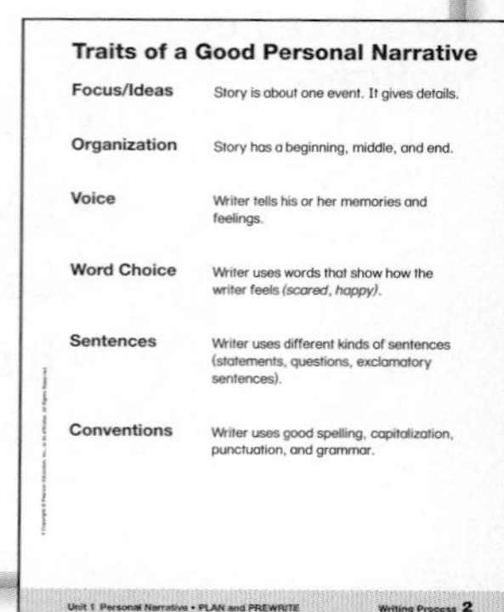

Traits of a Good Personal Narrative

Focus/Ideas	Story is about one event. It gives details.
Organization	Story has a beginning, middle, and end.
Voice	Writer tells his or her memories and feelings.
Word Choice	Writer uses words that show how the writer feels (*scared, happy*).
Sentences	Writer uses different kinds of sentences (statements, questions, exclamatory sentences).
Conventions	Writer uses good spelling, capitalization, punctuation, and grammar.

Unit 1 Personal Narrative • PLAN and PREWRITE Writing Process 2

Writing Transparency WP2
TR DVD

Generate ideas for writing

Reread the writing prompt to children. The writing prompt asks you to write about something funny that happened to you and an animal. Encourage children to generate ideas for their personal narratives using these strategies:

- ✔ Draw pictures of favorite animals. Tell about funny things the animals did.
- ✔ Share ideas with family members.
- ✔ Make a list of their best story ideas.

Corrective feedback

If... children have difficulty thinking of an animal to write about, **then...** name different animals and ask children about experiences they may have had with these animals.

Narrow topic

Have children ask themselves questions about the ideas on their list. They might ask: *Would this idea make an interesting story? Would a friend enjoy reading this story?* Model how to narrow the choices on a list to one topic using the example list shown below.

Think Aloud I thought of three ideas. Now I will choose one. I don't think the raccoon in the yard would make an interesting story because I saw it for only a second. A trip to the zoo is a big topic. I saw many animals there, but it would be best to write about only one animal. I can think of several funny stories about my cat Mack, including the way I got him.

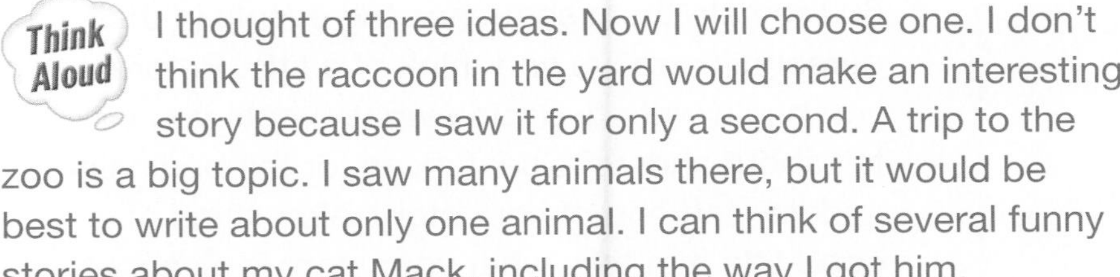

Topic Ideas
raccoon in the yard
trip to the zoo
my cat Mack

Write Guy
Jeff Anderson

Use Mentor Text

Help children remember a narrative they have read that uses the words *I* and *me* or *we,* such as *Animal Park* in this unit (which uses *we*). Children need to hear and remember writing that resembles what they are learning to do. Tell them that they will write a story about something that happened to them, using the words *I* and *me.*

Differentiated Instruction

Strategic Intervention

Alternative Writing Prompt Think about a time when an animal made you smile or laugh. Name the animal. Tell what happened and why you thought it was funny.

Advanced

Alternative Writing Prompt In your personal narrative, write one thing you said to the animal or another character. Remember to use quotation marks before and after the words you say.

Writing Process

Objectives

- Understand the criteria for an effective personal narrative.
- Plan a narrative by organizing ideas.
- Sequence ideas in sentences to prepare and write a first draft.

Plan and Prewrite

MINI-LESSON

Planning a First Draft

- **Use a Story Chart** Display Writing Transparency WP3 and read it aloud to children.

I write sentences about the events in my story in order on my story chart. I write what happened first in the Beginning box, what happened next in the Middle box, and what happened last in the End box. I think of a good title for my story and write that on the line at the top. Now I can start writing a first draft of my personal narrative.

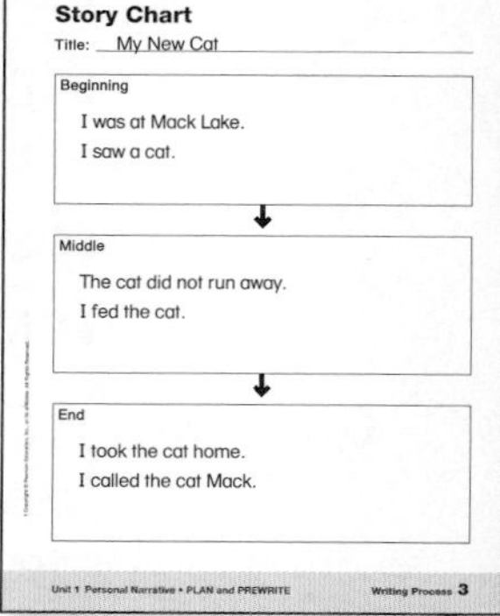

Story Chart
Title: My New Cat
Beginning
I was at Mack Lake.
I saw a cat.
Middle
The cat did not run away.
I fed the cat.
End
I took the cat home.
I called the cat Mack.

Writing Transparency WP3
TR DVD

- Have children use the Story Chart graphic organizer on *Reader's and Writer's Notebook* page 603 to help them sequence the events in their personal narrative and think of a title. Before you begin writing, decide what events you will tell about and write sentences for the beginning, middle, and end of your story. Also, think of a good title that tells what your story is all about.

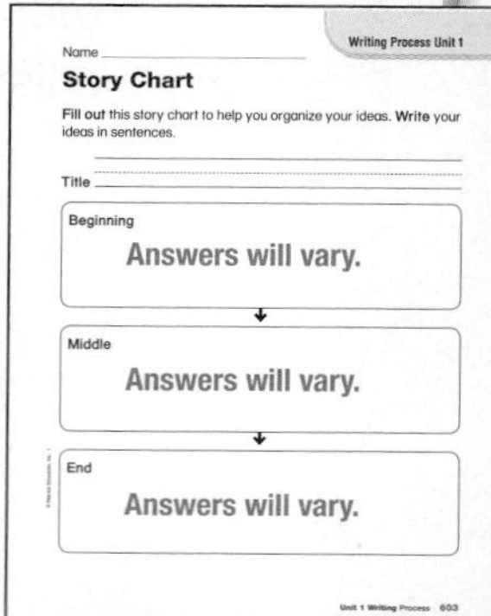

Writing Process Unit 1
Name
Story Chart
Fill out this story chart to help you organize your ideas. Write your ideas in sentences.
Title
Beginning
Answers will vary.
Middle
Answers will vary.
End
Answers will vary.

Reader's and Writer's Notebook, p. 603

Draft

Display rubric Display the Scoring Rubric WP1 from the Teacher Resource DVD-ROM. Read aloud and discuss with children the traits and criteria that you choose. Encourage children to think about these criteria as they develop drafts of their personal narratives. Tell them that rubrics such as this one are often used to evaluate and score writing.

Scoring Rubric: *Personal Narrative*

	4	3	2	1
Focus/Ideas	Reader can understand the story about you	Reader can understand part of the story about you	Reader cannot understand the story very well	Reader cannot understand the story
Organization	Has a good beginning, middle, and end	Has a beginning, middle, and end	Events are out of order	Does not have a beginning, middle, and end
Voice	Clearly shows how you feel	Shows a little about how you feel	Does not show very well how you feel	Does not show how you feel
Word Choice	Has words that help reader "see" the story	Some words help reader "see" part of the story	Words do not help reader "see" the story	Words are hard to read
Sentences	Sentences not all alike	Sentences are complete	Sentences are not complete	Sentences not complete or clear
Conventions	Uses good spelling and capitalization	Uses fair spelling and capitalization	Uses poor spelling and capitalization	Uses very poor spelling and capitalization

Prepare to draft Have children look at the story charts they worked on earlier. Ask them to make sure that their story charts are complete. If they are not, have children finish them now. Use your story chart as you write a draft of your personal narrative. You will have a chance to revise your draft later.

Corrective feedback

If... children do not understand how the Scoring Rubric can be used to evaluate writing,

then... show them how you can use the Scoring Rubric to evaluate and score one or more traits of the model personal narrative on Writing Transparency WP1.

Differentiated Instruction

Strategic Intervention

Plan a First Draft Some children will need additional guidance as they plan and write their stories. You might give them the option of writing a story with a partner under your supervision or pair them with more able writers who can help them with the process.

English Language Learners

Prepare to Draft Have children tell you what they want to include in their stories. Help them restate their ideas as complete sentences. Record the sentences on the board and have children copy them.

Objectives

- Choose words that tell about feelings.
- Write a first draft of a personal narrative.
- Revise a draft of a personal narrative.

2 DRAFT Draft

MINI-LESSON

Writing Trait: Voice

- **Use Words That Tell How You Feel** List feeling words on the board. Explain that these words name different emotions or feelings. Act out one of the emotions and have children name the correct feeling word. Remind them to use one or more of these feeling words or other words about feelings in their personal narratives. Explain that a writer should show how he or she feels about the events in a personal narrative.

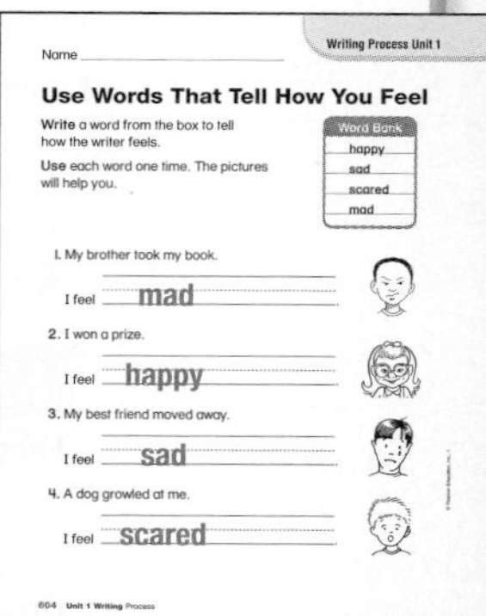
Writing Process Unit 1

Name ____________

Use Words That Tell How You Feel

Write a word from the box to tell how the writer feels.

Use each word one time. The pictures will help you.

Word Bank
happy
sad
scared
mad

1. My brother took my book.
   I feel mad.
2. I won a prize.
   I feel happy.
3. My best friend moved away.
   I feel sad.
4. A dog growled at me.
   I feel scared.

604 Unit 1 Writing Process

Reader's and Writer's Notebook, p. 604

Feeling Words
sad
happy
mad
tired
scared

- Have children use *Reader's and Writer's Notebook* page 604 to practice using words that tell about feelings.

Develop draft Remind children that when they write their first drafts, they just want to get their ideas down on paper. Suggest that they try these drafting strategies:

✔ Close their eyes and visualize the events in the story. Write sentences about what they see.

✔ Start at the beginning. Answer these questions in complete sentences: *Where were you? What were you doing? What happened first?*

Revise

MINI-LESSON

Writer's Craft: Adding a Word, Phrase, or Sentence

- Explain to children that when good writers revise, they often add words, phrases, or sentences. They may want to better describe someone or something. They may want to better show their feelings about their topic. Discuss these examples with children.

That is Tabby's food.	The dog lives with me.
That is Tabby's <u>favorite</u> food <u>for dinner.</u>	The <u>greatest</u> dog <u>in the world</u> lives with me.

- Have children identify the word, phrase, and sentence a writer added on *Reader's and Writer's Notebook* page 605. Then together discuss how these revisions make the writing more interesting.

Name ____________ Writing Process Unit 1

Adding a Word, Phrase, or Sentence

Read each set of sentences. Answer the question.

1. What word did the writer add? Write the word.
I saw a fish.
I saw a huge fish.
huge
2. What phrase did the writer add? Write the phrase.
The fish swam.
The fish swam into me.
into me
3. What sentence did the writer add? Write the sentence.
Then the fish swam away.
Then the fish swam away. I laughed.
I laughed.

Unit 1 Writing Process 605

Reader's and Writer's Notebook, p. 605

Teacher Tip

Segment the assignment into manageable pieces. To make sure children's writing is on track, check their work at regular intervals, such as after children complete their graphic organizers and after they write their first drafts.

Revise model Use Writing Transparency WP4 to model how to revise a personal narrative.

Think Aloud My first sentence clearly tells where my story takes place, but if I wanted readers to know exactly when my story takes place, I might add a phrase such as *Last month* to my first sentence. I added the adjectives *big* and *yellow* because I wanted readers to "see" the cat. Readers can certainly tell how I feel about him. I told about my feelings in this sentence: *He is a great cat.*

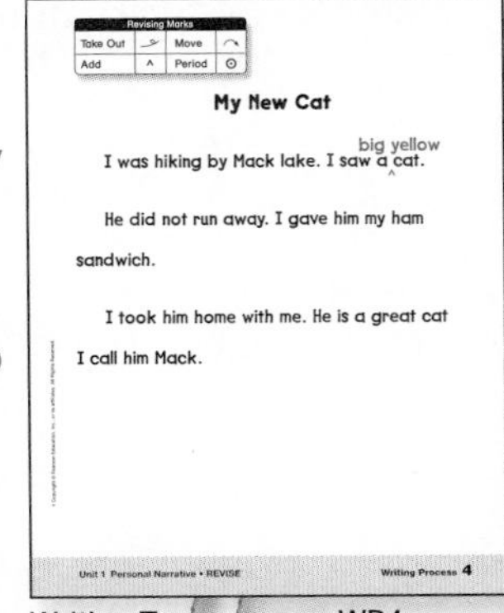

Revising Marks

Take Out		Move	
Add	^	Period	⊙

My New Cat

I was hiking by Mack lake. I saw a ^big yellow^ cat.

He did not run away. I gave him my ham sandwich.

I took him home with me. He is a great cat

I call him Mack.

Unit 1 Personal Narrative • REVISE Writing Process 4

Writing Transparency WP4
TR DVD

ELL

English Language Learners

Revise for Voice To help children improve voice in their writing, work with them to develop lists of words and details that show feelings. Encourage them to use beginning dictionaries, if available, to find new words to add to their lists. Children can refer to their lists when they are writing their personal narratives.

Writing Process

Objectives

- Revise a draft of a personal narrative.
- Edit a revised draft of a personal narrative to correct errors in grammar, punctuation, capitalization, and spelling.

Revise

Revise draft

We have written first drafts of our personal narratives. Now we will revise our drafts. When we revise, we try to make our writing clearer and more interesting to read.

Peer conferencing

Peer Revision Write the questions you choose from the Revising Checklist on the board. If you elect to use peer revision, help pairs of children exchange and read each other's drafts. Read aloud the checklist, one question at a time. Ask children to answer each question about their own draft or their partner's draft. Remind them to think about where a word, phrase, or sentence could be added to better describe or show feelings.

Help children revise their personal narratives using their own ideas or their partner's comments as well as what they have learned about personal narratives.

Revising Checklist

- ✔ Does the personal narrative tell about an interesting event in the writer's life?
- ✔ Does the story have a beginning, middle, and end?
- ✔ Does the title help tell what the story is all about?
- ✔ Does the writer use the pronouns *I, me,* and *my*?
- ✔ Does the writer use words that show how he or she feels about the event?
- ✔ Will adding a word, phrase, or sentence help make a description better?

Edit

MINI-LESSON

Editing Strategy: One Thing at a Time

- Explain this editing strategy to children: Look for one kind of mistake at a time. First look for spelling errors, then look for missing capital letters, and finally look for incorrect or missing punctuation. Model this strategy using Writing Transparency W5. If you elect to teach proofreading marks, explain what they mean and how they are used as you discuss the errors on the transparency.

First I look for spelling errors. Good, there are no misspelled words. Next I look for missing capital letters. The word *lake* in the first sentence should begin with a capital letter because it is part of a proper noun, Mack Lake. Last I look for incorrect or missing punctuation. The second-to-last sentence needs a period or an exclamation point at the end after the word *cat.*

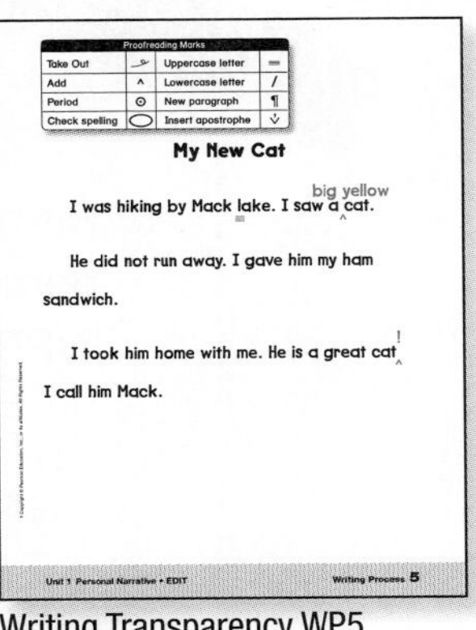

Proofreading Marks			
Take Out		Uppercase letter	
Add	^	Lowercase letter	/
Period	⊙	New paragraph	¶
Check spelling		Insert apostrophe	

My New Cat

I was hiking by Mack lake. I saw a big yellow cat.

He did not run away. I gave him my ham sandwich.

I took him home with me. He is a great cat!

I call him Mack.

Unit 1 Personal Narrative • EDIT Writing Process 5

Writing Transparency WP5
TR DVD

- Help children edit their own drafts. Have them check their spelling, grammar, punctuation, and capitalization. Make a simple rubric so children can use it to check the grammar, punctuation, spelling, and capitalization criteria you select for this writing.

Technology Tips

Children who type their personal narratives on computers may find this tip useful as they edit.

✔ Use the print preview or page layout feature when they finish typing. It will show them how their writing will look on a page before they print it.

Differentiated Instruction

Advanced

Apply Editing Skills As they edit their work, children can consider these ways to improve it.

- Make sure statements end with periods and questions end with question marks.
- Check that every sentence begins with a capital letter.
- Make sure they spelled the pronoun *I* as a capital *I*.

Write Guy
Jeff Anderson

Focus Their Editing

In the editing process, children can get bogged down by everything that needs to be fixed. Editing one aspect at a time helps them focus their efforts and concentrate on one task, while making it easier for you as a teacher to fully explain the concept, moving children toward correctness. Sometimes less really is more.

English Language Learners

Support Editing When reviewing a child's draft, focus on ideas more than errors. Keep in mind that a consistent grammatical error may reflect the writing conventions of the home language. Use the appropriate lessons in the *ELL Handbook* to explicitly teach the English conventions.

Objectives

- Write and present a final draft of a personal narrative.
- Evaluate one's own writing.

Publish

Present

After children have revised and edited their personal narratives, have them write a final draft. Offer them two ways to present their work:

Compile their personal narratives to make a class book titled *Stories About Us.* Place the book in the classroom library.	Illustrate their personal narrative with photographs, magazine pictures, or their own drawings. Share the final product with a friend.

MINI-LESSON

Evaluating Writing

- Prepare children to fill out a Self-Evaluation Guide about their personal narrative. Display and read aloud Writing Transparency WP6. Model the self-evaluation process.

Think Aloud In my personal narrative, I used some good words to describe and to show feelings and actions. I would mark *Yes* for numbers 1, 2, and 3 on my Self-Evaluation Guide. The best part, I think, is about Mack not running away from me. If I wrote this personal narrative again, I would tell about how hungry Mack was. I don't think he had eaten anything for a long time. He really made that sandwich disappear! That would be a good detail to add.

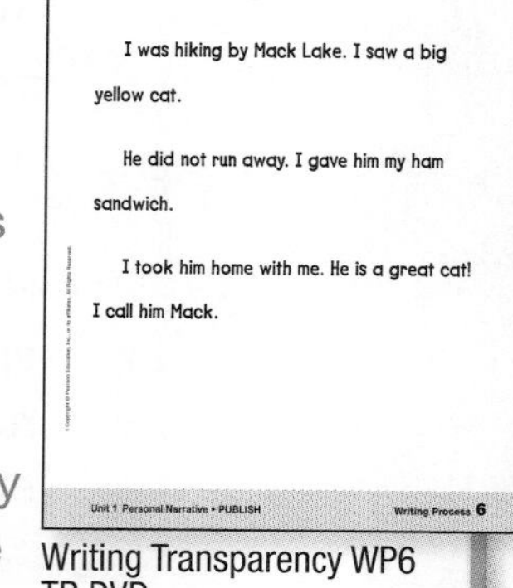

My New Cat

I was hiking by Mack Lake. I saw a big yellow cat.

He did not run away. I gave him my ham sandwich.

I took him home with me. He is a great cat! I call him Mack.

Unit 1 Personal Narrative • PUBLISH Writing Process 6

Writing Transparency WP6
TR DVD

- Have children complete the Self-Evaluation Guide on *Reader's and Writer's Notebook* page 606 to evaluate their personal narratives. They can save their Self-Evaluation Guides and their work in a portfolio to monitor their development as writers. Encourage them to build on their skills and to note areas to improve.

Reader's and Writer's Notebook, p. 606

Customize Literacy in Your Classroom

Table of Contents
for Customize Literacy

Customize Literacy is organized into different sections, each one designed to help you organize and carry out an effective literacy program. Each section contains strategies and support for teaching comprehension skills and strategies. *Customize Literacy* also shows how to use weekly text sets of readers in your literacy program.

Weekly Text Sets
to Customize Literacy

The following readers can be used to enhance your literacy instruction.

	Decodable Readers	Concept Literacy Reader	Below-Level Reader	On-Level Reader	Advanced Reader	ELD Reader	ELL Reader
Unit 1 WEEK 4	*Big Jobs; Packing Bags; Rocking and Kicking*	*We See Animals*	*Time for Dinner*	*Which Fox?*	*Baby Animals in the Rain Forest*	*Do Not Go Near*	*Do Not Go Near*
Unit 1 WEEK 5	*Jeff the Cat; Ted and Fran; The Sleds*	*Neighborhood Animals*	*At Your Vet*	*What Animals Can You See?*	*Cary and the Wildlife Shelter*	*Who Lives Here?*	*Who Lives Here?*
Unit 1 WEEK 6	*Duck Has Fun; At the Pond; Cub and Mom at the Pond*	*Wild Animals*	*Fun in the Sun*	*Which Animals Will We See?*	*Around the World*	*Animals of Africa*	*Animals of Africa*

Customize Literacy in Your Classroom

Customize Instruction
to Improve Reading Behaviors

Instruction in comprehension skills and strategies provides readers with avenues to understanding a text. Through teacher modeling and guided, collaborative, and independent practice, students become independent thinkers who employ a variety of skills and strategies to help them make meaning as they read.

Mini-Lessons for Comprehension Skills and Strategies

Unit R	Character, Setting, Plot, Realism and Fantasy, Questioning, Monitor and Clarify, Background Knowledge
Unit 1	Character, Setting, Plot, Main Idea and Details, Cause and Effect, Summarize, Important Ideas, Story Structure
Unit 2	Sequence, Cause and Effect, Author's Purpose, Compare and Contrast, Predict and Set Purpose, Inferring
Unit 3	Sequence, Compare and Contrast, Fact and Opinion, Author's Purpose, Draw Conclusions, Visualize, Text Structure
Unit 4	Draw Conclusions, Theme, Facts and Details, Cause and Effect, Important Ideas, Questioning
Unit 5	Literary Elements, Draw Conclusions, Compare and Contrast, Main Idea and Details, Sequence, Theme, Monitor and Clarify, Summarize

Envision It! A Comprehension Handbook

Envision It! Visual Skills Handbook
Author's Purpose
Categorize and Classify
Cause and Effect
Compare and Contrast
Draw Conclusions
Fact and Opinion
Generalize
Graphic Sources
Literary Elements
Main Idea and Details
Sequence

Envision It! Visual Strategies Handbook
Background Knowledge
Important Ideas
Inferring
Monitor and Clarify
Predict and Set Purpose
Questioning
Story Structure
Summarize
Text Structure
Visualize

Anchor Chart Anchor charts are provided with each strategy lesson. These charts incorporate the language of strategic thinkers. They help students make their thinking visible and permanent and provide students with a means to clarify their thinking about how and when to use each strategy. As students gain more experience with a strategy, the chart may undergo revision.

See pages 107–128 in the *First Stop on Reading Street* Teacher's Edition for additional support as you customize literacy in your classroom.

Good Readers DRA2 users will find additional resources in the *First Stop on Reading Street* Teacher's Edition on pages 110–111.

Contents

Pacing Guide

This chart shows the instructional sequence from *Scott Foresman Reading Street* for Grade 1. You can use this pacing guide as is to ensure you are following a comprehensive scope and sequence. Or, you can adjust the sequence to match your calendar, curriculum map, or testing schedule.

Grade 1 READING

UNIT R

	Week 1	Week 2	Week 3	Week 4	Week 5	Week 6
Phonemic Awareness	Match Initial Phonemes	Match Initial Phonemes	Match Final Phonemes	Isolate Final Phonemes	Isolate Phonemes	Isolate Medial Phonemes
Phonics	/m/ spelled *m*, /s/ spelled *s, ss* /t/ spelled *t*, /a/ spelled *a*	/k/ spelled *c*, /p/ spelled *p*, /n/ spelled *n*	/f/ spelled *f, ff*, /b/ spelled *b*, /g/ spelled *g*, /i/ spelled *i*	/d/ spelled *d*, /l/ spelled *l,ll* /h/ spelled *h*, /o/ spelled *o*	/r/ spelled *r*, /w/ spelled *w*, /j/ spelled *j*, /k/ spelled *k*, /e/ spelled *e*	/v/ spelled *v*, /y/ spelled *y*, /u/ spelled *u*, /kw/ spelled *qu*, /z/ *z, zz*
High-Frequency Words	*I, see, a, green*	*we, like, the, one*	*do, look, you, was, yellow*	*are, have, they, that, two*	*he, is, to, with, three*	*where, here, for, me, go*
Comprehension Skill	Character	Setting	Plot	Realism/ Fantasy	Plot	Realism/ Fantasy
Comprehension Strategy	Questioning	Predict and Set Purpose	Story Structure	Questioning	Monitor and Clarify	Background Knowledge
Fluency	Oral Rereading	Oral Rereading	Oral Rereading, Paired Reading	Oral Rereading, Paired Reading	Oral Rereading, Paired Reading	Oral Rereading, Paired Reading

UNIT 1

	Week 1	Week 2
Phonemic Awareness	Blend and Segment Phonemes	Blend and Segment Phonemes
Phonics	Short *a* Final *ck*	Short *i* Final *x*
High-Frequency Words	*on, way, in, my, come*	*take, up, she, what*
Comprehension Skill	Character and Setting	Plot
Comprehension Strategy	Monitor and Clarify	Summarize
Fluency	Accuracy	Accuracy

UNIT 3

	Week 1	Week 2	Week 3	Week 4	Week 5	Week 6
Phonemic Awareness	Segment Phonemes	Blend and Segment Words	Add Phonemes	Blend and Segment Syllables	Isolate Medial and Final Phonemes	Add Phonemes
Phonics	Vowel Sounds of *y* Long Vowels (CV)	Final *ng, nk* Compound Words	Ending *-es*, Plural *-es* *r*-Controlled *or, ore*	Inflected *-ed, -ing* *r*-Controlled *ar*	*r*-Controlled *er, ir, ur* Contractions *'s, 've, 're*	Comparative Endings *dge/j/*
High-Frequency Words	*always, become, day, everything, nothing, stays, things*	*any, enough, ever, every, own, sure, were*	*away, car, friends, house, our, school, very*	*afraid, again, few, how, read, soon*	*done, know, push, visit, wait*	*before, does, good-bye, oh, right, won't*
Comprehension Skill	Sequence	Compare and Contrast	Fact and Opinion	Author's Purpose	Fact and Opinion	Draw Conclusions
Comprehension Strategy	Summarize	Inferring	Monitor and Clarify	Visualize	Text Structure	Background Knowledge
Fluency	Accuracy/ Rate	Phrasing	Phrasing	Expression/ Intonation	Expression/ Intonation	Expression/ Intonation

UNIT 4

	Week 1	Week 2
Phonemic Awareness	Substitute Initial Phonemes	Substitute Final Phonemes
Phonics	Long *a: ai, ay* Possessives	Long *e: ea* Inflected Endings
High-Frequency Words	*about, give, enjoy, would, worry, surprise*	*colors, drew, over, sign, draw, great, show*
Comprehension Skill	Draw Conclusions	Theme
Comprehension Strategy	Monitor and Clarify	Visualize
Fluency	Expression/ Intonation	Accuracy/ Rate

Are you the adventurous type? Want to use some of your own ideas and materials in your teaching? But you worry you might be leaving out some critical instruction kids need? Customize Literacy can help.

Week 3	Week 4	Week 5	Week 6
Blend and Segment Phonemes	Blend and Segment Phonemes	Blend and Segment Phonemes	Blend and Segment Phonemes
Short *o* -*s* Plurals	Inflected Endings -*s*, -*ing*	Short *e* Initial Blends	Short *u* Final Blends
blue, little, get, from, help, use	*eat, her, this, too, four, five*	*saw, small, tree, your*	*home, into, many, them*
Character and Setting	Main Idea and Details	Main Idea and Details	Cause and Effect
Visualize	Important Ideas	Story Structure	Text Structure
Rate	Accuracy/ Rate	Phrasing	Phrasing

UNIT 2

Week 1	Week 2	Week 3	Week 4	Week 5	Week 6
Blend and Segment Phonemes	Blend and Segment Phonemes	Distinguish Long/Short Sounds	Distinguish Long/Short Sounds	Distinguish Long/Short Sounds	Distinguish Long/Short Sounds
Digraphs *sh, th* Vowel Sound in *ball*	Long *a* (CVCe) *c*/s/ and *g*/j/	Long *i* (CVCe) Digraphs *wh, ch, tch, ph*	Long *o* (CVCe) Contractions *n't, 'm, 'll*	Long *u*, long *e* (CVCe) Inflected Endings -*ed*	Long *e: e, ee* Syllables VCCV
catch, good, no, put, want, said	*be, could, horse, old, paper, of*	*live, out, people, who, work*	*down, inside, now, there, together*	*around, find, food, grow, under, water*	*also, family, new, other, some, their*
Sequence	Cause and Effect	Author's Purpose	Sequence	Author's Purpose	Compare and Contrast
Predict and Set Purpose	Monitor and Clarify	Important Ideas	Inferring	Background Knowledge	Questioning
Accuracy/ Rate	Phrasing	Phrasing	Accuracy/ Rate	Phrasing	Accuracy/ Rate

Week 3	Week 4	Week 5	Week 6
Substitute Phonemes	Substitute Phonemes	Segment Syllables	Blend and Segment
Long *o: oa, ow* Three-letter Blends	Long *i: ie, igh* *kn*/n/ and *wr*/r/	Compound Words Vowels *ew, ue, ui*	Suffixes -*ly*, -*ful* Vowels in *moon*
found, once, wild, mouth, took	*above, laugh, touch, eight, moon*	*picture, room, thought, remember, stood*	*told, because, across, only, shoes, dance, opened*
Facts and Details	Facts and Details	Theme	Cause and Effect
Important Ideas	Questioning	Story Structure	Predict and Set Purpose
Expression/ Intonation	Accuracy/ Rate/ Expression	Phrasing	Expression/ Intonation

UNIT 5

Week 1	Week 2	Week 3	Week 4	Week 5	Week 6
Delete Initial Phonemes	Blend and Segment Phonemes	Add Final Phonemes	Substitute Final Phonemes	Blend and Segment Phonemes	Delete Phonemes
Diphthongs *ow, ou* Syllables C + *le*	Vowel Patterns *ow, ou* Syllables V/CV, VC/V	Vowels in *foot* Inflected Endings	Diphthongs *oi, oy* Suffixes -*er*, -*or*	Syllable Patterns	Prefixes *un-*, *re-* Long Vowels *i, o*
along, behind, eyes, never, pulling, toward	*door, loved, should, wood*	*among, another, instead, none*	*against, goes, heavy, kinds, today*	*built, early, learn, science, through*	*answered, carry, different, poor*
Character, Setting, and Plot	Draw Conclusions	Compare and Contrast	Main Idea and Details	Sequence	Theme
Monitor and Clarify	Background Knowledge	Monitor and Clarify	Summarize	Text Structure	Inferring
Accuracy/ Rate/ Expression	Accuracy/ Rate/ Expression/ Phrasing	Expression/ Intonation	Phrasing	Expression/ Intonation	Phrasing

Pacing Guide

Grade 1

LANGUAGE ARTS

UNIT R

	Week 1	Week 2	Week 3	Week 4	Week 5	Week 6
Speaking, Listening, and Viewing	Participate in a Discussion	Share Ideas	Follow, Restate, Give Instructions	Give Instructions	Ask Questions	Retell
Research and Study Skills	Parts of a Book	Parts of a Book	Signs	Map	Calendar	Library/ Media Center
Grammar	Nouns: People, Animals, and Things	Nouns: Places	Verbs	Simple Sentences	Adjectives	Sentences
Weekly Writing	Sentences	Sentences	Sentences	Sentences	Sentences	Sentences
Writing						

UNIT 1

	Week 1	Week 2
Speaking, Listening, and Viewing	Ask Questions	Share Information and Ideas
Research and Study Skills	Parts of a Book	Media Center/ Library Resources
Grammar	Sentences	Subjects
Weekly Writing	Story/Voice	Fantasy Story/ Conventions
Writing		

UNIT 3

	Week 1	Week 2	Week 3	Week 4	Week 5	Week 6
Speaking, Listening, and Viewing	Relate an Experience	Share Information and Ideas	Give Descriptions	Present a Poem	Share Information and Ideas	Give Announce-ments
Research and Study Skills	Interview	Glossary	Classify and Categorize	Diagram	Technology: My Computer	Picture Graph
Grammar	Action Verbs	Verbs That Add *-s*	Verbs That Do Not Add *-s*	Verbs for Past and for Future	*Am, Is, Are, Was,* and *Were*	Contractions with *Not*
Weekly Writing	Realistic Story/ Organization	Comments About a Story/Voice	Summary/ Conventions	List/ Sentences	Captions and Pictures/ Focus/Ideas	Play Scene/ Sentences
Writing	Photo Writing/Expository Article					

UNIT 4

	Week 1	Week 2
Speaking, Listening, and Viewing	Give Descriptions	Share Information and Ideas
Research and Study Skills	Interview	Chart and Table
Grammar	Adjectives	Adjectives for Colors and Shapes
Weekly Writing	Letter/ Organization	Invitation/ Word Choice
Writing		

Week 3	Week 4	Week 5	Week 6
Give Introductions	Share Information and Ideas	Give Descriptions	Give Directions
Picture Dictionary	Chart	List	Notes
Predicates	Declarative Sentences	Interrogative Sentences	Exclamatory Sentences
Short Poem/ Sentences	Personal Narrative/ Voice	Realistic Story/ Organization	Brief Composition, Focus/Ideas
Keyboarding/Personal Narrative			

UNIT 2

Week 1	Week 2	Week 3	Week 4	Week 5	Week 6
Relate an Experience	Share Information and Ideas	Give Announce-ments	Informal Conversation	Share Information and Ideas	Follow Directions
Parts of a Book	Interview	Map	Periodicals/ Newsletters	Alphabetical Order	Picture Dictionary
Nouns	Proper Nouns	Special Titles	Days, Months, and Holidays	Singular and Plural Nouns	Nouns in Sentences
Friendly Letter/ Organization	Poster; Brief Composition/ Sentences	Explanation/ Conventions	Poem/ Organization	Description/ Voice	Expository Paragraph/ Focus/Ideas
Electronic Pen Pals/Letter					

Week 3	Week 4	Week 5	Week 6
Present a Poem	Purposes of Media	Purposes of Media	Purposes of Media
Bar Graph	Glossary	Technology: Using E-mail	Alphabetical Order
Adjectives for Sizes	Adjectives for What Kind	Adjectives for How Many	Adjectives That Compare
Poem/ Focus/Ideas	Realistic Story/Voice	Thank-You Note/ Conventions	Directions/ Organization
Story Starters/Realistic Story			

UNIT 5

Week 1	Week 2	Week 3	Week 4	Week 5	Week 6
Techniques in Media	Share Information and Ideas	Techniques in Media	Respond to Media	Techniques in Media	Respond to Media
Reference Sources/ Take Notes	Dictionary	Text Features	Picture Graph	Technology: Web Page	Encyclo-pedia
Imperative Sentences	Pronouns	Using *I* and *Me*	Pronouns	Adverbs	Prepositions and Prepositional Phrases
Animal Fantasy/ Voice	Letter/Voice	Questions/ Word Choice	Persuasive Ad/Focus/ Ideas	Autobiography/ Sentences	Poem/ Conventions
E-Newsletter/Short Report					

Teaching Record Chart

This chart shows the critical comprehension skills and strategies you need to cover. Check off each one as you provide instruction.

Reading/Comprehension	DATES OF INSTRUCTION		
Confirm predictions about what will happen next in text by "reading the part that tells."			
Ask relevant questions, seek clarification, and locate facts and details about stories and other texts.			
Establish purpose for reading selected texts and monitor comprehension, making corrections and adjustments when that understanding breaks down (e.g., identifying clues, using background knowledge, generating questions, re-reading a portion aloud).			
Connect the meaning of a well-known story or fable to personal experiences.			
Explain the function of recurring phrases (e.g., "Once upon a time" or "They lived happily ever after") in traditional folk and fairy tales.			
Respond to and use rhythm, rhyme, and alliteration in poetry.			
Describe the plot (problem and solution) and retell a story's beginning, middle, and end with attention to the sequence of events.			
Describe characters in a story and the reasons for their actions and feelings.			
Determine whether a story is true or a fantasy and explain why.			
Recognize sensory details in literary text.			

Tired of using slips of paper or stickies to make sure you teach everything you need to? Need an easier way to keep track of what you have taught, and what you still need to cover? **Customize Literacy** can help.

Reading/Comprehension	DATES OF INSTRUCTION		
Read independently for a sustained period of time.			
Identify the topic and explain the author's purpose in writing about the text.			
Restate the main idea, heard or read.			
Identify important facts or details in text, heard or read.			
Retell the order of events in a text by referring to the words and/or illustrations.			
Use text features (e.g., title, table of contents, illustrations) to locate specific information in text.			
Follow written multi-step directions with picture cues to assist with understanding.			
Explain the meaning of specific signs and symbols (e.g., map features).			
Establish purposes for reading selected texts based upon desired outcome to enhance comprehension.			
Ask literal questions of text.			
Monitor and adjust comprehension (e.g., using background knowledge, creating sensory images, re-reading a portion aloud).			
Make inferences about text using textual evidence to support understanding.			
Retell or act out important events in stories in logical order.			
Make connections to own experiences, to ideas in other texts, and to the larger community and discuss textual evidence.			

Main Idea and Details

Objectives:

- Tell the one big idea in a story or a selection.
- Tell what the child used to identify what a story or article is about.

Student Edition 1.1, p. EI•3

What is it? The **main idea** is what a story or nonfiction article is about. At Grade 1, children tell what the big idea in a story or article is after hearing it read aloud. They retell the story or are able to say in a word or two what the big idea of an article is.

How Good Readers Use the Skill Identifying and stating main ideas is a critical skill for readers because it helps them determine the important information in a text. At first, students think about what a story or selection is mostly about. They go on to select a statement of main idea, from a choice of statements or from the selection itself. They begin to identify details as pieces of information that enlarge on the main idea, help clarify the main idea, or give examples. Older readers are able to identify main ideas, stated or implied, and are able to frame main ideas in their own words.

Texts for Teaching

Student Edition

- *A Fox and a Kit,* 1.1, pages 102–111
- *Get the Egg! 1.1,* pages 128–137
- *Simple Machines,* 1.5, pages 138–155

Leveled Readers

- See pages 24–29 for a list of Leveled Readers.

Teach the Skill

Use the Envision It! lesson 1.1, on page EI•3 to visually review main idea and details.

Remind children that:

- the **main idea** is what a story or article is mostly about.

Practice

Have two pictures ready to show to children. Show one of the pictures and ask: What do you see in the picture? Is this picture mostly about [provide an incorrect answer] or [provide the correct answer]? Help children match the answer with what is shown in the picture. (For example, a picture of a forest may show lots of animals, but it is still mostly about a forest.) Show another picture and have children tell what it is mostly about without choices.

If... students have difficulty what a picture is mostly about, **then...** think aloud as you name the details that tell more about the big idea.

Apply

As children read on their own, have them look at the pictures to see what they are mostly about.

Writing

Tell children to draw a picture that shows what a place, such as a forest, is mostly about.

Mini-Lesson 2

Teach the Skill

Use the Envision It! lesson 1.1 on page EI•3 to visually review main idea and details.

Remind children that:

- the **main idea** is what a story or article is mostly about.

Practice

Read the following paragraph to children. Tell them to close their eyes and listen and make a picture in their minds as you read. Balloons can be red or yellow. Balloons can be green or blue. They can be purple, orange, or white. Balloons can be many colors. Ask: Do you have a picture in your mind? What do you see? Then ask: What are the sentences all about? Listen as I give you three choices. Are the sentences all about red things, toys, or balloons? Talk with children how they can figure it out by recalling that all of the sentences are about one thing: balloons. **If...** students have difficulty identifying the big idea, **then...** have them select from two choices, one of which is correct.

Apply

As children read, tell them to think about what the sentences are mostly about.

Writing

Have students write sentences that tell about puppies or other topic of their choice.

Mini-Lesson 3

Teach the Skill

Use the Envision It! lesson 1.1 on page EI•3 to visually review main idea and details.

Remind children that:

- the **main idea** is what a story or article is mostly about.
- they can use information in the story to tell what it is mostly about.

Practice

Read or retell a familiar tale or selection to children and have them listen and think about what the story is mostly about. (For example, *Goldilocks* is mostly about a girl who causes trouble in a bears' house.) When you are finished, talk about what the story is mostly about and ask: What helps us figure out what the story is mostly about? Help them understand that what happens in a story helps us figure this out. In *Goldilocks,* the little girl causes trouble by eating the porridge, breaking a chair, and by sleeping in a bed. We put these events together to see what the story is mostly about. **If...** children have difficulty telling what a story is mostly about, **then...** retell the story with them and then ask: What is this story mostly about?

Apply

As children read, tell them to think about the big ideas in the story.

Writing

Have children write a story and give it a title that tells what it is mostly about.

Objectives:

- Answer What happened? and Why did that happen?
- Identify cause-and-effect relationships.
- Understand that cause-and-effect relationships can be signaled by clue words.

Cause and Effect

Student Edition 1.1, p. EI•2

What is it? A **cause** is why something happens. An **effect** is the result of the cause. Not all causal relationships are stated directly or signaled by clue words, such as *because, so,* and *since.* In these cases, children must infer either cause or effect, using information in the text and their prior knowledge. At Grade 1, readers are identifying causal relationships by answering the questions: *What happened? Why did it happen?*

How Good Readers Use the Skill Children experience cause-and-effect relationships every day. To be successful, they need to recognize these relationships in fiction as well as in all content areas. The ability to do so will help them increase their understanding when dealing with longer, more difficult texts. Readers begin their understanding of causal relationships by asking *What happened? Why did it happen?* Children then learn that a cause may have multiple effects and one effect can have many causes and that sometimes clue words signal causal relationships.

Texts for Teaching

Student Edition

- *Animal Park,* 1.1, pages 154–163
- *The Farmer in the Hat,* 1.2, pages 52–65
- *Henry and Mudge and Mrs. Hopper's House,* 1.4, pages 198–217

Leveled Readers

- See pages 24–29 for a list of Leveled Readers.

Teach the Skill

Use the Envision It! lesson on 1.1, page EI•2 to visually review cause and effect.

Remind children that as they read they should:

- think about **what happens.**
- think about **why** that thing happens.

Practice

Write these sentences on the board and read them with students.

It was raining and I got wet.

Ask: What happened? (I got wet.) Why did that happen? (It was raining.)

Christie dropped a book and there was a loud noise.

Ask: What happened? (There was a loud noise.) Why did that happen? (Christie dropped a book.)

Use additional examples if necessary and have students identify what happened and why it happened.

If... students have difficulty identifying what happened and why it happened,

then... provide additional physical examples and ask *What happened?* and *Why did that happen?*

Apply

As students read, have them ask themselves: *What happened? Why did it happen?*

Writing

Students can work in pairs to write what happened and why sentences.

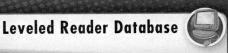

Teach the Skill

Use the Envision It! lesson on 1.1, page EI•2 to visually review cause and effect.

Remind children that:

- they should think about **what happens** as they read.
- they should think about **why** that thing happens.
- words such as *because* and *so* can make it easier to understand what happened and why.

Practice

Read aloud the following and have children listen for what happened and why it happened.

It rained all day yesterday, so it was very muddy. I took my dog on a walk. I walked on the sidewalk, but he walked in the mud. When we got home, I took off my boots. Since my dog doesn't have any boots, he tracked mud into the house. He made the floor very messy with his paws.

Ask: What happened? (It was muddy; the dog made the floor messy.) Why? (It rained; the dog walked in the mud and then on the floor.) Record their ideas on a chart.

What happened?	Why did it happen?

If... children have difficulty identifying it what happened and why, **then...** have children visualize the events in the story and ask specific *what happened* and *why* questions as you reread the passage.

Apply

As children read, have them think about what happens and why.

Writing

Have children complete a chart like the one here for a familiar story.

Teach the Skill

Use the Envision It! lesson on 1.1, page EI•2 to visually review cause and effect.

Remind children that:

- they should think about **what happens** as they read.
- they should think about **why** that thing happens.
- words such as *because* can make it easier to understand what happened and why.

Practice

Tell children that some words are clues to helping them figure out why things happened. One of these words is *because*. On strips of paper, write things that happened. Then have children complete them using *because*. Use everyday happenings, such as the following:

The cat yowled; The fence fell down; Marie beamed; The snowman melted.

Have children share their ideas.

If... children have difficulty finishing a sentence,
then... provide a clue word as a prompt.

Apply

As children read the assigned text, have them think about what happens and why that thing happens.

Writing

Children can take one of the finished sentences and write more about what happened and why it happened.

Objectives:

- Tell the one big idea in a story or selection.
- Tell what the child used to identify what a story or article is about.

Texts for Teaching

Student Edition

- *A Fox and a Kit,* 1.1, pages 102–111
- *Who Works Here?* 1.2, pages 86–95
- *A Trip to Washington, D.C.,* 1.4, pages 96–109

Leveled Readers

- See pages 24–29 for a list of Leveled Readers.

Important Ideas

Student Edition 1.1, p. EI•9

Understand the Strategy

Important ideas in text are the ones the author wants the reader to remember. In nonfiction, readers need to be able to distinguish important ideas from information that is interesting but not that important. Many texts have text features that help readers determine the important ideas.

Teach

Use the Envision It! on page EI•9 to visually introduce important ideas with children.

Tell children that the important ideas are the most important ones in a nonfiction selection. Show an informational book on a recognizable topic. Preview the book with children pointing out some of the text features that can be used to determine the important ideas. These include titles, headings, contents, captions, illustrations, photographs, and so on. Think aloud as you use these features. For example: This book is all about shadows. The first chapter tells what a shadow is. Then the book tells how to make hand puppets and stick puppets using shadows. There are lots of pictures of kids making different puppets. Then they put on a show. The most important idea, however, is not the puppets. The most important idea is that shadows form when an object, such as your hand or a puppet, blocks light—then you have a picture.

Practice

Read another informational book or have children select one to read on their own. Tell them to listen for words that are repeated because these words may be clues to the important idea. Together, decide on the important idea of the book. Talk about what children used to decide.

If... children have difficulty locating important ideas,
then... have them determine the important idea of a picture.

Apply

Have children recall information from a book they have read and use it to tell the important idea(s).

Anchor Chart

Anchor charts help children make their thinking visible and permanent. With an anchor chart, the group can clarify their thinking about how to use a strategy. Display anchor charts so readers can use them as they read. Here is a sample chart for important ideas.

Important Ideas

1. Preview before you read so you know what the topic is.
2. Look for key words. These might be in titles or in bold print. You can use key words to predict what the important ideas are.
3. Look at all the pictures. Read the captions. You might see some of the key words.
4. Read carefully.
5. Ask yourself:
   What are most of the sentences about?
   What is important to know?
6. Write down the most important idea. Try writing it in your own words.
7. Share your important ideas with others.

Anchor Chart

Objectives:

- Recognize that stories are organized in order from beginning to middle to end.
- Identify characters and plot as parts of a story.

Texts for Teaching

Student Edition

- *Tip and Tam,* 1.R, pages 70–79
- *Get the Egg!* 1.1, pages 128–137
- *Peter's Chair,* 1.4, pages 162–181

Leveled Readers

- See pages 24–29 for a list of Leveled Readers.

Story Structure

Student Edition 1.2, p. EI•14

Understand the Strategy

Story structure refers to how a story is arranged. This means understanding the basic elements of a story—characters, setting, and plot—and how the author presents them. Recognizing story structure helps readers understand, recall, and appreciate stories.

Teach

Use the Envision It! on page EI•14 to visually teach story structure with children.

Explain to children that stories are alike in some ways. Stories tell about events in order. In a story, there is a beginning, a middle, and an end. Ask children to name some favorite stories. Choose one and talk about who is in the story and what happens in the beginning, middle, and end. Model, if necessary, by thinking aloud. A story I like is Peter's Chair. Peter is the main character in the story. In the beginning, Peter is upset that all his baby things are going to his new baby sister. He decides to run away with his dog. In the end, he helps paint his baby chair for his sister after he realizes he has grown too big for it!

Story Sequence Chart
Beginning Peter is upset that his baby things are going to his little sister.
Middle He decides to run away with his dog.
End He can't fit into his baby chair and he paints it for his little sister.

Show what happens on a Story Sequence Chart. Talk about the importance of order in the story. What happened before Peter decided to paint his baby chair? Would it have made sense if Peter ran away after he and his Dad painted the chair? Why?

Practice

Have pairs of children choose a story and reread or retell it to each other. They can fill in a Story Sequence Chart and use it to retell the story to the class.

If... children have difficulty recognizing story structure,
then... write out events on sentence strips and have them put them in order.

Apply

Ask children to read a short story and record the events in order. They can check their order by retelling the story.

Anchor Chart

Anchor charts help children make their thinking visible and permanent. Display anchor charts so readers can use them as they read. Here is a sample chart for story structure.

Story Structure

1. Look over the story before you read. Ask yourself:
   What will this be about?
   Do I recognize any characters?
   What is going on in the pictures?

2. Read the story.

3. Think about the story. Ask yourself:
   What happens in the beginning?
   What happens in the middle?
   What happens at the end?

4. Write down the events on a *Story Sequence Chart.*

5. Use your chart to retell the story. Are the events in the right order?

6. Retell your story to someone. Tell why the order is important.

Anchor Chart

Using Multiple Strategies

Good readers use multiple strategies as they read. You can encourage students to read strategically through good classroom questioning. Use questions such as these to help students apply strategies during reading.

Questioning

- Who or what is this question about?
- Where can you look to find the answer to this question?
- What do you want to know about ________?
- What questions to do you have about the ________ in this selection? Use the words *who, what, when, where, why,* and *how* to ask your questions.
- Do you have any questions after reading?

Graphic Organizers

- What kind of graphic organizer could you use to help you keep track of the information in this selection?

Monitor and Clarify

- Does the story or article make sense?
- What don't you understand about what you read?
- Do you need to reread, review, read on, or check a reference source?
- Do you need to read more slowly or more quickly?
- What is a ________? Where could you look to find out?

Predict and Set Purpose

- What do you think this story or article will be about? Why do you think as you do?
- What do you think you will learn from this selection?
- Do the text features help you predict what will happen?
- Based on what has happened so far, what do you think will happen next?
- Is this what you thought would happen?
- How does ________ change what you thought would happen?

Preview

- What do the photographs, illustrations, or graphic sources tell about the selection?
- What do you want to find out? What do you want to learn?

Background Knowledge

- What do you already know about ________?
- Have you read stories or articles by this author before?
- How is this selection like others that you have read?
- What does this remind you of?
- How does your prior knowledge help you understand ________?
- Did the text match what you already knew? What new information did you learn?

Story Structure

- Who are the characters in this story? What is the setting?
- What is the problem in this story? How does the problem get solved?
- What is the point of this story?

Summarize

- What two or three important ideas have you read so far?
- How do the text features relate to the important ideas?
- Is there a graphic organizer that can help you organize the information before you summarize?

Text Structure

- How has the author organized the writing?
- What clues tell you that the text is structured ________?

Visualize

- When you read this, what do you picture in your mind?
- What do you hear, see, or smell?
- What do you think ________ looks like? Why do you think as you do?

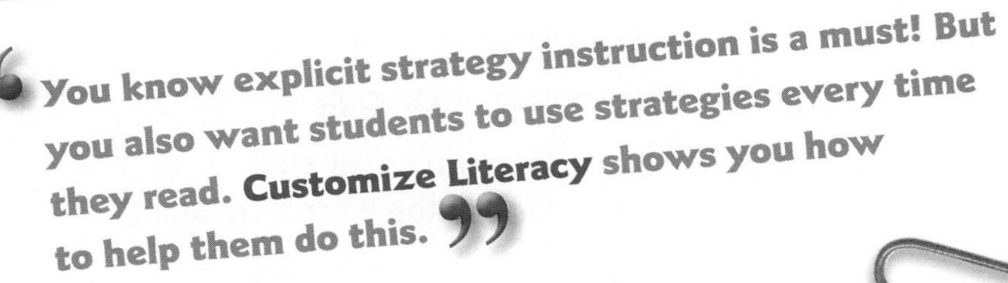

"You know explicit strategy instruction is a must! But you also want students to use strategies every time they read. **Customize Literacy** shows you how to help them do this."

Glossary of Literacy Terms

This glossary lists academic language terms that are related to literacy. They are provided for your information and professional use.

A

alliteration the repetition of a consonant sound in a group of words, especially in poetry

allusion a word or phrase that refers to something else the reader already knows from history, experience, or reading

animal fantasy a story about animals that talk and act like people

answer questions a reading strategy in which readers use the text and prior knowledge to answer questions about what they are reading

antonym a word that means the opposite of another word

ask questions a reading strategy in which readers ask themselves questions about the text to help make sense of what they read

author's point of view the author's opinion on the subject he or she is writing about

author's purpose the reason the author wrote the text

autobiography the story of a real person's life written by that person

B

background knowledge the information and experience that a reader brings to a text

biography the story of a real person's life written by another person

C

cause why something happens

character a person, an animal, or a personified object in a story

chronological order events in a selection, presented in the order in which they occurred

classify and categorize put things, such as pictures or words, into groups

climax the point in a story at which conflict is confronted

compare tell how things are the same

comprehension understanding of text being read—the ultimate goal of reading

comprehension strategy a conscious plan used by a reader to gain understanding of text. Comprehension strategies may be used before, during, or after reading.

conclusion a decision or opinion arrived at after thinking about facts and details and using prior knowledge

conflict the problem or struggle in a story

context clue the words, phrases, or sentences near an unknown word that give the reader clues to the word's meaning

contrast tell how things are different

D

details small pieces of information

dialect form of a language spoken in a certain region or by a certain group of people that differs from the standard form of that language

dialogue written conversation

diary a day-to-day record of one's activities and thoughts

draw conclusions arrive at decisions or opinions after thinking about facts and details and using prior knowledge

E

effect what happens as the result of a cause

etymology an explanation of the origin and history of a word and its meaning

exaggeration a statement that makes something seem larger or greater than it actually is

expository text text that contains facts and information. Also called *informational text.*

F

fable a story, usually with animal characters, that is written to teach a moral, or lesson

fact piece of information that can be proved to be true

fairy tale a folk story with magical characters and events

fantasy a story that could not really happen

fiction writing that tells about imaginary people, things, and events

figurative language the use of language that gives words a meaning beyond their usual definitions in order to add beauty or force

flashback an interruption in the sequence of events of a narrative to include an event that happened earlier

folk tale a story that has been passed down by word of mouth

foreshadowing the use of hints or clues about what will happen later in a story

G

generalize make a broad statement or rule after examining particular facts

graphic organizer a drawing, chart, or web that illustrates concepts or shows how ideas relate to each other. Readers use graphic organizers to help them keep track of and understand important information and ideas as they read. Story maps, word webs, Venn diagrams, and KWL charts are graphic organizers.

graphic source a chart, diagram, or map within a text that adds to readers' understanding of the text

H

historical fiction realistic fiction that takes place in the past. It is an imaginary story based on historical events and characters.

humor writing or speech that has a funny or amusing quality

hyperbole an exaggerated statement not meant to be taken literally, such as *I'm so hungry I could eat a horse.*

I

idiom a phrase whose meaning differs from the ordinary meaning of the words. *A stone's throw* is an idiom meaning "a short distance."

imagery the use of language to create beautiful or forceful pictures in the reader's mind

inference conclusion reached on the basis of evidence and reasoning

inform give knowledge, facts, or news to someone

informational text writing that contains facts and information. Also called *expository text.*

interview a face-to-face conversation in which someone responds to questions

irony a way of speaking or writing in which the ordinary meaning of the words is the opposite of what the speaker or writer is thinking; a contrast between what is expected and what actually happens

J

jargon the language of a special group or profession

L

legend a story coming down from the past about the great deeds of a hero. Although a legend may be based on historical people and events, it is not regarded as historically true.

literary elements the characters, setting, plot, and theme of a narrative text

M

main idea the big idea that tells what a paragraph or a selection is mainly about; the most important idea of a text

metacognition an awareness of one's own thinking processes and the ability to monitor and direct them to a desired goal. Good readers use metacognition to monitor their reading and adjust their reading strategies.

metaphor a comparison that does not use *like* or *as,* such as *a heart of stone*

meter the pattern of beats or accents in poetry

M

monitor and clarify	a comprehension strategy by which readers actively think about understanding their reading and know when they understand and when they do not. Readers use appropriate strategies to make sense of difficult words, ideas, or passages.
mood	the atmosphere or feeling of a written work
moral	the lesson or teaching of a fable or story
motive	the reason a character in a narrative does or says something
mystery	a story about mysterious events that are not explained until the end, so as to keep the reader in suspense
myth	a story that attempts to explain something in nature

N

narrative	a story, made up or true, that someone tells or narrates
narrator	the character in a selection who tells the story
nonfiction	writing that tells about real things, real people, and real events

O

onomatopoeia	the use of words that sound like their meanings, such as *buzz* and *hum*
opinion	someone's judgment, belief, or way of thinking
oral vocabulary	the words needed for speaking and listening
outcome	the resolution of the conflict in a story

P

paraphrase	retell the meaning of a passage in one's own words
personification	a figure of speech in which human traits or actions are given to animals or inanimate objects, as in *The sunbeam danced on the waves.*
persuade	convince someone to do or to believe something
photo essay	a collection of photographs on one theme, accompanied by text
play	a story that is written to be acted out for an audience
plot	a series of related events at the beginning, middle, and end of a story; the action of a story
poem	an expressive, imaginative piece of writing often arranged in lines having rhythm and rhyme. In a poem, the patterns made by the sounds of the words have special importance.
pourquoi tale	a type of folk story that explains why things in nature came to be. *Pourquoi* is a French word meaning "why."

P

predict tell what a selection might be about or what might happen in a text. Readers use text features and information to predict. They confirm or revise their predictions as they read.

preview look over a text before reading it

prior knowledge the information and experience that a reader brings to a text. Readers use prior knowledge to help them understand what they read.

prop an item, such as an object, picture, or chart, used in a performance or presentation

R

reading vocabulary the words we recognize or use in print

realistic fiction a story about imaginary people and events that could happen in real life

repetition the repeated use of some aspect of language

resolution the point in a story where the conflict is resolved

rhyme to end in the same sound(s)

rhythm a pattern of strong beats in speech or writing, especially poetry

rising action the buildup of conflicts and complications in a story

S

science fiction a story based on science that often tells what life in the future might be like

semantic map a graphic organizer, often a web, used to display words or concepts that are meaningfully related

sensory language the use of words that help the reader understand how things look, sound, smell, taste, or feel

sequence the order of events in a selection or the order of the steps in which something is completed

sequence words clue words such as *first, next, then,* and *finally* that signal the order of events in a selection

setting where and when a story takes place

simile a comparison that uses *like* or *as,* as in *as busy as a bee*

speech a public talk to a group of people made for a specific purpose

stanza a group of lines in a poem

steps in a process the order of the steps in which something is completed

S

story map a graphic organizer used to record the literary elements and the sequence of events in a narrative text

story structure how the characters, setting, and events of a story are organized into a plot

summarize give the most important ideas of what was read. Readers summarize important information in the selection to keep track of what they are reading.

supporting detail piece of information that tells about the main idea

symbolism the use of one thing to suggest something else; often the use of something concrete to stand for an abstract idea

T

tall tale a humorous story that uses exaggeration to describe impossible happenings

text structure the organization of a piece of nonfiction writing. Text structures of informational text include cause/effect, chronological, compare/contrast, description, problem/solution, proposition/support, and ask/answer questions.

theme the big idea or author's message in a story

think aloud an instructional strategy in which a teacher verbalizes his or her thinking to model the process of comprehension or the application of a skill

tone author's attitude toward the subject or toward the reader

topic the subject of a discussion, conversation, or piece of text

V

visualize picture in one's mind what is happening in the text. Visualizing helps readers imagine the things they read about.

Leveled Readers Skills Chart

Scott Foresman Reading Street provides more than six hundred leveled readers. Each one is designed to:

- Practice critical skills and strategies
- Build fluency
- Build vocabulary and concepts
- Develop a lifelong love of reading

Grade 1

Title	Level*	DRA Level	Genre	Comprehension Strategy
Bix the Dog	A	1	Realistic Fiction	Summarize
Time for Dinner	B	2	Realistic Fiction	Important Ideas
Sam	B	2	Realistic Fiction	Monitor and Clarify
Mack and Zack	B	2	Realistic Fiction	Monitor and Clarify
The Sick Pets	B	2	Realistic Fiction	Summarize
On the Farm	B	2	Realistic Fiction	Visualize
At Your Vet	B	2	Realistic Fiction	Story Structure
Fun in the Sun	B	2	Expository Nonfiction	Text Structure
We Are a Family	B	2	Nonfiction	Predict and Set Purpose
Where They Live	C	3	Realistic Fiction	Visualize
Which Fox?	C	3	Realistic Fiction	Important Ideas
Which Animals Will We See?	C	3	Realistic Fiction	Text Structure
Let's Go to the Zoo	C	3	Nonfiction	Predict and Set Purpose
A Play	C	3	Realistic Fiction	Monitor and Clarify
A Class	C	3	Nonfiction	Monitor and Clarify
Here in My Neighborhood	C	3	Nonfiction	Important Ideas
Look at My Neighborhood	C	3	Realistic Fiction	Important Ideas
Look at Dinosaurs	C	3	Expository Nonfiction	Inferring
Around the Forest	C	3	Nonfiction	Background Knowledge
Learn About Worker Bees	C	3	Expository Nonfiction	Questioning
In My Room	C	3	Nonfiction	Summarize
Hank's Song	C	3	Fantasy	Inferring
Gus the Pup	C	3	Realistic Fiction	Monitor and Clarify
What Animals Can You See?	D	4	Expository Nonfiction	Text Structure
The Dinosaur Herds	D	4	Expository Nonfiction	Inferring
People Help the Forest	D	4	Expository Nonfiction	Background Knowledge
Honey	D	4	Nonfiction	Questioning
Let's Build a Park!	D	4	Fiction	Summarize
Mac Can Do It!	D	4	Fantasy	Inferring
The Seasons Change	D	4	Nonfiction	Visualize

* Suggested Guided Reading Level. Use your knowledge of students' abilities to adjust levels as needed.

The chart here and on the next few pages lists titles of leveled readers appropriate for students in Grade 1. Use the chart to find titles that meet your students' interest and instructional needs. The books in this list were leveled using the criteria suggested in *Matching Books to Readers: Using Leveled Books in Guided Reading, Grades K–3* by Irene C. Fountas and Gay Su Pinnell. For more on leveling, see the *Reading Street Leveled Readers Leveling Guide.*

Target Comprehension Skill	Additional Comprehension Instruction	Vocabulary
Plot	Sequence	High-Frequency Words
Main Idea and Details	Compare and Contrast	High-Frequency Words
Character and Setting	Draw Conclusions	High-Frequency Words
Character and Setting	Main Idea and Details	High-Frequency Words
Plot	Draw Conclusions	High-Frequency Words
Character and Setting	Plot	High-Frequency Words
Main Idea and Details	Theme	High-Frequency Words
Cause and Effect	Author's Purpose	High-Frequency Words
Sequence	Draw Conclusions	High-Frequency Words
Character and Setting	Theme and Plot	High-Frequency Words
Main Idea and Details	Compare and Contrast	High-Frequency Words
Cause and Effect	Setting and Plot	High-Frequency Words
Sequence	Compare and Contrast	High-Frequency Words
Cause and Effect	Main Idea and Details	High-Frequency Words
Cause and Effect	Author's Purpose	High-Frequency Words
Author's Purpose	Draw Conclusions	High-Frequency Words
Author's Purpose	Compare and Contrast	High-Frequency Words
Sequence	Cause and Effect	High-Frequency Words
Author's Purpose	Cause and Effect	High-Frequency Words
Compare and Contrast	Sequence	High-Frequency Words
Sequence	Author's Purpose	High-Frequency Words
Compare and Contrast	Realism and Fantasy	High-Frequency Words
Fact and Opinion	Cause and Effect	High-Frequency Words
Main Idea and Details	Compare and Contrast	High-Frequency Words
Sequence	Draw Conclusions	High-Frequency Words
Author's Purpose	Cause and Effect	High-Frequency Words
Compare and Contrast	Draw Conclusions	High-Frequency Words
Sequence	Author's Purpose	High-Frequency Words
Compare and Contrast	Realism and Fantasy	High-Frequency Words
Author's Purpose	Draw Conclusions	High-Frequency Words

Leveled Readers Skills Chart *Continued*

Grade 1

Title	Level*	DRA Level	Genre	Comprehension Strategy
Animals Change and Grow	D	4	Nonfiction	Text Structure
Ready for Winter?	D	4	Expository Nonfiction	Background Knowledge
A Party for Pedro	D	4	Realistic Fiction	Monitor and Clarify
Space Star	D	4	Realistic Fiction	Visualize
Our Leaders	D	4	Nonfiction	Important Ideas
Grandma's Farm	D	4	Realistic Fiction	Questioning
A New Baby Brother	D	4	Realistic Fiction	Story Structure
My Babysitter	D	4	Narrative Nonfiction	Predict and Set Purpose
What Brown Saw	D	4	Animal Fantasy	Monitor and Clarify
Fly Away Owl!	D	4	Realistic Fiction	Background Knowledge
What A Detective Does	D	4	Realistic Fiction	Monitor and Clarify
The Inclined Plane	D	4	Expository Nonfiction	Summarize
Using the Telephone	D	4	Expository Nonfiction	Text Structure
A Garden for All	D	4	Nonfiction	Inferring
Big Wishes and Her Baby	E	6–8	Realistic Fiction	Monitor and Clarify
Plans Change	E	6–8	Realistic Fiction	Visualize
Let's Visit a Butterfly Greenhouse	E	6–8	Nonfiction	Text Structure
Seasons Come and Go	E	6–8	Expository Nonfiction	Background Knowledge
Special Days, Special Food	E	6–8	Expository Nonfiction	Monitor and Clarify
The Art Show	F	10	Realistic Fiction	Visualize
Treasures of Our Country	F	10	Nonfiction	Important Ideas
A Visit to the Ranch	F	10	Realistic Fiction	Questioning
My Little Brother Drew	F	10	Realistic Fiction	Story Structure
The Story of the Kids Care Club	F	10	Expository Nonfiction	Predict and Set Purpose
Squirrel and Bear	G	12	Animal Fantasy	Monitor and Clarify
Puppy Raiser	G	12	Expository Nonfiction	Background Knowledge
A Mighty Oak Tree	G	12	Expository Nonfiction	Monitor and Clarify
Simple Machines at Work	G	12	Expository Nonfiction	Summarize
Carlos Picks a Pet	H	14	Realistic Fiction	Monitor and Clarify
That Cat Needs Help!	H	14	Realistic Fiction	Summarize

* Suggested Guided Reading Level. Use your knowledge of students' abilities to adjust levels as needed.

You know the theory behind leveled books: they let you match books with the interest and instructional levels of your students. You can find the right reader for every student with this chart.

Target Comprehension Skill	Additional Comprehension Instruction	Vocabulary
Fact and Opinion	Sequence	High-Frequency Words
Draw Conclusions	Sequence	High-Frequency Words
Draw Conclusions	Author's Purpose	High-Frequency Words
Theme	Realism and Fantasy	High-Frequency Words
Facts and Details	Cause and Effect	High-Frequency Words
Facts and Details	Plot	High-Frequency Words
Theme	Realism and Fantasy	High-Frequency Words
Cause and Effect	Main Idea	High-Frequency Words
Character, Setting, and Plot	Realism and Fantasy	High-Frequency Words
Draw Conclusions	Cause and Effect	High-Frequency Words
Compare and Contrast	Cause and Effect	High-Frequency Words
Main Idea and Details	Cause and Effect	High-Frequency Words
Sequence	Author's Purpose	High-Frequency Words
Theme	Sequence	High-Frequency Words
Fact and Opinion	Setting	High-Frequency Words
Author's Purpose	Setting	High-Frequency Words
Fact and Opinion	Author's Purpose	High-Frequency Words
Draw Conclusions	Compare and Contrast	High-Frequency Words
Draw Conclusions	Author's Purpose	High-Frequency Words
Theme	Plot	High-Frequency Words
Facts and Details	Cause and Effect	High-Frequency Words
Facts and Details	Compare and Contrast	High-Frequency Words
Theme	Realism and Fantasy	High-Frequency Words
Cause and Effect	Author's Purpose	High-Frequency Words
Character, Setting and Plot	Realism and Fantasy	High-Frequency Words
Draw Conclusions	Main Idea	High-Frequency Words
Compare and Contrast	Draw Conclusions	High-Frequency Words
Main Idea and Details	Compare and Contrast	High-Frequency Words
Character and Setting	Compare and Contrast	Amazing Words
Plot	Sequence	Amazing Words

Leveled Readers Skills Chart *Continued*

Grade 1

Title	Level*	DRA Level	Genre	Comprehension Strategy
Loni's Town	H	14	Realistic Fiction	Visualize
Baby Animals in the Rain Forest	H	14	Expository Nonfiction	Important Ideas
Cary and the The Wildlife Shelter	H	14	Realistic Fiction	Story Structure
Around the World	H	14	Narrative Nonfiction	Text Structure
The Communication Story	H	14	Expository Nonfiction	Text Structure
Marla's Good Idea	H	14	Realistic Fiction	Inferring
Rules at School	I	16	Animal Fantasy	Predict and Set Purpose
School: Then and Now	I	16	Expository Nonfiction	Monitor and Clarify
Mom the Mayor	I	16	Realistic Fiction	Important Ideas
The Dinosaur Detectives	I	16	Expository Nonfiction	Inferring
All About Food Chains	I	16	Expository Nonfiction	Background Knowledge
Bees and Beekeepers	I	16	Expository Nonfiction	Questioning
A New Library	I	16	Narrative Nonfiction	Summarize
Paul's Bed	J	18	Traditional Tales	Inferring
Britton Finds a Kitten	J	18	Realistic Fiction	Monitor and Clarify
All About the Weather	J	18	Expository Nonfiction	Visualize
Learn About Butterflies	J	18	Expository Nonfiction	Text Structure
Monarchs Migrate South	J	18	Narrative Nonfiction	Background Knowledge
Cascarones Are for Fun	J	18	Expository Nonfiction	Monitor and Clarify
Jamie's Jumble of Junk	J	18	Realistic Fiction	Visualize
America's Home	K	20	Nonfiction	Important Ideas
Go West!	K	20	Legend	Questioning
Double Trouble Twins	K	20	Realistic Fiction	Story Structure
What Makes Buildings Special?	K	20	Expository Nonfiction	Predict and Set Purpose
Grasshopper and Ant	K	20	Fable	Monitor and Clarify
Ways to be a Good Citizen	K	20	Expository Nonfiction	Background Knowledge
Great Scientists: Detectives at Work	L	24	Expository Nonfiction	Monitor and Clarify
Simple Machines in Compound Machines	L	24	Nonfiction	Summarize
Over the Years	L	24	Expository Nonfiction	Text Structure
Cody's Adventure	L	24	Realistic Fiction	Inferring

* Suggested Guided Reading Level. Use your knowledge of students' abilities to adjust levels as needed.

You know the theory behind leveled books: they let you match books with the interest and instructional levels of your students. You can find the right reader for every student with this chart.

Target Comprehension Skill	Additional Comprehension Instruction	Vocabulary
Character and Setting	Theme	Amazing Words
Main Idea and Details	Author's Purpose	Amazing Words
Main Idea and Details	Sequence	Amazing Words
Cause and Effect	Main Idea	Amazing Words
Sequence	Compare and Contrast	High-Frequency Words
Theme	Sequence	High-Frequency Words
Sequence	Character	Amazing Words
Cause and Effect	Draw Conclusions	Amazing Words
Author's Purpose	Cause and Effect	Amazing Words
Sequence	Draw Conclusions	Amazing Words
Author's Purpose	Cause and Effect	Amazing Words
Compare and Contrast	Main Idea	Amazing Words
Sequence	Author's Purpose	Amazing Words
Compare and Contrast	Character	Amazing Words
Fact and Opinion	Setting	Amazing Words
Author's Purpose	Plot	Amazing Words
Fact and Opinion	Cause and Effect	Amazing Words
Draw Conclusions	Author's Purpose	Amazing Words
Draw Conclusions	Sequence	Amazing Words
Theme	Character, Setting, Plot	Amazing Words
Facts and Details	Cause and Effect	Amazing Words
Facts and Details	Theme	Amazing Words
Theme	Realism and Fantasy	Amazing Words
Cause and Effect	Draw Conclusions	Amazing Words
Character, Setting and Plot	Cause and Effect	Amazing Words
Draw Conclusions	Compare and Contrast	Amazing Words
Compare and Contrast	Compare and Contrast	Amazing Words
Main Idea and Details	Cause and Effect	Amazing Words
Sequence	Draw Conclusions	Amazing Words
Theme	Sequence	Amazing Words

Section 3 Matching Books and Readers

What Good Readers Do

You can use the characterstics and behaviors of good readers to help all your children read better. But what are these characteristics and behaviors? And how can you use them to foster good reading behaviors for all your children? Here are some helpful tips.

Good Readers enjoy reading! They have favorite books, authors, and genres. Good readers often have a preference about where and when they read. They talk about books and recommend their favorites.

Develop this behavior by giving students opportunities to respond in different ways to what they read. Get them talking about what they read, and why they like or dislike it.

This behavior is important because book sharing alerts you to students who are somewhat passive about reading or have limited literacy experiences. Book sharing also helps you when you select books for the class.

Good Readers read independently for longer periods of time.

Develop this behavior by taking note of the level of support students need during guided reading. Use this information to gauge independent reading time accordingly.

This behavior is important because students become better readers when they spend time reading many texts at their independent level.

Good Readers select books they can read.

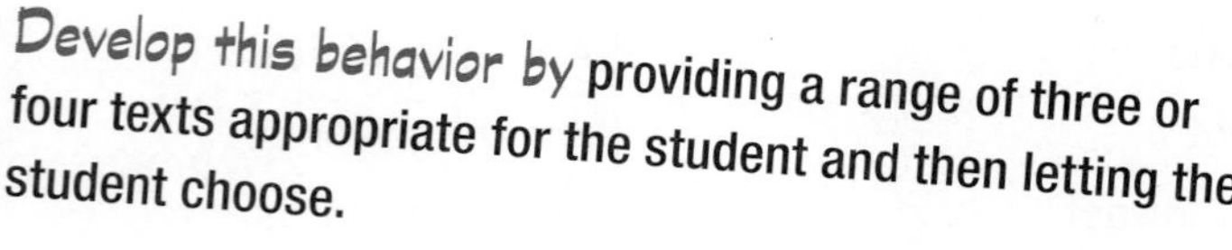

Develop this behavior by providing a range of three or four texts appropriate for the student and then letting the student choose.

This behavior is important because students gain control over reading when they can choose from books they can read. This helps them become more independent in the classroom.

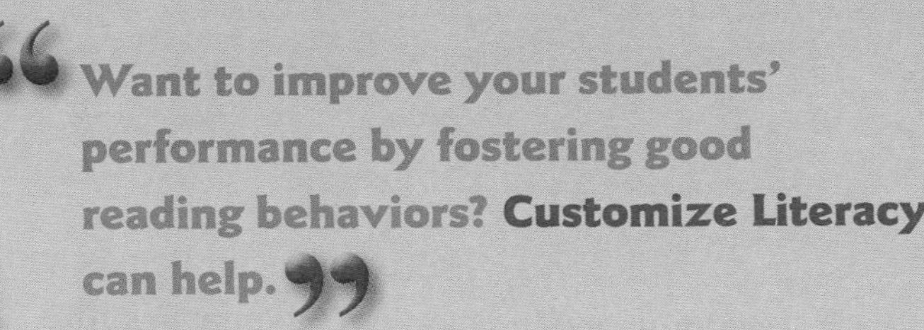

"Want to improve your students' performance by fostering good reading behaviors? Customize Literacy can help."

Good Readers use text features to help them preview and set purposes.

Develop this behavior by having students use the title and illustrations in fiction texts or the title, contents, headings, and other graphic features in nonfiction texts to make predictions about what they will be reading.

This behavior is important because previewing actually makes reading easier! Looking at features and sampling the text enables readers to predict and set expectations for reading.

Good Readers predict and ask questions before and while they read.

Develop this behavior by asking questions. After reading a passage, ask students what they think will happen next in a fiction text. Have them ask a question they think will be answered in a nonfiction text and read on to see if it is.

This behavior is important because when students predict and ask questions as they read, they are engaged. They have a purpose for reading and a basis for monitoring their comprehension.

Good Readers read aloud at an appropriate reading rate with a high percent of accuracy.

Develop this behavior by timing students' oral reading to calculate their reading rates. You can also record students' miscues to determine a percent of accuracy. This will help identify problems.

This behavior is important because when students read fluently texts that are "just right," they find reading more enjoyable. A fluent reader is able to focus more on constructing meaning and is more likely to develop a positive attitude toward reading.

Good Readers read meaningful phrases aloud with appropriate expression.

QU-

Develop this behavior by giving students lots of opportunities to read orally. As they read, note students' phrasing, intonation, and attention to punctuation and give help as needed.

This behavior is important because reading fluently in longer, meaningful phrases supports comprehension and ease in reading longer, more complex texts.

Section 3 Matching Books and Readers

QU-

ST-

Good Readers use effective strategies and sources of information to figure out unknown words.

Develop this behavior by teaching specific strategies for figuring out unknown words, such as sounding out clusters of letters, using context, reading on, and using references.

This behavior is important because when readers have a variety of strategies to use, they are more able to decode and self-correct quickly. Readers who do these things view themselves as good readers.

Good Readers construct meaning as they read and then share or demonstrate their understanding.

Develop this behavior by having students retell what they read or write a summary of what they read in their own words.

This behavior is important because the ability to retell or write a summary is essential for success in reading. It shows how well a student has constructed meaning.

Good Readers locate and use what is explicitly stated in a text.

Develop this behavior by asking questions that require students to go back into the text to find explicitly stated information.

This behavior is important because the ability to recall, locate, and use specific information stated in a text enables readers to respond to literal questions, as well as to support opinions and justify their responses.

Good Readers make connections.

Develop this behavior by asking questions to help students make connections: *What does this remind you of? Have you ever read or experienced anything like this?*

This behavior is important because making connections helps readers understand and appreciate a text. Making connections to self, the world, and other texts supports higher-level thinking.

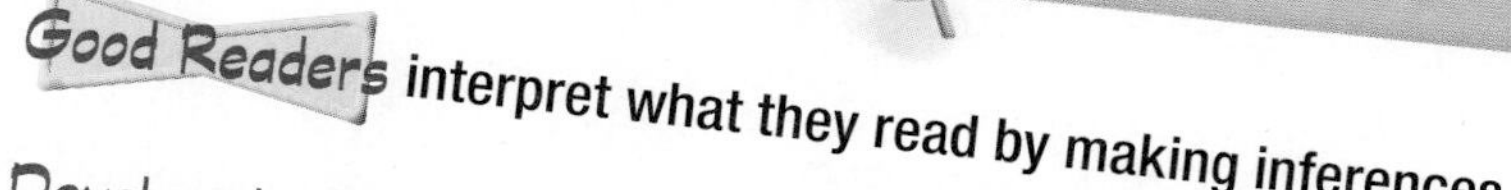

Good Readers interpret what they read by making inferences.

Develop this behavior by asking questions to help students tell or write about what they think was implied in the text: *Why do you think that happened? What helped you come to that conclusion?*

This behavior is important because the ability to go beyond the literal meaning of a text enables readers to gain a deeper understanding. When students make inferences, they use background knowledge, their personal knowledge, and the text to grasp the meaning of what is implied by the author.

Good Readers determine importance and evaluate what they read.

Develop this behavior by always having students identify what they think is the most important message, event, or information in a text.

This behavior is important because readers must be able to sort out important from interesting information. The ability to establish and/or use criteria and provide support when making judgments is an important critical-thinking skill.

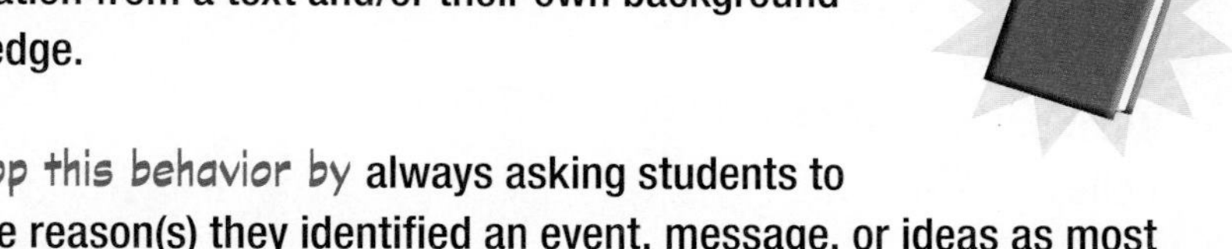

Good Readers support their responses using information from a text and/or their own background knowledge.

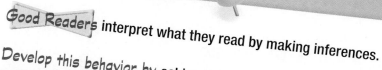

Develop this behavior by always asking students to give the reason(s) they identified an event, message, or ideas as most important.

This behavior is important because the ability to justify one's response is important for all learners. It enables others to know the basis for a decision and provides an opening for further discussion.

Conversation Starters

Asking Good Questions When children read interesting and thought-provoking books, they want to share! You can encourage children to think critically about what they read. Use questions such as the following to assess comprehension as well as evoke good class/group discussions.

Author's Purpose

- Who wrote this section?
- Why did the author write this piece?

Cause and Effect

- What is one thing that happens in the story? Why did it happen?
- Is there one thing that causes other things to happen?

Compare and Contrast

- What shows that the author is comparing people in this story?
- How are the characters and events in this story like and/or different from real people and events you know of?

Draw Conclusions

- Based on what you have read, seen, or experienced, what can you conclude about this event in the selection?
- This story seems to be a fantasy. Why might you conclude this?
- What can you decide about the characters?

Realism and Fantasy

- What parts of this story could be real? Why?
- What parts of this story could be make-believe? Why?

Graphic Sources

- This selection has many pictures. Which one or ones best help you understand the events or ideas in the selection? Why?

Literary Elements: Character, Setting, Plot, Theme

- Who are characters in the story? What are they like?
- Where does the story take place?
- What does the main character want at the beginning of the story?
- Retell the story, putting the things that happen in the right order.
- What is the big idea of the story? What lesson did you learn?

Main Idea

- What is this selection mostly about?
- What details tell more about the main idea?
- What might be another good title for this selection?

Sequence

- How is the sequence of events important in the text?
- Is the order of events important in this story? Why or why not?

Connecting Science and Social Studies

Scott Foresman Reading Street Leveled Readers are perfect for covering, supporting, or enriching science and social studies content. Using these books ensures that all students can access important concepts.

Grade 1 Leveled Readers

Science

Earth and Space Science

Nonfiction Books

- *All About the Weather*
- *The Communication Story*
- *Over the Years*
- *Ready for Winter?*
- *Using the Telephone*

Fiction Books

- *Cody's Adventure*
- *Marla's Good Idea*
- *What a Detective Does*

Life Science

Nonfiction Books

- *All About Food Chains*
- *Animals Change and Grow*
- *Around the Forest*
- *Around the World*
- *Baby Animals in the Rain Forest*
- *Bees and Beekeepers*
- *The Dinosaur Detectives*
- *The Dinosaur Herds*
- *Fun in the Sun*
- *Honey*
- *In My Room*
- *Learn About Butterflies*
- *Learn About Worker Bees*
- *Let's Go to the Zoo*
- *Let's Visit a Butterfly Greenhouse*
- *Look at Dinosaurs*
- *A Mighty Oak Tree*
- *Monarchs Migrate South*
- *People Help the Forest*
- *The Seasons Change*
- *Seasons Come and Go*
- *What Animals Can You See?*

Life Science

Fiction Books

- *Bix the Dog*
- *Britton Finds a Kitten*
- *Carlos Picks a Pet*
- *Cary and the Wildlife Shelter*
- *Mac Can Do It!*
- *Mack and Zack*
- *Plans Change*
- *Sam*
- *The Sick Pets*
- *Time for Dinner*
- *What Brown Saw*
- *Which Animals Will We See?*
- *Which Fox?*

Physical Science

Nonfiction Books

- *The Inclined Plane*
- *Simple Machines at Work*
- *Simple Machines in Compound Machines*

Grade 1 Leveled Readers

Social Studies

Citizenship

Nonfiction Books

- *A Class*
- *A Garden for All*
- *Great Scientists: Detectives at Work*
- *Here in My Neighborhood*
- *A New Library*
- *Puppy Raiser*
- *The Story of the Kids Care Club*
- *Ways to Be a Good Citizen*

Fiction Books

- *The Art Show*
- *At Your Vet*
- *Big Wishes and Her Baby*
- *Double Trouble Twins*
- *Fly Away Owl!*
- *Grasshopper and Ant*
- *Hank's Song*
- *Let's Build a Park!*
- *Look at My Neighborhood*
- *My Little Brother Drew*
- *On the Farm*
- *Paul's Bed*
- *A Play*
- *Rules at School*
- *Space Star*
- *Squirrel and Bear*
- *That Cat Needs Help!*

Culture

Nonfiction Books

- *Cascarones Are for Fun*
- *My Babysitter*
- *Special Days, Special Food*
- *We Are a Family*
- *What Makes Buildings Special?*

Fiction Books

- *Go West!*
- *Grandma's Farm*
- *Gus the Pup*
- *Jamie's Jumble of Junk*
- *A New Baby Brother*
- *A Party for Pedro*
- *A Visit to the Ranch*
- *Where They Live*

History

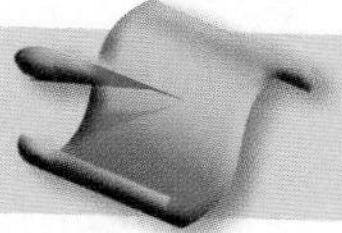

Nonfiction Books

- *School: Then and Now*
- *Treasures of Our Country*

Fiction Books

- *Loni's Town*

Government

Nonfiction Books

- *America's Home*
- *Our Leaders*

Fiction Books

- *Mom the Mayor*

Connecting Science and Social Studies

Need more choices? Look back to Grade K.

Grade K Leveled Readers

Science

Earth and Space Science	Life Science	Physical Science
Fiction Books • *We Can Do It!*	**Nonfiction Books** • *A Winter Home* • *What Can You Do?* • *The Trip* • *Pigs* • *Frog's New Home* • *A Small Trip* • *Safe Places for Animals* **Fiction Books** • *A Walk in the Forest* • *Looking for Animals* • *Skip and Run* • *Big Cats* • *My Pal Fran* • *Fun with Gram* • *They Will Grow* • *Sad and Glad*	**Fiction Books** • *Catch the Ball!* • *The Best Club Hut*

Grade K Leveled Readers

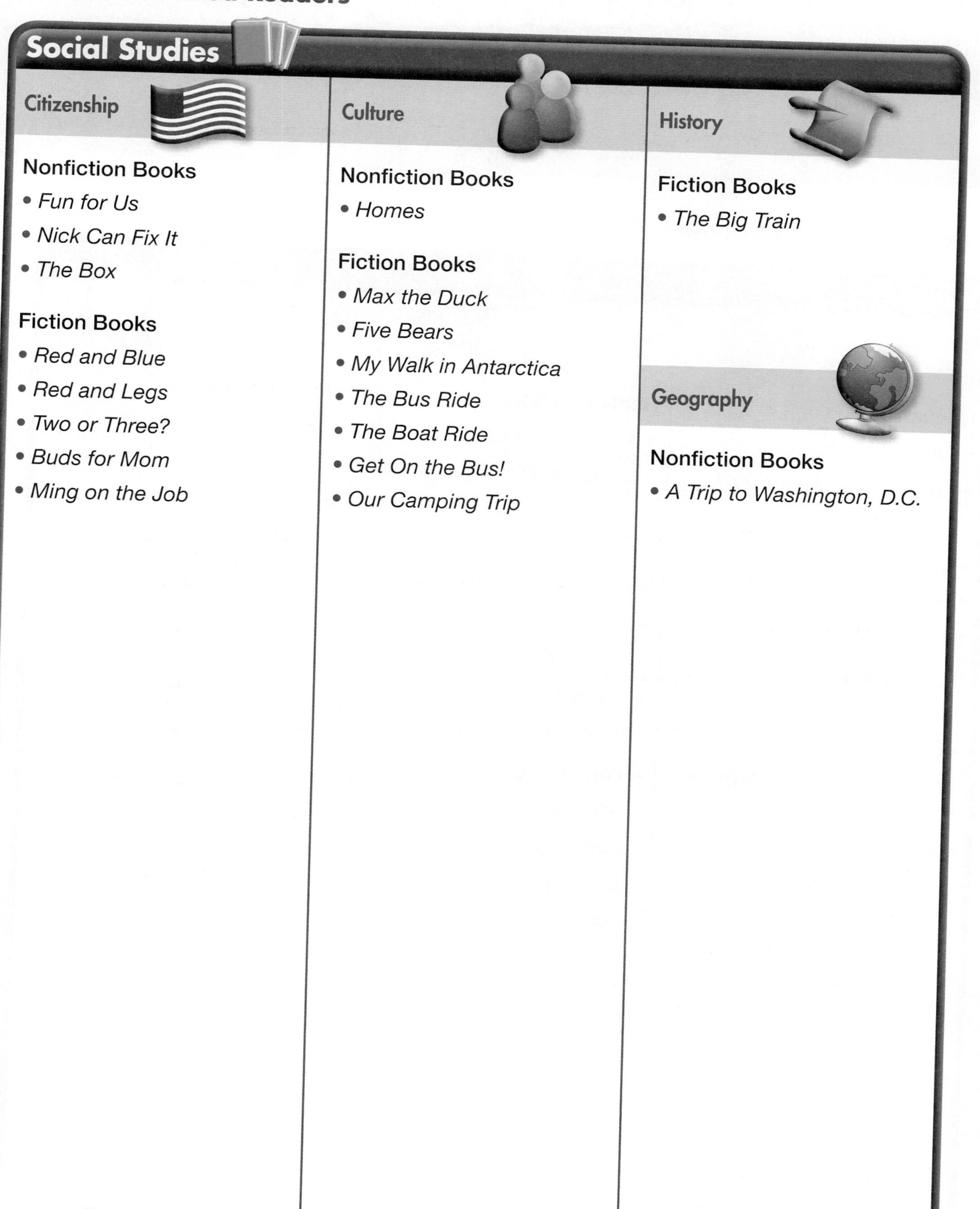

Social Studies

Citizenship

Nonfiction Books
- *Fun for Us*
- *Nick Can Fix It*
- *The Box*

Fiction Books
- *Red and Blue*
- *Red and Legs*
- *Two or Three?*
- *Buds for Mom*
- *Ming on the Job*

Culture

Nonfiction Books
- *Homes*

Fiction Books
- *Max the Duck*
- *Five Bears*
- *My Walk in Antarctica*
- *The Bus Ride*
- *The Boat Ride*
- *Get On the Bus!*
- *Our Camping Trip*

History

Fiction Books
- *The Big Train*

Geography

Nonfiction Books
- *A Trip to Washington, D.C.*

Connecting Science and Social Studies

Need more choices? Look ahead to Grade 2.

Grade 2 Leveled Readers

Science

Earth and Space Science

Nonfiction Books

- *All About Astronauts*
- *An Astronaut Space walk*
- *Desert Animals*
- *Deserts*
- *Hurricane!*
- *Look at Our Galaxy*

Fiction Books

- *Blizzard!*
- *Maggie's New Sidekick*
- *Rainbow Crow Brings Fire to Earth*
- *A Slice of Mud Pie*

Life Science

Nonfiction Books

- *Arachnid or Insect?*
- *Compost: Recycled Waste*
- *Farming Families*
- *How a Seed Grows*
- *How Can Animals Help?*
- *How Do Plants Grow?*
- *How to Grow Tomatoes*
- *Plants Grow Everywhere*
- *A Vet for All Animals*

Fiction Books

- *Annie Makes a Big Change*
- *Camping at Crescent Lake*
- *Growing Up*
- *Too Many Rabbit Holes*
- *Where Is Fish?*

Physical Science

Nonfiction Books

- *Many Types of Energy*
- *Sink or Float?*

Fiction Books

- *The Hummingbird*
- *Our School Science Fair*

Grade 2 Leveled Readers

Social Studies

Citizenship

Nonfiction Books

- *America's Birthday*
- *The Barn Raising*
- *Be Ready for an Emergency*
- *Everyone Can Make a Difference!*
- *Join an Adventure Club!*
- *Keeping Our Community Safe*
- *Protect the Earth*
- *The Rescue Dogs*
- *Service Workers*
- *Special Animal Helpers*
- *Using a Net*
- *What Can You Do?*
- *Working Dogs*

Fiction Books

- *Andrew's Mistake*
- *Camping with Pup*
- *Freda the Signmaker*
- *Hubert and Frankie*
- *Let's Work Together!*
- *Marty's Summer Job*
- *Sally and the Wild Puppy*
- *Stripes and Silver*
- *Too Many Frogs!*
- *Training Peanut*

Culture

Nonfiction Books

- *Celebrations and Family Traditions*
- *Living in Seoul*
- *Showing Good Manners*
- *Special Chinese Birthdays*
- *A World of Birthdays*

Fiction Books

- *Ana Is Shy*
- *The Camping Trip*
- *Country Friends, City Friends*
- *Dotty's Art*
- *The First People to Fly*
- *Glooskap and the First Summer: An Algonquin Tale*
- *Happy New Year!*
- *The International Food Fair*
- *Just Like Grandpa*
- *Living on a Ranch*
- *The New Kid in Bali*
- *Voting Day*

Economics

Nonfiction Books

- *Services and Goods*

Fiction Books

- *Country Mouse and City Mouse*
- *A Quiet Place*
- *Snakeskin Canyon*

History

Nonfiction Books

- *A Few Nifty Inventions*
- *The Hoover Dam*
- *Living in a Democracy*
- *Making Travel Fun*
- *Saint Bernards and Other Working Dogs*
- *Starting a New Life*
- *Women Play Baseball*

Fiction Books

- *At Home in the Wilderness*
- *A Class Play*
- *A Cowboy's Life*
- *Down on the Ranch*
- *Hank's Tortilla Factory*

Government

Nonfiction Books

- *Communicating Then and Now*
- *Let's Send a Letter!*

More Great Titles

Biography

- *American Revolution Heroes*
- *Baseball Heroes Make History*
- *Thomas Adams: Chewing Gum Inventor*
- *Three Great Ballplayers*

Planning Teacher Study Groups

Adventurous teachers often have good ideas for lessons. A teacher study group is a great way to share ideas and get feedback on the best way to connect content and students. Working with other teachers can provide you with the support and motivation you need to implement new teaching strategies. A teacher study group offers many opportunities to collaborate, support each other's work, share insights, and get feedback.

Think About It

A weekly or monthly teacher study group can help support you in developing your expertise in the classroom. You and a group of like-minded teachers can form your own study group. What can this group accomplish?

- Read and discuss professional articles by researchers in the field of education.
- Meet to share teaching tips, collaborate on multi-grade lessons, and share resources.
- Develop lessons to try out new teaching strategies. Meet to share experiences and discuss how to further improve your teaching approach.

Let's Meet!

Forming a study group is easy. Just follow these four steps:

1. **Decide on the size of the group.** A small group has the advantage of making each member feel accountable, but make sure that all people can make the same commitment!
2. **Choose teachers to invite to join your group.** Think about whom you want to invite. Should they all teach the same grade? Can you invite teachers from other schools? Remember that the more diverse the group, the more it benefits from new perspectives.
3. **Set goals for the group.** In order to succeed, know what you want the group to do. Meet to set goals. Rank goals in order of importance and refer often to the goals to keep the group on track.
4. **Make logistical decisions.** This is often the most difficult. Decide where and when you will meet. Consider an online meeting place where group members can post discussion questions and replies if people are not able to meet.

What Will We Study?

Use the goals you set to help determine what your group will study. Consider what materials are needed to reach your goals, and how long you think you will need to prepare for each meeting.

How Will It Work?

Think about how you structure groups in your classroom. Then use some of the same strategies.

- **Assign a group facilitator.** This person is responsible for guiding the meeting. This person comes prepared with discussion questions and leads the meeting. This could be a rotating responsibility dependent on experience with various topics. This person might be responsible for providing the materials.
- **Assign a recorder.** Have someone take notes during the meeting and record group decisions.
- **Use the jigsaw method.** Not everyone has time to be a facilitator. In this case, divide the text and assign each portion to a different person. Each person is responsible for leading the discussion on that particular part.

Meet Again

Make a commitment to meet for a minimum number of times. After that, the group can reevaluate and decide whether or not to continue.

"Have some great teaching tips to share? Want to exchange ideas with your colleagues? Build your own professional community of teachers. Customize Literacy gets you started."

Trial Lessons

Use your colleagues' experiences to help as you think about new ways to connect content and students. Use the following plan to create a mini-lesson. It should last twenty minutes. Get the support of your colleagues as you try something new and then reflect on what happened.

Be Creative! As you develop a plan for a mini-lesson, use these four words to guide planning: *purpose, text, resources,* and *routine.*

- **Purpose:** Decide on a skill or strategy to teach. Define your purpose for teaching the lesson.
- **Text:** Develop a list of the materials you could use. Ask your colleagues for suggestions.
- **Resources:** Make a list of the available resources, and consider how to use those resources most effectively. Consider using the Leveled Readers listed on pages CL24–CL29 and CL36–CL41 of Customize Literacy.
- **Routine:** Choose an instructional routine to structure your mini-lesson. See the mini-lessons in Customize Literacy for suggestions.

Try It! Try out your lesson! Consider audio- or videotaping the lesson for later review. You may wish to invite a colleague to sit in as you teach. Make notes on how the lesson went.

How Did It Go? Use the self-evaluation checklist on page CL45 as you reflect on your trial lesson. This provides a framework for later discussion.

Discuss, Reflect, Repeat Solicit feedback from your teacher study group. Explain the lesson and share your reflections. Ask for suggestions on ways to improve the lesson. Take some time to reflect on the feedback. Modify your lesson to reflect what you have learned. Then try teaching the lesson again.

Checklist for Teacher Self-Evaluation

How Well Did I ...	Very Well	Satisfactory	Not Very Well
Plan the lesson?			
Select the appropriate level of text?			
Introduce the lesson and explain its objectives?			
Review previously taught skills?			
Directly explain the new skills being taught?			
Model the new skills?			
Break the material down into small steps?			
Integrate guided practice into the lesson?			
Monitor guided practice for student understanding?			
Provide feedback on independent practice?			
Maintain an appropriate pace?			
Assess student understanding of the material?			
Stress the importance of applying the skill as they read?			
Maintain students' interest?			
Ask questions?			
Handle student questions and responses?			
Respond to the range of abilities?			

Books for Teachers

Children aren't the only ones who need to read to grow. Here is a brief list of books that you may find useful to fill your reading teacher basket and learn new things.

A Professional Bibliography

Adams, M. J. "Alphabetic Anxiety and Explicit, Systematic Phonics Instruction: A Cognitive Science Perspective." *Handbook of Early Literacy Research.* The Guilford Press, 2001.

Adams, M. J. *Beginning to Read: Thinking and Learning About Print.* The MIT Press, 1990.

Afflerbach, P. "The Influence of Prior Knowledge and Text Genre on Readers' Prediction Strategies." *Journal of Reading Behavior,* vol. XXII, no. 2 (1990).

Armbruster, B. B., F. Lehr, and J. Osborn. *Put Reading First: The Research Building Blocks for Teaching Children to Read.* Partnership for Reading, Washington, D.C., 2001.

Bear, D. R., M. Invernizzi, S. Templeton, and F. Johnston. *Words Their Way.* Merrill Prentice Hall, 2004.

Beck, I., M. G. McKeown, and L. Kucan. *Bringing Words to Life: Robust Vocabulary Instruction.* The Guilford Press, 2002.

Biemiller, A. "Teaching Vocabulary in the Primary Grades: Vocabulary Instruction Needed." *Vocabulary Instruction Research to Practice.* The Guilford Press, 2004.

Blachowicz, C. and P. Fisher. "Vocabulary Instruction." *Handbook of Reading Research,* vol. III. Lawrence Erlbaum Associates, 2000.

Cunningham, P. M. and J. W. Cunningham. "What We Know About How to Teach Phonics." *What Research Says About Reading Instruction,* 3rd ed. International Reading Association, 2002.

Daniels, H. *Literature Circles.* 2nd ed. Stenhouse Publishers, 2002.

Dickson, S. V., D. C. Simmons, and E. J. Kame'enui. "Text Organization: Instructional and Curricular Basics and Implications." *What Reading Research Tells Us About Children with Diverse Learning Needs: Bases and Basics.* Lawrence Erlbaum Associates, 1998.

Diller, D. *Making the Most of Small Groups: Differentiation for All.* Stenhouse Publishers, 2007.

Duke, N. K., V. S. Bennett-Armistead, and E. M. Roberts. "Bridging the Gap Between Learning to Read and Reading to Learn." *Literacy and Young Children: Research-Based Practices.* The Guilford Press, 2003.

Duke, N. K. and C. Tower. "Nonfiction Texts for Young Readers." *The Texts in Elementary Classrooms.* Lawrence Erlbaum Associates, 2004.

Ehri, L. C. and S. R. Nunes. "The Role of Phonemic Awareness in Learning to Read." *What Research Has to Say About Reading Instruction.* 3rd ed. International Reading Association, 2002.

Fountas, I. C. and G. S. Pinnell. *Guided Reading: Good First Teaching for All Children.* Heinemann, 1996.

Fountas, I. C. and G. S. Pinnell. *Matching Books to Readers: Using Leveled Books in Guided Reading,* K-3. Heinemann, 1999.

Harvey, S. and A. Goudvis. *Strategies That Work: Teaching Comprehension to Enhance Understanding.* 2nd ed. Stenhouse Publishers, 2007.

Hiebert, E. H. and L. A. Martin. "The Texts of Beginning Reading Instruction." *Handbook of Early Literacy Research.* The Guilford Press, 2001.

Indrisano, R. and J. R. Paratore. *Learning to Write, Writing to Learn. Theory and Research in Practice.* International Reading Association, 2005.

Juel, C., G. Biancarosa, D. Coker, and R. Deffes. "Walking with Rosie: A Cautionary Tale of Early Reading Instruction." *Educational Leadership* (April 2003).

National Reading Panel. *Teaching Children to Read.* National Institute of Child Health and Human Development, 1999.

Pressley, M. *Reading Instruction That Works: The Case for Balanced Teaching,* 3rd ed. The Guilford Press, 2005.

Smith, S., D. C. Simmons, and E. J. Kame'enui. "Word Recognition: Research Bases." *What Reading Research Tells Us About Children with Diverse Learning Needs: Bases and Basics.* Lawrence Erlbaum Associates, 1998.

Snow, C., S., Burns, and P. Griffin, eds. *Preventing Reading Difficulties in Young Children.* National Academy Press, 1998.

Vaughn, S., P. G. Mathes, S. Linan-Thompson, and D. J. Francis. "Teaching English Language Learners at Risk for Reading Disabilities to Read: Putting Research into Practice." *Learning Disabilities Research & Practice,* vol. 20, issue 1 (February 2006).

WEEK 4 Oral Vocabulary for

A Fox and a Kit

Let's Learn Amazing Words

Definitions, examples, and **applications** to use with the Oral Vocabulary in each lesson.

Amazing Words Oral Vocabulary Routine

wild

1. If an animal is *wild*, it lives in nature and is not taken care of by people.
2. **Examples** Foxes are *wild* animals. *Wild* animals often live in the woods. If an animal is *wild*, it takes care of itself.
3. **Apply to the instruction** Name one kind of *wild* animal. Tell where it lives.

parent

1. A mother or a father is a *parent*.
2. **Examples** A *parent* takes care of its young. The male sea horse is the *parent* who cares for its young. When they are born, some baby animals do not look like their *parents*.
3. **Apply to the instruction** What is something a *parent* might do for a child?

canopy

1. A *canopy* is a cover that hangs over something.
2. **Examples** A *canopy* can help shade you from the sun. A *canopy* in the rain forest is like a roof. The tallest trees make a *canopy* in the rain forest. The *canopy* provides shelter for many animals in the rain forest.
3. **Apply to the instruction** If you were standing, would you look up or down to see a *canopy?*

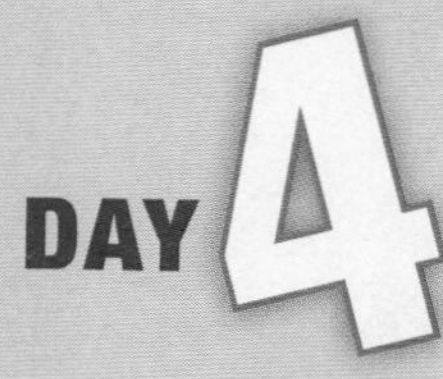

reserve

1. A *reserve* is a place set aside for special use.
2. **Examples** An animal *reserve* is a park for animals. A *reserve* provides a safe place for wild animals to live. Endangered animals may be protected in a *reserve*.
3. **Apply to the instruction** What are some things you might see in a *reserve?*

Oral Vocabulary for

Let's Learn Amazing Words

Get the Egg!

DAY 1

Amazing Words Oral Vocabulary Routine

hatch

1. *Hatch* means "to come out of an egg."
2. **Examples** To *hatch*, a baby chick breaks out of its egg. Snakes and turtles *hatch* from eggs. Some insects *hatch* from eggs.
3. **Apply to the instruction** If any of the things I name can *hatch*, say *hatch*. If not, say nothing: a train, a chicken, a jar of jam, a snake, a turtle.

survive

1. *Survive* means "to stay alive."
2. **Examples** We hoped the cat would *survive* after it fell from the tree. The man was thankful to *survive* the car accident. Some plants can *survive* with little water.
3. **Apply to the instruction** Name a word that means the opposite of *survive*. Name a word that means about the same as *survive*.

Oral Vocabulary for

Definitions, examples, and applications to use with the Oral Vocabulary in each lesson.

Animal Park

Amazing Words Oral Vocabulary Routine

forest

1. A *forest* is many trees growing together that cover a large area of land.
2. **Examples** A *forest* might have oak trees and maple trees. Wild animals like squirrels live in the trees in a *forest*. Other wild animals, like foxes, live in dens in the ground of the *forest*.
3. **Apply to the instruction** Name a kind of tree or animal that you might find in a *forest*.

world

1. *World* is the name for the earth.
2. **Examples** People live in different parts of the *world*. A globe is a model of the *world*. Ships can sail around the *world*.
3. **Apply to the instruction** Tell something about another part of the *world* that you have read in a book or seen on TV. Use the word *world* when you tell about it.

chatter

1. To *chatter* means "to talk quickly" or "to make quick, sharp sounds."
2. **Examples** Monkeys *chatter*. The *chatter* of the birds made it hard for me to think. The children *chattered* away on the bus ride home.
3. **Apply to the instruction** Demonstrate how a person or a monkey might *chatter*.

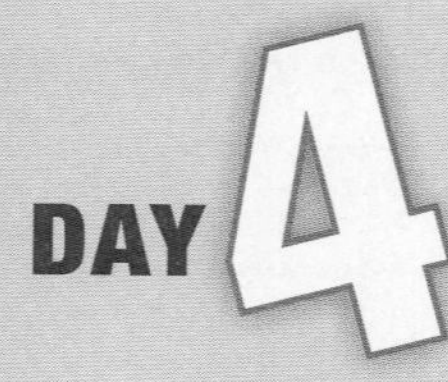

poisonous

1. Something that is *poisonous* is harmful to your health or life.
2. **Examples** If you eat something *poisonous*, you can get very sick. Some kinds of berries are *poisonous*. Certain animals are *poisonous*.
3. **Apply to the instruction** Explain why you would not want to eat or touch something *poisonous*.

Acknowledgments

Teacher's Edition

Text

KWL Strategy: The KWL Interactive Reading Strategy was developed and is used by permission of Donna Ogle, National-Louis University, Skokie, Illinois, co-author of *Reading Today and Tomorrow*, Holt, Rinehart & Winston Publishers, 1988. (See also the *Reading Teacher,* February 1986, pp. 564–570.)

Understanding by Design quotes: Wiggins, G. & McTighe, J. (2005). *Understanding by Design.* Alexandria, VA: Association for Supervision and Curriculum Development.

Illustrations

Cover Daniel Moreton

Running Header Steven Mach

Photographs

Every effort has been made to secure permission and provide appropriate credit for photographic material. The publisher deeply regrets any omission and pledges to correct errors called to its attention in subsequent editions.

Unless otherwise acknowledged, all photographs are the property of Pearson Education, Inc.

Student Edition

Acknowledgments

Text

Grateful acknowledgment is made to the following for copyrighted material:

Page 168: "Raccoon" from *Animal Snackers* by Betsy Lewin. © 1980, 2004 by Betsy Lewin. Reprinted by permission of Henry Holt and Company, LLC.

Page 169: Excerpt from "The Hippo" in *Mammalabilia*, text copyright © 2000 by Douglas Florian, reprinted by permission of Harcourt, Inc. This material may not be reproduced in any form or by any means without the prior written permission of the publisher.

Note: Every effort has been made to locate the copyright owner of material reproduced on this component. Omissions brought to our attention will be corrected in subsequent editions.

Illustrations

Cover Daniel Moreton

14 Robbie Short

20-29, 46-56, 74-83 Janet Stevens

34, 35 Maribel Suarez

40 Marilyn Janovitz

62, 63 Lindsey Gardiner

68 Paul Meisel

98 Ariel Pang

102-111 Charles Santore

116, 117 Jaime Zollars

126 Carol Koeller

128-141 Bernard Adnet

154 Victor Rivas

Photographs

Every effort has been made to secure permission and provide appropriate credit for photographic material. The publisher deeply regrets any omission and pledges to correct errors called to its attention in subsequent editions.

Unless otherwise acknowledged, all photographs are the property of Pearson Education, Inc.

Photo locators denoted as follows: Top (T), Center (C), Bottom (B), Left (L), Right (R), Background (Bkgd)

10 (B) ©Larry Williams/Corbis

36 ©DK Images

38 ©Picture Partners/Alamy Images

65 Getty Images, Joe McDonald/Corbis, Peter Arnold/Getty Images

66 (B) ©Chris Marona/Photo Researchers, Inc.

88 (BL) Getty Images

89 (TL) Mark Richards/PhotoEdit

90 (BR) Peter Olive/Photofusion Picture Library/Alamy Images

91 (TR) A. Ramey/PhotoEdit, (TL) Copyright Bryan & Cherry Alexander Photography/Bryan and Sherry Alexander Photography, (C) Dallas and John Heaton/Corbis

93 Daryl Balfour/Getty Images

94 (B) ©San Diego Zoo/Handout/Reuters/Corbis

118 (TR) Getty Images

121 ©Aristide Economopoulos/Star Ledger/Corbis

145 American Images Inc/Getty Images, Frank Lukasseck/Getty Images, Joel Sartore/Getty Images, Purestock/Getty Images

146 ©Frans Lanting/Corbis

147 ©Heidi & Hans-Jurgen Koch/Minden Pictures

154 (TL) Getty Images, (Bkgd) Tim Davis/Corbis

156 (BR) Craig Lovell/Corbis, (Bkgd) Photo Researchers, Inc.

157 (TR, BR) Digital Stock, (CR) Digital Vision, (L) Staffan Widstrand/Corbis

158 (TC) Jupiter Images, (Bkgd) Tom Nebbia/Corbis

159 (CC) Art Wolfe/Art Wolfe Inc., (TC) Tom Brakefield/Corbis

160 (TC) Beverly Joubert/NGS Image Collection, (BC) Peter Johnson/Corbis

162 (T) ©Theo Allofs/Getty Images

163 (TL) Brand X Pictures, (BL) David Young-Wolff/Alamy Images, (Bkgd) Digital Vision, (CL) Norbert Rosing/NGS Image Collection

171 Mira/Alamy Images, Phil Schermeister/Getty Images.

188

Student Edition p. 188

Teacher Notes

Teacher Notes

UNIT 1

Teacher Notes

Teacher Notes

UNIT 1

Teacher Notes

Teacher Notes

UNIT 1

Teacher Notes

Teacher Notes

UNIT 1

Teacher Notes

Teacher Resources

Looking for Teacher Resources and other important information?

In the First Stop on Reading Street

- Dear First Grade Teacher
- Research into Practice on Reading Street
- Guide to Reading Street
- Assessment on Reading Street
- Customize Writing on Reading Street
- Differentiated Instruction on Reading Street
- ELL on Reading Street
- Customize Literacy on Reading Street
- Digital Products on Reading Street
- Teacher Resources for Grade 1
- Index

Teacher Resources

Looking for Teacher Resources and other important information?

In the First Stop on Reading Street